RELIGION AND IDENTITY IN SOUTH ASIA AND BEYOND

Cultural, Historical and Textual Studies of South Asian Religions

The volumes featured in the Anthem **Cultural, Historical and Textual Studies of South Asian Religions** series are the expression of an international community of scholars committed to the reshaping of the field of textual and historical studies of religions. Titles in this series examine practice, ritual, and other textual religious products, crossing different area studies and time frames. Featuring a vast range of interpretive perspectives, this innovative series aims to enhance the way we look at religious traditions.

Series Editor

Federico Squarcini, University of Florence, Italy

Editorial Board

Piero Capelli, Ca' Foscari University of Venice, Italy
Vincent Eltschinger, ICIHA, Austrian Academy of Sciences, Austria
Christoph Emmrich, University of Toronto, Canada
James Fitzgerald, Brown University, USA
Jonardon Ganeri, University of Sussex, UK
Barbara A. Holdrege, University of California, Santa Barbara, USA
Sheldon Pollock, Columbia University, USA
Karin Preisendanz, University of Vienna, Austria
Alessandro Saggioro, Sapienza University of Rome, Italy
Cristina Scherrer-Schaub, University of Lausanne and EPHE, France
Romila Thapar, Jawaharlal Nehru University, India
Ananya Vajpeyi, University of Massachusetts Boston, USA
Marco Ventura, University of Siena, Italy
Vincenzo Vergiani, University of Cambridge, UK

RELIGION AND IDENTITY IN SOUTH ASIA AND BEYOND

ESSAYS IN HONOR OF PATRICK OLIVELLE

Edited by Steven E. Lindquist

ANTHEM PRESS
LONDON · NEW YORK · DELHI

Anthem Press
An imprint of Wimbledon Publishing Company
www.anthempress.com

This edition first published in UK and USA 2013
by ANTHEM PRESS
75-76 Blackfriars Road, London SE1 8HA, UK
or PO Box 9779, London SW19 7ZG, UK
and
244 Madison Ave. #116, New York, NY 10016, USA

First published in hardback by Anthem Press in 2011

Cover photograph courtesy of Lisa N. Owen

British Library Cataloguing-in-Publication Data
A catalogue record for this book is available from the British Library.

Library of Congress Cataloging-in-Publication Data
A catalog record for this book has been requested.

ISBN-13: 978 1 78308 067 0 (Pbk)
ISBN-10: 1 78308 067 1 (Pbk)

This title is also available as an ebook.

mātur agre vijananaṃ dvitīyaṃ mauñjibandhane |
atrāsya mātā sāvitrī pitā tv ācārya ucyate ||

The first birth is from the mother and the second is at the student's girding. At the latter birth, the Sāvitrī verse is his mother, while the teacher is said to be his father.

Vasiṣṭhadharmasūtra 2.3

Contents

STEVEN E. LINDQUIST
Introduction: Patrick Olivelle and Indology 9
Major Publications of Patrick Olivelle 15

I. WORD, TEXT, CONTEXT

TIMOTHY LUBIN
The Elusive Snātaka 23

JARROD L. WHITAKER
Who Gets to Live Forever in Ancient India?
Rethinking ā́yus *("life") in the* R̥gveda 41

STEVEN E. LINDQUIST
One Yājñavalkya... Two? On the (Questionable) Historicity of a Literary Figure 69

ROBERT A. GOODDING
A Theologian in a South Indian Kingdom: The Historical Context of the Jīvanmuktiviveka *of Vidyāraṇya* 83

BRIAN BLACK
The Rhetoric of Secrecy in the Upaniṣads 101

II. CUSTOM AND LAW

ROBERT A. YELLE
Punishing Puns: Etymology as Linguistic Ideology in Hindu and British Traditions 129

Donald R. Davis, Jr.
Matrilineal Adoption, Inheritance Law, and Rites for the Dead among Hindus in Medieval Kerala 147

Federico Squarcini
Punishing in Public: Imposing Moral Self-Dominance in Normative Sanskrit Sources 165

III. Buddhists and Jains as Selves and Others

Oliver Freiberger
How the Buddha Dealt with Non-Buddhists 185

Daniel Boucher
Sacrifice and Asceticism in Early Mahāyāna Buddhism 197

Lisa N. Owen
Text and Image: Identifying Ellora's Jain Deities 225

IV. (Re)considering Geographical and Conceptual Boundaries

Devin DeWeese
Spiritual Practice and Corporate Identity in Medieval Sufi Communities of Iran, Central Asia, and India: The Khalvatī/'Ishqī/Shaṭṭārī Continuum 251

Jason BeDuhn
Digesting the Sacrifices: Ritual Internalization in Jewish, Hindu, and Manichaean Traditions 301

Manu Bhagavan
The Hindutva Underground: Hindu Nationalism and the Indian National Congress in Late Colonial and Early Postcolonial India 321

Laura R. Brueck
Marking the Boundaries of a New Literary Identity: The Assertion of 'Dalit Consciousness' in Dalit Literary Criticism 347

Karline McLain
Young Śvetaketu in America: Learning to be Hindu in the Diaspora 369

List of Contributors 391

Steven E. Lindquist

*Introduction: Patrick Olivelle and Indology**

I have always thought it was an unfortunate cliché to start an introduction to a well-known individual by stating that such a person "needs no introduction." More than once, when someone has ventured forth with this sort of beginning, I have silently asked, "Then why are you here?" Of course, the irony of all armchair criticism is that it turns itself on the accuser should he or she be placed in a similar position and that position, I can firmly attest, is uncomfortable indeed.

If Patrick Olivelle himself does not need an introduction to the reading audience, this volume certainly does. It would be disingenuous, however, to separate the two and simply avoid the difficulty of introducing a person who is so well known, as each contributor in this volume has been directly influenced by Olivelle both personally and professionally. All of the contributors in this volume have worked directly with Olivelle in some fashion, most having done so in the classroom. I am sure these contributors could all share anecdotes of Olivelle's soft reproaches to a mangled Sanskrit translation, his parental sternness when grammar or historical context is misunderstood, his magnanimous attitude in advice and criticism, and his unflagging support for his students, whether they are aspiring Sanskritists or whether their research specializations lay elsewhere. The few contributors who were not directly Olivelle's students have known him through his numerous publications and have similarly sought his academic expertise and guidance in their work.

In the conception of this volume, it was decided early on that the most fitting tribute to this great scholar was not a *Festschrift* of senior Sanskrit scholars (itself, a long-standing and noble tradition), but a

* I would like to thank the series editor, Federico Squarcini, for his support and encouragement for this volume. The authors also deserve acknowledgment, not only for their fine contributions, but also for their diligence and patience.

volume which reflects his diverse influence as both a scholar and a teacher of a younger generation. Many participants in this volume are new professionals in their respective fields and their influence on the field of Asian Studies is fast emerging. The more senior participants come not only from South Asian Studies, but also Central and East Asian Studies, and are firmly established in their own rights.

Olivelle, Sanskrit, and the Study of South Asia

With my own accusatory question in the back of my mind, coupled with the fact that introductions always rehearse at least some information that is well known, I will not attempt to "introduce" Patrick Olivelle to the audience of this volume.[1] Rather my goal is simply to augment and remind the audience of what it already knows. I do not think it is hyperbole to state that Olivelle's work is known to anyone and everyone working on ancient and classical India as well as to those who teach religions of India more broadly. Whether that knowledge is through his monographs, his five critical editions, his eleven erudite and flowing book-length translations,[2] his five edited volumes, or his more than fifty articles (not to mention dozens of encyclopedia and dictionary entries), those working in the history, language, and religion of early India are well aware of his work.[3] Olivelle is not only exceptionally prolific and wide-ranging in his interests, but he is also a model scholar who can speak to different audiences, yet remain historically sensitive, philologically rigorous, and thematically relevant to the expanse of Indological and religious inquiry.

While the term "Indology" has fallen out of fashion as of late—sometimes dismissed as an obscure facet of historical linguistics or otherwise criticized as a regionally specific subset of Orientalism[4]—Olivelle's work stands solidly in a European intellectual lineage of professional Indology, exemplified in the historical and philological rigor of his training, first at Oxford University and then at the University of Pennsylvania under the tutelage of Ludo Rocher. This rigor is most clearly seen in his several critical editions of *dharmaśāstra* texts and his scholarly editions of other texts, such as the Upaniṣads. While editions

[1] A short biography and an appraisal of Olivelle's work through 1999 is already the subject of a detailed review (Olson 2000).

[2] In particular, see his work in the Oxford Classics series, where he has published seminal translations, often accompanied by separate scholarly editions with the Sanskrit originals on opposing pages. Such translations should be a model for both specialized and popular translations—straightforward, but detailed introductions that do not oversimplify, accurate and clear translations with a flair for readability, and finally copious notes that are up to date and academically rigorous, yet do not intrude on the easy readability of the text as a whole.

[3] A bibliography of Olivelle's major works is found at the end of this introduction.

[4] For example, see Inden (1990). Inden's work, however, has been the subject of criticism (e.g., Halbfass 1997; Smith 2005), not the least of which is that his definition of Indology variously encompasses professional academic Indologists, Western philosophers without significant training in India, and British amateur Indophiles.

of these texts have been available in some fashion to Western scholars for a long time, their importance within their respective traditions and in the history of early India is hard to overstate. It has become clear in retrospect, as Olivelle notes in several of his introductions and articles, that most of these previous editions are less than ideal—scholars have sometimes emended the texts against manuscript evidence, have relied upon previous editions and very few manuscripts, have not properly constituted a critical apparatus, or have produced translations that have not stood the test of time as readable and accurate. Olivelle's critical editing of texts, particularly of the *dharma* literature, is unparalleled in the number of manuscripts collated (the most important marker of quality of a critical edition), the care with which he considers variations and their significance, and his close analysis of problematic passages in light of the manuscript evidence and the latest scholarly exegesis.[5] Olivelle's *Manu's Code of Law* (2005) should be a model, albeit extremely difficult to emulate, of not only the care and hard work needed to construct such an edition, but also the revolutionary benefits that arise from that labor (such as Olivelle's novel argument about Manu as an author or the dating and interrelation of various *dharma* texts). Clearly, such fundamental work by Olivelle will be, like much of the work by his predecessors that he builds upon, the benchmark for work in these areas for the next several generations of scholars. I suspect that Olivelle's general humble nature, evidenced in his critical respect towards the generations of scholars that came before him, would compel him to add that he fully expects his own translations to be superseded in the course of time. Similar, though, to Olivelle's *Manu's Code of Law* appearing well over a century after Bühler, it will be longer than this before there is any perceived need for new comprehensive translations of many of these works. His critical editions are definitive and will certainly remain so.

Though Olivelle has focused a significant amount of his scholarly endeavors on the painstaking work of critical editing, his popularity beyond Indology comes from his ability to speak to a wide range of audiences while maintaining a faithfulness to his Indological lineage. In this sense, his work is the best of what Indology has to offer to the wider academic disciplines concerned with South Asia. The appreciation of Olivelle's work is easily seen in the number of accolades he has received from the academy at large: the Association of Asian Studies'

[5] One broad criticism of critical editions is that such editions privilege a particular version of the text over another and are thus inherently suspect and perhaps should be abandoned. There is no doubt that a critical edition privileges the reconstituted text based on the assumption of an *Urtext* from which other versions are thought to have emerged, but to suggest that critical editions should thus not be undertaken is seriously misguided. Unlike non-critical editions and translations, the main scholarly benefit of a critical edition is the critical apparatus (along with a *stemma codica*), a means by which *several versions of a text are simultaneously made publicly available.* The problem then, to my mind, is not with critical editions themselves, but rather with how some people use them.

A.K. Ramanujan Prize for Translation (1998), the American Academy of Religion's Award for Excellence in the Study of Religion in the Historical category (1994), several fellowships (including the National Endowment for the Humanities, the Guggenheim, the American Institute of Indian Studies, the Smithsonian Institution, and the American Council of Learned Societies) and various visiting positions. Represented in the prestigious awards that Olivelle has received, the dizzying array of conferences he presents at, and the various offices he has held in learned societies, Olivelle's work has directly impacted not only linguistics and religious studies of South Asia, but also history, anthropology, and the social sciences.

If there has been any significant criticism of the field of Indology from South Asian area studies more broadly, it has been that philologically-oriented studies of India have tended to produce works of intense specialization which have remained, at least in classical studies, rather immune to recent theoretical trends in academia, particularly in terms of theory or application of modern and post-modern European or North American philosophical thinking. With the rise of Area Studies, and more recently Cultural Studies, there has been a progressive blurring of the lines of disciplinary boundaries and an increased emphasis on theory. No doubt this is a positive development in many ways, as regional expertise cannot be confined by parochial limitations of a region, language, or religion, but it also cannot and should not be confined by theoretical approaches. A rise in an emphasis on method and theory and a decline in the "nuts and bolts" of cultural study (i.e., language and history), however, could lead to the "throwing of the baby out with the bath water."[6] This fear, at least for some, is that the increasing emphasis on theory and the blurring of disciplinary boundaries could lead to destruction of those lines altogether, where "culture" can be taken as some sort of universal, and context is given a secondary role at best.

Olivelle has always been open to new methods and theories, but has placed the most value in those which have direct practical application in the investigation of historically situated texts and practices. He began his career in the Department of Religious Studies at Indiana University, Bloomington (1974-1991, Chair from 1984-1990), as the only South Asianist among a diverse crowd of religionists. It is in this context, I imagine, that he learned to speak to a broad audience of colleagues, while advocating for the importance and distinctiveness of Indian traditions and history.

Olivelle shifted in 1991 to Texas and his leadership within the Department of Asian Studies at The University of Texas at Austin is a

[6] The declining importance of philology, albeit defined much more broadly than most who call themselves "philologists" would probably prefer, has recently and cogently been discussed by Pollock (2009). It is important to note, however, that philology has not suffered a universal decline in the disciplines as it retains a more secure position in Religious Studies than in other fields.

testament to the blurring of boundaries in the study of Asia, but in a way that retains the distinctiveness and value of the different disciplines brought together under one institutional roof. Olivelle served as the Chair of the Department of Asian Studies from 1994-2007 as well as the Director of the Center for Asian Studies (now the South Asia Institute) from 1994-2000. During this period, the program grew swiftly, hiring approximately twenty professors and lecturers and expanding the language offerings from six to ten. The University of Texas at Austin's program now includes forty specialists in these languages during all time periods, and includes seventeen affiliated faculty from ten departments and colleges. The University of Texas at Austin's Department of Asian Studies now houses one of the largest South Asian Studies programs in all of North America and much of that is thanks to the leadership of Olivelle. It is known not only as a premiere center for the study of Sanskrit, but also for history, art history, anthropology, and literature of South Asia. While Olivelle would be the first to say that it is the faculty that has made the program what it is, his own hand was central in what it has become.

Olivelle's Scholarship and This Volume

In terms of texts, Olivelle's body of work is largely concerned with two broad categories of Sanskrit literature: texts concerned with asceticism and those concerned with law (*dharma*). Another way to view his body of work is that there is an overriding theme of investigating the constitution and constraint of the individual body (particularly in regard to asceticism, but also gender) and the constitution and constraint of the social body (from the householder up to the king). Such a characterization, though, could be misleading if it was not clearly understood that, for Olivelle, defining the individual or the social is, at its base, a historically situated task, not just within a limited time span or region, but within particular communities or authors that are composing such texts. In particular, one of Olivelle's driving motivations appears to be getting "behind the texts" to explore and elucidate the social and ideological world constructed by real people "on the ground."

All of the papers in this volume, in some sense, build on the themes that have concerned Olivelle throughout his career. Like the best of all teachers, however, Olivelle neither guided his students to simply replicate his own interests nor was his assistance to younger scholars limited to classical India or even South Asia. The contributors in this volume stand as a testament to the diversity of his influence. As such there has been no conscious attempt at thematic unity in this volume, but a unity of sorts has emerged on its own, which seems to me fittingly appropriate to what will become known as Olivelle's legacy. In particular, all contributions to this volume are committed to linguistic and historical rigor, combined with a sensitivity to how the study of Asia has been changing over the several decades since Olivelle began his long and illustrious career. It is clear in all cases that these contributions build on the long and distinguished work of those who came before them and, rather than jettisoning their predecessors' hard work, move the ideas, theories, and areas of study forward.

Many of the contributions of this volume are concerned with the construction of religious and cultural identity (whether among Brahmins, Buddhists, Dalits, or Muslims of Iran and Central Asia). Several are concerned particularly with the problem of historical reconstruction and textual interpretation (whether of a figure like Yājñavalkya, the identification of Jain deities, the linguistic role of *mantras*, the literary function of secrecy, or the role of the *snātaka* or "bath-graduate"). Some focus on the earliest material (such as the *Ṛg* and *Atharvaveda*), while others are decidedly more recent (such as the rise of Hindutva ideology or a newly formulated version of an Upaniṣadic story). Law and asceticism are reoccurring topics throughout the volume.

The volume begins, in a sense, where Olivelle's career began and spreads out geographically and temporally from there. Section I, "Word, Text, and Context," consists of a series of papers concerned with the intersection of the literary and the historical especially in ancient India, but also in the medieval ascetic text of Vidyāraṇya. Section II, titled "Custom and Law," more clearly represents Olivelle's scholarly emphasis on *dharma* traditions since the late 1990s. Section III, "Buddhist and Jain Selves and Others," points to Olivelle's influence in the study of ascetic traditions outside of classical Hinduism. The final section, "(Re)considering Geographical and Conceptual Boundaries," branches the furthest out, both temporally and geographically, considering not only Sufi, Jewish, and Manichaean traditions, but also nationalism, Dalit literary criticism, and the Hindu diaspora.

Dallas, August 2010

Bibliography

Halbfass. W. (1997), "Research and Reflection: Responses to my Respondents. I. Beyond Orientalism? Reflections on a Current Theme" in *Beyond Orientalism: The Work of Wilhelm Halbfass and its Impact on Indian and Cross-Cultural Studies*, ed. E. Franco and K. Preisendanz, Poznan Studies in the Philosophy of the Sciences and the Humanities, vol. 59 (Atlanta: Rodopi), 1-25.

Inden, R. (1990), *Imagining India* (Cambridge MA: Basil Blackwell).

Olson, C. (2000), "Recent Contributions of Patrick Olivelle to Indology," *Religious Studies Review* 26.2: 157-163.

Pollock, S. (2009), "Future Philology? The Fate of a Soft Science in a Hard World," *Critical Inquiry* 35.4: 931-961.

Smith, D. (2003), "Orientalism and Hinduism" in *The Blackwell Companion to Hinduism*, ed. Gavin Flood (Oxford: Blackwell Publishing), 45-63.

Major Publications of Patrick Olivelle

Books

2009a, *Viṣṇu's Code of Law: A Critical Edition and Translation of the Vaiṣṇava-Dharmaśāstra*. Harvard Oriental Series, no. 73 (Cambridge, MA: Harvard University Press).

2009b, (Edited volume) *Dharma: Studies in Its Semantic, Cultural, and Religious History* (Delhi: Motilal Banarsidass). Expanded new edition of 2004a.

2009c, (Edited volume) *Aśoka in History and Historical Memory* (Delhi: Motilal Banarsidass).

2009d, *Collected Essays I: Language, Texts, and Society* (Florence: University of Florence Press), 2008. New edition of 2006a.

2009e, *Collected Essays II: Ascetics and Brahmins* (Florence: University of Florence Press), 2008. New edition of 2007.

2008, *Life of the Buddha: Buddhacarita by Aśvaghoṣa*. The Clay Sanskrit Library (New York: New York University Press).

2007, *Ascetics and Brahmins: Studies in Ideologies and Institutions* (Florence: University of Florence Press).

2006a, *Language, Texts, and Society: Explorations in Ancient Indian Culture and Religion* (Florence: University of Florence Press).

2006b, (Edited volume) *Between the Empires: Society in India 300 BCE to 400 CE* (New York: Oxford University Press).

2006c, *Five Discourses on Worldly Wisdom* (Text and Translation of the *Pañcatantra*). The Clay Sanskrit Library (New York: New York University Press).

2005a, *Dharmasūtra Parallels* (Delhi: Motilal Banarsidass).

2005b, *Manu's Code of Law: A Critical Edition and Translation of the Mānava-Dharmaśāstra* (New York: Oxford University Press).

2004a, (Edited volume) *Dharma: Studies in Its Semantic, Cultural, and Religious History*. Special double issue of *Journal of Indian Philosophy*, vol. 32.

2004b, *The Law Code of Manu* (based on the critical edition). Oxford World's Classics (Oxford: Oxford University Press).

2000, *The Dharmasūtras of Āpastamba, Gautama, Baudhāyana, and Vasiṣṭha*. Sanskrit editions and annotated translations. Sources of Indian Law, ed. Patrick Olivelle (Delhi: Motilal Banarsidass).

1999, *Dharmasūtras: The Law Codes of Ancient India* (annotated translation of the Dharmasūtras of Āpastamba, Gautama, Baudhāyana, and Vasiṣṭha). Oxford World's Classics (Oxford: Oxford University Press).

1998, *The Early Upaniṣads: Annotated Text and Translation.* (Sanskrit editions with variants, translation, and notes) South Asia Research Series (New York: Oxford University Press).

1997, *Pañcatantra: The Book of India's Folk Wisdom.* Oxford World's Classics (Oxford: Oxford University Press).

1996, *The Upaniṣads* (annotated translation of 12 early Upaniṣads). Oxford World's Classics (Oxford: Oxford University Press).

1995, *Rules and Regulations of Brahmanical Asceticism* (critical edition and translation of Yādava Prakāśa's *Yatidharmasamuccaya*) (Albany: State University of New York Press).
* Reprint: Sri Garib Dass Oriental Series no. 208 (Delhi: Indian Books Centre), 1997.

1993, *The Āśrama System: History and Hermeneutics of a Religious Institution* (New York: Oxford University Press).
* Reprint: New Delhi: Munshiram Manoharlal, 2004.

1992, *The Saṃnyāsa Upaniṣads: Hindu Scriptures on Asceticism and Renunciation* (New York: Oxford University Press).

1987, *Renunciation in Hinduism: A Medieval Debate.* Volume II: The Viśiṣṭādvaita Argument (Vienna, Austria: Institute for Indology, University of Vienna).

1986b, *Saṃnyāsapaddhati of Rudradeva.* Critically edited with introduction and notes (Madras: The Adyar Library and Research Center).

1986a, *Renunciation in Hinduism: A Medieval Debate.* Volume I: The Debate and The Advaita Argument (Vienna, Austria: Institute for Indology, University of Vienna).

1977, *Vāsudevāśrama Yatidharmaprakāśa. A Treatise on World Renunciation.* Part II: Annotated English Translation. Critically edited with introduction, annotated translation, and appendices (Vienna, Austria: Institute for Indology, University of Vienna).

1976, *Vāsudevāśrama Yatidharmaprakāśa. A Treatise on World Renunciation.* Part I: Sanskrit Text. Critically edited with introduction, annotated translation, and appendices (Vienna, Austria: Institute for Indology, University of Vienna).

1974, *The Origin and the Early Development of Buddhist Monachism* (Colombo, Sri Lanka: M.D. Gunasena).

Articles

2010a, "Dharmaśāstra: A Literary History" in *Cambridge Handbook of Law and Hinduism,* ed. T. Lubin and D. Davis (Cambridge: Cambridge University Press), 28-57.

2010b, "Āśrama and Saṃnyāsa" in *Brill's Encyclopedia of Hinduism,* ed. Knut A. Jacobsen, vol. 2 (Leiden: Brill).

2010c, "Āraṇyakas and Upaniṣads" in *Brill's Encyclopedia of Hinduism,* ed. Knut A. Jacobsen, vol. 2 (Leiden: Brill).

2010d, "Dharmaśāstra" in *Brill's Encyclopedia of Hinduism,* ed. Knut A. Jacobsen, vol. 2 (Leiden: Brill).

2009a, "Hindu Law: The Formative Period, 400 BCE-400 CE" in *Oxford International Encyclopedia of Legal History,* ed. Stanley N. Katz, vol. 3 (New York: Oxford University Press), 151-155.

2009b, "Manusmriti" in *Oxford International Encyclopedia of Legal His-*

tory, ed. Stanley N. Katz, vol. 4 (New York: Oxford University Press), 144-145.

2009c, "The Living and the Dead: Ideology and Social Dynamics of Ancestral Commemoration in India" in *The Anthropologist and the Native: Essays for Gananath Obeyesekere*, ed. H.L. Seneviratne (Florence: Società Editrice Fiorentina), 65-74.

2009d, "The Temple in Sanskrit Legal Literature" in *Archaeology and Text: The Temple in South Asia*, ed. H.P. Ray (Delhi: Oxford University Press).

2009e, "Study of South Asia in the American University," *Cracow Indological Studies*, nb. 10: 167-170.

2008a, "Celibacy in Classical Hinduism" in *Celibacy and Religious Traditions*, ed. Carl Olson (New York: Oxford University Press), 151-164.

2008b, "Orality, Memory, and Power: Vedic Scriptures and Brahmanical Hegemony in India" in *Theorizing Scriptures: New Critical Orientations to a Cultural Phenomenon*, ed. Vincent L. Wimbush (New Brunswick: Rutgers University Press), 214-219.

2007a, "Manu and Gautama: A Study in Śāstric Intertextuality" in *Expanding and Merging Horizons: Contributions to South Asian and Cross-Cultural Studies in Commemoration of Wilhelm Halbfass*, ed. K. Preisendanz. Österreichische Akademie der Wissenschaften (Vienna: Austrian Academy of Sciences Press), 681-692.

2007b, "The Term *vikrama* in the Vocabulary of Aśvaghoṣa" in *Pramāṇakīrtiḥ: Papers Dedicated to Ernst Steinkellner on the Occasion of his 70th Birthday*, ed. B. Kellner, et al., 2 volumes. Wiener Studien zur Tibetologie und Buddhismuskunde (Vienna: Arbeitskreis für Tibetsche und Buddhistische Studien), 587-595.

2007c, "On the Road: The Religious Significance of Walking" in *Theatrum Mirabiliorum Indiae Orientalis: A Volume to Celebrate the 70th Birthday of Professor Maria Krzysztof Byrski. Rocznik Orientalistyczny* 50: 173-187.

2007d, "The Date and Provenance of the *Viṣṇu-Smṛti:* On the Intersection between Text and Iconography," *Indologica Taurinensia* 33: 149-164.

2006a, "The Ascetic and the Domestic in Brahmanical Religiosity" in *Critics of Asceticism: Historical Accounts and Comparative Perspectives*, ed. Oliver Freiberger (New York: Oxford University Press), 25-42.

2006b, "Explorations in the Early History of Dharmaśāstra" in *Between the Empires: Society in India 300 BCE to 400 CE*, ed. Patrick Olivelle (New York: Oxford University Press), 169-190.

2006c, "Heart in the Upaniṣads," *Rivista di Studi Sudasiatici* (University of Rome), 1: 51-67.

2005, "Rebirth and Karma in Cross-Cultural Context." Gananath

Obeyesekere Volume in The Midweek Magazine of THE ISLAND. Wednesday 2, February 2005.

2004a, "Manu and the *Arthaśāstra:* A Study in Śāstric Intertextuality," *Journal of Indian Philosophy* 32: 281-91.

2004b, "Hair" in *Encyclopedia of Buddhism*, ed. Robert E. Buswell, 2 vols. (New York: Macmillan Reference), 313.

2004c, "Rhetoric and Reality: Women's Agency in the *Dharmaśāstras*" in *Encounters with the Word: Essays to Honour Aloysium Pieris*, ed. R. Crusz, M. Fernando, and A. Tilakaratne (Colombo: Ecumenical Institute for Study and Dialogue), 489-505.

2004d, "The Semantic History of *Dharma*: The Middle and Late Vedic Periods" in *Dharma: Studies in Its Semantic, Cultural, and Religious History*, ed. Patrick Olivelle. Special issue of *Journal of Indian Philosophy* 32: 491-511.

2003, "The Renouncer Traditions" in *The Companion to Hinduism*, ed. Gavin Flood (Oxford: Blackwell), 271-87.

2002a, "Structure and Composition of the *Mānava Dharmaśāstra*," *Journal of Indian Philosophy* 30: 535-74.

2002b, "*Abhakṣya* and *abhojya:* An Exploration in Dietary Language," *Journal of the American Oriental Society* 122: 345-54.

2002c, "Food for Thought: Dietary Regulations and Social Organization in Ancient India." 2001 Gonda Lecture (Amsterdam: Royal Netherlands Academy of Arts and Sciences).

2002d, Three essays on *Karma, Mokṣa*, and *Upaniṣads* in new edition of the Encyclopedia Brittanica.

2002e, "On Meat-Eaters and Grass-Eaters: An Exploration of Human Nature in Kathā and Dharma Literature" in *Holy War: Violence and the Bhagavad-gītā*, ed. Steven J. Rosen (Hampton, Virginia: Deepak Publishing), 99-116.

1999a, "Sanskrit Commentators and the Transmission of Texts: Haradatta on Āpastamba Dharmasūtra," *Journal of Indian Philosophy* 27: 551-74.

1999b, "Young Śvetaketu: A Literary Study of an Upaniṣadic Story," *Journal of the American Oriental Society* 119: 46-70.

1998a, "Caste and Purity: A Study in the Language of the Dharma Literature," *Contributions to Indian Sociology* 32: 190-216.

1998b, "Unfaithful Transmitters: Philological Criticism and Critical Editions of the Upaniṣads," *Journal of Indian Philosophy* 26: 173-87.

1998c, "Hair and Society: Social Significance of Hair in South Asian Traditions" in *Hair: Its Power and Meaning in Asian Cultures*, ed. Alf Hiltebeitel and Barbara D. Miller (New York: State University of New York Press), 11-49.

1997a, "*Amṛtā:* Women and Indian Technologies of Immortality," *Journal of Indian Philosophy* 25: 427-49.

1997b, "Orgasmic Rapture and Divine Ecstasy: The Semantic History of *ānanda*," *Journal of Indian Philosophy* 25: 153-80.

1996, "*Dharmaskandhāḥ* and *Brahmasaṃsthaḥ*: A Study of *Chāndogya Upaniṣad* 2.23.1," *Journal of the American Oriental Society* 116: 205-19.

1995a, "Hindu Asceticism" in *HarperCollins Dictionary of Religion*, ed. Jonathan Z. Smith (San Francisco: HarperCollins).

1995b, "Deconstruction of the Body in Indian Asceticism" in *Asceticism*, ed. Vincent L. Wimbush and Richard Valantasis (New York: Oxford University Press), 188-210.

1995c, "Ascetic Withdrawal or Social Engagement: The Inner Conflict in Indian Religions" in *Sources of Indian Religions*, ed. Donald S. Lopez (Princeton: Princeton University Press), 533-46.

1995d, "Food in India: A Review Essay," *Journal of Indian Philosophy* 23: 367-80.

1991, "From Feast to Fast: Food and the Indian Ascetic" in *Rules and Remedies in Classical Indian Law*, ed. Julia Leslie, Panels of the VIIth World Sanskrit Conference, vol. 9 (Leiden: E.J. Brill), 17-36.

1990, "Village vs. Wilderness: Ascetic Ideals and the Hindu World" in *Monasticism in the Christian and Hindu Traditions: A Comparative Study*, ed. Austin B. Creel and Vasudha Narayanan (Lewiston: Edwin Mellen Press), 125-160.

1987a, "King and Ascetic: State Control of Asceticism in the Arthaśāstra" in *Festschrift Ludo Rocher, Adyar Library Bulletin* 50: 39-59.

1987b, "Gananath Obeyesekere and the Study of Religion," *Contributions to Indian Sociology* (n.s.), 21: 29-35.

1986a, "Saṃnyāsa" in *The New Encyclopedia of Religion*, ed. Mircea Eliade, vol. 13 (New York: Macmillan & Co), 51-53.

1986b, "Rites of Passage: The Hindu Rites" in *The New Encyclopedia of Religion*, ed. Mircea Eliade, vol. 12 (New York: Macmillan & Co), 387-392.

1984a, "Function of Textual Tradition in *Sannyāsin* Orders" in *Identity and Division of Cults and Sects in South Asia*, ed. Peter Gaeffke and David A. Utz (Philadelphia: Dept. of South Asia Regional Studies, University of Pennsylvania), 45-57.

1984b, "Renouncer and Renunciation in the Dharmaśāstras" in *Studies in Dharmaśāstra*, ed. Richard Larivière (Calcutta: Firma KLM), 81-152.

1981a, "Ānandatīrtha's *Saṃnyāsapaddhati*: A Handbook for Madhvaite Ascetics," *Adyar Library Bulletin* 44-45: 293-303.

1981b, "Contributions to the Semantic History of *Saṃnyāsa*," *Journal of the American Oriental Society* 101: 265-274.

1981c, "*Praṇavamīmāṃsā*: A Newly Discovered Work of Vidyāraṇya," *Annals of the Bhandarkar Oriental Research Institute* 62: 75-101.

1980, "*Pañcamāśramavidhi*: Rite for Becoming a Naked Ascetic," *Wiener Zeitschrift für die Kunde Südasiens* 24: 129-145.

1978a, "Ritual Suicide and the Rite of Renunciation," *Wiener Zeitschrift für die Kunde Südasiens* 22: 19-44.

1978b, "The Integration of Renunciation by Orthodox Hinduism," *Journal of the Oriental Institute* 28: 27-36.
1976, "Odes of Renunciation," *Wiener Zeitschrift für die Kunde Südasiens* 20: 91-100.
1975, "A Definition of World Renunciation," *Wiener Zeitschrift für die Kunde Südasiens* 19: 75-83.
1974, "The Notion of Āśrama in the Dharmaśāstras," *Wiener Zeitschrift für die Kunde Südasiens* 18: 27-35.

I. Word, Text, Context

Timothy Lubin

The Elusive Snātaka[1]

Over a decade ago, Patrick Olivelle (1993: 220-221) drew attention to the fact that, with the general acceptance of the classical '*āśrama* system' in the *Manusmṛti* (ca. 2nd-3rd c.), the status of the *snātaka*, the graduate of Veda study who has taken the ritual bath that concludes studentship, was eclipsed.According to this system, the distinct 'occupations' (*āśrama*), such as student, householder, hermit, or wandering ascetic, were restricted to a fixed set of four and prescribed as a sequence of 'stages of life.' This meant that Veda study should properly be followed by marriage, which is the prerequisite for fulfilling the ritual obligations of the adult Ārya male.[2] Thus, although he was treated with deference and reverence, the *snātaka*, if he remained too long unmarried, ran the risk in later times of being condemned as an *anāśramin* (one without an *āśrama*). In fact, the notion of the *snātaka* as an unmarried graduate of Vedic study was ephemeral; the title soon came to be used to refer to a rather different status.

The *snātaka* appears in many types of sources in many periods; this article can only deal with a few, mainly Śāstric sources on domes-

[1] I take this opportunity to thank Patrick Olivelle for his advice and assistance over the past several years, and for the model he has provided for all who work on Dharmaśāstra; this article is presented in place of a *madhuparka*. A brief version was presented at the 216th Meeting of the American Oriental Society, where I received useful suggestions from him, as well as from Alf Hiltebeitel, Ashok Aklujkar, and others. The research was supported by a Fulbright-Hays research fellowship and a National Endowment for the Humanities fellowship, and was partly conducted while in residence as an affiliated researcher at the Institut français de Pondichéry.

[2] On the extension of the requirement of initiation and at least nominal Vedic study to all three of the upper *varṇas* as the justification of Ārya householder status, see also Lubin (2005; 2010).

tic ritual and *dharma*, plus some passages from the *Mahābhārata* (MBh). This is sufficient to document the ambiguity about this ritual and social role, and the process by which the distinct status of the *snātaka* became obscured in most of these sources, mainly on account of the success of the classical *āśrama* system, even as the *snātaka* ideal lived on as the type of the especially pious householder.[3]

The Ritual Construction of a Snātaka

In certain Gṛhyasūtras and in the Dharmasūtras,[4] the *snātaka* is set apart for special treatment. A long list of rules govern his conduct; some of these resemble the rules of *brahmacarya*, but the rules governing the *snātaka*—the *snātaka-vratāni* or *snātaka-dharmāḥ*—are distinctive in many respects. For example, according to the Dharmasūtras the *snātaka*, like the *brahmacārin*, obtains food by asking for it from others, but this is meant to be uncooked foodstuffs rather than true *bhikṣā* (which is the remnants of cooked food). The texts state that he may beg for food only from the king—or from a pupil (VDhS 12.2), or from gods, elders, and the righteous (GDhS 9.63)—unless he is really languishing (*avasīdet*) from hunger (VDhS 12.3-4).

The *snātaka* is assigned different equipment, including a turban, a water pot, sandals, and parasol; he should wear a double sacred thread, and his staff should be of bamboo. The turban however is also a distinctive attribute of the *dīkṣita*, who like the student undergoes an initiation (*dīkṣopāyana*) similar in many ways to the *upanayana/upāyana* rite, and who must adhere to a strict regimen. In fact, PGS 2.8.9 says that a *soma-dīkṣita* observes the same *vrata*s as a *snātaka.* Unlike the *brahmacārin*, the *snātaka* is allowed to anoint and adorn himself, though not when he will appear in public. He should maintain his own worship fire (*aupāsana agni*), in which he should offer the new and full moon services, etc.

The sanctity of the *snātaka* is ensured by a long list of restrictions on his speech and conduct. These restrictions are not organized in any particular order, but considered as a group they imply that the *snātaka* is vulnerable to dangers both to his bodily person, his sacred purity, and his social status. To ensure his bodily safety, he must not climb onto a cart or into a tree, climb up to or down from precarious spots (*viṣamārohaṇāvarohaṇa*), cross a river by swimming

[3] Even as a literary trope, the *snātaka* is absent in several landmark works, including the Vālmīka *Rāmāyaṇa*.

[4] The following Sūtra and Śāstra works are cited below (with abbreviations in parentheses): *Kāṭhakagṛhyasūtra* (KGS), *Mānavagṛhyasūtra* (MGS), *Baudhāyanagṛhyasūtra* (BGS), *Baudhāyanagṛhyaparibhāṣāsūtra* (BGPS), *Āgniveśyagṛhyasūtra* (ĀgGS), *Pāraskaragṛhyasūtra* (PGS), *Gobhilagṛhyasūtra* (GGS), *Jaiminīyagṛhyasūtra* (JGS), *Vaikhānasasmārtasūtra* (VaiSmS), *Āpastambadharmasūtra* (ĀpDhS), *Gautamadharmasūtra* (GDhS), *Baudhāyanadharmasūtra* (BDhS), *Vasiṣṭhadharmasūtra* (VDhS), *Mānavadharmaśāstra* (Manu), *Yājñavalkyasmṛti* (YājñSm).

or in an unsafe boat, submerge his head in water, descend into wells, use dangerous roads, or even crack his knuckles.[5] New-moon days present a special risk because at that time the sun (which protects creatures during the day) and the moon (which does so at night) dwell together; he should call on Rudra as Vāstoṣpati, 'Lord of the Dwelling-Place,' for protection if he enters the village by a dangerous road (ĀpDhS 1.31.19-21).

Other rules are intended to protect his purity (covering the head at night and when answering the call of nature) and his austere self-control (avoiding dancing, singing, and "anger or other faults that bring suffering to creatures," *krodhādīṃś ca bhūtadāhīyān doṣān varjayet,* ĀpDhS 1.31.23). He may not go to a sacrifice unless asked to officiate (VDhS 12.42), although attending as a spectator (i.e., without seeking food or gifts) is allowed. He should avoid using sacred grass or wood for profane purposes such as covering his feces or picking his teeth.

In some cases it seems just a matter of etiquette: he should not boast in his teacher's presence, make noise with his mouth while eating (VDhS 12.20), extend his feet toward fire, water, brahmin, cow, image, door, or into wind, appear in public with garland or anointed (GDhS: unless a garland of gold). He must be especially circumspect as regards the sun and cows: he must not look at the sun as it rises or sets, or bathe after sunset. He must not touch brahmins or cows with his foot, or even with his hand without good cause, and he should not step over a calf's tether.

In order to avoid association with impure, vulgar, or disreputable people, a *snātaka* must not visit gambling houses, fairs, markets, cities, or anywhere where bad people are. He should always behave like an Ārya, adhering to the rules of purification (GDhS 9.69, 71). This means not losing control (GDhS 9.50, 73) and never hurting any creature.

Especially notable in these lists of rules are the taboos, both general and specific, on his speech. General restrictions include a ban on speaking harshly about gods, the king, or cows, even to report a cow causing damage or suckling her calf (at a time when her milk is wanted for human consumption). He should not spread gossip (GDhS 9.53). ĀpDhS 1.32.22-24 even discourages him from resolving a dispute, since if he resolves it wrongly (*durvivaktṛ*) it can harm his own interests.[6]

Specific restrictions include a glossary of prescribed euphemisms. He should say:

sraj ('garland,' a Vedic and thus high-register term) instead of *mālā* (a word perhaps of Dravidian origin);

[5] ĀpDhS 1.32.25-27; VDhS 12.25-26; GDhS 9.51.

[6] *praśnaṃ ca na vibrūyāt;* Olivelle (2000: 73) renders this as 'Neither should he elucidate a question,' but the following stanza (supported by Haradatta's commentary, also cited by Olivelle) makes it clear that *praśnaṃ vi-brū-/vi-vac-* has the technical sense 'to settle a dispute or resolve a point of contention.'

bhagāla ('earthen cup') instead of *kapāla* ('earthen cup; skull'), the latter of which can have an inauspicious meaning;[7]

puṇya ('holy') or *praśāsta* ('commendable') instead of *bhadra* ('good'), which may be a case of using a more dignified-sounding word in place of a common one;

maṇidhanus ('jewel-bow, i.e., rainbow') instead of the synonym *indradhanus*, perhaps to avoid using Indra's name casually;

dhenubhavyā ('cow that is going to give milk') instead of *adhenu* ('non-milk-giving cow').

He should not call his adversary a *sapatna* ('adversary'), lest he make of him a true rival who hates him (*dviṣantaṃ bhrātṛvyam*) (ĀpDhS 1.31.15). Nor should he pronounce the name of a god while he is impure. All of these circumlocutions are meant to preserve the dignity and auspiciousness of the *snātaka*.

This special dignity is exhibited in the fact that he is generally listed as a potential recipient of the *madhuparka* (a mixture of honey with milk, curd, or water) and *arghya* (scented water), offerings due to worthy guests. The lists of recipients for each of these tend to be similar; one of the older examples: "There are six individuals worthy of the *arghya*: a teacher, a priest, a king, a suitor, a friend, a *snātaka*" (*ṣaḍ arghyārhā bhavanty ācārya ṛtvig rājā vivāhyaḥ priyaḥ snātaka iti*, KGS 24.1).[8] BGS 1.2.65 has a longer list, which adds father-in-law, paternal uncle, maternal uncle, and guest (*tathaite arghyā ṛtvik śvaśuraḥ pitṛvyo mātula ācāryo rājā vā snātakaḥ priyo varo 'tithir iti*).[9]

While the Dharmasūtras all recommend that those invited to partake of a *śrāddha* offering be pious and learned brahmins, preferably unrelated to the offerer,[10] BDhS 2.14.2-4 makes special mention of the *snātaka* as a suitable choice, along with men distinguished by extraordinary learning or the most advanced forms of ritual practice: those who maintain five fires, who recite the various sets of mystical verses, who perform a 'head regimen,' or who have studied the six subjects ancillary to the Veda. The 'one who knows the secret texts' is offered as an alternative. The *snātaka*, like the others mentioned, deserves to receive the invitations because of the principle that "the verses, formulas, and songs [of the three Vedas] are what makes the *śrāddha* great; therefore, he should feed a man who knows these, even if he is a relative."[11] The

[7] Burrow (1982: 188); *bhagāla* acquires the meaning 'skull' only later, in imitation of the secondary meaning of *kapāla*. However, the older, more basic sense of both words is probably meant in the ritual codes and Dharmasūtras, *pace* Olivelle, commenting on GDhS 9.21 (2000: 544).

[8] Cf. (with different sequences): MGS 1.9.1; PGS 1.1.3; VDhS 11.1. Some lists omit the *snātaka*: e.g., GDhS.

[9] The placement of the word *vā* in the edition suggests that the last three items in the list were an addition.

[10] ĀpDhS 2.17.4-15, 2.18.9-16, 2.20.2; GDhS 15.6-20; BDhS 2.14.6; VDhS 11.17-35.

[11] *trimadhus triṇāciketas trisuparṇaḥ pañcāgniḥ ṣaḍaṅgavic chīrṣako jyeṣṭhasāmakaḥ snātaka iti paṅktipāvanāḥ || tadabhāve rahasyavit || ṛco yajūṃṣi sāmānīti śrāddhasya mahimā | tasmād evaṃvidaṃ sapiṇḍam apy āśayet ||*

other individuals listed here are men who have studied secret, mystical doctrines and mantras, and who have consequently subjected themselves to special *vratas*. These accomplishments confer upon them the capacity to purify the lineages of those who feed them.

Similarly, in describing the *baliharaṇa*, BGS 2.9.17 (and ĀgGS 2.6.5, which is parallel here) lists the *snātaka* alongside "one who follows the same mode of life as one's guru, a *vaikhānasa*, or a righteous king." Into this list, BGS adds a householder, a forest-dweller, a wandering mendicant, or a wealthy man,[12] thus making it clear that it distinguishes between the *snātaka* and the householder. Moreover, in terms of venerability, the *snātaka* compares favorably with even the most august of worldly figures, for VDhS 13.59 goes so far as to say: "If a king and a *snātaka* meet, the king should give way to the *snātaka*" (*rājasnātakayor samāgame rājñā snātakāya deyaḥ*).[13]

Classes of Snātaka

Some Gṛhyasūtras distinguish three categories of graduate: the 'graduate of the Veda' (*vidyā-snātaka* or *veda-snātaka*), the 'graduate of the Regimen' (*vrata-snātaka*), and the 'graduate of the Veda and the Regimen' (*vidyā-vrata-snātaka* or *veda-vrata-snātaka*; e.g., BGPS 1.15.1 and also ĀpDhS 1.30.1-5). GGS 3.5.21-23 (cited by JGS 1.19) further specifies that, "of these, the last is best, while the former two are equal" (*teṣām uttamaḥ śreṣṭhas tulyau pūrvau*). This acknowledges the two relevant factors that give the *snātaka* his high status: his sacred expertise and his ritual, disciplinary accomplishments. Although they are meant to go together, this precept acknowledges the real possibility that someone might succeed in one but not the other. The ideal of course is the third type—one who has done both. Nevertheless, it seems that any one of the three 'counts' as a *snātaka* for the purposes of rites like *madhuparka* or *baliharaṇa*, even if the fruits of honoring them vary in degree according to the degree of learning (*śruti*) and discipline (*samādhi*) of the recipient.[14]

The Snātaka *as Distinct from the Householder*

The passages I have mentioned so far treat the *snātaka* as distinct from the householder. A couple more might be cited. In the *Śrāddhasūtra*, a *pariśiṣṭa* (appendix) to the PGS, *snātakas* are men-

[12] BGS 2.9.21 also inserts an alternate rule: "One should welcome all who come calling, including dogs and Cāṇḍālas" (*sarvebhyo 'bhyāgatebhya ā śvacāṇḍālebhyaḥ svāgataṃ kāryam*).

[13] Following Olivelle's translation. Some version of this rule may be the basis for the *Kāśikāvṛtti*'s citation (ad *Aṣṭādhyāyī* 2.2.31) of *snātakarājānau* as a recognizable illustration of a *dvandva* compound.

[14] ĀpDhS 1.30.4-5: *teṣu sarveṣu snātakavad vṛttiḥ | samādhiviśeṣāc chrutiviśeṣāc ca pūjāyāṃ phalaviśeṣaḥ |*

tioned—along with "ascetics (*yati*), or virtuous householders, who are aged, learned (*śrotriya*), and blameless, and devoted to their proper activities"—as suitable to be invited to a *śrāddha* offering, according to some: *yad ahaḥ saṃpadyeta tad ahar brāhmaṇān āmantrya pūrve dyur vā | snātakān eke yatīn gṛhasthān sādhūn vā śrotriyān vṛddhān anavadyānt svakarmasthān* | (Bākre 1917: 423). The *snātaka* is thus distinguished both from the professional ascetic (*yati*) and the virtuous householder (*gṛhastha*).[15] Even Gadādhara, ca. 1500, could regard the option of inviting *snātaka*s as an exception to the prohibition on inviting unmarried guests (*ayaṃ cāpatnīkanimantraṇapratiṣedhe pratiprasavaḥ*; he cites the rule of Atri [Bākre 1917: 427]).

We find a rare instance of an explicit definition of the *snātaka*'s separate status, between student and householder, in BGPS 1.15.10: "Until being united with a wife, they are 'graduates' (*snātaka*s); after that, 'householders' (*gṛhastha*s), so that there be no gap" (*ā jāyāsaṅgamāt snātakā bhavanty ata ūrdhvaṃ gṛhasthā avicchedāya*).[16] The distinctions between them, and the notion that the *snātaka* is an intermediate or even liminal status between student and householder, is suggested by the different modes of worship in the three states:

> BGPS 1.16.4-7:
> *yasminn agnāv upanayati tasmin vratacaryaṃ tasmin samāvartanaṃ tasmin pāṇigrahaṇaṃ tasmin gṛhyāṇi karmāṇi kriyante tasmin kāmyāni karmāṇi tasmin prajāsaṃskārā ity eke* |
> *sa eṣa upanayanaprabhṛti vyāhṛtibhiḥ samidbhir hūyata ā samāvartanāt* |
> *samāvartanaprabhṛty ājyena vyāhṛtibhir eva hūyata ā pāṇigrahaṇāt* |
> *pāṇigrahaṇaprabhṛti vrīhibhir yavair vā* |
>
> 4. The fire in which the initiation rite is performed is the fire in which the student's regimen-duties, the going-home rite, the wedding, and all the householder rites are performed. Some add: wish-fulfilling rites and childhood consecrations [are performed] in it.
> 5. It is this in which, beginning with the initiation, offerings are made with the Utterances and with kindling sticks, up until the *samāvartana*.

[15] The subsequent adjectives apparently are meant to qualify those members of all three classes who might be considered worthy invitees.

[16] The next sentence seems to propose an alternative to marriage (BGPS 1.15.11): "Or else he should pass his time by [observing] *vedavrata*s, e.g. [the *vrata*] of Kumāra, Maheśvara, [or] Dhanvantari" (*vedavratair vā viharet kaumāreṇa māheśvareṇa dhānvantareṇeti*). In the Mysore edition (all versions), this sentence begins *avicchedāya vedavratair vyavaharet*, but Muddudīkṣita's 1905 Grantha edition prints *vā viharet*. A check of two manuscripts at hand—Natl. Arch. Kathmandu 5-657 (Devanagari, f. 45v) and Mysore ORI P4559 (Nandinagari, f. 57v)—supports this reading. The position of *vā* suggests that *avicchedāya* must belong to the preceding sentence, as the 1905 edition indeed has it. Without comment or warrant, Gonda (1977a: 181) seems to translate *devavratair* instead of *vedavratair*: "For the sake of continuity he should carry on observances with regard to gods, viz. Kumāra, Maheśvara, (and) Dhanvantari." The sequence *kaumāreṇa māheśvareṇa dhānvantareṇeti* looks to have been inserted, perhaps later, as a clarification or set of examples of possible *vrata*s that might be followed by a *snātaka* who was a votary of one of these deities. A *vidyā-vrata-snāta* is said to observe the *kaumāraṃ vratam* at MBh 3.93.16, though here it is probably a synonym for *brahmacarya*.

6. Beginning with the *samāvartana*, offerings are made with ghee and with the Utterances, up until the wedding.
7. Beginning with the wedding, [offerings are made] with rice or barley.

The devotions of the student consist only of the holy Utterances *oṃ bhūr bhuvaḥ svaḥ*, with the firewood serving as an offering to Agni, the 'Lord of the Vrata.' The *snātaka* makes simple homas with ghee and the Utterances, but only the married householder is entitled to make the full grain offerings.

Here we should note the similarity of the *snātaka*'s ritual practice to that of certain other vocations, the *vānaprastha* or the *yati*, in which the Vedic rites may take a simplified and partly interiorized form. A *prayoga* of the Vaikhānasa tradition prescribes that the *prāṇāgnihotra*, an interiorized, spiritual *agnihotra*, be performed by a *naiṣṭika-snātaka*, a 'perpetual *snātaka*,'[17] which reminds us of the better-known *naiṣṭika-brahmacārin*, who spends his life under the tutelage and in the service of a teacher.

The Married Snātaka *(and the Benefits of Adult Education Rejected)*

Intimations of a married *snātaka* begin to appear in the latest Gṛhyasūtras and in the Dharmasūtras. VaiSmS 5.9 prescribes the 'cremation-in-distress' (*āpad-dāhya*) for a list of persons who ordinarily would not qualify for cremation. The intent seems to be to compensate for the misfortune that attends those who, for various reasons, are excluded from ordinary sacrificial performances. The list begins with the *snātaka* and also includes a widower, a newly tonsured or recently teethed boy, a prepubescent or otherwise childless widow, a woman who has died in pregnancy or childbirth, an amenorrheic woman, one who has aborted a fetus, a woman responsible for the death of her husband or son, a woman abandoned by a *dīkṣita*, and various other sufferers of misfortune.

The same passage may also acknowledge that a *snātaka* might be married. It proposes, for "a Self-worshiping *snātaka* who has not yet reached the householder state, or one whose wife has died" (*ātmayājī snātako 'prāptagṛhavṛtto mṛtadāro vā*), as well as for an unmarried woman, a token marriage to be performed before the cremation "so that his *brahman* may not be fruitless for him" (*tasya ha vai tad brahma viphalaṃ mā bhūd iti*).[18] In this case, the author

[17] *Vaikhānasagṛhyaprayogavṛtti* 8.3, cited by Gonda (1977b: 563).

[18] Caland (1929) understands this sequence of nominatives to denote three different subjects: a *yati* (mentioned already in 5.8), an unmarried *snātaka*, and a widower. While there is admittedly some possibility of ambiguity here, the two final adjectival compounds must mark a distinction between two conditions of the same class of person (Caland supplies *gṛhastha* as referent of the second in his translation), and, as Caland recognizes, *aprāptagṛhavṛtto* must modify *snātako*. Furthermore, although the word *ātmayājin* is applied to the *yati* in 5.8, it also applies to the *snātaka* (as per 2.18).

seems to recognize the word *snātaka* as applicable equally to an unmarried or a married graduate—unless *mṛtadāraḥ* is meant to designate some other person than the *snātaka*. In any case, it would seem that the 'fruit of *brahman*' here means offspring, as if the expected sequel to Veda study is marriage and procreation.

ĀpDhS 1.13.18-20 quotes Śvetaketu stating that even after marriage, a graduate may (if he wish) spend two months of the year in the teacher's home, continuing his studies. "For by that means I managed to study more of the Veda than during the time I was a student." "But," the Sūtra goes on to point out, "that is forbidden by authoritative texts." For the ĀpDhS, the duties of the householder, even though he be a *snātaka*, are restricted to offering fire sacrifices and hospitality.

The Position of the Snātaka *Rules in the Dharma Literature*

The Dharmasūtras seem to reflect divergent and inconsistent assumptions about the *snātaka*. ĀpDhS, perhaps the oldest,[19] presents the rules on the *snātaka* (1.30-32) after the discussion of studentship and immediately before the marriage rules. Despite leaving the home of the teacher, the *samāvṛtta* was in some respects still subject to the rules governing students. For example, ĀpDhS 1.7.31-1.8.1 states that, "even after he has returned home, the accepted practice is that he should behave towards these individuals [viz., the teacher, the teacher's family, and senior students] in exactly the same manner as a student" (*samāvṛttasyāpy etad eva sāmayācārikam eteṣu | yathā brahmacārino vṛttam*). But from his dress it is clear that the *snātaka*, with his sandals and turban, is understood. ĀpDhS 1.32 contains several references to marriage and sexual relations (that he should not sleep in a woman's bed through the night, but that he should adorn himself at night for his wife). This section applies to one engaged in teaching, and to Veda recitation; it is not explicit that the *snātaka* is the intended subject.

BDhS 1.5-7 includes a short description of the *snātaka* (dwelling at length on the water pot) immediately after the rules of studentship, but then there follow, from 1.8, purity rules of general applicability. The *snātaka* is not mentioned again until a section headed '*snātakavratāni*' (2.5.10-2.6.42) appears in the midst of a chapter on the duties of a householder. This *snātaka* section seems to have been included here simply because the preceding *sūtra*s concern bathing (2.5.1-7). After this apparent insertion, the description of householder rites associated with bathing continues (2.7-10).

VDhS 12 takes it as a matter of course not only that the *snātaka* may have licit sexual relations (which is implied in the specific

[19] On the relative chronology of the Dharmasūtras, see Olivelle (2000: 4-10).

prohibition of sex with certain types of women), but that he will be married and begetting children:[20]

> VDhS 12.21-24:
> *ṛtukālagāmī syāt parvavarjaṃ svadāreṣu || nātīrtham upeyāt || athāpy udāharanti |*
> *yas tu pāṇigṛhītāyā āsye kurvīta maithunam |*
> *bhavanti pitaras tasya tanmāsaṃ retaso bhujaḥ |*
> *yā syād anaticāreṇa ratiḥ sā dharmasaṃśritā ||*
> *api ca kāṭhake vijñāyate | api naḥ śvo vijaniṣyamāṇāḥ patibhiḥ saha śayīrann iti strīṇām indradatto vara iti ||*
>
> He should engage in sexual intercourse with his wife during her [fertile] season, avoiding the days of the moon's change. Let him not have intercourse in a place other than the vagina. Now, they also quote:
> "If a man performs the sex act in the mouth of a woman he has married, during that month his ancestors will feed on his semen. Intercourse performed without going beyond (the vagina) is in conformity with Dharma."
> It is moreover, stated in the *Kāṭhaka*: "May we lie with our husbands even when we are going to give birth the following day." This is the wish granted to women by Indra (cf. VDhS 5.8).

GDhS 9 likewise seems explicitly to treat the *snātaka*-rules as subsidiary to those of the householder:

> GDhS 1.9.1-2:
> *sa vidhipūrvakaṃ snātvā bhāryām adhigamya yathoktān gṛhasthadharmān prayuñjāna imāni vratāny anukarṣet |*
> [*snātako*][21] *nityaṃ śuciḥ sugandhiḥ snānaśīlaḥ* | ...
>
> That man, after he has completed his studies, should bathe according to the rules, marry a wife, and, as he continues to observe the Laws proper to a householder described above, subject himself to the following vows: [a *snātaka*], constantly pure, sweet-smelling, regularly bathed ...

What follows is a version of the usual set of rules for the *snātaka*. The fact that these rules are introduced after the rules of the householder was, perhaps, perceived as potentially confusing. The intention in so ordering them may indeed be reflected in the transition sentence, which situated the *snātaka* rules in relation to the marriage and householder rules. Even the insertion of the word '*snātaka*'—not found in all manuscripts—suggests a felt need to clarify the relevance of the rules that follow.

[20] The *Kāśikāvṛtti* ad *Aṣṭādhyāyī* 6.2.1 offers *snātakaputra* ('son of a snātaka') as an example of a *tatpuruṣa* compound.

[21] This word, omitted by Stenzler, appears in the commentaries of both Maskarin and Haradatta (the latter in fact reading *snātakaś ca*), in quotations in the *Mitākṣarā* and *Kṛtyakalpataru* digest, and in the Ānandāśrama edition.

The commentators' uncertainty over this passage is telling. Maskarin takes the word *snātaka* as closing the first *sūtra*, explaining that "the householder who should perform the observances that are about to be discussed is called '*snātaka*'" (*snātaka ity asyopādānaṃ saṃjñārthaṃ yo vakṣyamāṇavratāny anutiṣṭhed asau gṛhasthaḥ snātaka ity ucyata iti* | *anyathā sa vidhipūrvaṃ snātvety anenaiva siddhatvān na vaktavyam*). Haradatta, by contrast, adds the word 'and,' thus indicating that the following rules apply to two distinct classes of individual.[22] Olivelle, agreeing with Maskarin, states that "a Snātaka is not always different from a householder but is a very specific type of householder" (2000: 543 n. 9.2), and adopts the *Mitākṣarā*'s view, reading *snātako* as the first word of the second *sūtra*.

The notion that the *snātaka may* be and ultimately *should* be married is probably the reason why the *snātakadharma* section comes where it does in the GDhS. But we should also recognize that it forms a coherent unit, tied to the preceding discussion of the householder life by a single crucial transitional statement, while in other works it stands between the sections on studentship and householdership.

To summarize, in the Dharmasūtras, the rules pertaining to the *snātaka*, though connected in the first instance to the sections on studentship, tend to be treated as applying to pious householders generally. As an originally distinct status, however, the *snātaka* necessarily ends up overlapping with the category of the householder, and the rules themselves get patched together in such a way that it is no longer easy to tell whether a distinction between the two is still recognized.

In the *Mānavadharmaśāstra* (4.13-257), the subsuming of the *snātaka* rules within the householder framework is formally completed. Chapter 4 as a whole contains a complex interleafing of *snātaka* rules and other prescriptions on brahmin conduct in general. The net effect is to recast the *snātaka*'s distinctive traits as a special, supererogatory part of householder piety.

The "transitional verses" (as Olivelle calls them), which open and close this section, knitting it into the larger program of the work as a whole, clearly state that the contents of this chapter pertain to the twice-born *gṛhastha*. Those stanzas in Manu that actually parallel the *snātaka-vrata* sections of the Gṛhyasūtras and Dharmasūtras are framed by blocks of verses speaking of householder virtues more generally.

The special significance of the *snātaka-dharma*s is specified in the penultimate stanza of the chapter:

Manu 4.259:
eṣoditā gṛhasthasya vṛttir viprasya śāśvatī |
snātakavratakalpaś ca sattvavṛddhikaraḥ śubhaḥ ||

[22] Bühler adopts this view in his translation (1879: 218-219).

> This, the constant mode of life of a brahmin householder, has here been explained, and the splendid practice of the *snātaka*-rule, which increases his purity.

This promiscuous mingling of *snātaka-dharma*s and general rules of brahmin conduct thus reflects the stages by which the *snātaka*'s status got subsumed within that of the *gṛhastha*. The outcome of this process can be seen in commentators' remarks on the *snātakadharma* sections. The *Mitākṣarā* begins this section by observing:

> *Mitākṣarā* ad YājñSm 1.129:
> *evaṃ śrautasmārtāni karmāṇy abhidhāyedānīṃ gṛhasthasya snānād ārabhya brāhmaṇasyāvaśyakartavyāni vidhipratiṣedhātmakāni mānasasaṃkalpāṇi snātakavratāny āha* |
>
> After thus setting forth the *śrauta* and *smārta* rites, [Yājñavalkya] now states the observances of the *snātaka*, which consist of injunctions and prohibitions, are given form by a mental resolution, and are indispensable duties of [every] brahmin, beginning with the bath of a householder.

Similarly, Harihara, commenting (before 1250 CE) on the prescription of a special three-night *vrata* to follow the graduation bath (PGS 2.8.1), says of all the preceding rules, which are the general rules governing the *snātaka*:

> *evaṃ snātakasya samāvartanaprabhṛti* ***yāvad gārhasthyaṃ*** *kartavyatvena varjanīyatvena ca nṛtyagītādīny abhidhāya ...*
>
> Thus, beginning with the returning-home of the *snātaka*, [rules about] such things as dancing and singing are indicated by prescriptions and prohibitions, **as long as householdership continues**.

In this view, he is followed also by Gadādhara (ca. 1500 CE).

Later digests even generalize the *snātaka*'s virtues more broadly. For a single instance, Gopīnātha Dīkṣita, in discussing the rules for the clothing and accoutrements of the *snātaka*, remarks that "where there is no impediment, these should be considered the general duties of students, householders, etc." (*asati bādhaka ete dharmā brahmacārigṛhasthādisādhāraṇā jñeyāḥ*).[23]

A Special Type of Pious Householder

On the other hand, the many allusions, from the Gṛhyasūtras onward, to the special sanctity and piety of a *snātaka* require us to doubt that this status was ever simply merged with that of an ordinary householder in the Dharmaśāstra. The impression that the

[23] *Saṃskāraratnamālā* (Bhaṭṭagopīnāthadīkṣita 1899: 388).

word denotes something different and special is reinforced when we look to other types of sources. Outside of the Sūtras and Śāstras, the *snātaka* in fact seems to represent a specially self-disciplined householder who observes supererogatory *vratas*.

The *Agnipurāṇa* (364.10b) defines the word thus: "a *snātaka* is one who, having bathed, observes *vratas*" (*snātakaś cāplutavratī*).[24] The particularly close association between the rites of the householder and the regimen of the *snātaka* is reinforced in this work in the section on expiations, which prescribes that "not eating [is the expiation] if one violates the *snātaka* regimen, for that is the abandonment of the ritual duties [of a householder]" (*snātakavratalope ca karmatyāge hy abhojanaṃ*, 170.14ab).

The term is used in precisely this sense in the *Mahābhārata* (MBh). For instance, as the despondent Drupada wanders the world, he comes to the forest hermitage of Yaja and Upayaja:

> MBh 1.155.6:
> *tatra nāsnātakaḥ kaś cin na cāsīd avratī dvijaḥ* |
> *tathaiva nāmahābhāgaḥ so 'paśyat saṃśitavratau* ||
>
> In that place, there was no brahmin who was not a *snātaka*, no one who did not observe *vratas*, and who was not most distinguished. He saw those two who strictly followed their regimen.

Snātakas in the MBh are often said to be *gṛhasthas* and *gṛhamedhins* ('performing the domestic offerings').[25]

The most revealing epic testimony comes from the episode of the 'killing of Jarāsandha' (*Jarāsandhavadha*) in MBh 2.18-22.[26] Arjuna and Bhīma present themselves, with Kṛṣṇa, as brahmin *snātakas* before King Jarāsandha, who duly welcomes them with foot-washing water and *madhuparka* (2.19.29). In stanzas that follow in the southern recension, it is noted that Arjuna and Bhīma are observing a *vrata* of not speaking before midnight, perhaps reflecting the rule of not giving instruction until that time.[27]

Alf Hiltebeitel has recently hypothesized that Aśvaghoṣa may have consciously modeled his account in *Buddhacarita* 10-11 on the *Jarāsandhavadha* (Hiltebeitel 2006). In both cases, the story involves kṣatriyas disguising themselves as holy men, entering the capital of Magadha, and meeting the king. In Aśvaghoṣa's poem, it is the Bodhisattva, in the attire of a monk, who is confronted by King Śreṇya-Bimbisāra and enters into a debate on Dharma. Hiltebeitel judges Aśvaghoṣa to have made a "close and critical reading" of the

[24] This and the surrounding stanzas are reproduced with little variation in the *Amarakośa*: *snātakas tv āpluto vratī*, 2.6.900b.

[25] MBh 12.1.5; 2.45.17 = 2.48.39 = 3.222.41.

[26] Ten of the twenty-three instances of the term *snātaka* in the MBh occur in Book 2.

[27] E.g., ĀpDhS 1.32.14: *ūrdhvam ardharātrād adhyāpanam*.

Jarāsandha episode. If this were indeed the case, it is striking that he would seem to have considered the *snātaka* a Brahmanical analogue of the Buddhist monk, that is, as personifying the ideal of Dharma, so as to be the paradigmatic recipient of respectful offerings.

The significance which he finds in that context is borne out by the fact that in many of the other instances in this epic, *snātaka*s are repeatedly specified to be brahmins.[28] Likewise, as brahmins, they are also spiritual and moral exemplars, formulaically described as 'possessing a great soul' (*mahātman*), once with the further attribute of 'eating alms-food' (*bhikṣābhuj*).[29] This rule that *snātaka*s were generally expected to be brahmins is confirmed, in a way, by the development of the *Jarāsandhava* episode. The king perceives (MBh 2.19.37-40) that these *snātaka*s must not be brahmins, since they are wearing colored clothes and are adorned with sandal paste and garlands (*virāgavasanā bahirmālyānulepanāḥ*).[30] He also notes that they entered the city through the wrong gate,[31] and that, "bearing a martial vigor" (*bibhrataḥ kṣātram ojaḥ*) rather than a priestly demeanor, their hands are marked by the bowstring. He reproaches them for disguising themselves (*vigarhamāṇaḥ* ... *veṣagrahaṇakāraṇāt*), saying:

> MBh 2.19.38:
> *na snātakavratā viprā bahirmālyānulepanāḥ* |
> *bhavantīti nṛloke 'smin viditaṃ mama sarvaśaḥ* ||
>
> I know that everywhere in this world of men brahmins observing the *snātaka-vrata*s do not openly wear garlands and ointment.

Kṛṣṇa, admitting that they are kṣatriyas, insists that they are *snātaka*s all the same, offering a pseudo-Śāstric analysis that is at once mocking and dripping with irony:

[28] *brāhmaṇa*: MBh 1.11.8; 2.18.22; 2.19.31; 3.47.6; 12.45.5; *vipra*: 2.19.38; 13.98.20. Besides these, the adjective *dvija* or *dvijāti* is sometimes used; this conceivably could include any of the upper *varṇa*s, but it is typically used as a synonym for 'brahmin' (Lubin 2005: 87-88): 12.1.5; 13.98.20; see 1.155.6, discussed above. Only stanzas included in the main text of the Poona critical edition are used here.

[29] MBh 1.11.8 (*snātakānāṃ* ... *bhikṣābhujāṃ brāhmaṇānāṃ mahātmanāṃ*); 3.47.6; 4.65.16; 12.1.5-6; 12.45.5; 12.124.11. Only BDhS 1.5.10 allows the *snātaka* to seek or receive *bhaikṣa*, i.e., cooked food sought as alms; otherwise he may obtain only uncooked food (BDhS 1.5.9-9); VDhS 12.2-4 sanctions only asking the king or one's pupil for the means of subsistence. However, in general terms, *bhikṣā* is the emblem of the pious vocation—hence the general term for a Buddhist monk: *bhikṣu*.

[30] This reasoning is supported, with strikingly similar wording, by ĀpDhS 1.30.10 and 1.32.5: "As regards clothes, he should avoid any that are colored ... He should not appear in public garlanded or anointed" (*sarvān rāgān vāsasi varjayet* ... *anāviḥsraganulepaṇaḥ syāt*). There is no indication that this applies only to brahmins, although there may be an tacit assumption that *snātaka*s are, in practice, brahmins.

[31] Perhaps an allusion to the rule that *snātaka*s should enter a settlement by the east or north (e.g., ĀpDhS 1.30.7).

MBh 2.19.45-50:
snātakavratino rājan brāhmaṇāḥ kṣatriyā viśaḥ |
viśeṣaniyamāś caiṣām aviśeṣāś ca santy uta ||
viśeṣavāṃś ca satataṃ kṣatriyaḥ śriyam arcati |
puṣpavatsu dhruvā śrīś ca puṣpavantas tato vayam ||
kṣatriyo bāhuvīryas tu na tathā vākyavīryavān |
apragalbhaṃ vacas tasya tasmād bārhadrathe smṛtam ||
svavīryaṃ kṣatriyāṇāṃ ca bāhvor dhātā nyaveśayat |
tad didṛkṣasi ced rājan draṣṭāsy adya na saṃśayaḥ ||
advāreṇa ripor gehaṃ dvāreṇa suhṛdo gṛham |
praviśanti sadā santo dvāraṃ no varjitaṃ tataḥ ||
kāryavanto gṛhān etya śatruto nārhaṇāṃ vayam |
pratigṛhṇīma tad viddhi etan naḥ śāśvataṃ vratam ||

45. Those who observe the *snātaka-vratas* [may be] brahmins, kṣatriyas, or vaiśyas. They follow special rules as well as rules in common.
46. A kṣatriya who observes the special rules honors Prosperity (*Śrī*), and śrī always wears flowers, so we wear flowers!
47. And the kṣatriya has mighty arms, not mighty words; that is why his words are not considered arrogant, son of Bṛhadratha.
48. The Creator placed his own might in the arms of kṣatriyas—if you want to see it, king, you'll see it today, no doubt!
49. The pious always enter the house of an enemy by a wrong door, and the house of a friend by the proper door; hence [your] door is forbidden to us.
50. Know that since we come to [your] home with a purpose, we may not accept worship from an enemy—this is our perpetual *vrata*.

Thus the rule (that *snātaka*s are generally brahmins) is honored in the breach. Kṛṣṇa can take refuge in the fact that the *kṣatriya-snātaka* status is "on the books," even if rarely put into practice. The "special rules" however are a piece of ad hoc religious jurisprudence that riffs on the theological and ritual hermeneutics of orthodox Śāstrins.

Almost a Forest-Dweller

In prescribing the correct time for the bathing a Kṛṣṇa image, *Brāhmapurāṇa* 65.10 enumerates four distinct categories of Kṛṣṇa-worshippers: householders, *snātaka*s, ascetics (*yati*), and *brahmacārins* (*gṛhasthāḥ snātakāś caiva yatayo brahmacāriṇaḥ | snāpayanti tadā kṛṣṇaṃ mañcasthaṃ sahalāyudham*). This fourfold classification recalls the sequence of *āśrama*s as first defined in Manu: *brahmacārin, gṛhastha, vānaprastha, yati.* Could it be that the *Brāhmapurāṇa* regards '*snātaka*' to be synonymous with '*vānaprastha*'?

There is some Śāstric basis for such a view. Manu introduces the topic of the *vānaprastha* as follows:

Manu 6.1:
evaṃ gṛhāśrame sthitvā vidhivat snātako dvijaḥ |
vane vaset tu niyato yathāvad vijitendriyaḥ ||

> After living thus in the householder's order according to the rule, a twice-born *snātaka* should duly live in the forest, with his senses under control.

It is particularly striking that the word *snātaka* was not used in the parallel transition-stanza, Manu 4.1, despite the fact that the topic being introduced there was precisely the commencement of the householder's life soon after graduation from Veda-study!

Olivelle entitles chapter 4 "The Bath-Graduate," yet the stanzas pertaining to the *snātaka* begin only at 4.13. The discussion of marriage and the householder's duties actually precedes, in chapter 3. One might imagine that the sequentially logical place to introduce the rules for the *snātaka* would be immediately following the description of the rites for the end of brahmacarya, including the concluding bath. This is in fact the arrangement in the ĀpDhS, BDhS, and VDhS; only in the GDhS do the rules for marriage and domestic observances intervene, as in Manu. Hence, I hypothesize that, during the redaction of Manu, the *snātaka* section was (somewhat awkwardly) inserted between the *gṛhastha* and *vānaprastha* sections precisely because it had come to be understood as a status somehow between the two: a special form of the *gṛhastha* that was the precursor to the hermit.

Conclusion

As we have seen, the sections on the *snātaka* and on the *gṛhastha* in the Dharmaśāstra literature are quite independent in their content and relative position in the texts, despite the fact that according to the classical *āśrama*-system, all 'householders' (in the technical sense of married twice-born Āryas who pay the three 'debts' to the gods, sages, and ancestors) should also have been graduates of Veda study, and thus *snātaka*s. In fact, the principle that Veda study is the duty of all male kṣatriyas and vaiśyas, as well as all brahmins, was an innovation introduced in the Gṛhyasūtras (Lubin 2005; 2010) and probably never borne out in actual practice.

The fact that these two statuses were never collapsed into one strongly suggests that it was never taken for granted that all householders were in practice *snātaka*s, whether in the sense of having completed the study of the Veda, or of having successfully observed the rules of studenthood for the full period, or both. The *snātaka* was always regarded as something more than a mere householder. The status consisted not merely in having undergone the concluding bath, but in adhering scrupulously to a rigorous set of supplemental rules (*vratāni, dharmāḥ*) that caused one to be perceived as especially pious and venerable.

In the Dharmaśāstra, but even more strikingly in the epic and Purāṇic sources, it is presumed that *snātaka*s are always (or almost always) brahmins. A similar presumption seems to inform usage of the label *dvija*, for precisely the same reason: Veda study in practice was pursued only (or almost only) by brahmins.[32] It was this extreme and exemplary devotion to Veda recitation and ritual practice that sets the *snātaka* apart from, and above, the ordinary householder, and makes him an authority for the sanctification of other householders. For example, in choosing auspicious times for the consecration a king (the *ghṛtakambala*), *Atharvavedapariśiṣṭa* 33.4.2 suggests that "a discerning man should perform it at the conclusion of a *taptakṛcchra vrata*, or at the end of any *kṛcchra vrata*, or at whatever [time] *snātaka*s specify" (*taptakṛcchrāvasāne vā sarvakṛcchrasya cāntataḥ* | *yasmin vā snātakā brūyus tatra kuryād vicakṣaṇaḥ* ||)

Hence, Manu 6.1 can be understood to imply that the householders who might be expected to become *vānaprastha*s are precisely those who were already *snātaka*s—i.e., those who were learned in the Veda and observant of the special rules of piety incumbent upon Veda-graduates. The *snātaka* as depicted in the *Mahābhārata* (and in the story literature) is not very different in habits from a *vānaprastha*: of austere appearance and disciplined conduct, to be seen with *kuśa* grass in hand, ever reciting the Veda and making offerings.[33] We even find the suggestion that *snātaka-dharma*s are aimed at something higher than the worldly fruits of householder piety. In a couple places, the knowledge of the *ātman* and the way to seek it is referred to as "this doctrine of the *snātaka*s" (*snātakānām idaṃ śāstraṃ*, MBh 12.238.15a = *Brāhmapurāṇa* 237.36a).

Bibliography

Amarasiṃha. (1984), *Nāmaliṇgānuśāsanaṃ, nāma, Amarakoṣaḥ*, ed. V.L. Paṇaśīkaraḥ (Delhi: Caukhambā Saṃskṛta Pratiṣṭhāna).

Bākre, M.G. (1917), *Grihya-Sūtra by Paraskar with Five Commentaries of Karka Upādhyāya, Jayarām, Harihar, Gadādhar and Vishvanāth* (Bombay: Gujari Printing Press; rep. Delhi: Munshiram Manoharlal, 1982).

Bhattacharya, C. (1936), *Gobhilagṛhyasūtram with Bhaṭṭanārāyaṇa's Commentary* (Rep. Delhi: Munshiram Manoharlal, 1982).

[32] On the use of the term *dvija*, see Lubin (2005: 87).

[33] Among the eight occasions on which the word *nahātaka* (= Skt. *snātaka*) appears in the Pali literature, it twice describes a *tapassin* (*Dīghanikāya* 3); the formula *nahātakasatāni* repeated in an enumeration (in *Dīghanikāya* 2) recalls the similarly repeated *sahasrāṇi snātakānām* (and the like) scattered through the MBh (3.47.6, 3.222.41, 4.65.16, 7.87.60, 12.45.5, 12.124.11, etc.).

Bhaṭṭagopīnāthadīkṣita. (1899), *Saṃskāraratnamālā Bhaṭṭagopīnāthadīkṣita-viracitā* (Puṇe: Ānandāśramagranthālayaḥ).

Bolling, G.M., and J. von Negelein. (1909-1910), *The Pariśiṣṭas of the Atharvaveda*, vol. 1, parts 1 and 2 [all published] (Leipzig: Harrassowitz).

Bühler, G. (1879, 1882), *Sacred Laws of the Āryas*. Sacred Books of the East 2 and 14 (Oxford: Clarendon Press; rep. Delhi: Motilal Banarsidass).

Burrow, T. (1982), Review of *Vedic Ritual: The Non-Solemn Rites* by J. Gonda, *Bulletin of the School of Oriental and African Studies* 45.1: 187-188.

Caland, W. (1922), *The Jaiminigṛhyasūtra belonging to the Sāmaveda, with Extracts from the Commentary, Edited with an Introduction and English Translation*. Punjab Sanskrit Series 2 (Lahore; rep. Delhi: Motilal Banarsidass, 1991).

_____. (1925), *The Kāṭhakagṛhyasūtra* (Lahore).

_____. (1927), *Vaikhānasasmārtasūtram: The Domestic Rules and Sacred Laws of the Vaikhānasa School Belonging to the Black Yajurveda*. Bibliotheca Indica 242 (Calcutta; rep. Delhi, MLP, 1989).

_____. (1929), *Vaikhānasasmārtasūtra: The Domestic Rules and Sacred Laws of the Vaikhānasa School Belonging to the Black Yajurveda*. Bibliotheca Indica 251 (Calcutta; rep. Delhi: Ramanand Vidya Bhavan, 1982).

Gonda, J. (1977a), "The Baudhāyana-Gṛhya-Paribhāṣā-Sūtra" in *Beiträge zur Indienforschung: Ernst Waldschmidt zum 80. Geburstag gewidmet*, ed. H. Härtel (Berlin: Museum für Indische Kunst), 169-190.

_____. (1977b), "Religious Thought and Practice in Vaikhānasa Viṣṇuism," *Bulletin of the School of Oriental and African Studies* 40.3: 550-571.

_____. (1980), *Vedic Ritual: The Non-Solemn Rites*. Handbuch der Orientalistik 2.4.1 (Leiden: E.J. Brill).

Hiltebeitel, A. (2006), "Aśvaghoṣa's *Buddhacarita*: The First Known Close and Critical Reading of the Brahmanical Sanskrit Epics," *Journal of Indian Philosophy* 34: 229-286.

Johnston, E.H. (1935-1936), *The Buddhacarita; or, Acts of the Buddha*, 2 vols. (Calcutta: Baptist Mission Press).

Lubin, T. (2005), "The Transmission, Patronage, and Prestige of Brahmanical Piety from the Mauryas to the Guptas" in *Boundaries, Dynamics and Construction of Traditions in South Asia*, ed. F. Squarcini (Firenze: Firenze University Press), 77-103.

_____. (2010), "The Householder Ascetic and the Uses of Self-Discipline" in *Asceticism and Power in South and Southeast Asia*, ed. P. Flügel and G. Houtman, Royal Asiatic Society Books (London: Routledge).

Mitra, R. (1870-1879), *Agni-Purana*. Bibliotheca Indica, 65.1-3 (Calcutta: Asiatic Society of Bengal).

Muddudīkṣita, M., (ed.) (1905), *Maharṣibodhāyanapraṇītaḥ smārta-kalpasūtragranthaḥ* (Cennanagara [Madras]: Jñānasāgara Mudrākṣaraśālā).
Nārāyaṇa Śāstrī Khiste and Jagannātha Śāstrī Hośiṅga. (1930), *The Yājñavalkya Smṛti with Vīramitrodaya, the Commentary of Mitra Miśra and Mitāksharā, the Commentary of Vijñāneśvara.* Chowkhamba Sanskrit Series 322, 335, 344, 348, 353, 363, 373, 378, 382, 388, and 399 (Benares: Chowkhamba).
Olivelle, P. (1993), *The Āśrama System* (New York: Oxford University Press).
_____. (2000), *Dharmasūtras: The Law Codes of Āpastamba, Gautama, Baudhāyana, and Vasiṣṭha* (Delhi: Oxford University Press).
_____. (2005), *Manu's Code of Law: A Critical Edition and Translation of the* Mānava-Dharmaśāstra (New York: Oxford University Press).
Rangaswami Aiyangar, K.V. (1941-1958), *Kṛtyakalpataru of Lakṣmīdhara* (Baroda: Oriental Institute).
Ravi Varma, L.A. (1940), *Āgniveśyagṛhyasūtra.* Trivandrum Sanskrit Series 146 (Trivandrum: University of Travancore).
Rhys Davids, T.W. and J.E. Carpenter. (1889), *Dīgha-nikāya*, vol. 1 (London: Pali Text Society).
Sastri, R.H. (1926), *Mânavagṛhyasûtra of the Maitrâyaṇîya Śâkhâ with the Commentary of Aṣṭâvakra*, Government Oriental Series 35 (Baroda: Central Library).
Shama Sastri, R. (1920), *Bodhâyana Gṛihyasutra.* Oriental Library Publications Sanskrit Series 32/55 (Mysore: Government Branch Press).
Sharma, A. (1969-1985), *Kāśikā: A Commentary on Pāṇini's Grammar by Vāmana and Jayāditya* (Hyderabad: Osmania University, Sanskrit Academy).
Stenzler, A.F. (1876), *The Institutes of Gautama* (London: Trübner).
Sukthankar, V.S., et al. (1927-1972), *The Mahābhārata* (Poona: Bhandarkar Oriental Research Institute).
Vaikhānasagṛhyaprayogavṛtti of Sundararāja. Manuscript (Government Oriental Manuscript Library, no. 1610).

JARROD L. WHITAKER

Who Gets to Live Forever in Ancient India? Rethinking ā́yus *("life") in the* Ṛgveda*

Introduction

The Sanskrit term *ā́yus* ("life, lifetime") maintains a fairly stable meaning throughout Indian history. This is evident in its earliest appearance in the *Ṛgveda*,[1] its use in the classical Indian medical tradition of *Āyurveda* ("Science of Life/Longevity"),[2] and through to its modern Hindi manifestation as *āyu* ("lifespan, age"). While "life" may be one of the most basic social constructs and realities, the interpretation of *ā́yus* in its earliest manifestation in the *Ṛgveda* is not without its shortcomings. The term *ā́yus* has been squarely situated within a problematic set of interpretative categories dubbed *Daseinsmächte*, which are supposedly "energy/power-substances" that can be manipulated by magical, ritual techniques (see Oldenberg 1919; Gonda 1952, 1957).[3] The ramifications of this

* It is with the greatest respect and gratitude that I write this paper for Dr. Patrick Olivelle, whose profundity in thought and volume has greatly advanced the field of Sanskrit studies and our understanding of South Asian religion, history, and culture. Versions of this paper were read at the *217th Meeting of the American Oriental Society* (March 2007), and at the *New England Conference of the Association for Asian Studies: Magical Practice and Magical Thinking in Asian Culture* (November 2006, *in absentia*)

[1] For examples of *ā́yus* as "life, lifetime" in the *Ṛgveda*, see ṚV 3.49.2cd, to Indra: *inátamaḥ sátvabhir yó ha śūṣaíḥ pṛthujráyā aminād ā́yur dásyoḥ.* "Ever staunch, far-reaching with his impetuous fighters, he has destroyed the barbarian's life." ṚV 10.27.7a, to Indra: *ábhūr v aúkṣīr vy ù ā́yur ānaḍ.* "You have come into being, grown strong, and gained a life." ṚV 10.144.5c, 6c, to Indra: *enā́ váyo ví tāry ā́yur jīváse-... krátvā váyo ví tāry ā́yuḥ sukrato.* "Thereby, your health, your life is lengthened in order to live ... Through resolve, your health, your life is lengthened, O one of good resolve."

[2] See Wujastyk (1998: 3).

[3] Geib (1975: 269, n.1) summarizes past translations of *ā́yus*, such as "life force (*force vitale, Lebenskraft*), life, lifetime, time, and epoch." See Watkins (2000: 2) and Mayrhofer (EWA 1: 171-172) for a brief discussion of the etymology of *ā́yus* (PIE *h_2óįu-s*).

methodological disposition led scholars such as Thieme (1952) and Geib (1975) to the conclusion that ancient Indians believed they could manipulate reality through ritual performances in order to prolong their lives or protect them from danger.[4] The obvious problem with this is that early Vedic ritual rhetoric and activity—apart from accidental injury—cannot affect the biological lifespan of humans. Do we accept then that ancient Indians acted irrationally or were intellectually unable to recognize that their rituals did not in fact lengthen their biological lifespans?

In order to address these concerns, this paper will reconsider *ā́yus* from a sociological and cultural studies perspective so as to situate the term within a coherent, yet discursive R̥gvedic worldview. It will show that this worldview is embedded in a complex set of ritualized processes, ideologies, and relationships that make lengthening life in R̥gvedic *sóma* rituals meaningful, rational, and normative. It will also show that these factors reflect the realities of being human.[5] I take my theoretical lead from Foucault (1972, 1977) and Bourdieu (1977). On the one hand, Foucault's work makes us focus on discourse as a key strategy through which individuals define appropriate ways of thinking and acting. As we will see, the idioms bound up in the use of *ā́yus* function as a "discursive formation" that works to construct and circumscribe the identities and practices of ritual participants in the early Vedic ritual tradition. On the other hand, Bourdieu asks us to see the multifaceted ways in which such practices and ideologies are inherently "interested" since they are directed strategically towards the monopoly of material and symbolic capital. Such strategies often remain unarticulated or "misrecognized" in society as this better serves the political and hierarchical ends of interpersonal or group relationships. In this vein, this paper seeks to explain the diverse benefits—material and symbolic—that

[4] In a future work, I plan to lay out the ways in which theories of magic and power have influenced Indologists. For now, let me briefly state that Jan Gonda's major influences come from the phenomenological approaches of Otto (1917) and Van der Leeuw (1933), who in turn were reacting to and incorporating various theories of magic and religion proposed by scholars such as Frazer (1911), Mauss (1972 [1902-03]), and Marett (1914). One of the dominant threads throughout the writings of all these scholars is that "power" underlies magic, which is considered a "pseudo-science" that attempts to manipulate reality (Vedic rituals were considered to be inherently "magical"). Power was normally an appropriation of the Melanesian term *mana*—a concept introduced into anthropological discourse by Codrington (1891). Theorists of magic and Indologists freely (and in scholarly exchange with each other) interpreted the class of *-as* stem nouns (= *Daseinsmächte*) in Sanskrit literature as examples of *mana* in Indian culture. See Whitaker (2004: 568, n.11) for a summary of Indologists who have uncritically adopted this theoretical stance.

[5] For in-depth discussion on the problematic nature of the terms "belief" and "rationality," see Wilson (1971), Stoller (1998), and Ruel (2005). For criticism of the use of the word "rational" in social science debates, see Buchowski (1986), Bunge (1987), and Banner (1990). See also Strawson (1992), who nicely discusses the relationships between belief, rationality, and lived reality.

individuals can gain in the process of lengthening life through early Vedic ritual practices. An understanding of how early Vedic Āryans encode, constrain, and give meaning to the concept of *ā́yus* will thus highlight one of the many ways by which such individuals reproduce and legitimize their ritual tradition, while conveying a heavily ritualized way in which they should understand their identities and place in early Vedic society. In other words, in the face of experience and lived reality, why did ancient Indians continually assert in their hymns that they could gain life and prolong it through ritual performances?

Interpreting prá √tr̥̄ ā́yus

Let us begin by considering a stanza where twin rescuer gods, the Aśvins, lengthen the life of an old man by replacing his skin:

> R̥V 1.116.10: *jujurúṣo nāsatyotá vavrím prā́muñcataṃ drāpím iva cyávānāt, prā́tirataṃ jahitásyā́yur dasrā́d ít pátim akr̥ṇutaṃ kanī́nām.*
>
> O Nāsatyas, you two removed the covering from the aged Cyavāna as if a garment. O wondrous deed-doers, you prolonged the life (*ā́yus*) of the forsaken one and thereupon made him the husband of maidens.

Cyavāna's rejuvenation appears to function as a paradigmatic allegorical story that incorporates important cultural and ritual values pertaining to youth and marriage.[6] As attested in this stanza, the term *ā́yus* features in a standard formula with the verb *prá √tr̥̄*, which is typically translated as "to extend, lengthen, prolong."[7] Geib (1975) argues that *prá √tr̥̄* actually means "to bring through, carry across [*hindurchbringen*]," and the formula *prá √tr̥̄ ā́yus* denotes that life is brought through some form of life-threatening danger. In relation to the above stanza, Geib (1975: 273) states that the aged Cyavāna's lifetime was carried across his old age (that is, across certain death) and by a miracle the Aśvins made him young again. While Geib's interpretation is plausible here, he nevertheless furnishes in parenthesis "through old age" (*durch das Alter*) in order to account for the apparent danger and to justify his new translation of the verb. Indeed, in numerous other cases, Geib liberally supplies in parenthesis the hypothetical, life-threatening danger as the object of the preposition

[6] For detailed consideration of Cyavāna in later literature, see Goldman (1977).

[7] See Geib (1975: 270, esp. n.3) for a summary of past translations of *prá √tr̥̄* as "to lengthen, etc." For examples of this formula, see R̥V 1.25.12c (= R̥V 4.39.6d and R̥V 10.186.1c): *prá ṇa ā́yūṃṣi tāriṣat.* R̥V 1.94.16b: *asmā́kam ā́yuḥ prá tirehá deva.* R̥V 1.119.6d: *prá dīrghéṇa vándanas tāry ā́yuṣā.* R̥V 8.48.4d: *prá ṇa ā́yur jīváse soma tārīḥ.* R̥V 10.59.5b: *jīvā́tave sú prá tirā na ā́yuḥ.* R̥V 10.95.10d: *prórvā́śī tirata dīrghám ā́yuḥ.* "Urvaśī extends her/his long lifetime." R̥V 10.100.5b: *bŕ̥̥haspate pratarītā́sy ā́yuṣaḥ.* Cf. R̥V 10.14.14d: *dīrghám ā́yuḥ prá jīváse.* See also the single use of *prá √sr̥* with *dīrghám ā́yus* at R̥V 3.7.1cd.

"*durch.*" In some instances that danger is apparent, yet does not need to be supplied with a parenthetical prepositional clause, or indeed, a new translation of the verb. In many other instances no danger exists.[8]

Geib also ignores another stanza from the Cyavāna hymn where the poet desires to gain *ā́yus* so that he can live to a ripe old age:

> R̥V 1.116.25: *prá vāṃ dáṃsāṃsy aśvināv avocam asyá pátiḥ syāṃ sugávaḥ suvī́raḥ, utá páśyann aśnuván dīrghám ā́yur ástam ivéj jarimā́ṇaṃ jagamyām.*
>
> I have proclaimed your wondrous deeds, O Aśvins. Possessing good cattle and good warriors, I would be lord of this (wealth). Perceiving and obtaining a long life (*dīrghám ā́yus*), may I go to old age just as one goes home.

The hymn in which both stanzas appear certainly documents the Aśvins' "wondrous deeds" (*dáṃsas-*), many of them involving saving figures from danger. Likewise, in the *R̥gveda* the noun *ásta* ("home") refers to a secure place to which individuals should return/dwell, and the simile "just as one goes home" (*ástam iva ít* √*gam*) suggests that the poet should go to old age in a safe manner.[9] While this stanza agrees with Geib's general thesis, avoiding danger and living to a ripe old age are tantamount to the same thing. Consider another example:

> R̥V 4.12.6 (= R̥V 10.126.8): *yáthā ha tyád vasavo gauryàṃ cit padí ṣitā́m ámuñcatā yajatrāḥ, evó ṣv àsmán muñcatā vy áṃhaḥ prá tāry agne pratarā́ṃ na ā́yuḥ.*
>
> Just as you, O good ones worthy of worship, released even the cow tied by the foot, even so, release us from constraint. Let our life (*ā́yus*) be extended more extensively, O Fire.

Geib (1975: 279) states that the lifetime of each ritual participant is brought through the constraint (*áṃhas*). This is once again a reasonable interpretation, yet it sidesteps the use of *pratarā́m* ("more extensive/-ly"; Geib's *weiterhin*), which suggests that the ritual participants' *ā́yus* has been allowed to continue in a tempo-

[8] Geib (1975: 271) even admits that the life of the ritual participant is lengthened at R̥V 8.79.6c: *prém ā́yus tārīd átīrṇam.* "He (Soma) prolongs an unprolonged lifetime." Cf. R̥V 1.127.5, for the hapax legomenon *áprāyus* "the one whose lifetime is not extended." The adjective *áprāyu* appears at R̥V 1.89.1d (*áprāyuvo rakṣitā́raḥ*), R̥V 5.80.3b, and R̥V 8.24.18c (*áprāyubhir yajñébhiḥ*). For a brief discussion of these forms, see Geldner (1951 1: 177).

[9] I would like to thank George Cardona (pers. comm. March 2007), who suggested that the simile may refer to the standard idiom for the setting sun as a metaphor for the end of life, since in later Vedic literature *ásta* frequently appears with the sun and verbs meaning "to go" (√*i*, √*yā*, √*gam*).

ral sense.[10] Consider two other stanzas ignored by Geib in which *prataráṃ* appears:

> R̥V 10.18.2-3: *mr̥tyóḥ padáṃ yopáyanto yád aíta drā́ghīya ā́yuḥ prataráṃ dádhānāḥ, āpyā́yamānāḥ prajáyā dhánena śuddhā́ḥ pūtā́ bhavata yajñiyāsaḥ. imé jīvā́ ví mr̥taír ā́vavr̥trann ábhūd bhadrā́ deváhūtir no adyá, prā́ñco agāma nr̥táye hásāya drā́ghīya ā́yuḥ prataráṃ dádhānāḥ.*
>
> While effacing the footprint of Death, you (gods) have come, establishing a longer more extensive lifetime (*ā́yus*). Increasing with progeny and wealth, be cleansed and pure, O you all who are worthy of sacrifice. The living have separated themselves from the dead. Our invocation to the gods has been auspicious today. We have gone eastward for dance and laughter, establishing a longer more extensive lifetime (*ā́yus*).

Geldner (1951, 3: 152) suggests that the hymn in which these stanzas appear was used in a funeral service (*Leichenfeier*). The use of √*dhā* ("to establish") plays on the same issues as the use of *prá* √*tr̥̄* elsewhere. In stanza 2, it is the gods who ultimately possess the ability to remove death and grant long life, and stanza 3 suggests that the living want to outlive the dead. The poet at once recognizes that the deceased have not been saved from death and that the *ā́yus* of the living should continue. Moreover, this process is contingent on the presence of the gods and on ritual measures directed towards them. The ritual participants do ritually separate themselves from the dead and death itself, but this is only half the equation in that they also celebrate the fact that they will live a long god-given life.

Prolonging life and avoiding death are thus not mutually exclusive ideas. Sustaining *ā́yus* through some danger is the equivalent of saying that the ritual participants will live longer.[11] While many of Geib's interpretations warrant merit, he overstates his point and

[10] See also R̥V 1.53.11: *yá udŕ̥cīndra devágopāḥ sákhāyas te śivátamā ásāma, tvā́ṃ stoṣāma tváyā suvī́rā drā́ghīya ā́yuḥ prataráṃ dádhānāh.* "O Indra, (our) herdsmen are gods: we will be your most auspicious friends at the conclusion (of the sacrifice). Through you, we, who have good warriors, will praise you as we establish for ourselves a longer more extensive lifetime." And R̥V 10.115.8, to Agni: *ū́rjo napāt sahasāvann íti tvopastutásya vandate vŕ̥ṣā vā́k, tvā́ṃ stoṣāma tváyā suvī́rā drā́ghīya ā́yuḥ prataráṃ dádhānāḥ.* "Saying (*íti*): 'O vigorous son, O dominating one', the bull, the speech of a celebrant celebrates you. Through you, we, who have good warriors, will praise you as we establish for ourselves a longer more extensive lifetime."

[11] Another good example of this is R̥V 8.44.30: *purā́gne duritébhyaḥ purā́ mr̥dhrébhyaḥ kave, prá ṇa ā́yur vaso tira.* "O Fire, O sage, prolong our lifetime away from bad courses and negligent ones, O treasure." Cf. also R̥V 1.34.11: *ā́ nāsatyā tribhír ekādaśaír ihá devébhir yātam madhupéyam aśvinā, prā́yus tā́riṣṭaṃ nī́ rápāṃsi mr̥kṣataṃ sédhataṃ dvéṣo bhávataṃ sacābhúvā.* "O Nāsatyas, with the thirty three gods travel here to the honey drinking, O Aśvins. Prolong life; wipe away defects; drive away hostility; and be (our) two companions." Cf. Geib (1975: 275). Note lines cd = R̥V 1.157.4cd. In one stanza Soma actually increases (√*vr̥dh*) the *ā́yus* of ritual participants by conquering any potential threats, rather than avoiding them. R̥V 3.62.15: *asmā́kam ā́yur vardháyann abhímātīḥ sáhamānaḥ, sómaḥ sadhástham ā́sadat.* "Increasing our lifetime, dominating those of hostile intentions, Soma has taken his seat at his abode."

often fabricates the life-threatening danger (so readily supplied in parentheses). He tries unsuccessfully to reinterpret the formula *prá* *√tṝ ā́yus* so as to make it functional and pragmatic; that is, an immediate ritual response to perceived or real danger. In the end, Geib essentially quibbles over semantics.[12] As we will see, Ṛgvedic poets repeatedly assert that the *ā́yus* of ritual participants is lengthened in a temporal sense. In addition, in many cases in which the formula appears, poets are not concerned with any form of danger. The verb does not intrinsically indicate that *ā́yus* is brought through some form of peril (though this does not preclude it from being used in such a context). In rejecting Geib's interpretation of *prá √tṝ*, the verb can still be meaningfully translated as "to lengthen, prolong, extend". Poets deploy it to indicate that *ā́yus* is either sustained through a specific time period (night, summer heat, some immediate danger, or death), or, more frequently, in an indefinite temporal sense; that is, through the rest of an individual's lifetime.

It is also crucial to consider another ramification of Geib's interpretation of *ā́yus*—one that relates to the theoretical legacy of magic that still haunts academia in general (see Styers 2004), and Vedic studies in particular. Geib explains the relevance of the formula *prá √tṝ ā́yus* by appropriating the conclusions of scholars such as Malinowski (1955). In this vein, the formula reflects an early Vedic form of cathartic wish-fulfillment. The problem with this line of thinking is that Malinowski reduces ritual practices (in his case "magic") to a simple pragmatic belief system or psychological device that alleviates stress and anxiety in times of uncertainty or danger (which in reality can apply to many forms of propaganda or inspirational speech). Hence, ancient Indians try to affect their lives through rituals in order to alleviate their fear and anxiety about dying young or death in general. Mary Douglas (1966: 59) sarcastically critiques Malinowski's presentation of ritual-cum-magical practices as "a kind of poor man's whiskey, used for gaining conviviality and courage against daunting odds." We obviously cannot accept that every time ancient Indians performed their rituals they were wracked with anxiety. As Van Baal (1971: 69) so scathingly remarks with regard to this issue: "Primitive [*sic*] people know as well as we do that a wish is not fulfilled by wishing more ardently, and that fair words butter no parsnips."[13] Consequently, a Malinowskian interpretation of ritual/magical efficacy fails to explain the complex dis-

[12] I would like to thank Boris Oguibénine (pers. comm. May 2007) for pointing out that Lazzeroni (1988) offers a favorable interpretation of Geib. Regrettably, I have been unable to consult this work.

[13] Belmont (1982: 18) offers a similar criticism in relation to Frazer's insistence that magic is mistaken science: "...agrarian rituals exist alongside agrarian techniques. People must therefore have been perfectly capable of telling technical effectiveness from magical effectiveness."

cursive factors and relationships—symbolic, social, economic, and political—that give value and meaning to why early Vedic Āryans sought to lengthen their lives through ritual practices.[14]

Lengthening Life

Let us return to the concept of *ā́yus* with an understanding that Ṛgvedic poet-priests employ an idiomatic form of rhetoric that envisions a process whereby life is lengthened. As would be expected, physical life indicates living through time. This temporal aspect of *ā́yus* is expressed in numerous examples. One of the clearest statements (conveniently ignored by Geib) appears in the following stanza to the goddess Uṣas, who, according to Kuiper (1960), is the personification of the first dawn of the new year:

> ṚV 1.92.10: *púnaḥ-punar jā́yamānā purāṇī́ samānáṃ várṇam abhí śúmbhamānā, śvaghnī́va kṛtnúr víja āminānā́ mártasya devī́ jaráyanty ā́yuḥ.*
>
> As she is born again and again, the ancient one, beautifying herself with her usual color, like a skillful gambler diminishing the stakes, the goddess (Dawn) is causing the lifetime (*ā́yus*) of a mortal to age.

The poet implies that with the dawning of each new day, or more likely each new year, Uṣas (herself then a symbol of time) whittles away life.[15] The gambling simile suggests that in the sacrificial context the ritual participant is trying to sustain, if not replenish, his lifetime through a ritual performance, as if his *ā́yus* were a "stake"—though the poet is clearly self-conscious of the futility of this endeavor as the "house" (read: Dawn), so to speak, always wins. Another stanza to Uṣas offers a similar idea about ritual participation and prolonging life:

> ṚV 1.113.16: *úd īrdhvaṃ jīvó ásur na ā́gād ápa prā́gāt táma ā́ jyótir eti, ā́raik pánthāṃ yā́tave sū́ryāyā́ganma yátra pratiránta ā́yuḥ.*

[14] For similar criticisms of Malinowski, see Nadel (1957: 197), Tambiah (1990: 72), and Bell (1992: 71). For more profound interpretations of magic, or better, ritual practices, see Beattie (1971), Tambiah (1968, 1973), and MacDonald (1984-1986, 1995). In relation to this issue, Bourdieu (1977: 115) nicely observes: "Rites take place because and only because they find their *raison d'être* in the conditions of existence and dispositions of agents who cannot afford the luxury of logical speculation, mystical effusions, or metaphysical anxiety. It is not sufficient to ridicule the more naive forms of functionalism in order to have done with the question of the practical function of practice ... But, contrary to appearances, scarcely more understanding is derived from a structural analysis which ignores the specific functions of ritual practices and fails to inquire into the economic and social conditions of the production of the dispositions generating both these practices and also the collective definition of the practical functions in whose service they function."

[15] Cf. ṚV 8.48.7cd: *sóma rājan prá ṇa ā́yūṃṣi tārīr áhānīva sū́ryo vāsarā́ṇi.* "O king Soma, extend our lives as the sun (extends) the mornings into days."

> Rise up! The enlivening force (*jīvá ásu*) has come to us. Darkness has gone away and light draws near. She (Dawn) has left behind a path for the sun to travel. We have come to where they prolong life (*ā́yus*).[16]

With regard to this stanza, Geldner (1951, 1: 149) suggests that each new day issues in a new phase in life. Geib (1975: 276) argues that the liftime of each ritual participant is brought safely through the dark and deadly night and allowed to continue in an unbroken succession. In saying this, the place where *ā́yus* is prolonged appears to be the ritual ground and the context alludes to the sacrificial offerings made in the early morning. As Kuiper (1960: 235) points out, as the first dawn of the new year, Uṣas symbolizes the rebirth of the cosmos and the "rebirth of life itself." The process of lengthening *ā́yus* is thus symbolically marked and enacted through a yearly ritual performance, whether the night posed any actual threat.

As would be expected, the temporal aspect of *ā́yus* appears elsewhere. For example:

> R̥V 6.16.27: *té te agne tvótā iṣáyanto víśvam ā́yuḥ, táranto aryó árātīr vanvánto aryó árātīḥ.*
>
> These ones of yours are prospering throughout their whole lifetime (*ā́yus*), aided by you, O Fire; overcoming a stranger's hostilities, vanquishing a stranger's hostilities.

The poet here seems to play on the standard formula as *ā́yus* and √*tr̥̄* (without *prá*) straddle the caesura of the two hemistiches.[17] Although overlooked by Geib, this highlights his argument as *ā́yus* is placed in relation to the danger posed by the stranger. However, in contrast to Geib, the central idea plays on temporal matters, not the danger *per se*. The same notion of a "whole/complete/full lifetime" (*víśvam ā́yus*) appears in another hemistich to Agni, the deified ritual Fire:

> R̥V 2.38.5ab: *nā́naúkāṃsi dúryo víśvam ā́yur ví tiṣṭhate prabhaváḥ śóko agnéḥ.*
>
> Fire's overwhelming household heat spreads through various dwellings throughout one's whole lifetime (*ā́yus*).

The last two examples indicate that *ā́yus* not only signals physical life but also life experienced throughout time.[18] While there is noth-

[16] Note line d = R̥V 8.48.11d. The "enlivening force/living life" (*jīvá ásu*) appears to qualify the goddess Dawn (for ásu, see Bodewitz 1991: 30-49). For Uṣas and *ā́yus*, see also R̥V 7.77.5 and R̥V 7.80.2. Cf. R̥V 3.53.16cd.

[17] The verb √*tr̥̄* means "to overcome, pass/cross over; to withstand/endure".

[18] See also R̥V 10.85.42b (*víśvam ā́yus vy àśnutam*). Cf. R̥V 7.34.11b: *ánuttam asmai kṣatrám̐ viśvā́yu.* "Dominion throughout his whole life has been conceded to him (Varuṇa)." The compound *viśvā́yu* appears 28 times in the *R̥gveda*. Cf. R̥V 1.37.15c, to the Maruts: *víśvaṃ cid ā́yur jīváse.* "(Prolong our) whole lifetime in order to live."

ing revealing in my interpretation here, it nevertheless sets in place the basic parameters of the use of *ā́yus*. This necessitates then an explanation of the meaning of *ā́yus* in ritual and symbolic contexts as these examples are saying more than just the obvious fact that Fire heats the home. An Āryan's lifetime is intimately connected with the god Agni, whose presence signals and demands correct ritual participation. The following stanza makes this explicit:

> ṚV 4.4.7: *séd agne astu subhágaḥ sudā́nur yás tvā nítyena havíṣā yá ukthaíḥ, píprīṣati svá ā́yuṣi duroṇé víśvéd asmai sudínā sā́sad iṣṭíḥ.*
>
> O Fire, let him be of generous portion and of excellent gift, who desires to please you with his own oblation and with praises during his own lifetime (*svá- ā́yus*) and in his home. May there be only splendid days for him. This will be his desire.

Another stanza to the wealth-giving (*draviṇodā́*) Agni clarifies the relationship between the ritual Fire and *ā́yus*:

> ṚV 1.96.8: *draviṇodā́ dráviṇasas turásya draviṇodā́ḥ sánarasya prá yaṃsat, draviṇodā́ vīrávatīm íṣaṃ no draviṇodā́ rāsate dīrghám ā́yuḥ.*
>
> The (material) wealth giver (Agni) will hold out to us surpassing (material) wealth. The (material) wealth giver will hold out to us (material) wealth that comes with men. The (material) wealth giver will bestow on us refreshment that comes with warriors. The (material) wealth giver will bestow a long life (*ā́yus*) on us.[19]

At its most basic, this example underscores the idea that wealth and brave progeny facilitate a long life (*dīrghám ā́yus*), and ritual participants clearly express their desire to obtain this good life from the ritual Fire.[20] Since Agni is such a dominant symbol of Āryan social, ritual, and political relationships,[21] then the well-being of a ritually-active man is symbolically enmeshed in divine realities and his life receives validation at economic, social, and biological levels through ritual performances. Consider another stanza:

> ṚV 3.17.3: *tríṇy ā́yūṃṣi táva jātavedas tisrá ājā́nīr uṣásas te agne, tā́bhir devā́nām ávo yakṣi vidvā́n áthā bhava yájamānāya śáṃ yóḥ.*
>
> You have three lives (*ā́yus-*), O Jātavedas, three dawns are your birth givers, O Fire. With these procure by sacrifice the favor of the gods. Then, as one who knows, become prosperity and life (*śáṃ yóḥ*) for the sacrificer.

[19] Cf. ṚV 10.36.14d: *savitā́ no rāsatāṃ dīrghám ā́yuḥ.*

[20] For a metaphorically rich hemistich to Agni, see ṚV 3.1.5cd: *śocír vásānaḥ páry ā́yur apā́ṃ śríyo mimīte bṛhatī́r ánūnāḥ.* "Clothing himself entirely in flame, in the lifetime of the waters, he measures his beauties, lofty and unfailing." For the same "clothing" metaphor, see ṚV 10.16.5c and ṚV 10.53.3c. Cf. ṚV 4.58.11.

[21] See Proferes (2007).

Here Agni's three lives most likely refer to the three separate fires which are kindled on the ritual ground and collectively constitute the god's presence.[22] The three fires allow Agni, as the officiating priest (*hótṛ*), to establish a relationship between the gods and human sacrificer (*yájamāna*) in order to procure sacrificial rewards. Another hemistich underscores Agni's function to contact the gods so as to lengthen a sacrificer's life:

> ṚV 1.44.6cd, to Agni: *práskaṇvasya pratiránn ā́yur jīváse namasyā́ daívyaṃ jánam.*
>
> Prolonging Praskaṇva's life (*ā́yus*) in order to live, offer salutations to the divine tribe.

Ṛgvedic poets equally apply the concept of *ā́yus* to gods, especially the ritual Fire, and human sacrificers, who must perform rituals to the Fire throughout their lives in order to obtain rewards from the gods.[23] This highlights the fundamentally ritualized way in which *ā́yus* is conceived and the fact that it is inextricably connected with ritual and divine realities. In one stanza, the gods even make Agni's life unaging (*ā́yur ajáram*) so that Fire will always provide them with their sacrificial oblations.[24] Agni subsequently lays claim to the sacrificial offerings and responds to the gods:

> ṚV 10.51.8d: *agnéś ca dīrghám ā́yur astu devāḥ.*
>
> Let Fire's lifetime (*ā́yus*) be long, O gods.

It seems then that sustained ritual activity keeps Agni alive, and this implies that only by maintaining and interacting with the constantly burning ritual Fire can the Āryan communities sustain themselves over time.

Let me briefly return to ṚV 3.17.3d (cited above) in which the fixed formula *śám yóḥ* conveys the meaning "prosperity/welfare and well-being" or simply "luck and life." According to Szemerényi (1991), the second member *yós* is etymologically connected with *ā́yus*.[25] In addition, the initial component *śám* has several possible

[22] Sāyaṇa states that *tríṇi ā́yūṃṣi* refers to the three eatables; i.e., fat/butter, plants and *sóma* (Geldner 1951, 1: 353). Cf. ṚV 9.66.19: *ágna ā́yūṃṣi pavasa ā́ suvórjam íṣaṃ ca naḥ, āré bādhasva duchúnām.* "O Agni, you purify your own lifetimes (*ā́yus*-), and impel invigoration and refreshment for us. Drive misfortune far away!"

[23] See also ṚV 10.45.8b, where Agni's *ā́yus* is "unmistakable" (*durmárṣam*).

[24] ṚV 10.51.7.

[25] See also Mayrhofer (EWA 2: 420-421). In addition, Burrows (1955: 157) and Beekes (1995: 39) connect *yós* ("welfare") with Avestan *yaoš-* and Latin *iūs* ("law"), while Szemerényi (1991: 1736-1737) outright rejects the possibility of the latter equation. It is with deepest sorrow that I offer my belated thanks to Mark R.V. Southern for his advice on *śám yóḥ* (pers. comm. October 2002).

etymologies, either from √*śū* "to swell; prosper" (Szemerényi 1991: 1738ff.) or √*śam* "to be ritually active."[26] If the former is the case then the formula equates a state of thriving with living the good life; while if the latter is the case then it aligns ritual activity with life. Both possibilities have already been encountered in stanzas featuring *ā́yus*.

The close relationship between *ā́yus*, ritual activity, and Agni equally applies to Indra. In one stanza, ritual participants directly align their unsatisfactory lives with Indra's cosmic responsibilities:

> R̥V 7.23.2: *áyāmi ghóṣa indra devájāmir irajyánta yác churúdho vívāci, nahí svám ā́yuś cikité jáneṣu tā́níd áṃhāṃsy áti parṣy asmā́n.*
>
> The shout akin to the gods was offered up, O Indra, when the ritual gifts direct themselves (forward) in the verbal contest. Since their own lifetime (*svám ā́yus*) is not satisfactory to people, take us beyond just these constraints.[27]

In this case, the lives of ritual participants are placed under the auspices of Indra and mediated through ritual performances. The rhetoric envisions that Indra can remove the constraints (*áṃhas-*) that occur throughout life. The poet accepts that Indra alone makes opportunities available, and it is Indra who betters the lives of his worshippers beyond what they would normally be able to achieve if they did not foster a ritual relationship with the war-god. The solution appears to invoke Indra's prime duty to eliminate obstacles (*vr̥trá-*) that stand in the way of Āryan concerns. Another poet succinctly expresses the idea that Indra works for the benefit of the entire community, while also emphasizing that *ā́yus* is intrinsically wedded to the war-god's activity:

> R̥V 8.54.7b: *índra ā́yur jánānām.*
>
> In Indra is the lifetime (*ā́yus*) of the tribes.

The point here is that the most appropriate way in which early Vedic Āryans can better themselves is to interact with their war-god Indra—the rhetoric implies that their lives depend on it—and this is obviously done through ritual performances.

All the examples presented so far highlight the desires, if not basic needs, of ritually-inclined Āryans for prosperity, progeny, security, victory, and of course a long life. Ritual participants repeatedly align their desires with certain deities, thereby placing authority for the realization of such wishes directly in the gods' hands.[28] As Bourdieu

[26] See Mayrhofer (EWA 2: 609-610).

[27] For *svá- ā́yus-*, cf. R̥V 4.4.7c.

[28] Cf. R̥V 6.52.15cd: *té asmábhyam iṣáye víśvam ā́yuḥ kṣápa usrā́ varivasyantu devā́ḥ.* "Let

(1977) points out, the sustained reproduction of such ritualized statements serves conceptually and cosmically to intertwine fundamental needs with ritual practices. This process functions to reaffirm and legitimize the expectation to participate in rituals, while the idiomatic discourse about life and its prolongation conveys a clear message to Āryans; that is, their lives are naught without ritual performances and the gods.[29] We have then some parameters in which the concept of *ā́yus* is deployed. It functions as a basic marker of physical and temporal life, yet consistently signifies a close ritual relationship with various early Vedic gods. It is this ritual relationship with the gods that needs to be examined more in depth because it will bring into sharp focus the primary function of *ā́yus* in the *R̥gveda*.

Living a Hundred Years

Ritual participants repeatedly envision that they should live an idealized length of time of a "hundred autumns" (*śatá śarád, śatáśārada*) or a "hundred winters" (*śatá himā́, śatáhima*), yet only a god can make this possible. For example:

> R̥V 1.73.9: *árvadbhir agne árvato nŕ̥bhir nr̥̄́n vīraír vīrā́n vanuyāmā tvótāḥ, īśānā́saḥ pitr̥vittásya rāyó ví sūráyaḥ śatáhimā no aśyuḥ.*
>
> O Fire, may we win race horses with race horses, men with men, and warriors with warriors, aided by you: Being masters of wealth acquired by their fathers, may our patrons of a hundred winters obtain (this).
>
> R̥V 6.4.8cd, to Agni: *tā́ sūríbhyo gr̥ṇaté rāsi sumnám mádema śatáhimāḥ suvī́rāḥ.*
>
> Grant these to patrons and benevolence to the singer. May we find exhilaration as ones destined for a hundred winters, as ones who possess good warriors.[30]

In both cases, Fire determines whether or not ritual patrons (*sūrí*) will live to see a century. It seems that being ritually identi-

the gods grant us space (to roam) throughout (our) whole lifetime for refreshment by night and red dawn/day."

[29] Bourdieu (1977: 116) rightly suggests that the metonymic relationships set up between humans, their desires, and the physical or supernatural world serve only to foster specific and imitative modes of ritual and practical behavior ("mimesis"). Bourdieu highlights this point by referring to a fertility rite, which connects cooking grain, pregnancy, and germination. Strathern (1996: 28) expands on Bourdieu by critiquing Malinowski's (1935) interpretation of garden magic: "…when a Trobriand garden magician mimics the actions of yams growing in a garden and says, 'The belly of my garden swells,' he transfers the scheme of pregnancy in the human body over to the scheme of garden fertility, thereby setting up a correspondence that reenergizes both contexts … What is involved here is not just symbolic action based on metaphor but also the bringing together of two separate spheres, which thereby become cosmically fused."

[30] Cf. R̥V 2.33.2.

fied as one who possesses a lifetime of a hundred autumns/winters is also a marker of ritual patronage or an outcome of it. This label signals then the correct ritual behavior of socially important individuals, who presumably strive to maintain their social positions through staging rituals. The first stanza also underscores the genealogical continuity between patrons and their forefathers. Consider a similar example where ancient precedents establish the model of long life:

> R̥V 2.27.10: *tvám̐ víśveṣām̐ varuṇāsi rā́jā yé ca devā́ asura yé ca mártāḥ, śatám̐ no rāsva śarádo vicákṣe 'śyā́mā́yūm̐ṣi súdhitāni pū́rvā.*
>
> You are the ruler of all, O Varuṇa, both those who are gods, O Asuric-lord, and those who are mortals. Allow us to see a hundred autumns. We would obtain the well-established lifetimes (*ā́yus-*) of old.

Here the kingly god Varuṇa has authority over the well-established past lifetimes (*ā́yūm̐ṣi súdhitāni pū́rvā*) of ritual participants and the stated length of time is a "hundred autumns" (*śatám śarád-*). In order to live a hundred years, ritual participants must maintain a benevolent relationship with various gods. This same idea appears elsewhere:

> R̥V 3.36.10cd: *asmé śatám̐ śarádo jīváse dhā asmé vīrā́ñ cháśvata indra śiprin.*
>
> In us, establish one hundred autumns in order to live, in us (establish) endless warriors, O mustached Indra.[31]

In this hemistich Indra, the other kingly god of early Vedic culture, grants his worshippers longevity and warriors (or male children expected to be brave).[32] Another hemistich highlights the role of gods in this process:

> R̥V 5.54.15cd: *idám̐ sú me maruto haryatā váco yásya tárema tárasā śatám̐ hímāḥ.*
>
> O Maruts, delight in this speech of mine, through its endurance may we endure a hundred winters.

The poet here asks the Maruts to accept his ritual speech (*vácas*) so that its "endurance" (*táras* < $\sqrt{}$*tr̥̄*) will allow all parties to live long.

[31] For Indra, see also R̥V 8.48.10cd: *ayám̐ yáḥ sómo ny ádhāyy asmé tásmā índram pratíram emy ā́yuḥ.* "This *sóma* here which has been placed in us, for it I go to Indra to prolong life."

[32] At R̥V 10.161.1-5, Indra and Agni, among several other gods, are asked to cure a disease (*yákṣma*), and the hymn naturally revolves around living for a hundred years. See esp. R̥V 10.161.3-4, where the abbreviated form "hundred lifetimes" (*śatā́yus*) appears. For *śatā́yus*, see also R̥V 6.2.5d.

As this poet recognizes, sustained and sustaining ritual speech plays a key role in confirming a long life.

In stark contrast, failure to maintain a relationship with gods comes with negative repercussions as they can detrimentally affect the lives of ritual participants:

> ṚV 1.89.9: *śatám ín nú śarádo ánti devā yátrā naś cakrā́ jarásaṃ tanū́nām, putrā́so yátra pitáro bhávanti mā́ no madhyā́ rīriṣatā́yur gántoḥ.*
>
> Only a hundred autumns are now before us, O gods, where you have set the (old) age of the body, where sons become fathers. Do not hurt our lifetime (*ā́yus*) in the midst of its course.

As Geib (1975: 269) observes, ritual participants ask the gods not to negatively affect the natural course of their lives. Like previous examples, time is appropriately marked when sons become fathers and when presumably they assume their ritual duties to various gods. It seems then that lengthening life connects ritual participants with their genealogical past, while mapping out their future in a continuous unbroken succession marked by ritual performances. Ritual activity thus verifies familial, ritual, and social ties.[33]

While we cannot outright reject the possibility that a few ancient Indians may have lived for a hundred years, the idiom "hundred autumns/winters" more realistically signifies a cultural ideal afforded to socially important individuals who seek a long healthy life through ritual activity and divine providence. This ideal places authority over the lives of Āryans squarely in the hands of the gods and underscores the responsibility of men to interact ritually with their gods throughout the course of their lives.

The Ritualized Struggle for Life

As we have repeatedly seen, Ṛgvedic poet-priests deploy a circumscribed form of discourse wherein the gods have authority over the lives of Āryans and the only way to maintain a relationship with them is to perform early Vedic rituals. Sustained ritual activity is, in my view, the key to understanding *ā́yus*. Ritualized practices confirm the process whereby *ā́yus* is lengthened, and in turn lengthening *ā́yus* affirms ritual participation. In order to substantiate this observation let us consider other examples in more detail. In one case, both Indra and Varuṇa control the well-being and lives of sacrificers (*yájamāna-*):

> ṚV 8.59.7: *índrāvaruṇā saumanasám ádṛptaṃ rāyás póṣaṃ yájamāneṣu dhattam, prajā́m puṣṭím bhū́tim asmā́su dhattaṃ dīrghāyutvā́ya prá tirataṃ na ā́yuḥ.*

[33] See Heesterman (1993) for a similar assessment of the social function of Vedic rituals.

O Indra and Varuṇa, establish among the sacrificers uncomplicated benevolence and an abundance of wealth. Establish among us progeny, prosperity, and potential. Let the two of you prolong our lifetime (*ā́yus*) in order to live long (*dīrghāyutvá-*).[34]

R̥gvedic poet-priests and their clientele thus share a reciprocal relationship with regard to their gods' demeanor, the financial and familial outcomes of ritually interacting with them, and the acquisition of a long and fruitful life. The lifelong maintenance of this relationship would have been crucial for economic prosperity and the social standing of men eligible to stage rituals.

In saying this, another stanza from the Cyavāna hymn highlights the important role of a sacrificer's wife in acquiring *ā́yus*:

R̥V 1.116.19: *rayíṃ sukṣatráṃ svapatyám ā́yuḥ suvī́ryaṃ nāsatyā váhantā, ā́ jahnā́vīṃ sámanasópa vā́jais trír áhno bhāgáṃ dádhatīm ayātam.*

O Nāsatyas, conveying wealth, good dominion, a lifetime (*ā́yus*) with good offspring (and) good warriors: with prizes you thoughtfully came to Jahnu's wife, who was establishing a portion (of the sacrifice) three times a day.

While he anticipates that the Aśvins will bestow on Jahnu's wife rewards and a life full of brave progeny, it is telling that the poet emphasizes her involvement in ritual practices thrice daily (perhaps an allusion to the morning, midday, and evening offering sessions during a *sóma* sacrifice).[35] Consider a similar stanza:

R̥V 10.85.39: *púnaḥ pátnīm agnír adād ā́yuṣā sahá várcasā, dīrghā́yur asyā yáḥ pátir jī́vāti śarádaḥ śatám.*

Fire has returned the wife along with life (*ā́yus*) and lustre (*várcas*). Her husband, possessing a long lifetime (*dīrghā́yus*), will live a hundred autumns.

In this stanza from a wedding hymn both husband and wife receive *ā́yus* from Agni at a certain point in the ritual.[36] In addition, the sac-

[34] Cf. R̥V 10.170.1ab, to Sūrya: *vibhrā́ḍ br̥hát pibatu somyám mádhv ā́yur dádhad yajñápatāv ávihrutam.* "Let the lofty radiant one drink the sóma honey, establishing an intact life upon the lord of the sacrifice." See also R̥V 10.18.5-6.

[35] For a similar statement about parents, progeny, and *ā́yus*, see R̥V 8.31.8. For other statements about gods, progeny, and *ā́yus*, see R̥V 1.113.17d, to Dawn: *asmé ā́yur ní didīhi prajā́vat.* "Shine down on us a lifetime full of progeny." R̥V 8.18.18, to the Ādityas: *tucé tánāya tát sú no drā́ghīya ā́yur jīváse, ā́dityāsaḥ sumahasaḥ kr̥ṇótana.* "For the sake of offspring and descendants, make our life longer in order to live, O very great Ādityas." See also R̥V 1.66.1, R̥V 1.93.3, R̥V 1.125.1cd, R̥V 1.132.5d, and R̥V 2.41.17.

[36] See Jamison (1996: 222-224) for consideration of this hymn, and the role of the sacrificer's wife. Jamison has recently presented two papers (13th World Sanskrit Conference, July 2006, Edinburgh, Scotland; 4th International Vedic Workshop, May 2007, Austin, TX) on the late, innovative appearance of the sacrificer's wife in the *R̥gveda*.

rificer is afforded the labels "hundred autumns" (*śarádaḥ śatám*) and "long life" (*dīrghā́yus*). The standing of the sacrificer and his wife depends then in part on this poet's ritual performance whereby Fire acknowledges their *ā́yus* and *várcas* ("lustre"); the latter term could equally be translated as "prestige."[37] Elsewhere, a wife even strives to outperform other wives in *várcas* (ṚV 10.159.5). Olivelle (1997: 435) aptly observes that it is not just any person who has access to *ā́yus*:

> ...it is a married male possessing the ritual fires as the head of a household. A wife is an absolute necessity for performing ritual functions; she is as much a sacrificial instrument as the priests, spoons, knives, and fires, an instrument in assuring her husband's *āyus*.

The juxtaposition of *ā́yus* and *várcas* also highlights the social importance of both concepts as forms of "symbolic capital" (Bourdieu 1977; cf. Whitaker 2004). Symbolic capital refers to accumulated and redeemable conceptualizations of prestige, celebrity, knowledge, or honor that are highly contested within a culture. This capital serves to legitimize certain individuals or groups and in turn allows them to impose legitimation, while also demarcating exactly what or who is illegitimate. The sacrificer and his wife have access to lustre (*várcas*) and life (*ā́yus*) because they perform rituals and maintain a beneficial relationship with the gods. A ritually-endorsed long life functions then as a mark of reputation within early Vedic society.

We have consistently seen that an Āryan's lifetime (*ā́yus*) cannot be prolonged without a strict ritual relationship with the gods. This fact should not be disregarded as a consequence of the purely ritual nature of the *Ṛgveda*. Although everything is filtered through a ritual lens, this obvious fact could be too easily trivialized in the case of *ā́yus*. The consistent aligning of *ā́yus* with ritual activity is the key to understanding its social and symbolic importance. Gods are given the responsibility of prolonging and protecting an Āryan's life because the primary way an Āryan can access the gods and be credited with such longevity is through the never-ending performance of early Vedic rituals. This dominant theme highlights the implications of *ā́yus* in ritual and social spheres, and also indicates in lived reality

[37] Cf. ṚV 1.23.23cd-24ab (note line 23d = ṚV 10.9.9d). *Várcas* conveys the notion of Fire's lustre or brilliance. Figuratively, it denotes some form of social or ritual prestige, which in later literature is especially associated with Brahmans (see Mayrhofer EWA 2: 516). Outside of compounds, *várcas* only appears 13 times in the *Ṛgveda* and of these only 3 occur in the core family books. The term appears to be late to Vedic diction. See, e.g., ṚV 9.65.18: *ā́ naḥ soma sáho júvo rūpáṃ ná várcase bhara, suṣvāṇó devávītaye.* "O Soma, bring here to us dominance, speed, as if a symbol/sign for lustre/prestige, you who are being pressed for the pursuit of the gods." *Várcas* is bestowed on the conveyor of the sacrifice at ṚV 3.8.3cd (note line d = ṚV 3.24.1d), to Vanaspati: *súmitī mīyámāno várco dhā yajñávāhase.* "Being fixed with the correct fixture, establish lustre for the one who conveys the sacrifice." For *yajñávāhas*, see Insler (1996: 178-182), who argues that *vā́has* actually means "respect" and this compound means "receiving or offering the respect of sacrifice".

one way in which ritual participants constantly struggle for ritual and social recognition. The following examples underscore this point:

> ṚV 1.89.2: *devā́nām bhadrā́ sumatír ṛjūyatā́ṃ devā́nāṃ rātír abhí no ní vartatām, devā́nām sakhyám úpa sedimā vayáṃ devā́ na ā́yuḥ prá tirantu jīvā́se.*
>
> Let the auspicious benevolence of the gods be for those who are upright. Let the gift of the gods return downward to us. We courted the friendship of the gods: Let the gods prolong our lifetime (*ā́yus*) in order to live.
>
> ṚV 1.89.8d: *vy àśema devā́hitaṃ yád ā́yuḥ.*
>
> May we obtain a lifetime (*ā́yus*) established by the gods.
>
> ṚV 10.62.11cd: *sā́varṇer devā́ḥ prá tirantv ā́yur yásminn áśrāntā ásanāma vā́jam.*
>
> Let the gods prolong Sāvarṇi's life (*ā́yus*), beside whom we, being unwearied, have won the prize.

The last hemistich foregrounds the sacrificer's acquisition of *ā́yus*. In addition, the poet-priests emphasize their successful and arduous ritual endeavors to contact the gods in order to achieve this, while also underscoring their desire to receive a prize (*vā́ja*), which here refers to the payment for performing the ritual (*dákṣiṇā*).[38] The process of lengthening life thus involves a significant economic component. Two stanzas make this explicit:

> ṚV 1.125.6: *dákṣiṇāvatām íd imā́ni citrā́ dákṣiṇāvatāṃ diví sū́ryāsaḥ, dákṣiṇāvanto amṛ́tam bhajante dákṣiṇāvantaḥ prá tiranta ā́yuḥ.*
>
> These bright things are only for those who give the sacrificial fee. The suns in the sky are only for those who give the sacrificial fee. The sacrificial fee givers enjoy freedom from death (*amṛ́ta*) and the sacrificial fee givers prolong their lifetime (*ā́yus*).
>
> ṚV 10.107.2: *uccā́ diví dákṣiṇāvanto asthur yé aśvadā́ḥ sahá té sū́ryeṇa, hiraṇyadā́ amṛtatvám bhajante vāsodā́ḥ soma prá tiranta ā́yuḥ.*
>
> Those who offer sacrificial fees have stood on high in the heaven. Those who gift horses have stood along with the Sun. Those who gift gold enjoy for themselves deathlessness (*amṛtatvám*). Those who gift garments prolong their lifetime (*ā́yus*), O Soma.

In both cases the individuals who prolong their lives are those who offer the sacrificial fee (*dákṣiṇāvant-*); that is, ritual patrons and sacrificers. In addition, the acquisition of *amṛtatvám* ("deathlessness")

[38] ṚV 10.62.8-11 is a praise (*dānastuti*) of Sāvarṇi's sacrificial payment (*dákṣiṇā*).

goes hand-in-hand with prolonging *ā́yus*.[39] In order to lengthen their lives, ritual patrons offer their poets and gods sacrificial rewards, presumably in the form of horses, gold, and garments. In order to receive the sacrificial fee (*dákṣiṇā*), poet-priests must have proved their worth by successfully staging ritual performances in order to contact the gods. Both parties enact and negotiate their relationships with each other in a ritual performance in order to benefit at symbolic and socio-economic levels. This system of reciprocal exchange represents then a field of struggle in which ritual participants vied for material and symbolic recognition and capital.[40]

In saying this, one poet states in no uncertain terms the realities of this process:

> ṚV 8.18.22: *yé cid dhí mṛtyúbandhava ā́dityā mánavaḥ smási, prá sū́ na ā́yur jīváse tiretana.*
>
> Since we humans are indeed bound to death, O Ādityas, may you prolong our life (*ā́yus*) in order to live.

This poet is clearly self-conscious of one single truth: he, like all humans, is going to die.[41] His request then is for a prosperous, fruitful, and healthy life, and the dative infinitive *jīváse* ("in order to live"), which frequently appears in stanzas featuring *ā́yus*, conveys this notion. Lengthening life is thus not a statement of anxiety-laden wish-fulfillment or about ultimately avoiding death. While ritual participants repeatedly articulate their concern with premature death, this concern overlaps with other cultural expectations for progeny, wealth, and security.[42] The standardized and idiomatic use of *ā́yus*,

[39] See Thieme (1952: 15ff.). It is interesting that the concept *amṛ́ta* ("freedom from death, deathlessness") is conspicuously absent from nearly all examples featuring *ā́yus*, bar the two presented here (ṚV 1.125.6 and ṚV 10.107.2). This suggests that prolonging life and gaining a state of *amṛ́ta* involve overlapping, yet different ritual processes. This may be due to the fact that becoming "deathless" is primarily connected with drinking *sóma*. However, for *sóma* and *ā́yus*, see ṚV 8.48.4, 10, 11, and also ṚV 9.80.2, where the divine draught extends the lifetime of patrons (*maghávan-*). Cf. also ṚV 9.93.5c and ṚV 9.96.14d. For consideration of the later Vedic meaning and use of *amṛ́ta*, see Olivelle (1997: 428ff.), who states "The term *amṛta* does not always mean immortal in the sense we usually attach to it ... it is a full and prosperous life and all things that sustain and promote such a life, including food, drink, cattle, and medicine. *Amṛta* can thus denote both life/immortality, as well as instruments that sustain life and ward off death. The two terms *amṛta* and *āyus* (long and full life) are often juxtaposed and form a single complex of meanings."

[40] Cf. ṚV 8.31.8: *putríṇā tā́ kumāríṇā víśvam ā́yur vy àśnutaḥ, ubhā́ híraṇyapeśasā.* "Those two (parents; *dámpatī-*) obtain a complete lifetime with sons and children, and both are ornamented in gold."

[41] Cf. Geib (1975: 274), who explains this stanza away by stating that only a few individuals (namely Cyavāna and the Moon) are afforded the privilege of avoiding death.

[42] In saying this, a poet rescues a dying or deceased man in two stanzas from a hymn in which Indra is asked to cure a disease (*yákṣma*). ṚV 10.161.2: *yádi kṣitā́yur yádi vā páreto yádi mṛtyór antikáṃ nī́ta evá, tám ā́ harāmi nírṛter upásthād áspārṣam enaṃ śatáśāradāya.* "If his life has expired (*kṣitā́yus*), if he has departed, or if he has descended into the presence of Death, I bring him here from the lap of Destruction. I have recovered him for a hundred

especially with *prá* √*tr̥*, communicates, promotes, and reinforces the responsibility of Āryans to perform rituals throughout their entire lives—immortality only comes in the afterlife and through male children and prosperity in this life. Consequently, when ritual participants lengthen *ā́yus* they performatively communicate to themselves and their wider community that they are living the correct ritually-endorsed and ritually-active life.

This conclusion is further attested in cases where a failure to correctly interact with the gods through rituals can be ruinous. We have already seen at R̥V 1.89.9 (cited above) that ritual participants ask the gods not to impede their lifetime during its natural idealized course. This also appears in the following stanza:

> R̥V 1.24.11: *tát tvā yāmi bráhmaṇā vándamānas tád ā́ śāste yájamāno havírbhiḥ, áheḷamāno varuṇehá bodhy úruśaṃsa mā́ na ā́yuḥ prá moṣīḥ.*
>
> Celebrating you with a formulation, I implore you for that (lifetime): the sacrificer hopes for that (lifetime) through his oblations. O Varuṇa, be here without animosity, O widely praised one, do not steal our lifetime (*ā́yus*).

The implication of this stanza is much the same as many of the others already encountered; that is, a god, in this case Varuṇa, has authority over the sacrificer's life, and, in anger, could take it away. The poet-priest expresses his concern for the ritual to succeed and for his sacrificer (*yájamāna*) to acquire *ā́yus*. In order to ensure this, he ritually mediates the demeanor of Varuṇa and his patron's desire for a long life, while capitalizing on the fact that the process is not a sure thing; that is, Varuṇa could take away the sacrificer's *ā́yus*. This prefigures then a ritual strategy wherein poet-priests can successfully demonstrate their ritual abilities and worth in order to ensure that their clients receive *ā́yus*. Ritualists thus wield considerable symbolic power over individuals eligible to participate in sacrifices. The basis for this power comes from the fact that ritually affirming *ā́yus* is an appropriate, if not demanded, act in the course of a man's life as it confirms his participation in the ritual arena, reaffirms his social status as a lifelong patron/sacrificer, and of course ritually communicates his desire to live a full life.[43] We can see then a reciprocal, yet strategically negotiated, exchange of economic and symbolic capital between ritual experts, patrons, and their gods.[44]

---

autumns." R̥V 10.161.5: *ā́hārṣaṃ tvā́vidaṃ tvā púnar ā́gāḥ punarnava, sárvāṅga sárvaṃ te cákṣuḥ sárvam ā́yuś ca te 'vidam.* "I have fetched you, I have found you: you will return once more, O renewed one. I have found your entire sight, and your entire lifetime, O you who have a complete body." See also R̥V 10.59.1.

[43] See Olivelle (1997: 434) for consideration of the refrain "he will live his full life span" (*sarvam āyur eti*) at the conclusion of later Vedic rites.

[44] Cf. R̥V 3.53.7 (d = R̥V 7.103.10d): *imé bhojā́ áṅgiraso vírūpā divás putrā́so ásurasya vīrā́ḥ, viśvā́mitrāya dádato maghā́ni sahasrasāvé prá tiranta ā́yuḥ.* "The hospitable ones,

This process constitutes a form of "redemptive hegemony" (Bell 1992: 83-88), whereby participants privilege themselves over others through the performance of rituals, yet they must constantly struggle to maintain their positions of power in the same manner in order to recreate and restate anew their social, economic, and political interests and investments.

Given all the evidence presented so far, let us consider one final stanza to the Moon:

> ṚV 10.85.19: *návo-navo bhavati jā́yamānó 'hnāṃ ketúr uṣásām ety ágram, bhāgáṃ devébhyo ví dadhāty āyán prá candrámās tirate dīrghám ā́yuḥ.*
>
> Constantly being born anew, he is the banner of the days and he goes ahead of the dawns. As he comes, he distributes a portion to the gods. The Moon prolongs his long lifetime (*ā́yus*).

Geib (1975: 275) translates the final line as *Hindurch (durch die Neumondnacht) bringt der Mond seine lange Lebenszeit*; that is, the moon brings his *ā́yus* through the new moon night. What Geib casually overlooks is that the penultimate line states that the Moon offers a portion of the early morning sacrificial offerings to the gods. The Moon's role in this stanza is one intimately connected with correct ritual activity. Like his human counterparts, the Moon here "prolongs his long life" by appropriately carrying out his ritual responsibilities. This stanza is a clear example of the formulaic context in which *ā́yus* appears. It also highlights the fact that like humans, a god's life depends on ritual performances.[45]

Conclusion

There is some gratifying irony in the fact that I only became aware of Patrick Olivelle's (1997: 435) almost identical conclusions about *ā́yus* in the later Vedic context after I had finalized my own with regard to the *Ṛgveda*:

> ... humans cannot achieve their full life span naturally; it is the outcome of ritual activity and ritual knowledge ... within the ancient Indian context of ritual persona, living a long life is rooted within a ritual/familial context and is bound up with fame, riches, children, and social position. It would have seemed absurd to associate *āyus* or *amṛta* with a poor, low-class, and ignorant man.

Aṅgirases of different kinds, sons of heaven, warriors of the Asuric-lord, bestowing bounties on Viśvāmitra at the pressing accompanied by a thousand (cows), they extend (his) lifetime."

[45] Cf. ṚV 2.32.1cd to Heaven and Earth: *yáyor ā́yuḥ pratarám̐ té idám purá úpastute vasūyúr vām mahó dadhe.* "Of you two whose lifetime is extensive, I, seeking treasure, establish eastward you two in greatness when praised."

In bringing this paper to a close, I want to consider in depth some of the underlying social and ritual processes implicit in the use of *ā́yus*. Let me frame this with perhaps the most basic of questions: Did ancient Indians *believe* that they could lengthen their lives through performing rituals? In short, the only answer I can provide is "maybe." Foucault (1972) argues that discursive formations work to circumscribe specific forms of knowledge, specific ways of knowing, and restricted ways of enacting that knowledge. The R̥gvedic tradition would obviously have been successful in ensuring that its ideologies and practices were dominant and normative if individuals accepted fully (read: "believed") that their life was prolonged because of ritual participation. However, even this begs many questions since the very concept of "belief" is fraught with problems. Ruel (2005: 261-263) argues that it is too simplistic, if not analytically untenable, to identify belief and be done with it. One of the few comparable notions in early Vedic culture is *śrád* √*dhā/kr̥* or *śraddhā́* ("to place trust; have faith in"), yet this is late to R̥gvedic diction.[46] In addition, R̥gvedic poets never use it in the context of lengthening life. In saying this, the fundamental task is to identify the object of that belief, the status that object holds in society, and the ideologies and practices that lend authority and meaning to it in the first place. As Lopez (1998) points out, statements of belief, especially in Christianity, have a distinct performative element in that they function to declare allegiance and identity. Before equating a statement of belief with an all-encompassing, discrete mindset, its function as a rhetorical and cultural strategy needs to be determined. For this reason, it is a mistake to think that belief is, in Ruel's (2005: 262) words, "fundamentally an interior state, a psychological condition." Sharf (1998: 114) puts it best when he states "all attempts to signify 'inner experience' are destined to remain 'well-meaning squirms that get us nowhere.'" Indeed, in the ancient Indian context we have little or no access to the psychological makeup of individuals. The point here is that a reductionist emphasis on what goes on in people's minds distracts from the primary task of explaining the complex social realities and relationships that affect, constrain, and give meaning to the agency and identities of individuals. Whether aware of it or not, people constantly negotiate, balance, and are motivated by institutional and self-interested ideologies, (pre) dispositions, symbolic networks of inference, and coercive actions. Belief, faith, and the related concept of cathartic wish-fulfillment are little more than generalized and uncritical abstractions. Individual or group belief cannot therefore be cited as sufficient evidence for the basis of human values and behavior (Ruel 2005: 261).[47]

[46] See, e.g., R̥V 10.151.1-5.

[47] Needham (cited in Ruel 2005: 257) states that "... the notion of belief is not appropriate to an empirical philosophy of mind or to an exact account of human motives and

In order to incorporate a cognitive basis for human actions in early Vedic culture, rather than reducing such practices to "belief," it is more fruitful to talk in terms of practical and interested dispositions that strategically negotiate and reproduce ritualized values, while accepting such values as worthwhile in the first place. Bourdieu's (1977: 21-22, 172-183) notion of "misrecognition" goes a long way towards illuminating such dispositions and the social and political processes that motivate ancient Indians to lengthen their lives through rituals.[48] In responding to ritual ideals, rules, and expectations, early Vedic Āryans must have possessed a practical sense of how to negotiate and align their desires for a long life with ritual and social advantages in the form of prestige, respect, and wealth. It may have been the case that a sacrificer was content with the ritual's outcome because, like his ritually-active compatriots, he too continued to grow old. However, poets are quick to point out that various gods can threaten a sacrificer's *ā́yus* and, throughout the *R̥gveda,* Indra is repeatedly instructed to kill individuals who do not perform rituals ("miser" *paṇí,* "non-presser" *ásuṣvi/ásunvant,* "barbarian" *dā́sa/dásyu*).[49] In failing to perform rituals, such people become legitimate targets for sustained violence: this is a powerful ethical and symbolic incentive for ritual participation. We can speculate then that when early Vedic Āryans ritually lengthened their lives they would have "*put themselves in the right*" by creating an appearance of "ethical impeccability" (Bourdieu 1977: 22; emphasis in original). The ritualized process of lengthening life thus constitutes a symbolically and ethically charged field of struggle. The point here is that the misrecognition of the arbitrary nature of these purposes (prestige, wealth, ethical/ritual correctness) supports and legitimizes a coherent, yet discursively self-interested worldview wherein life can be rhetorically and ritually lengthened. Since no poet openly questions the stated goals of the ritual, this suggests that ritual participants are motivated by, in Bourdieu's words, a "*pure, disinterested* respect for the rule" (emphasis in original); or to turn this formulation on its head, an unwavering performative commitment to the ritual's figurative efficacy. We can certainly postulate that poet-priests would have been concerned with correct ritual recitation and performance in order to receive social and ritual recognition and economic rewards from their peers, patrons, and of course the gods. They also promote their sacrificial patron's life in order to ensure his sustained investment in ritual endeavors over long periods of time—a fact underscored by the exchange of the sacrificial fee (*dákṣiṇā*). Ritual patrons most likely engaged in

conduct. Belief is not a discriminable experience, it does not constitute a natural resemblance among men, and it does not belong to 'the common behaviour of mankind'."

[48] See also Bell (1992: 114-117).

[49] On these terms, see Whitaker (2007).

the appropriate ritualized behavior for many of the same reasons; that is, to negotiate and monopolize material and symbolic benefits, to satisfy any ritualized demands, to ensure that their poet-priests correctly perform rituals, to keep themselves in favor with the gods, and ultimately to maintain their lifelong standing in society as patrons. The ritualized process of lengthening life reflects a complex set of reciprocal relationships between poet-priests, patrons, gods, and the wider community. In lengthening life, all parties exercise their practical sense of how to monopolize, challenge, or capitalize on economic, social, ethical, and political advantages. It would have been ritually and politically detrimental, if not absurd—to extend Olivelle's critique—to undermine the rhetorical goals of the ritual because one would be jeopardizing one's access to various economic and symbolic benefits, if not undermining one's status and membership in Vedic society.

The close relationship between *ā́yus* and the body offers another insight into the way in which such dispositions, behaviors, and relationships were shaped and learned. The early Vedic body certainly functions as a "natural symbol" (Douglas 1973),[50] or better yet that "three bodies"—the individual, social, and political—are melded in a complex relationship with each other (Scheper-Hughes and Lock 1987).[51] The point here is that the physical self and representations of such are discursively embedded in institutions of social and political power (LaFleur 1998: 45). Conceptualizations of the body reproduce and map social and political values onto the body. This process serves to naturalize such values and makes them appear to be intrinsic factors in one's biological/physical makeup and individual and social identity. This is not merely symbolic, as it produces appropriate behavior and socialized bodies (Connerton 1989; Strathern 1996). In the case of *ā́yus*, ritual responsibility is symbolically mapped onto the body and this serves to naturalize ritual participation, thereby making it an inherent factor in living the correct, ritually-endorsed, god-given lifestyle. To appropriate Stoller's (1998: 252) useful concept of "embodied rationality" for the early Vedic context, it is not that ritual participants master life through

[50] Douglas (1973: 137-139) argues that the body serves as a symbol of society, and the powers and prohibitions associated with the social structure are reproduced on the human body. Various types of bodily symbolism grant certain individuals influence in society.

[51] To counter the separation of mind from body in Cartesian dualism, Scheper-Hughes and Lock (1987), taking their cue from Douglas (1966, 1973), cogently forward three perspectives from which the body can be interpreted: 1) The "individual body," the "lived self," which refers to the phenomenological body that experiences; 2) the "social body," which refers to the way in which the body is conceived and represented with regard to social, natural, supernatural, and spatial relations; and 3) the "body politic," which refers to the way in which social, political, and legal systems regulate, condition, and control physical bodies. For an astute presentation and evaluation of the works of Mauss, Scheper-Hughes and Lock, Douglas, Bourdieu, and Connerton, see Strathern (1996: 1-39).

ritualized practices, but rather that such practices directed towards prolonging life master ritual participants. This process thus reflects a potent embodied ideology which ensures that people perform early Vedic rituals throughout their ritually-defined lives.

Let me push this interpretation even further. We have repeatedly seen that lengthening life is only possible within a R̥gvedic ritual context. J.Z. Smith (1982: 64-65) persuasively argues that rituals take place within predictable, yet ultimately artificial arenas in which the potential exists for all the variables of life to be symbolically "factored out"; rituals are (often) unlike everyday life. This sheds some light on the contextual use of *ā́yus* in the *R̥gveda*. While I do not want to reify early Vedic rituals as somehow distinct or different from the everyday hustle and bustle of life, we can postulate that only within this symbolically charged, ritualized, and "perfected" world, so to speak, can R̥gvedic poets talk and act as if life is lengthened and danger is avoided. As a performative speech act, "lengthening life" gains its symbolic efficacy only through ritual practices. Conversely, this indicates a "realistic assessment" on the part of early Vedic Āryans that rituals cannot in fact lengthen their biological lifespans and that injury and death are ever-present realities.

To sum up, in the face of experience and lived reality, "lengthening life" is better understood as a heavily ritualized, discursive formation and cultural trope. When R̥gvedic poet-priests prolong their patrons' *ā́yus*, they publicly re-affirm both parties' allegiance to the early Vedic ritual tradition, while underscoring the ritual responsibility to offer sacrifices to gods as a social constant. Lengthening *ā́yus* represents then a badge of membership within early Vedic society as it is tantamount to declaring a commitment to the endless performance of rituals. Longevity is a matter of social and ritual inclusion. The use of *ā́yus* in the *R̥gveda* functions as one of the many cultural strategies that reproduce the importance of sustained ritual participation, in this case throughout an Āryan's entire life. In early Vedic culture, life is not conceived of as separate to or apart from ritual participation. Moreover, ritual rhetoric suggests that to remain a member of early Vedic society Āryan men and their wives must patronize and perform sacrifices to gods over and again. The process involved in prolonging *ā́yus* does not appear to be a one-time deal. In order to maintain an unbroken sequence of *ā́yus*, Āryans need to constantly perform rituals. The extension of life would only be as good as one's last ritual performance.[52] The process thus indicates that an individual is getting older in the correct, ritually-endorsed

[52] This appears to be suggested at R̥V 1.10.11: *ā́ tū́ na indra kauśika mandasānáḥ sutám piba, návyam ā́yuḥ prá sū́ tira kr̥dhī́ sahasrasā́m ŕ̥ṣim.* "O Indra, (god of) Kuśika, becoming exhilarated, drink up our pressed offering (of *sóma*). Prolong (our) lifetime anew and make the sage win thousands (of cattle)." Cf. also R̥V 10.59.1a: *prá tāry ā́yuḥ pratarám návīyaḥ-*. "His extensive lifetime has been prolonged anew." The terms *návya* and *návīya*

way. This idea is further confirmed by the fact that at death the ritual Fire of a sacrificer (*yájamāna*) is put out; that is, his life is no longer connected to the ritual.[53] Extinguishing the ritual Fire symbolically and socially disconnects the sacrificer from his duties to the gods. Premature or natural death is not the failure of the ritual, only a statement that the individual will no longer participate in the ritual tradition. The use of *ā́yus* in the *Ṛgveda* thus highlights a complex set of strategies at the micro-political level of early Vedic society; that is, in lived reality, in which ritual participants constantly embody, reproduce, and give value to their lives in a heavily ritualized way.

Bibliography

Baal, J. van. (1971), *Symbols for Communication* (Assen: Van Gorcum).

Banner, M.C. (1990), *The Justification of Science and the Rationality of Religious Belief* (Oxford: Clarendon Press).

Beattie, J.H.M. (1971), "On Understanding Ritual" in *Rationality,* (ed.) B.R. Wilson, (New York: Harper Torchbooks, Harper and Row, 1971), 240-268.

Beekes, R.S.P. (1995), *Comparative Indo-European Linguistics: An Introduction* (Amsterdam/Philadelphia: John Benjamins).

Bell, C. (1992), *Ritual Theory, Ritual Practice* (New York: Oxford University Press).

Belmont, N. (1982), "Superstition and Popular Religion in Western Societies" in *Between Belief and Transgression: Structuralist Essays in Religion, History, and Myth,* (ed.) M. Izard and P. Smith, trans. by J. Leavitt (Chicago: The University of Chicago Press), 9-23.

Bodewitz, H.W. (1991), *Light, Soul and Visions in the Veda* (Poona, India: Bhandarkar Oriental Research Institute).

Bourdieu, P. (1977), *Outline of a Theory of Practice* (Cambridge: Cambridge University Press).

Buchowski, M. (1986), "The Controversy Concerning the Rationality of Magic," *Ethnologia Polona* 12: 157-167.

Bunge, M. (1987), "Seven Desiderata for Rationality" in *Rationality: The Critical View,* (ed.) J. Agassi and I.C. Jarvie (Dordrecht: Martinus Nijhoff), 5-15.

("anew, once again") highlight the continual nature of this process. Geib (1975: 275) translates *návya* as "junge."

[53] Later Vedic literature indicates that the sacrificer's Fire is extinguished at his death, specifically after his cremation, and this custom appears to be practiced in the Ṛgvedic period. On this issue, see Heesterman (1993: 33-39; 111-141, esp. 115) and Olivelle (1993: 40-41). See also ṚV 10.16.13 and Geldner (1957, 3: 149).

Burrow, T. (1955), *The Sanskrit Language* (London: Faber and Faber).
Codrington, R.H. (1891), *The Melanesians: Studies in their Anthropology and Folk-Lore* (Oxford: Clarendon Press).
Connerton, P. (1989), *How Societies Remember* (New York: Cambridge University Press).
Douglas, M. (1966), *Purity and Danger: An Analysis of Concepts of Pollution and Taboo* (New York: Praeger).
_____. (1973), *Natural Symbols: Explorations in Cosmology* (New York: Vintage Books). [Orig. pub. New York: Pantheon Books, 1970.]
Foucault, M. (1972), *The Archaeology of Knowledge* (New York: Pantheon Books).
_____. (1977), *Discipline and Punish: The Birth of the Prison* (New York: Pantheon Books).
Frazer, J.G. (1911), *The Golden Bough: A Study in Magic and Religion*, 3rd edition, 12 vols. (London: Macmillan). [Orig. pub. 1890 in 2 volumes.]
Geib, R. (1975), "Die Formel *ā́yus prá tṝ* im Ṛg-Veda," *Indo-Iranian Journal* 16.4: 269-283.
Geldner, K.F. (1951), *Der Rig-Veda: Aus dem Sanskrit ins Deutsche übersetzt und mit einem laufenden Kommentar versehen.* 4 vols., Harvard Oriental series, vols. 33-36 (Cambridge: Harvard University Press, 1951-57). [Orig. pub. vol. 1 as vol. 12 of the series *Quellen der Religionsgeschichte* (Göttingen: Vandenhoeck and Ruprecht, 1923).]
Goldman, R.P. (1977), *Gods, Priests, and Warriors: The Bhṛgus of the Mahābhārata* (New York: Columbia University Press).
Gonda, J. (1952), *Ancient-Indian* ojas, *Latin* *augos *and the Indo-European nouns in* -es/-os (Utrecht: A. Oosthoek).
_____. (1957), *Some Observations on the Relation between 'Gods' and 'Powers' in the Veda, a propos of the Phrase* Sūnaḥ Sahasaḥ ('s-Gravenhage: Mouton).
Heesterman, J.C. (1993), *The Broken World of Sacrifice* (Chicago: University of Chicago Press).
Insler, S. (1996), "Avestan *vāz* and Vedic *vāh*" in *Festschrift für Paul Thieme. Studien zur Indologie und Iranistik* 20: 169-186.
Jamison, S.W. (1996), *Sacrificed Wife/Sacrificer's Wife: Women, Ritual, and Hospitality in Ancient India* (New York: Oxford University Press).
Kuiper, F.B.J. (1960), "The Ancient Aryan Verbal Contest," *Indo-Iranian Journal* 4.4: 217-281.
LaFleur, W.R. (1998), "Body" in *Critical Terms for Religious Studies*, (ed.) M.C. Taylor (Chicago and London: The University of Chicago Press), 36-54.
Lazzeroni, R. (1988), "Il nettare e l'ambrosia: su alcune rappresentazioni indoeuropee della morte," *Studi e Saggi Linguistici* 28: 177-199.
Leeuw, G. van der. (1933), *Phänomenologie der Religion* (Tübingen: J.C.B. Mohr (Paul Siebeck)). [*Religion in Essence and Manifestation*, trans. J.E. Turner, 2 vols. (London: Allen and Unwin, 1938).]

Lopez, D.S., Jr. (1998), "Belief" in *Critical Terms for Religious Studies*, ed. M.C. Taylor (Chicago and London: The University of Chicago Press), 21-35.

MacDonald, M.N. (1984-1986), "An Interpretation of Magic," *Religious Traditions: A Journal in the Study of Religion* 7-9: 83-104.

_____. (1995), "Magic and the Study of Religion," *Religiologiques* 11 (Spring): 137-153.

Malinowski, B. (1935), *Coral Gardens and their Magic: A Study of the Methods of Tilling the Soil and of Agricultural Rites in the Trobriand Islands*. 2 vols. (London: George Allen and Unwin; New York: American Book).

_____. (1955), *Magic, Science and Religion* (Garden City, N.Y.: Doubleday, Doubleday Anchor Books). [Orig. pub. in *Science, Religion and Reality*, ed. J. Needham (New York: Macmillan, 1925).]

Marett, R.R. (1914), *The Threshold of Religion*, 2nd ed. (London: Methuen [1909]).

Mauss, M. (1972), *A General Theory of Magic*, trans. R. Brain (London and Boston: Routledge and Kegan Paul). [Orig. pub. as H. Hubert and M. Mauss, (1904), "Esquisse d'un théorie générale de la magie," *Année sociologique* 7 (1902-1903): 1-146.]

Mayrhofer, M. (1986-1996), EWA. *Etymologisches Wörterbuch des Altindoarischen*, 2 vols. (20 issues) (Heidelberg: Carl Winter, Universitätsverlag).

Nadel. S.F. (1957), "Malinowski on Magic and Religion" in *Man and Culture: An Evaluation of the Work of Bronislaw Malinowski*, ed. R. Firth (London: Routledge and Kegan Paul), 189-208.

Oldenberg, H. (1919), *Vorwissenschaftliche Wissenschaft: Die Weltanschauung der Brāhmana-Texte* (Göttingen: Vandenhoeck and Ruprecht).

Olivelle, P. (1993), *The Āśrama System: The History and Hermeneutics of a Religious Institution* (New York: Oxford University Press).

_____. (1997), "Amṛtā: Women and Indian Technologies of Immortality," *Journal of Indian Philosophy* 25: 427-449.

Otto, R. (1917), *Das Heilige: Über das Irrationale in der Idee des Göttlichen und sein Verhältnis zum Rationalen* (Breslau: Trewendt and Granier). [*The Idea of the Holy*, trans. J.W. Harvey (London: Oxford University Press, 1923).]

Proferes, T.N. (2007), *Vedic Ideals of Sovereignty and the Poetics of Power*, American Oriental Series, vol. 90 (New Haven, Connecticut: American Oriental Society).

Ruel, M. (2005), "Christians as Believers" in *Ritual and Religious Belief: A Reader*, ed. G. Harvey (New York: Routledge), 242-264. [Orig. pub. M. Ruel, *Belief, Ritual and the Securing of Life: Reflexive Essays on a Bantu Religion* (Leiden: E.J. Brill, 1997).]

Scheper-Hughes, N. and M.M. Lock. (1987), "The Mindful Body: A Prolegomenon to Future Work in Medical Anthropology," *Medical Anthropology Quarterly*, n.s. 1.1: 6-41.

Sharf, R.H. (1998), "Experience" in *Critical Terms for Religious Studies*, ed. M.C. Taylor (Chicago and London: The University of Chicago Press), 94-116.

Smith, J.Z. (1987), *To Take Place: Toward Theory in Ritual* (Chicago: The University of Chicago Press).

Stoller, P. (1998), "Rationality" in *Critical Terms for Religious Studies*, ed. M.C. Taylor (Chicago and London: The University of Chicago Press), 239-255.

Strathern, A.J. (1996), *Body Thoughts* (Ann Arbor: The University of Michigan Press).

Strawson, P.F. (1992), *Analysis and Metaphysics: An Introduction to Philosophy* (Oxford: Oxford University Press).

Styers, R. (2004), *Making Magic: Religion, Magic, and Science in the Modern World* (Oxford: Oxford University Press).

Szemerényi, O. (1991), "Vedic šam, šaṃ yoḥ, and šaṃ (ča) yošča" in *Oswald Szemerényi: Scripta Minora* 4 (Innsbruck): 1725-1750. [Orig. pub. in *Indian Linguistics*, vol. 4 (1978/1979): 159-184.]

Tambiah, S.J. (1968), "The Magical Power of Words," *Man: Journal of the Royal Anthropological Institute*, n.s., 3.2 (June): 175-208.

_____. (1973), "Form and Meaning of Magical Acts: A point of View" in *Modes of Thought: Essays on Thinking in Western and Non-Western Societies*, ed. R. Horton and R. Finnegan (London: Faber and Faber), 199-229.

_____. (1990), *Magic, Science, Religion, and the Scope of Rationality* (Cambridge: Cambridge University Press).

Thieme, P. (1952), "Studien zur indogermanischen Wortkunde und Religionsgeschichte" in *Berichte über die Verhandlungen der Sächsischen Akademie der Wissenschaften zu Leipzig. Philologisch-historische Klasse* 98.5 (Berlin): 1-77.

Watkins, C. (2000), *The American Heritage Dictionary of Indo-European Roots*, 2nd ed. (Boston: Houghton Mifflin).

Whitaker, J.L. (2004), "Ritual Power, Social Prestige, and Amulets (*maṇí*) in the *Atharvaveda*" in *The Vedas: Texts, Language, and Ritual. Proceedings of the Third International Vedic Workshop, Leiden 2002*, ed. A. Griffiths and J.E.M. Houben (Groningen: Egbert Forsten), 565-580.

_____. (2007), "Does Pressing *Sóma* Make You an Āryan? A Brief Review of *súṣvi-* and *ásuṣvi-* in the *R̥gveda*," *Zeitschrift der Deutschen Morgenländischen Gesellschaft* 157.2: 417-426.

Wilson, B.R., (ed.) (1971), *Rationality* (New York: Harper Torchbooks, Harper and Row).

Wujastyk, D. (1998), *The Roots of Āyurveda: Selections from Sanskrit Medical Writings* (London: Penguin Books).

Steven E. Lindquist

One Yājñavalkya... Two? On the (Questionable) Historicity of a Literary Figure

Yājñavalkya is a popular figure within the Hindu tradition, both because of his association with key Hindu doctrines such as *karma*, rebirth, and the relationship of *ātman* and *brahman*, but also because of the "liveliness" of his persona found in the *Śatapatha Brāhmaṇa* (ŚB) and the *Bṛhadāraṇyaka Upaniṣad* (BĀU). His importance within the academic tradition is central in the reconstruction of early Indian religious and philosophical history. While the Hindu tradition has generally assumed the historical veracity of this figure across the literature, a principal concern of scholarship has been to determine when he may have lived and what doctrines or ideas are historically attributable to this specific individual. A general assumption of scholarship has been that there is a "historical core" to this figure which has been progressively elaborated in the tradition into legend or myth (cf. Bronkhorst 2000, 2007; Fišer 1984; Horsch 1966; Ruben 1947; Witzel 2003).[1] A principal intellectual problem for such scholars then has been determining where history ends and legend begins or, to put it another way, whether there is one, two, or more Yājñavalkyas.

The significance of identifying the historical period of Yājñavalkya is partially due to the importance placed on the dating of the historical Buddha, Siddhārtha Gautama. Based on inscriptions commissioned by Aśoka Maurya, we are able to estimate, with a relative degree of reliability, a rough time period for the life of the Buddha. It is universally agreed that the Buddha lived for eighty

[1] Recent exceptions to this view include Black (2007) and Lindquist (2008, forthcoming a & b).

years, but precisely which eighty years is open to debate.[2] It would not be an understatement to say that the dating of Siddhārtha Gautama is the basic benchmark for dating all other literature in early Indian history. As is well known, the dating of early Sanskrit literature is principally dated based on comparative linguistics to construct a relative chronology of texts. While comparison with the Avestan materials allows for a rough *terminus post quem* of the earliest Vedic material, without a relatively firm date for the Buddha, the relative chronology of other early literature would be without an anchor.

For the purposes of Upaniṣadic scholarship, the importance of the date of the historical Buddha is principally to determine whether certain Upaniṣadic texts or doctrines are contemporaneous with or fall before or after the historical Buddha. Once this is determined, comparative linguistics and comparative literary analysis is used to further fine tune the relative distance from his lifetime.[3] A fairly straightforward way to attempt this is by analyzing whether an Upaniṣadic text seems aware of certain Buddhist concepts or terms and to what degree; this can then be compared to other dating schemes within Buddhist studies. This is clearly an imprecise science as no early Upaniṣad mentions Buddhism directly and there is a significant amount of "reading between the lines." There is also the possibility that Upaniṣadic composers intentionally avoid direct mention of Buddhist concepts and terms, even if they are familiar with them.

Such dating, in general, is complicated because it is always predicated on the dating of something else, which is further predicated on similar educated guesses. As Olivelle has noted, dating individual Upaniṣads with more precision than a couple centuries "is as stable as a house of cards" (Olivelle 1998: 12). At least, though, a date for the Buddha gives a rough basis from which to begin.

The point of this article is not to argue that the search for more precise dates of Yājñavalkya is without merit, particularly in the broad, but it is the argument of this paper to point out that recent attempts to do so have had only very limited interpretive success. Further, I suggest, there are fruitful avenues in approaching Yājñavalkya and other such figures as literary objects, rather

[2] Though the debate generally focuses on specific dating, the argument that Siddhārtha Gautama as we know him is wholly legendary occasionally appears. Buddhologists, though, have generally assumed the historicity of the Buddha and the debate over the exact dates for him is confined to about a two hundred year period (see the extensive bibliography in Bechert 1991).

[3] To a degree, archeological evidence can also aid in anchoring such texts (e.g., Bechert's 1981 study of the Buddha in comparison with Erdosy's 1993 archaeological analysis). Such mutually reinforcing types of evidence, particularly when both types of evidence are sparse, come with their own limitations since independent verification of interpretation is difficult, if not often impossible.

than as historical agents, and that such studies may be necessary precursors to attempting more specific dating. Such literary studies in biblical scholarship are fairly common and there are similar approaches employed in later Sanskrit literature, such as the epics and Purāṇas.[4] However, such an approach is all too rare in Vedic and late-Vedic material.[5]

Much of the scholarship on Yājñavalkya has been focused on determining what can be historically situated in these narratives, particularly in regards to what is indicative of an actual person. From this core, then, scholars hypothesize, sometimes implicitly, how certain narrative elements that strike them as fantastic, mythic, or ahistorical accumulate onto this core. At the center of this methodological approach is the notion that a text can reflect an "authentic" person—one which is historically verifiable and original.[6] In the case of Yājñavalkya, like certain other literary figures, the situation is complicated because authorship, person, and literary object are intertwined. In the case of Yājñavalkya and the texts ascribed to him we are put into an interpretive circle—the proclaimed "author" of some of our texts is also the principal subject.[7] Even if we do not accept the traditional ascription of authorship, and historically there is good reason not to, the search for an "authentic" person and "authentic" text cannot be separated.

Recent Approaches to Yājñavalkya

I will take two recent works (Fišer 1984; Witzel 2003) which, in varying degrees and with different levels of sophistication, make claims about a "real" Yājñavalkya. Further, each posits reasons (the one implicitly and the other more explicitly) why the portrayal of Yājñavalkya should or should not be thought of as "authentic" in different parts of the early literature. In this paper, I am not arguing for a particular historical view of Yājñavalkya as much as I am using this as a platform to discuss the problems of correlating a historical person with narrative within the confines of the early material. I will then argue why it can be important and useful to avoid the entire question of a "real" Yājñavalkya altogether. As such, I suggest, we can

[4] For example, in epic studies of figures such as Arjuna (Katz 1989) and Vyāsa (Sullivan 1999).

[5] One reason for this is that later material is dominated by stories, and thus more generally accepted as "myth" or "legend" that makes it more often the object of literary (instead of historical) analysis. It is, however, this notion that "story" somehow perverts history that has dominated our understanding of Yājñavalkya and casts suspicion on any form of story (see below). A notable exception to this trend is a forthcoming issue of *Journal of the American Academy of Religion* devoted to a literary analysis of characters in early South Asia, notably Śaunaka, Yājñavalkya, Mahāvīra, and the Buddha, among others.

[6] "Authenticity" can also denote a value judgment, suggesting that an "authentic" text or person is proper, warranted, or worthy of the value placed in it by the tradition.

[7] The White YV, ŚB, and YS, though not the MBh or Purāṇic accounts.

view the Yājñavalkya narratives as reflective of tradition through time and thus develop a more sophisticated understanding of late-Vedic narrative. By not viewing Yājñavalkya directly as a historical agent, but by using Yājñavalkya and the narratives as *a means* to uncover a literary and cultural history, we may be in a better position to develop a more sophisticated approach to the historicity of this literary figure.

Both Fišer and Witzel have argued for a "real" Yājñavalkya within the early literature, but have come to conclusions that are quite different from each other. In brief, for Fišer the "real" Yājñavalkya is the figure who appears in the earliest material, books 1-5 of the ŚB, while for Witzel, the historical Yājñavalkya is the figure found throughout the ŚB and BĀU. While both scholars have significantly advanced our understanding of this material and the figure of Yājñavalkya, I contend that neither view of a historical individual is persuasive. I will discuss the methodological and interpretive problems that I find in their endeavors, not to propose my own alternative history of Yājñavalkya, but with the goal of complicating the relationship of text and history surrounding one figure.

Fišer

Ivo Fišer (1984), in his study of Yājñavalkya, is one of the few scholars who attempts to take the "personality" of Yājñavalkya seriously as a criteria for determining his historicity.[8] Like others, however, Fišer's goal is to demarcate a "real" (versus "legendary") Yājñavalkya in the late-Vedic material. As is well known, Yājñavalkya first appears in the ŚB as a figure whose authority is referred to on several ritual matters. In the early books of the ŚB (books 1-5), Yājñavalkya's name usually appears in a list of opinions on a particular matter. In many, but not all cases, his name appears at the end and his position is taken as authoritative.[9] Fišer is careful to distinguish authoritative passages from certain passages where Yājñavalkya's opinion is in question or contrary to tradition. The later books of ŚB follow a similar pattern, but here the passages in question become more detailed and sometimes contain very short narratives (and, in one case, a longer narrative) rather than singular pronouncements.

In contrast, BĀU chapters 3-4 is a clustered set of stories bound into a unit by the figure of Yājñavalkya and is known traditionally as the *Yājñavalkyakāṇḍa*. Chapter 3 is the famous debate at Janaka's court, where Yājñavalkya bests eight interlocutors. Chapter 4 contains three "Janaka stories," where Yājñavalkya discusses various phil-

[8] Cf. also Renou (1948).

[9] For an extensive discussion of each passage in the ŚB where Yājñavalkya appears, see Lindquist (forthcoming a).

osophical matters with the famous King of Videha and this chapter concludes with a dialogue between Yājñavalkya and his wife Maitreyī.[10]

Fišer's criteria for distinguishing the "real" Yājñavalkya from a legendary one is never clearly argued in his work, but his consistent use of such a distinction suggests two main criteria: (1) the change of narrative forms found between the ŚB books and the BĀU (including the longer narratives in ŚB book 11) and (2) the particularities of language usage in the text, specifically the words attributed to Yājñavalkya (1984: 60-61). In the first case, Fišer is neither explicit about what those changes in form are nor when a line is crossed into ahistorical narrative. However, it is clear that to him a line has been crossed.

After discussing the role of Yājñavalkya's authority in the ŚB, Fišer (1984: 60) states

> The gap between Yājñavalkya's quotations in the ŚB, and those preserved in BU [BĀU], is a significant feature of Yājñavalkya's 'biography'.

This, of course, cannot be denied, but the significance and role of this "gap" is never explored in detail. Instead, Fišer repeatedly makes claims about the ahistorical nature of ŚB 11 and the BĀU (1984: 70):

> The material contained in Book 11 of ŚB, and the corresponding passages in JB [*Jaiminīya Brāhmaṇa*], might be characterized as the birth of the Yājñavalkya legend, i.e. it represents a transition from the isolated and impersonal remembrances to the 'classical' record of BU [BĀU], full of previously unknown details. Yet, it was the stories of King Janaka of Videha and his disputes with Yājñavalkya and other brahmanic teachers which captivated the imagination and almost caused plain facts to fall into oblivion.

and

> Yājñavalkya's encounters with Janaka are of no real historical relevance…

In both cases, Fišer does not go into the details of his claims, details which he sees as either unnecessary or extraneous.[11] In one sense, this is a strange move on his part as these details are fundamental to his argument about the historicity of the early Yājñavalkya. In another sense, though, it seems that Fišer takes the ahistorical nature of the later Yājñavalkya as so obvious that it only needs cursory men-

[10] BĀU 4.1 and 4.2 can be read as a linear set or independently, whereas 4.3-4 and 4.5 are clearly separate narratives. There are good reasons, however, to see the whole of BĀU 3-4 as a literary unit, where each narrative thematically and structurally builds off of the preceding ones (Lindquist forthcoming a).

[11] Cf. Fišer 1984: 60 & 70.

tion. Fišer's criteria for the "legendary" status of the later material seems based on the fact that the form of the passages has changed, coupled with his own subjective notion that these stories *simply cannot be true.* Further, Fišer seems to take *any narrative* as inherently ahistorical. Regarding BĀU, he states (p. 77) that

> ... [t]here is neither logical sequence in the arrangement of the disputes, nor is Yājñavalkya presented as a historical figure. The contents of the discussions and the gradation of the importance of the ideas expressed in them obviously determined the arrangement of the dialogues in which Yājñavalkya is conceived as a great sage of the past, beyond the reach of memory, who is an undisputed authority.[12]

How exactly Yājñavalkya can be "presented as a historical figure" according to Fišer is unclear. Fišer's own language, however, is suggestive: "impersonal" and "isolated" (1984: 70) statements, presumably here meaning the short pronouncements found in the ŚB, carry historical weight whereas narrative (ŚB 11 and BĀU) is questionable or dismissed.

A series of subjective reader-response type interpretations pepper the rest of Fišer's article. Presumably, the debate in BĀU 3 up until the questions from the lone female, Gārgī, is "monotonous" (p. 78). Gārgī appears twice in the narrative and the second instance is an "incongruous interpolation" (p. 79) which is "unusually pompous" (p. 80). Yājñavalkya treats Śākalya, his final interlocutor in the debate, "exceptionally haughtily" (p. 80).[13] The composers of BĀU, according to Fišer, are showing Yājñavalkya's absolute authority out of "zeal" and ascribe "rather unnecessarily boastful words" to him (p. 81). Fišer concludes by stating that the dialogue between Yājñavalkya and his wife (4.5) as well as the lineage (*vaṃśa*) that concludes the text (4.6) must also be completely "legendary" (p. 83ff.).

Fišer is direct in that he sees the BĀU as "legendary," even if his criteria for saying so is more opaque. This directness, though, more pointedly indicates the problems with his position. First, there are several basic questions that must be addressed in distinguishing factual versus non-factual narrative: when is a narrative a "legend" instead of a historical narrative? How does a text present someone, to use Fišer's words (p. 77), as "a historical figure" and how does it not? There is nothing in this text that could not, at least in theory, be historical (such as clearly impossible situations or miraculous events), so why are narratives dismissed as ahistorical?

[12] Fišer's claim that there is no "logical sequence" in the debates and that the episodes are arranged as a gradation of discourse is obviously contradictory. In fact, as I argue elsewhere (Lindquist forthcoming a), there is a very specific and complicated logical sequence in this text, but that arrangement does not necessarily prove that what is said by the individuals is not historically accurate.

[13] On Śākalya's role in this text, see Lindquist (forthcoming b).

What seems to trouble Fišer is narrative itself—extended interactions between characters and contexts that take on formal features of storytelling (e.g., framing, character development, thematic continuity, or foreshadowing). But at what point are narrative structures and devices a signal that a narrative is ahistorical? Are we to define "legend" based on the accumulation of narrative structures and devices in a text? How many of these devices constitute a "legend?" One? Two? A dozen? Are certain devices (such as a "gradation" of ideas) to be weighted more heavily as indicative of legend? It is true that the nature of some passages in ŚB 11 and BĀU have changed—they are proper narratives, rather than singular pronouncements—but why should a genre shift indicate a shift away from history? Must historical remembrance be a simple listing of facts, one that is "impersonal" and "isolated?" Such questions are not rhetorical, but rather they are fundamental if we wish to avoid idiosyncratic reader-responses based solely on subjective impressions.

While Fišer discusses Yājñavalkya's character, especially his sarcastic persona, he uses this trait in an attempt to attribute a motive ("zeal") to the author of BĀU and to dismiss this portrayal of Yājñavalkya. As I have shown elsewhere (Lindquist forthcoming a), there is a historical development of Yājñavalkya's sarcasm across texts and it has different effects in different contexts. Attributing this development to the "zeal" of the composer or seeing it as unnecessary or superfluous literary flair ignores *what* the texts are saying, the *reasons* they are saying it, and *how* they are saying it. These are precisely the questions that need to be addressed. While there is a development and increase across texts in the sarcasm attributed to Yājñavalkya, this could simply be because a shift from pronouncements to longer narratives allows for more opportunities. Further, an increase in Yājñavalkya's apparent authority across these texts can be more simply explained as a "rise to authority" of a figure within a literary tradition that *may or may not* correlate with a historical human individual. As far as I can tell, there is no definitive way to tell the difference between historically accurate remembrance or literary fantasy in these texts. Formal narrative structures and devices are signs of good storytelling, rather than historical inaccuracy.

Finally, Fišer also suggests that the language used in the texts helps in determining the historical veracity of the figure portrayed. In particular, he states repeatedly that the existence of *hapax legomena* in the BĀU shows that the Yājñavalkya portrayed in the BĀU is not connected directly to the Yājñavalkya of the ŚB. Fišer's argument is that the continued use of *hapax* in the BĀU indicates the linguistic needs of a newer tradition, needing new linguistic forms for their doctrines that are then placed into the mouth of an established mythical figure for authority.

The logic in this argument is highly specious. The use of *hapaxes*, as far as I can see, has nothing to do with distancing the BĀU from the ŚB accounts. Fišer himself points to *hapaxes* in both the ŚB and BĀU (suggesting similarity, rather than difference, between the texts). As Witzel (2003: 125ff.) has shown, the use of *hapaxes* and novel compounded forms could equally indicate that the text is portraying a single historical Yājñavalkya using a "personalized speech" and is not a "legendary" attribution of speech and ideas to a revered mythical figure.[14]

In any event, if Fišer wants us to see *hapaxes* in BĀU as indicating that the Yājñavalkya of BĀU is fundamentally distinct from the Yājñavalkya of ŚB, logic would require us to view *anything* in BĀU not prefigured in the ŚB to be a new and unconnected innovation. Such a view requires a strict consistency between texts, patently at odds with even a highly-evolved oral literature. More problematic is that such a view asks us to take a text (or part of a text) as a closed unit, rather than as a textual instantiation of a dynamic cultural milieu that historically changes.

Witzel

While Fišer argues for a fundamental historical disconnect between an early (historical) Yājñavalkya in the ŚB and a later (legendary) one in ŚB 11 and BĀU, Witzel (2003) argues that Yājñavalkya's portrayal across these texts is indicative of a single historical individual. Witzel's approach is novel, even if it is not necessarily more compelling than Fišer's. His argument is based on two criteria—that the portrayal of the character of Yājñavalkya is relatively consistent across the texts and that there is similarity in speech-use that suggests, to Witzel, a "personalized speech" of a single individual. In this way, Witzel's focus on language and personality parallels Fišer, but he does not take a change in narrative form across texts as indicative of a change in the historical veracity of the figure.

> It should also be noted that the 'different' types of Yājñavalkyas appearing in the early part of ŚB (1-5) and the later one (ŚB 11-13) are due to the content of the texts, not to a difference in personality. The later parts deal with additional material and discuss it in a more speculative way, often in form of dialogues (*brahmodya*), than the ritualistic sections in ŚB 1-5. (2003: 106)

Witzel extends this to include the BĀU, taking into account its more "mystical" context. As such, Witzel takes Yājñavalkya to be a complex individual who is simultaneously a ritual specialist, a Upaniṣadic thinker, and even a mystic on certain occasions. This portrayal of Yājñavalkya is more compelling since it is more sensi-

[14] However, there are logical problems with this argument as well (see below).

tive to concerns of genre and, from a historical point of view, that individuals themselves are not one-dimensional.

While I agree that there are a number of means by which the pronouncements and the narratives of Yājñavalkya attempt consistency, particularly with regards to Yājñavalkya's personality, the general topic matter, etc., there is a significant problem in accepting Witzel's suggestion that consistency suggests "historical fact." Religious narratives centered on a literary individual would favor consistency as consistency creates a continuity between literary portrayals. As such, if there was not an attempt at a certain consistency, a listening audience would not find such a narrative compelling or "believable."[15]

Of course, the need and degree of consistency varies case by case based on a number of factors—the degree of reverence a text or person may have or may strive for, the historical needs at the time for a particular group and how those needs may be embodied in a narrative, or the ideological position of a particular genre. This is not to say that such literary portrayals are universally consistent or that they may not be intentionally inconsistent (particularly when an inconsistency is a theme in the narrative). Indeed, the complex history of the oral transmission of early Sanskrit literature means that a certain inconsistency is to be expected. This does not mean that innovation does not happen at all or happen often, but rather when that innovation is put into the context of an established authority (which Yājñavalkya is, *even in the early ŚB*), it is likely to be "naturalized" within the discourse by connecting that innovation to already established tropes, themes, personalities, and doctrine.[16] In this sense, particularly when narratives are centered around a personality, a certain consistency or "cultural logic" is employed to make such personalities historically and culturally believable. Even in the case where such literary figures seem radically removed from a particular context, a consistency is still often attempted if it is culturally thought necessary. In this light, one could see the early Yājñavalkya pronouncements/stories as forming a "template" of Yājñavalkya's personality which is later employed, manipulated, and even modified according to the needs of a particular community at a particular time.[17]

[15] I have argued elsewhere (Lindquist forthcoming a) that in one particular portrayal of Yājñavalkya in the MBh book 12 what defines Yājñavalkya as a literary character has all but disappeared. In that case, the passage is immediately followed by the first extended hagiography of how Yājñavalkya received the White Yajurveda from the Sun. This narrative is tacked on, I argue, precisely because it fills in the possible gap of associating this figure with his literary past.

[16] This, of course, does not mean we cannot notice particular innovations within a tradition nor that "naturalization" is necessarily absolute, but that the degree of "naturalizing" innovation must be assessed on a case-by-case basis. On one particular literary innovation in the BĀU, see Lindquist (forthcoming b).

[17] But this does not mean in the early texts that the teachings themselves are necessarily of one person or not, only that the form of the narrative is constructed in a way to serve certain ends.

Witzel further argues that the speech attributed to Yājñavalkya is indicative of a single personality that binds the different literary portrayals together. For example, he notes parallels in the fashion that Yājñavalkya dismisses other ritual interpretations other than his own (2003: 119-121) or his view of himself and Brahmins as a group (2003: 121-123). In doing so, Yājñavalkya can be seen as a compelling figure, both to scholars and to those within the Hindu tradition.

But how does one demarcate such speech as a personal language in these texts? In a fashion opposite of Fišer, Witzel (2003: 124ff.) argues that the continuous use of *hapax*, the use of old words in new ways (particularly in constructing novel compounds), and the repeated use of *svid* and *evāham* in his discourses indicate that Yājñavalkya is a single historical person in the ŚB and the BĀU. He also points out that many of Yājñavalkya's statements are witty, straightforward, almost common-sense responses and that such consistency of his speech across the ŚB and BĀU points to a single, historical individual.

Witzel's attempt at demarcating a "personal language" is the most novel approach to Yājñavalkya's historicity to date, but it again raises a series of problems that must be addressed before it can be taken in any way as conclusive. First and foremost, while Fišer's argument is marred by not distinguishing "legend" from "history" in narratives, Witzel similarly does not draw a distinction between "individual" and "shared" speech. Is it even possible or desirable to speak of such categories within the limited number of stories we have of Yājñavalkya? What of others' speech within the same or related texts? How can Witzel demarcate *an individual's* speech, if he does not do so with the speech of others in the same texts, as a form of counterpoint?[18]

Another problem, not dissimilar to those mentioned above, is how do we theoretically and practically demarcate individualized speech and stereotyped speech? Since Yājñavalkya appears rather unique in the Vedic sources for his provocative statements and his irreverent personality, it is equally likely that Yājñavalkya himself became a template, even quite early, for a tradition that needed a particular type of spokesman to promulgate and legitimize newly emerging ideas in contestation with other established traditions. In this way, it is equally possible that the tradition at the time had a stereotyped notion of Yājñavalkya and the way that he was thought to talk. Certainly, a stereotyped notion of "his" speech could easily be imitated in other stories.

Further, as Witzel himself acknowledges, a detailed analysis of other teachers' speech of and around this time period would need

[18] Witzel himself suggests that this needs to be carried out, yet still draws the conclusion that, for example in BĀU 4.3 Yājñavalkya's "...way of expression is a very *personal* one, fit for this quasi mystical chapter" (2003: 132; italics original).

to be carried out, but it is again unclear how such data could be used to isolate a historical person from a narrative tradition by means of the words employed. For example, Witzel argues (2003: 124-125) that *svid* and *evāham* are common in the speech that is attributed to Yājñavalkya. However, as Thompson (1997: 30ff.) has shown, *svid* is used more than 40 times in the *Ṛgveda* and at least 12 of those appear to be in *brahmodya*-like or riddling settings.[19] While *svid* itself does not necessarily mark an interrogative statement (though it often goes along with them), it does, according to Thompson, function "to mark the passage in which it occurs as emphatic, i.e., marked, charged, or of special significance" (1997: 30). Thompson contends that *svid* is probably commonly used in *brahmodya*-like settings because it "suggests that *brahmodyas* are perceived to be a form of charged discourse" (1997: 30), which is certainly the case with Yājñavalkya in the BĀU. The dramatic rise in the use of *svid* that Witzel points out from the early ŚB, to the later ŚB, to the BĀU can easily be explained by the fact that it is in the later books that we are more often faced with the context of *brahmodyas*. Even in the BĀU, there are others who use the particle and it is not limited to Yājñavalkya (BĀU 3.1.1 by Janaka; BĀU 3.2.10 by Jāratkārava Ārtabhāga)—so how, then, is it personal? It is important to note that in all cases in the *Yājñavalkyakāṇḍa*, *svid* is used in interrogative sentences (rhetorically at 3.9.17) and Yājñavalkya only uses the particle in two situations—in insulting Śākalya (3.9.17) and multiple times in his final question/riddle to the assembled Brahmins (3.9.28). The particle does not appear to be used outside of the *brahmodya*-setting at all (i.e., in BĀU 4).[20]

While Witzel has put forth the most detailed study of Yājñavalkya, and has suggested a novel means to investigate the language attributed to Yājñavalkya, there are questions that need to be addressed if we are to consider "language" as a marker of a personal—and in this case, historical—identity. How can one tell the difference between a community attempting continuity in their literary tradition and an actual, single, historical individual? What criteria are being used to demarcate the language of one person versus the language of others (versus the language of the community that is maintaining these traditions)? While Witzel's project holds out interesting possibilities, they are, for now, only that.

[19] Thompson also states that there are 10 other suggestive, but less certain, instances (1997: 30).

[20] Witzel's *eva + aham* of Yājñavalkya in the ŚB occurs only at BĀU 4.3.20 where Yājñavalkya is describing/imitating someone else's speech (cf. also Gārgī's speech at BĀU 3.8.1 which includes *hantāham eva* and, at 3.8.2, *evāham*). Outside of direct speech, *svam eva* at 3.1.2 emphasizes that Yājñavalkya alone (probably indicating arrogance) claims the cows meant for the victor in the debate.

Conclusion

I have, up until this point, critiqued two opposing positions about the historicity of Yājñavalkya in ŚB and BĀU, one which takes only the earliest ŚB material as historical (Fišer) and the other which takes the combined early literature as historical (Witzel). Both have greatly expanded our understanding of Yājñavalkya, particularly in the use of language in this material. However, as I hope I have shown, neither is particularly persuasive in regards to what constitutes a historical figure. I have attempted to illuminate some of the problems that must be addressed should scholars continue the endeavor to demarcate a "real" Yājñavalkya in early Indian literature, particularly if no new literary material comes to light to definitively settle this matter.

None of this has been done with the intention of saying that such historical studies should be abandoned altogether, but it has been done with the intent to show that much more sophisticated theoretical models need to be developed if this sort of inquiry is to bear fruit. In particular, what is necessary is an analysis of how narrative and history are interrelated as well as an explicit discussion about the criteria used to determine if something is historical fact or literary imagination. As I have suggested, neither of these attempts have been able to conclusively demarcate a "real" Yājñavalkya—more often than not, the logic employed to do so can simply be turned on itself or equally compelling interpretive alternatives can be given.

Further, a more sophisticated view of literature must be adopted as regards the notion of "narrativity;" that is the development of structures, themes, and so on that transform simple speech-acts into narratives. Any narrative (whether told for the first time or repeated for generations) takes on formal literary characteristics which do not necessarily say anything about historicity. This is to say something that should in itself be obvious: narrative is ever affected by narrativity. This does not mean that what is being told is historically true or not, but it does mean that the speech is motivated towards various ends and literary characteristics are employed to support those ends. As Roland Barthes (1972) has shown, we are always surrounded by narrativity whether it be in our speech acts, our justice practices, our view of our own individual lives, or in our various cultural productions.

The textual evidence as we have it does not appear to lend itself, as far as I can determine, to drawing an objective line regarding the historicity of Yājñavalkya in the early literature. Clearly by the time of the epics, where, for example, Yājñavalkya is portrayed as simultaneously functioning as the *adhvaryu* priest for Indra in heaven and for Yudhiṣṭhira on earth (MBh II), we have crossed into the realm of literary and religious imagination at least in this particular case. But in the early material, no such sharp line between historical remembrance and literary imagination exists. By taking a figure like Yājñavalkya as a literary, rather than historical, figure we can move beyond subjective reader-response interpretations about the "authenticity" of a figure and turns towards investigating the literary nature of this figure and the value placed in him by the tradition.

Bibliography

Barthes, R. (1972), *Mythologies*, trans. A. Lavers (New York: Hill and Wang).
Berchert, H. (ed.) (1991-1997), *The Dating of the Historical Buddha (Die Datierung des Historischen Buddha)*, 3 vols. (Göttingen: Vandenhoech & Ruprecht).
_____. (1981), "The Date of the Buddha Reconsidered," *Indologica Taurinensia* 10: 29-36.
Black, B. (2007), *The Character of the Self in Ancient India: Priests, Kings, and Women in the Early Upaniṣads* (Albany: State University of New York Press).
Bronkhorst, J. (2007), *Greater Magadha: Studies in the Culture of Early India* (Leiden: Brill).
_____. (2000), *The Two Traditions of Meditation in Ancient India* (New Delhi: Motilal Banarsidass).
Erdosy, G. (1993), "The Archaeology of Early Buddhism" in *Studies on Buddhism in Honour of Professor A.K. Warder*, ed. N.K. Waglc and F. Watanabe (Toronto: University of Toronto), 40-56.
Fišer, I. "Yājñavalkya in the Śruti Tradition of the Veda," *Acta Orientalia* 10: 55-87.
Horsch, P. (1966), *Die vedische Gāthā- und Śloka-Literatur* (Bern: Francke Verlag).
Katz, R. (1989), *Arjuna in the Mahabharata: Where Krishna is, There is Victory* (Columbia: University of South Carolina Press).
Lindquist, S. (2008), "Gender at Janaka's Court: Women in the Olivelle, P. (1998), *The Early Upaniṣads: Annotated Text and Translation* (New York: Oxford University Press).
_____. (forthcoming a), *Creating a Sage: The Literary Life of Yājñavalkya* (Albany: State University of New York Press).
_____. (forthcoming b), "Literary Lives and a Literal Death: Yājñavalkya, Śākalya, and an Upaniṣadic Death Sentence," *Journal of the American Academy of Religion*, online pre-publication, Nov. 2010, doi: 10.1093/jaarel/lfq060
Renou, L. (1948), "La relation du Śatapathabrāhmaṇa avec la Bṛhadāraṇyakopaniṣad et la personalité de Yājñavalkya," *Indian Culture* 14: 75-89.
Ruben, W. (1947), *Die Philosophen der Upaniṣaden* (Bern: A. Francke).

Sullivan, B. (1999), *Seer of the Fifth Veda: Kṛṣṇa Dvaipāyana Vyāsa in the Mahābhārata* (New Delhi: Motilal Banarsidass).

Thompson, G. (1997), "The *Brahmodya* and Vedic Discourse," *Journal of the American Oriental Society* 117.1: 13-37.

Witzel, M. (2003), "Yājñavalkya as Ritualist and Philosopher, and His Personal Language" in *Paitimāna: Essays in Iranian, Indo-European, and Indian Studies in Honor of Hanns-Peter Schmidt*, ed. S. Adhami (Costa Mesa: Mazda Publishers), 103-143.

Robert A. Goodding

A Theologian in a South Indian Kingdom: The Historical Context of the Jīvanmuktiviveka *of Vidyāraṇya*

Authorship of the Jīvanmuktiviveka

Vidyāraṇya, also known as Mādhava, composed the *Jīvanmuktiviveka* (JMV) in ca. 1380 CE,[1] toward the end of his life after he had entered the *saṃnyāsāśrama* and had become the pontiff of the Śṛṅgeri *maṭha* in southwestern Karnataka. This *maṭha*, or monastic institution, still endures today. The text is a novel work in Advaita Vedānta, though Vidyāraṇya places himself in line with the earlier Advaitins Śaṅkara, Sureśvara, and Padmapāda, whom he calls teachers[2] (JMV 2.9.9-14 and 2.3.64).[3] Like his predecessors, Vidyāraṇya defines the renouncer's goal as the attainment of the nondual "knowledge" (*jñāna, vidyā*). The Śaṅkaran Advaitins understood that this experiential knowledge of the equivalence of the Self and Brahman is sufficient for the attainment of liberation. Although Vidyāraṇya is careful to incorporate the basic positions of his teachers, he departs from the earlier Advaita of Śaṅkara by prescribing in addition to knowledge a program of yogic discipline based on such texts as the *Bhagavad Gītā*, the *Pātañjalīya Yogasūtras*, the *Gauḍapādīya Kārikās*, and the *Laghu-Yogavāsiṣṭha*. He inte-

[1] The date 1380 is given by J.F. Sprockhoff in the first part of his thorough study of the JMV (1964: 225). He assigned it to 1350 in an earlier article (1962: 202).

[2] Andrew Fort (1996, 1998) has characterized Vidyāraṇya's contribution as "Yogic Advaita," stating that the JMV is syncretic. Elsewhere Fort (1999: 377-378) analyzes Vidyāraṇya's use of the *Yoga Sūtras* in his text but maintains that Vidyāraṇya still believed that "ultimately there is no doubt that knowing *brahman* is the essential element for full liberation."

[3] Citations of the JMV refer to my own edition and translation of the text, where I have given a new numbering system. See Goodding (2002).

grates the structures of thought from the Śaṅkaran Advaita and the Pātañjalīya Yoga systems into one system bearing on the life and goal of the renouncer.

The JMV is thus a constructive synthesis of models from Indian thought and in this way stands as a novel contribution to the history of the idea of liberation-in-life (*jīvanmukti*). Nevertheless, Vidyāraṇya does not claim to say anything that is not already in the revealed Vedic truth of *śruti* or in the tradition of *smṛti*. The work became well-known in India, but I believe it was composed for a limited, internal audience participating in the debates in medieval Vedānta theology. Earlier in his career, Vidyāraṇya (under the name Mādhava) had composed a legal digest and commentary on the *Pārāśarasmṛti* known as the *Pārāśara-Mādhavīya* (PāM) and, within that work, included a separate treatise on renunciation. There he deals with the first three of the four types of renouncers: the *kuṭīcaka*, the *bahūdaka*, and the *haṃsa*.[4] In the JMV, Vidyāraṇya focuses on the highest type of renouncer, the *paramahaṃsa*.

Despite all that has been written about the sage Vidyāraṇya, we have little reliable data about his identity. First I want to consider the clues available in Vidyāraṇya's own writings. In the beginning of the JMV itself, the author outlines the plan of his book, naming the four types of renouncers, and says "Now, the practices of these (renouncers) have been described by us in the commentary on the *Pārāśarasmṛti*. Here the *paramahaṃsa* is described" (1.0.11). These words by themselves are the single best evidence we have that Vidyāraṇya, the author of the JMV, is the same as Mādhava the author of the PāM. We find in the introductory verses 6-7 of the PāM that the author was the son of Māyaṇa and Śrīmatī, brother of Sāyaṇa and Bhoganātha. He was the disciple of the Śaṅkarācāryas Vidyātīrtha and Bhāratītīrtha. These verses also mentions Śrīkaṇṭhanātha, who may have been his family's preceptor. He studied the *Black Yajurveda* and the *Baudhāyana Dharmasūtra* and belonged to the Bhāradvāja-gotra.[5] His date of birth is unknown; however, according to an inscription preserved at the Śṛṅgeri *maṭha*, we may be certain he died in 1386.[6]

While in his *pūrvāśrama*, i.e., before he had renounced as an old person, Vidyāraṇya contributed widely during his career to the separate branches of Sanskrit literature under the name Mādhava. In

[4] See PāM, vol. 1, (1973-1974: 530 ff). The terms refer to types of renouncers and their increasing levels of intensity of renunciation. The *kuṭīcaka* is a renouncer living in a hut, the *bahūdaka* lives near a *tīrtha* or pilgrimage site, and the *haṃsa* begins entering the higher intensity away from society.

[5] See PāM vol. 1, (1973-1974: 3), verses 6-7: *śrīmatī jananī sukīrtir māyaṇaḥ. sāyaṇo bhoganāthaś ca manobuddhī sahodarau. yasya baudhāyanaṃ sūtraṃ śākhā yasya ca yājuṣī, bhāradvājaṃ kulaṃ yasya sarvajñaḥ sa hi mādhavaḥ.*

[6] The inscription has been translated and published in *Vidyāraṇya* (1985: 112-117). It records a grant made by Harihara II to the *maṭha* upon Vidyāraṇya's death and is dated May 26, 1386.

addition to the his digest of civil and religious law in the PāM already mentioned, another related work is the *Kālanirṇaya*. This work falls within the general category of astrology and astronomy and treats the nature of time and how it is divided in the Hindu calendar. But the *Kālanirṇaya* also relates to dharmaśāstra in that it discusses the auspicious times to perform rituals, and the author specifically mentions that he composed it after his commentary on *Pārāśarasmṛti*.[7] Vidyāraṇya as Mādhava also composed the well-known work on the fundamentals of Pūrvamīmāṃsā, the *Jaiminīyanyāyamālāvistara*. Vidyāraṇya is mostly known for his philosophical works in Advaita Vedānta. However, from these works earlier in his career on the dharmaśāstric legal literature, ritual performance, and the Pūrvamīmāṃsā, we gather that his understanding of ritual action and Advaitic knowledge does not place the two in some conflict as one might assume they are. There seems to be no indication that before he renounced, Vidyāraṇya as Mādhava was himself married with children. Nevertheless, from these aforementioned works on ritual such as the *Kālanirṇaya*, we see that he was sensitive to the standards of social and religious life of the wider householder population who formed the ritual-performing collective. We can deduce, furthermore, that he recognized that the Advaitic knowledge prescribed for the renouncer, which was the focus of his literary efforts leading up to the JMV, was not for everyone. I argue that Vidyāraṇya in the JMV attempts to lessen the tension between the householder community and the renouncer by clarifying the renouncer's duties, or *dharmas*, and the purposes, or *prayojanas*, of liberation-in-life, making them more identifiable to the householder community. I will address this point further in the section on the context of the JMV.

Earlier on, Vidyāraṇya as Mādhava was involved also in the philosophical debates between the different *darśanas*, or philosophical schools. His *Sarvadarśanasaṃgraha* is an arrangement of the various positions in Indian philosophy that Mādhava knew starting from the materialist Cārvākas and Buddhists that he thought had the least validity, up to the Pātañjalīya Yoga system and Śaṅkara's Advaita that is the highest expression of the truth. The introduction of this text mentions the author "Sāyaṇa-Mādhava," which led A.C. Burnell to believe that Mādhava and his brother were the same person. Without any other internal or independent evidence, we may only presume the work is his because the view expressed in this text is consistent with those of the later Vidyāraṇya the Advaitin. We also can speculate that Mādhava and Sāyaṇa collaborated and that Mādhava had some involvement in Sāyaṇa's *Vedabhāṣya*.[8] Vidyāraṇya also composed works

[7] See *Kālamādhava*, (1989: ii), verse 4: *vyākhyāya mādhavācāryo dharmān pārāśarānatha, tadanuṣṭhānakālasya nirṇayaṃ kartum udyataḥ*.

[8] P.V. Kane believed Sāyaṇa must have collaborated (vol. 1, pt. 2, 3d ed. 1997: 781): "It should not be supposed that Sāyaṇa single-handedly composed the Vedabhāṣyas. He

from the Advaita standpoint such as the *Bṛhadāraṇyakavārtikasāra*, which is a commentary on Śaṅkara's *Aparokṣānubhūti*, his own commentaries on the *Aitareya*, *Chāndogya*, *Kaivalya*, *Nṛsiṃhottaratāpini*, and *Taittirīya Upaniṣads*, as well as a metrical work on the philosophy of the Upaniṣads, the *Anubhūtiprakāśa*. Other philosophical works include the *Vivaraṇaprameyasaṃgraha* and his most important work on Advaita, the *Pañcadaśī*, which became a standard work of the Vivaraṇa school of post-Śaṅkaran Advaita. The tradition attaches Vidyāraṇya's name to the *Vivaraṇaprameyasaṃgraha* and also to the hagiographical work, the *Śaṅkaradigvijaya*, but these may not be his works. This confusion also has led to controversy over identifying Vidyāraṇya with Mādhava[9] and added to the confusion over Mādhava-Vidyāraṇya's political role in the founding of the Vijayanagara kingdom. T.M.P. Mahadevan accepted the identity of Mādhava and Vidyāraṇya, and Mādhava's political activities in the founding of Vijayanagara, but believed that the *Pañcadaśī* and the *Vivaraṇaprameyasaṃgraha* were works of Vidyāraṇya's preceptor, Bhāratītīrtha,[10] suggesting Vidyāraṇya may have been a surname of both men. In the JMV itself, Vidyāraṇya cites the *Pañcadaśī* as an authority and yet does not explicitly treat the text as his own. I will deal with the *Śaṅkaradigvijaya* more below in regard to Vidyāraṇya's supposed political activity in the founding of Vijayanagara.

Controversy over Vijayanagara and Vidyāraṇya

Some historians in the twentieth century would have us understand the character of Vidyāraṇya as a unique blend of religious renouncer and secular politician active in guiding the founders of the Vijayanagara kingdom in the early and middle parts of the fourteenth century. His cultural, intellectual, and political contributions mark the beginning of what many believe went on to become the last great Hindu empire in South India. In another, bolder interpretation of Vidyāraṇya's career, Paul Hacker suggested that Vidyāraṇya, "in a sort of deliberate Hindu cultural politics" (Hacker, cited in Halbfass, 1995: 29), carried out his literary and institutional activities against the effects of the incursions of the Central Asian Turkish

was probably the chairman of the committee of scholars fathered for carrying out the work of several bhāṣyas."

[9] Historians in series of articles carried on this debate in the 1930s. R. Rama Rao (1931: 78-92) denied this identity, while K. Markandeya Sarma (1932: 611-614) rejoins Rao and cites the same evidence given here from PāM. M.A. Doraiswamy Iyengar (n.d.: 241-250) rejects the identity and would "reduce Vidyāraṇya from the position of a world-figure to that of an insignificant ascetic who presided over the Śṛṅgeri Maṭh from c. 1377 to 1386 A.D." (243). My own view here is that they are the same, but Mādhava-Vidyāraṇya's political role is less clear than the historians of the twentieth century want to ascribe to him. I would not, however, call him "an insignificant ascetic."

[10] See Mahadevan (1957: 1-8).

Muslims into South India in the late thirteenth and early fourteenth centuries, creating a new orthodoxy of Brahmanism. It is true that the Vijayanagara state was founded after the incursions of the Delhi Sultanate destabilized the existing political networks of the South Indian peninsula, leading to the collapse or decline of the previous kingdoms. However, whatever role Vidyāraṇya played in the founding of this kingdom is not certain, even though many scholars have presumed it.

Standard historical works dealing with the question of the founding of Vijayanagara have repeated the same story, which would lead readers to believe this story's general acceptance among experts. One can take, for instance, K.A. Nilakanta Sastri's *A History of South India* (1976: 237-39) and N. Venkataramanayya's contribution to *The Delhi Sultanate* (1960: 272-273).[11] The fact that this version of the history of the founding of Vijayanagara, which represents the Andhra or Telugu version, was chosen to appear in such a major work as Bharatiya Vidya Bhavan's *History and Culture of the Indian People* volume 6 on the Delhi Sultanate, excluding the differing views of the Kannada historians, indicates its wide acceptance by many historians in the twentieth century. Subsequently, this story found its way into many standard works on Indian history. One of the problems with the Andhra version is that it draws heavily on the later Sanskrit textual accounts such as the *Vidyāraṇya-kālajñāna*, *Vidyāraṇya-vṛttānta*, and the *Vidyāraṇya-śaka* that were composed some 200 years after the events in question. According to the Andhra version, the founding Saṅgama brothers, Harihara I and Bukka I, were retainers of the Kākatīya royal house and were captured by the Turkish Muslims during their attack on Warangal, the Kākatīya capital in Andhra. The brothers were taken to Delhi and converted to Islam. They were then sent back to the south as administrators of the Sultanate and met Vidyāraṇya, who saw fit to convert them back to the Hindu Dharma. They then are supposed to have broken away from the Sultanate and to have begun forming their own kingdom in ca. 1336. The scholars who published the *Vijayanagara Sexcentenary Commemoration Volume* (1936) then erroneously agreed upon this date of 1336. According to this version, drawing as it does on later Sanskrit sources that purport to relate Vidyāraṇya's activities, Vidyāraṇya is thus given a key role in the founding of Vijayanagara. The Saṅgamas supposedly were successful in founding their glorious Hindu kingdom only after they received Vidyāraṇya's blessing.

Against the Andhra or Telugu version, the adherents of a Karnatic origin of the Saṅgamas argue that Harihara and Bukka were already in the service of the Hoysaḷas. The city called Hosapaṭṭaṇa or Virūpākṣapaṭṭaṇa had already been built on the site of the future

[11] See also Venkataramanayya (1990: 59-90).

Vijayanagara by Ballāla III, and was known also by its name still used currently, Hampi. The early date of 1336 for the foundation of the new kingdom is discarded also because, in the view first proposed by Father Henry Heras, it is based only on spurious copperplate inscriptions made in the sixteenth century. This theory states these copperplate inscriptions were forged by the Śṛṅgeri *maṭha* at a time when the Vijayanagara kings shifted their interest from the Śaivite *maṭha* to the Vaiṣṇava sect, and the leaders of the *maṭha* wanted to reassert their prestige by connecting themselves directly with the foundation of the empire.

For their part, Heras and others favored the date 1346 for the founding of the kingdom, pointing to an inscription recording what is called either the *mahotsava*, or "great festival," of the brothers held at the Śṛṅgeri *maṭha*.[12] This inscription does not mention any role of Vidyāraṇya and thus his political activities, if any, do not even figure in the founding of the kingdom. The actual founding of the capital would have been decades later, owing to a dynastic continuity between the Saṅgamas and the Hoysaḷas through marriage alliances. The picture is more one of a smooth transition of power from the Hoysaḷas to the Saṅgamas. The controversy over the origins of the Saṅgama brothers and the founding of the city and empire continued for the better part of the twentieth century, without resolution between the two factions.

Revised Views of Vidyāraṇya's Career

Sufficient research has appeared in recent decades to give a very different account from what historians had written previously about the theologian Vidyāraṇya's role in early Vijayanagara and the Śṛṅgeri *maṭha*. This research may allow us to further delineate the scope of Vidyāraṇya's activities and perhaps more accurately infer some of his intentions. From the epigraphical work of Vasundhara Filliozat (1973, 1999) and the article drawing from Filliozat's work by Hermann Kulke (1985), as well as the study by Phillip Wagoner (2000) treating the Sanskrit text sources such as the *Vidyāraṇya-kālajñāna* and the others mentioned, we may derive the following conclusions:

(1) Vidyāraṇya had no involvement in the politics of founding Vijayanagara; at least there is no contemporary epigraphical or textual evidence naming him in connection with these events. Phillip Wagoner (2000: 304-305) interprets the later Sanskrit textual accounts, where Vidyāraṇya is mentioned and which is datable to the sixteenth and seventeenth centuries, as a "political foundation myth, an ideological attempt to represent the authority of the Vijayanagara

[12] Father Henry Heras (1929) and B.A. Saletore (1934) both proposed this view.

state as deriving directly *from that of the Sultanate.*" It was meant to cast Vijayanagara as a legitimate successor state to Delhi among the other sultanates in the Deccan. The role played by Vidyāraṇya in the founding of Vijayanagara as political and religious advisor to Harihara I and Bukka I was probably imagined at least 200 years afterward, and Vidyāraṇya's name was used presumably to give these events legitimacy and prestige.

(2) The earlier notions of Vidyāraṇya's political stature derive in part from the misidentification of his former pre-renunciation name, Mādhava, with Mādhavamantrin who was a minister to the Saṅgama brother Mallapa I. We cannot infer that Mādhava-Vidyāraṇya carried out any political activities in his early career similar those attributed to Mādhavamantrin.

(3) Mādhava is not mentioned in any inscriptions before 1374, but only the prior *jagadgurus* of Śṛṅgeri Vidyātīrtha and Bhāratītīrtha are mentioned. Therefore, the earlier role of Mādhava in Śṛṅgeri and his ascension to *jagadguru* as Vidyāraṇya cannot be confirmed before 1374. We can only presume that he was present in 1346 at the Saṅgamas' *mahotsava* at Śṛṅgeri, although he is not mentioned.

The key event in the founding of Vijayanagara that the historians favoring the Kannada version have pointed to is the *mahotsava* that the Saṅgama rulers are said to have held at the Advaita Vedānta *maṭha* at Śṛṅgeri in 1346. Śṛṅgeri is one of the monastic institutions that the Advaitin tradition believes was founded by the great Śaṅkara. We may consider this *mahotsava*, or "great festival," a historical event because it was recorded with an inscription found at Śṛṅgeri. Here, in 1346, the new Vijayanagara sovereigns began a patronage relationship with the Śaṅkarācārya and Vidyātīrtha. They received his legitimizing blessing for their kingdom and Śṛṅgeri received the surrounding lands as a land grant, or *agrahāra*. Śṛṅgeri is in Karnataka, near the border with Kerala, and it appears that the Saṅgamas' relationship with it lends more credence to the Kannada version of the founding of Vijayanagara kingdom, according to which the Saṅgamas were retainers to the Hoysaḷa royal house in Karnataka and not the Kākatīyas in Andhra. For the Kannada version, the date 1346 then marks the inheritance of the Hoysaḷa domains by the new Saṅgama dynasty.

(4) From the time of this *mahotsava* in 1346 until Vidyāraṇya's ascension to the role of *jagadguru* in c. 1374, the lands and money granted to Śṛṅgeri by the Vijayanagara rulers greatly increased. Therefore, when Vidyāraṇya actually became the *jagadguru*, Śṛṅgeri was a very different place from what it had been just 30 years earlier. We may surmise that the influence attached to the role of *jagadguru* had increased as well.

It is not clear exactly what characterized this increased influence or what degree of secular power was vested in it. One can at least say this influence allowed for a further promulgation of Advaitin views as they were being taught at Śṛṅgeri at this time under the *jagadgurus* Vidyātīrtha, Bhāratītīrtha, and Vidyāraṇya, as well as provided the environment for the commentaries on the Veda carried out by Sāyaṇa and his workers. Vidyāraṇya himself had presumably already completed his PāM and his *Sarvadarśanasaṃgraha* before he had become *jagadguru* in ca. 1374 and perhaps at some time shortly before this he took the name Vidyāraṇya upon formally renouncing. It was after this that he composed the JMV, some time between 1380 and his death in 1386.[13]

To return to Paul Hacker's thesis, given what I have outlined from the work of Filliozat and Kulke, I pose the following questions: (1) In what sense may we say the activities of Vidyāraṇya constitute a "deliberate Hindu cultural politics?" (2) What was his intention? (3) At whom or what was it directed? Was it prompted by the Islamic presence in South India in the fourteenth century, or by other factors? In presenting his thesis, Hacker ascribes to Vidyāraṇya the responsibility for creating the myth in the *Śaṅkaradigvijaya* (ŚDV) of Śaṅkara and Śaṅkara's founding of Śṛṅgeri and the other Advaitin *maṭhas*. Jonathan Bader (2000: 55-56; n. 75) has shown in a full-length study of all the Śaṅkaran hagiographical works that Mādhava-Vidyāraṇya was not the author of the ŚDV. This work was composed at the earliest sometime between 1650 and 1798 and was therefore wrongly attributed to Mādhava-Vidyāraṇya. If this is the case, an attempt to infer Vidyāraṇya's "cultural politics" is made more ambiguous and must be revised.

It is also evident, as was noted by Kulke, that the oldest inscriptions at Śṛṅgeri date to the twelfth century and identify a Jaina presence. Kulke believes this "does not yet permit an established theory of a Jaina origin of Śṛṅgeri" (1985: 133), but for the purpose of this study, the inscriptions at Śṛṅgeri show that the establishment had been taken as the residence of the Advaitin *jagadgurus* at least by the Saṅgama *mahotsava* in 1346. Afterward, in 1356, Bukka I designated lands near Śṛṅgeri as an *agrahāra*. However, the epigraphical evidence makes no reference to Śaṅkara himself.

Bader (2000: 56) notes that Mādhava, the author of the ŚDV (not Mādhava-Vidyāraṇya), venerates the *jagadguru*, Vidyātīrtha: "Because Vidyātīrtha is considered the greatest guru in the Śṛṅgeri lineage, it is not surprising for him to be evoked by the author of the ŚDV, who, we may assume, was affiliated with that tradition." Without the supporting evidence of a contemporary hagiographical work composed by Mādhava-Vidyāraṇya in the fourteenth century, it is only on the basis of the epigraphical evidence and the literary production of Mādhava-Vidyāraṇya and Sāyaṇa that we may still suppose Śṛṅgeri *jagadgurus* initiated a Hindu cultural politics sometime in the second half of the

13 See above, n.1.

fourteenth century. I think the intention behind such a program was more limited than Paul Hacker had speculated. The literary activities of Mādhava-Vidyāraṇya and Sāyaṇa were surely meant to promote a sort of orthodox Brahmanism based on Advaita, though I doubt that political and cultural pressure due to the Islamic presence prompted it. The most we can say is that the presence of Muslim intellectuals on the subcontinent contributed to the overall intellectual climate and that Vidyāraṇya and Sāyaṇa produced their novel works within this climate. Patronage given to them by the Vijayanagara sovereigns for their literary productions also cannot be simply presumed to promote "Hinduism" versus a Muslim presence. We must be careful in assessing the "Hindu" nature of the Vijayanagara state. The changing situation of religious and political affilations and alliances in Vijayanagara is well-stated by Anila Vergese:

> Earlier writers have interpreted titles such as 'supporters of dharma' or 'upholders of the ancient constitutional usage' too literally. Such titles constitute an important part of the traditional pedigree of the kings of ancient India and 'protection of dharma' formed part of the coronation oath of Hindu kings. It is true that wars against the Bahmanī sultāns were frequent. But their cause was more political and economic rather than religious. It was but a revival of the ancient feud that had existed between the Deccan and south India under the earlier Hindu sovereigns, e.g., between the Chālukyas of Badami and the Pallavas, the Chālukyas of Kalyāṇi and the Chōḷas, the Yādavas and the Hoysaḷas. Besides, the major victims of the Vijayanagara arms were not always the Muslims. The expansion and maintenance of the Vijayanagara Empire also necessitated military expeditions against less powerful Hindu rulers, such as the Śaṁbuvarāyas, the Reḍḍis of Koṇḍavīdu, the Velamas and the Gajapatis. Also, Muslim soldiers played an important part in the successes of the Vijayanagara army. Therefore, the Hindu nature of the Vijayanagara state should not be overstressed. (1995: 2-3)

To give some provisional answer to the third question I posed above, it is more likely that Vidyāraṇya promoted his Advaita Brahmanism in response to the Śrīvaiṣṇava sectarian presence in neighboring Andhra and Tamil Nadu, rather than in response to some Islamic presence. The sharply increasing patronage the Saṅgamas made available to Śṛṅgeri allowed for a never-before-realized institutional growth and the formation of a *maṭha* based in Advaita teachings. Had there been a *maṭha* at Śṛṅgeri previous to 1346, it was most likely not a public institution with far-reaching influence in its teachings and did not garner much patronage. I argue, then, that when the *jagadgurus* of Śṛṅgeri Vidyātīrtha, Bhāratītīrtha, and Vidyāraṇya started securing greater patronage in the second half of the fourteenth century, and bestowing some sacred legitimacy on their Saṅgama patrons, they could begin to compete for the patronage of other areas that had previously been under the control of other sovereigns. It is unlikely that they would have approached Islamic sovereigns for such patronage.

I argue that the Advaitin *jagadgurus* looked to other territories to promote their Advaitin theology in the political vacuum created by the collapse of institutions in the early part of the fourteenth century after the Turkish incursions into South India. When the newly legitimated Saṅgama dynastic kings filled this political vacuum and began expanding to other territories, the Advaita *jagadgurus* also looked to other territories whose sovereigns and local leaders were responsible for the management of temples and who had long patronized the Śrīvaiṣṇava sectarians.[14] Even if territories—say in the vicinities of Śrīraṅgam in Tamil Nadu or Tirupati in Andhra—were not yet under the control of the Vijayanagara sovereigns in the middle of the fourteenth century, the Śṛṅgeri *jagadgurus* could at least look to these areas traditionally populated by adherents to Śrīvaiṣṇavism as a place to promote their Advaitin teachings. It is in this limited sense, then, that I would use the idea of a "deliberate cultural politics." There were also other competing groups in fourteenth-century South India, most notably the Śaiva Kālamukhas and the Vīraśaivas. The Śṛṅgeri Advaitins surely would have been acquainted with these other groups and would have competed with them for support. But the textual evidence to my knowledge does not mention them as serious opponents of the Advaitin theological views. Therefore, the Śṛṅgeri Advaitins would have limited the scope of their theological programs for the most part to the Śṛīvaiṣṇava Viśiṣṭādvaitins, who could argue with them on the same theological grounds. It is in this milieu, then, that I would like to place the appearance of Vidyāraṇya's JMV.

At about the time that Vidyāraṇya became the *jagadguru* of Śṛṅgeri in ca. 1374, the Vijayanagara sovereigns expanded their control to territories that were traditionally inhabited by Śrīvaiṣṇava adherents in Tamil Nadu and Andhra in 1371 CE. In his study of the *Koil Olugu*, the chronicle of the Śrīvaiṣṇava temple complex at Śrīraṅgam, George W. Spencer (1978:23-26) discusses the motives for the Telugu generals of the Saṅgama sovereigns of Vijayanagara who took over authority and restored order to this temple.[15] Drawing on the work of Arjun Appadurai on king/temple relations, Spencer believes that aside from piety or material gain, they patronized this temple in order to have it confer on them its legitimation and sought the ceremonial honors. Based on the coincidences of these dates and the expansion enjoyed by the Advaitins of Śṛṅgeri since 1356 under the initial patronage of the Vijayanagara sovereigns, I suggest that Vidyāraṇya, as the new Śaṅkarācārya of Śṛṅgeri, saw these new territories subsumed under Vijayanagara authority as a new opportunities

[14] For a theory of the power structure of South Indian temple complexes in the premodern South Indian state, see Appadurai (1978: 47-73). Those who actually carried out the operations of the temple complexes such as Śrīraṅgam and Tirupati were not the theologians like Rāmānuja and Vedānta Deśika.

[15] See also Appadurai's later discussion of the restoration of Śrīraṅgam (1981: 83-84).

for the promotion of Advaita. If we can place anything about the JMV in time and space and consider Vidyāraṇya's motives beyond teaching his own Advaitin followers, his deliberate cultural politics were to promote Advaita among sectarian Śrīvaiṣṇava laypeople in these newly controlled territories and defend the idea of liberation-in-life (*jīvanmukti*) against the Śrīvaiṣṇava theologians.

The Jīvanmuktiviveka *in Context*

The leading theologian of the Śrīvaiṣṇava Viśiṣṭādvaitin school in the fourteenth century, and worthy opponent of Vidyāraṇya, was Vedānta Deśika.[16] Deśika's *Śatadūṣaṇī* directly attacks the Advaitin positions. One can point to a couple of obvious cases of refutations that Vidyāraṇya then countered with his broad program in the JMV. The 31st refutation of the *Śatadūṣaṇī*, titled the *Jīvanmuktibhaṅgavāda*, rejects the Advaitin notion of *jīvanmukti* in particular. The 65th refutation, titled the *Alepakamatabhaṅgavāda*, deals specifically with the validity of Advaitin renunciation as an *āśrama* and rejects it as antinomian libertinism (Olivelle 1987: 97-158).

It is probable that Vedānta Deśika presumed the rules for renouncers as set out by the *Yatidharmasamucaya*, a legal digest composed in the second half of the eleventh century by Yādava Prakāśa. This text emerged out of the sectarian Śrīvaiṣṇava theological context. The views in this text differed greatly from the ascetic tradition of the Advaita. It retained the main rules for the Brahmanical householders and, indeed, integrated the ascetical life of the renouncer into the ritual life of the householder. Olivelle states in the introduction to his edition of the *Yatidharmasamucaya* that, for the Śrīvaiṣṇava tradition, the renouncer is really something more of "a very exalted type of Brahmanical householder rather than a figure who contradicts the value system represented by domestic life." (1995: 17-18) This tradition was much more concerned with preserving ritual boundaries of purity and impurity, especially concerning the body. Vidyāraṇya, however, specifically states in the second chapter of the JMV there is no possibility of cleansing the body, and the desire to do so is another latent tendency, or *vāsanā*, that should be dissolved: "Through its nine open-

[16] The Śrīvaiṣṇava *prabhāvam* literature relates a story of a meeting between the two great Ācāryas, where Vidyāraṇya invited Deśika to become a court poet at the newly founded Vijayanagara capitol, which Deśika refused. The Śrīvaiṣṇava authors wished show their teacher rejecting mere earthly wealth and honors, while conversely the Advaitin Vidyāraṇya was lacking such detachment. Whether the two teachers met or not, the Vaṭakalai Śrīvaiṣṇava authors portrayed a tension and rivalry focused in these two figures. For a study of this literature on the life of Vedānta Deśika, see Hopkins (2002: 48-75). The Madhvite Dvaita Vedāntins also remember a debate between Vidyāraṇya and the disciple of Madhva, Akṣobhya Tīrtha. Vedānta Deśika is said to have been the arbiter in this dispute and pronounced Akṣobhya Tīrtha the winner. See Sharma (1961: 229-230).

ings filth constantly oozes out; through its innumerable pores it is covered with sweat—who indeed is able even with the greatest effort to wash the body?" (2.4.80)[17] Such a concern for the purification of the body shows us the basically conservative and communal view of the Śrīvaiṣṇavas, who admitted the ancient and classical values of the ascetic traditions, but fully subsumed them within the householder mainstream.

In medieval times, although renunciation was presented in the Brahmanical law books as a value common to all Brahmins, or twice-born classes, the reality was that the ascetic tradition became organized into monastic establishments divided along sectarian lines. Interestingly, although we can be sure that Vidyāraṇya was the head of just such a monastic establishment, the Śṛṅgeri *maṭha*, he mentions the term *maṭha* only once, late in the fifth chapter of the JMV. This mention is in the context, moreover, of an extended discussion of the definition of the highest type of renouncer, the *paramahaṃsa yogin*. The term *maṭha* is mentioned by way of commentary on the *Paramahaṃsa Upaniṣad* 4, where it states: "the mendicant remains homeless." Vidyāraṇya comments: "If he (i.e., the *paramahaṃsa yogin*) were to come to some monastery (*maṭha*) in order to have a permanent residence, then, given that he feels a sense of ownership with regard to it, its decline and growth would distract his mind" (5.4.11).[18] Why then, would Vidyāraṇya compose a book at the time when he was head of the Śṛṅgeri *maṭha* defining an individual who, Vidyāraṇya seems to believe, did not belong in his own monastic establishment?

The reason is, again, that Vidyāraṇya was responding to refutations given by the Viśiṣṭādvaitins, in particular that *jīvanmukti* is not a valid possibility. For Vedānta Deśika, Advaitin renunciation is not a valid *āśrama* institution, nor is it valid to say it is beyond the *āśramas*, as some Advaitins, including Vidyāraṇya, tried to argue. First of all let us deal with the latter objection. One of the first arguments made in JMV concerns the nature of *vividiṣāsaṃnyāsa*, or "renunciation out of the desire for knowledge." Vidyāraṇya cites the appropriate *pramāṇas*, or authoritative scriptural passages, from the Upaniṣads such as *Bṛhadāraṇyaka Upaniṣad* 4.4.22: "Desiring this alone as their world, the renouncers undertake the life of wandering" (1.1.6).[19] He then defines *vividiṣāsaṃnyāsa* as twofold: "the one consisting only in the abandonment of rites and the like, which produces rebirth; the other constitutes an order in society (*āśrama*) that is connected with carrying a staff and the like, which are pre-

[17] *navachidrair nirantaraṃ sravatsu maleṣu romakūpair asaṁkhyātaiḥ svinne gātre ko nāma khedena prakṣālayituṃ śaknuyāt?*

[18] *yadi niyatanivāsārthaṃ kaṃcin maṭhaṃ saṃpādayet tadānīṃ tasmin mamatve sati tadīyahānivṛddhyoś cittaṃ vikṣipyeta.*

[19] *etam eva pravrājino lokam icchantaḥ pravrajanti.*

ceded by uttering the *praiṣa* ritual formula" (1.1.11).[20] This is a very important distinction that is assumed in the rest of the text.

Roger Marcaurelle (2000: 188-194) in his study of Śaṅkara's views on renunciation terms these two types "informal" and "formal" renunciation. Vidyāraṇya also later refers to a distinction between "Vedic" and "common" (*laukika*) in this regard. Renunciation out of the desire for knowledge (*vividiṣāsaṃnyāsa*) can be an informal, inward, mental abandonment of rites and wandering mendicancy for the attainment of knowledge. The other type is a formal *āśrama*, or public order in society, that is entered fulltime and involves emblems of this institution like carrying a staff and a public declaration of the intention to renounce. It is here, then, that Vidyāraṇya extends the entitlement to this kind of renunciation, the informal type to members of the other *āśramas* by saying: "When, for whatever reason, Vedic students, householders, and forest-dwellers are prevented from entering the renunciant order, there is nothing to prevent the mental abandonment of rites and the like for the purpose of knowledge, even while they remain performing the duties (*dharma*) of their own order, because we see many such knowers of truth in the Śrutis, Smṛtis, Itihāsas, and Purāṇas" (1.1.14).[21] Then, in conclusion to this section, he comments "Since the order of the *paramahaṃsa*, which is the cause of knowing and consists in carrying the staff and the like, has been treated at length in many ways by earlier teachers. Therefore, we will not deal with it" (1.1.15).[22]

For Vidyāraṇya, the knowledge of *brahman* may then be realized in either way. This realization, however, necessarily leads to the *vidvatsaṃnyāsa*, or renunciation-of-the-knower. While both *vividiṣāsaṃnyāsa* and *vidvatsaṃnyāsa* are under the rubric of *paramahaṃsa*, Vidyāraṇya says that they each have different duties or *dharmas*. The *vividiṣāsaṃnyāsin* is to perform the means of knowledge in order to realize *brahman*; the *vidvatsaṃnyāsin* must perform the means that allow the knower to safeguard that realization, i.e., by means of yogic practices. This is not an *āśrama*, *per se*. Nonetheless it seems there is some ambiguity here, because in the fifth chapter Vidyāraṇya says that renunciation-of-the-knower has characteristics of both types of renunciation out of the desire for knowledge. Given that the renunciation-of-the-knower is basically a modification of renunciation-for-knowledge, it carries with it all the details pertaining to the prototype, according to the hermeneutic maxim: "The

[20] *ayaṃ ca vedanahetuḥ saṃnyāso dvividhaḥ, janmāpādakakarmādityāgamātrātmakaḥ, praiṣo-ccāraṇapūrvakadaṇḍadhāraṇādyāśramarūpaś ceti.*

[21] *brahmacārigṛhasthavānaprasthānāṃ kenacin nimittena saṃnyāsāśramasvīkāre pratibaddhe sati, svāśramadharmeṣv anuṣṭhīyamāneṣv api vedanārtho mānasaḥ karmādityago na virudhyate, śrutismṛtītihāsapurāṇeṣu loke ca tādṛśāṃ tattvavidāṃ bahūnām upalambhāt.*

[22] *yas tu daṇḍadhāraṇādirupo vedanahetuḥ paramahaṁsāśramaḥ sa pūrvair ācāryair bahudhā prapañcita ity asmābhir uparamyate.*

modification should conform to the archetype" (5.1.39).[23] That is to say, the ritual details of the archetype ritual must all carry over to the modification: "This is just as in the case of the *Agniṣṭoma Soma* sacrifice, where the ritual details pertaining to it are applicable to the modified rites such as the *Atirātra*. Therefore, as in the other type of renunciation, here too one should declare the intention to give up sons, friends, etc., with the *praiṣa* ritual formula" (5.1.39).[24] However, the means of knowledge then become subsidiary for the renouncer who is a knower and the yogic practices become primary (2.3).

For the more conservative householder community of the Śrīvaiṣṇava Viśiṣṭādvaitins, ambiguity in regard to religious life could not be tolerated. Did a renunciant have a place in society or not? Vidyāraṇya took the view that once an individual renunciant realizes the liberating knowledge of *brahman*, he should continue living a renunciant lifestyle as a yogin. Vidyāraṇya believed that the knowledge of Self (*ātman*) as *brahman* in classical Advaita philosophy is not enough to completely root out suffering and *prārabdha-karma*, or operative action, which causes future births. Liberation also requires a lifelong commitment to the yogic practices of the eradication of latent tendencies (*vāsanākṣaya*) and elimination of the mind (*manonaśa*). To be liberated in this lifetime, a *jīvanmukta*, the individual who realizes the equivalence of self and *brahman*, must sustain further yogic discipline and a renunciant lifestyle for the rest of his life, renouncing even the fact that he is a knower of Brahman. The Yoga Sūtras of Patañjali were by this time already very ancient, originating as early as perhaps the second century BCE. Yoga philosophy had permeated the religious life of Indians in various forms, including by this time the Kuṇḍalinī Yoga of Tantric cults and the Haṭha Yoga of the Nath ascetics. Given Vidyāraṇya's sociopolitical context that I have outlined here, I argue that he went back to the earlier Yoga of Patañjali and integrated it with Śaṅkara's philosophy of the liberating knowledge was to accommodate the conservative Śrīvaiṣṇava view of Vedānta Deśika. Making the renouncer responsible for further moral perfection beyond the attainment of knowledge puts him above all reproach by the householder community. Indeed, one of the purposes of liberation-in-life that Vidyāraṇya treats in the fourth chapter of the JMV is the

[23] *prakṛtivad vikartavyaḥ kartavyāḥ*. Cf. *Arthasaṃgraha of Laugākṣi Bhāskara*, (1998: 19): "Where there is a specification or mention of all subsidiaries, that (is) the arche-type, as the new moon and full moon sacrifices and others. For, in their context all subsidiaries are mentioned. Where all subsidiaries are not specified, that (is) the modification, as the oblation to the sun (*saurya*). There some subsidiaries become available (*prāpta*) by means of extended application."

[24] *yady apy atra śrāddhādikaṃ nopadiṣṭaṃ tathāpy asya vidvatsaṃnyāsasya vividiṣāsaṃnyāsavikṛtitvāt "prakṛtivad vikṛtiḥ kartavyā" iti nyāyena tadīyā dharmāḥ sarve 'py atra prāpnuvanti yathāgniṣṭomasya vikṛtiṣv atirātrādiṣu tadīyadharmaprāptis tadvat. tasmād itarasaṃnyāsavad atrāpi praiṣamantreṇa putramitrādityāgaṃ saṃkalpayet.*

"absence of opposition" (*visaṃvādābhāvaḥ*) to the master yogin by members of varying sects (4.3). His virtue would be obvious to everyone and no argumentative opposition is needed.

Viewed from a sociopolitical standpoint, Vidyāraṇya wanted to mitigate the ambiguity of the individual renouncer's position in the mainstream community by directing him to sustain the path toward his spiritual goal, even after attaining knowledge and liberation from desire. Vidyāraṇya preserved the possibility of complete liberation in this lifetime, while not disturbing the conventional religious social order. In following Vidyāraṇya's teaching, the individual who renounces society lessens the resulting tension by maintaining an identifiable lifestyle, and the highest moral standards, with conventional ascetical practices. He does not compromise his position but remains an ascetic outside of, while still recognized by, the householder society.

Granted, this may not have satisfied the Śrīvaiṣṇava community. The interpretation and reinterpretation of normative texts and teachings, and the appropriation of legitimate views of opposing sides continues still. It is in this sense we can see why Walter Slaje believes that Vidyāraṇya's JMV is "tendentious" (2000: 171), though I don't think Vidyāraṇya is "naive" (Slaje 1998: 103). Part of the business of theologians is to look for ways to interpret their normative textual tradition in order to apply it to their contemporary situations. We do not hear scholars criticizing Thomas Aquinas for changing anything in his new treatment of Aristotle. It may well be that Vidyāraṇya changed ideas in his normative textual tradition, though all the while not admitting he had made anything new.

Bibliography

Primary Sources

Arthasaṃgraha. (1998), ed. A.B. Gajendragadkar and R.D. Karmarkar. *Arthasaṃgraha of Laugākṣi Bhāskara*, orig. pub. 1934 (Delhi: Motilal Banarsidass).

Bṛhadāraṇyaka Upaniṣad. (1998), ed. and tr. P. Olivelle. *The Early Upaniṣads: annotated text and translation* (New York: Oxford University Press).

Kālanirṇaya. (1989), ed. B.K. Swain. *Kālamādhava*, Kashi Sanskrit Series 45 (Varanasi: Chaukambha Sanskrit Sansthan).

Paramahaṃsa Upaniṣad. (1912), ed. F.O. Schrader. *The minor Upanisads, critically edited for the Adyar library (Theosophical society)* (Madras: Adyar Library).

Pārāśara-Mādhavīya. (1973-1974), ed. C. Tarkalankara. *Pārāśarasmṛt-*

Pārāśara Mādhava, orig. pub. 1893, 3 vols. (Calcutta: The Asiatic Society).

Jīvanmuktivivekaḥ. (2002), ed. and tr. R.A. Goodding. *The Treatise on Liberation-in-Life: Critical Edition and Annotated Translation of the Jīvanmuktiviveka of Vidyāraṇya.* Ph.D. Diss. (Austin: University of Texas at Austin).

Vidyāraṇya. (1985), prepared by Uttankita Sanskrit Vidyā-Araṇya Trust, Uttankita Sanskrit Vidyā-Aranya Epigraphs. Vol. 1. (Bombay: Bharatiya Vidya Bhavan).

Yatidharmasamuccaya. (1995), ed. and tr. P. Olivelle. *Rules and Regulations of Brahmanical Asceticism: Yatidharmasamuccaya of Yādava Prakāśa* (Albany: State University of New York Press).

Secondary Sources

Appadurai, A. (1978), "Kings, Sects, and Temples in South India: 1350-1700 A.D." in *South Indian Temples: An Analytical Reconsideration,* ed. B. Stein (New Delhi: Vikas Publishing House Pvt. Ltd), 47-73.

_____. (1981), *Worship and Conflict under Colonial Rule: A South Indian Case* (Cambridge: Cambridge University Press).

Bader, J. (2000), *Conquest of the Four Quarters: Traditional Accounts of the Life of Śaṅkara* (Delhi: Aditya Prakashan).

Doraiswamy Iyengar, M.A. (n.d.), "The Mādhava-Vidyāraṇya Theory," *Journal of Indian History* 12: 241-250.

Filliozat, V. (1973), *L'Épigraphie de Vijayanagar du Début à 1377,* vol. 91 (Paris: École Francaise d' Extrême-Orient).

_____. (ed.) (1999), *Vijayanagar as seen by Domingos Paes and Fernao Nuniz (16 Century Chroniclers) and others,* orig . pub. 1977, rev. ed. (New Delhi: National Book Trust).

Fort, A.O. and P.Y. Mumme (1996), *Living Liberation in Hindu Thought* (Albany: State University of New York Press).

Fort, A.O. (1998), *Jīvanmukti in Transformation: Embodied Liberation in Advaita and Neo-Advaita* (Albany: State University of New York Press).

_____. (1999), "On Destroying the Mind: The *Yogasūtras* in Vidyāraṇya's *Jīvanmuktiviveka,*" *Journal of Indian Philosophy* 27: 377-378.

Hacker, P. (1995), "On Śaṅkara and Advaitism" in W. Halbfass, *Philology and Confrontation: Paul Hacker on Traditional and Modern Advaita (*Albany: State University of New York Press), 27-32.

Heras, H. (1929). *Beginnings of Vijayanagara History* (Bombay: Indian Historical Research Institute).

Hopkins, S.P. (2002), *Singing the Body of God: The Hymns of Vedāntadeśika in Their South Indian Tradition* (Oxford: Oxford University Press).

Kane, P.V. (1977-1997), *History of Dharmaśāstra,* orig. pub. 1930-

1962. 2nd and 3rd rpt. editions (Pune: Bhandharkar Oriental Research Institute).
Kulke, H. (1985), "Maharajas, Mahants, and Historians: Reflections on the Historiography of Early Vijayanagara and Ṣringeri" in *Vijayanagara-City and Empire: New Currents of Research*, ed. A. Dallapiccola and S.Z. Lallemant (Stuttgart: Steiner Verlag Wiesbaden), 120-143.
Mahadevan, T.M.P. (1957), *The Philosophy of Advaita with special Reference to Bhāratītīrtha-Vidyāraṇya* (Madras: Ganesh and Co. Pvt. Ltd).
Marcaurelle, R. (2000), *Freedom through Inner Renunciation: Śaṅkara's Philosophy in a New Light* (Albany: State University of New York Press).
Markandeya Sarma, K. (1932), "Identity of Vidyāraṇya and Mādhavācārya," *Indian Historical Quarterly* 8: 611-614.
Nilakanta Sastri, K.A. (1976), *A History of South India from Prehistoric to the Fall of Vijayanagar*, orig. pub. 1947. Rpt. ed. (Delhi: Oxford University Press).
Olivelle, P. (1986-1987), *Renunciation in Hinduism: A Medieval Debate.* De Nobili Research Library, vols. 13-14 (Vienna: University of Vienna Institute for Indology).
Rama Rao, R. (1931), "Origin of the Mādhava-Vidyāraṇya Theory," *Indian Historical Quarterly* 7: 78-92.
Saletore, B.A. (1934), *Social and political life in the Vijayanagara empire (A.D. 1346-A.D. 1646)* (Madras: B.G. Paul & Co.).
Sharma, B.N.K. (1961), *History of the Dvaita School of Vedānta and its Literature* (Delhi: Motilal Banarsidass).
Slaje, W. (1998), "On Changing Others' Ideas: The Case of Vidyāraṇya and the Yogavāsiṣṭha," *Indo-Iranian Journal* 41: 103-124.
_____. (2000), "Liberation from Intentionality and Involvement: On the Concept of *Jīvanmukti* according to the Mokṣopaya," *Journal of Indian Philosophy* 28: 171-194.
Spencer, G.W. (1978), "Crisis of Authority in a Hindu Temple under the Impact of Islam" in *Religion and the Legitimation of Power in South Asia*, ed. B.L. Smith (Leiden: E.J. Brill), 14-27.
Sprockhoff, J.F. (1962), "Zur idee der Erlösung bei Lebzeiten in Buddhismus," *Numen* 9: 201-227.
_____. (1964), "Der Weg zur Erlösung bei Lebzeiten, ihr Wesen und Wert, Nach dem Jīvanmuktiviveka des Vidyāraṇya," *Weiner Zeitschrift für die Kunde Südasiens* 8: 224-262.
Venkataramanayya, N. (1960), "The Kingdom of Vijayanagara" in *The Delhi Sultanate*, ed. R.C. Majumdar, The History and Culture of the Indian People, vol. 6 (Bombay: Bharatiya Vidya Bhavan), 271-325.
_____. (1990), *Vijayanagara: Origin of the City and Empire*, orig. pub. 1933 (New Delhi: Asian Educational Services).
Verghese, A. (1995), *Religious Traditions at Vijayanagara as Revealed*

Through its Monuments, Vijayanagara Research Project Monograph Series, vol. 4 (New Delhi: Manohar, American Institute of Indian Studies).

Vijayanagara Sexcentenary Commemoration Volume. (1936), (Dharwar: Published under the auspices of the Vijayanagara Empire Sexcentenary Association and Karnatak Historical Research Society).

Wagoner, P.B. (2000), "Harihara, Bukka, and the Sultan: The Delhi Sultanate in the Political Imagination of Vijayanagara" in *Beyond Turk and Hindu: Rethinking Religious Identities in Islamicate South Asia*, ed. D. Gilmartin and B.B. Lawrence (Gainesville: University Press of Florida), 300-326.

Brian Black

The Rhetoric of Secrecy in the Upaniṣads[1]

Introduction

Among Patrick Olivelle's many contributions to scholarship on ancient Indian religion and culture has been his appreciation for the literary dimension of Sanskrit texts. In his excellent article about the young Śvetaketu (1999), Olivelle demonstrates that the different portrayals of shared characters in the *Bṛhadāraṇyaka* and *Chāndogya Upaniṣads* (BU, CU) are connected to the competing political agendas of these two texts and the scholastic traditions to which they belonged. Building on some of Olivelle's insights, in this paper I would like to explore the literary dimension of secrecy in the Upaniṣads.

It is well known that the Upaniṣads are considered to be secret texts. The secrecy associated with their teachings is one of their most alluring characteristics and has been part of their appeal to modern audiences.[2] Yet, despite the general acknowledgement that the Upaniṣads are in some sense secret texts containing secret teachings, the rhetorical dimensions of secrecy have not been analysed closely. How is secrecy conveyed by the texts? Who shares the secrets and who are they guarded from? What are some of the possible reasons for why the Upaniṣads characterize themselves and their teachings in this way? As we will see, there are a number of metaphors, modes of

[1] I would like to thank Daud Ali, Kunal Chakrabarti, Kumkum Roy, and Romila Thapar for their comments and suggestions when an earlier version of this paper was presented at Jawaharlal Nehru University in January 2008. I would also like to thank Patrick Olivelle for taking an interest in my work on the Upaniṣads and whose own work continues to inspire.

[2] Indeed, perhaps indicating the connotations of the word *upaniṣad* itself, the Upaniṣads have been regarded as secret texts since their first known translation into a non-Indian language, as the Persian translation of the Upaniṣads initiated by Dārā Shūkōh was titled *Sirr-i Akbar*—"The Great Secret" (see Müller [1900] 2000: lvii-lxii; Halbfass 1988: 33-35).

expression, and literary situations through which the Upaniṣads convey their teachings as secret. While some of these literary devices are common tropes of secrecy—also found in secret texts and esoteric traditions from other cultures and historical periods—I will argue that the Upaniṣads employ a rhetoric of secrecy specific to their historical context in order to present their teachings as superior to those of competing traditions and as distinct from the content of previous Vedic texts.

Preliminary Remarks: Secrecy and Rhetoric

In the past decade there have been numerous studies on secrecy in religious traditions.[3] A brief survey of such studies makes it clear that there are a variety of types of secrecy, not to mention differing opinions for how to define secrecy and how to determine what constitutes a secret. In this paper I will explore two aspects of secrecy that are particularly relevant to the Upaniṣads:

1) A secret as information or knowledge that is not observable or not immediately apparent

2) A secret as information or knowledge that is intentionally concealed by a person or group of people

As we will see, these distinct, yet interconnected, aspects of secrecy are conveyed in different ways in the Upaniṣads. The first notion of secrecy—that the truth is either beyond observation or extremely difficult to detect—tends to be communicated through a number of metaphors and modes of expression that characterize teachings as hidden, concealed, and inexpressible through conventional language. The second aspect of secrecy—what we might call the social dimension of secrecy—is expressed through the many literary scenes that depict the transmission of knowledge from teachers to students. These two aspects of secrecy are distinct in the sense that they are not mutually dependent and, as we will see, they tend to be conveyed through different rhetorical techniques; yet these aspects of secrecy are also indelibly intertwined because, at least in the Upaniṣads, they represent two ways of presenting the same secrets.

When looking at these two aspects of secrecy, this paper will be more concerned with the formal features of secrecy than in attempting to uncover the secrets themselves. As Hugh Urban has argued, this does not mean that the content of secrets is meaningless or "semantically empty," but rather that there is often more to say about the "forms and the strategies through which secret information is concealed, revealed and exchanged" (2001: 20). Thus, rather

[3] The *Journal of the American Academy of Religion*, for example, recently dedicated an entire issue to the topic 'Religion and Secrecy' (74 (2), June 2006). Other notable studies include articles by Faivre (1999) and Campany (2006), as well as a number of publications by Urban (e.g., 2001, 2006).

than "search for the ever-elusive hidden content" (2001: 20), this paper will examine the ways by which the Upaniṣads present their teachings as secret, or what we might call the 'rhetoric of secrecy.' By using the term 'rhetoric,' I am not suggesting that the secrecy in the Upaniṣads is an empty claim—i.e., I am not suggesting that the secrecy is *mere* rhetoric. Rather I aim to bring attention to the literary mechanisms through which the Upaniṣads portray their teachings as secret. Moreover, I will argue that secrecy in the Upaniṣads is rhetorical in the sense that it is not merely descriptive, but that it is directed towards particular audiences and is addressed within the context of particular social situations. This inherently social and interactive quality of rhetoric has been described recently by Michael Carrithers: "Through the glass of rhetoric we can see that, in any moment of interaction, some act to persuade, others are the targets of persuasion" (2005: 578). In this paper, I will not only discuss the rhetorical devices—the acts to persuade—through which the Upaniṣads convey their teachings as secret, but I will also consider the possible targets of persuasion and potential reasons for why the Upaniṣads would opt to present their teachings as secret.

The Hidden Nature of Reality

The secrecy of the Upaniṣads is closely intertwined with the meaning of the word *upaniṣad* itself, as well as through a number of related terms the texts use in association with some of their core teachings. According to Harry Falk (1986), in its earliest textual contexts the word *upaniṣad* is used to describe a connection between things, often presented in a hierarchical relationship. In such contexts *upaniṣad* is employed in a similar way as the term *bandhu*, which is used to designate equivalences between components of different realms of reality. Such connections were not considered observable by the senses, but required a special knowledge or understanding. On one occasion, in the BU, the word *upaniṣad* is equated with the formulation *satyasya satyam* (BU 2.2.20)—"the truth behind the truth"—an expression suggesting that there is a truth or reality beyond that which appears to be true. When *upaniṣad* is used in this way, it refers to something that is not immediately perceptible, but remains concealed or obscured. Olivelle has surmised that, due to the hidden nature of an *upaniṣad* as an equivalence or connecting power, it "came to mean a secret, especially secret knowledge or doctrine" (1996: liii). On several occasions *upaniṣad* seems to be used in exactly this way, as designating a secret teaching (i.e. CU 1.1.10; 1.13.4; 8.8.4; BU 2.1.20; 4.2.1; 5.5.3-4; TU 1.3.1; 1.11.4; 2.9.1; 3.10.6). This designation is reinforced by other formulations such as *guhya ādeśa* ("hidden instruction"; CU 3.5.2). The word *guhya*, which means "to be covered or concealed or hidden or kept secret" derives from √*guh*, which means "to cover, conceal, hide, keep secret" (Monier-Williams [1899]: 360).

Related images of hiding and concealment appear frequently. In the *Kaṭha Upaniṣad* (KaU; 2.20), for example, Yama teaches Naciketas that the self lies "hidden in the cave" (*nihito guhāyām*). While commentators have taken the cave metaphor, which appears on several occasions (KaU 2.12; 3.1; TU 2.1.1; MuU 3.1.7), to refer to the space within the heart, Jonardon Ganeri has suggested that perhaps "the allusion to a cave is not to be taken quite so literally but rather simply as a metaphor for the idea that the self is hidden" (2007: 21). This more general sense of concealment, with suggestions of physical inaccessibility, resonates with other metaphors that describe the truth as tantalisingly near, yet remaining unnoticed because it is obscured, hidden, or buried. The CU, for example, compares the world of *brahman* to a hidden treasure of gold: "Just as those who do not know the field (*kṣetra*), pass over a golden treasure again and again, and do not find it; so all creatures here go to the world of *brahman* every day and do not find it, because they are pushed away by falsehood" (8.3.2).[4]

As this metaphor suggests, the true teaching is passed over every day, but remains undetected.[5] This paradox, that the truth is both near and far, recurs on a number of occasions. An earlier passage in the same section of the CU describes the truth as being very small, thus remaining indiscernible by the senses: "Now, here in the city of *brahman* is a small lotus house; within it is a tiny space. What is within there, that should be searched for, because that is what one should try to understand" (8.1.1).[6] Such metaphors, portraying *ātman* or *brahman* as hidden, concealed, or too small to detect, connote the sense that the truth is difficult to obtain, just out of reach. As such, the type of secrecy evoked by these images is not one of intended concealment—it is not a secret created by social relations—but rather points to a secret that lies hidden within the structure of reality.

Besides their physical inaccessibility, the Upaniṣads present their teachings as being difficult to explain or describe. As such, a crucial part of the concealment or inaccessibility of the knowledge is that it is beyond language. Yājñavalkya repeatedly describes *ātman* using negation, implying that the self cannot be described in words: "About the self (*ātman*), one can only say *neti, neti*" (BU 3.9.26; 4.2.4; 4.4.22).[7] The linguistic, or indeed conceptual, limitations for conveying the truth also comes across in the repeated use of paradox and contradiction. The *Īśā Upaniṣad* (ĪU), for example, uses paradoxical language

[4] *tad yathāpi hiraṇyanidhiṃ nihitam akṣetrajñā upary upari sañcaranto na vindeyuḥ* | *evam evemāḥ sarvāḥ prajā ahar ahar gacchantya etam brahmalokaṃ na vindanty anṛtena hi pratyūḍhāḥ* || Translations of passages from the Upaniṣads are my own.

[5] In a similar metaphor, the *Maitrī Upaniṣad* compares seeking *brahman* to searching for minerals in a mine (6.28).

[6] *atha yad idam asmin brahmapure daharaṃ puṇḍarīkaṃ veśma daharo 'sminn antarākāśaḥ*| *tasmin yad antas tad anveṣṭavyaṃ tad vāva vijijñāsitavyam iti* ||

[7] *sa eṣa neti nety ātmā* |

when discussing the Lord: "It moves, it does not move; it is far, yet it is near. It is within everything, yet it is outside everything" (ĪU 5).[8] Similarly, Śāṇḍilya describes *ātman* through paradox: "This self of mine within the heart is smaller than a grain of rice, or a barley corn, or a mustard seed, or a millet grain, or the kernel of a millet grain. This self of mine within the heart is greater than the earth, greater than the middle region, greater than the sky, greater than these worlds" (CU 3.14.3).[9] Joel Brereton has suggested that the Upaniṣads "use paradox to bring together things that appear to be separate in order to create a larger whole" (1990: 130).

I would only add that paradox, as well as other rhetorical techniques such as contradiction and negation, are used to characterize the teachings of the Upaniṣads as beyond conventional description: they are employed to express that the ultimate reality is beyond language, beyond distinction, beyond conceptual thought. The Upaniṣads, then, combine these techniques that point to the ineffable nature of the truth, with the use of words associated with secrecy and with metaphors of concealment, to characterize their teachings as unique and valuable. There are also indications that the Upaniṣads revel in their own secrecy, such as the repeated claim: "the gods love what is secret" (*parokṣapriyā hi devāḥ*; ŚB 6.1.1.1-15; BU 4.2.2; AU 1.3.14). Beyond any descriptive aspect of these modes of expression, the rhetoric of secrecy is used, at least in part, to create a secret. Charles Malamoud has made a similar observation: "The gods' secret ...is an artificial one: it proceeds, not from a will to protect a mystery, but rather, that of creating one" (1996: 206).

Tropes of Secrecy

That the Upaniṣads characterize their teachings in this way is perhaps not so surprising when we consider that secret knowledge is an aspect of a number of religious texts and traditions. Some scholars even claim that secret knowledge is the basis of all religions. Kees Bolle, for example, proclaims that secrecy is "the mystery at the heart of all religions" (1987: 4), that any religion "has its central secret, its mysterum magnum" (1987: 5). While Bolle's statements might be helpful in pointing out that the Upaniṣadic claim to secrecy is by no means unique among religious texts, such descriptions of secrecy, as Urban observes, are "disappointingly vague" (2006: 360) and are examples of what Steven Wasserstrom calls the 'esocentrism' of the study of religions—"a privileging of the mystical, secret, elitist

[8] *tad ejati tan naijati tad dūre tad v antike | tad antar asya sarvasya tadu sarvasyāsya bāhyataḥ ||*

[9] *eṣa ma ātmāntarhṛdaye 'ṇīyān vrīher vā yavād vā sarṣapād vā śyāmākād vā śyāmākataṇḍulād vā | eṣa ma ātmāntarhṛḍaye jyāyān pṛthivyā jyāyān antarikṣāj jyāyān divo jyājān ebhyo lokebhyaḥ ||*

aspects of religion, often to the neglect of their more mundane 'exoteric' aspects" (2006: 360, referring to Wasserstrom 1999). Urban proposes that secrecy, rather than being portrayed as universal, should be examined in its specific social and political contexts.

In exploring the contextual dimensions of secrecy in the Upaniṣads, the narratives featuring teachers and students have particular relevance. While the language, metaphors, and rhetorical techniques tell us that Upaniṣadic teachings are hidden and difficult to know, the narratives put the secrecy in a social context by depicting teachers who guard their teachings closely and by portraying students who endure trials in their quest to learn; thus, besides describing secrecy as a 'natural phenomenon'—part of the nature of reality—the Upaniṣads also present a social dimension to secrecy, one in which hierarchies are established between those who know and those who do not, and strict procedures are outlined regarding the concealment and revelation of knowledge. As we will see, there are a number of shared literary tropes throughout these scenes that contribute to characterizing the teachings as secret, while also adding authority to those who possess the teachings.

(a) The Reluctant Teacher

In the opening scene of the *Maitrī Upaniṣad* (MtU 1.2) King Bṛhadratha, who had been practising severe austerities for one thousand days, asks the sage Śākāyanya to teach him about the self. Śākāyanya, however, implores the king not to ask this question because it is too "difficult" (*duḥśaka*) to achieve, and he tells the king to choose another wish. Śākāyanya's initial refusal to teach is comparable to the hesitation of a number of other teachers in the Upaniṣads. In a dialogue from the KaU (1-2) Yama, the god of death, is similarly cast as the reluctant teacher, describing his knowledge as subtle and not discernible (*na suvijñeya*; KaU 1.21). Instead of teaching him, he offers the young brahmin a number of gifts—including sons and grandsons, livestock and elephants, horses and gold, and a lifespan as long as he chooses—in an attempt to avoid disclosing what he knows. Naciketas does not accept these material rewards, saying that these things cannot make him happy. In another example, from a story that appears in both the BU (6.2.1-16) and the CU(5.3.1-5.10.10), King Pravāhaṇa Jaivali attempts to persuade Uddālaka Āruṇi to take wealth, rather than disclose to the eminent brahmin the knowledge of the five fires (*pañcāgnividyā*).

The figure of the hesitant teacher is depicted again in a dialogue from the CU (8.7-12) in which the creator-god Prajāpati is cast as the teacher, with the Ṛgvedic figures Indra and Virocana taking the roles of his students. Initially, both Indra and Virocana live as *brahmacārins* for twelve years before Prajāpati offers to give them instruction. Even after thirty-two years, Prajāpati asks Indra and Virocana what they wanted when they came to him in the first place (CU 8.7.3). When

Prajāpati finally gets around to giving his first lesson, he imparts false knowledge, telling Indra and Virocana that the self that one sees in the eye, in the water, and in a mirror is the true *ātman*—all three descriptions conveying the sense that appearance or reflection is the true self. Prajāpati then sends them on their way thinking that this is the true teaching. However, Indra soon recognizes that this teaching is false, or at least incomplete, and, before arriving back with the other gods, he returns to Prajāpati in order to learn more. Prajāpati tells him that if he stays for another thirty-two years he will teach him further, but again Prajāpati conveys false knowledge, and again Indra returns to him, realizing that his true teaching has not yet been revealed. This pattern continues several times, until Indra's tenure as a student adds up to one hundred and one years. At the end of the story, Prajāpati finally reveals his true teaching about the self.

In this scene Indra and Virocana are both tested by having to wait several years for their instruction, only to be given a false teaching. While Indra shows he is a worthy student by realizing the limitations of Prajāpati's initial teaching, he is still asked to prove himself on several further occasions before finally being entrusted to the true teaching. Along with posing the challenge of determining the true teaching from false or incomplete disclosures, Prajāpati's method of imparting his knowledge in 'carefully timed' increments is a pedagogical method similar to other knowledge exchanges in secret or esoteric traditions. Indeed, Prajāpati's teaching style is even reminiscent of recent practices among secret societies. Lamont Lindstrom, for example, in the context of his anthropological work in the South Pacific explains:

> Knowers, rather than destroying all their secrets in some impressive flow of information, carefully time their revelations so that these last from conversation to conversation. Here, secret tellers may indicate to auditors that they are holding back the real truths of their knowledge, although they communicate enough to convince people of the existence of their secrets to make these conversationally conspicuous (1990: 120).

Similarly, by communicating false teachings, Prajāpati reveals that there is more to learn, thus increasing the value of the knowledge he withholds.

(b) Difficult and Dangerous

While both Yama and Pravāhaṇa are reluctant to share their knowledge because it is the source of their power, Śākāyanya hesitates with the warning that his teaching is difficult. The toils associated with learning, in fact, come across in a number of cases, suggesting that the inclusion of trials and tests were standard aspects of the Upaniṣadic curriculum: Naciketas has to stay in isolation in the house of Yama for three nights (KaU 1.9); Satyakāma has to tend cows for several years on his own (CU 4.4.5); Upakosala is abandoned by his teacher and not allowed to leave his teacher's house, even though his classmates were permitted to go home (CU 4.10.1), and, although his austerities are not directly part of his tutelage under Śākāyanya, Bṛhadratha practices asceticism for a thousand days, yet is still not immediately ready to learn about the self (MtU 1.2). Thus, along with the hesitancy of the teacher, the narratives suggest that students have to endure tests or perform challenging tasks in order to earn their right to learn. In the case of Naciketas there is the additional dynamic that by approaching Yama, who is the personification of death, the young brahmin is risking his life—that in addition to the difficulty of attaining the truth, the path to knowledge is potentially dangerous. The combination of difficulty and danger comes across again in the KaU in the well known metaphor of the razor's edge, which compares the path of knowledge to treading along the fine edge of a blade: "[As] the sharp edge of a razor is difficult to cross; difficult to traverse is this path, the poets say" (3.14).[10]

Perhaps the most striking example of the potential danger surrounding the type of knowledge contained in the Upaniṣads is the famous head-shattering episode that takes place during a debate in the court of King Janaka. In this scene, which appears in the BU (3), Yājñavalkya is challenged by eight opponents, with the debate ending dramatically as the head of Śākalya, the final interlocutor, shatters apart because he cannot answer Yājñavalkya's question. The Upaniṣads do not tell us how incomplete or false knowledge can lead to such dangerous outcomes. Nevertheless, the repeated use of the head-shattering motif in debating episodes clearly illustrates that high stakes are involved when it comes to Upaniṣadic teachings. Although this is the only scene where the threat ends with fatal consequences, the threat appears on a number of occasions in the Brāhmaṇas and Upaniṣads, and is indeed one of the distinguishing features of debating scenes (see Black 2007: 64-65; 80-88).[11] Through such warnings, these scenes reveal the limitations of both questions and answers, and they convey the rule that one must already know in order to be allowed to ask. As such, they ward off uncontrolled questioning that may threaten the distribution of knowledge. While a number of dialogues depicting teachers and students advertise the secrecy of the knowledge, this *brahmodya* episode offers the warning: handle with care. We might also suggest that the potential dangers of the teachings highlight the power of the knowledge, thus contributing to its value and desirability.

[10] *kṣurasya dhārā niśitā duratyayā durgaṃ pathas tat kavayo vadanti* ||

[11] For further discussions on the trope of head shattering, see Witzel (1987), Insler (1989-90), and Lindquist (forthcoming).

(c) Disclosure

While concealment, reluctance to teach, and warnings of the difficulties and dangers of the teachings are central features of these episodes, an equally important aspect is the ultimate disclosure of knowledge. Despite their initial hesitations, the teachers in the Upaniṣads do eventually reveal what they know: as we have seen, Prajāpati does finally deliver his true teaching at the end. Similarly, Śākāyanya does teach Bṛhadratha; Yama does ultimately grant Naciketas his wish to learn about death; and Pravāhaṇa does eventually tell his secret to Uddālaka.[12] Additionally, in an episode that takes place during the debate in King Janaka's court (BU 3.2), Yājñavalkya takes Ārtabhāga outside, explaining to his interlocutor that he can only answer his question about what happens after death in private. Although Yājñavalkya's reply is beyond the earshot of other participants in the debate, the narrative voice still reveals the gist of his teaching. As a consequence, although it is kept secret from the audience in King Janaka's court, his teaching is revealed to the receivers of the text. Revelation, it seems, is integral to these scenes. Indeed, as some scholars suggest, revelation is integral to secrecy itself. Antoine Faivre, for example, has defined secrecy as "a practice of intentional concealment, or more interestingly, as a theme of discourse in which concealment and unveiling sometimes intertwine" (1999: 156). Similarly, in the pedagogical episodes in the Upaniṣads, despite the repeated emphasis on the subtlety and scarcity of the knowledge, revelation is as essential to secrecy as concealment.

(d) Inconclusive Narratives

Yet, even though teachers reveal their knowledge, many narratives leave a sense of mystery because the scenes end inconclusively. We rarely learn how, or if, the teachings transform those who learn them. Unlike comparable scenes in the Pāli Canon, for example, that relate what happens to those who listen to the Buddha's teachings, the narratives in the Upaniṣads do not reveal the soteriological outcome of its characters. The Upaniṣads, in other words, give us no indication as to whether students such as King Bṛhadratha, Indra, or Uddālaka are transformed by the teachings that they learn. A rare exception is the KaU, which returns to the frame dialogue at the end of the text, relating that Naciketas "reached *brahman*; became free from passion, from death. And so may any other who knows this concerning the self" (6.18).[13] In most cases, however, the narratives in the

[12] Additionally, the answer to the riddle that appears after the debate in Janaka's court (BU 3.9.28) could be seen as a disclosure. As Lindquist (2004) argues, the inclusion of the solution to this riddle is perhaps an attempt to tack on an answer to what might have otherwise been considered to be an inconclusive ending.

[13] *brahmaprāpto virajo 'bhūd vimṛtyur anyo 'py evaṃ yo vid adhyātmam eva* ||

Upaniṣads introduce the teachings, but seldom continue after them.[14] By contrast, in the *Dīgha* (DN) and *Majjhima Nikāyas* (MN), almost all the encounters between the Buddha and non-Buddhists end with the Buddha's interlocutor converting to Buddhism, either as a lay supporter or as a member of the *saṃgha*, with many *suttas* including details such as the Buddha's interlocutor attaining the Dhamma-eye, or, in some cases, achieving *nibbāna*.[15] Thus, an important component of early Buddhist literature is depicting the effect that the Buddha's teachings have on those who hear them. Considering some of the similarities between the narratives in the Upaniṣads and the Pāli Canon (see Manné 1992, Gombrich 1996, Black forthcoming a), the lack of closure in the Upaniṣads is noteworthy.

This indirect and inconclusive character of the narratives also implies that there may be more to be known; despite revealing some of their knowledge teachers give very little, if anything, away. As such, the narratives suggest that establishing the teacher as the one who knows is as important as expressing what the teacher knows. In this way, the Upaniṣads create their own mystique by claiming to contain secret teachings, yet at the same time implying that the teachings they reveal are only partial or incomplete, that there may be more to be learned. Moreover, because the secrets are not only characterized by their exclusivity, but also by their profundity, even when teachings are revealed, they continue to be elusive.

Demonstrations of Secret Knowledge

As many studies of secrecy have noted, there are a number of tendencies shared by esoteric traditions, such as the concealment of knowledge from public dissemination, restricting knowledge to a small number of people, and strict initiation procedures that include trials and ordeals for students (e.g. Simmel [1906] 1974; Tiryakian 1974). In his analysis of esoteric traditions in medieval China, for instance, Robert Campany (2006) examines a number of features that are reminiscent of the secrecy described in the Upaniṣads, including: the aloof teacher; the difficulty involved in learning the teachings; the 'self-esotericizing' character of the texts; and the

[14] This non-closure is a feature of a number of texts that are presented in the form of a dialogue. For example, as Minkowski notes, there is no real attempt to close the Ugraśravas frame story in the *Mahābhārata* (1989: 405). Similarly, Olivelle comments that the frame dialogue in the *Mānava Dharmaśāstra* "fizzles out; there is no conclusion to the narrative" and that this is also a feature of the frame dialogue in the *Pañcatantra* (2004: xxv).

[15] Both Pokkharasāti (DN 3) and Kūṭadanta (DN 5), for example, become lay supporters and attain the Dhamma-eye. Sela and his three hundred brahmin students become *arahants* (MN 92). Brahmāyu becomes a lay supporter after his encounter with the Buddha, but when he dies the Buddha declares that he reached *nibbāna* (MN 91). Dhānañjāni dies and reappears in the Brahma world (MN 97). For a full list of the outcomes of Buddhist suttas in the Nikāyas, see Chakravarti (1996: Appendix C).

instructions for keeping teachings secret. However, Campany also notes that many texts contain "displays of wondrous results" in which "adepts flaunted their abilities" (2006: 323). Such demonstrations of the power of knowledge include the abilities to transform oneself into vapour, to travel long distances instantaneously, to submerge oneself into rocks and stones, to swallow knives and swords. As Campany points out, the performance of such feats functions as "a test of authenticity" (2006: 323), with an integral feature of these episodes being the performance of special powers in front of an audience: "Much was done to call attention to the existence, possession, and power of these secret methods; access to them was carefully managed, but part of that management was the incessant announcement of the methods' existence and of the possibility of assessing them given the right qualifications and conditions" (2006: 317).

While the Upaniṣads do not appear to feature any individuals performing comparable supernatural acts as evidence of their knowledge, one incident that we might be tempted to call a wondrous demonstration is the head-shattering incident in the BU. As we have seen, this scene seems to characterize the power of the knowledge, rather than the power that individuals can gain from the knowledge. At the same time, there does seem to be some agency attributed to Yājñavalkya. As I have argued elsewhere (2007: 87-88), the BU—in contrast to a similar scene which appears in the ŚB (11.6.3.11) in which Yājñavalkya merely predicts Śākalya's death and in which the cause of Śākalya's death is unstated—depicts Yājñavalkya as assuming the role of the interrogator and as explicitly threatening Śākalya. To say that Yājñavalkya kills Śākalya would perhaps be too strong of a claim, but he certainly creates the circumstances for his opponent's death to occur. That his other opponents seem to recognize Yājñavalkya's role in bringing about Śākalya's death is suggested by the fact that none of them dare to oppose him further when Yājñavalkya invites more challenges after his encounter with Śākalya. While the head-shattering episode may not be exactly the type of personal demonstration of one's abilities that appear in the stories that Campany examines from medieval China, one of the features of the debate in Janaka's court is that it is a public display of the power of knowledge and those who have attained it.[16]

Other possible examples of the outward display of knowledge come from two scenes from the CU (4.4.1-5), which we will examine in more detail below. Both episodes depict brahmin students whose appearance is changed by what they learn—to the point that their teachers recognize that they "shine" ($\sqrt{}$*bhās*) like one who knows *brahman*. Although it is clear that in both cases the young brahmins go

[16] See Lindquist (forthcoming) for a discussion about the death of Śākalya and survival of Yājñavalkya within BU's teaching on immortality.

through a physical transformation that is observed by their respective teachers, in neither scene is their physical transformation public, nor, as we shall see, is it the emphasis of the story, as both students return to their teachers for further instruction—indeed, in both cases the shine they attain functions more as a demonstration that they are ready to learn more, rather than as evidence that they have already achieved knowledge.

Thus, while these examples from the BU and CU show that knowledge can lead to demonstrable powers or changes in one's appearance, it is also the case that the narratives in the Upaniṣads do not emphasize the publicly verifiable aspects of knowledge nearly as much as other traditions. In the early Buddhist literature, for example, the outward displays of the Buddha's knowledge, such as his supernatural powers or the thirty-two marks on his body, are often more convincing to potential converts than his doctrines (see Black forthcoming b; McClintock forthcoming). Yet in the Upaniṣads, rather than through the display of miraculous powers, the teachers seem to attract audiences mostly through word of mouth. Although most narratives do not reveal how students came to know of the teachers that they approach, on a few occasions we learn that teachers are approached because of their reputations. Uddālaka Āruṇi, for example, suggests to the householders who approach him to learn about *ātman* that they all go to Aśvapati Kaikeya because he is studying about the self (CU 5.11.4). We do not know how Uddālaka knows this about Aśvapati, but clearly his decision to take the householders to approach him is based on information he has learned about him. Also, when Uddālaka goes to learn from Pravāhana Jaivali, it is because his son Śvetaketu has just been asked questions by the king that the young brahmin could not answer. While in the BU and CU versions of this story we do not know why Śvetaketu goes to the king in the first place,[17] it is clear that Uddālaka subsequently approaches Pravāhaṇa because of the knowledge the king has demonstrated in his earlier interaction with Śvetaketu. Indeed, the most consistent demonstration of one's knowledge throughout the narratives in the Upaniṣads is the delivering of a teaching. In other words, rather than performing special powers to demonstrate their knowledge, the teachers in the Upaniṣads are more likely to display their knowledge through the revelation of the knowledge itself.

One additional external indication of knowledge seems to be wealth, as those characters who are considered knowledgeable are consistently portrayed as accumulating material possessions. Characters such as Raikva (CU 4.1-2) and Uṣasti Cākrāyaṇa (CU 1.10-

17 In the *Kauṣītaki Upaniṣad* (1.1) the king, who is here called by the name Citra Gāṅgyānani, is about to perform a sacrifice and had chosen Uddālaka Āruṇi as his officiating priest. Uddālaka, however, sends Śvetaketu on his behalf.

11) demand large fees for their knowledge, while Yājñavalkya claims the prize after the debate in Janaka's court and later wins thousands of cows from Janaka for his private instructions (BU 4.3-4). As I have explored previously (2007: 88-92), much of the wealth mentioned in the Upaniṣads is for the sake of highlighting the material value of the knowledge, particularly in relation to the fees for performing sacrifices. But we also might suggest that wealth is an external display of the power of learning a secret teaching: it is the most clear indication of what one can attain through knowledge.[18] Although many of the teachings promise immortality, or knowledge of *ātman* or *brahman*, the narratives rarely tell us if knowers achieve their soteriological goals. However, almost every scene mentions the wealth that one can attain through knowledge, thus rendering material goods an external indicator for those who know.

Secrecy and Scholastic Rivalry

While others have brought attention to the secrecy in the Upaniṣads (e.g. Deussen 1906; Radhakrishnan 1953), there has been very little attempt to place this secrecy into a social and historical context. As Campany has suggested in his exploration of secrecy in medieval China: secrecy is a "stance towards the wider society, not the absence of any relation to society" (2006: 317). My intention in bringing attention to the rhetoric of secrecy has been to make a similar point: the secrecy in the Upaniṣads is not just a way of describing knowledge, but is a stance towards the world. But if this is the case, then what type of stance are the Upaniṣads taking? Who are the Upaniṣads trying to convince that their teachings are secret?

It is generally assumed that the early Upaniṣads were composed during the time of dynamic changes in North India. As Olivelle describes, there were "five major elements in the socioeconomic changes of the sixth century: food surplus, increase in population, trade, monarchical states, and, above all, cities" (1992: 30; see also Thapar 1993). It is perhaps too speculative to claim that we can detect all of these changes within the texts, but the Upaniṣads nevertheless portray a number of more specific social changes in the narratives, particularly shifts in the role and function of brahmins, in attitudes towards the Vedic sacrifice, and in the interactions among priests affiliated with different Vedas (see Black 2007: 12-16).

All of these changes, as we will see, are related to the secrecy claimed by the texts, but of particular relevance is the intense rivalry that is often depicted between brahmins from different traditions of

[18] Material possessions have similar functions in other religious literature. In the context of Mahāyāna narrative literature, as Osto has demonstrated, wealth can function "as a sign of both ethical development and spiritual power" (2008: 74).

transmission. The most illustrative example of such rivalries is the debate in King Janaka's court where Yājñavalkya's opponents represent competing Vedic texts and traditions, with most of his challengers coming from the western Kuru-Pañcāla region and having affiliations with the Ṛgveda (ṚV) and Black Yajurveda; in contrast, Yājñavalkya, through Janaka, is closely associated with the eastern city of Videha and belongs to the White Yajurveda.[19] The BU (4.1) also contains another scene in which Yājñavalkya counters the opinions of six other brahmins, again with most of his opponents representing different regions and different textual traditions. In addition to scenes depicting individual brahmins in conflict with each other, textual rivalries are also borne out in the different theological claims, the different literary styles and conventions, and the different practices portrayed by individual Upaniṣads (Olivelle 1999). Recently, Signe Cohen has claimed that the secrecy of the Upaniṣads can be seen in the context of such textual rivalries. As Cohen suggests, secrecy is "a natural extension of a closed system of textual transmission ... Through secrecy a sense of community is imparted to the members of the *śakhā* [school] and a sense of the authority of the tradition is communicated to those who are not members" (2008: 12).[20]

One of the ways that knowledge is linked to particular traditions of transmission is through the repeated insistence on learning from the proper teacher. This is illustrated in two scenes from the CU (4.4.1-5), both of which depict brahmin students learning about *brahman* from non-traditional sources. In the first example (CU 4.4.1-5) the teacher Hāridrumata gives his student Satyakāma four hundred emaciated cows and asks him to look after them. Satyakāma accepts them, promising not to return until he has a thousand cows. After a number of years Satyakāma fulfills his promise by increasing the number of cows to one thousand. Soon after this a bull begins to instruct him about *brahman*. Subsequently, Satyakāma is taught by a fire, a goose, and a cormorant. When Satyakāma finally returns to his teacher's house, Hāridrumata notices that his student shines ($\sqrt{}$*bhās*) like a man who knows *brahman* (CU 4.9.2). When Hāridrumata questions Satyakāma about where he has learned about *brahman*, Satyakāma replies that it was not from humans. After acknowledging that non-humans had taught him, Satyakāma adds that he wants to learn it from Hāridrumata because he has heard from people like him that knowledge learned from one's teacher attains the best results.

Satyakāma reiterates this point when he later becomes a teacher himself. He receives Upakosala as his student, but then embarks on

[19] See Witzel (1997: 319-20).

[20] Although I generally agree with Cohen that secrecy developed in the context of emerging textual rivalries between different traditions of transmission, it is not clear from her book whether these rivalries are between *śākhās* (schools) or, more generally, between different Vedas.

a journey before ever teaching him. When he is away, his student, like Satyakāma himself, receives instruction from unlikely sources. In this case, his teachers are the household fire, the southern fire, and the offering fire. When Satyakāma returns he recognizes that now his own student shines like a man who knows *brahman*. However, when he learns that the fires taught Upakosala, he promises to teach him himself. That both Satyakāma and Upakosala are described as "shining like a man who knows *brahman*" suggests that their knowledge led to a physical transformation that was discernible to their respective teachers, yet in both cases the students return to their teachers and continue their education, suggesting that even knowledge that led to an externally verifiable change was considered less valuable than instruction from a proper teacher.

Along with highlighting the prestige of individual teachers, the Upaniṣads also emphasize the authority of particular lines of transmission. This comes across in the three genealogies in the BU (2.6.1-3, 4.6.1-3, 6.5.1-4), as well as in the many passages that contain instructions for how knowledge should be transmitted. In the BU, at the end of a description of how to make a mixture for attaining greatness, the narrative records several moments of instruction as this teaching had been passed down from Uddālaka Āruṇi to Yājñavalkya, to Madhuka Paiṅgya, to Cūla Bhāgavitti, to Jānaki Āyasthūṇa, to Satyakāma, and to his students. After recording these moments of instruction the text warns that this knowledge should not be shared with anyone who is not a son (*putra*) or a student (*antevāsin*; 6.3.12). The CU (3.11.4) instructs that a father should only impart a teaching of *brahman* to his eldest son (*jyeṣṭha putra*) or a worthy pupil (*praṇāyya antevāsin*), and never to anyone else (See also ŚU 6.22; MuU 3.2.11; MtU 6.29). By means of outlining to whom knowledge should be shared, the narratives establish hierarchies of authority and normative practices through which knowledge can be disseminated. The narratives about teachers and students, combined with the instructions for sharing knowledge, rehearse how discourses should be taught, and how they should be learned; how students should ask questions, and how teachers should answer them. Taken together, these details contribute to limiting and controlling those who have access to knowledge.

The notion that teachings should only be revealed to some people and in only specific situations is perhaps what is going on in an exchange between Yājñavalkya and Jāratkārava Ārtabhāga in the debate in King Janaka's court (BU 3.2). After asking Yājñavalkya about graspers (*graha*) and over-graspers (*atigraha*), Ārtabhāga asks Yājñavalkya questions about the nature of death, and then returns to this subject in his final question: "When a man (*puruṣa*) dies, and his speech goes into fire, his breath into wind, his sight into the sun, his mind into the moon, his hearing into the cardinal directions, his body into the earth, his self (*ātman*) into space … then where is that man (*puruṣa*)" (3.2.13).[21] To this question Yājñavalkya does not answer, but rather replies: "Take my hand good man, Ārtabhāga. Only the two of us will know of this, it is not for us (to discuss) in public" (3.2.13).[22]

A number of scholars have commented upon this curious response. Sarvepalli Radhakrishnan, for example, supposes that Yājñavalkya takes Ārtabhāga outside due to the sensitivity of the subject matter: "When the question of man's final destiny was raised, Yājñavalkya took his pupil aside and whispered to him the truth" ([1953] 1992: 19-20). More recently, Cohen has proposed that because both bramins are affiliated with the Yajurveda, Yājñavalkya can teach Ārtabhāga in secret: "Perhaps it is Ārtabhāga's affiliation with the Yajurveda, Yājñavalkya's own tradition, that leads to his preferential treatment and his ultimate initiation into the secret teachings about karma, a concept introduced in this passage as an esoteric idea not suitable for public discussion" (Cohen 2008: 77-78). But while Cohen is right to point out that both Yājñavalkya and Ārtabhāga are connected to the same Veda, it is not the case that the brahmins belong to the same *śākhā* (school), as Yājñavalkya is affiliated with the White Yajurveda, while Ārtabhāga is aligned with the Black Yajurveda. As such, if Yājñavalkya does indeed initiate Ārtabhāga because of their mutual connection with the Yajurveda, then it would demonstrate that secrets could be shared within the same Veda, and not necessarily limited to a particular school. There does, nonetheless, seem to be good reason to assume that Yājñavalkya formally initiates Ārtabhāga. As I have pointed out elsewhere (2007: 77) Yājñavalkya takes Ārtabhāga's hand as they go outside—a gesture reminiscent of the *upanayana*, the initiation ceremony for a brahmin student.[23] By suggesting that Ārtabhāga was initiated before receiving Yājñavalkya's secret teaching, this scene reinforces the Upaniṣadic emphasis on maintaining lineages and the proper modes of transmission.

While the Upaniṣadic emphasis on secrecy seems to coincide with its depictions of rivalries between individual brahmins, as well as between regions and textual traditions, it is also important to acknowledge that the rhetoric is perhaps stronger than the reality. As Cohen points out, a number of quotations appear in the Upaniṣads across scholastic boundaries, reflecting that the Upaniṣads "were known outside their respective traditions of recitation" (2008: 10). Also, because many Upaniṣads refute the ideas contained in other Upaniṣads affiliated with different Vedas, they must have had some ideas of the texts and teachings in those rival traditions: "The Upaniṣadic teachings, although not accessible to all, were probably

[21] *yatrāsya puruṣasya mṛtasyāgnim vāg apyeti vātaṃ prāṇaś cakṣur ādityaṃ manaś candraṃ diśaḥ śrotraṃ pṛthivīṃ śarīram ākāśam ātmā … kvāyaṃ tadā puruṣo bhavati* |

[22] *āhara somya hastam ārtabhāga* | *āvām evaitasya vediṣyāvo na nāv etat sajana …* |

[23] Similarly, Ajātaśatru takes Dṛpta-Bālāki by the hand when he receives him as a student (BU 2.1.15).

kept less secret than some of the passages ... would suggest" (2008: 10-11). Moreover, in a recent presentation, Steven Lindquist (2006) has proposed that the appearance of literary characters and stories from the Upaniṣads in later texts such as the epics and Purāṇas—texts which claim to appeal to a wide-ranging, rather than restricted, audience—may imply that at least some of the content of the Upaniṣads was relatively well known, or at least not nearly as restrictive as they claim it to be. In other words, the inclusion of stories with characters such as Yājñavalkya, Janaka, Uddālaka Āruṇi, and Śvetaketu in subsequent texts suggests that they were already recognizable figures.

This tension between the exclusive and shared aspects of the Upaniṣads also comes across in some of the narratives. Returning once again to the debate in King Janaka's court, it is perhaps noteworthy that while Yājñavalkya is discreet with his teachings during the initial stages, he shares his knowledge more freely as the debate unfolds. Although Yājñavalkya does not repeat exactly what he says to Ārtabhāga in his subsequent arguments during the debate, he does voice some of the same teachings in the public debate he otherwise reveals in private instruction with Janaka (cf. 3.9.26 with 4.2.4 & 4.4.22; 3.5.1 with 4.4.22) and his wife Maitreyī (cf. 3.4.2, 3.7.23, & 3.8.11 with 4.5.14; cf. 3.9.26 with 4.5.14). This entire episode, thus, presents us with an interesting juxtaposition of private and public, with the debate itself portrayed as an occasion on which knowledge is disseminated across boundaries of textual affiliation. Paradoxically, while secrecy may have emerged in a context in which different Vedas claimed to have doctrines distinct from each other, one of the central ways in which their rivalries were expressed—namely, debate—created the conditions for such secrets to be shared.

This paradox—that knowledge is both concealed and publicly known—comes across vividly in the scene where Uddālaka Āruṇi learns a secret teaching from King Pravāhaṇa. In both the BU and CU versions of this episode, the king explicitly portrays his teaching as a secret that has never been known to brahmins before, thus highlighting the scarcity of his knowledge. The CU account makes an even stronger claim, maintaining that the *kṣatriya* monopoly on political power is founded on the exclusive possession of this knowledge: "Prior to you, this knowledge has not gone to the brahmins. Therefore, in all the worlds, government has belonged only to the *kṣatriyas*" (5.3.7).[24]

Pravāhaṇa's claim has led many scholars to suggest that the knowledge of the five fires (*pañcāgnividyā*) was literally authored by *kṣatriyas*.[25] However, as H.W. Bodewitz (1973: 216) and Dermot

[24] *yatheyaṃ na prāk tvattaḥ purā vidyā brāhmaṇān gacchati* | *tasmād u sarveṣu lokeṣu kṣatrasyaiva praśāsanam abhūd* ... ||

[25] See Black (2007: 103-5) for a discussion about the authorship debate. The most recent scholar to make the argument that Pravāhaṇa's teaching is of non-Vedic origins is Bronkhorst (2007: 112-126).

Killingley (1997) have illustrated, Pravāhaṇa's teaching, as well as other discourses spoken by *kṣatriya* characters, had appeared earlier in Vedic literature, but then were re-presented as the speech of a *kṣatriya* in the Upaniṣads.[26] For example, Pravāhaṇa's teaching also appears in the *Jaiminīya Brāhmaṇa* (JB; 1.45-6), but without the context of a dialogue between a *kṣatriya* and a brahmin. Also, alternative versions of this discourse appear in the *Aitareya Āraṇyaka* and the ŚB. Taking this into account, Pravāhaṇa's claim that this teaching is only known by *kṣatriyas* is clearly not a factual representation, but rather can be seen as part of the text's characterization of its teachings as secret knowledge.[27] In this way, Pravāhaṇa's claim seems to be more about creating a sense of mystery than about preserving a secret.

Moreover, it is noteworthy, if not a bit ironic, that this passage, which is perhaps the most well-known example of secrecy in the Upaniṣads, appears in more than one Upaniṣad (i.e. in both the BU (6.2.8) and the CU(5.3.6)). In other words, the very passage that is the most explicit example of secrecy in the Upaniṣads is itself not a secret, but a story that is shared across different and competing textual traditions. Almost all the surviving Vedic Upaniṣads, in one way or another, make claims to secrecy in terms of protecting knowledge within a particular line of transmission. Yet, as we have seen, some of the same teachings that claim to be secret, as well as some of the same stories that characterize them as secret, are shared across textual traditions. These instances indicate that despite using secrecy as a way of distinguishing one's own texts and traditions from others, the Vedic lines of transmission were not examples of secret societies cut off from each other and from other social groups, but rather that secrecy was a way for different Vedic traditions to make claims for themselves that were directed towards each other, as well as towards possible patrons. As Urban suggests: "Secrecy ... is a tactic which functions to transform certain knowledge into a rare and valuable commodity, a scarce resource, which in turn enhances the status and prestige ... of its possessor" (2001: 12).

From Esoteric Discourse to the Rhetoric of Secrecy

Another crucial aspect of secrecy in the Upaniṣads is how the texts present themselves in relation to previous Vedic material. It is

[26] Bodewitz also has a more recent article (1996) in which he explores the development of the *pañcāgnividyā*, again demonstrating that this teaching originally appeared in texts without the frame narrative.

[27] Olivelle has commented: "It is naive, therefore, to accept the literary evidence of the Upaniṣads regarding their Kṣatriyas authorship at face value and as historical fact ... The most we can say is that some segments of the Brahmanical community must have perceived it as advantageous to present doctrines they favored as coming from the royal elite" (1996: xxxv).

important to note that the lines between different genres of Vedic texts—Saṃhitās, Brāhmaṇas, Āraṇyakas, Upaniṣads—are often fuzzy, so any attempt to characterize differences between them are generalities, not absolute distinctions. Nonetheless, the Upaniṣads, despite containing much material that is almost indistinguishable from the Brāhmaṇas and Āraṇyakas, do position themselves on several occasions in contrast to other sections of the Vedas. This is illustrated, for example, by both Nārada (CU 7.1.1-3) and Śvetaketu (CU 6.1.1) who approach their teachers after having received a formal Vedic eduction, yet not having learned about the self. Such passages claim to present teachings that are both absent from and superior to any and all of the knowledge contained in other Vedic sources. I would suggest that the rhetoric of secrecy can be seen as part of the same general tendency in which the Upaniṣads criticize a number of aspects of traditional Vedic ideas and practices, while presenting themselves as containing a new type of knowledge, which is not only superior, but also more closely guarded.

Intriguingly, however, much of the earlier Vedic material also has dimensions of secrecy. As a number of scholars have demonstrated, many sections of the Saṃhitās and Brāhmaṇas can be characterized as an esoteric discourse that is only known by very few. Joel Brereton (1999) and Stephanie Jamison (2004), for example, have examined riddle hymns in the ṚV that pose questions that are left unanswered, the clues only apparent to those who know the discourse. As George Thompson comments, such riddles test "a candidate's knowledge of a restricted cultural, i.e., shared, code. It is metalinguistic in function, just as the riddle in general is. Here the Vedic 'language of gods' is directly juxtaposed with 'the language of men'" (1997: 16). Contrary to Norman Brown's view that the riddles of the ṚV would have been understood "with relative ease" (1968: 199) by those familiar with the discourse during the Vedic period, Thompson contends—I believe correctly—that some hymns were deliberately obscure and that "even a relatively 'expert audience' might have been baffled by significant portions of the hymn" (1997: 35).

Besides the deliberate obscurity of much of the material in the Saṃhitās and Brāhmaṇas, it is also well known that the process of learning these texts, especially the ṚV, was highly complex and sophisticated, requiring years of formal education (Scharfe 2002). Students would not only memorize the Vedic texts, but learn to recite them with the aid of mnemonic manuals such as the *padapāṭha*, *kramapāṭha*, and *jaṭāpāṭha*, along with accompanying head movements and hand gestures. Although the early Vedic texts do not contain descriptions of or narratives about the transmission and dissemination of texts, the attention to the finest details of memorization and recitation, as evinced by the existence of such mnemonic manuals, combined with the transcendental value placed on the Vedas themselves, indicates that the practices of transmission would have involved strict initiation procedures and would have been limited to a relatively small number of people.

When we consider the esoteric nature of much of Vedic discourse in the context of the strict and time-consuming practices inherent in learning the texts, we might describe the Vedas as intrinsically restrictive: they were so complicated and laborious to learn that they were only ever available to a specific and limited group of people. Taking these two aspects of pre-Upaniṣadic Vedic material into account—1) the controlled access and strict procedures involved in the transmission of knowledge; and 2) the hidden meanings that are deliberately obscured from even other initiated members of the community—we might justifiably call some sections of the Saṃhitās and Brāhmaṇas 'secret' texts. As will become clear, it is not my intention to make the argument for categorizing the early Vedic material in this way, but by bringing attention to the secretive dimension of the Saṃhitās and Brāhmaṇas, we can see that an interesting aspect of the secrecy in the Upaniṣads is that it does not oppose itself to knowledge that is universal or widely available; rather it opposes itself to knowledge that also has characteristics of secrecy. Indeed, we might even suggest that these earlier texts are more inherently secretive than the Upaniṣads. While the Upaniṣads might describe their teachings as secret, it is possible to see them as less cryptic or enigmatic as compared to the esoteric language of the riddle hymns and *brahmodya*s of earlier Vedic material. The Upaniṣads might present their central ideas, such as *ātman*, *brahman*, or *puruṣa*, as beyond description, yet this very point—that the nature of reality is ineffable—is made quite straightforwardly; although rhetorical flourishes such as paradox and negation are employed, the language itself is neither encoded nor technical. In contrast, as Thompson argues, the riddle hymns of the ṚV could bewilder even those who had learned the rarefied discourse. We might imagine, then, that compared to the esoteric discourses of the Saṃhitās and Brāhmaṇas, the teachings of the Upaniṣads were considered more readily attainable and more easily appropriated by rival lines of transmission. Seen in this way, composers of the Upaniṣads might have felt the need of finding a new means of restricting access, such as presenting their texts and their ideas as secret.

When considering how they position themselves vis-à-vis previous texts, it is important to keep in mind that the Upaniṣads characterize their teachings as being learned in addition to other Vedic material, rather than as an alternative discourse. Students such as Nārada and Śvetaketu learn teachings about the self after they have received a formal eduction, not as a substitute for the Vedas. Nonetheless, through the rhetoric of secrecy, the Upaniṣads characterize themselves as an elite section of Vedic learning, even if other sections of Vedas appear to be more intrinsically esoteric.

Another crucial factor in comparing the Upaniṣads with earlier Vedic material is the change in outlook towards the Vedic sacrifice.

As a number of scholars have argued, the Vedic sacrifice is not nearly as central of a practice in the Upaniṣads, with a number of passages suggesting that some members of the brahmin community were quite critical of sacrifice and were looking for ways to reframe Vedic knowledge for new contexts. Ryūtaro Tsuchida explains this process:

> When śrauta-ritualism gradually lost its actuality in the life of the average twice-born, Vedic learning also had to change its orientation. The separation of Vedic learning from ritual practice, however, had no negative effect up on the authority of the Veda and Vedic scholars. It helped Vedic learning to become, as it were, more self-existent and introversive. The study of the Veda now was made into something to be practised essentially for its own sake, and more stress was laid on erudition, itself, than on its ritual application (1991: 69-70).[28]

But while Tsuchida is perhaps correct that the process of detaching Vedic texts from their ritual application had no negative effect on the authority of the Vedas, I would suggest that this was only the case because brahmins continually sought to recontextualize, reframe, and reformulate their texts in ways that presented them as not only relevant, but indispensable to changing times, new contexts, and different audiences. The rhetoric of secrecy, it seems to me, was one of several ways that the Upaniṣads portrayed their teachings as unique and valuable in a situation in which the significance of Vedic texts was less directly tied to ritual application.

Conclusion

By way of conclusion, I would like briefly to make a comparison between secrecy in the Upaniṣads and how it is presented in the *Bhagavad Gītā* (BhG). As a number of scholars have pointed out, the BhG has several passages in common with the Upaniṣads. Indeed, Cohen has recently made the argument that the BhG, along with the KU, *Śvetāśvatara*, and *Muṇḍaka* Upaniṣads, belonged to a "metatextual complex" as all these texts "borrow extensively back and forth from each other" (2008: 201). In addition to the many passages that these texts have in common,[29] the BhG also presents itself as an Upaniṣad in the colophons of the text. According to Thomas Coburn: "the testimony of the colophons is that the Gītā is of a piece with the Upaniṣads, for, at the end of the first chapter, out of the fifty-three manuscripts used to constitute the Gītā portion of the Bhiṣmaparvan,

[28] It is important to note, however, that this was only one of several processes going on simultaneously. As Patton brings to attention, while brahmin composers of the Upaniṣads may have challenged the institution of sacrifice, the brahmin composers of the Gṛhyasūtras continued to perform Vedic rituals, all the while investing them with new meanings and purposes (2005: 185).

[29] See Zaehner (1969) for an index of Upaniṣadic passages that are found in the *Bhagavad Gītā*.

forty-seven read *bhagavadgītāsu upaniṣatsu*, 'in the songs (verses) of the Blessed One, which are Upanisads'" (1984: 448-9). Considering the intimate connection between the Upaniṣads and the BhG, it is noteworthy that the BhG also claims to contain secret teachings. Kṛṣṇa, on three occasions, uses the word *guhya*, which, as we have seen, is often used to denote secrecy in the Upaniṣads.[30] While none of these passages appear to be direct quotations from previous sources, it is possible that Kṛṣṇa's claim to secrecy is one of the ways that the BhG links itself with the Upaniṣads.

But if there is a paradox of secrecy in the Upaniṣads, then there is even more of one in the BhG, as Kṛṣṇa claims to deliver a universal message available for women and *śūdras* (9.32). Moreover, the text itself is embedded within the *Mahābhārata*, which makes its own claims to universality. How, then, is it possible to consider Kṛṣṇa's teaching as secret? This is a question to which I hope to return on another occasion, but for now, I would just like to suggest briefly that one of the implications of secrecy in the BhG is not so much that Kṛṣṇa's teaching should continue to be protected—indeed, it should be shared with everyone—but rather that it has not been known until now. Perhaps like the golden treasure in the CU, it has been around for a while, passed by day after day, but remained unnoticed because it was hidden (*guhya*) from view; but now, through Kṛṣṇa's revelation, it has become manifest. In contrast to the BhG, though, the Upaniṣads are much more exclusive in who they address, never making such universal claims. It may be the case, however, that one of the aspects of Upaniṣadic secrecy, like the secrecy proclaimed by Kṛṣna, is not so much an attempt to protect its teachings, but to make them more popular.

Bibliography

Black, B. (2007), *The Character of the Self in Ancient India: Priests, Kings, and Women in the Early Upaniṣads* (Albany: State University of New York Press).

_____. (forthcoming a), "Ambaṭṭha and Śvetaketu: Literary Connections between the Upaniṣads and Early Buddhist Narratives," *Journal of the American Academy of Religion*.

_____. (forthcoming b), "Rivals and Benefactors: Encounters between Buddhists and Brahmins in the Nikāyas," *Religions of South Asia*.

[30] Kṛṣṇa uses this term on three occasions. He calls his teaching the "highest secret" (*guhyatamam*; 9.1); the "highest secret teaching" (*guhyatamaṃ śāstram*; 15.20); and "the most secret of secrets" (*guhyād guhyataram*; 18.63).

Bodewitz, H.W. (1973), *Jaiminīya Brāhmaṇa: I, 1-65 : Translation and Commentary. With a Study: Agnihotra and Prāṇāgnihotra* (Leiden: E.J. Brill).

_____. (1996), "The Pañcāgnividyā and the Pitṛyāna/Devayāna" in *Studies on Indology: Professor Mukunda Madhava Sharma Felicitation Volume*, ed. A.K. Goswain and D. Chutia, Sri Garib Das, Oriental Series, no. 201 (Delhi: Sri Satguru Publications).

Bolle, K. (1987), "Secrecy in Religion" in *Secrecy in Religion*, ed. K. Bolle (Leiden: Brill).

Brereton, J. (1990), "The Upanishads" in *Approaches to the Asian Classics*, ed. Wm. T. de Bary and I. Bloom (New York: Columbia University), 115-135.

_____. (1999), "Edifying Puzzlement: Ṛgveda X.129 and the Uses of Enigma," *Journal of the American Oriental Society* 119: 248-260.

Bronkhorst, J. (2007), *Greater Magadha: Studies in the Culture of Early India* (Leiden: Brill).

Brown, W.N. (1968), "Agni, Sun, Sacrifice, and Vāc: A Sacerdotal Ode by Dīrghatmas (Rig Veda 1.164)," *Journal of the American Oriental Society* 88.2: 199-218.

Campany, R.F. (2006), "Secrecy and Display in the Quest for Transcendence in China, Ca. 220 BCE - 350 CE," *History of Religions* 45.4: 291-336.

Carrithers, M. (2005), "Why Anthropologists Should Study Rhetoric," *Royal Anthropological Institute* 11: 577-583.

Chakravarti, U. (1996), *The Social Dimension of Early Buddhism* (New Delhi: Munshiram Manoharlal).

Coburn, T.B. (1984), "Scripture in India: Towards a Typology of the Word in Hindu Life," *Journal of the American Academy of Religion* 52: 439-459.

Cohen, S. (2008), *Text and Authority in the Older Upaniṣads* (Leiden: Brill).

Faivre, A. (1999), "The Notions of Concealment and Secrecy in Modern Esoteric Currents since the Renaissance (A Methodological Approach)" in *Rending the Veil: Concealment and Secrecy in the History of Religions*, ed. E.R. Wolfson (New York: Seven Bridges Press).

Falk, H. (1986), "Vedisch upaniṣád," *Zeitschrift der Deutschen Morgenländischen Gesellschaft* 136: 80-97.

Ganeri, J. (2007), *The Concealed Art of the Soul: Theories of Self and Practices of Truth in Indian Ethics and Epistemology* (Oxford: Oxford University Press).

Gombrich, R.F. (1996), *How Buddhism Began: The Conditioned Genesis of the Early Teachings* (London: Athlone).

Halbfass, W. (1988), *India and Europe: An Essay in Understanding* (Albany: State University of New York Press).

Insler, S. (1989-90), "The Shattered Head Split in the Epic Tale of Shakuntala," *Bulletin d'Etudes Indiennes* 7-8: 97-139.

Jamison, S. (2004), "Poetry and Purpose in the Rigveda: Structuring Enigmas" in *The Vedas. Texts, Language and Ritual: Proceedings of the Third International Vedic Workshop, Leiden 2002*, ed. A. Griffiths and J.E.M. Houben, Groningen Oriental Studies Volumen XX (Groningen: Egbert Forsten), 237-249.

Killingley, D. (1997), "The Paths of the Dead and the Five Fires" in *Indian Insights: Buddhism, Brahmanism and Bhakti: Papers from the Annual Spalding Symposium on Indian Religions*, ed. P. Connolly and S. Hamilton (London: Luzac Oriental).

Lindquist, S. (2004), "Yajnavalkya's Riddle (BĀUK 3.9.28)" in *Problems in Sanskrit and Vedic Literature: Felicitation Volume in Honor of Dr. G.U. Thite*, ed. M. Deshpande (Delhi: New Indian Book Center), 192-211.

_____. (2006), "Creating a *Ṛṣi*: The Later Literary Life of Yājñavalkya." Paper presented at the American Academy of Religion annual meeting, Washington, D.C.

_____. (forthcoming), "Literary Lives and a Literal Death: Yājñavalkya, Śākalya, and an Upaniṣadic Death Sentence," *Journal of the American Academy of Religion.*

Lindstrom, L. (1990), *Knowledge and Power in a South Pacific Society* (Washington: Smithsonian Institute Press).

Malamoud, C. (1996), *Cooking the World: Ritual & Thought in Ancient India* (Delhi: Oxford University Press).

Manné, J. (1992), "The Dīgha Nikāya Debates: Debating Practices at the Time of the Buddha," *Buddhist Studies Review* 9.2: 117-136.

Minkowski, C. (1989), "Janamejaya's *Sattra* and Ritual Structure," *Journal of the American Oriental Society* 109: 401-420.

McClintock, S. (forthcoming), "Compassionate Trickster: The Buddha as a Literary Character in the Narratives of Early Indian Buddhism," *Journal of the American Academy of Religion.*

Monier-Williams, M. [1899] (1993), *A Sanskrit-English Dictionary, Etymologically and Philologically Arranged with Special Reference to Cognate Indo-European Languages, Revised Edition* (Delhi: Motilal Banarsidass).

Müller, F.M. (tr.) [1900] (2000), *The Upanishads, Part I* (Delhi: Motilal Banarsidass).

Ñāṇamoli, B. and Bodhi, B. (trs.) (1995), *The Middle Length Discourses of the Buddha: A Translation of the Majjhima Nikāya* (Boston: Wisdom Publications).

Olivelle, P. (tr.) (1992), *Saṃnyāsa Upaniṣads* (New York: Oxford University Press).

_____. (tr.) (1996), *The Upaniṣads: A New Translation* (Oxford: Oxford University Press).

_____. (tr.) (1998), *The Early Upaniṣads: Annotated Text and Translation* (New York: Oxford University Press).

_____. (1999), "Young Śvetaketu: A Literary Study of an Upaniṣadic Story," *Journal of the American Oriental Society* 119.1: 46-70.

_____. (tr.) (2004), *The Law Code of Manu: A New Translation* (Oxford: Oxford University Press).

Osto, D. (2008), *Power, Wealth and Women in Indian Mahāyāna Buddhism: The Gaṇḍavyūha-sūtra* (Abingdon: Routledge).

Patton, L.L. (2005), *Bringing the Gods to Mind: Mantra and Ritual in Early Indian Sacrifice* (Berkeley: University of California Press).

Radhakrishnan, S. (tr.) [1953] (1992), *The Principal Upaniṣads: Edited with Introduction, Text, Translation and Notes* (New Jersey: Humanities Press).

Roebuck, V. (tr.) (2003), *The Upaniṣads* (London: Penguin Classics).

Scharfe, H. (2002), *Education in Ancient India* (Leiden: Brill).

Simmel, G. [1906] (1974), "The Sociology of Secrecy and of Secret Societies" trans. A.W. Small in *On the Margins of the Visible: Sociology, the Esoteric, and the Occult,* ed. E. Tiryakian (New York: John Wiley and Sons), 79-92.

Thapar, R. (1993), "Sacrifice, Surplus, and the Soul," *History of Religions* 33.4: 305-324.

Thompson, G. (1997), "The Brahmodya and Vedic Discourse," *Journal of the American Oriental Society* 117.1: 13-37.

Tiryakian, E. (1974), "Toward the Sociology of Esoteric Culture" in *On the Margins of the Visible: Sociology, the Esoteric, and the Occult,* ed. E. Tiryakian (New York: John Wiley and Sons), 257-280.

Tsuchida, R. (1991), "Two Categories of Brahmins in the Early Buddhist Period," *Memoirs of the Research Department of the Toyo Bunko* 49: 51-95.

Urban, H.B. (2001), *The Economics of Ecstasy: Tantra, Secrecy, and Power in Colonial Bengal* (Oxford: Oxford University Press).

_____. (2006), "Fair Game: Secrecy, Security, and the Church of Scientology in Cold War America," *Journal of the American Academy of Religion* 74.2: 356-389.

Walsh, M. (tr.) (1995), *The Long Discourses of the Buddha: A Translation of the Dīgha Nikāya* (Boston: Wisdom Publications).

Wasserstrom, S. (1999), *Religion After Religion: Gershom Scholem, Mircea Eliade, and Henry Corbin at Eranos* (Princeton: Princeton University Press).

Witzel, M. (1987), "The Case of the Shattered Head," *Studien zur Indologie und Iranistik* 13/14: 363-415.

_____. (1997), "The Development of the Vedic Canon and its Schools: The Social and Political Milieu" in *Inside the Texts, Beyond the Texts,* ed. M. Witzel, (Columbia, MO: South Asian Books), 255-345.

Zaehner, R.C. (1969), *The Bhagavad-Gītā, with commentary based on the original sources* (Oxford: Oxford University Press).

II. Custom and Law

Robert A. Yelle

Punishing Puns: Etymology as Linguistic Ideology in Hindu and British Traditions

The Problem of So-Called "Folk" Etymologies

The study of etymologizing—of the techniques and theories of word-derivations in different cultures—as distinct from the study of etymologies themselves, might appear, to an outsider, a dull if necessary aspect of linguistics and critical philology. However, closer examination of some of the varying uses of etymologies and related forms of wordplay in different cultures, and of the divergent views of language that these uses encode, reveals that the topic is far from trivial. On the contrary, such linguistic forms tell us much about the ways in which language, the physical world, and especially the relation between the two have been conceived. The present essay compares and contrasts etymologizing and some related forms of language in the classical Hindu and modern British traditions as a preliminary effort toward understanding the differences between the "linguistic ideologies" of those traditions.[1]

Scholars of ancient Indian languages have paid greater attention recently to the function of etymologizing and para-etymological word manipulations within the traditions they study, in part because these represent such prominent and distinctive features of these traditions, and in part to correct earlier dismissals of such verbal forms by Western scholars. Friedrich Max Müller's (1823-1900) statement that "a sound etymology has nothing to do with sound" (Müller 1877: 59), although directed at unscientific linguists in Europe, also captured

[1] "Linguistic ideology" or "language ideology" is a term that has become popular in linguistic anthropology and sociolinguistics to denote the theory of the nature and functions of language current in a culture. See Kroskrity (2000) and Schieffelin, Woolard & Kroskrity (1998).

an attitude common among earlier European scholars, including Müller himself, toward some of the etymological speculations within the Hindu tradition. Beginning in the Brāhmaṇas, certain forms of Hinduism used adventitious resemblances among words to argue for deeper connections among the things these words denoted. For example, *Chāndogya Upaniṣad* (CU) 1.4.2 states:

> When the gods feared death, what they did was to enter the triple Veda. They covered it with the meters. The fact that the gods covered (*chad*) it with them gave the name to and discloses the true nature of the meters (*chandas*). (Trans. Olivelle 1998: 175)

The broader phenomenon of reliance on coincidental phonetic analogies to disclose the true meaning of a word has been called "fictitious etymologizing." To some degree, of course, what counts as "fictitious" is in the eye of the beholder. As some have pointed out, Müller's own etymological analyses of the names of deities sometimes relied on false phonetic analogies. Eivind Kahrs has even argued that Müller's predilection for such etymologies may have constituted an imitation of some of the Sanskrit texts he studied (see Bronkhorst 2001: 153). However, this conclusion seems unlikely for several reasons. The first is Müller's contempt for this aspect of the Indian tradition. Second, the use of fraudulent and far-fetched phonetic resemblances to argue for the identity of the names of deities had been a part of the European tradition of comparative mythology long before Müller arrived on the scene, as his own criticism of such etymologizing—quoted previously—suggests.[2]

Disputing such earlier views, which tended to dismiss such Hindu etymologies out of hand, more recent scholarship has done much to show that these etymologies were not simply mistaken attempts to reconstruct the historical relations among words, crude anticipations of modern etymological science. They were instead deliberate attempts to exploit the poetic properties of language for philosophical and ritual purposes. Referring to the cosmological connections (*bandhu*) that were a key part of the esoteric knowledge communicated in the Upaniṣads, as in the earlier Brāhmaṇas, Patrick Olivelle has argued that

> An important basis for these connections ... is the phonetic similarity between the Sanskrit words for two things or even the fact that the two terms may have the same number of syllables. One finds with an almost annoying frequency such "etymological" connections in these documents ... These are clearly not "folk" etymologies; the authors of these documents were learned men, and these documents themselves

[2] This reflected a very old tradition in European comparative mythology, which, shortly before Müller's time, reached an apogee with Constantin-François Volney's identification of Christ with Krishna ("Christna"; Volney 1796: 292).

> demonstrate that the science of grammar had already reached a high degree of sophistication. These men clearly knew the philological etymologies of the terms they deal with, but their quest was not for such common and well-known connections but for deeper and hidden ones, and they found in the sounds of the names a clue to those connections. (Olivelle 1998: 25)

For reasons similar to those that lead Olivelle to reject the pejorative term "folk etymologies" to describe such linguistic devices, Johannes Bronkhorst, who has proposed a theory of such devices in Indian culture and beyond, prefers to call them "semantic etymologies," which "connect one word with one or more others which are believed to elucidate its meaning" (Bronkhorst 2001: 148). Both scholars make clear that, within the Indian tradition at least, these devices were not regarded as true, historical etymologies in the strict sense. Consequently, they were not failed attempts to discover etymological relationships, but culturally successful attempts to argue poetically for relationships that extended deeper than the verbal level, into cosmology and the structure of the world itself. Indeed, the very use of the term "etymology" to describe such linguistic devices may be inherently misleading. It would be more accurate to say that we are talking about a range of uses of phonetic resemblances among words that, at first glance, appear to exhibit kinship with modern etymologies. Part of the purpose of this essay is to explore such devices in order to achieve a more accurate characterization of their range and function than the dismissive label of "folk etymology" allows.

One can immediately suggest a range of functions for such devices, such as: revealing a true (historical) etymology; defining or fixing the meaning of a word; developing poetic associations; arguing, whether seriously or facetiously, for a point (i.e., functioning rhetorically); producing humor, as in the case of puns; serving memory, as with an acronym; and exploiting a connection of imitation or resemblance for magical purposes, as do so many rituals of the type called "sympathetic magic" (see Bronkhorst 2001: 183-191). Only the first coincides with modern practices of etymologizing. The range of forms and functions that such devices may take in Hinduism has not been explored fully. In the next section of this essay, I propose to broaden our consideration of such devices in Hinduism beyond the Brāhmaṇas and the *nirvacana* ("etymological") tradition that are the main focus of Bronkhorst's analysis, by including some related forms found in the later Tantric tradition. This will lead to an examination of the linguistic ideology underlying and encoded in these devices. Later sections of this essay will explore, for purposes of comparison, the etymological theories and linguistic ideology of the early modern British linguistic tradition, especially as this came into contact with the Hindu tradition in the person of Friedrich Max Müller. As we shall see, some of the features that distinguished Müller's views of etymologizing from Hindu views on the subject are directly traceable to earlier British nominalist thinkers, such as Thomas Hobbes (1588-1679) and John Locke (1632-1704), who employed etymological analysis as a tool for the purification of language by tracing words back to their concrete roots in matter and purging metaphysical terminology from our vocabulary.

"Semantic" Etymologies and Related Forms in Sanskritic Hinduism

We begin with Bronkhorst's important contribution to the understanding of the function of semantic etymologies in different premodern traditions. Bronkhorst argues that these are nearly universal devices that are meant to exploit and enhance the relations of meaning among different words. His emphasis on the contribution of such devices to the enhancement of meaning leads him to term them "semantic" etymologies. However, Bronkhorst also argues that such devices have often been connected with magic, and may therefore do more than create meaning by contributing to the efficacy of ritual performance. Indeed, in the early Upaniṣads, it is often said that "For one who knows thus" (*ya evam veda*), i.e., understands the *bandhu* or cosmological associations of the ritual, the ritual will be effective. As Bronkhorst explains, "The practical advantage of these etymologies is that they allow man to obtain knowledge about these connections with the hidden reality. This knowledge—the texts emphasize it repeatedly—is of great importance: it can convey a number of advantages to him who knows" (2001: 155).

Bronkhorst's account coincides with two important discoveries of modern linguistic theory. The first concerns the manner in which phonetic resemblances may produce meaning, even when such resemblances are artificial or constructed. Ferdinand de Saussure (1966: 126) maintained that "associative relations" among words could be formed on the basis of such phonetic resemblances alone. Roman Jakobson (1960) showed further how, in poetry and poetic uses of language, such resemblances may be exploited to create meaning. Secondly, like Bronkhorst, modern linguistic theory places emphasis on the performative or pragmatic dimensions of language, or on "How to Do Things with Words" (see Austin 1975). Poetic relations among words may be exploited not only for semantic, but also for pragmatic purposes, which partly explains the prevalence of poetic devices in many rituals, including those of the magical variety (Yelle 2003: 75-106). Bronkhorst recognizes the connection of such devices with magical ritual. However, he argues that "semantic etymologies are not performative acts and have no persuasive validity, as far as I can see; they certainly don't in early and classical Indian literature" (2001: 191). Although this may be true in a narrow sense, in the later tradition, there are, as we shall see, some examples of such forms of wordplay, including some Tantric *mantras*, that do function as true performatives: that is, they are thought to bring about, by virtue of being uttered and as if by magic, the state of affairs that they declare and describe.

A theory of the function of etymologies and related forms of wordplay in Hinduism should properly grow out of an empirical consideration of their different types and functions. Bronkhorst's main case is Yāska's *Nirukta*, a text that codified, systematized, and to some degree modified a style of etymologizing prevalent in the Brāhmaṇas. I propose to introduce for our additional consideration a variety of linguistic devices used in later texts, and especially the Tantras. Bronkhorst specifically addresses the connection of the Indian etymological tradition with the Tantras, which represented, as he states, the "apogee" of a tradition that "attribute[d] a specific metaphysical significance to every sound of the Sanskrit language" (2001: 163). However, he argues that there are some major differences between the *nirvacana* tradition and the Tantric analysis of the meaning of sounds, which is largely concerned not with ordinary words but with *bījas*, literally the "seed" *mantras* that are the most efficacious part of the *mantras*, and the sounds out of which *bījas* and other *mantras* are composed. Despite some resemblances between the ideas and uses of language found in the Tantric tradition and the earlier *nirvacana* tradition, Bronkhorst emphasizes the differences between those traditions. By contrast, Eivind Kahrs (1998: 55-97) provides an extensive analysis of *nirvacana*-type analyses in the Tantric tradition of Kashmiri Śaivism, and emphasizes the continuities between the Vedic and Tantric traditions in this regard.

A closer perusal of such linguistic devices in Tantra suggests that the continuities are more important than the differences. In the Tantras, a number of different linguistic devices are employed that bear a distinct resemblance to the etymologies found in the Brāhmaṇas and early Upaniṣads, as well as in the *Nirukta*. In the first place, the use of semantic etymologies of the very sort that Bronkhorst describes can be found with regularity. For example, the entire seventeenth chapter of the *Kulārṇava Tantra* (KT) consists of such etymologies. Many of these explicate the various implements or technical terminology of Tantric ritual, such as chanting (*japa*), esoteric gestures (*mudra*), and sacred designs (*maṇḍala*). The etymology for *mantra* in KT 17.54—"It is called '*mantra*' because, from contemplating (*mananāt*) the true form of the deity, which is boundlessly radiant, it preserves (*trāyate*) one from all fears" (*mananāt tattvarūpasya devasyāmita tejasaḥ trāyate sarvabhayatas tasmān mantra itīritaḥ*; my trans.)—echoes that found in a number of other Tantras. We can presume that some of these etymologies were traditional, and not idiosyncratic to the KT.

Apart from such more or less direct continuations of earlier practices of *nirvacana*, we find a number of other, related practices in which the phonetic relations among words are exploited or words are analyzed down to their component sounds. The *Śatanāmas* and *Sahasranāmas*, lists of a hundred or a thousand names of the deity common in the Purāṇas and Tantras, occasionally use wordplay, as at

Lalitāsahasranāma 777-79: "She who is worshipped by heroes (*vīra*), She who is the cosmogenetrix (*virāj*), She who is without stain (*virajas*)" (my trans.). Wordplay involving the name of the deity is also found in certain *bīja mantras* in which the first letter of the name of the deity (e.g., "g" for *Gaṇapati*) is converted into a *bīja* (e.g., *gaṃ*) and prefixed to the name of the deity invoked by the *mantra*: e.g., *oṃ gaṃ* (or *gāṃ gīṃ gūṃ*) *gaṇapataye namaḥ* ("reverence to *Gaṇapati*").[3] *Lakṣmī Tantra* 21.22-25 specifically instructs that a *bīja* may be formed from the first letter of a word in this way. What is important about such examples is the cosmological theory that underlies them: the idea that sound, more specifically language or the alphabet that is the matrix (*mātṛkā*) out of which the universe evolved, is ontologically prior to physical reality and may be manipulated as a means of altering that reality. Within the structural sequence of a *mantra*, the *bīja* is the seed or semen (*bīja* can literally mean either of those things) out of which physical reality—whether the objective form of the deity or some other physical manifestation—evolves (Yelle 2003: 36-47).

Another example of such devices is the Tantric *haṃsa mantra*, *haṃsaḥ so 'ham* ("I am that divine bird"). This *mantra* is, at the level of the syllables or *bīja*s employed, a near-palindrome that is intended to imitate, and harness the power of, the cosmic cycle of creation, stability, and destruction (see Yelle 2003: 28-30). The two syllables, "ha" and "sa," stand for the god Śiva and the goddess Śakti respectively. The *haṃsa mantra* moves from the god to his consort and back again, diagramming his entry into and exit from the natural world. The *mantra* resembles the so-called Great Sayings (*mahāvākya*) of the Upaniṣads, such as the famous "Thou art that" (*tat tvam asi*) of CU 6, in that it expresses the connection (*bandhu*) between the supreme principle or Brahman (*haṃsaḥ*) and the essential self or *Ātman* (*so 'ham*). Like other cosmic connections expressed by semantic etymologies or verbal definitions, the *haṃsa mantra* exploits phonetic associations to make a philosophical point. Although the precise origins of the *haṃsa mantra* may be unknown, it recalls the male-to-female-back-to-male patterns expressed in *Ṛgveda* 10.90.5 and especially *Bṛhadāraṇyaka Upaniṣad* (BAU) 6.4.20: "I am he, you are she; you are she, I am he" (*amo 'ham asmi sā tvaṃ sā tvam asy amo 'ham*; my trans.), which even uses similar syllables. BAU 1.3.22 provides a semantic etymology related to the latter formula: "And [the breath] is also the *Sāman*. The *Sāman*, after all, is Speech. 'It is both she (*sā*) and he (*ama*)'; this gave the name to and discloses the true nature of the *Sāman*" (trans. Olivelle 1998: 43).[4]

As these examples indicate, there appears to be significant continuity between the Vedic tradition of *nirvacana* and later Tantric

[3] Yelle (2003: 14, 42-44) refers to these as "acronymic *bījas*."

[4] See Yelle (2003: 49-53) for an analysis of these issues.

verbal manipulations. Moreover, Bronkhorst's evaluation of the function of such forms of wordplay in the Vedas is true also of the Tantras: knowledge of the deeper connections revealed by such surface phonetic associations contributes to the efficacy of the ritual. This is true of all of the *bījas*, including the *haṃsa mantra*, which is employed occasionally as a means of making *mantras* successful or effective (*siddha*). This, indeed, appears to be the paramount function of these devices, which supports Bronkhorst's contention that such devices are, for lack of a better word, "magical." The Vedic and Tantric uses of such linguistic devices, then, exhibit a fundamental similarity, which is evident in the continued use of the *nirvacana* form in the Tantras, but even more in the ritual uses to which such devices are put and the underlying conception of the relationship between language and reality that they encode. Words are not "mere" words, but clues to a hidden reality that is, ultimately, both divine and physical. There is a continuum, rather than a sharp distinction, between language and physical reality. This is suggested already by the personification and deification of Speech (*Vāc*) at *Ṛgveda* 10.125. Much later, Tantric *mantras* attempt to convert this belief in the ontological priority of speech by imitating, in their sequence of *bījas*, the evolution of the deity from the letter of the alphabet with which its name begins (e.g., *gaṃ gaṇapataye*), or the production of a real-world objective from the alphabet, conceived as the matrix of not only language but also the entire creation. Arthur Avalon (Sir John Woodroffe) correctly identified Tantra as a theory of "natural name" (Avalon 1998: 70-81), although he did not recognize the extent of influence this idea had on the very structure of Tantric *mantras*. Without an appreciation of this underlying linguistic ideology, it is impossible to understand fully the uses of semantic etymologies and related devices within the Hindu tradition.

Like other traditions, of course, the Hindu tradition was not monolithic in its views of language. Mīmāṃsā, for example, held that Sanskrit, or at least the language of the Vedas, was not conventional and created, but rather eternal or without origin (*autpattika*; *Mīmāṃsāsūtra* 1.5). However, Śabara's commentary distinguishes this claim from the erroneous view that, upon the pronunciation of a word, the thing denoted by that word will be physically produced. The rejected view sounds suspiciously close to the later Tantric view of *mantras* and *bījas*. Other Hindus used etymological wordplay for polemical, political, or satirical purposes. Kahrs (1998: 95) provides two examples from Kṣemarāja's *Deśopadeśa* 8.3: "'*Guru*' is so called because he is devoid of qualities (*guṇa*) and always lusting (*rutakārī*) after the wives of his students. '*Dīkṣā*' (initiation) is so called because it leads to the loss (*kṣayakaraṇād*) of money (*dīnāra-*; i.e. costs money)" (*guṇarahito rutakārī śiṣyavadhūnāṃ sadā gurur gaditaḥ dīnārakṣayakaraṇād dīkṣety uktā kṛtā tena*; my trans.). As Kahrs points out, these examples resemble the parody of the names of the *varṇas* in the Buddhist *Aggañña Sutta*, where such etymologizing serves a clear polemical purpose. Such cases were likely the exception, rather than the rule, in Tantra and most of the rest of the Hindu ritual tradition. Nothing like this transgressive, satirical use of semantic etymologizing occurs in KT, where at 17.7-9 we find more reverent etymologies of guru.

From Nature to Culture: Etymology and the Problem of Arbitrariness in Plato's Cratylus and British Nominalism

The linguistic ideology thus revealed by means of semantic etymologies in the Hindu tradition is remarkably different from the views of language affirmed by modern, Western linguistics, where language is treated by and large as an arbitrary social institution, which is created rather than creative. However, the dream of a natural language, i.e., one that has a direct and immediate connection with reality, as reflected in its etymology, was not uncommon in European culture also prior to modernity, and even into modernity as an increasingly marginalized minority opinion. Bronkhorst points to the *locus classicus* of such theories, Plato's *Cratylus*, which debates whether language is dependent on nature (*phusis*) or human laws (*nomos*). Like Yāska's *Nirukta*, the *Cratylus* engages in extensive use of semantic etymologies to reveal the "natural" meanings of Greek words, although in the process the text casts doubt upon the validity of such etymologies, and it is never entirely clear where Socrates, or rather Plato, stands with respect to the central question of the natural status of language. This would appear to reinforce the conclusion that Indian and Greek views on language were similar, though with Plato being perhaps a bit more critical than Yāska, and certainly more than the authors of the Brāhmaṇas and Tantras.

However, the Indian and Greek, or rather Brahmanical and Platonic views, may have been further apart than at first appears. Bronkhorst notes that, unlike the Brahmans, the Greek philosophers did not regard their language as the only true one (2001: 169). He does not note, however, the deeper levels of irony in Plato's dialogue, which pokes fun at the theory of a natural correspondence between language and reality. The very name of one of the interlocutors, Hermogenes, means "born of Hermes," i.e., a rich person, but the man himself is poor (*Cratylus* 384c). Friedrich Nietzsche later exploited this very example in the course of arguing that language is always inherently unnatural, artificial and misleading, a "metaphor of a metaphor."[5] Already when it occurs in Plato, this example suggests a deeper suspicion toward the deceptive potentialities of language than anything we have observed in Hindu theorizing about

[5] See Nietzsche (1989: 248) and the discussion in Yelle (2003: 64-66, 146-47).

language. Moreover, in Plato the magical potential of wordplay is specifically attacked and excluded as a false form of rhetoric. In his *Encomium of Helen*, the fifth century BCE Sophist, Gorgias, extensively employed rhyming endings (*homoioteleuton*), which he associated with magical incantations. Plato, in his *Republic*, accepted the association among poetry, magic, and rhetoric, yet condemned and sharply delimited their use. Therefore, on the key question of the magical or performative efficacy of such wordplay, there was a wider gap, and at some points even a diametrical opposition, between the Hindu and Platonic traditions.

Despite this, as Bronkhorst notes, Neoplatonists and other groups in the ancient and medieval Mediterranean and European environments employed word magic along with other types of magic, neglecting the more skeptical Platonic views that suggested language was not merely unnatural, but potentially misleading. The modern doctrine of the conventional status of language was elaborated in the sixteenth and seventeenth centuries partly in order to refute magicians who exploited the supposedly natural status of language (Bronkhorst 2001: 182; cf. Aarsleff 1982: 24-26). Bronkhorst does not develop an account of these movements, which produced what amounted to a disenchantment of language. However, a sketch of British nominalism from Thomas Hobbes to F. Max Müller will illustrate the importance to this movement of controlling both etymology and, through this, language itself. The linguistic ideology of this movement was in some respects directly opposed to that of Hindu Tantra, and in other respects exhibited some interesting parallels to that tradition.

The main tradition of British linguistics inaugurated by Francis Bacon (1561-1626), Thomas Hobbes, and John Locke was both nominalist and empiricist in its orientation. Its nominalism was reflected in the critique of the habit of "taking words for things," or believing that the abstract entities denoted by some words enjoyed a real, rather than merely verbal, existence.[6] Its empiricism was reflected in the complementary insistence that our words should be made to conform, so far as possible, to the real world. Science, or empirical investigation, was to purge language of metaphysical notions and approach the goal of a language that reflected the world perfectly. This tradition tended to overemphasize the role of substantives, or nouns, in language, in part because such words could be identified with concrete entities in the real world. Jeremy Bentham (1748-1832), in some of his later prose, even attempted to divest his language of verbs, replacing many complex verbs with simpler verbs combined with nominal phrases.

Etymology played an important role in these projects of linguistic purification. Hobbes, for example, employed etymological

[6] For an account of these aspects of the British linguistic tradition, see Yelle (2005).

analysis as one of the main supports for his nominalist reduction of metaphysical language. Significantly, he selected the terms "spirit" and "angel" for his analyses. Tracing each back to its Latin roots revealed a concrete meaning: *spiritus* originally denoted breath; *angelus*, a messenger. All language ultimately referred to the physical world. At the same time, Hobbes was a strong proponent of the view that linguistic reference is a matter of convention, equivalent to an act of legislation. In both of these positions—his empiricism and his nominalism—Hobbes was largely followed by Locke and subsequent British theorists.

The linguistic ideology of the British tradition as thus outlined constituted both a radical break with the earlier, magical idea of a natural language and, paradoxically, a continuation of this idea (cf. Aarsleff 1982: 249). Language was decidedly not "natural," in the twin senses that it did not conform to the reality of the world, and was a product of social legislation. However, language could be made to conform to reality, through empirical investigation and philosophical fiat. As in magical versions of the ideal of a natural language, the goal of the new, scientific ideal was eminently practical, as it would facilitate the manipulation of nature. There was also a soteriological dimension to such projects, which endeavored to remove the "curse of Babel" that had introduced the diversity and confusion of tongues (Stillman 1995: 15-16).

F. Max Müller on Mythology and Etymology

Müller reflected the British tradition, which he combined with German Romanticism, comparative philology, and observations gleaned from his study of Sanskrit and other languages. In the course of his writings, and especially in the *Lectures on the Science of Language* (1861) and the *Science of Thought* (1887), Müller invoked with approval Bacon, Locke, and above all Hobbes, who appears to have been the main inspiration for his *Science of Thought*. Müller termed his new science "Nominism" to associate it with as well as to distinguish it from ordinary nominalism. Like that of some of his British predecessors, Müller's nominalism was most conspicuous in his etymological analysis of the names of deities, which traced these back to substantive terms (*nomina*) that, in course of time, had been mistaken for the names of gods (*numina*). As there is precedent for all of this in the British tradition,[7] it is unnecessary to assume, as Kahrs does, that Müller's etymologizing was taken from the Vedic texts that were his prime object of study. Indeed, Müller dismissed many of these Vedic

[7] The precise identification of *numina* (spirits) as *nomina* (names), as well as several other formulas used by Müller, can be found in earlier comparative mythologists, including Gerard Vossius (1577-1649) and John Selden (1584-1654), who were, after all, writing in Latin.

etymologies as unscientific, although he also acknowledged the great contributions the ancient Indian grammarians had made to linguistic science. Following these grammarians, Müller also refocused his account of the origins of language, away from the substantives that were the main focus of the British empiricists, and toward the verbal roots that, as the Indian tradition had concluded, were the true historical source of language. The original names of gods were formed from verbal roots, e.g., the word for "heaven," *divya*, was formed from the verb "to shine" (*div*). However, like the British empiricists, Müller argued that the bases of these verbal roots were themselves ultimately concrete, material, or experiential.

Müller's theory of language and mythology represented the survival, albeit in attenuated form, of the dream of a natural language (Aarsleff 1982: 32, 36-37, 290). Although language *per se* was not natural except in a very limited sense, it could be traced back through scientific etymology to a limited number of roots that were, in some sense, based in the natural or physical world. And these etymological meanings were, for Müller, still the key to understanding language and especially mythology, which etymology served to debunk. Müller was, of course, familiar with Plato's *Cratylus* (see, e.g., Müller 1972: 147; 1895: 65-66; 1892a: 375), and with more contemporary Western theories affirming the natural origin of words or language. However, he subjected most of these theories to intense criticism, referring to them derisively as the "bow wow" and "pooh pooh" theories (Müller 1877). These were, respectively, the theories that words were derived originally from the imitation of animal cries and other natural sounds, or from the instinctive cries or interjections of human beings in certain situations. Müller did not reject the possibility that some words were derived in this way. However, he objected to the notion that many words could have been so derived, particularly because this would have contradicted his alternative theory of the derivation of words from verbal roots that were, themselves, based in physical experience, and even, on occasion, possibly onomatopoetic.

"Purity" and "Punishment": An Illustration of Contrasting Ideologies of Etymology

Consideration of a particular set of examples involving the Sanskrit roots *pū* (to cleanse) and *pūy* (to stink) will help to elucidate the differences in the understanding of etymology, and in the idea of a natural language, between Hindus and British. Although, as we have seen, Bronkhorst rejected the idea that etymologies were used as speech acts in the Hindu tradition, the *Divyatattva*, a sixteenth-century Sanskrit Dharmaśāstra text authored by the Bengali Raghunandana Bhattacharya, employs etymologies in the operative portion of its rituals of ordeal (*divya*, Yelle 2002: 261-62). One of these is the invocation of fire in the ordeal of carrying the heated iron ball (*Divyatattva* 216): "You are called 'purifier' (*pāvaka*) because you purify (*punāsi*) sin (*pāpam*)" (*pāpaṃ punāsi vai yasmāt tasmāt pāvaka ucyate*; trans. Larivière 1981: 200). The form of the invocation, which is taken from Pitāmaha (whom P.V. Kane places between 400 and 700 CE), refers to a real etymological connection between "purifier" (*pāvaka*) and "purify" (*punāsi*) through the verbal root "to purify" (*pū*). It also exploits the resemblance in sound between *pāvaka* and *pāpam*, or sin. Overall, the formula is supposed to disclose the "truth" about fire so that fire, personified as a god, will reveal the "truth" about the guilt or innocence of the person undergoing the ordeal. The etymology invokes the presence of the god of fire and requests his contribution to the efficacious operation of the ceremony. It therefore functions as a kind of performative utterance, by establishing an identification between the rites of purification in which fire is employed, and the moral purity of the agent in question, thus affirming for morality a basis that is, at once, both natural and divine.

By comparison, this sort of thinking was antithetical to much of British nominalism. In his critique of linguistic fictions, Jeremy Bentham singled out for opprobrium various abuses of the word "purity," and especially "the inference that has been made of the existence of moral impurity from that of physical impurity—of impurity in a moral sense, from that of impurity in a physical sense" (Ogden 1959: cxxiii). The connections of this with Protestant anti-ritualism cannot be explored here. However, what is clear already from this quote is Bentham's heightened, indeed exaggerated awareness of the rhetorical potentialities of language, and of its deeply metaphorical or fictional status, a fact he deplored deeply.

The classicist Theodor Gomperz (1832-1912) addressed the case of "purity" and related words in the course of a discussion of ancient Greek theories of the natural basis of language, including the *Cratylus*. Gomperz's chief example of the natural basis of some words was the Indo-European root *pū*, meaning "to cleanse:"

> If we employ the mouth itself, the organ of speech, to perform an act of cleansing, this is done by blowing away the particles of dust, straw, etc., which cover and pollute any superficial plane. If we do this energetically by a determined narrowing of our protruded lips, we produce sounds like *p*, *pf*, or *pu*. In this way the last-named sound might at least have obtained its primitive significance. Presuming our conjecture to be correct, a definite position and movement of the organs of speech formed in this instance, as doubtless in countless others, the bond between sound and meaning. (1949: 399)

However, with the passage of time, more and more words, including Latin *purus* (pure) and *pœna* (punishment), would be derived from this root through the admixture of purely arbitrary cultural elements, until at last, as with the modern English word "punishment," the relationship to the natural root had become so attenuated as to be unrecognizable to anyone except an etymologist (1949: 399-400). Closer to the origins of language, however, grew up a range of uses that were somehow, given their proximity to their source, more natural: "the conception of punishment as a religious atonement or purification would be more appropriately expressed by the derivatives of *pu* than by descendants of other roots ..." (1949: 400). Thus far, Gomperz's attempt to rehabilitate some portion of the traditional, natural theory of language origins resembles somewhat the *Divyatattva*'s ritual invocation of *pū* and, more broadly, the Hindu tradition's approach to etymology. However, Gomperz immediately adds that, even assuming a natural basis for some linguistic forms, that basis may lead in conflicting directions: the same operation of blowing may constitute an act of cleansing or, conversely, an expression of disgust, as in *pooh-pooh* or *pfui*, as reflected in verbal derivatives such as "putrid." Both, diametrically opposed uses of onomatopoeia occur in his pun, "I pooh-pooh the purity of your intentions" (1949: 401). Gomperz cites Heraclitus' observation that the "same" word (the homonyms βῐος and βιός) could mean opposite things, in this case, both life (βῐος) and the bow (βιός) that shoots arrows that cause death (1949: 395). Bronkhorst notes the same example (2001: 149), but for him it is just another instance of semantic etymology. As with the example of Hermogenes in the *Cratylus*, we sense in this example a skepticism concerning the ability of language to signify naturally, a skepticism that, although not uniquely Western, contrasts sharply with the sort of thinking found in the *Divyatattva*, the Vedas, and the Tantras.

Although he does not name Müller as his target, Gomperz's extended discussion of *pū* was intended as a comment on and partial refutation of his predecessor's dismissal of theories of language as onomatopoetic, including the "pooh pooh" theory. Müller addressed the examples of *pū* and *pūy* and their derivatives again and again in his writings on language. He rejected the attempt to derive many words from their immediate resemblance to certain, supposedly natural interjections such as *pu*, *piff* and *pfui* (1877: 102-03; 1887: 200-203; 1901: 20-21). The proper connection was an indirect one, through historical etymology, which took into account the transformation of words over time so that their connection with their original, historical roots was often no longer recognizable, but could be known only through the established laws of comparative etymology: "Sound etymology has nothing to do with sound" (1877: 259). Müller allowed only that, at the basis of all of these far-flung derivatives, "the root PŪY was very likely the residuum of a number of sounds accompanying the acts of primitive men when rejecting something unpleasant and expressing their disgust" (1887: 202).

On the other hand, Müller on several occasions emphasized that the etymological connection of the root *pū* with the notions of both purity and punishment "shows us that when the word *pœna* was first framed, punishment was conceived from a higher moral and religious point of view, as a purification from sin ..." (1895: 217):

> Do we want to know what was uppermost in the minds of those who formed the word for punishment, the Latin *pœna*, or *punio*, to punish; the root "pû" in Sanskrit, which means to cleanse, to purify, tells us that the Latin derivative was originally formed, not to express mere striking or torturing, but cleansing, correcting, delivering from the stain of sin. In Sanskrit many a god is implored to cleanse away ("punîhi") the sins of men, and the substantive "pâvana," though it did not come to mean punishment, ... took in later times the sense of purification and penance. Now, it is clear that the train of thought which leads from purification to penance or from purification to punishment reveals a moral and even a religious sentiment in the conception and naming of *pœna*; and it shows us that in the very infancy of criminal justice punishment was looked upon, not simply as a retribution or revenge, but as a correction, as a removal of guilt. ... And here we perceive the difference between etymology and definition, which has so often been overlooked. The etymology of a word can never give us its definition; it can only supply us with historical evidence that at the time when a word was formed, its predicative power represented one out of many characteristic features of the object to which it was applied. We are not justified in saying that because *punire* meant originally to purify, therefore the Roman conception of punishment was exclusively that of purification. All we can say is that one aspect of punishment, which struck the earliest framers of the language of Italy, was that of *expiation*. (1892b: 254-56)

Müller affirmed the value of etymology, which reveals the historical meaning of words. However, he maintained that, although some roots may have a basis in nature, including instinctive human reactions, they are inevitably cultural constructs. Moreover, the value of etymology is limited, as it cannot reveal the true or current definition or meaning of a word, although it may point to one of its original meanings. All of this shows how far Müller's attitude is from that of the *Divyatattva*, despite his recognition of the religious and moral dimensions of purification. Indeed, Müller's debunking of mythological language elsewhere focused on the same Sanskrit root:

> The name of Pan is connected with the Sanskrit name for wind, namely, "pavana." The root from which it is derived means, in Sanskrit, to purify ... [w]e have from "pû," to purify, the Greek "Pân," "Pânos," the purifying or sweeping wind, strictly corresponding to a possible Sanskrit form "pav-an." ... It is thus that mythology arose ... (1892b: 157-58)

Mythology proceeded through a mistaken personification of terms that had originally a natural reference. This etymological reduction of Pan is entirely in keeping with Müller's nominalism, which echoed Hobbes's in contending that spirit "meant originally no more than a puff or whiff, a breeze, a breath" (1898: 87). A true science of etymology would reveal, not that nature is divine, but that so much of what we regard as divine is merely natural, or rather human and linguistic. For Müller as for some other nominalists, the project of purifying language of its demons assumed religious, indeed soteriological dimensions. However, his idea of a natural language was, in other ways, diametrically opposed to that of much of the Hindu tradition prior to modernity.

Conclusion

This essay has attempted to show several things. First, the historical study of earlier theories of etymologizing often tells us much about the linguistic ideologies of the cultures that produced such theories. The study of such theories therefore remains relevant as a branch of cultural history long after earlier practices of etymologizing have been rendered obsolete by the advances of modern linguistic science. Second, there was a profound continuity in linguistic ideology among many branches of the Hindu tradition, and especially between the Vedas and Tantras. This shared ideology affirmed that language, or at least particular, especially sacred forms of language were in some sense "natural," in the double sense that they both reflected the world (or ultimate reality) and were even, on occasion, capable of influencing it through ritual speech acts. Third, this ideology parallels a significant minority opinion in European traditions that lasted well into modernity, at which point, in the seventeenth century in England among other places, the foundations of the modern view that language is strictly arbitrary were laid. Finally, the examples of F. Max Müller and of the divergent interpretations of the etymology of words for "purity" illustrate the historical convergence and philosophical contrast among traditional Hindu and modern European linguistic traditions. This convergence is still occurring, and the contrast that it describes promises to shed further light on the linguistic ideology of modernity, as well as on that of its past.

Bibliography

Aarsleff, H. (1982), *From Locke to Saussure: Essays on the Study of Language and Intellectual History* (Minneapolis: University of Minnesota Press.).

Austin, J. (1975), *How to Do Things with Words* (Cambridge: Harvard University Press).

Avalon, A. [J. Woodroffe] (ed.) (1965), *Kulārṇava Tantra* (Madras: Ganesh & Co.).

_____. (1998), *The Garland of Letters* (Madras: Ganesh & Co.).

Bronkhorst, J. (2001), "Etymology and Magic: Yāska's *Nirukta*, Plato's *Cratylus*, and the Riddle of Semantic Etymologies," *Numen* 48: 147-203.

Gomperz, T. (1949), *Greek Thinkers: A History of Ancient Philosophy* (London: John Murray).

Gupta, S. (trans.) (2000), *Lakṣmī Tantra* (Delhi: Motilal Banarsidass).

Jakobson, R. (1960), "Closing Statement: Linguistics and Poetics" in *Style in Language*, ed. T. Sebeok (Cambridge: MIT Press), 350-77.

Jha, Ganganatha. (1916), *The Pūrvamīmāṃsāsūtras of Jaimini: Chapters I-III* (Allahabad)

Kahrs, E. (1998), *Indian Semantic Analysis: The* Nirvacana *Tradition* (Cambridge: Cambridge University Press).

Kroskrity, P. (ed.) (2000), *Regimes of Language: Ideologies, Polities, and Identities* (Sante Fe: School of American Research Press).

Larivière, R. (1981), *The Divyatattva of Raghunandana Bhattacharya: Ordeals in Classical Hindu Law* (New Delhi: Manohar).

Müller, F.M. (1877), *Lectures on the Science of Language*, 9th ed., 2 vols. (London: Longmans, Green & Co.).

_____. (1887), *The Science of Thought*, 2 vols. (New York: Charles Scribner's Sons).

_____. (1892a), *Natural Religion*, 2d ed. (London: Longmans, Green & Co.).

_____. (1892b), *Chips from a German Workshop*, vol. 2 (New York: Charles Scribner's Sons).

_____. (1895), *Chips from a German Workshop*, vol. 4 (New York: Charles Scribner's Sons).

_____. (1898), *Three Introductory Lectures on the Science of Thought* (Chicago: Open Court).

_____. (1901), *Last Essays*, first series (London: Longmans, Green & Co.).

_____. (1972), *Introduction to the Science of Religion*, reprint ed. (Varanasi: Bharata Manisha).

Nietzsche, F. (1989), "On Truth and Lying in an Extra-Moral Sense" in *Friedrich Nietzsche on Rhetoric and Language*, ed. S. Gilman, C. Blair, and D. Parent (New York: Oxford University Press), 246-57.

Ogden, C. (1959), *Bentham's Theory of Fictions* (Paterson, NJ: Littlefield, Adams & Co.).

Olivelle, P. (ed. and trans.) (1998), *The Early Upaniṣads* (Oxford: Oxford University Press).

Sastry, R.A. (1988), *Lalitā Sahasranāma* (Madras: Adyar Library).

de Saussure, F. (1966), *Course in General Linguistics*, trans. W. Baskin (New York: McGraw-Hill).

Schieffelin, B., K. Woolard & P. Kroskrity, (eds.) (1998), *Language Ideologies: Practice and Theory* (New York: Oxford University Press).

Stillman, R. (1995), *The New Philosophy and Universal Languages in Seventeenth-Century England: Bacon, Hobbes, and Wilkins* (Lewisburg: Bucknell University Press).

Volney, C.-F. (1796), *The Ruins, or A Survey of the Revolutions of Empires*, 3d ed. (London).

Yelle, R. (2002), "Poetic Justice: Rhetoric in Hindu Ordeals and Legal Formulas," *Religion* 32: 259-72.

_____. (2003), *Explaining Mantras: Ritual, Rhetoric, and the Dream of a Natural Language in Hindu Tantra* (New York and London: Routledge).

_____. (2005), "Bentham's Fictions: Canon and Idolatry in the Genealogy of Law," *Yale Journal of Law & the Humanities* 17: 151-79.

DONALD R. DAVIS, JR.

*Matrilineal Adoption, Inheritance Law, and Rites for the Dead among Hindus in Medieval Kerala**

The Hindu law of adoption provides an exemplary case of the interaction of religion and law in traditional Indic discourse. According to classical Hindu jurisprudence, there are two reasons behind an adoption. The first, a religious reason, ensures that a man will receive the ancestral offering called *śrāddha* after his death.[1] The adoptee offers the *śrāddha* which sustains a man in the afterlife and, without which, his soul may potentially be lost forever (Derrett 1977: 40-1). The second motive for an adoption, a legal one, is to provide an heir for a family's property.

These two motives are by no means unique to the Hindu tradition as both form part of a common pattern in many parts of the Eurasian world up to the modern period (Goody 1976). Evidence from Rome, Greece, and China suggests that issues surrounding both inheritance and ancestral rites were at the heart of adoption.[2]

* I gratefully acknowledge the following colleagues and friends for their help and suggestions for this essay: Kesavan Veluthat, Tom Trautmann, Richard Larivière, Jay Krishnan, and Madhav Deshpande. I must also thank the Center for South Asian Studies at the University of Michigan for a US/ED Academic Sharing Program Grant which provided access to their wonderful library collections. Finally, it is a testimony to my deep indebtedness to Prof. Olivelle to acknowledge that he, too, made suggestions for a paper written in his honor by reading with me the sometimes opaque text of the *Laghudharmaprakāśikā*.

[1] For a complete description of the *śrāddha* rite on the basis of Hindu legal texts, see Kane (1962-75: 4.334ff). See also, the brief description and bibliography on *piṇḍa* (rice-ball) offerings and *śrāddha* in Rocher (2002: 27, n. 5). For additional information on *śrāddha* in broader Hindu contexts, see Knipe (1977), Nicholas (1981), and Sand (1986).

[2] Cicero and Demosthenes represent the Roman and Greek positions, respectively, with Cicero declaring, "And these adoptions, like others, more than I can count, were followed by the inheritance of the name and property and sacred rites of the family" (*De Domo Sua* 13 in Yonge 1891). Demosthenes' linking of adoption, inheritance, and ancestral rites is found in his *Pros Leochares* 31-33 (Murray 1939).

Neither Jewish law nor Islamic law, by contrast, accept adoption in a fully legal sense and both thus serve as useful contrasts. In both the latter systems, however, fosterage or guardianship was permitted without any change in the legal status of the child.[3] The comparative approach to adoption reveals the important, though often elided, difference between adoption and fosterage, the latter being a more precise term for the charitable acceptance of orphans, whether or not they be also legally adopted. Adoption then "involves the transfer of an individual from one filial relationship to another, from a 'natural' relationship to a 'fictional' one, but one which is in most respects legally equivalent" (Goody 1976: 69). As in most legal traditions of the premodern world, therefore, adoption in Hindu law was emphatically not concerned with children's welfare, but rather with the perpetuation of family lineages and the preservation of family ancestral rites.

These same two purposes behind adoption in Hindu law are clear and uniform throughout the texts on religious jurisprudence known as Dharmaśāstra, and both purposes are fulfilled in the single person of the adopted son, at least in patrilineal contexts considered normative in most Dharmaśāstra texts. Kane (1962-75: 3.665) cites the following verse from the *Dattakacandrikā* which demonstrates the importance of both purposes:

> *aputreṇa sutaḥ kāryo yādṛk tādṛk prayatnataḥ* | *piṇḍodakakriyāhetor nāmasaṃkīrtanāya ca* ||
>
> A man without a son should do whatever it takes to produce a son for the sake of the rites of the *piṇḍa* balls and water and for the [continued] glorification of his name.[4]

Nearly all Dharmaśāstra texts presume a patrilineal context because patriliny was and is by far the most common mode of reckoning kin relationships in India. In fact, until now scholars believed that all Dharmaśāstra presumed a patrilineal kinship system when dealing with laws relating to the family and imagined only the adoption of males as capable of fulfilling the purposes stated. How then might the specifics of an actual adoption vary if the prevailing kinship system were matrilineal, as was the case for a large proportion of the

[3] An excellent survey of religious perspectives on adoption in the so-called Abrahamic traditions can be found in Pollack, et al. (2004). For a general review of adoption in Islamic law, see Sobol (1995). A more nuanced and ethnographically situated study of adoption in Islamic society is found in Bargach (2002), which also considers the classic Islamic legal prohibitions of adoption.

[4] The more recently published critical edition of the *Dattakacandrikā* (Pāṇḍeya 1980: 3) reads somewhat differently: *aputreṇaiva kartavyaḥ putrapratinidhiḥ sadā* | *piṇḍodakakriyāhetor yasmāt tasmāt prayatnataḥ* (A man without a son should constantly make/find a substitute for a son with all diligence for the sake of the rites of the *piṇḍas* and water).

populace of medieval Kerala? Typically, matrilineal kinship systems as well as the possible adoption of females were held to be part of the "customary law" of India. For example, in his discussion of the role of customary law in the history of adoption, Derrett writes:

> To this day customs are given the force of law, notwithstanding the Hindu law on the point, which enable either sex to adopt, which enable daughters or orphans to be adopted, and daughters' sons, and even sons-in-law, *positions not considered by the Dharmaśāstra* (1977: 31, emphasis added).[5]

It turns out that Derrett was mistaken and that he probably overlooked a relatively recent Dharmaśāstra text that does in fact discuss these issues because he views most later Hindu legal texts as "spurious" or "apocryphal" (see Larivière 2004: 619-622 for a critical discussion). In this essay, I intend to show the profound historical value and "genuine" character of this later Hindu legal text.

Contrary to Derrett's assertion, a 16th or 17th century CE Dharmaśāstra text from Kerala entitled *Laghudharmaprakāśikā* (LDhP), "The Shorter Illumination of Religious Law," includes an explicit and extended discussion of the adoption of females specifically and adoption among matrilineal groups generally.[6] The unusual regional specificity of this Dharmaśāstra text makes it particularly interesting as a source for the representation of social history in normative texts and as a case-study in the compositional inputs of

[5] Derrett's assertion follows the principal line of thought in Dharmaśāstra, summarized neatly in the *Vyavahāramayūkha* as follows: *dattakaś ca pumān eva bhavati na kanyā* (An adoptee must be male, never female; cited in Kane 1962-75: 3.674). However, Kane does cite three texts that permit the adoption of a daughter, but only with reference to mythological contexts (3.675).

[6] The LDhP goes by the more popular name *Śāṅkarasmṛti* in Kerala, and has regularly been attributed to the great Hindu philosopher Śaṅkara, though such an attribution has been unanimously rejected by scholars. Recently, a new edition of the text, based on several manuscripts, was published in Unni (2003), though the older edition of Tamburān (1906) is still useful, particularly because of its modern Malayalam commentary/paraphrase. Unfortunately, Unni's translation is also more a paraphrase than a translation and cannot always be trusted to reliably convey the precise meaning of the sometimes strange Sanskrit used in the LDhP. Both Unni (2003) and Parpola (2001) date the LDhP to the 14th century, but their reasoning is not persuasive. Unni merely states, "This work seems to be a product of the 14th century as can be gleaned from the system of administration dealt with in the text" (23), but no clear historical link to a particular form of polity in Kerala can be established from the LDhP because administrative details Unni mentions correspond to later periods as well. Similarly, references to the *janmi* system of landholding in Kerala are similarly not conclusive as to the date. Moreover, references to any author are external to the text itself and are not reliable. If we look rather to those portions of the text that self-consciously acknowledge an awareness of Kerala as distinct, we may note that the Namputiri community seems to have produced an increasing number of Kerala-specific texts beginning the early 16th century. The LDhP would indeed be anomalous if it were dated prior to 1500 because the regional consciousness demonstrated in the text makes little sense before this date, or at least the other textual evidence for an awareness of "Kerala" dates from this later period. On these grounds, I prefer a more conservative dating in the 16th or even 17th century CE.

medieval Hindu legal texts. In other words, we may learn something both about the history of the social institution of matrilineal adoption and the presentation of that history in a śāstric form. In what follows, I will first provide some background information on matriliny in Kerala and show how the LDhP's discussion of adoption in matrilineal groups challenges certain colonial and modern ethnographic interpretations of matriliny in Kerala—specifically, the idea that matriliny, despite the etymology of the English term, centered on women, at least in a legal sense. I will then discuss matrilineal adoption in more detail as it is presented in the LDhP, with an emphasis on describing the imagined legal permutations of adoption. Finally, I will assess the value of this description of adoption in matrilineal communities of medieval Kerala for what it reveals about the relationship of legal text and legal practice in Hindu law. I will argue in fact that this poignant example elucidates in a textual form the process of localization in Hindu law and that this presentation of matrilineal adoption in the idiom of Dharmaśāstra takes us to the heart of Hindu law in practice.

Aspects of Matriliny in Medieval Kerala

Matriliny, or *marumakkattāyaṃ* (Mal.), literally "inheritance by the sister's son," in Kerala was found among Brahmins from Payyanūr village, Sāmantas, Nāyars, Tiyyas (Iḻavas) and other castes in Kerala.[7] Although most modern anthropologists focus on the lineage of women in matrilineal societies,[8] Kerala society explained matriliny from the perspective of the men in those communities. The head of the *taṟavāṭŭ* (Mal.), or the joint family and its property, was called the *kāraṇavan* (Mal.) and was always male.[9] However, the *kāraṇavan* was not the husband of the eldest female, as one might expect, but rather the oldest male related fraternally to the oldest living female in the family, i.e. her oldest brother. According to Balakrishnan, "The eldest male member of a Malabar family or Tarwad as it was termed, was called the Karanavan in whom was vested actually, though in theory in the females, all the property movable and immovable

[7] Balakrishnan (1981: 255) lists 27 castes that followed the *marumakkattāyaṃ* system, according to the colonial gazetteers from Malabar. Most of the information on matriliny in Kerala has come from two sources: colonial legal documents (court decisions, legislated acts, commissioned studies, etc.; see Balakrishnan 263ff.) and ethnographic accounts. Both of these sources pertain primarily to the last two hundred years or so of India's history and cannot tell us much about matriliny in Kerala prior to 1800. As a result, the LDhP's several references to matriliny, though not concerned with describing or explaining *marumakkattāyaṃ* as such, provide rare insight into the structure and motivations behind *marumakkattāyaṃ* as a whole prior to the colonial period in India.

[8] For Kerala, see Fuller (1976), as well as the work of Gough, Mencher and others cited therein.

[9] Under extraordinary circumstances, it was possible for a woman to take up *temporary* management of the *taṟavāṭŭ* as the *kāraṇavati* (Mal.). See Balakrishnan (1981: 41).

belonging to the Tarwad" (1981: 39). Thus, despite the fact that we are dealing with a "matrilineal" kinship system, we are still in a man's world (cf. Moore 1985: 527 and Jeffrey 2001: 25, 35).

Marumakkattāyaṃ provides a means of assessing which kin relationships are important and why. Marriage in Kerala's matrilineal communities, a contentious topic among scholars,[10] was attenuated and, consequently, consanguineous relationships came to the fore. The most important of these relationships were between a man and his sister, and between a man and his sister's son. These two kin relationships were the foundation of the more public manifestations of *marumakkattāyaṃ*, the property dealings and the rituals of the *taṟavāṭŭ*.

In the LDhP, ideas about family lineage (*kula*) and kinship (*saṃbandha*)[11] recur. These references indicate that medieval *marumakkattāyaṃ* communities considered biological descent and kinship relations important[12] because, echoing the general pattern of kinship-based motivations for adoption outlined above, the key elements of Kerala's matrilineal system as depicted in the LDhP were inheritance (*dāya*) and rites for the dead (*śrāddha*).[13] Although the kinship and marital patterns among *marumakkattāyaṃ* communities may have differed from patrilineal communities, kinship and lineage were equally important to both communities in terms of their religious obligations, legal obligations, and even in the realm of politics (especially of royal lineages in Kerala).[14]

In terms of inheritance law, control over the *taṟavāṭŭ* passed from a man to his sister's son, not to his own son as in patrilineal, or *makkattāyaṃ*, communities. A question arises here as to the legal owner of the joint family property in this matrilineal system. Was the *kāraṇavan* merely a "manager" of the *taṟavāṭŭ* property or was he

[10] For a discussion of the weakness of marriage in matrilineal communities in Kerala, including both *tālikeṭṭŭ* and *saṃbandham* "marriages," see Trautmann (1981: 209ff.) and Fuller (1976: 99-115).

[11] Despite its more generic uses, *saṃbandha* is used in a technical sense throughout the excerpted passage to refer to a kinship relation established either naturally or by means of the ritual of adoption. Moreover, it is not used in the text to refer to the so-called *saṃbandham* marriage among matrilineal groups in Kerala. For more on *saṃbandham* marriage, see Trautmann (1981: 209ff).

[12] This is *contra* Moore (1985) who rejects kinship as a significant basis of the *taṟavāṭŭ*. However, Moore's denial of kinship and descent as relevant to *marumakkattāyaṃ* contradicts more than a hundred years of scholarly research on matriliny in Kerala and betrays the limitations of her isolated ethnography.

[13] On *śrāddha* rites among the matrilineal Nayars, see Gough (1959: 240-272). Gough describes the *śrāddha* as one of three cults of the dead among Nayars and contrary to the LDhP, states that "A Nāyar woman's chief mourner is her eldest son; that of a man, the man next junior to him in the property group. But all males of the *taravād* junior to the deceased make subsidiary *bali* offerings to him in the period of pollution" (255). The LDhP makes no mention of mourners for a woman and is clear that the sister's son is a man's chief mourner.

[14] On the place of *marumakkattāyaṃ*, at least among Nayars, in the broader scheme of South Indian kinship, see Trautmann (1981: 167-72, 208-214); and on kinship and politics in medieval Kerala, see 417-425.

also the legal owner? In the early to mid-twentieth century, women were regularly considered the legal owners of the joint family property, though a drive toward abolishing matriliny in Kerala gradually dismantled their status as property holders (Fuller 1976: 71 and Jeffrey 2001: 35). In Anglo-Hindu law, *taṟavāṭŭ* property was held to be vested "in the family and not in individuals" (Derrett 1962: 353). In this view, joint family property was collectively owned by all the members of the household, and the *kāraṇavan* could theoretically only alienate *taṟavāṭŭ* property with the consent of *all* its members (Fuller 1976: 56 and Jeffrey 2001: 38). Questions and complaints about alienations made by *kāraṇavans* plagued the colonial courts in Kerala and became proverbial in Kerala folklore and literature, precisely on the grounds of non-consent. It is unclear whether political, legal, and moral pressures of the British exacerbated and formalized practices that might have been commonplace in early periods, but that were now redefined as not in the family interest and downright greedy or corrupt. In any event, the present scholarly consensus (clearly presented in Fuller 1976: 56-72) argues that an increasing separation of descent group from property group in matrilineal families resulted in a breakdown of the joint family and its collective property and a concomitant rise in individual property.

Several verses in the LDhP, however, suggest that legal ownership of family property was vested in the *kāraṇavan* as an individual and not in the family as a whole nor in the women of the family. In the technical language of the text, it is the man's sister's son (*bhāgineya*) who inherits the property in fact and, one presumes, also in law. LDhP 1.1.23-4, for example, states:

> *samantrasaṃskriyādye syād api cānyatra dṛśyate* | *rāmakṣetre tu nāsty anye bhāgineyā hi dāyinaḥ* || *abrāhmaṇānāṃ prāyeṇa tasmād dharmo vibhidyate* |
>
> Sacramentary rites should be accompanied by mantras among the first (i.e. Brahmins) and this is known elsewhere as well. But in the land of Paraśurāma (i.e. Kerala), it is not so because the other [i.e. in other communities] inheritors (*dāyinaḥ*) are sisters' sons. Mostly for non-Brahmins, therefore, the law (*dharma*) diverges.[15]

The emphasis here challenges the idea that it was either the family or women who legally inherited property in the *marumakkattāyaṃ* system. Similarly, in LDhP 6.2.26 and 6.2.37, the term *bhāgineyātmadāyāda*, "one whose personal heir is his sister's son," describes the nephew as the inheritor, employing the technical legal

[15] Cf. Unni (2003: 173) which follows the modern Malayalam commentary in Tamburān (1906) by including Kṣatriyas among those who recite mantras at sacramentary rites. The text itself says only *ādye* "in the first," and does not justify including kings in this list. Moreover, many royal families in medieval Kerala followed *marumakkattāyaṃ* and would, therefore, fall into the second group described.

term *dāyāda*.[16] Another piece of corroborating evidence comes from the twelfth-century Malayalam commentary on *Arthaśāstra* 1.14.2.[17] Glossing the phrase *svadharmād dāyādād vā uparuddhaḥ* [one who is hindered from doing his own duty or receiving his inheritance], the commentator states,

> *svadharmmam āvitu dākṣiṇātyarkku mātulakanyāvivāhādikaḷ | dāyādam āvitu dākṣiṇātyarkkē tammāmandhanaṃ marumakkaḷ koḷḷumatu |*
>
> By 'own duty' is meant that among people of the South there are people who marry their maternal uncle's daughter; by 'inheritance' is meant that among certain people of the South sisters' sons inherit the property of their maternal uncle (Sambasiva Sastri 1972: 115).

Though not conclusive, the three verses from the LDhP and the statement of the *Bhāṣākauṭilīyaṃ* do indicate the probability that legal ownership was vested in the *kāraṇavan* and his lineage as reckoned through his sister's son.

Another early witness to the fact that males were conceived as the inheritors of family property as reckoned through the female line is the sixteenth-century *Tuḥfatu'l-Mujāhidīn* of Sheikh Zainu'd-Dīn, a history of Muslim communities in Kerala in the wake of Portuguese colonial expansion in the region. He writes:

> The laws of inheritance amongst the Nairs, and other castes allied to them, make property to *descend to the brothers* from the mother, and to the children of their sisters and maternal aunts, and to all who are descended from the mother, and not to the immediate offspring. And this peculiarity of excluding the immediate offspring, has been adopted by the greater part of the Mahomedans of Cannanore, and those who are dependent on them in the neighbourhood of that place. (Rowlandson 1833: 62-63, emphasis added)

Clearly, for Zainu'd-Dīn, a native of Kerala not a visitor, inheritance and family property were possessed by the males in matrilineal families, even though the female line was used to determine succession.

Finally, in a telling recollection of traditional life in a *taravāṭŭ*, the reformer Mannath Padmanabhan (Mannam) in 1914 "called for legal recognition of patriliny so that a man's property descended to his wife and children, not his nephews" (Jeffrey 2001: 41). The perspective on ownership in Mannam's memory thus also indicates that property belonged to a man and passed to his sister's sons, exactly the image of succession presented in the LDhP. It is obvi-

[16] Unni (2003: 239) fails to translate the term in either of these verses. It is noteworthy that the Malayalam commentary glosses the term simply as *marumakkattāyakār*, "those who practice inheritance of the sister's son."

[17] For a short introduction to the *Bhāṣakauṭilīyaṃ*, see Ezhuthachan (1975).

ous that females are not irrelevant to inheritance because they are connected with the family lineage (*kulatantu*, see LDhP 6.2.27 and 6.2.40) and are said to "produce the honor" (*mānaḥ saṃbhāvyate tayā*) for the males in the family (LDhP 6.2.64). However, it appears likely that matrilineal kinship in medieval Kerala was merely a mode of reckoning inheritance among males. This fact does not deny the special privileges and relatively high autonomy accorded females in Kerala society, but does call into question their legal status as heirs and centerpieces of the joint family, except in a nominal sense as placeholders for the males of the *taṟavāṭŭ*.

As with inheritance, rites for the dead also rely on the relationship a man has with his nephew, because in the *marumakkattāyaṃ* system it was a man's sister's son who must perform his *śrāddha*, not his own son. The importance of these *śrāddha* rites is signaled in the opening verse of the LDhP's discussion of adoption:

> *yeṣāṃ tu bhāgineyāḥ syuḥ piṇḍadās tair api svayam* | *apramattair yathākālaṃ bhāvyam atrārthagauravāt* ||
>
> Those for whom the sister's sons are the ones who make the ancestral offerings should themselves also diligently bring about [an adoption] at the appropriate time because of the importance of the goal in this case. (6.2.23)

If a man's sister does not have a son, then, he must make sure that a son is adopted to her/by her in order to secure the performance of his *śrāddha* rites after death, not to mention to inherit the family property, as described. Modern ethnographic accounts confirm the importance of this religious motivation for adoption even among "lower" castes (Gough 1959: 254-7 and Moore 1985: 529).[18] The fact that the discussion of matrilineal adoption in the LDhP begins with an imperative to adopt nephews in order to guarantee the continuation of *śrāddha* rites further confirms the rather nominal, placeholding role played by females in the text. In addition, it places the issue of *śrāddha* rites for the dead in a position of greater importance than the issue of inheritance (for which a female may be adopted as a conduit to a nephew for the adopted male). Thus, the principal concerns of LDhP are: 1) to ensure that a nephew-less man adopt a *piṇḍada*, an offerer of the ancestral rites, and 2) to ensure the preservation of his lineage (*kulatantu*) through the adoption of a niece, who will ultimately provide the man's nephew with a nephew of his own. Therefore, in ways that sometimes challenge the present knowledge of the history of matriliny in Kerala, the evidence of the LDhP suggests that in medieval Kerala *marumakkattāyaṃ* was a kinship system

[18] *Śrāddha* and *piṇḍa* rites are performed by Nayars in Kerala (technically a *śūdra* caste) and evidence for this practice among Nayars can be found as early as the 16th century *Ādhyātma-Rāmāyaṇaṃ* of Eḻuttaccan.

centered both on the inheritance of landed property controlled, and possibly owned, by the head of the joint family and on the performance of rites for the dead.

A Detailed Description of Matrilineal Adoption in the LDhP

In the context of *marumakkatāyaṃ*, if a man's sister lacks either a daughter, a son, or both, the fact that inheritance was traced through the female line might necessitate the adoption of a female, while performance of the *śrāddha* rites might require the adoption of a male. Comparing *marumakkattāyaṃ* adoptions to patrilineal adoptions, we see that the participants in an adoption change in this matrilineal context. Matriliny was not a mirror of patriliny in Kerala. In the patrilineal communities of Kerala, a sonless man who adopted a son, known as the *dattaka* or "given" son, fulfilled both goals of adoption simultaneously and in the same person of the adopted son. In the matrilineal context, by contrast, it should be clear that a man himself did not need to adopt any child. Rather, he must ensure that his sister either gave birth herself to both a daughter and a son or that she adopted a male or female or both for the proper preservation of the family in both a legal and religious sense.

The LDhP describes adoption in matrilineal communities in some detail. Despite many problems and obscure passages, the discussion is clear enough to glean the basic concerns of the text and to draw conclusions from its contents. In terms of context, the discussion of matrilineal adoption in the LDhP comes between a discussion of the importance of having a son (*putramahātmya*) and a discussion of adoption in patrilineal communities. The end of the *putramahatmya* introduces the subject of adoption:

> *tasmād aputro dattena putravantam yathāvidhi* | *sādhayet tvarayātmānaṃ prāptaṃ kālam alaṅghayan* || *punnāmanarakād yasmāt trāyate 'to 'bhidhīyate* | *putra ity auraso jātyā datto mantraprabhāvataḥ* ||
>
> Therefore, a man without a son, not transgressing the proper time [for having children], should, by means of an adoption, quickly cause himself to become a man with a son in accordance with the proper procedures. A son (*putra*) is called so because he saves (tra=*trai*) a man from the hell called Put—the natural son (*aurasa*), by means of birth; the given (adopted) son, by the power of the mantra (spoken at the adoption rite). (6.2.21-22, cf. *Mānava-Dharmaśāstra* 9.138)

The succeeding verses (6.2.23-4), however, equate the importance of adopting a son in patrilineal communities with adopting a sister's son in matrilineal communities, at least in terms of performing the *śrāddha*. Throughout the discussion, therefore, the nephew (*bhāgineya*) takes on this role of the son (*putra*).

In general, the text puts forth three basic scenarios regarding matrilineal adoptions as well as several limitations to, elaborations on, or qualifications of these scenarios. The text does not follow a strictly logical arrangement and the scenarios and limitations have been abstracted from the occasionally convoluted and/or corrupt text. Throughout the discussion, the hypothetical subject, Devadatta, is presumed to already have a sister (either by blood or by adoption).[19] It is fair to assume, though it is nowhere stated explicitly, that Devadatta is also the *kāraṇavan*, or head of the joint family. The following is a general outline of the contents of the discussion in the LDhP:

> 6.2.23-24 *Scenario 1:* If Devadatta's sister has no son, then a male must be adopted for the performance of the *śrāddha*.
> 6.2.25-38 *Scenario 2:* If Devadatta's sister has no children at all, then both a male and a female must be adopted to her.
> 6.2.27, 39-41 *Scenario 3:* If Devadatta's sister already has a son, then a female may be adopted by herself.[20]
> 6.2.42-45 Rules for *śrāddha*, marriage, and adoption in matrilineal communities who wear the sacred thread (*sūtrin* and *samantraka*)
> 6.2.46-53 Further explanation of why a man needs both a sister's son & sister's daughter
> 6.2.53-56 Adoptions among those not permitted to say mantras (*mantrahīna*)
> 6.2.57-67 Unbreakable bond and continuing legal relationship between an adopted female and her natural children prior to adoption.

The principal concerns of the text seem to be: 1) the necessity for Devadatta to have both a sister's son and a sister's daughter, and 2) the nature and kinds of females who can be adopted into a matrilineal family. These two concerns guide the overall plan of the text.

From these three basic scenarios, the LDhP provides rules for a number of possible complications associated with each of the scenarios. What if the female to be adopted already has children, for example? Should the male and female to be adopted be children of the same mother? Such questions are handled in the text with additional rules and hierarchical classifications of preferences (see, for example, 6.2.33-4 and 6.2.54-5) in typical Dharmaśāstra style.

Scenario 1, adopting a sister's son, is the most straightforward. In this case, the text focuses on the fact that the sister's son will perform the *śrāddha* rite for his maternal uncle (6.2.23-4). The basic rule for this kind of adoption states,

[19] Readers of the LDhP should not be misled by the text's use of the term *bhaginī* to refer to the sister of the natural or adopted nephew and not to the sister of Devadatta. The text is explicit at 6.2.29-30 that the *bhaginī* and *bhāgineya* are brother and sister, or legally become so through adoption. One would normally expect *bhāgineyī*, not *bhaginī*, in order to keep the perspective of the example consistent.

[20] Though Scenario 3 in a strict sense seems to be limited to three verses, much of what is said in other verses regarding the preferences and procedures in adopting females should be understood to apply to both Scenario 2 and 3, because both involve the adoption of a female.

> *svīkāryo bhāgineyas tair dattaḥ putra ivānyataḥ* |
>
> They should adopt a sister's son from another [household] as though he were an adopted (given) son" (6.2.24ab).

As noted previously, the text here creates a parallel between the son in patrilineal communities and the sister's son in matrilineal communities. Beyond this, however, the text does not provide any other information about possible complications or restrictions of this scenario, such as preferred *jāti* (caste), *gotra* (family), or *sapiṇḍa* (inheritance group) statuses. Perhaps the most important point to take away, however, is the prominent place given to the religious motivation for adopting a male in these circumstances.

Scenario 2, adopting both a male and a female, introduces the range of concerns over what kind of females should and/or can be adopted. Many preferences are discussed regarding the adoption of both a male and female, but few incontrovertible rules are established. For example, adopting a brother and sister of the same mother is preferred to adopting the children of different mothers, but both adoptions are considered legal and religiously efficacious (6.2.29-32). Even if the sister is already married, she, her children (if they exist), and her brother may be adopted into the new *taṟavāṭŭ* (6.2.32-33). In fact, in cases where both a male and female are required, not adopting both the brother and sister nullifies the rite and requires an expiation (6.2.45-6). This is true whether a family has adopted a male without a female or a female without a male (6.2.51-52). The stated preference, therefore, is to adopt a natural brother and sister who will become a man's sister's son and the sister's daughter, respectively (6.2.28-30).

Scenario 3, adopting a female, illustrates the concern felt in the LDhP for the female's role in the preservation of the family lineage. In the case where a man's sister already has a son, i.e. a natural *bhāgineya* (*sati svabhāgineye* in 6.2.39) the general rule from the LDhP (also given as an exception to Scenario 2 at 6.2.27) permitting the adoption of a female alone reads:

> *sahodarīvihīno 'yaṃ yato na kulatantave* | *prasūtāṃ sahasantānaṃ dadyāt gṛhṇīta cedṛśīm* ||
>
> Because this male without a sister cannot continue his family line, one should adopt even such a woman who has already given birth, along with her children. (6.2.40)

In this verse, the first hemistich, lit. "because that male without a sister is not for the family lineage," provides the reason for the second. The next verse, moreover, extends the concern for having both a sister's daughter and a sister's son even to the next generation beyond the original adoptees:

tatsantāneṣu puruṣo nāsti ced itaraḥ pumān | *dātavyaś ca pratigrāhyas tayā sākam iti sthitiḥ* ||

If there is no male among her children, then still another male should be adopted along with her. This is the rule. (6.2.41)

This verse seems to describe a new situation. If an adopted female has children but no son, then a son should be adopted to her as well, as part of her adoption rite. Otherwise, as the text implies, Devadatta's sister's son (*bhāgineya*) will have no *bhāgineya* himself to perform his own ancestral rites. The text here anticipates possible future problems that may arise from the adoption of a female who is already a mother, but who has not delivered a male. *Marumakkattāyaṃ* adoption, therefore, may involve not only the immediately succeeding generation, but the generation after that as well. The importance of both the male and female to the system should be clear from the care with which both are discussed in the text.

Moving from the three basic scenarios to more general concerns of the text, at first glance it appears that the LDhP restricts what kind of female may be adopted. Ideally, the female should be a virgin (6.2.45-46) and the ritual of her adoption should be accompanied by mantras, if appropriate (6.2.25, 6.2.37, 6.2.53-54, and see below for a discussion of mantras). The characteristics are merely preferences, however, as the text proceeds to include both married[21] women without children and married women with children (6.2.32-33, 6.2.40). In the end, the LDhP permits almost any female to be legally adopted, preferences notwithstanding. The text does prescribe adopting a female from a good family (see *tadanvayodbhavāṃ kanyāṃ* at 6.2.45), but it does not explicitly mention concerns over caste, purity, or physical appearance which might factor, for instance, in the selection of prospective brides.[22] Presumably, adoptions would preferably have taken place when the adoptees were children (cf. Kane 1962-75: 3.679ff.), but the LDhP also envisions and permits the adoption of adult married women with children as well. The lack of rigid restrictions appears to signal the importance attached to ensuring the fulfillment of both goals of adoption. Moreover, the near desperation implied by this flexible approach to adoption indicates either that the adoption was so important as to supersede normal rules of social interaction or that these rules were implied and considered unworthy of mention by the author of the LDhP.

[21] Though the LDhP describes an orthodox marriage rite which includes mantras at 6.2.43-45 and says that a woman from a family who observes this rite is acceptable for adoption, the discussion of adoption among communities who do not use mantras in their rites (*mantrahīna*) suggests that the text also intends to speak to a variety of matrilineal communities (see discussion of adoption in *mantrahīna* communities below).

[22] See Larivière (1996: 163-172). See also the list of preferred choices for adoptees in Derrett (1977: 53ff.).

The text also introduces another distinction between adoption in communities permitted to recite mantras in their rites (*samantraka*) and those that are not (*mantrahīna*). Most of the rules specified for *samantraka* communities are repeated in the discussion of *mantrahīna* adoptions, e.g. the adoption of a married woman with or without children is permissible, although inferior to the adoption of a virgin in both communities (6.2.32-33 for *samantraka* and 6.2.54-55 for *mantrahīna*). The inclusion of communities that were not permitted to recite mantras signals that the LDhP was not composed for an exclusively Brahmin audience. In fact, its prescriptions probably derived from both Brahmin groups and lower castes as well. It is impossible to specify exactly which castes the author of the LDhP had in mind, but given the paucity of Kṣatriya and Vaiśya castes in Kerala, the LDhP almost certainly intended Nayars and perhaps even lower castes as well.

The issue of mantras is connected with the question of which adoptee, the male or the female, is more important. For the LDhP, the male is more important in terms of the procedures of the adoption itself. The text declares that in the adoption of both a male and a female, the rite of adoption with mantras for the male should be considered effective for the female as well (6.2.34-38). The Malayalam commentary to the text explicitly states,

> *dattiṉṟe kāryyattil prādhānyaṃ puruṣannu mātram* |
>
> The male is in reality the important [person] in an adoption (6.2.31).

When adopting a brother and sister or mother and son, the rite of adoption for the male appears technically to depend on the recitation of appropriate mantras at the ritual, whereas the adoption of the female depends in a technical sense on her connection with the male being adopted, i.e. her brother or son (6.2.50-51). Presumably in cases in which only a female is being adopted or in *mantrahīna* communities, the rite is effective despite the absence of mantras. The text, however, is silent on this point.

The final verses of the discussion (6.2.57-67) contain a largely rhetorical description of the importance and unbreakability of the bond between a mother and a son. Because the LDhP makes possible the adoption of a female who already has children, the author seems to feel compelled to explain why her children, especially her son, must go with her as part of the adoption. The issue behind the text in this case seems to be that a son born to a female in *marumakkattāyaṃ* might be the sister's son for the *kāraṇavan* of her natal *taṟavāṭŭ*. If she is adopted into a different *taṟavāṭŭ*, then, the original family may feel that they have a claim to her son who could potentially serve an important role in his natal family. The LDhP dismisses these possible objections outright by stating, *bhaved eva tayā pūrvaṃ saṃbandho yādṛśo 'sya tu tasya dānāt paraṃ* |

Whatever his relationship with her was before (the adoption), however, should hold for after the adoption (6.2.60).

In general, this concluding discussion emphasizes the unbreakable legal connection an adopted woman has to her natural son and intends thereby to thwart her natal family's possible objections to her children being adopted along with her.

Although the actual procedures of an adoption are not described in detail in the LDhP, the importance of "properly" performing the rite of adoption is repeatedly emphasized because the ritual creates new kinship bonds and preserves both the inheritance line and the necessary rites for the dead required in the family. In terms of general procedures, Golapchandra Sarkar seems to be correct in saying that the ceremony of adoption in India is related to the ceremony of marriage because both consist of the gift (*dāna*) of a child (1891: 368, cf. LDhP 6.2.25, 6.2.43-48). A *dāna* ceremony always involves the following elements: gift, acceptance, and a pouring of water. At both a marriage and an adoption, a Vedic rite, called *dattahoma* in the case of adoption, and a series of Vedic mantras also accompany the ceremony.[23] Although Sarkar (1891: 377-9) argues that religious rites and recitations are not required to effect a legal adoption, the fact that most Dharmaśāstra texts on adoption give considerable space to a discussion of the rites and mantras associated with adoption suggests that the religious elements were inseparable from the legal considerations, or indeed that they are the same. As Derrett writes: "It was not seriously considered that the adoption might be valid for spiritual purposes and invalid for secular purposes" (1977: 48); the reverse is perhaps also true. It is the ritual, therefore, that makes the adoption effective as a legal act (cf. Derrett 1977: 64).

In summary, perhaps the most striking aspect of the LDhP's discussion of adoption in *marumakkattāyaṃ* is its inclusiveness. While preferences are given in terms of whom should be adopted, whether male or female, a near totalizing variety of forms of adoption in matrilineal communities is described and declared to be effective legally and religiously for the man and his family.[24] As long as proper procedures are followed, the text permits almost anyone to be adopted, male or female, married or unmarried, child or adult. The range of

[23] For a thorough description of the *dattahoma* rites according to Śaunaka and Baudhāyana, see Kane (1962-75: 3.687-9).

[24] This perspective is corroborated by the *Tuḥfatu'l-Mujāhidīn*: "In the event of the failure of rightful heirs, or of any scarcity of them, they make choice of a stranger (provided he be a person advanced in age) to succeed, instead of the son, or brother, or nephew; and after this adoption they make no distinction between him and a lawful heir. And this custom prevails with all the pagans of Malabar, whether in the succession to kingdoms and high dignities, or to the most inconsiderable patrimonies; a perpetuity of heirs being thus secured to them" (Rowlandson 1833: 66).

possible adoptees seems boundless. It seems reasonable to conclude, therefore, that the motivations of adoption were so strong as to permit adoptions that necessarily involved otherwise prohibited social exchanges, if no other solutions were available.

The Localization of Hindu Law in Practice

The discussion of matrilineal adoption in the LDhP sheds light on two crucial issues in the history of Hindu law—the process of creating Dharmaśāstra texts and the localization of Dharmaśāstra rules in practical legal systems in India. First, we clearly see that the claim by Derrett and others that adopting females was either not possible or not recognized by Dharmaśāstra texts must be set aside in view of the evidence from the LDhP. Furthermore, the LDhP cannot be dismissed as an anomalous or aberrant deviation from classical Dharmaśāstra texts on adoption because it preserves both the legal and religious motivations for adoption[25] and employs the interpretive strategies of Dharmaśāstra to incorporate the local Kerala practice of matriliny into an acceptable legal form. In this case, while faithfully holding on to the classic Dharmaśāstra motivations and procedures of adoption, the LDhP changes the focus of the adoption from a man's son to his sororal niece and nephew and modifies the legal procedures accordingly. The patrilineal presumptions of classic Dharmaśāstra had to be "translated" into a matrilineal context while preserving the fundamental and necessary motivations for legal adoption. Although the LDhP explicitly recognized that its prescriptions often deviated from the standard patrilineal context of most Dharmaśāstra texts,[26] the resulting solutions arrived at in the LDhP maintained the jurisprudential structure of Dharmaśāstra while providing a legal foundation for the adoption of females in Kerala. In this way, the LDhP exemplifies one prominent way in which the authors of Dharmaśāstra texts both preserved and innovated tradition as they struggled to keep the *dharma* literature relevant.

If we extrapolate from the example of the LDhP, I think we learn something about the way Dharmaśāstra texts must have come into existence. It appears that Kerala Brahmins felt compelled to compose this text in the idiom of Dharmaśāstra and its jurispru-

[25] This is *contra* Balakrishnan (1981: 165) who incorrectly states, "The spiritual background of adoption is not present in the Marumakkathayam law and it is purely of a secular nature. It is based entirely on secular motives and is akin to the Krithrima form of adoption ..." The evidence from the LDhP conclusively shows that adopting a male in the *marumakkattāyaṃ* system was based on a religious motivation, namely providing a *piṇḍada*. Moreover, several verses (e.g. 6.2.31, 6.2.34, 6.2.42) suggest that, in fact, the religious motivation was more important than the legal motivation of providing an "heir."

[26] Several passages in the LDhP explicitly limit its prescriptions to Kerala, called Bhārgavakṣetra or (Paraśu)rāmakṣetra in the text. See, for examples, LDhP 1.1.23, 1.1.28, 1.2.17, 1.3.12, 12.4.1.

dence—a fact which suggests the influence and the relevance of Dharmaśāstra to the living legal and religious systems in Kerala at the time. Furthermore, despite different social and historical contexts, the similarities between the LDhP and other Hindu legal texts suggests that the motivations and intentions of a text like the LDhP were not different in kind from other *smṛti* texts including Manu, Yājñavalkya, Nārada, etc. The point here is the same as one which Richard Larivière (2004) recently made in his critique of Derrett's notion of "apocryphal *smṛti*s," namely that these so-called "late," "spurious," or "peripheral" Dharmaśāstra texts are not unusual at all. In fact, they represent a continuing tradition of *smṛti* composition and accommodation of changing legal and religious standards into the Dharmaśāstra idiom.

Tradition and innovation must co-exist in any sustainable legal system and the case of the LDhP shows that Indian jurists never stopped using the tension between tradition and innovation in intelligent and meaningful ways in their legal practice. The example of matrilineal adoption is, I admit, unusual, but unusual in what way? Is it unusual that Dharmaśāstra ideals have clearly been translated into local practice, or rather only that such a legal translation has been textualized in the form of another Dharmaśāstra text? I would argue strongly for the latter. The LDhP is valuable as a source for social and legal history precisely because it exposes the process of creating Hindu law in practice, and specifically exemplifies a continuous process of accommodating and translating idealized, yet incomplete Dharmaśāstra rules into a system of positive, practicable laws. The cultural diversity of India is proverbial, but documenting that diversity in action has been difficult as an historical matter. What I imagine here are myriad other legal issues, beyond the accommodation of matriliny, that must have been practically handled with a deference to both Hindu legal texts and local norms without leaving a trace of the accommodation process in a textualized form. Though some may accuse me of making too much of one text,[27] I would nevertheless stake my claim that the LDhP, and especially its discussion of matrilineal adoption, displays the essence of Hindu law in its practical operation.

Stated generally, in the Hindu legal tradition, Dharmaśāstra rules from classic texts are neither dismissed outright nor accepted at face value. Instead, the motivations, procedures, and the notions of justice and religious efficacy of the Dharmaśāstra are translated into localized social, political, religious, and economic ways of life. To the extent that these local legal traditions touch Dharmaśāstra, they are Hindu traditions, but inherent in the system is a tremendous vari-

[27] A similar example would be Mādhava's defense of cross-cousin marriage in South India in his commentary on the *Parāśarasmṛti*. See Trautmann (1981: 438-446) for a translation and discussion.

ability and capacity for molding rules and ideas into different temporal or geographic contexts. Moreover, we see that this is a constant two-way process in that the LDhP, itself influenced by Dharmaśāstra, also captures local legal practice in a Dharmaśāstra idiom, a process that cannot be unique to this text. Usually, we do not see textual descriptions of this bilateral process of legal translation, and this is the special value of the LDhP. It offers historical evidence for the processes involved in the formation of positive law in the Hindu tradition—processes that must have been repeated for a plethora of legal issues in the innumerable localities of medieval India, but rarely set down in a textual, historically recoverable, form.

Bibliography

Balakrishnan, P.V. (1981), *Matrilineal System in Malabar* (Cannanore: Satyavani Prakashan).

Bargach, J. (2002), *Orphans of Islam: Family, Abandonment, and Secret Adoption in Morocco* (Lanham, MD: Rowman & Littlefield).

Derrett, J.D.M. (1977), "Adoption in Hindu Law" in *Essays in Classical and Modern Hindu Law*, Vol 3. (Leiden: Brill).

_____. (1962), *Introduction to Modern Hindu Law* (Bombay: Oxford UP).

Ezhuthachan, K.N. (1975), "The *Bhāṣākauṭilīyaṃ*" in *Sanskrit and Indological Studies: Dr. V. Raghavan Felicitation Volume.* ed. R.N. Dandekar, et al (Delhi: Motilal Banarsidass), 105-111.

Fuller, C.J. (1976), *The Nayars Today* (Cambridge: Cambridge UP).

Goody, J. (1969), "Adoption in Cross-cultural Perspective," *Comparative Studies in Society and History* 11: 55-78, reprinted in *Production and Reproduction: A Comparative Study of the Domestic Domain.* Cambridge Studies in Social Anthropology 17 (Cambridge: Cambridge UP, 1976), 66-85.

Gough, E.K. (1959), "Cults of the Dead Among the Nāyars" in *Traditional India: Structure and Change*, ed. M. Singer (Philadelphia: The American Folklore Society), 240-272.

Jeffrey, R. (2001), *Politics, Women, and Well-being: How Kerala Became 'A Model,'* new ed. (Delhi: Oxford UP).

Kane, P.V. (1962-75), *History of Dharmaśāstra*, 5 vols. (Poona: BORI).

Knipe, D.M. (1977), "*Sapiṇḍīkaraṇa*: The Hindu Rite of Entry into Heaven" in *Religious Encounters with Death*, ed. F.E. Reynolds and E.H. Waugh (University Park: Pennsylvania State UP).

Larivière, R.W. (1996), "Never Marry a Woman with Hairy Ankles" in *Festschrift für Dieter Schlingloff*, ed. F. Wilhelm (Munich: Orientalistische Fach Publicationen, Reinbek), 163-172.

_____. (2004), "Dharmaśāstra, Custom, 'Real Law,' and 'Apocryphal' Smṛtis," *Journal of Indian Philosophy* 32.5-6: 611-627.

Moore, M. (1985), "A New Look at the Nayar Taravad," *Man*, n.s., 20.3: 523-541.

Nicholas, R.W. (1981), "Śrāddha, Impurity, and Relations between the Living and the Dead," *Contributions to Indian Sociology* 15.1/2: 367-379.

Pāṇḍeya, R.P. (ed.) (1980), *Dattakacandrikā* (Varanasi: BHU).

Parpola, M. (2001), *Kerala Brahmins in Transition. A Study of a Namputiri Family* (Studia Orientalia 91; Helsinki: Finnish Oriental Society).

Pollack, D., et al (2004), "Classical Religious Perspectives of Adoption Law," *Notre Dame Law Review* 79: 693-753.

Rocher, L. (2002), *Jīmūtavāhana's Dāyabhāga: The Hindu Law of Inheritance in Bengal* (Oxford: OUP/ Center for Asian Studies, University of Texas at Austin).

Rowlandson, M.J. (trans.) (1833), *Tohfut-ul-Mujahideen: an Historical Work in the Arabic Language* (London: John Murray).

Sambasiva Sastri, K. (1930), *Kauṭilīyaṃ Bhāṣāvyākhyānasahitaṃ*. 2nd ed. (Trivandrum: Dept of Publications, Univ. of Kerala. Reprinted in 1972).

Sand, E.R. (1986), "The Śrāddha (Ancestor Ritual) According to Some Important Purāṇas: Some Facets" in *South Asian Religion and Society*, ed. A. Parpola and B.S. Hansen (Copenhagen: Scandinavian Institute of Asian Studies), 97-107.

Sarkar, G. (1891), *Hindu Law of Adoption* (Calcutta: Thacker, Spink & Co.).

Sonbol, A.E. (1995), "Adoption in Islamic society: A Historical Survey" in *Children in the Muslim Middle East*, ed. E.W. Fernea (Austin: University of Texas Press), 45-67.

Tamburān, K.K. (ed.) (1906), *Śāṅkarasmṛti* (*Laghudharmaprakāśikā*) (Tṛśśivapērūr: Bhāratavilāsaṃ).

Trautmann, T.R. (1981), *Dravidian Kinship* (Cambridge: Cambridge UP).

Unni, N.P. (2003), *Śāṅkarasmṛti* (*Laghudharmaprakāśikā*) (Corpus Iuris Sanscriticum IV, Torino: CESMEO).

Federico Squarcini

Punishing in Public: Imposing Moral Self-Dominance in Normative Sanskrit Sources

This essay will explore the socio-political and semiotic functions ascribed to specific forms of punishment by the author of the *Mānavadharmaśāstra*, a classical Sanskrit text which contains the first articulated discourse on the need for shaming punishment and brutal executions in public places.[1] I will argue that we need to view this specific form of novelty in Sanskrit normative discourse as related to, and justified by, an historical and political necessity for controlling and restraining certain practices and intellectual attitudes of "inferior classes" (*avaravarṇa*)[2] and other specific social strata. Hence, with this work I want to show how this discourse on public punishment is guided by the author's clear political awareness about the need to establish a thorough moral discipline in order to achieve social stability.

Moving from such premises, I suggest taking Manu's[3] doctrine of public punishment as a key element of a broader cultural struggle

[1] See *Mānavadharmaśāstra* (MDhŚ) 8,193; 8,334; 8,352; 8,370-372; 9,248; 9,262-263; 9,288; 9,291. Throughout this essay, I'll try to highlight the importance of the juridical novelty introduced by the *Mānavadharmaśāstra*, mentioning when the particular stanzas I am referring to are not present in precedent normative and juridical texts (*dharmasūtras*) available to us. The acronym NPP*dh* ("Not present in precedent *dharmasūtras*") inserted after the reference numbers of the *Mānavadharmaśāstra* will recall such novelty.

[2] See MDhŚ 9,248 (NPP*dh*).

[3] Apart from being the author of the *Mānavadharmaśāstra*—and its main protagonist—Manu is also a famous mythical progenitor, known since ancient Vedic *saṃhitās*. His role as expounder of the *Mānavadharmaśāstra* is an important literary innovation within Sanskrit legal tradition. This innovation has probably been the result of the agonistic relationship with the early Buddhist traditions, which introduced the figure of Buddha as a truly historical truth-claimer. See, on Manu and the authorship of the *Mānavadharmaśāstra*, Olivelle (2005: 18-25).

intended to institute, or preserve, a specific form of "proper social/ritual conduct" (*sadācāra*). A struggle meant to produce, through norms and law, a self-balanced social world that, as such, does not exist.[4]

First of all, in order to become aware of the epistemic potential of such forms of social control, we need to briefly revisit the history of the Sanskrit discourse on punishment.

1. *A short social and political history of the classical Sanskrit discourse on punishment*

The genesis and the form of a theory of punishment ought necessarily to be conceived inside a socio-systemic dynamism made of social relations and political interests which influence the configuration and the developments of that very theory. It is also important to notice that the nature of the Sanskrit normative and juridical *corpus* does not legitimate any direct de-contextualization of its descriptive data, mainly due to its prescriptive and normative intent. In fact, while the topic of the "doctrine of penal prescriptions" (*daṇḍanīti*) is often present in normative treatises, we have different variants of such a doctrine. A punctual reflection on the chronology of these materials is, consequently, very important.

Recently Werner Menski, willing to revise the existing scholarly periodizations, re-presented the idea of the two stages of the Sanskrit normative *corpus*: an ancient stage, in which the primacy of uses and customs (*ācāra, sadācāra, saṃstayā*) is favored, and a successive stage, in which normative texts dealt mostly with codified norms and deterrent intents.[5] Although this two-fold classification has merits on its own, it becomes much richer if we consider the rise of specific normative texts (i.e., the genre of *śāstra*s) as a turning point. Indeed, the *Mānavadharmaśāstra*, with its new formulation of the "doctrine of penal prescriptions,"[6] has to be seen as a major innovation within the South Asian classical normative tradition. This to say that the *Mānavadharmaśāstra* plays a strategic role inside the chronology of *dharma* literature.

[4] Here I want to draw attention to the performative power of law, which utilizes a descriptive form of discourse to prescribe moral and behavioral patterns (see Lange 2002).

[5] See Menski (2003: 79-83; 107-130 and 1989: 7-8).

[6] Which is not the only novelty introduced with this treatise. The *Mānavadharmaśāstra*'s construction or re-elaboration of notions like *āpaddharma* (10,1-131), *sanātanadharma* (4,138; 7,98; 9,64), *varṇasaṃkara* (10,1-73), *dvijottama* (2,49; 2,166; 3,124; 3,183; 3,190; 3,213; 3,283; 4,44; 4,153; 5,21; 5,100; 5,108; 8,73; 11,34; 11,95; 11,128; 11,130; 11,134; 11,163; 12,92; 12,113), *āryāvarta* (2,17-24), *vaidika* (see Squarcini 2007: 115-136) and *kaṇṭakoddharaṇa/kaṇṭakāśodhana* (9,252-293), are some other indicators of its innovative intention. Further *Mānavadharmaśāstra*'s important innovations pertain to textual morphology: "Manu introduces two major innovations in comparison to the previous literature of the *dharma* tradition. First, he composed his text entirely in *śloka* verse. Second, he set his text within a narrative structure that consists of a dialogue between an exalted being in the role of teacher and others desiring to learn from him" (Olivelle 2002: 549).

Nevertheless, hints about the existence of a codified system of punishments and penal prescriptions can be traced back to one of Aśoka's (r. 270-230 B.C.E.) edicts, which deals with the proxy for penal matters allotted by the king to his solicitors and which discusses the death penalty.[7] However, classical definitions of *daṇḍanīti* vary from the etymological one of *Gautamadharmasūtra*,[8] to the paradigmatic one of the *Mahābhārata*.[9] Many more definitions could be quoted,[10] as well as a good number of modern studies.[11]

According to classical sources, the doctrine of penal prescription came from the alliance between two main social powers (*brahman* and *kṣatra*).[12] It is a doctrine that merges together the symbolic and regulative power of *dharma*—with its guarantors—and the necessity to preserve it concretely, even with political coercion (*kṣatra*).[13] This new alliance linked the "norm" (*dharma*) and its guardians (*brāhmaṇa*) with "punishment" (*daṇḍa*) and "punishers" (*kṣatriya*), evoking the idea of a divine origin of punishment and of the "natural" relation that exists between the administration of punishment and the *kṣatriya* class.[14]

The author of the *Mānavadharmaśāstra*, however, was a staunch promoter of a wider and reinvigorated doctrine of penal prescription.[15] His aim was to reinforce the tie between "norm" (*dharma*) and "punishment" (*daṇḍa*) by including it within the formal scheme of the "administration of justice" (*vyavahāra*). In this way, the compulsive and deterrent aspects of punishment were molded in the same juridical doctrine on the grounds that it was a social necessity. This was a conception later legitimated by classical sources with the claim that in previous times, with the absence of violations of the norm, no legal procedure nor punishment was needed:

> When men had *dharma* as their sole purpose and were speakers of the truth, then there was no legal procedure, no enmity, and no selfishness. Legal procedure came into being at the time when *dharma* was lost

[7] See *Pillar Edict*, IV [Delhi-Toprā] and Norman (1975).

[8] "The word 'punishment' [*daṇḍa*], they say, is derived from 'restrain' [*damana*]." *Gautamadharmasūtra* (GDhS) 11,28 in Olivelle (2000).

[9] "That which leads this [world on the right path] by *daṇḍa*, or which carries [or set forth] the rod of punishment, this is called *daṇḍanīti*, which rules over the universe" *Mahābhārata* (MBh) 12,59,78.

[10] Yāska *Nirukta* 2,2; Kauṭilya *Arthaśāstra* 1,4,1-16; MDhŚ 7,14-31; 9,262-263; Kāmandakī *Nītisāra* 2,15-16; 2,36-44.

[11] See Lubin (2007), Menski (2003: 107-111), Lingat (1999: 207-242), Kangle (1997: 3-5; 237-239), Glucklich (1994: 213-238), and Day (1982: 53-66).

[12] See GDhS 11,28.

[13] See MDhŚ 9,243-247 (NPP*dh*).

[14] A relation clearly described in MBh 12,122,11-55.

[15] Apart from Olivelle's important reflections about the authorial intent in the *Mānavadharmaśāstra* (Olivelle 2005: 5-37), I have also elaborated on notion of authoriality in classical South Asia—and specifically in the *Mānavadharmaśāstra*—in Squarcini (2004).

among men. The overseer of legal procedures is the king; he has been made the rod-bearer.[16]

In any case, the first expanded and detailed narration of a mythical genesis of the doctrine of penal prescriptions is found in Manu's treatise:

> 2. A Kṣatriya who has received the vedic consecration according to rule has the obligation to protect this whole world in accordance with the norms; 3. for when people here were without a king and fleeing in all directions out of fear, to protect this whole world the Lord created the king 4. by extracting eternal particles from Indra, Wind, Yama, Sun, Fire, Varuṇa, Moon, and the Lord of wealth. [...] 14. For the king's sake, the Lord [*īśvara*] formerly created Punishment [*daṇḍa*], his son—the Law and protector of all beings—made from the energy of Brahman [*brahmatejomayaṃ*]. 15. It is the fear of him that makes all beings, both the mobile and the immobile, accede to being used [*bhayād bhogāya kalpante*] and do not deviate from the Law proper to them [*svadharmān na calanti ca*]. 16. The king should administer appropriate Punishment on men who behave improperly, after examining truthfully the place and the time, as well as their strength and learning. 17. Punishment is the king; he is the male; he is the leader; he is the ruler; and, tradition tells us, he stands as the surety for the Law with respect to the four orders of life. 18. Punishment disciplines all the subjects, Punishment alone protects them, and Punishment watches over them as they sleep—Punishment is the Law, the wise declare [*daṇḍaṃ dharmaṃ vidur budhāḥ*]. 19. When he is wielded properly after careful examination, he gives delight to all the subjects; but when he is administered without careful examination, he wreaks total havoc.[17]

These important stanzas are placed at the beginning of the seventh *adhyāya* of the *Mānavadharmaśāstra*, which is dedicated to the enumeration of the duties of the king (*rājadharma*) and which, from what can be seen from concordances and parallels,[18] is one of the most innovative sections of the text. Here the king is first linked to *dharma* and then to punishment (*daṇḍa*), thus indicating that he is the *locus standi* in which *dharma* and *daṇḍa* cohabit. Indeed, according to Manu, by punishing or killing the guilty the king is performing a sort of sacrifice.[19] Later sources maintain that the convergence of the spiritual/symbolic power and the secular arm happen even earlier: "It is in the past that the form of *daṇḍa* is given to *dharma* by the *brāhmaṇa*."[20] This suggests an ancient bond of subordination between Varuṇa, the

[16] *Nāradasmṛti* 1,1-2 in Larivière (1989). This is a clear example of the coercive use of the discourse on punishment. Also, *Bṛhaspatismṛti* 1,1,1-4 and MDhŚ 7,3.

[17] MDhŚ 7,2-4 (NPP*dh*) and 7,14-19 (with the exception of 7,16, all these stanzas are NPP*dh*) in Olivelle (2005). Also, MDhŚ 7,25-28.

[18] See Olivelle (2005: 1022-1024).

[19] See MDhŚ 8,306 (NPP*dh*). It is interesting to read this *śloka* in relation with *Āpastambadharmasūtra* (ADhS) 2,26,18-20.

[20] *Yājñavalkyasmṛti* 1,354.

"lord of punishment" (*īśo daṇḍasya varuṇo*), the rod of punishment, and the king.[21] Charles Malamoud aptly speaks of interdependence between *dharma*, the king and the doctrine of punishment.[22]

The structural convergence between *rājan*, *dharma* and *daṇḍa* is largely agreed upon by the dominant *doxa* of classical periods, since it appears in texts mainly concerned with rituals,[23] as well as in the epics.[24] Here, for example, the god Rāma says to his foe Khara, brother of the demonic Rāvaṇa: "I come as king, night-stalker, to end the life of evildoers and all who wish the world ill."[25]

The *Mānavadharmaśāstra* undoubtedly endorses this synthesis between political and juridical functions of punishment and the idealized principles of *daṇḍa*,[26] as proven by the large number of stanzas devoted to the king's duties.[27] To establish this necessity, its author maintains that not applying punishment would expose the entire society to dire consequences. In fact, says the *Mānavadharmaśāstra*,

> 20. If the king fails to administer Punishment tirelessly on those who ought to be punished [*yadi na praṇayed rājā daṇḍaṃ daṇḍyeṣvatandritaḥ*], the stronger would grill the weak like fish on a spit [*śūle matsyān ivāpakśyan durbalān balavattarāḥ*]; 21. Crows would devour the sacrificial cakes; dogs would lap up the sacrificial offerings; no one would have any right of ownership; and everything would turn topsy-turvy [*pravartetādharottaram*].[28]

Here a common enemy, represented by disorder and insubordination, unites the interests of *brāhmaṇa* and *kṣatriya* classes and binds together *dharma*, *daṇḍa* and *rājan*. The perceived threats and social conflict represented in the quoted stanzas also explain why the *Mānavadharmaśāstra*—largely concerned with political issues and relations between social powers (*brahman*, *kṣatra*, etc.)—resorts to a repressive ideology of punishment which, as far as cruelty goes, has no rivals in former texts.[29] Punishment here is not only meant to fulfill "objective" goals within the frame of a particular legal doctrine, but also to build an environment where submission, self-discipline and self-government can be nurtured.

Such a political vision leaves no room for alternatives and implies a stern verdict, in which a socially molded form of *daṇḍanīti* is clearly oriented toward stressing and endorsing social divisions:

[21] See MDhŚ 9,245 (NPP*dh*).
[22] See Malamoud (1994: 210).
[23] See Joshi (1973: 114-334).
[24] See MBh 12,38,6-9; 12,121,34-49 and Yamazaki (1999: 18-31).
[25] *Rāmāyaṇa* 3,28,10 in Pollock (1991). Furthermore MDhŚ 7,3.
[26] See MDhŚ 7,14-31; 8,119-130; 8,299-385; 9,229-293.
[27] See MDhŚ 7,1-226; 8,1-402; 9,1-325.
[28] MDhŚ 7,20-21 (NPP*dh*) in Olivelle (2005).
[29] See Squarcini (2003: § 6.2).

22. The whole world is subdued through Punishment, for an honest man is hard to find; clearly, it is the fear of Punishment that makes the whole creation accede to being used [*jagadbhogāya kalpate*]. 23. Gods, demons, Gandharvas, fiends, birds, and snakes—even these accede to being used [*te 'pi bhogāya kalpante*] only when coerced by Punishment [*daṇḍenaiva nipīḍitāḥ*]. 24. All the social classes [*sarvavarṇāś ca*] would become corrupted, all boundaries would be breached, and all the people would revolt, as a result of blunders committed with respect to Punishment. 25. Wherever Punishment, dark-hued and red-eyed, prowls about as the slayer of evildoers, there the subjects do not go astray—so long as its administrator ascertains correctly.[30]

As a proof of the persuasiveness of such discourse we may consider that much later elements of this doctrine of penal prescription came to be incorporated in devoted digests (*nibandha*). Later historical samples are the works of Vardhamāna Upādhyāya (*Daṇḍaviveka*, part of his *Smṛtitattvaviveka*, 15th century) and Śambhurāja (*Daṇḍanītiprakaraṇa*, part of his *Nītimañjarī*).

But, in order to further illustrate the logic of my interpretative proposal, I wish to present some of the theoretical reasons behind my hermeneutical effort.

2. *Reasons to put classical Sanskrit juridical doctrines in context*

To believe that socio-political history and the history of law are deeply connected means that we are also ready to accept that there are tight relations between the genealogy of a norm and the socio-semiotic function of punishment.[31] As a consequence, one can argue that the discourse about punishments inflicted on the transgressors of a given norm serves, *in primis*, to legitimize and to justify the norm itself. One reason why is that to be perceived as truly effective, a norm often turns to coercion and deterrence.

All the discourses of norm-makers and norm-givers are, in fact, based on the fundamental assumption that society becomes stable and tidy only when all its components are loyal to rules and abide by the norm. The more they do so voluntarily—because they perceive a norm as the "natural" way of behaving—[32] the more the society will become stable and non-conflictual. Obviously, the norm-makers know—more or less explicitly—that, in order to be long-lasting, the will to observe rules cannot be imposed but has to rise from the individual itself, who should understand that to follow a given rule is the most convenient among the possible choices.

[30] MDhŚ 7,22-25 (NPP*dh*) in Olivelle (2005).

[31] See Assmann (1997: 190-215). It is necessary, therefore, to speak about a sociology of the juridical field. See Bourdieu (1987) and Pavarini (1996).

[32] This logic of "naturalization" of justice has very much to share with the ones presented in other cultural contexts. See, for example, Cartuyvels and Tulkens (1993), and van de Kerchove (1993).

To achieve this goal, classical normative discourses developed strategies for social suasion, so that a rule—born from specific social conditions and historical contexts—would not appear as intimately bound to mundane facts, but more like the natural condition of things.

The privileged tool to enact such a complex operation is what Pierre Bourdieu defined as "symbolic violence," a long-lasting strategy of oblivion that works quite in depth and without the explicit assent of the social agents. In the words of the French sociologist,

> [...] la violence symbolique est cette coercition qui ne s'institue que par l'intermédiaire de l'adhésion que le dominé ne peut manquer d'accorder au dominant (donc à la domination) lorsqu'il ne dispose, pour le penser et pour se penser ou, mieux, pour penser sa relation avec lui, que d'instruments de connaissance qu'il a en commun avec lui et qui, n'étant que la forme incorporée de la structure de la relation de domination, font apparaître cette relation comme naturelle; ou, en d'autres termes, lorsque les schèmes qu'il met en oeuvre *pour se percevoir et síapprécier* ou *pour apercevoir et apprécier les dominants* (élevé/bas, masculin/féminin, blanc/noir, etc.) sont le produit de l'incorporation des classements, ainsi naturalisés, dont son être social est le produit.[33]

According to Bourdieu, the forms of coercion exercised through symbolic violence are invisible to the individual, who, under the effect of this cognitive device, *perceives*, *values* and *judges* himself—and others—according to the "natural" model to which he has been "violently" exposed. In fact, besides what he has to do, social norms teach him how to know what he should abstain from, while explaining that it is always to his advantage to do so.

It is clear that such a process of embodiment of a norm happens neither spontaneously nor rapidly. It comes with the primary social forms of "cultivation" (from the Latin verb *colĕre*), which transform the "unwrought" (Latin *rudis*) individual into an educated (Latin *cultus*, "prepared for the crops") citizen.

Similar forms of symbolic violence work when they are applied to simple social scenarios, whereas they lose efficacy in complex and pluralistic societies, where a univocal normative structure seems to be unable to steadily discipline their members. It is at this point that the producer of a norm must turn to different forms of sanction, which increase in number and intensity according to the degree of social disorders arising. In such social contexts, punishment develops not only as a repressive instrument but also as a communicative[34] and self-regulative *dispositif*.[35]

[33] Bourdieu (2003: 245-246; italics are mine) and Bourdieu (1998: 41). See, on the "politics of perception" of the *Mānavadharmaśāstra*, Squarcini (2003: § 6.1.1).

[34] See *infra*.

[35] Punishment, with its variations—like shaming punishment—, is often viewed

If this is the rationale that justifies the development of a penal system, then now I have some more reasons to argue that the discourses about the necessity of public punishment presented in classical Sanskrit normative sources—and in the *Mānavadharmaśāstra* in particular—are mainly motivated by the rise of social agonism within specific historical contexts.[36] Historical contexts to which we have to return,[37] if we want to understand the logic that shaped Sankrit classical normative texts.

3. Punishment is meant to communicate and establish moral self-regulation: on brahmanical justifications for punishment and penal prescriptions

Classical South Asian authors of normative treatises were quite aware of the need to publicly justify legal doctrine and principles. This is clear from the questions they pose to themselves while compiling legal treatises, questions that can be paraphrased as "is the exercise of punishment a useful deterrent for criminal tendencies?" or "is the legitimacy of its practice related to its effectiveness?" These are crucial issues for any legal doctrine,[38] and the ancient texts on *dharma* are no exception. Although the authors of the *dharmasūtras* take various positions on the justification or legitimization of punishment and expiation,[39] it is only with Manu's treatise that the theme is given a crucial role. In his *dharmaśāstra,* he explicitly asks whether punishment is efficacious or not and answers affirmatively.[40] He even says that "When men who have committed sins are punished by kings, they go to heaven immaculate, like virtuous men who have done good deeds,"[41] expressing the same extreme conviction displayed in other parts of the treatise extensively dedicated to punitive and penitential acts.[42]

The author of the *Mānavadharmaśāstra* is so fond of punishment as the best way to establish a moral self-dominance—in the flesh of the people—that he specifies the ten parts of the body on which

as a strong self-regulative device. See Braithwaite (1989); Garvey (1998). In order to critically explore this aspect it is necessary to understand how and if shame works (see Scheff 2000).

[36] An agonistic situation not only related to political or economical power, but also—if not mainly, at least for the producer of normative forms of knowledge—to semiotic power, as I have argued in Squarcini (2005).

[37] See, for latest descriptions and dating of *Mānavadharmaśāstra*'s historical context, Olivelle (2005: 18-41). Further, for broader studies on that very same historical and political context, see Olivelle (2006) and Witzel (2006).

[38] See, for very recent and less recent studies on the need and possibility to justify legal punishment, Honderich (2006), Cavalla (1979), and Mathieu (1978). Furthermore, on the European history of punishment and its justification, see Cattaneo (1990), Padovani (1981), and Cattaneo (1974).

[39] See GdhS 19,2-10; *Baudhāyanadharmasūtra* (BDhS) 3,10,1-18; *Vasiṣṭhadharmasūtra* (VDhS) 22,1-7.

[40] See MDhŚ 7,14-31; 9,318; 11,44-54.

[41] MDhŚ 8,318 in Olivelle (2005).

[42] See MDhŚ 8,119-130; 8,299-301; 8,314-343; 9,229-249; 11,1-265.

punishments are to be inflicted.[43] He operates lexical distinctions between the different types of corporal punishment, such as maiming, injuring, beating, traumatizing, torturing, etc. Moreover, he precisely distinguishes between a broader use of "corporal punishment" (*vadha*) and "capital punishment" (*prāṇānta*).[44] Apart from that, he is the first author who explicitly formulates a discourse on the legitimate use of punishment, giving a striking example of the coercive and inhibitory role attributed to it.

He enjoins that the administrator of justice must provide for various typologies of corporal punishment:

> 129. He should employ first the punishment of verbal reprimand [*vāgdaṇḍa*]; next a public denunciation [*dhigdaṇḍa*]; third, a fine [*dhanadaṇḍa*]; and finally, corporal punishment [*vadhadaṇḍa*]. 130. If he is unable to restrain them even with corporal punishment, then he should impose on them all these four.[45]

Furthermore, the *Mānavadharmaśāstra* marks a distinction between punishments consisting in tortures and mutilations (*vikṛtaṃ prāpnuyādvadham*),[46] and ferocious but immediate punishments such as beheading on the spot (*śuddhavadhena vā*).[47]

The complexity of this discourse implies that the surrounding social context forced experts on *dharma* (i.e. *dharmaśāstrakāra, dharmaśāstrin, dharmavid, dharmakovida*)[48] to give explanations and justifications regarding the structure of their discourse on the penal system.

This invites a reflection on the fact that—also in South Asia—the motives for questioning the efficacy of punishment are strictly related to the pressure exerted on the legal experts by the surrounding social context and the various detractors. Thus, in a normative text, the study of a section which deals with the purpose of a specific form of

[43] See MDhŚ 8,124-125.

[44] On *vadha*, see MDhŚ 8,129-130; 8,193; 8,310; 8,320-325; 9,248-249; 10,56; on *prāṇānta*, MDhŚ 8,34; 8,359; 8,377; 8,379.

[45] MDhŚ 8,129-130 (NPP*dh*) in Olivelle (2005).

[46] See MDhŚ 9,291 (NPP*dh*).

[47] See MDhŚ 9,279 (NPP*dh*).

[48] This is to say that we still need to work in order to reconstruct the actual social context of the normative and juridical production in classical South Asia. In fact, although normative treatises describe in details courtroom, legal proceedings and various aspects related to witnesses admitted to juridical contentions (see, respectively, MDhŚ 8,1-3; 8,9-46; 8,61-118), we are far from firmly attesting the concrete existence of courts in classical times and, therefore, from definitely establishing the relationship between textually codified judicial practices (Joshi 1937: 1-598) and the factual legal practice employed by real people. However, this is not condemning us to silence. By reading legal textual sources that deal, e.g., with codified forms of penal doctrine delivered through the king, together with other statements urging for a correct administration of justice (MDhŚ 8,386-387) to avoid political ruin (MDhŚ 8,344-347), it is possible to shape a frame where different social agents can be put in context. Setting classical legal doctrines in action can promote a better understanding of the reality of mutual influences played between social fields and political and normative spheres.

punishment (i.e., whether it can serve to discourage criminal activity and help to correct and reintegrate criminals in society) allows an understanding not only of the morphology and the nature of a penal system, but also of its building technique and the reasons of its durability. Although by doing so we can grasp some of the reasons why certain penal systems developed, we still need to understand why a penal system continued to impose forms of punishment that proved unable to produce the desired results. This is to say that there were other motives for persevering such practices, motives related to other aspects of social and political *Lebenswelt.* So, even though a form of punishment would not prevent certain crimes, it would serve other ends, such as the affirmation of the cultural supremacy—or *presumed* supremacy—of a value system.

As a matter of fact, recent studies argue that it is not enough to explain the institution of punishment as the univocal response to the criminal act, as proponents of a retributive view tried to do.[49] Rather, it is necessary to include in our analysis of punishment all collateral effects that are aimed at when punishing. Hence, the institution of punishment has to be seen as composed of various elements, which means that in interpreting its own characteristics and the arguments made to legitimate and justify it one must consider such complexity.

Similar proposals are apt for the context of the *Mānavadharmaśāstra*, in which, through punishment, the juridical authority is not only trying to rehabilitate the offender or to prevent future crimes, but is engaged in a communicative and political act.[50] Here too punishment and social sanction are, if anything, powerful means to communicate certain values, moral and practical.[51]

Throughout the stanzas of the *Mānavadharmaśāstra* it is clear that, while punishing an offender, a specific group of social agents communicates something by means of the juridical authority. It communicates not only to the offender himself, but to all the individuals who relate to him, and, lastly, to the society in its entirety.

Punishment, therefore, serves the purpose of specifying, explaining, reaffirming and transmitting to a large number of individuals certain moral values, which are perceived as a necessary condition for maintaining a specific social and moral apparatus. Within this

[49] A view that is today sharply criticized (see Honderich 2006: 170-201, Eusebi 1990, and Eusebi 1983).

[50] Communicating to the public through symbolic means was not new in classical times, as we can see from the display of idols during public processions under the Kuṣāna period (see Schopen 2005). If Schopen (2005: 299) is right in assuming that the materials that constitute this *Vinaya* text are from, or around, the Kuṣāna period, then we can safely refer to it as an example of ancient public communication.

[51] The conception of punishment as a communicative and expressive act has been, and still is, an object of debate within contemporary philosophy of law. See von Hirsch (2000), von Hirsch (1993), Primoratz (1989), Duff (1986, 1996, 2001) and Feinberg (1970).

communicative perspective, the different components of the institution of punishment can be interpreted as part of a linguistic world, a world of meanings in which a normative communication takes place.[52] Of course, since normative communication always implies social disparity, the choice of communicating norms through the institution of punishment has to be understood as a form of social conditioning, which duly obeys the logic of symbolic violence.

4. *The role of symbolic violence in the imposition of moral norms*

While exploring the social and communicative dimensions to which the practice of punishment is related, it is relevant to understand the meaning and value of symbolic aspects within the struggle to impose specific moral norms. To be efficacious a norm has to be perceived and recognized by every social agent, whose acceptance of its "natural" status has to be unquestionable, if not embodied. As specified by Pierre Bourdieu,[53] the establishment of every moral norm implies the use of various forms of symbolic violence, that is not directly perceived as a violation and that operates through learning and socialization processes.

One of the pieces of evidence for the existence of various forms of structural violence within Sanskrit normative culture is the use of particular terms very rich in symbolic value. One of these words, which I have already quoted, is *daṇḍa*. The word literally means "stick," "rod," "sceptre,"[54] all instruments connected with various forms of control and chastisement, as referred to by the god Kṛṣṇa as well: "Of punishers, I am the rod."[55]

It is clear here that a stick raised in a threatening way is the image through which the text wants to influence the reader, persuading him not to commit crimes or to violate norms. And, in effect, the fear of punishment, so vividly represented by the symbol of the stick, is one of the reasons why the subject accepts and interiorizes the norm, finally obeying a given moral principle "spontaneously." This is why there is a symbolic tie between social regulations, "divine" justice and weapons, a tie already present in the image, given in a *dharmasūtra*,[56] of the "twice-born" (*dvija*) that "holds the sword of Veda" (*vedakhaḍgadhara*).[57]

The author of the *Mānavadharmaśāstra* follows and elaborates these symbolic evocations, establishing the rod of punishment as the

[52] See, for a careful analysis of some crucial notions of this "linguistic world" Conte (2001: 659-667; 987-1000).

[53] See *supra* n. 33.

[54] See Minkowski (1991: 141-154).

[55] *Bhagavadgītā* 10,38.

[56] See BDhS 1,1,13.

[57] Furthermore, the epic literature offers a long list of "para-synonyms" of *daṇḍa* having a strong symbolic content. See MBh 12,59,20-23.

central axis of the government of society.[58] Such form of analogical communication aims to develop a specific "politics of perception," a full-fledged socio-cognitive strategy meant to establish—through the communicative and epistemic effects of public punishment—codified forms of self-perception and self-evaluation.[59]

In this way, the rod of punishment becomes the *super partes* principle that everyone—except the *brāhmaṇas*—must obey, from the gods in the sky to reptiles on earth.[60] A vivid image, with a strong and significant communicative power.

5. Punishment in public: the best way to impose self-regulation and self-dominance

When the communicative function of punishment encounters the socio-cognitive power of symbolic violence, it reaches the pinnacle of its strength. A fatal *connubium*, with the potential to produce a durable social consensus.

Nevertheless, as with any result achieved through social negotiation, this consensus does not last forever. To be maintained, it requires a constant effort towards coherence and persuasion, an effort that, to be socially successful, needs recourse to various forms of social conditioning. Indeed, amongst these forms, public punishment deserves special attention, since it presents a noteworthy synthesis of different factors.

It is not surprising, therefore, that the author of the *Mānavadharmaśāstra* himself attributes a remarkable socio-political function to public punishment. Justified by the need to preserve social order,[61] in the *Mānavadharmaśāstra* the king is advised to keep the military forces at his disposal and to instill fear and awe in those who do not address him with reverence. The same king, brandishing the rod of punishment, must keep all the citizens under subjection.[62] He is informed that a mostly effective tool of intimidation is the resort to punishment, or even to brutal executions, in public places.[63]

In different textual contexts, the display of cruel punishments is repeatedly linked with, and justified by, the political necessity of social control and repression of certain individuals within the lower classes (*avaravarṇa*), as explicitly stated:

[58] See MDhŚ 7,15-19 (with the exception of 7,16, all these stanzas are NPP*dh*).

[59] See MDhŚ 9,288 (NPP*dh*).

[60] See MDhŚ 7,22-23 (NPP*dh*); 7,28-29 (NPP*dh*). A good example of the strong social and political implications imbibed in this rod-axis symbolical nexus is also the long discussion between Bhīṣma and Yudhiṣṭhira on the role and primacy of punishment (Mbh 12,121,1-60 [in part. 34-36]).

[61] See MDhŚ 7,20 (NPP*dh*).

[62] See MDhŚ 7,102-103 (NPP*dh*).

[63] See MDhŚ 8,193; 8,334; 8,352; 8,370-372; 9,248; 9,262-263; 9,288; 9,291 (with the exception of 8,370-372, all these stanzas are NPP*dh*).

248. If a man of a lower class [*avaravarṇaja*] deliberately torments Brahmins [*brāhmaṇān bādhamānaṃ tu kāmād avaravarṇajam*], the king should kill him using graphic modes of execution that strike terror into men [*hanyāc citrair vadhopāyair udvejanakarair nṛpaḥ*].[64]

By saying so, the *Mānavadharmaśāstra* presents a discipline of public punishment that also confronts problems of penal doctrine and social stability. For example, while exhorting the king to practice the "eradication of thorns" (*kaṇṭakāśodhana*), the author of the treatise offers a decisive example of his "policy of perception":

288. He should locate all prisons along the royal highway [*bandhanāni ca sarvāṇi rājamārge niveśayet*] where people will see the criminals, grieving and mutilated [*duḥkhitā yatra dṛśyeran vikṛtāḥ pāpakāriṇaḥ*].[65]

Here the *dispositif* of public punishment is presented as an efficacious method to impose forms of moral self-dominance on the individual and then to achieve the stability of the entire society.

For the author of the *Mānavadharmaśāstra* there is nothing preventing him from prescribing forms of punishment that, like a pillory, displays to the public the pitiable condition of criminals stricken by the firm hand of the law. Relevant, in this regard, is the prescription to brand criminals with fire or with ink,[66] a symbolic practice rarely mentioned by juridical authorities before the *Mānavadharmaśāstra*.[67] These forms of punishments are indeed considered by the *Mānavadharmaśāstra* as an efficacious deterrent to check various forms of moral decay, especially the feared "mixing of classes" (*varṇasaṃkara*). This important social phenomenon was perceived as a serious threat and cruel public punishment was invoked in order to deal with it:

352. When men violate the wives of others, the king should disfigure their bodies with punishments that inspire terror and then execute them [*udvejanakarair daṇḍaiś cihnayitvā pravāsayet*]; 353. for such violations give rise to the mixing of social classes among the people, creating deviation from the Law that tears out the very root and leads to the destruction of everything [*yena mūlaharo 'dharmaḥ sarvanāśāya kalpate*].[68]

This proves that for the author of the *Mānavadharmaśāstra* everything has to be done in order to keep the society arranged under a strict hierarchy and, therefore, under control.

Of course, such is the view of punishment given by a prescriptive treatise and is not to be read as a precise blueprint of the func-

64 MDhŚ 9,248 (NPP*dh*) in Olivelle (2005).
65 MDhŚ 9,288 (NPP*dh*) in Olivelle (2005).
66 See MDhŚ 9,235-239 (with the exception of 9,237, all these stanzas are NPP*dh*).
67 See GDhS 12,47; BDhS 1,18,18.
68 MDhŚ 8,352-353 (NPP*dh*) in Olivelle (2005).

tion of punishment in the society of those days.[69] Nevertheless, the social phenomena of that time were truly present in the mind of the author of *Mānavadharmaśāstra,* who was seriously concerned for the future of his society. This is why, in his view, public punishment and preservation of "proper social conduct" (*sadācāra*) are intimately connected and mutually justified:

> 371. When a woman, arrogant because of the eminence of her relatives and her own feminine qualities, becomes unfaithful to her husband, the king should have her devoured by dogs in a public square frequented by many [*tāṃ śvabhiḥ khādayed rājā saṃsthāne bahusaṃsthite*]. 372. He should have the male offender burnt upon a heated iron bed [*pumāṃsaṃ dāhayet pāpaṃ śayane tapta āyase*]; they should stack logs and burn up that villain [*pāpakāt*] there.[70]

I hope that within these pages I have been able to show how much, also in this context, socio-political conditions and normative discourses are much more interrelated than any simple formula would suggest. So, if it is true that "[...] law is not just an isolated, culture-neutral phenomenon,"[71] then Sanskrit legal discourse about

[69] The true extent of the application of punishments and of their use in a judicial venue has been object of a long-lasting debate (see Larivière 1997). The scarcity of archaeological, epigraphic and literary testimonies has frustrated many attempts to produce a convincing solution to this important problem. Nonetheless, various hypotheses have been presented (Lubin 2007; Olivelle 2004: xxxviii-xli; Menski 2003: 71-130; Davis 1999; Rocher 1993; Menski 1989: 6-7) which can be reduced basically to two positions: some consider these gruesome systems of punishment as an aspect of "penal codes" truly applied within royal courts of realms sufficiently large to deserve the name of "state;" others consider them as mere prescriptive exhortations to rectitude promoted by Brahmanical legal circles and by specialists of *dharma* (a corporation that, in this view, was never capable to seriously affect local usage and customary practices—individual and collective—concerning the administration of justice). To that I ought to add a certain hesitancy to read South Asian textual materials *vis à vis* to historical and political issues, therefore committing—as Duncan Derrett stated—the "[...] error to suppose that the State in ancient India did not have an important sacral and ritual side, or that this side did not have a part to play" (Derrett 1999: 562). Furthermore Sherman (2010). In order to tackle these issues, it is necessary first of all to deal with a very important, and still unexplored, subject: the actual nature and the reality of the "courtrooms" (*sabhā*) and "juridical corporations" (*pariṣad*) in the classical period. See, for classical sources on these themes, Joshi (1937: 20-66) and further, Davis (2007), Sharma (1996: 105-117), Sharma (1986: 335-361), Veluthat (1985), Chakrabarti (1980), Solomon (1976: 23-31). Indeed, sources spoke of these two as the standard places of administration and exercise of the law (MDhŚ 8,1-3; 8,9-46; 8,61-118; Kauṭilya *Arthaśāstra* 3,1-3,20). Interpreters, functionaries, tutors and guarantees of the legal doctrine met within these contexts, giving life to a certain variety of legal institutions and juridical agencies, both royal and private (see Lingat 1999: 222-256; Sharan 1978: 15-79; Mazzarella 1909: 51-550). Furthermore, the extensive literature and the lexical variety which specifies roles and responsibilities in the political, administrative, legal and judicial activity performed within the *sabhā* (Kane 1990: 975-1007) strengthen the hypothesis that legal experts did indeed gathered within actual structures to perform their professional duties, characterized according to specific assignations.

[70] MDhŚ 8,371-372 in Olivelle (2005) and MDhŚ 11,104-105. Similar practices are mentioned in GDhS 23,14-15, VDhS 21,1-3.

[71] Menski (2003: 236-237).

punishment must be understood, within its due context, as a part of complex systems of social relations, connecting it to political, economical and symbolic fields of interest.

Bibliography

Assmann, J. (1997), *La memoria culturale. Scrittura, ricordo, e identità politica nelle grandi civiltà antiche* (Torino: Einaudi).

Bourdieu, P. (1987), "The Force of Law: Toward a Sociology of the Juridical Field," *Hastings Law Journal* 38.5: 814-853.

_____. (1998), *La domination masculine* (Paris: Seuil).

_____. (2003), *Méditations pascaliennes* (Paris: Seuil).

Braithwaite, J. (1989), *Crime, Shame and Reintegration* (Cambridge: Cambridge University Press).

Cartuyvels, Y., Tulkens, F. (1993), "La naturalisation des crime dans le pensée classique" in *Images et usages de la nature en droit,* ed. P. Gérard, F. Ost, and M. van de Kerchove, (Bruxelles: Facultés universitaires Saint-Louis), 231-254.

Cattaneo, M.A. (1974), *La filosofia della pena nei secoli XVII e XVIII.* (Ferrara: Edizioni Universitarie).

_____. (1990), *Pena, diritto e dignità umana. Saggio sulla filosofia del diritto penale* (Torino: Giappichelli).

Cavalla, F. (1979), *La pena come problema. Il superamento della concezione razionalistica della difesa sociale* (Padova: CEDAM).

Chakrabarti, S.C. (1980), "Sabhā in the Vedic Literature" in *A Corpus of Indian Studies,* ed. AAVV (Calcutta: Sanskrit Pustak Bhandar), 61-68.

Conte, A.G. (2001), *Filosofia del linguaggio normativo. III* (Torino: Giappichelli).

Davis, D.R. (1999), "Recovering the Indigenous Legal Traditions of India: Classical Hindu Law in Practice in Late Medieval Kerala," *Journal of Indian Philosophy* 27.3: 159-213.

_____. (2007), "Maxims and Precedent in Classical Hindu Law," *Indologica Taurinensia* XXXIII: 33-55.

Day, T.P. (1982), *The Conception of Punishment in Early Indian Literature* (Waterloo: Wilfrid Laurier University Press).

Derrett, J.D.M. (1999), *Religion, Law and the State in India* (Delhi: Oxford University Press).

Duff, R.A. (1986), *Trials and Punishments* (Cambridge: Cambridge University Press).

_____. (1996), "Penal Communications: Recent Work in the Philosophy of Punishment" in *Crime and Justice: A Review of Research,* ed. M. Tonry (Chicago: University of Chicago Press), 1-97.

_____. (2001), *Punishment, Communication, and Community* (New York: Oxford University Press).

Eusebi, L. (1990), *La pena in crisi: il recente dibattito sulla funzione della pena* (Brescia: Morcelliana).

_____. (1983), "La nuova retribuzione. Pena retributiva e teoria preventiva" in *Rivista Italiana Diritto e Procedura Penale*.

Feinberg, J. (1970), "The Expressive Function of Punishment" in *Doing and Deserving*, ed. J. Feinberg (Princeton: Princeton University Press), 95-118.

Garvey, S.P. (1998), "Can Shaming Punishment Educate?" *University of Chicago Law Review* 65: 733-794.

Glucklich, A. (1994), *The Sense of Adharma* (New York: Oxford University Press).

Honderich, T. (2006), *Punishment: The Supposed Justifications Revisited* (London: Pluto Press).

Joshi, L. (ed.) (1937), *Dharmakośa*. Vol. 1 (*vyavahāramātṛkā*), pt. 1 (Wai: Prājña Pāṭhaśāḷā Maṇḍaḷa).

_____. (ed.) (1973), *Dharmakośa*. Vol. 4 (*rājanītikāṇḍa*), pt. 1 (Wai: Prājña Pāṭhaśāḷā Maṇḍaḷa).

Kane, P.V. (1990), *History of Dharmaśāstra*. Vol. 3 (repr. Poona: Bhandarkar Oriental Research Institute).

Kangle, R.P. (ed. and trans.) (1997), *The Kauṭilīya Arthaśāstra*. Vol. 3 (repr. Delhi: Motilal Banarsidass).

Lange, B. (2002), "What does law know? –Prescribing and describing the social world in the enforcement of legal rules," *International Journal of the Sociology of Law* 30.2: 131-150.

Larivière, R.W. (1997), *Dharmaśāstra, Custom, "Real" Law and "Apocryphal Smṛtis"* in *Law, State, and Administration in Classical India*, ed. B. Kölver (Munich: R. Oldenbourg), 97-109.

_____. (trans.) (1989), *The Nāradasmṛti*. Vol. 2 (Philadelphia: University of Pennsylvania).

Lingat, R. (1999), *The Classical Law of India* (repr. Delhi: Oxford University Press).

Lubin, T. (2007), "Punishment and Expiation: Overlapping Domains in Brahmanical Law," *Indologica Taurinensia* XXXIII: 93-122.

Malamoud, Ch. (1994), *Cuocere il mondo* (Milano: Adelphi).

Mathieu, V. (1978), *Perché punire?* (Milano: Rusconi).

Mazzarella, G. (1909), *Studi di etnologia giuridica*. Vol. 2 (Catania: Tipografia Eugenio Coco).

Menski, W.F. (1989), *Diritto dell'India* in *Enciclopedia giuridica*, ed. AAVV (Italiana, Roma: Istituto della Enciclopedia), 6-7.

_____. (2003), "Hindu Law in Modern India: Can the Duty not to Talk about Dharma be Conducive to Justice?" in *Liberty, Equality and Justice: Struggles for a New Social Order*, ed. S.P. Sathe (Lucknow: Eastern Book Company), 236-237.

_____. (2003), *Hindu Law: Beyond Tradition and Modernity* (Delhi: Oxford University Press).

Minkowski, C.Z. (1991), *Priesthood in Ancient India: A Study of the Maitrāvaruṇa Priest* (Vienna: Publications of the De Nobili Research Library).
Norman, K.R. (1975), "Aśoka and Capital Punishment: Notes on a portion of Aśoka's Fourth Pillar Edict, with an Appendix on the Accusative Absolute Construction," *Journal of the Royal Asiatic Society* 1: 16-24.
Olivelle, P. (2002), "Structure and Composition of the Mānava Dharmaśāstra," *Journal of Indian Philosophy* 30.6: 535-574.
_____. (ed. and trans.) (2000), *Dharmasūtras: The Law Codes of Āpastamba, Gautama, Baudhāyana and Vasiṣṭha* (Delhi: Motilal Banarsidass).
_____. (ed. and trans.) (2005), *Manu's Code of Law: A Critical Edition and Translation of the Mānava-Dharmaśāstra* (New York: Oxford University Press).
_____. (ed.) (2006), *Between the Empires: Society in India 300 BCE to 400 CE* (New York: Oxford University Press).
Padovani, T. (1981), *L'utopia punitiva. Il problema delle alternative alla detenzione nella sua dimensione storica* (Milano: Giuffrè).
Pavarini, M. (1996), *I nuovi confini della penalità: introduzione alla sociologia della pena* (Bologna: Martina Editore).
Pollock, S. (trans.) (1991), *The Rāmāyaṇa of Vālmīki, Vol. III Araṇyakāṇḍa* (Princeton: Princeton University Press).
Primoratz, I. (1989), "Punishment as Language," *Philosophy* 64: 187-205.
Rocher, L. (1993), "Law-Books in an Oral Culture," *Proceedings of the American Philosophical Society* 137.2: 254-267.
Scheff, T.J. (2000), "Shame and the Social Bond: A Sociological Theory," *Sociological Theory* 18.1: 84-99.
Schopen, G. (2005), "Taking the Bodhisattva into Town: More Texts on the Image of 'the Bodhisattva' and Image Processions in the *Mūlasarvāstivāda-vinaya*," *East and West* 55.1-4: 299-311.
Sharan, M.K. (1978), *Court Procedure in Ancient India* (Delhi: Abhinav Publications).
Sharma, R. (1986), *A Socio-political study of the Vālmīki Rāmāyaṇa* (Delhi: Motilal Banarsidass).
Sharma, R.S. (1996), *Aspects of Political Ideas and Institutions in Ancient India* (repr. Delhi: Motilal Banarsidass).
Sherman, T.C. (2010), *State, Violence and Punishment in India* (London : Routledge).
Solomon, E.A. (1976), *Indian Dialectics: Methods of Philosophical Discussion*, vol. 1 (Ahmedabad: Gujarat Vidya Sabha).
Squarcini, F. (2003), *Violenza, norma, immaginativa politica. Fra costruzione identitaria e violenza simbolica nel Mānava-dharmaśāstra* (Doctoral Thesis, University of Bologna).
_____. (2004), "Testi senza autore, autori senza testa. Appunti rispetto all'odierno dibattito sulla condizione autoriale nel campo

letterario sudasiatico classico," *Rivista degli Studi Orientali* 78: 1-24.

_____. (2005), "Traditions against Tradition: Criticism, Dissent and the Struggle for the Semiotic Primacy of Veridiction" in *Boundaries, Dynamics and Construction of Traditions in South Asia*, ed. F. Squarcini (Firenze: Firenze University Press - Delhi: Munshiram Manoharlal), 437-484.

_____. (2007), "To be Good is to be *vaidika*. On the Genesis of a Normative Criterion in the *Mānavadharmaśāstra*" in *Tradition, Veda and Law. Studies on South Asian Classical Intellectual Traditions*, ed. F. Squarcini (Firenze - Delhi: Società Editrice Fiorentina - Manohar), 115-136.

van de Kerchove, M. (1993), "La naturalisation des peines" in *Images et usages de la nature en droit*, ed. P. Gérard, F. Ost and M. van de Kerchove (Bruzelles: Facultés universitaires Saint-Louis), 255-285.

Veluthat, K. (1985), "The Sabhā and Pariṣad in Early Medieval South India: Correlation of Epigraphic and Dharmaśāstraic Evidences," *Tamil Civilisation* 3.2-3: 75-82.

Von Hirsch, A. (1993), *Censure and Sanctions* (Oxford: Oxford University Press).

_____. (2000), "Punishment, Penance and the State" in *Punishment and Political Theory*, ed. M. Matravers (Oxford: Hart Publishing), 69-82.

Witzel, M. (2006), "Brahmanical Reactions to Foreign Influences and to Social and Religious Change" in *Between the Empires: Society in India between 300 BCE and 400 CE*, ed. P. Olivelle (Oxford: Oxford University Press), 457-499.

Yamazaki, G. (1999), "Kingship in Ancient India as Described in Literary Sources and Inscriptions" in *Kingship in Indian History*, ed. N. Karashima (Delhi: Manohar), 18-31.

III. Buddhists and Jains as Selves and Others

Oliver Freiberger

How the Buddha Dealt with Non-Buddhists

The implausible combination of incredible scholarly productivity, high-quality research, administrative efficiency, personal accessibility for students, colleagues, and virtually everyone, friendliness, generosity, and humor makes Patrick Olivelle rather suspicious as a person. Astonished observers have denoted this combination of qualities as super-human, concluding that Olivelle must be an *avatāra* that has manifested himself in our world to restore the *dharma* of scholarship on India. One characteristic feature of his work that makes such a conclusion rather unlikely is his own critical, historical approach toward Indian (and other) traditional theology and ideology. In his work, he constantly reminds us of the fact that the sources (not only) from ancient India, which we use for our historical inquiries, were created in particular historical, cultural, and socio-political contexts, within particular, mostly élite, circles that had their own internal disputes. Given that this tiny window into history poses an enormous obstacle for historical research, Olivelle's work demonstrates how we are nevertheless able to get a glimpse of social reality, by reading between the lines, by trying to understand the perspectives and motives of the authors, and by critically analyzing their truth-claims about religion and society.

The following is but a humble exercise in reading ancient Indian texts in what I would call an "Olivelle spirit." Whether or not he will agree to this I do not know, and the reader may decide whether the exercise is valuable at all. It seems to me that one of Bruce Lincoln's "theses on method" expresses well the aspect of Patrick Olivelle's approach that I refer to here.

> The same destabilizing and irreverent questions one might ask of any speech act ought be posed of religious discourse. The first of these is "Who speaks here?" i.e., what person, group, or institution is respon-

> sible for a text, whatever its putative or apparent author. Beyond that, "To what audience? In what immediate and broader context? Through what system of mediations? With what interests?" And further, "Of what would the speaker(s) persuade the audience? What are the consequences if this project of persuasion should happen to succeed? Who wins what, and how much? Who, conversely, loses?" (Lincoln 1996: 225f.).

By posing some "destabilizing and irreverent questions," the present article examines the ways in which the Buddha dealt with non-Buddhists. I confess that I chose the chapter's title primarily for its irresistible brevity, being aware that the formulation may be misleading. Let me clarify at the outset that I do not believe that our sources provide fully reliable historical information about the person known as the Buddha, let alone about his personal thoughts or his social behavior. Equally, the term "non-Buddhist" is, as a descriptive category, problematic and hard to define, unless one assumes an "essence" of Buddhism, which would go beyond historical analysis. Thus a more precise (but totally unattractive) title would read like "How the Buddha, as certain texts portray this person, dealt, according to some sources, with persons that those passages construct as being non-Buddhist." As we will see, this is not a fashionable and useless deconstruction that deliberately complicates matters, but rather is a conclusion of the research.

In the following, I first present some categories and theoretical frameworks that have been applied in analyzing the issue. By examining a few selected passages from the Pāli canon, I point at some advantages and disadvantages those categories may have. Finally, I suggest an approach that has its starting point in the analysis of the actual techniques of dealing with "the other." Reflecting upon early Buddhist religious identity, I also suggest that "the other" is not necessarily non-Buddhist.

Categories and Theoretical Frameworks

Scholars have used various categories and theoretical frameworks for analyzing the ways in which early Buddhists dealt with other religions. Perhaps the first category that comes to mind is tolerance—Buddhism is known for its alleged tolerance and peacefulness. Modern Buddhist authors trace this attitude back to the historical Buddha himself. The well-known modern Buddhist philosopher Kulatissa Nanda Jayatilleke, for example, begins a lecture on *The Buddhist Attitude to Other Religions* with the statement: "The Buddhist attitude to other religions has from its very inception been one of critical tolerance" (Jayatilleke 1966: 1). Similarly, the Buddhist scholar Phra Khantipālo states in a book on this topic: "Without fear of contradiction, one may say that Buddhadharma is the only one of the world's major religions in which deep faith and true tolerance coexist." (Khantipālo 1964: 19). Although both authors emphasize the tolerant nature of Buddhism, by speaking of "critical" tolerance and its combination with "deep faith," they also stress that the Buddhist attitude of tolerance is accompanied by a distinctive religious stance. This implicit reservation reveals the impreciseness of the term tolerance, which has—at least—two dimensions: dogmatic tolerance and social or institutional tolerance.[1] The former refers to ways of integrating beliefs of other religions into one's own religious framework, methods that are more precisely described as inclusivism and pluralism (see below). The latter, social or institutional tolerance, refers to the refusal to use force against—or to persecute—the adherents of other religions. If early Buddhists used physical violence against others, there is, to my knowledge, no textual evidence of it. With regard to persecution we must keep in mind that the early Buddhist community was merely one among many ascetic groups and movements present in North India during that period. Even if they would have strived for it, Buddhists were simply not in a position that provided sufficient political power to enforce persecution; or, for that matter, to deliberately refuse it. Thus, for analyzing the ways in which early Buddhists dealt with non-Buddhists who operate on a more or less equal level, the term tolerance appears to be of little use. A theoretical framework that goes back to John Hick may be more suitable for dealing with the issue (Hick 1983).[2] This model, which has been used primarily in the Christian "theology of religions," distinguishes exclusivist, inclusivist, and pluralist approaches. For our purposes, quoting Hick's short definition will suffice.

> By exclusivism I mean the view that one particular mode of religious thought and experience (namely one's own) is alone valid, all others being false. By inclusivism I mean the view ... that one's own tradition alone has the whole truth but that this truth is nevertheless partially reflected in other traditions. ... And by pluralism I mean the view ... that the great world faiths embody different perceptions and conceptions of, and correspondingly different responses to, the Real or the Ultimate ... (Hick 1983: 487).

I have not found a concept of pluralism in the canonical Pāli texts yet, but the other two categories may be useful for the analysis. While in the majority of cases, identifying an exclusivist attitude is relatively easy, inclusivist approaches are more difficult to define. In a recent article, Kristin Beise Kiblinger describes the term more specifically.

> [Inclusivism] casts a wide net, allowing many different methods and warrants for inclusions. All that is required is that there is acknowledgement of a provisional, subordinate, or supplementary place within the

[1] See Berner (1993), with a summary of the discussion on this term in Religious Studies including additional references.

[2] See the first application of this model in Race (1983).

> home religious system for some element(s) from one or more alien traditions. Inclusivists deliberately look for the potential contributions of religious others to the home tradition and use their own system as a filter for selecting borrowings from the outside, borrowings that will not disrupt the coherence of the home system or obstruct its aims. (Kiblinger 2003: 81)

In her article, Kiblinger shows how modern "inclusivist-minded" Buddhists use certain passages from Buddhist texts to justify their inclusivist approach.[3] As I will try to demonstrate below, identifying an inclusivist attitude in the canonical texts themselves is more difficult. A term often used for what some may call an inclusivistic strategy is skill-in-means. The concept of skill-in-means (*upāya-kauśalya*) was further elaborated in Mahāyāna Buddhism (see Pye 2003) but scholars use it as a descriptive category also for early Buddhism. Thomas William Rhys Davids' description of the skill-in-means the Buddha displays when dealing with non-Buddhists is a classic example.

> [The Buddha] puts himself as far as possible in the mental position of the questioner. He attacks none of his cherished convictions. He accepts as the starting-point of his own exposition the desirability of the act or condition prized by his opponent ... He even adopts the very phraseology of his questioner. And then, partly by putting a new and (from the Buddhist point of view) a higher meaning into the words; partly by an appeal to such ethical conceptions as are common ground between them; he gradually leads his opponent up to his conclusion. This is, of course, always Arahatship ... There is both courtesy and dignity in the method employed. But no little dialectic skill, and an easy mastery of the ethical points involved, are required to bring about the result. (Rhys Davids 1899: 206f.)

This passage was written more than a century ago and still captures well a view that is widely accepted among Buddhist scholars. Recently Richard Gombrich quoted the passage, admitting that he could not improve on it (Gombrich 2002: 17f.). The Buddha's (allegedly) non-aggressive, intellectual attitude, full of sympathy for the opponent and quite the opposite of certain Christian missionary methods that aggressively demand faith, has contributed much to the positive image of Buddhism in the West. We are so fond of this image of the Buddha that we rarely question it. But as I intend to show, when basing our analysis on the personal skills of an individual, we can easily overlook less flattering attitudes and methods of interaction in the texts. In fact, even the broader categories of exclusivism and inclusivism may not cover all the ways in which early Buddhists dealt with non-Buddhists.Therefore, I prefer to speak of inter-religious hermeneutics, a term borrowed from Andreas Grünschloß (Grünschloß

[3] See also her book-length study (Kiblinger 2005).

1999). It is broad enough to include the Buddhists' perception of non-Buddhists and the techniques they apply in responding to them. In the following, I examine a few selected passages from the canonical Pāli texts to identify some of those perceptions and techniques.

The Exclusivity Approach

In the texts, one method of dealing with others is well represented: strict repudiation. When talking to his monks, the Buddha often speaks about the inferiority of non-Buddhist ascetics. They are portrayed as being blind, ignorant, and naïve. Their doctrines are either false or insignificant, their practices useless or even harmful.[4] In the *Brahmajāla Sutta* of the *Dīghanikāya* (DN), the Buddha points out that even when other ascetics praise Buddhism, the monks should not take them seriously because those ascetics praised merely the monks' outward behavior, not the deeper meaning of the Buddhist doctrine. The Buddha declares that in either praise or accusation, other ascetics do not know what they are talking about (DN I 1-3).

We find this attitude of superiority also in the *Sarabha Sutta* of the *Aṅguttaranikāya* (AN I 186-188), in which the Buddha has to handle a fairly delicate issue. Here Sarabha, an ascetic who had been a Buddhist monk but quit the Buddhist order, tells other ascetics that he had understood the Buddhist worldview and had therefore—we may add, because he was not convinced by it—left the Buddhist community. This is, of course, a serious matter that could affect the public image of Buddhism, so the Buddha himself goes to visit Sarabha to take him to task. He confronts him with his claims, asks him to explain how he views the *dhamma,* and offers to complete his understanding if necessary. After having questioned Sarabha three times without getting an answer, the Buddha addresses the other ascetics standing around. He states that when he questions a person who accuses him of ignorance, he usually gets one of three responses: "Either (the person) would shelve the question by another, and direct the talk to an alien subject; or he would display anger, malignity, and sulkiness; or he would sit silent, confused, hanging his head, looking downwards, a disappointed man, unable to make reply, just as now does Sarabha the Wanderer" (AN I 186f.). After the Buddha has left, the other ascetics poke fun at Sarabha, portraying him as a "decrepit jackal in the great forest, thinking to utter a lion's roar," and as a "poor little hen (that) thinks to crow like a cock" (AN I 187f.).[5]

The message of this story seems obvious. Sarabha would not have abandoned Buddhism if he had fully understood the *dhamma.* As a result of his ignorance, he turns out to be inferior even to non-

[4] I discuss this in greater detail elsewhere (Freiberger 2000: 99-115).
[5] Translations taken from Woodward (1932: 169f).

Buddhist ascetics. The listener or reader of this text may infer that a person who has the chance to receive the *dhamma* in the presence of the Buddha but abandons it nonetheless, is so stupid that even other ascetics lose all respect for him. And by describing the three helpless reactions of those who question the Buddha's status—evasion, aggressiveness, and depressiveness—the text effectively demonstrates the superiority of Buddhism.

Straw-Men, Skillfully Instructed

We encounter the exclusivistic view that non-Buddhist ascetics are blind and inferior primarily in the Buddha's internal instructions to the saṅgha. When he communicates with non-Buddhists about doctrinal questions, we might receive a different impression. I wish to discuss two accounts of the Buddha conversing with the non-Buddhist ascetics Kassapa and Nigrodha, respectively. In the first dialogue, the *Kassapa-Sīhanāda Sutta* (DN I 161-177), the naked ascetic Kassapa asks the Buddha whether he condemned all rigorous ascetic practices. For those of us who are familiar with the concept of the Middle Way, the Buddha's answer may come as a surprise. He responds that with his superhuman Buddha vision he could see that ascetics who had performed extreme practices were reborn in lower as well as in higher states. For those who lead a less extreme life, he predicts equally diverse forms of existence. The Buddha concludes that given this fact, he could not condemn all rigorous asceticism on principle (DN I 161f.). Then the ascetic Kassapa comes up with a long list of ascetic practices. The Buddha responds that if a man performed these practices without attaining a state at which greed and delusion are destroyed, he was not a true ascetic (DN I 167). We see that the Buddha does not explicitly reject the extreme practices but puts them into perspective. They are worth nothing if they do not help overcome greed and delusion.

Kassapa is impressed. He remarks that it must be very hard to become a true ascetic. The Buddha agrees but states that this is not due to the ascetic practices. "It would be quite possible for a householder, or for the son of a householder, or for anyone, down to the slave girl who carries the water-jar" to perform these practices. In contrast, overcoming greed and delusion was really hard (*sudukkaraṃ*), and those true ascetics are also much harder to recognize (DN I 169f.). What follows is a stock description of Buddhist conduct, meditation and insight. This convinces Kassapa. He joins the Buddhist order.

This dialogue seems to be a good example of the Buddha's skill-in-means. He appears sensitive toward the views of the opponent. He does not condemn his practices, but merely puts them into perspective, and he presents an alternative way of asceticism that he labels harder than the other practices—a description certainly attractive for ascetics who seek hardships. But if we take a closer look at this dialogue, several (irreverent) questions arise. Why does the ascetic Kassapa accept every argument the Buddha brings up? Why does he believe him when he claims that ascetic practices have no effect on the next life? Why does he agree when the Buddha polemically declares that the extreme ascetic practices were so undemanding that they could be performed even by a slave girl? Why does he accept with no objections the Buddha's concept of the true ascetic? And why does he, a naked ascetic himself, allow the Buddha to completely ignore the aims and objectives of those rigorous ascetic practices? The answer to these questions seems fairly obvious: the character "Kassapa" as he appears in this story can be viewed as a mere straw-man, a fictive dialogue partner created to affirm the Buddha's argument. This is not to say that such ascetic characters were entirely imaginary and would not correspond to the real-life opponents that Buddhists had to deal with. Yet in this dialogue, Kassapa's character appears to be shaped for the purpose of reinforcing the Buddhist worldview. But if his opponent is not a real person in need for guidance, the dialogue can hardly be taken as evidence of the Buddha's skillfulness in means. One does not need particular skills to beat a fictive character.

This example demonstrates that the term skill-in-means is not only descriptive; it also carries our admiration for a person—the Buddha—who is gifted in guiding others successfully through his argument. The term inclusivism is equally problematic here. Do we assume that the Buddha "includes" the ascetic practices merely because he refuses to reject them right away? By re-interpreting the term asceticism, he rather replaces them with his mode of conduct. In consequence, the rigorous practices are dismissed, even if this is not explicitly stated. Thus, for our analysis, it seems more promising to focus on the actual techniques of dealing with "the other" that are applied here. These are: (1) the re-interpretation of the concept of asceticism by claiming that it solely consisted of overcoming greed and delusion; (2) the avoidance of condemning rigorous ascetic practices on principle, combined with an internalization/ethicization strategy that replaces austerities with moral behavior, meditation, and insight; (3) the use of polemics to disparage and belittle the hardships of other ascetics. This last method in particular we could have missed if we had looked only through the lenses of skill-in-means or inclusivism.

Vain Negotiations and the Hardships of the Religious Market

The second dialogue I wish to discuss, the *Udumbarikā-Sīhanāda Sutta* (DN III 36-57) has a similar plot. Here the wandering ascetic Nigrodha asks the Buddha to explain the Buddhist worldview. The Buddha remarks that his doctrine was very difficult to understand, suggesting that Nigrodha question him about the practices he and his fellow ascetics perform. Nigrodha is very pleased. He asks the Buddha how the fulfillment of their rigorous ascetic practices was attained (DN III 40).

Let me interrupt the dialogue for a moment. This introductory passage is a good example of how the bias of the Buddhist texts manipulates our judgment more frequently than we expect. At first glance, the Buddha's behavior can be considered as skill-in-means. Even when asked for it, he does not insist on preaching his own doctrine but rather offers to be questioned about the ascetic's practices. But again we may ask: why does Nigrodha agree? Why is he even pleased when the Buddha suggests this? Does he not realize that the Buddha takes advantage of discussing Nigrodha's doctrine instead of his own? Why does he not insist that the Buddha answer his question about Buddhism? From Nigrodha's perspective, the Buddha could easily appear to be acting exactly in one of the three before-mentioned ways that were ascribed to non-Buddhists: "shelving the question by another, and directing the talk to an alien subject," that is, evasion.[6] In the *Sarabha Sutta*, the Buddha's analysis of the three responses appeared so precise and plausible that we implicitly assumed that he and his followers would never respond that way. This passage is a counter-example. And it suggests that other ascetics could have analyzed the Buddha's responses in a similar way.

But let us return to the dialogue between the Buddha and Nigrodha, which evolves in a way similar to the dialogue with Kassapa. The Buddha is careful not to condemn extreme austerities but presents his own practice as true asceticism. But then we encounter an interesting twist in the text. The Buddha continues by claiming that if he were to instruct a student, it would take the student only seven years to attain liberation. No, he says, it would take him only six years, or five years, or four years. Thus the Buddha shortens the time-span and ends with the claim that a serious student, instructed by him, would take only seven days to attain liberation (DN III 55f.). This seems odd. It almost resembles the behavior of a car dealer who continuously reduces the price until eventually the skeptical customer buys the car.

And the text continues oddly. After reducing the price—that is, the time-span needed for attaining liberation—the Buddha emphasizes that his aim was not to gain pupils and to make others secede from their teachers, their doctrines, and their modes of livelihood, but only to help them overcome suffering (DN III 56f.).[7]

[6] See the *Sarabha Sutta* discussed above (AN I 186-188). Just to mention this in passing, there are also accounts in which the Buddha remains silent when questioned, which from the perspective of the questioner must look just like the former monk Sarabha who did not respond to the Buddha's question. See, for example, the *Uttiya Sutta* (AN V 193-195).

[7] At first glance, this statement expresses religious tolerance and almost reminds us of the current Dalai Lama's encouragement to remain in one's own religious tradition. On

Compared to the earlier arguments of the Buddha, both these final passages, the "price reduction" and the Buddha's affirmation that he was not out to make converts, appear rather defensive, if not weak. The Buddha is not the skilful teacher who masterly guides an opponent through an argument anymore, but the salesman who desperately wishes to sell his product. The very end of the sutta confirms this impression. It reports that none of the ascetics who listened to this dialogue converted to Buddhism. The Buddha's final thoughts are: "Every one of these foolish men is pervaded by the Evil One, so that to not even one of them will the thought occur: come, let us now live the holy life taught by the Samaṇa Gotama, that we may learn to know it. What does an interval of seven days matter?"(DN III 57).[8] As it is unlikely that the Buddhist redactors would have forged such a feeble and miserable ending, the account of the Buddha failing seems to reflect an actual historical situation in which Buddhists had a hard time "selling" their religion to non-Buddhists.[9]

The two techniques, reducing the "price" for attaining liberation and offering to maintain one's own religious affiliation, can be described as expressions of concession. One is more ready to employ them when arguing from a weak position. In the sutta, the last words of the Buddha are: "What does an interval of seven days matter?" because the other ascetics are responsive not even to this almost unbeatable offer: liberation in seven days! This seems to refer to a social context in which Buddhists, debating with other ascetic groups, could easily end up in the inferior position. The Buddhist text describes the other ascetics as being pervaded by Māra, the Evil One, but in fact, they prevailed. Although offered liberation for a substantial discount, they are not interested. Apparently the liberation offered by the Buddhists was rather unattractive for some.

Who is a Non-Buddhist?

Finally, I wish to touch upon another issue that becomes relevant when we examine the ways in which Buddhists dealt with non-Buddhists: religious identity. The assumption that sometimes the Buddha's dialogue partners were mere fictive characters raises the question whether the debate about those topics was always a debate between Buddhists and non-Buddhists. It seems useful to reconsider the question, who is a Buddhist and who is a non-Buddhist?

the other hand, the text implies that if one really wants to end suffering, one would have to follow the Buddha's way, which inevitably means to give up doctrines, life-styles, and teachers that are incompatible with it.

[8] Translation taken from Rhys Davids (1921: 52).

[9] The redactors of the texts were aware of this situation. It is not relevant to the argument put forward here whether this was during the Buddha's lifetime or anytime later. Nor is it relevant here if in the composition of the sutta formerly separate sections were joined together.

I mention here merely one facet of this broad issue which I have examined in greater detail elsewhere (Freiberger 2006). Reading the texts closely, one finds that the ascetic practices, rejected implicitly in the above-mentioned suttas and explicitly in others, are, surprisingly, approved of and endorsed by the Buddha in other passages. The canonical texts are heterogeneous in this respect. It seems that some of the ascetics who practiced severe austerities were, in fact, Buddhist monks. But another faction of the Buddhist community, which became the prevailing mainstream, rejected those austerities and defined Buddhism in a different way, in particular by developing and applying the polemical concept of the Middle Way. Therefore it may well be that some textual accounts of dialogues between Buddhists and non-Buddhists actually reflect an inner-Buddhist debate.

If this conclusion is correct, the canonical texts lack a uniform definition of Buddhist religious identity. What follows is that we must also question our umbrella term: inter-religious hermeneutics. Drawing a definitive dividing line between Buddhism and other religions seems as problematic for the canonical texts as it is anywhere else. Thus inter-religious hermeneutics can also be intra-religious hermeneutics. It consists of the perception of "the other" and of the techniques applied in dealing with "the other"—whoever the "other" may be, whether a member of a different religious group or a fellow monk.

Concluding Remarks

Having posed "irreverent and destabilizing" questions, what do we gain from this brief study? First, we saw that categories such as tolerance, the Buddha's skill-in-means, or inclusivism are problematic because they carry an inherent (positive) value judgment that obstructs the analytical view, or they fail to include certain aspects. Instead of using those abstract categories, I wish to suggest an approach that has its starting point in identifying and analyzing the actual techniques of dealing with "the other." In the examined passages, we came across the following: (1) Strictly rejecting other beliefs and practices; (2) Re-interpreting terms; (3) Internalizing and ethicizing practices; (4) Using polemics to disparage others; (5) Employing concessions of several sorts. Not even these five would have been entirely covered by any of the before-mentioned categories and we may be able to find more techniques in the texts. Even the broadest category, inter-religious hermeneutics, has to be modified to include inner-Buddhist debates, as well. Reducing our analysis to one of those categories involves the risk of ignoring other, particularly less-flattering, ways of dealing with non-Buddhists, such as the use of polemics and concessions. The analysis of those techniques shows that in the tough competition of the religious market, sometimes early Buddhists were far from occupying a superior position, as the canonical texts usually want us to believe.

Bibliography

Aṅguttaranikāya [AN] (1885-1900), ed. R. Morris and E. Hardy, 5 vols. (London: Pali Text Society).

Berner, U. (1993), "Toleranz und Intoleranz in den nichtchristlichen Weltreligionen" in *Die Anfänge der Inquisition im Mittelalter*, ed. P. Segl (Köln: Böhlau), 269-284.

Dīghanikāya [DN] (1890-1911), ed. T.W. Rhys Davids and J.E. Carpenter, 3 vols. (Oxford: Pali Text Society).

Freiberger, O. (2000), *Der Orden in der Lehre: Zur religiösen Deutung des Saṅgha im frühen Buddhismus* (Wiesbaden: Harrassowitz).

_____. (2006), "Early Buddhism, Asceticism, and the Politics of the Middle Way" in *Asceticism and Its Critics: Historical Accounts and Comparative Perspectives*, ed. O. Freiberger, (New York: Oxford University Press), 235-258.

Gombrich, R. (2002), *How Buddhism Began: The Conditioned Genesis of the Early Teachings*, 2nd ed. (New Delhi: Munshiram Manoharlal).

Grünschloß, A. (1999), *Der eigene und der fremde Glaube: Studien zur interreligiösen Fremdwahrnehmung in Islam, Hinduismus, Buddhismus und Christentum* (Tübingen: Mohr Siebeck).

Hick, J. (1983), "On Conflicting Religious Truth Claims," *Religious Studies* 19: 485-492.

Jayatilleke, K.N. (1966), *The Buddhist Attitude to Other Religions* (Colombo: Public Trustee Department).

Khantipālo, P. (1964), *Tolerance: A Study from Buddhist Sources* (London: Rider).

Kiblinger, K.B. (2003), "Identifying Inclusivism in Buddhist Contexts," *Contemporary Buddhism* 4: 79-97.

_____. (2005), *Buddhist Inclusivism: Attitudes Towards Religious Others* (Burlington: Ashgate).

Lincoln, B. (1996), "Theses on Method," *Method and Theory in the Study of Religion* 8: 225-227.

Pye, M. (2003), *Skilful Means: A Concept in Mahāyāna Buddhism*, 2nd ed. (London: Routledge).

Race, A. (1983), *Christians and Religious Pluralism: Patterns in the Christian Theology of Religions* (London: SCM Press).

Rhys Davids, T.W. (tr.) (1899), *Dialogues of the Buddha*, vol. 1 (Oxford: Pali Text Society).

Rhys Davids, T.H. and C.A.F. Rhys Davids (tr.) (1921), *Dialogues of the Buddha*, vol. 3 (Oxford: Pali Text Society).

Woodward, F.L. (tr.) (1932), *The Book of the Gradual Sayings*, vol. 1 (Oxford: Pali Text Society).

Daniel Boucher

*Sacrifice and Asceticism in Early Mahāyāna Buddhism**

It goes without saying that any study of asceticism in Indian religion owes a great debt to the work of Patrick Olivelle. In addition to making many of the classic texts available in masterful translation, Olivelle has sharpened our reflection on the purposes of brahmanical renunciation and its inherent conflicts with the social, religious, and political landscape from which it emerged. The study of Buddhist renunciation is similarly enhanced by his work, and it is in the spirit of honoring my former teacher that I would like to make a small contribution here toward better understanding the motifs of sacrifice and asceticism in the early Mahāyāna tradition specifically.

Of course, Buddhism seldom calls to mind the notions of either sacrifice or severe asceticism. The historical Buddha's purported rejection of both is well known. For example, in the *Kūṭadanta-sutta*, the Buddha counsels the brahmin Kūṭadanta, who plans to offer a great sacrifice consisting of hundreds of bulls, rams, and goats. The Buddha describes for the brahmin his advice to a king for a bloodless sacrifice in a former life. Kūṭadanta wants to know if there is an even more profitable sacrifice, and naturally the Buddha replies that there is. Gifts given to the *saṅgha* are more fruitful than other kinds of sacrifice, but even more profitable still is going for refuge to the Buddha, the Dharma, and the *Saṅgha*, undertaking the moral precepts, and attaining direct insight into the nature and cessation of the manifold defilements.[1]

* This paper was written as part of another project on a Mahāyāna text entitled the *Rāṣṭrapālaparipṛcchā-sūtra*. The fruits of that research have now been published (Boucher 2008). This contribution in honor of my former teacher represents a small part of that larger project.

[1] The *Kūṭadanta-sutta* can be found at *Dīrgha-nikāya* I: 127-149 and in the Chinese *Dīrghāgama*, T 1, 1: 96c-101b. All references to Pāli sources are to Pali Text Society editions.

The Buddha's rejection of extreme austerities is famously connected to his own initial but fruitless attempt to win liberation. In the *Mahāsīhanāda-sutta*, the Buddha recounts his numerous mortifications: extreme fasting, wearing only rags, pulling his hair out by the roots, standing or squatting for long durations, and lying on a bed of thorns, among others. All of these efforts failed to bring him closer to the realization he sought:

> And yet, Sāriputta, by this deportment, by this conduct, by this performance of austerities I did not attain excellence in the gnosis and insight of the truly ennobled by means of superhuman qualities. Why was that? Because of my lack of attainment of the very noble wisdom which is a noble wisdom that when attained is noble and liberating and leads the practitioner thereof to the complete destruction of suffering (*Majjhima-nikāya* I, 81).

Despite these explicit rejections of sacrifice and asceticism here and elsewhere in the Buddhist canons, I will argue that these two motifs function as powerful analogues for other behaviors that are prescribed in some genres of Buddhist literature, both Mainstream and Mahāyāna. More particularly, I will attempt to demonstrate how the extreme sacrifices of the Buddha during his former lives, as narrated prominently in the *jātaka* tales, came to be homologized with the intensified, ascetic-like path of the forest-dwelling monk in the rhetorical strategy of one Mahāyāna text, the *Rāṣṭrapālaparipṛcchā-sūtra*. My analysis here will focus upon these motifs within this text in particular, but with due attention to the ways in which the *Rāṣṭrapāla* was clearly participating within a broad set of developments within the Mahāyāna tradition.[2]

The *Rāṣṭrapāla* stands out among Mahāyāna works as a strongly polemical tract. Its authors criticized their monastic contemporaries as no longer following the rigorous ideal of the first Buddhist communities, an ideal which, for some in the Mahāyāna, self-consciously imitates the disciplines and sacrifices of the Buddha's own bodhisattva career. For the contemporary bodhisattva, this path finds its best expression in the practice of the *dhutaguṇas*, the twelve or thirteen rigorist practices which classically define the lifestyle of the hardcore, forest-dwelling monk. My goal here will be to show how the authors of the *Rāṣṭrapāla* drew upon the arduous, multi-life bodhisattva career of the Buddha in the service of their own reactionary response to the state of Buddhist monasticism of their day.

"T" throughout this paper refers to *Taishō shinshū daizōkyō* (Takakusu and Watanabe, eds. 1924-1935); texts are referred to by serial number followed by volume, page, register, and line numbers where appropriate.

[2] References to the *Rāṣṭrapāla* will be to Finot's Sanskrit edition (1901), modified at times by my own reading of the Nepalese ms upon which his edition is based. For a fuller discussion of the manifold sources available for the study of this *sūtra* and a fuller fleshing out of the rhetorical strategy of the text, see Boucher (2008).

The Bodhisattva's Sacrifices

As is well known, the hagiography of the Buddha begins not with his birth, but with his many former lives undergone in pursuit of his supreme attainment. Given the fact that the biographical literature of the early post-Aśokan period must have provided the model for the bodhisattva path that became central to Mahāyāna self-understanding, it is not surprising that we find allusions to these former life narratives in a number of Mahāyāna texts. The *Rāṣṭrapāla*, the focus of our concern here, in fact contains a versified list of references to fifty of these former lives in its first chapter.

One of the most prominent themes repeatedly cited among the *jātaka*s referred to in the *Rāṣṭrapāla* is *dehadāna*, "the gift of the body." In these cases, the bodhisattva, intent upon giving every conceivable thing asked of him, offers his eyes, hands, head, or other parts, including sometimes his entire body, in response to the entreaty of some interlocutor. This motif in Buddhist narrative literature has recently been dealt with at great length and with great profit by Reiko Ohnuma, and I am in many ways indebted to her work in my own discussion of several examples from this genre.[3] I will here briefly summarize and discuss only a few examples of 'gift of the body' narratives cited in the *Rāṣṭrapāla*. These will be adequate for understanding the general thrust of such stories in the larger agenda of the text.

The *Sarvaṃdada-jātaka*, known to a variety of Buddhist sources and collections, is among the more famous tales of self-sacrifice.[4] This narrative describes the time when Śākyamuni was formerly a king named Sarvaṃdada ("All Giver"). Despite being well known for his generosity, he was attacked by a king from a nearby realm out of greed. Sarvaṃdada, mindful of both the dangerous follies of kingship and the benefits of renouncing life in the world, retired to the forest rather than resist his usurper:

> "When shall I abandon the household, unpleasant because it is crowded with hundreds of evil deeds, and live in the forest, pleasing because

[3] See Ohnuma (1997, 1998, 2000a, 2000b, 2001, and 2007).

[4] My summary and discussion is based upon the version found in the *Avadānasāra-samuccaya*; the Sanskrit is edited and translated into English on facing pages in Handurukande (1984: 58-87). At least two different versions of this story are known in early Chinese sources, one in the *Liu du ji jing* (T 152, 3: 5a.20-6a.20) and the other in the *Za piyu jing* (T 207, 4: 530a.13-c.12), both translated in Chavannes ([1910-1934] 1962, I: 38-45 and II: 59-61 respectively). Other variations to the same basic story also exist in these collections. Another version of the story of Sarvaṃdada is known from the *Mahāvastu* (Senart 1882-1897, III: 250-54; trans. in Jones 1949-1956, vol. 3: 239-42), but it differs in a number of ways from the above accounts. The placement of the events of this story in the sacred geography of Buddhist India is noted by the Chinese pilgrim Xuanzang in his travel account (T 2087, 51: 883a; Li 1996: 86). For additional citations, see Handurukande (1984: 20-23).

> of the joy and bliss of tranquility?"—those deliberations of my mind, which existed over a long time, have fortunately come to fruition without delay, on meeting this king.[5]

Sarvaṃdada feels great relief in the forest, released now from the burdens of kingship and surrounded by sylvan beauty.

A brahmin, driven by poverty, journeyed to Sarvaṃdada's kingdom, knowing that the king was renowned for his generosity. The brahmin encountered Sarvaṃdada in the forest en route to his kingdom, at which time Sarvaṃdada befriended the brahmin while informing him that the king he seeks has renounced the throne to perform austerities (*tapas*) in the forest. Seeing that the brahmin was distraught, Sarvaṃdada suggests that the brahmin take him as ransom to the usurping king, who longed to extinguish any threat to his rule. The brahmin accepts his plan, and the Bodhisattva (Sarvaṃdada) enters the city in bondage, striking awe in those who see him with his glorious features—features often used to describe the Buddha:

> Seeing him, pure like gold, tall as Mount Sumeru, bright with the best of marks (*lakṣaṇaratnacitram*), having the gait of an elephant in rut, wearing a piece of bark as his garment and having long, matted hair, the enemy king trembled on account of his own spinelessness.[6]

The usurping king, overcome by the sight of the Bodhisattva, rebukes the brahmin for his evil deed and offers to return the kingdom to Sarvaṃdada. Sarvaṃdada accepts his offer, despite his strong inclination to continue his renunciant life:

> Bodhisattvas are beings who are not seized by attachment to the pleasures of the senses, even in the household as in the forest. Like ascetics, they are inclined to dwell in the forest regions, living alone with a fondness for tranquility.[7]

The enemy king submitted to Sarvaṃdada, and having been so disciplined by the Bodhisattva's example, returned to his own former kingdom. The reannointed Sarvaṃdada then gave the brahmin wealth beyond his desires.

As in the more famous *Viśvantara-jātaka*, the Sarvaṃdada narrative also represents gifting as an expression of renunciation. In both cases the Bodhisattva offers something of comparatively little worth (his family or self) for something of infinitely greater value: progress toward enlightenment, expressed as an opportunity "to extract the essence from his worthless body."[8] He leaves behind his foul, polluted

[5] Handurukande (1984: 67, v. 23).
[6] Handurukande (1984: 79, v. 63, with modifications).
[7] Handurukande (1984: 82, v. 78, my translation).
[8] *kāyād asārād aham adya sāraṃ bhavantam āsādya samujjihīrṣuḥ* (Handurukande

body, which is subject to decay and death, so as to obtain a glorified body "bright with the best of marks." Ohnuma argues that the physical body here serves as a template for spiritual qualities: *dehadāna* allows for the exchange of one for the other, "resulting in a corresponding 'dharma-body' favored over the ordinary physical body" (Ohnuma 1997: 174). She continues:

> By giving away his body, the bodhisattva denigrates physical existence as being completely worthless and expresses a wish for some form of immaterial, non-embodied existence. This existence may be spoken of in terms of 'body', but the body imagined is wholly non-physical, and the emphasis is on getting rid of all the shortcomings of physical existence: 'Body' is used metaphorically here to stand for 'non-body' (Ohnuma 1997: 175).[9]

The *Rāṣṭrapāla* moves in a very different direction. It clearly wants to celebrate the glorified *physical* body of the Buddha, a body that contemporary bodhisattvas can also achieve if they undergo the practice of ascetic discipline, which substitutes for the Buddha's extreme self-sacrifice. The contrast is not between absence/transcendence and presence/immanence, but between ordinary embodiment—with all its imperfections—and superior embodiment, which overcomes the limitations of the flesh by means of the bodhisattva's long career of self-sacrifice. The corporeal and the ethereal are not opposed, but exist along a continuum, with the Buddha at the far end.

The bodhisattva's gift of his body is most often no mere ransom of his person. In many stories it involves the outright sacrifice of a body part or body as a whole. One of the better known of these tales is the story of King Śibi (Pāli Sivi). There are several variations on this narrative, some in which the bodhisattva makes a gift of his eyes, others where he donates flesh from his thigh, still others where he gives his head or entire body.[10] My paraphrase and partial transla-

1984: 76, v. 53). On this cliché of "extracting the essence from a worthless body," see Strong (1983: 148-55); Silk (1994: 353-54, n. 1, where he notes the occurrence of this phrase in both the *Ratnarāśi* and *Ugraparipṛcchā*); Pagel (1995: 381-82, contrasting the non-substantial physical body of the bodhisattva with the substantial body of the Tathāgata); Ohnuma (1997: 170, n. 34, which also records several additional references); and Nattier (2003: 227-28, n. 120).

[9] Ohnuma (1998) also makes a similar connection between the bodhisattva's gift of his physical body and the Buddha's gift of the dharma, though I fail to see how the Buddha's gift of the dharma constitutes an act of self-sacrifice as she has argued (esp. 345-55).

[10] The Śibi *jātaka* involving the bodhisattva's gift of his eyes can be found, among other places, in Pāli *Jātaka* no. 499 (trans. in Cowell [1895] 1994, vol. IV: 250-56) and *Jātakamālā* no. 2 (Kern 1891: 6-14; trans. in Khoroche 1989: 10-17). The version in which King Śibi offers flesh from his thigh to save a dove (in reality the god Śakra in disguise) from being eaten can be found in the *Pusa bensheng man lun* (T 160, 3: 333b.10-334a.13) and the *Da zhidu lun* (T 1509, 25: 87c.28-89c.27; trans. in Lamotte 1944-80, T. I: 255-60), to mention only two. Parlier (1991) has discussed this narrative in relationship to parallel

tion here is drawn from the version in the *Xianyu jing* (*Scripture on the Wise and the Foolish*):[11]

Countless aeons ago, the Buddha was a king named Śibi, who lived in a prosperous capital called *Dīpavatī. King Śibi governed 84,000 small kingdoms in Jambudvīpa and possessed a huge retinue of wives, concubines, princes, and ministers, over whom he exercised great compassion.

At that time the lord of the gods Śakra, declining in strength and life-force, grew melancholic. The god Viśvakarman saw Śakra lamenting and inquired as to his malady. Śakra replied with a host of depressing observations: he was approaching death; the [presumably former] Buddha's Dharma had disappeared; and there are no great bodhisattvas in the world in whom to take refuge. Viśvakarman reported that there is a great king in Jambudvīpa named Śibi who follows the bodhisattva path. "You should go and take refuge in him; he will certainly be able to save you."

Śakra retorted: "If he is a bodhisattva, first we should test him to see whether or not he is really sincere. You transform yourself into a pigeon; I will change into a falcon and will chase you, after which we will go to where the king is seated. Then you will seek his protection so as to test him. This will be sufficient to know if he is a genuine or fake."

Viśvakarman transformed himself into a pigeon and Śakra changed into a falcon. After pursuing the pigeon, he was about to seize hold of it and eat it when the pigeon anxiously flew under the king's arm for refuge. The falcon perched itself in front of the palace and addressed the king: "Now this pigeon is my meal. Though he has come by the king's side, you should hasten to return him to me. My hunger is severe."

The king replied: "My former vow was to save all who come to me for refuge. I cannot, alas, give him to you."

The falcon retorted: "Great king, today you say that you will save all beings. If you cut me off from food, my life will not be saved. Are those like me not among 'all beings'?"

The king asked the falcon to accept another kind of meat—meat from the king's own thigh that would not require him to sacrifice other lives.

The falcon was duly impressed by the king's generosity, but remarked that if he were to accept his flesh in exchange for the pigeon, he would have to receive a comparable portion of meat. The king ordered his attendants to bring in a scale. On one side he placed the pigeon; on the other, he placed the flesh cut from his thigh. Because this latter side was lighter than the pigeon, he cut additional flesh from his two arms and from both sides of his trunk. The flesh from his body still did not equal the pigeon in weight. Then the king lifted himself up, about to put his whole body on the scale pan when his strength

narratives from brahmanical sources, in particular the *Mahābhārata*, as well as to expressions of the Śibi tale in Buddhist art. Another version of the Śibi *jātaka* occurs in Jain sources as well; see Granoff (1991: 226 and n. 10). Additional references can be found in Lamotte (1944-80, T. I: 255-56, n. 1) and Grey (2000: 391-97). A comprehensive study of this narrative, including a discussion of its various incarnations in Indian and especially Chinese sources and their relationship to one another, can now be found in Meisig (1995).

[11] *Xianyu jing* (T 202), 4: 351c.5-352b.18.

failed and he fell to the ground unconscious. Coming to after a long time, he reproached himself: "I have long been fatigued transmigrating through the triple world, undergoing sorrow and hardship without merit. Today is the time to be zealously established in practice; it is not the time for sloth."

Emboldening himself, he got up on the scale, joyous as he realized the virtue in this. At that time heaven and earth quaked in six ways. The heavenly mansions all shook up to the gods of the Form Realm. At the same time the gods came down to within the atmosphere, from where they watched the bodhisattva afflict his body with austerities, his mind pledged to the great Dharma without regard for his own life. Every god shed tears like a torrential downpour, raining down celestial flowers in homage.

Then Śakra returned to his original form and went before the king saying: "Today you carried out such a difficult-to-fulfill course. What do you seek? Do you seek to become a *cakravartin* king, a Śakra, or a Brahmā? What do you seek within the triple world?

The bodhisattva replied, "What I seek cannot be met with among the pleasures esteemed in the triple world. The meritorious reward for what I have done is directed toward enlightenment."

Śakra then inquired if the bodhisattva had any regrets in so destroying his body. He replied that he did not. Śakra wondered aloud who could believe the king's assertion while looking at his trembling body. The king reiterated his vow: "From the beginning until today, I have been without any regret, even as large as a hair breadth. The vow that I have sought to fulfill will certainly succeed. If this is true, not false, as I say, may my body be restored."

Having performed this Act of Truth, the king's body was immediately restored, even more excellent than before. Gods and men both exclaimed, "Extraordinary!" as they jumped for joy. King Śibi was none other than the Buddha himself.

"Blessed One, formerly you were without regard for body and life for the sake of sentient beings .... Why do you now abandon all sentient beings and enter nirvāṇa?" Then Brahmā appeared before the Blessed One and stated that the Buddha had offered his head a thousand times in the past for sentient beings as he sought the Dharma. At Brahmā's request, the Buddha proceeded to the Deer Park in Benares where he turned the wheel of Dharma, thus manifesting the three jewels in the world to the delight of all.

In such cases of extreme giving, we are confronted with an unavoidable tension: to what extent is the bodhisattva, by his sacrifice, a model of the ideal donor, a benefactor who gives without regard to personal consequences, and to what extent may his act be inimitable, a literary exaltation that places the Buddha in a transcendent category? As with gifts offered in other tales, the Bodhisattva's sacrifice of his physical body stands in place of world renunciation, for his world has not yet a buddha nor the Dharma, and therefore, no institutional monasticism. For a contemporary Mainstream audience, Śākyamuni's dispensation makes such extreme acts of giving no longer necessary, for a devout lay person now has available the supreme field of merit: the *saṅgha* headed by the Buddha. In a post-

Śākyamuni world, the deeds of the bodhisattva are ideal only in the past.[12] Members of living bodhisattva traditions in the Mahāyāna, on the other hand, may well have taken these sacrifices more literally, as we will see below.

Objections to the Sacrifice

A number of Buddhist sources are critical of such extreme forms of giving or at least felt the need to substantially qualify them. For example, after describing King Śibi's gift of his flesh to save the pigeon as the fulfillment of the perfection of generosity, the *Da zhidu lun* (*Great Treatise on the Perfection of Wisdom*) qualifies its previous statement from the point of view of the perfection of wisdom.[13] If giving mere material goods constitutes an inferior gift, giving one's body is still only a medium gift. The superior gift is achieved when one makes the donation with utter detachment. When asked why King Śibi's sacrifice represents a medium gift when it was previously said to express the fulfillment of the perfection of generosity, the commentator points out that King Śibi's thoughts were impure—he failed to perceive that neither he nor what he gave exist in any inherent way. Lacking wisdom, his thoughts are attached to false notions of donor, gift, and recipient. While such a gift entitles King Śibi to meritorious recompense in this world, it cannot lead directly to buddhahood.

I should note, however, that while such a critique of ordinary notions of giving is common in some genres of Mahāyāna literature, the *Rāṣṭrapāla* itself offers no such qualification of giving vis-à-vis the doctrine of emptiness. For the authors of the *Rāṣṭrapāla*, the purity of the bodhisattva's intention appears to have been assumed: he gave without regret or limitation, feeling no distress as he strove to accomplish the spiritual perfections that would result in complete enlightenment.

Other Buddhist authors, however, were disconcerted by the disparity between the extremity of such a gift and the worthiness of the recipient. For example, Śāntideva, in his *Bodhicaryāvatāra*, declares:

> The body serves the True Dharma. One should not harm it for some inferior reason. For it is the only way that one can quickly fulfill the hopes of living beings.

[12] Cf. Ohnuma (2000b: 66): "The *jātakas* constitute a Buddha-centered genre that praises and exults in the idealistic deeds of the bodhisattva. In large part, the reader of the *jātakas* is encouraged to worship and show devotion toward the Buddha rather than to imitate him directly."

[13] For the initial statement concerning King Śibi, see T 1509, 25: 87c.27-88c.27 (trans. in Lamotte 1944-80, T. 1: 255-60). The counter statement can be found at 25: 92c.12-28 (trans. in Lamotte 1944-80, T. 1: 297-98). See also the discussion on this passage in Ohnuma (2000b: 63).

> Therefore one should not relinquish one's life for someone whose disposition to compassion is not as pure. But for someone whose disposition is comparable, one should relinquish it. That way, there is no overall loss (Crosby and Skilton 1995: 41-42).

There can be no doubt that Śāntideva was himself well aware of such gift of the body narratives, for he records several in his compilation, the *Śikṣāsamuccaya.*[14] Śāntideva's view then is unexpected here, for over and over again, *dehadāna* stories portray the bodhisattva as making his sacrifice to a recipient who is often not only his spiritual inferior, but who may even harbor evil intentions for the gift.

There is an illustrative story in the *Da zhidu lun* concerning Śāriputra's earlier attempt to fulfill the perfection of generosity.[15] Sixty aeons ago, while he formerly trod the bodhisattva path, Śāriputra was approached by a beggar who demanded his eye. Asked why he wanted the eye instead of his body or his personal property, the beggar replied, "I don't need your body or your goods; I only want your eye. If you really practice generosity, you will give it to me." Śāriputra took out one of his eyes and gave it to the beggar. The beggar took the eye, and in Śāriputra's presence, sniffed it and spit on it, then threw it to the ground and stepped on it. Śāriputra thought to himself how difficult it would be to save such a malicious person. Despite having no use for the eye, he requested it, and when it was given to him, he threw it to the ground and stepped on it. "Such people are impossible to save. Better to train oneself and more quickly escape from *saṃsāra.*" Henceforth Śāriputra left the path of the bodhisattva and returned to the Lesser Vehicle.

The point here for this Mahāyāna commentator is that Śāriputra's failing—unlike those who remain zealously committed to the bodhisattva path—was to regret his gift on account of the recipient's lack of appreciation or worth. Generosity is only perfected when there is not the slightest reservation. Śāntideva's cost-benefit analysis, that one should not destroy one's life for someone of lesser spiritual qualities, seems by contrast designed to inhibit his potentially overzealous contemporaries from imitating the bodhisattva's heroic deeds too literally. Despite clear canonical precedent, it is not unlikely that such extreme acts of self-sacrifice were unsettling to a domesticated Mahāyāna establishment of Śāntideva's age (ca. 7th-8th cent.). If the late seventh-century Chinese pilgrim Yijing is to be believed, there may indeed have been grounds for this concern in medieval India at a time roughly contemporaneous with Śāntideva.

[14] For example, he cites *dehadāna* tales from the *Nārāyaṇaparipṛcchā-sūtra* (Bendall 1897-1902: 21.1-22) and from the *Vajradhvaja-sūtra* (Bendall 1897-1902: 23.13-26.3). In both cases the bodhisattva is called upon to offer of himself whatever is asked to anyone who petitions him, always without hesitation or regret.

[15] T 1509, 25: 145a.18-29 (my summary and translation); see also Lamotte (1944-80, T. II: 701-702). I am indebted for this reference to Ohnuma (2000b: 58-59).

Yijing (635-713) travelled to India from China in 671 by boat via Sumatra, where he stayed to study Sanskrit. He continued his travels to east India in 673 before making his way to Nālandā and other famous centers of learning in north India. He left India in 687 and returned again via Sumatra, where he wrote an account of his travels sometime before 691. He returned to China in 695, after which he began translating the Indic texts he acquired into Chinese.

The two chapters of this travelogue most relevant to our discussion are Chapter 38: "Burning the Body is Not Acceptable" and Chapter 39: "Bystanders Are Guilty Too."[16] Here Yijing wrestles with a hermeneutical dilemma: how should a monk properly regard the sacrifice of the body motif clearly lauded in scripture against the *vinaya* regulations that appear to forbid monks from harming the body? In this regard he is especially concerned with young, impressionable monks being led astray:

> For those within the assembly of renunciants, there is but one path. Those who are at the beginner level tend to be hardcore; they are not yet trained in the scriptural canon. They put their faith in their predecessors, using the burning of fingers as a way to make extreme efforts, and they regard the burning of the flesh as a great blessing. They do this solely in accordance with their own feelings, making judgments on the basis of their own thoughts. As is made clear in scripture, these activities belong to the realm of the laity. If they (the laity) are exhorted to offer even their own bodies, how much more the rest of their "external" wealth. Therefore [this practice] is only referred to in the scriptures if people have generated the aspiration for enlightenment. [The scriptures] do not make reference to the assembly of renunciants [participating in this practice]. The reason is that people who have left the household are restricted by the *vinaya-piṭaka*.

His solution then is clear: scriptural accounts of bodhisattvas offering their bodies in sacrifice are possible only for laymen who aspire to complete awakening. Monks have taken on a different calling:

> However, [the bodhisattva] Sarvasattvapriyadarśin, who was a layman, burned his arm as an offering—truly that was appropriate.[17] It was possible for the Bodhisattva to give away his male and female children.[18] So should we have monks seek children in order to give them away? The Mahāsattva destroyed his eyes, destroyed his body,

[16] *Nanhai ji gui nei fa zhuan* [*Account of Buddhism Sent Back Home from the Southern Seas*], T 2125, 54: 231a.28-c.16. A complete translation of these chapters can be found in Boucher (2008: 35-38).

[17] The bodhisattva Sarvasattvapriyadarśin's burning his arm is described in Chapter 22 of the *Saddharmapuṇḍarīka-sūtra* (Kern and Nanjio [1908-12] 1970: 411.6 ff.). Sarvasattvapriyadarśin, desiring to pay homage to the relics of the recently departed Buddha Candravimalasūryaprabhāsaśrī, lit his own arm on fire before *stūpas* containing the buddha's ashes as an act of heroic worship. A similar tale is alluded to in the *Rāṣṭrapāla* (Finot 1901: 23.1-2).

[18] A clear reference to the story of Viśvantara.

> but suppose that we required mendicants to use their bodies or their eyes to practice giving! King *Ṛṣinanda killed people, but how could this be the practice of one who adheres to the vinaya?[19] Maitrībala sacrificed his body, but this is not what a monastic disciple should do.[20]
>
> I have recently heard that youngsters, valiantly aspiring for enlightenment, think that if they burn their bodies, they will achieve highest enlightenment. As a result, they follow one after another in this practice, flippantly throwing away their bodies.... They should comply with and firmly observe the *prātimokṣa*, requite the four benevolences we receive,[21] and steadfastly engage in meditation in the hope of extracting themselves from the three realms of existence.... To hastily cut off one's own life—truly I have yet to hear a reason for this. The sin of suicide is second only to [the violations of] the first section (i.e., the *pārājika* offenses). When I examine the *vinaya-piṭaka*, I do not see any license for this practice.... There certainly are those who practice the bodhisattva training and who do not accept the precepts and regulations. They disregard their own lives to save others. They are necessarily beyond our discussion here.

And Yijing makes clear that the practice of sacrificing one's body as an act of religious zeal was not a literary relic from hoary antiquity but a recurring practice of medieval Indian Buddhism:

> In the Ganges River, any number of people are killed daily [by self-drowning]. In the vicinity of the hill at [Bodh-]gāya, those who kill themselves are not few. Some don't eat, starving themselves. Others climb trees and throw themselves down. These behaviors are misguided. The Blessed One judged such actions to be heretical. Furthermore, there are some who castrate themselves—this is profoundly contrary to the *vinaya*. Even those who regard such action as wrong fear committing a violation themselves and so do not dare admonish others. But if one sacrifices one's life for this reason, then one mistakes the fundamental point of one's whole life. This is why the Buddha forbade it. With regard to the above-mentioned persons, the broadly learned do not themselves consent to this practice.

The fact that Yijing was an eyewitness to contemporary practice in India makes his discussion of *dehadāna* particularly illuminating.[22]

[19] Xianyu was one of the Buddha's former lives as a king. According to the *Mahāyāna-Mahāparinirvāṇa-sūtra* (T 374, 12: 434c.8-21), King Xianyu was devoted to the Mahāyāna scriptures. When he heard that 500 brahmins reviled them, he had them executed. These brahmins were reborn in hell as a result of their impiety.

[20] The story of King Maitrībala can be found in, among other places, *Jātakamālā*, Chapter 8.

[21] Lists of the four benevolences vary, but often include parents, sentient beings, kings, and the three jewels.

[22] It is worth pointing out, however, that this is not always the case. Gregory Schopen has noted on more than one occasion that there are a number of passages in Yijing's travel record that in fact constitute citations from the *Mūlasarvāstivāda-vinaya*, not eyewitness reports. See Schopen (1992: 25-26, n. 19) and Schopen (1995: 119, n. 4). The failure to recognize this has occasionally misled scholars who took these passages as records of actual practice and not as the normative prescriptions they were.

Yijing was clearly concerned that young, impressionable monks would be misled by their elders, some of whom apparently took the scriptural passages concerning the gift of the body literally. The *dehadāna* narratives frequently proclaim the body to be worthless, which affords the bodhisattva an opportunity to "extract the essence from his insubstantial body" by sacrificing it for others. Yijing by contrast emphasizes the rarity of a human rebirth. It would be foolish from his point of view for a monk to squander the opportunity to use his body for spiritual advancement.

In fact, Yijing is principally concerned with adherence to the *vinaya*, since it was the desire to acquire *vinaya* texts that motivated his journey to India from the start. He therefore is emphatic that those who have left the household must first and foremost submit to monastic law—and this most definitely prohibits suicide and encouraging others to destroy their flesh. But it is also interesting that Yijing admits that such extreme acts of giving would be appropriate for *lay* bodhisattvas, i.e., those individuals, as he says, "who practice the bodhisattva training and who do not accept the precepts and regulations."

We see in these statements a profound ambivalence. Clearly he is aware of the scriptural precedent for this form of self-sacrifice, a precedent that a number of monks in medieval India apparently took to heart. But at the same time he wants to declare that ordained recluses, regardless of their spiritual orientation, must adhere to a different norm. The hermeneutical principle is clear: if there is a perceived conflict between *sūtra* and *vinaya*, *vinaya* wins. Moreover, it is also clear that Yijing is equally concerned with this practice among Chinese monks, who had long engaged in the custom of burning the flesh—particularly the fingers—as an act of heroic devotion.[23] We are, in the end, left with the impression that the sacrifice of the body in pursuit of enlightenment was not perceived as a perverse oddity from an ancient era. It had remained, ironically, a living option for those on the fast track toward enlightenment, yet one that made representatives of the monastic establishment more than a little uncomfortable.

In the *Rāṣṭrapāla* the extreme sacrifice of the *dehadāna* stories represented a model of bodhisattva behavior—not necessarily to be imitated literally, but homologized in the sacrifices entailed by

[23] On the practice of self-immolation among medieval Chinese monks, see Gernet (1960), Jan (1965), and more recently, Kieschnick (1997: 35-50), and Benn (1998, 2001, and 2007). Chinese monks were also motivated by scriptural precedent, especially the tale of Sarvasattvapriyadarśin in the Lotus Sūtra (see Gernet 1960: 536 ff., Benn 2001: 287-331, and 2007: 54-77). Nevertheless, this was a matter of considerable debate in Chinese Buddhist circles, often couched as a choice between the priority of Mahāyāna virtues and "Hīnayāna" discipline. Benn (1998: 312-16) has argued convincingly that the apocryphal *Shoulengyan jing* (T 945), which advocates burning the body so as to eliminate karmic defilements, may well have been composed in direct response to Yijing's critique of the practice.

ascetic discipline. Immediately after finishing the list of references to the fifty previous life stories, the author of the *Rāṣṭrapāla* has the Buddha state:

> Formerly doing hundreds of such difficult to carry out acts, I felt no distress at that time while seeking the highest pure enlightenment.
>
> There is nothing internal or external which I have not given when I trained in morality, tolerance, exertion, meditation, stratagems, and wisdom.
>
> I gave the flesh, skin, marrow, and blood from my very own body. When I was living in caves in the hinterlands, my body was drained.
>
> The vehicle of ascetic discipline (*dhutayāna*) taught by the Victors is the one in which they applied themselves and became the Victors. In that ascetic discipline I constantly exerted myself when I was steadfastly training in the past.
>
> Such are the lofty vows which I observed while I was training. Hearing about the training for them, [the bodhisattva] has no desire for even a single word more (Finot 1901: 27.11-28.2).

The vehicle of ascetic discipline, manifested in the practice of the *dhutaguṇa*s, represented the proper sacrifice of the bodhisattva, the only means by which his goal of supreme, perfect enlightenment could be achieved as it was achieved by all buddhas.

Buddhist Asceticism: the Dhutaguṇas

The *dhutaguṇa*s, literally "qualities of purification," are the traditional set of ascetic disciplines in both Mainstream and Mahāyāna literature which came to characterize, or rather standardize, the rigorous life of the forest-dwelling monk. They are variously listed as twelve or thirteen, although some texts further reduce or expand the list.[24] Despite such variations, there is considerable overlap in the various formulations. One of the standard thirteen member lists is as follows:

[24] For various lists of the ascetic disciplines, see Ehara et al. (1961: 27-38), Bapat (1964), Dantinne (1991), and Ray (1994: 292-323). Bapat (1964: xxi) and Ray (1994: 297) suggest that the twelve-member list belongs to Mahāyāna literature while the thirteen-member list became standard in Pāli (i.e., Theravādin) sources. Although there is some truth to this pattern, the situation is somewhat more complicated. For example, Dantinne has noted (1991: 64-55, nn. 29-30) that the Mahāyāna text, the *Akṣobhyatathāgatavyūha*, has a twelve-member list in one of its Chinese translations (T 310 [6], 11:102b.28-c.2) but a thirteen-member list in its Tibetan translation (cf. also Dantinne 1983: 87-88), suggesting that the precise formulation of the list remained fluid even within one textual tradition. Moreover, the Chinese *Ekottarāgama-sūtra* (*Zengyi ahan jing*, T 125, 2: 557b.8-9) also knows a list with twelve members, indicating that not all Mainstream sources can be contrasted with Mahāyāna traditions.

1. *piṇḍapātika*: one who subsists only upon alms and relinquishes accepting invitations to eat in lay households
2. *sāvadānapiṇḍapātika*: one who goes on alms rounds systematically, without showing preference for some houses over others
3. *ekāsanika*: one who eats in one sitting only
4. *khalupaścādbhaktika*: one who does not eat after the appropriate time (i.e., midday)
5. *traicīvarika*: one who wears only the three monastic robes
6. *nāmatika*: one who wears a woolen garment
7. *pāṃsukūlika*: one who wears refuse-rag robes, i.e., does not accept donations of cloth from patrons
8. *āraṇyaka*: one who dwells in the wilderness
9. *vṛkṣamūlika*: one who lives at the foot of a tree
10. *ābhyavakāśika*: one who dwells in the open air, i.e., without roof or cover
11. *śmāśānika*: one who dwells in cremation grounds
12. *naiṣadika* (*naiṣadyika*): one who remains in the sitting posture without lying down
13. *yathāsaṃstarika*: one who accepts whatever seat is offered[25]

Pāli sources usually include *pattapiṇḍika*, "one who eats only a single bowl of food,"[26] in place of *nāmatika*. Although the thirteen-member list tends to appear only in relatively late Pāli literature, a number of the items show up throughout the canon and in other Mainstream texts.[27]

In his detailed discussion of the forest orientation across Buddhist traditions, Reginald Ray argues that texts like the *Vimuktimārga* "provide us with a glimpse of life in the forest," constituting "a description of thirteen *dhutaguṇas*, much as they must have been practiced by forest renunciants" (Ray 1994: 298). There is a danger, however, in confusing normative textual expressions with actual practice. In fact, their very standardization within the literature into twelve or thirteen item lists may suggest an attempt to domesticate a potentially subversive movement, to contain the threat such practices represented to the sedentary monastic establishment. Such a threat could be neutralized by co-option—adopting but weakening the ascetic impulse—or by restriction, a tightening of the ranks of those who qualify for such strictures.

[25] See Dantinne (1991: 5) and Bapat (1964: 5-7) for this list of thirteen, with some variation as to order. The Chinese translation of the *Vimuktimārga* also includes a list of thirteen members (*Jietuo dao lun*, T 1648, 32: 404b.20-406c.20). This text has been linked with the Abhayagiri fraternity in Sri Lanka; it subsequently became lost in Pāli when the Mahāvihāra attained supremacy. For arguments on this affiliation, see Bapat (1964: xxviii-xxix) and Norman (1983: 113-14).

[26] See, e.g., *Visuddhimagga* 2.39 (Warren and Koasambi [1950] 1989) and Dantinne (1991: 15).

[27] Complete lists in Pāli include the *Parivāra* (*Vinaya-piṭaka*, V, 131 and 193), *Milindapañha* (359), *Visuddhimagga*, Chap. 2. An alternative and almost certainly earlier list which incorporates the thirteen practices can be found in the *Theragāthā* (vv. 842-865); on this list see Ray (1994: 308-310).

Buddhaghosa's *Visuddhimagga* may be an example of the former strategy. After listing and describing the thirteen classic *dhutaṅgas* ("limbs of purification") in Chapter Two of his classic fifth-century compendium, Buddhaghosa notes that there are three degrees of conformity to the actual practice: those who are strict in their observance of the discipline, those who are mediocre in adherence, and those whose commitment is "mild" (*Visuddhimagga* 2.20 ff.).[28] For example, Buddhaghosa describes the manifold ways that one who observes the practice of wearing only refuse-rag robes might obtain materials with which to make his garment. Such a monk could obtain them from cremation grounds, from the street, or from a piece that has been gnawed by animals, but he may not accept cloth as a personal gift from a householder. Nevertheless, Buddhaghosa observes, there are gradations of adherence:

> The *grades* are these. There are three kinds of refuse-rag wearers: the strict, the medium, and the mild. Herein, one who takes it only from a charnel ground is strict. One who takes one left [by someone, thinking], 'One gone forth will take it' is medium. One who takes one given by being placed at his feet [by a bhikkhu] is mild (Ñāṇamoli [1975] 1999: 63).

In other words, Buddhaghosa allows that an ascetic practitioner remains faithful to his discipline even though he accepts a gift of robes from a fellow monk. While Ray wants to see in Buddhaghosa's casuistry the culmination of a long process of monasticization of the forest tradition, I am more inclined to see here an intra-monastic struggle. Buddhaghosa's solution allows him to maintain a normative place for settled monasticism while at the same time domesticating this more radical threat to its authority.

In the *Milindapañha* we see a similar praise of the ascetic disciplines. The monastic protagonist Nāgasena goes so far as to say that anyone, including a layman, who has achieved *nibbāna* has done so by the practice of the *dhutaguṇas* in former lives.[29] But Nāgasena also reminds King Milinda that there are individuals who are not worthy to undertake these special vows:

> Furthermore, whichever person, Great King, who undertakes the ascetic disciplines but has evil desires, is overcome with covetousness, is hypocritical, greedy, gluttonous, desirous of profit, desirous of fame, desirous of renown, undisciplined, unaccomplished, unsuitable, unworthy, unbefitting [of the *saṅgha*], he incurs a double punishment and incurs the destruction of all virtues (*Milindapañha* 357).

[28] Warren and Kosambi ([1950] 1989).

[29] *Milindapañha* 353: *na mahārāja dhutaguṇesu pubbāsevanaṃ vinā ekissa yeva jātiyā arahattaṃ sacchikiriyā hoti* ("There is no realization of arhatship in one lifetime without the former adherence to the ascetic disciplines").

Nāgasena goes on to say that such an individual will be ridiculed by and expelled from the monastic community in this life and will suffer torments in the Avīci Hell in the next.

Again, Ray, consistent with his thesis on the estrangement of forest dwellers from sedentary monastics, sees in such statements an attempt to restrict the *dhutaguṇa*s to monks in good standing with the establishment:

> Like the *Parivāra*, then, the *Milindapañha* says that only monastics, and among these only those deemed worthy, are permitted to practice the *dhutaguṇas* without incurring negative consequences. For the *Milindapañha*, only a select few have the right to practice them, and the text explicitly mentions only virtuous members of the monastic order as qualified. It seems, moreover, that they may retire to the forest only when their obligations to the monastic order are fully in order (that is, they remain in good standing) ... It may be noted how easily this restriction can provide a basis for the repudiation of Buddhist renunciants following the *dhutaguṇa*s who may not be *prātimokṣa*-following *bhikṣus* at all or who are otherwise deemed unfit according to canons of settled monasticism (Ray 1994: 305).

Ray has, in my opinion, conflated two separate issues. It is almost certain that wilderness-dwellers were always members of established monastic orders, and as monks, they would very probably have been expected to fulfill a number of the obligations incumbent on Buddhist renunciants generally. Certainly the *Rāṣṭrapāla* assumes as much, and so do many other texts, Mainstream and Mahāyāna alike. In fact, the restrictions pressed for by the *Milindapañha* make little sense unless one assumes an ongoing relationship between different but connected monastic orientations. Rather than representing an attempt to repudiate forest dwelling *per se*, the *Milindapañha* may be more concerned with reining in "irregular" practitioners: those who are motivated by base concerns—a topic the *Rāṣṭrapāla*'s authors harp on endlessly—as well as, perhaps, forest monks whose relationship with the *saṅgha* had become more distant than its senior members were comfortable with. In other words, I see no evidence for a pre-monastic or non-monastic *dhutaguṇa* tradition in Buddhist literature as assumed by Ray. The practice of these additional ascetic disciplines is in my view a reformist movement within Mainstream Buddhism, one that was co-opted also in some Mahāyāna circles and continues to this day among Theravādin monastics.[30]

[30] Many scholars, Ray included, would like to see the *dhutaguṇa* tradition as representing the original Buddhist lifestyle practiced by the Buddha and his immediate disciplines, a lifestyle that was eventually lost as later generations of monks became increasingly sedentary (see more recently this assumption in Bailey and Mabbett 2003: 161 ff.). Such scholars may be right. But I would argue that we have no direct evidence for the lifestyle of the Buddha and his earliest followers. We should not, therefore, mistake polemic from later *dhutaguṇa* factions as historical statements of fact.

Asceticism in the Rāṣṭrapāla

There can be no doubt that living in the wilderness in order to practice a rigorous form of reclusion was central to the orientation of the *Rāṣṭrapāla*. Over and over again the authors of the *Rāṣṭrapāla* exhort those on the bodhisattva path to "take pleasure in the wilderness" and "dwell alone like a rhinoceros"; to "not abandon residence in the wilderness"; to take "pleasure in lodging in secluded hinterlands"; to "always dwell in forests and caves"; and to "frequent the wilderness and manifold hinterlands." Specific *dhutaguṇa* practices are listed in the story of Prince Puṇyaraśmi's going forth after the death of the Buddha in Chapter Two: "Having gone forth (from the household), he became a wearer of the three robes; he always practiced begging for alms, and he only sits (never lying down)" (Finot 1901: 57.10-11). When the Buddha describes the sacrifices he made lifetime after lifetime in pursuit of enlightenment, the *dhutaguṇas* are clearly placed center stage:

> The vehicle of ascetic discipline (*dhutayāna*) taught by the Victors is the one in which they applied themselves and became the Victors. In that ascetic discipline I constantly exerted myself when I was steadfastly training in the past (Finot 1901: 27.17-18).

Here the vehicle of ascetic discipline (*dhutayāna*) is identified with the vehicle of the bodhisattva, that is, with the Mahāyāna itself. All buddhas who have come before have followed this discipline and all who hope to achieve complete and perfect enlightenment in the future will have to as well. In addition, the authors of the *Rāṣṭrapāla* assumed that bodhisattvas who engaged in such rigorous discipline would not be welcome at established monasteries near towns and villages and would as a result have to resort to the forest:

> Even when they are reviled on all sides, these sons of mine, remembering my words during the final period (of the Dharma), will dwell in forests in the hinterland at that time (Finot 1901: 31.13-14).

> Those who are disciplined in morality and virtue will be despised in the last period (of the Dharma). Abandoning villages, kingdoms, and cities, they will dwell in the wilderness and forest (Finot 1901: 31.17-18).[31]

World renunciation is most centrally defined by sexual abstinence. Thus, one of the common traits of the ascetic orientation within Buddhist texts, indeed for ascetic factions in a great many religious traditions, is a disdain for women as temptresses who threaten the chastity of male recluses. Here again, the *Rāṣṭrapāla* is no exception.

[31] There are other stories of bodhisattvas being expelled from towns and kingdoms and forced to dwell in forests in the hinterland. See, for example, Chapter 35 of the *Samādhirāja-sūtra* (Dutt [1939-1959] 1984, II, pt. 3: 491.6 ff.).

In a long discussion in Chapter Two between King Arciṣmat and the young prince Puṇyaraśmi, whom we learn later is a former incarnation of Śākyamuni Buddha, Puṇyaraśmi rejects his father's attempts to shower him with every possible sensual pleasure:

> "Your majesty, no one has done anything unpleasant to me; but I have no desire today for sensual pleasures. All that are dear are like enemies, unfit for attachment, which causes one to fall into the abyss of the defilements and unfortunate destinies.
>
> "These women are pleasing to ignorant, stupid people. They are great pitfalls, bound by the noose of Māra. They are always condemned by the (spiritually) ennobled. How can I cherish those who are the source of affliction in the hells and unfortunate destinies?
>
> "These women are beautiful and pleasurable only on the surface. On account of its impurities, I have no interest in this contraption of sinews and bones. Oozing of excretions—blood, urine, and excrement—how can I delight in what are surely only suitable for a cemetery? (Finot 1901: 43.14-19).

Such misogynist passages have increasingly made it difficult to affirm the inclusive spirit of the early Mahāyāna in contradistinction to the monastic elitism so often ascribed to Mainstream authors. For example, the following remarks by Nancy Schuster are typical:

> There are many Mahāyāna Buddhist *sūtras* which have something to say about women. Some are quite hostile; many of these uphold the old clerical biases against women which have cropped up from time to time in the various Buddhist sects ... But there are many Mahāyāna scriptures which insist that only the ignorant make distinctions between the religious aspirations and intellectual and spiritual capacities of men and women. This position is the only one which is consistent with the Mahāyāna doctrine of the emptiness of all phenomenon (Schuster 1981: 25).

Alan Sponberg (1992) has offered, in my view, a more nuanced appreciation of the multiplicity of voices operating in Buddhist literature with regard to the status of women. He sees essentially four major attitudes expressed: beginning with soteriological inclusiveness (nirvāṇa/arhatship available to all), a somewhat later institutional androcentrism developed that privileged male authority, and this view co-existed with a more negative ascetic misogyny that projected the psychological distress of celibacy upon women, now seen as objectified desire. Lastly, a soteriological androgyny developed in the much later Vajrayāna tradition which positively revalorized the feminine in dramatic fashion. Sponberg summarizes his view of the development of misogynous attitudes thus:

> The most blatantly misogynous texts of the Pali literature are found in the *jātaka* stories, an (originally) noncanonical Buddhist appropria-

> tion of popular animal tales and hero legends. This relative (even if not exclusive) contrast between views in the *sutta* literature versus those in the more popular genres further supports my thesis that misogyny initially was resisted by the early tradition, but eventually found more of a home among those later factions of the community who defined their soteriological goals more in terms of ascetic purification than in terms of psychological enlightenment (Sponberg 1992, 35, n. 29).

On the one hand, Sponberg's thesis is confirmed by what we see in the *Rāṣṭrapāla*, which not only defined its goals in terms of ascetic discipline, but drew upon a wealth of *jātaka* stories to lend support for these goals. However, I think it would be overstating the case to see these different attitudes in terms of temporal development. Sponberg's advocacy for a multiplicity of voices almost certainly applies to Buddhist literature of all periods. Clearly some very early texts express a sharply misogynous message. Consider, for example, this passage from the *Aṭṭhakavagga*, put in the mouth of the Buddha:

> Looking upon Craving, Aversion, and Passion (i.e., the daughters of Māra), I have not the least desire for sexual intercourse. What is this thing, full of urine and feces? I would not wish to touch it even with my foot (*Sutta-nipāta* v. 835).

These sentiments, as we just saw, are echoed in the *Rāṣṭrapāla*. I would also take issue with Sponberg's view that virulent misogyny only appears in *later* Mahāyāna literature as it developed its own ascetic wing within the *saṅgha*: "Although the early Mahāyāna reaffirmed the basic principle of soteriological inclusiveness with its universalization of the bodhisattva path, a religious ideal it held open to all—men and women, monastic and lay—this rejection of institutional androcentrism did not entail a corresponding rejection of ascetic misogyny."[32] We see very little evidence in the *Rāṣṭrapāla*—or in other early Mahāyāna texts we will consider—for the kind of soteriological inclusiveness Sponberg and others so often refer to.[33]

[32] Sponberg (1992: 21).

[33] In this regard it is also worth noting the observations by Gregory Schopen, based on his survey of the inscriptional records of donor activity from the earliest times through the Gupta period: "Although the full details have yet to be worked out, it appears that the appearance or presence of monks calling themselves *śākyabhikṣus* everywhere in the fourth-fifth century C.E. occurs in conjunction with the marked decline or disappearance of the participation of nuns in recorded Buddhist religious activity. The fact that these *śākyabhikṣus* are almost certainly Mahāyāna monks may seem curious, but it appears that the emergence of the Mahāyāna in the fourth-fifth century coincided with a marked decline in the role of women of all kinds in the practice of Indian Buddhism. What is important for us to note here, however, is that until that time—contrary to Oldenberg—nuns, indeed women as a whole, appear to have been very numerous, very active, and, as a consequence, influential in the actual Buddhist communities of early India" (Schopen 1988-89: 165). As if to confirm these observations, it is worth pointing out that nowhere does the *Rāṣṭrapāla* refer to the order of nuns, either in its injunctions or in its critiques. They are for all intents and purposes invisible within this text.

On the contrary, we will see a sharp narrowing of bodhisattva membership in favor of a highly selective, wilderness-dwelling fraternity of monks who had little room for women or the laity.

Wilderness Dwelling and the Dhutaguṇas *in Other Mahāyāna Texts*

Distinct echoes of the *Rāṣṭrapāla* and its predilection for wilderness asceticism can be found in a number of Mahāyāna *sūtras*, with, as one might expect, varying degrees of enthusiasm. Few are more fervid, however, than the *Ratnarāśi* (RR), a text made more readily accessible recently by Jonathan Silk's superb edition, translation, and study (1994).[34] From the very start, its authors make clear their bias in favor of the *śramaṇa* who "follows the yogic practice of cultivating the path," "who delights in dwelling in the wilderness," "who abides in the *dhutaguṇas*," and "who wanders alone like a rhinoceros."[35] The true monk—and there can be no doubt again that such an individual is part of a monastic community[36]—is described as "alone, unaccompanied, with nothing on which to rely, without possessions, without chattels" (RR V.6). He is entreated to take his alms systematically, in conformity with standard *dhutaguṇa* practice, showing no preference for generous patrons or disfavor toward those who give nothing (RR V.11). Although he practices alms begging, he should refrain from being intimate with specific patrons or dropping hints as to what he might prefer in his bowl (RR VI.10-11). Moreover, the ideal monk is one who is content to acquire his robes from the refuse heap, taking no delight in adorning his body with new clothing (RR VII.1).

Closely related to the *Ratnarāśi* is the *Kāśyapa-parivarta*, a text also within the *Mahāratnakūṭa* collection of the Chinese and Tibetan canons.[37] The *Kāśyapa-parivarta* (KP) overlaps with the *Ratnarāśi* along a number of thematic lines, but it also exhibits considerably more polemic in its overtly pro-Mahāyāna and anti-Hīnayāna stance. Nevertheless, it too is clearly in the pro-forest camp. The *Kāśyapa-parivarta* assumes that a true bodhisattva "will delight in the wilderness without wantonness" (KP §17) or "without deceit" (KP §19); "he dwells in the forest with great enthusiasm" (KP §25).[38] This *sūtra* is particularly sensitive to duplicity, charg-

[34] My references to the RR are by the section and sub-sections used by Silk in his edition and translation. Translations are his unless otherwise stated.

[35] RR I.2 (numbers 47, 56, 58, and 61 in Silk; translation slightly modified).

[36] Cf. RR V.7: "If he is a dweller in the wilderness abode, he should be bound by the vows of the monastic disciplinary rule."

[37] On the relationship between these two texts, see esp. the remarks in Silk (1994: 23 ff). References to the *Kāśyapa-parivarta* are to Staël-Holstein ([1926] 1977).

[38] Skt. *satkṛtyāraṇyavāsaḥ*. The sense of *satkṛtya* here is much stronger than "piously" or "respectfully." The authors intend, I think, to suggest something of a zealous, even fanatical, commitment to life in the wilderness, though, of course, they mean this in a positive sense.

ing that all too many renunciants engage in seemingly disciplined behavior—including the rigorous practices of the *dhutaguṇas*—only to elicit the admiration of others.[39]

If the *Ratnarāśi* and the *Kāśyapa-parivarta*, along with the *Rāṣṭrapāla*, can safely be placed within the sub-genre of texts espousing wilderness dwelling for the monastic bodhisattva, then we might be somewhat surprised to discover that another text ostensibly dedicated to the household dwelling bodhisattva, the *Ugra-paripṛcchā*, also belongs within this corpus.[40] The first two-thirds of the text describe at length the practices of the lay bodhisattva, only to provide repeated opportunities to expose the faults of household life and the desirability of leaving it behind. Having soundly deconstructed the house dwelling option as a viable path toward buddhahood, the author delivers his *coup de grâce*:

> There has never been a bodhisattva who dwells in the household and who has awakened to unexcelled, perfect enlightenment. They all, moreover, having gone forth from the household, fixed their thoughts on the wilderness with a predilection toward the wilderness. Having gone to the wilderness, they awakened to unexcelled, perfect enlightenment. And [it is there that] they acquired the prerequisites (Skt. *saṃbhāra*) [for enlightenment; i.e., merit and gnosis].[41]

This passage unequivocally makes renunciation of the household a necessity for the bodhisattva intent upon eventual enlightenment. Clearly the goal of the *Ugra-paripṛcchā* is not merely to asceticize the laity, but also to argue for the ultimate incompatibility of the spiritual orientation of the Mahāyāna with life in the household, a life which places far too many demands upon one who is setting out for a goal as ambitious as complete buddhahood. In fact, mere renunciation is not enough. The lay bodhisattva must leave behind not only the comforts of the household, but, having gone forth as a *bhikṣu*, he must also relinquish the sedentary habits of the monastery. Here we see clear parallels with the wilderness orientation which we find loudly proclaimed in the *Rāṣṭrapāla*:

> I should examine the matter as follows: "I came to the wilderness on account of being afraid of such frightening and terrifying things [as inauspicious rebirths, etc. as mentioned in a previous passage]. I cannot be freed from such frightening and terrifying things as these

[39] See esp. KP §§121-126 on the various caliber of *śramaṇas*.

[40] The linking of these four texts into a single sub-genre is not merely the result of my own random search through the Buddhist canon. The seventh/eighth-century Indian monk Śāntideva quotes from all four of these texts, together with the *Samādhirāja-sūtra*, in Chapter 11 ("Praise of the Wilderness") of his *Śikṣāsamuccaya* (Bendall 1897-1902: 193-201). Thus in some monastic minds within the classical Indian Buddhist world, these texts were explicitly associated with the *āraṇyaka* vocation.

[41] Stog Palace Manuscript, vol. 39 (Ca), 24a.3-5. See also Nattier (2003: 265-66).

by living in the household, by living in company (with others), or by living without exerting myself, without applying myself diligently to yoga, or by thinking distractedly. All bodhisattvas *mahāsattva*s who appeared in the past were delivered from every fear by dwelling in the wilderness; in this way they obtained the fearlessness which is unexcelled, perfect enlightenment. All bodhisattvas *mahāsattva*s who will appear in the future will be delivered from every fear by dwelling in the wilderness; in this way they will obtain the fearlessness which is unexcelled, perfect enlightenment. All bodhisattvas *mahāsattva*s who appear in the present and who have obtained unexcelled, perfect enlightenment are delivered from every fear by dwelling in the wilderness; in this way they obtained the fearlessness which is unexcelled, perfect enlightenment. Therefore, I too, frightened and terrified here, and desiring to transcend every fear and attain the fearless state, should dwell in the wilderness."[42]

When we start to look for it explicitly, we begin to notice how wide-ranging the wilderness-dwelling motif is within Mahāyāna *sūtra* literature, even when it is not the central preoccupation of any given text. In fact, wilderness dwelling shows up in places where we might least expect it, including texts which are overtly hostile to the monks who practice it.[43] That even some Mahāyāna *sūtra*s qualify or oppose the wilderness for its members reminds us that we are witnessing one dimension of the dialectic of tradition.

The Dialectic of Tradition

Buddhist reclusion has long struggled between two poles: the untamed renunciant on the outermost fringes of human civilization, an ascetic who earned his reputation from years of austerity; and the domesticated monk, sedentary and respectable, perhaps scholarly, but more often a ritual specialist attuned to the needs of the laity. These two poles, of course, are essentially coterminous with Weber's charismatic and bureaucratic modes of leadership. Buddhist monks come down at various places along this continuum, to some degree in response to the socio-economic milieu in which they find themselves.[44] A fully domesticated *saṅgha* must reject the forest option. The former simply cannot hold their own against the latter when it comes to securing lay patronage. And the *Rāṣṭrapāla* makes it clear that patronage was never far from the minds of their contemporaries.

[42] Stog Palace Manuscript, vol. 39 (Ca), 37a.6-b.6. See also Nattier (2003: 298). On wilderness dwelling in the *Ugra-paripṛcchā* more generally, see Nattier (2003: 130-31).

[43] See Boucher (2008: 56-61) for a discussion and translation of Mahāyāna texts which express concern if not contempt for the presumed spiritual superiority of the wilderness-dwelling vocation.

[44] See Tambiah (1984: 329-34) for an important qualification of Weber's typology, a qualification essentially confirmed by my sources as well.

However, it was the very success of wilderness-dwelling monks in acquiring patronage that eventually compromised this ascetic thrust. This dialectic—reform, domestication, and renewed reform—is a recurring pattern in monastic culture everywhere:

> As is well known, monastic wealth became a major source of corruption and relaxation of ascetic standards. Paradoxically, laymen tended to bestow donations and protection on monasteries or orders that they perceived as purer or holier, in a process usually leading to further monastic slackening and need for reform.[45]

The authors of the *Rāṣṭrapāla* are themselves aware of wilderness dwellers whose motives they regarded as thoroughly compromised:

> Even among those who dwell in the forest, their thoughts will be preoccupied with the village. The mind of those who burn with the fire of the defilements is not steady.
>
> Forgetting all the virtues of the Buddha as well as the rules of training, the ascetic disciplines, and stratagems, those full of pride, arrogance, and conceit fall to the dreadful Avīci Hell (Finot 1901, 30.13-16).

These wilderness dwellers are judged to be hypocrites because they have adopted this lifestyle expressly for the elevated status it conferred and the accompanying patronage such a status generated.

The *Rāṣṭrapāla* for its part wants to have it both ways. Its authors clearly sought to co-opt the charismatic power of the genuine wilderness ascetic, distant, aloof, and therefore unbeholden to patrons. In fact, for these bodhisattva critics, it is precisely the status quo relationship between monks and the laity, a relationship founded on the exchange of material and symbolic commodities, that had become disordered.[46] Corrupt monks, from their point of view, were in the habit of coaxing undeserved patronage from unsuspecting donors, thereby depriving the latter of the full fruits of their investment. The wilderness-dwelling faction for their part sought to reestablish the mutually beneficial relationship between donors and proper fields of merit. Thus the *Rāṣṭrapāla* and like-minded texts were in part engaged in a fundamentally conservative agenda: the purification from the *saṅgha* of renunciants who had deceitfully undermined the foundations of this transaction. But they also intended to locate the wilderness monk's power within the structure and authority of

[45] Silber (1995, 148-49); see also her comments on this pattern and the role of virtuoso radicalism in it (42-43 and 53-54).

[46] I am reminded here of the remarks of Ivan Strenski, who argued—rightly, I think—that the process of the domestication of the *saṅgha* was not, contra Weber and Weberians, a degeneration from a purer, peripatetic life, but was instead a natural outgrowth of the system of non-reciprocal, generalized exchange between the laity and the monastic establishment, be they sedentary or forest dwelling (Strenski 1983).

the monastic institution. If they have to live in the forest now, it's because the conditions in the monastery do not make it possible to live as real monks otherwise. At no point, however, do we sense that the wilderness life was understood to obviate the disciplinary strictures of classical Buddhist monasticism. I would go so far as to say that the authors of the *Rāṣṭrapāla* may not even have been able to envision a non-monastic version of the bodhisattva path. They could, however, envision a version of monastic life which differed considerably from that which surrounded them.

Bibliography

Bailey, G. and I. Mabbett. (2003), *The Sociology of Early Buddhism* (Cambridge: Cambridge University Press).

Bapat, P.V. (1964), *Vimuktimārga Dhutaguṇa-Nirdeśa. A Tibetan Text Critically Edited and Translated into English* (New Delhi: Asia Publishing House).

Bareau, A. (1988/89), "Etude du bouddhisme" in *Annuaire de collège de France*: 533-47.

_____. (1991), "Les agissements de Devadatta selon les chapitres relatifs au schisme dans les divers *Vinayapiṭaka*," *Bulletin de l'Ecole française d'Extreme-Orient* 78: 87-132.

Bendall, C. (ed.) (1897-1902), *Śikṣāsamuccaya. A Compendium of Buddhistic Teaching Compiled by Śāntideva Chiefly from Earlier Mahāyāna-Sūtras*. Bibliotheca Buddhica 1 (St. Petersburg; Rpt. Osnabrück: Biblio Verlag, 1970).

Benn, J.A. (1998), "Where Text Meets Flesh: Burning the Body as an Apocryphal Practice in Chinese Buddhism," *History of Religions* 37.4: 295-322.

_____. (2001), "Burning for the Buddha: Self-Immolation in Chinese Buddhism," Ph.D. dissertation (University of California, Los Angeles).

_____. (2007), *Burning for the Buddha: Self-Immolation in Chinese Buddhism*. Kuroda Institute Studies in East Asian Buddhism 19 (Honolulu: University of Hawai'i Press).

Boucher, D. (2008), *Bodhisattvas of the Forest and the Formation of the Mahāyāna: A Study and Translation of the Rāṣṭrapālaparipṛcchā-sūtra*. Studies in the Buddhist Traditions (Honolulu: University of Hawai'i Press).

Chavannes, E. (1910-1934), *Cinq cents contes et apologues extraits du Tripitika chinois*, 4 vols. (Paris: Ernest Leroux; Rpt. Adrien-Maisonneuve, 1962).

Cowell, E.B. (gen. ed.) (1895-1913), *The Jātaka or Stories of the Buddha's Former Births*, 6 vols. (Cambridge: Cambridge University Press; Rpt. Delhi: Motilal Banarsidass, 1994).
Crosby, K. and A. Skilton. (1995), *Śāntideva. The Bodhicaryāvatāra* (Oxford: Oxford University Press).
Dantinne, J. (1983), *La splendeur de l'inébranlable (Akṣobhyavyūha)*, Tome I (Chapitres I-III), Les auditeurs (Śrāvaka) (Louvain-La-Neuve: Institut Orientaliste).
_____. (1991), *Les qualités de l'ascète (Dhutaguṇa): Etude sémantique et doctrinale* (Brussels: Thanh-Long).
Dutt, N. (1939-1959), *Gilgit Manuscripts*, 4 vols. (Srinagar; Rpt. Delhi: Sri Satguru Publications, 1984).
Ehara, N.R.M., S. Thera, and K. Thera. (1961), *The Path of Freedom by the Arahant Upatissa* (Colombo).
Finot, L. (1901), *Rāṣṭrapālaparipṛcchā. Sūtra du Mahāyāna* (St. Petersburg: Academy of Sciences; Rpt. 'S-Gravenhage: Mouton & Co., 1957).
Gernet, J. (1960), "Les suicides par le feu chez les bouddhistes chinois du Ve au Xe siècle," *Mélanges publiés par l'Institut des Hautes Études Chinoises* 2: 527-58.
Granoff, P. (1991), "The Sacrifice of Maṇicūda: The Context of Narrative Action as a Guide to Interpretation" in *Kalyāṇa-Mitta: Professor Hajime Nakamura Felicitation Volume*, ed. V.N. Jha (Delhi: Sri Satguru Publications), 225-39.
Grey, L. (2000), *A Concordance of Buddhist Birth Stories*, 3rd ed. (Oxford: The Pali Text Society).
Handurukande, R. (1984), *Five Buddhist Legends in the Campū Style. From a Collection named Avadānasārasamuccaya* (Bonn: Indica et Tibetica Verlag).
Horner, I.B. (1952), *The Book of Discipline (Vinaya Piṭaka)*, vol. V (Cullavagga) (Oxford: The Pali Text Society, Rpt. 1988).
Jan, Y.H. (1965), "Buddhist Self-Immolation in Medieval China," *History of Religions* 4.2: 243-65.
Jones, J.J. (1949-1956), *The Mahāvastu*, 3 vols. Sacred Books of the Buddhists, vols. 16, 18, and 19 (London: Luzac & Company, Ltd.).
Kern, H. (ed.) (1891), *The Jātaka-Mālā or Bodhisattvāvadāna-Mālā Ārya-Śūra*. Harvard Oriental Series 1 (Boston: Ginn & Company).
Kern, H. and B. Nanjio. (eds.) (1908-12), *Saddharmapuṇḍarīka*. Bibliotheca Buddhica X (St. Petersburg: Imperial Academy; Rpt. Osnabrück: Biblio Verlag, 1970).
Khoroche, P. (1989), *Once the Buddha Was a Monkey: Ārya Śūra's Jātakamālā* (Chicago: University of Chicago Press).
Kieschnick, J. (1997), *The Eminent Monk: Buddhist Ideals in Medieval Chinese Hagiography*. Kuroda Institute. Studies in East Asian Buddhism 10 (Honolulu: University of Hawai'i Press).

Lamotte, E. (1944-1980), *Le Traité de la grande vertu de sagesse de Nāgārjuna*, 5 vols. (Louvain: Université de Louvain, Institut Orientaliste [vols. I and II rpt. Louvain-La-Neuve, 1981]).

Li R.X. (1996), *The Great Tang Dynasty Record of the Western Regions*, trans. by the Tripiṭaka-Master Xuanzang under Imperial Order. BDK English Tripiṭaka 79 (Berkeley: Numata Center for Buddhist Translation and Research).

Meisig, M. (1995), *König Śibi und die Taube. Wandlung und Wanderung eines Erzählstoffes von Indien nach China*. Studies in Oriental Religions, vol. 35 (Wiesbaden: Harrassowitz Verlag).

Ñāṇamoli, B. (1975), *The Path of Purification (Visuddhimagga)* (Kandy, Sri Lanka: Buddhist Publication Society; Rpt. Seattle: BPS Pariyatti Editions, 1999).

Nattier, J. (2003), *A Few Good Men: The Bodhisattva Path According to the 'Inquiry of Ugra' (Ugraparipṛcchā-sūtra)*. Studies in the Buddhist Traditions (Honolulu: University of Hawai'i Press).

Norman, K.R. (1983), *Pāli Literature. Including the Canonical Literature in Prakrit and Sanskrit of All the Hīnayāna Schools of Buddhism*. A History of Indian Literature, vol. VII, fasc. 2 (Wiesbaden: Otto Harrassowitz).

Ohnuma, R. (1997), "Dehadāna: The 'Gift of the Body' in Indian Buddhist Narrative Literature" (Ph.D. dissertation, University of Michigan).

_____. (1998), "The Gift of the Body and the Gift of Dharma," *History of Religions* 37.4: 323-59.

_____. (2000a), "The Story of Rūpāvatī: A Female Past Birth of the Buddha," *Journal of the International Association of Buddhist Studies* 23.1: 103-45.

_____. (2000b), "Internal and External Opposition to the Bodhisattva's Gift of His Body," *Journal of Indian Philosophy* 28: 43-75.

_____. (2001), "Woman, Bodhisattva, and Buddha," *Journal of Feminist Studies in Religion* 17.1: 63-83.

_____. (2007), *Head, Eyes, Flesh, and Blood: Giving Away the Body in Indian Buddhist Literature* (New York: Columbia University Press).

Pagel, U. (1995), *The Bodhisattvapiṭaka: Its Doctrines, Practices and their Position in Mahāyāna Literature*. Buddhica Britanica. Series Continua V (Tring, U.K.: The Institute of Buddhist Studies).

Parlier, E. (1991), "La légende du roi des Śibi: du sacrifice brahmanique au don du corps bouddhique," *Bulletin d'études indiennes* 9: 133-60.

Ray, R. (1994), *Buddhist Saints in India: A Study in Buddhist Values & Orientations* (New York: Oxford University Press).

Schopen, G. (1988/89), "On Monks, Nuns and 'Vulgar' Practices: The Introduction of the Image Cult into Indian Buddhism," *Artibus Asiae* 49.1-2: 153-68.

_____. (1992), "On Avoiding Ghosts and Social Censure: Monastic

Funerals in the *Mūlasarvāstivāda-Vinaya*," *Journal of Indian Philosophy* 20: 1-39.

_____. (1995), "Monastic Law Meets the Real World: A Monk's Continuing Right to Inherit Family Property in Classical India," *History of Religions* 35.2: 101-23.

Schuster, N. (1981), "Changing the Female Body: Wise Women and the Bodhisattva Career in Some *Mahāratnakūṭasūtras*," *Journal of the International Association of Buddhist Studies* 4.1: 24-69.

Senart, E. (1882-1897), *Le Mahāvastu*, 3 vols. (Paris: Imprimerie Nationale).

Silber, I.F. (1995), *Virtuosity, Charisma, and Social Order: A Comparative Sociological Study of Monasticism in Theravada Buddhism and Medieval Catholicism* (Cambridge: Cambridge University Press).

Silk, J.A. (1994), "The Origins and Early History of the Mahāratnakūṭa Tradition of Mahāyāna Buddhism with a Study of the Ratnarāśisūtra and Related Materials" (Ph.D. dissertation, University of Michigan).

Sponberg, A. (1992), "Attitudes toward Women and the Feminine in Early Buddhism" in *Buddhism, Sexuality, and Gender*, ed. J.I. Cabezón (Albany: State University of New York Press), 3-36.

Staël-Holstein, B.A. Wilhelm von. (ed.) (1926), *The Kāçyapaparivarta. A Mahāyānasūtra of the Ratnakūṭa Class Edited in the Original Sanskrit in Tibetan and in Chinese* (Shanghai: Commercial Press; Rpt. Tokyo: Meicho-Fukyū-kai, 1977).

Strenski, I. (1983), "On Generalized Exchange and the Domestication of the *Sangha*," *Man*, n.s., 18: 463-77.

Strong, J.S. (1983), *The Legend of King Aśoka: A Study and Translation of the* Aśokāvadāna (Princeton: Princeton University Press).

Takakusu J. and K. Watanabe. (eds.) (1924-1935), *Taishō shinshū daizōkyō* [*The Complete Buddhist Canon Newly Edited during the Taishō Reign Period*], 100 vols. (Tokyo: Daizōkyō Publication Committee).

Tambiah, S.J. (1984), *The Buddhist Saints of the Forest and the Cult of Amulets: A Study in Charisma, Hagiography, Sectarianism, and Millennial Buddhism.* Cambridge Studies in Social Anthropology 49 (Cambridge: Cambridge University Press).

Warren, H.C. and D. Kosambi. (eds.) (1950), *Visuddhimagga of Buddhaghosâcariya* (Cambridge: Harvard Oriental Series; Rpt. Delhi: Motilal Banarsidass, 1989).

Lisa N. Owen

Text and Image: Identifying Ellora's Jain Deities

Perhaps the most widespread approach to the study of Indian sculpture is through an examination of iconography. In fact, the majority of the earliest published works on Indian sculpture are iconographical studies. Works such as T.A. Rao's *Elements of Hindu Iconography* (1914), B. Bhattacharya's *The Indian Buddhist Iconography* (1924) and B.C. Bhattacharya's *The Jaina Iconography* (1939) reveal an attempt to record, describe, and identify various forms of Hindu, Buddhist, and Jain sculpture. These publications rely heavily on textual descriptions, citing information from selected Purāṇas, Āgamas, and Tantras. In the study of Jain art, such iconographical studies have continued well into the 1980s by such esteemed scholars as U.P. Shah (1987), M.N.P Tiwari (1983), and J. Jain and E. Fischer (1978). In their studies, these scholars have turned to medieval and early modern Jain texts to assist them in their identifications, descriptions, and visual analyses of images of Jinas and Jain deities. For example, according to iconographical texts dating from the twelfth through sixteenth centuries, Jina images can be differentiated through a number of elements.[1] In general, these include: a specific pair of attendant *yakṣa*s (identified as *śāsanadevatā*s), a certain color for the Jina's body, a specific type of tree (*caityavṛkṣa*) which is associated with the Jina's *kevalajñāna* (attainment of omniscience), and a special emblem or mark (*lāñchana*) depicted on the base of sculptures. Some of the iconographical texts also provide descriptions of the *śāsanadevatā* pairs and their accompanying identifiable attributes, including color, number of arms, type of objects

[1] Most scholars cite, either directly or indirectly, the sixth chapter of the sixteenth-century text *Rūpamaṇḍana*.

held, and their supportive vehicle (*vāhana*). While these lists are clearly attempts at systematizing the Jain pantheon, it is important to note that they have limited applicability to the actual production and presentation of images.

What is curious, however, is that many scholars constantly refer to these texts in their identification and description of much earlier Jina images. For example, in A. Ghosh's edited volume, *Jaina Art and Architecture* (1974), the contributing authors have included a list of the twenty-four Jinas (along with their identifying color, *lāñchana*, *śāsanadevatās*, and places of birth and final liberation) in the second chapter titled "The Background and Tradition." Its placement and employment throughout the survey sets up an erroneous association between what a Jina image is in early modern iconographical texts versus what a Jina is in the art historical record. Unfortunately, this is not an isolated case, as a large number of publications featuring Jain art approach the material in this fashion.[2]

The Jina images at Ellora have not escaped this kind of treatment either. As examples of ninth-century sculpture, it is often assumed that Ellora's rock-cut Jinas are differentiated. For example, according to Tiwari (1983: 6):

> Jina images reached the final stage of iconographic development in c. ninth-tenth century A.D. The fully developed Jina images invariably contain distinguishing emblems, *Yakṣa-Yakṣī* pairs, *aṣṭaprātihāryas*, *dharmacakra* with worshippers, diminutive Jina figures and at times *navagrahas*, Vidyādevīs, elephants lustrating the Jinas and some other figures.

However, the vast majority of Ellora's ninth-century Jinas are *not* carved with even a few of these attributes. This has resulted in a number of attempts to identify Ellora's Jinas based solely on the central element carved on the Tīrthaṅkara's throne. These elements, which at Ellora typically include a lion or a wheel, are not *lāñchanas per se*, but are merely the traditional emblems often carved on throne bases for Buddhist, Hindu, and Jain imagery. Nonetheless, scholars continue to identify Jinas seated on lion-thrones (*siṃhāsanas*) as images of Mahāvīra, as this Jina's *lāñchana* in later texts is the lion.

The identification of Ellora's Jinas as images of Mahāvīra also typically results in the identification of the many sculptures of Jain deities as Mahāvīra's specific *śāsanadevatās*. In this essay, I will not only challenge this identification, but also suggest other ways that we can identify and come to a better understanding of who these deities are and the reasons for their representation within the caves. With this

[2] See for example Tiwari (1983: 124-6). This approach is even found in exhibition catalogs of Jain art. For example, in *The Peaceful Liberators: Jain Art from India* the identity of the Jina (and whether or not there is a visible *lāñchana* and/or pair of *śāsanadevatās*) is almost always the central concern in the catalog entries (see Pal 1994: cat. nos. 18, 20, 23, 26, 27, 29, 34, 35, 36, 39, 40, 42, 45, 47, 48, 50, and 52).

approach, we can go beyond issues of iconography and consider how these images played an integral role in establishing a sacred environment. Moreover, a consideration of *what* they represent, rather than *who* they represent, will shed more light on their role in devotional activities at the site.

Sculptures of Jain deities at Ellora can be found either inside the main halls or carved on the verandas. These figures are non-liberated beings and their ties to both earthly and divine realms are often highlighted in their full-bodied forms and their rich ornamentation. Seated under large canopies of foliage and holding items such as a citron or a tree-branch, these figures are presented as *yakṣa*s and *yakṣī*s—divinities associated with trees and the natural world. In medieval Jain art and literature, *yakṣa*s and *yakṣī*s are commonly portrayed as bestowers of well-being—deities who are capable of granting their devotees the means to an enriched, spiritual life (Cort 1983; Granoff 1993: 182-8). They are also typically associated with the creation and protection of sacred structures, ranging from miraculous towns and palaces to the celestial assembly hall of a Jina. Thus, reasons as to why such deities are included in Ellora's Jain caves can be investigated from many angles.

At Ellora, two deities (one male and one female) are commonly represented in the caves. Although individual sculptures will be examined in detail below, in general, the male figure sits upon an elephant and grasps a citron and a mongoose-skin purse used to hold coins. A large banyan tree, identifiable through its cluster of broad leaves and small oval fruits, is typically carved overhead. The female figure at Ellora is invariably presented underneath a mango tree. She is seated on a lion and often holds a bunch of mangos or a branch from the tree in her proper right hand. She is also depicted with a small child who either sits on her lap or stands near her. Both deities at Ellora have oval halos and are usually accompanied by attendants. They are also often seated against an elaborate bolster and throne crossbar.

Although the Archaeological Survey of India has recognized five Jain complexes at the site (numbered Caves 30-34), there are in actuality twenty-three individual excavations. This larger figure, which follows the numbering system used by Pereira (1977), takes into account the number of excavated spaces that have shrines or Jina images carved into their back wall and thus provide a place for worship activities.[3] Out of these twenty-three excavations, seventeen contain large-scale sculptures of this *yakṣa*/*yakṣī* pair.[4] These deities

[3] The caves include J4, J6, J8, J10-26, and three excavations in the Choṭa Kailāsa complex (CK 1-3).

[4] The seventeen excavations are: CK 3, J6, J10-J14 and J17-J26. It should be noted that while J16 has an image of the *yakṣa* on its rear wall, only a niche for the accompanying *yakṣī* was carved.

are not, however, presented together in the same panel or architectural niche, but are carved as complementary figures that either face each other at opposite ends of the veranda or flank the shrine doorway. In the latter location, they visually serve as attendants to the Jina housed inside the shrine, with the male *yakṣa* on the viewer's left (when facing the sanctum) and the *yakṣī* on the right. Some of these figures are raised on pedestals, elevating them from the floor of the cave. In other sculptures, the deities are framed by elaborate *toraṇa*s (archways) that visually link them to the shrine Jina who is also crowned by this element.

The presentation of this pair as "attendant" deities to the Tīrthaṅkara follows a sculptural convention that emerged in the mid-sixth century (Shah 1961). Although earlier Jina images may be flanked by fly-whisk bearers or even Brahmanical deities (Leoshko 1999), sculptures produced during the mid-sixth through tenth centuries often include this specific *yakṣa/yakṣī* pair as attendants. Identified in contemporary texts as *śāsanadevatā*s, these figures protect and preserve the teachings (*śāsana*) of the Tīrthaṅkara. According to Shah (1955-56 and 1959), the earliest Jina images to include this pair are among the metal sculptures found in the Akoṭā and Vasantagadh hoards. The female *yakṣī* (*śāsanadevī*) is typically seated to the proper left of the Tīrthaṅkara on an open lotus. She supports a small child on her lap with her left hand and holds a branch from a mango tree in her right. In some seventh and eighth-century bronzes, she is shown seated on a lion. These attributes—the child, mango, and the lion *vāhana*—accord with later descriptions of the Jain goddess Ambikā, also known as Kūṣmāṇḍinī.[5] In addition to her presentation as a *śāsanadevī* to the Jina, Ambikā/Kūṣmāṇḍinī appears to have been popular as an independent deity, as individual images of this goddess (or goddess-type) can also be dated to the sixth century (Shah 1940; Tiwari 1989).

In individual images of Ambikā/Kūṣmāṇḍinī and in her presentation as a *śāsanadevī*, aspects of fertility and fecundity are expressed through her physical form as she is invariably portrayed with round, large breasts and wide hips that literally support the child she cradles in her lap. The branch of mangos that she holds is also symbolic of

[5] A number of texts dating from the eighth through sixteenth century provide iconographical descriptions of the goddess Ambikā/Kūṣmāṇḍinī. For selected passages from texts such as the *Caturviṃśatikā* of Bappabhaṭṭisūri, Pādaliptasūri's *Nirvāṇakalikā*, Hemacandra's *Triṣaṣṭiśalākāpuruṣacaritra*, the *Pravacanasāroddhāra* of Nemicandrasūri, Vasunandin's *Pratiṣṭhāsārasaṃgraha*, Jinaprabhasūri's *Vividhatīrthakalpa*, Āśādhara's *Pratiṣṭhāsāroddhāra*, and the *Rūpamaṇḍana* of Sūtradhāramaṇḍana see Tiwari (1989: 25-33). For an English translation of the story in Jinaprabhasūri's *Vividhatīrthakalpa* which explains Ambikā's attributes and her lion *vāhana* see Granoff (1993: 182-4). A Digambara version of this legend is recorded in a palm-leaf manuscript of the *Puṇyāśravakathā* which is currently housed in the Vardhamāna temple in Kāñcīpuram. This account is discussed in Ramachandran (1934: 157-60).

reproduction and fertility due to the high volume of fruit produced by this type of tree. Ambikā's presentation with a branch from the mango tree also suggests her relationship to *śālabhañjikās*, a specific type of *yakṣī* who is able to cause a tree to blossom or produce fruit by touching its branches.

The male *śāsanadevatā* on metal Jina images dating from the mid-sixth through tenth centuries is a pot-bellied *yakṣa* who wears a small, conical crown, earrings, necklace, and armlets. He is generally portrayed seated on an open lotus or on an elephant. In his proper right hand he holds a fruit, or citron, and in his left, he grasps a mongoose-skin purse. In a number of images, he holds the purse up high near his shoulder, mimicking the gesture of Ambikā holding the branch of mangos. The elevation of the purse not only creates a sense of balance and symmetry between the two attendant figures, but it also draws attention to this particular attribute, a sign of financial well-being and general abundance. The citron he holds, as well as his corpulent physique, further contribute to notions of sustenance and nourishment.

Unlike the rather straightforward identification of the *śāsanadevī* as some form of Ambikā/Kūṣmāṇḍinī, there has been some speculation over the specific identity of the male attendant on these metal sculptures. Shah (1987: 215-6) identifies the figure as either a form of Sarvānubhūti or Sarvāhṇa *yakṣa* based on an unpublished sixth-century auto-commentary by Jinabhadragaṇi Kṣamāśramaṇa on his text titled the *Viśeṣāvaśyaka Bhāṣya*. According to Shah, this is the earliest literary evidence for *śāsanadevatās* as the text makes reference to both Amba-Kūṣmāṇḍī and Sarveṇe—the latter being what Shah calls "a scribal error for Sarvāhṇa *yakṣa*." Shah also notes a verse addressed to Sarvāhṇa *yakṣa* (identified as Sarvānubhūti) in the Śvetāmbara *Pañcapratikramaṇasūtra*. In this text, specifically in the *Snātasyā Stuti*, the *yakṣa* Sarvānubhūti is described as a two-armed deity who rides an elephant.[6]

Complicating the task of identifying this *yakṣa* are descriptions of Sarvāhṇa/Sarvānubhūti found in later texts (ca. twelfth through sixteenth century) that diverge from earlier accounts. Rather than explaining or repeating the known attributes of this *yakṣa* (as in the general case of Ambikā/Kūṣmāṇḍinī) these descriptions in essence create new iconographical forms for this figure. For example, in medieval Digambara accounts, the *yakṣa* Sarvāhṇa is described as having three heads and at least six attributes, including an axe, a rod, and a flower.[7] Śvetāmbara descriptions describe him as having one to three heads and a minimum of fourteen attributes.[8]

[6] For an English translation of the verse, see Pereira (1977: 60).
[7] See the description in Ramachandran (1934: 208).
[8] For the list of attributes see Pereira (1977: 61).

Moreover, some Śvetāmbara texts, such as the *Vividhatīrthakalpa* and the *Triṣaṣṭiśalākāpuruṣacaritra*, provide a description of a *yakṣa* who holds a citron and a mongoose-skin purse, however the *yakṣa* is identified as the four-armed Kapardin and the Śvetāmbara *śāsanadevatā* Mātaṅga, respectively.[9] Although this *yakṣa* takes on a variety of physical forms and names within later Jain textual traditions, it is significant that his representation in the art historical record during the mid-sixth through tenth century remains fairly constant. This constancy in form attests to the importance of the concepts of wealth and well-being that this *yakṣa* symbolizes.

The problems associated with identifying the male *yakṣa* on early medieval Jina images also extend to Ellora's Jain caves. A number of scholars who have examined the site tend to identify the male *yakṣa* as Mātaṅga—the specific *śāsanadevatā* for the Jina Mahāvīra (Gupte and Mahajan 1962: 221-24; Dhavalikar 2003: 86-96). This identification seems to be based primarily on the assumption that all of Ellora's shrine images are representations of Mahāvīra; a claim that is supported solely by the inclusion of a lion-throne beneath the Jina. Another difficulty is the fact that Ellora's ninth-century *yakṣa*s only correspond to twelfth-century Śvetāmbara textual descriptions of Mātaṅga. Since Ellora is considered to be a Digambara site based on the nudity of its Jina images, the identification of this figure as the Śvetāmbara Mātaṅga is problematic. Medieval Digambara texts further complicate the matter as Mātaṅga is typically described as a four-armed *yakṣa* who makes the gesture of *varadamudrā* or *añjali* with his lower hands and touches the top of his crown with the upper hands (Ramachandran 1934: 211). Finally, the identification of Ellora's *yakṣa* as any form of Mātaṅga is not viable when we consider the image as part of a *pair*, since the *śāsanadevī* coupled with Mātaṅga in later iconographical texts is *not* Ambikā/Kūṣmāṇḍinī but Siddhāyikā—a four-armed goddess found in much later imagery. Although this is the case, images of Ellora's *yakṣī*s are often identified as Siddhāyikā by default even though they clearly do not exhibit this goddess's iconographical features.[10]

Other scholars, such as Pereira (1977) and Chatham (1996), identify the pair at Ellora as Ambikā and Sarvānubhūti based in part on Shah's identification of the attendants on the mid-sixth through tenth-century Western bronzes. However, the majority, if not all of the images from the Akoṭā and Vasanatagadh hoards are also Śvetāmbara and thus these appellations may not necessarily be applicable to Ellora's Digambara carvings. A more appropriate identification for Ellora's pair might be Kūṣmāṇḍinī and Sarvāhṇa—the

[9] For the story of the *yakṣa* Kapardin, see Granoff (1993: 185-6). For a description of Mātaṅga from the *Triṣaṣṭiśalākāpuruṣacaritra* see Johnson (1931-62, vol. 6: 125).

[10] For images of Siddhāyikā see Shah (1972).

corresponding Digambara names for these deities. The popularity of Sarvāhṇa *yakṣa* at other contemporary Digambara sites, such as Śravaṇa Beḷgoḷa, also lends support to this identification.[11]

Although the specific identities of Ellora's Jain deities are important, I do not want to be limited by this concern in my examination of the site's carvings. By focusing on *what* these deities represent and *how* these images convey meaning, we can begin to understand why these two deities are included in almost all of Ellora's Jain caves and how they function within the temple setting. Indeed, unlike the *śāsanadevatās* on metal and stone sculptures, Ellora's *yakṣa/yakṣī* pairs are presented in an *architectural* context. While they *visually* serve as attendants to the Tīrthaṅkara inside the shrine, it is important to note that these two deities are never actually included within that sacred space. They are found *outside* the sanctum, flanking the door. Their inclusion at liminal spaces—next to doorways and at the ends of verandas—suggests that they may serve a protective function for the temple itself. Moreover, their location at these architectural junctures creates a power of place. In other words, they provide both protection and glorification to areas in the cave-temple that precede the main shrine. Thus, rather than merely serving as *śāsanadevatās*, this pair functions in more complex ways within Ellora's Jain caves.

Images of the Jain Yakṣa *and* Yakṣī *at Ellora*

With the exception of Chatham's stylistic analysis of these figures (1996), there has been little serious study of Ellora's *yakṣī* and *yakṣa* sculptures. While they are included in Pereira's book on Ellora's Jain caves (1977), he does not discuss them individually nor does he consider their roles within the excavations. He simply reiterates the later narratives constructed about these deities that explain certain iconographical features. Pereira also provides a list of the various elements that are included in Ellora's *yakṣa/yakṣī* carvings such as halos, parts of the throne, attendant figures, and held attributes. While such a list can be useful, it does not facilitate an in-depth understanding of these sculptures and the aesthetic choices that were made by the artists. Nor does it allow for close comparative analyses between different images. Pereira is not alone in this approach, as other art historians who have written about Ellora's Jain deities also tend to discuss them collectively as if all of the images are the same from cave to cave (Shah 1940;

[11] According to Settar (1971), the majority of *yakṣa* images at Śravaṇa Beḷgoḷa in Karnataka are representations of Sarvāhṇa. This *yakṣa*, who rides an elephant and holds a flower and a citron, is also often rendered at the top of *mānastambhas* (pride pillars) preceding Digambara temples. At Ellora, there is a *mānastambha* that is crowned with a fourfold *yakṣa* sculpture. However, in the nineteenth century, the pillar collapsed, thereby damaging the carving. As a result, it is difficult to determine whether or not the *yakṣas* held attributes or had a specific *vāhana*. Nonetheless, their ornamentation and physique is similar to the larger *yakṣa* images within Ellora's Jain caves.

Tiwari 1989; and Dhavalikar 2003). However, a close examination of these sculptures reveals that there is a great amount of variety in their presentations. This is particularly true for Ellora's *yakṣī* images.

Perhaps the largest and most elaborate presentation of the *yakṣī* at Ellora is the sculpture carved in J18 (Figure 1).[12] Measuring over fourteen feet in height, this image is carved on the right (east) end of the veranda and is located at the stairwell which provides access to this upper-story cave. The image is carved in high-relief and is only elevated from the cave floor by a few inches. The paws of her lion *vāhana* stretch out towards the viewer, its claws hanging over the lower edge of the panel. Although the head of the lion is completely damaged, it would have directly faced the viewer. The *yakṣī* is seated in *lalitāsana* under a lush mango tree. A child sits on her proper left knee and she gently supports him with her left hand. In her proper right hand, which is slightly damaged, she grasps a bunch of mangos—the foliage and the stem of the branch hangs down over her wrist. She is accompanied by four other figures: two females holding *cāmara*s (fly-whisks) and two males who stand at her side. In the corners of the niche, above the mango tree, are pairs of peacocks—symbols of fertility, courtship, and the rainy season. The *yakṣī*'s Jain affiliation is indicated by a small seated Jina carved in her headdress and a painted Tīrthaṅkara on the lintel above the niche.

Narratives about this goddess-type (identified as Kūṣmāṇḍinī or Ambikā) were written in the fourteenth through sixteenth centuries to explain her iconography and her role as *śāsanadevī* to the twenty-second Jina, Neminātha. While Śvetāmbaras and Digambaras have their own versions of this story, the turn of events leading to her transformation from mortal to goddess are quite similar in both traditions. According to the Digambara *Puṇyāśravakathā* and the Śvetāmbara *Vividhatīrthakalpa*, Kūṣmāṇḍinī (Śvet. Ambikā) was initially married to an orthodox brahmin and they had two children together.[13] One day, Kūṣmāṇḍinī's husband invited some local brahmins to visit so that they could perform a *śrāddha* ceremony for his ancestors. Kūṣmāṇḍinī and her mother-in-law prepared the food for this ritual as well as a feast for the brahmins. However, when Kūṣmāṇḍinī found herself alone, a Jain monk showed up at the house to beg for alms so that he could break his month-long fast. As this was an extremely auspicious moment and Kūṣmāṇḍinī was pure of heart and conduct, she offered the monk the first serving of food that she had prepared. When Kūṣmāṇḍinī's mother-in-law

[12] J18 is more commonly known as the upper-story cave of the Indra Sabhā complex.

[13] In the *Puṇyāśravakathā*, the names of her children are Śubhaṅkara ("one who makes [things] auspicious") and Prabhaṅkara ("one who makes [things] splendid/bright"), see Ramachandran (1934: 157-60). In the *Vividhatīrthakalpa*, they are Siddha ("Liberated") and Buddha ("Enlightened"), see Granoff (1993: 182-4).

and husband found out what she had done, they were irate, as the remaining food was now considered to be polluted.

Kūṣmāṇḍinī was forced out of the house with her two children. As they wandered homeless, her children became hungry and thirsty. Kūṣmāṇḍinī became distraught and did not know what to do, so she sat down to rest. Miraculously, a mango tree (or a wish-fulfilling tree) appeared and a dry tank (or lake) filled with water. Thus, she could provide nourishment for herself and her children. Meanwhile, back in town, some miracles occurred that convinced Kūṣmāṇḍinī's husband and mother-in-law that her actions were indeed honorable.[14] Kūṣmāṇḍinī's husband then decided to retrieve his wife and children but when he tried to do so, Kūṣmāṇḍinī thought that he was coming to do her more harm and so she tried to hide. Kūṣmāṇḍinī died in the process[15] and was reborn as a *yakṣī* and *śāsanadevī* to the Jina Neminātha. Her husband also died soon afterwards, and was reborn as her lion *vāhana*.

The *yakṣī* images at Ellora clearly display the attributes commonly associated with this goddess, namely the mango tree (seen overhead and in a branch held in her hand), the lion, and a child. Six of Ellora's sculptures, including the carving in J18, depict Kūṣmāṇḍinī with a child seated on her proper left knee.[16] Other examples show the child standing next to the *yakṣī's vāhana*.[17] In these images, the goddess makes the gesture of *varadamūdra* with her proper left hand and displays a small round object in her palm, perhaps a mango, jewel, or citron. While it is difficult to discern the object in Ellora's images, a number of tenth through thirteenth-century sculptures from Maharashtra and Karnataka portray her with a branch of mangos in her proper right hand and a citron in her proper left.[18] The inclusion of the citron in these later images clearly continues her association with the pot-bellied Jain *yakṣa* who invariably holds this item.

[14] In the *Puṇyāśravakathā*, various gods who had witnessed Kūṣmāṇḍinī's banishment became angry and burned down the entire town with the exception of Kūṣmāṇḍinī's house. On seeing this, the brahmins and the townspeople realized that her house was spared due to her meritorious act of feeding the Jain monk. The brahmins then decided to partake in the food that was once considered polluted but was now divine, see Ramachandran (1934: 158). In the *Vividhatīrthakalpa*, the miracles that occurred in town include a magic restoration of the food that was given to the Jain monk and the leaves that served as plates were transformed into gold platters, see Granoff (1993: 184).

[15] The *Vividhatīrthakalpa* refers to two legends of how she died. In one version, she jumped into a well and in the other she jumped off of a cliff. In both instances, she died with her mind fixed on the best of Jinas and glad that she made the offering to the Jain monk. In the *Puṇyāśravakathā*, she died after falling from a precipice into a cave below.

[16] The other five are in CK3, J6, J14, J17, and J22.

[17] These are found in J11, J12, J13, J19, J20, J21, J23, J24 and J26. The image in J10 is too damaged to determine the position of the child. In J25, two children are depicted: one in her lap and the other standing next to her proper right knee.

[18] For illustrations of both metal and stone images of Kūṣmāṇḍinī from Maharashtra and Karnataka, see Tiwari (1989: figs. 19, 59, 61, 68-70, 79 and 80).

In addition to the citron, there are other elements that are included in Ellora's *yakṣī* images that are not necessarily associated with the narratives described above—thereby giving us additional information about this figure. For example, female *cāmara* bearers are carved behind the *yakṣī* in J18 and also in J17, J20, J21, J23, J24 and J25. These attendants are included to demonstrate her elevated status as a Jain goddess. Like the Tīrthaṅkara in the shrine, this goddess is also worthy of veneration and the attendant figures highlight her position as an important deity. The *cāmara* attendants also point to her royal status—an aspect which is expressed further through her rich ornamentation. In all of Ellora's images, the *yakṣī* wears a jeweled girdle and necklace, earrings, armlets, bracelets, and anklets. Her hair is usually piled up in an elaborate chignon and crowned with a gem-studded diadem.

The male attendants who flank the *yakṣī* in J18 are also quite interesting as they are not simply male versions of the female *cāmaradhara*s. Although the male on her proper right holds a long-stemmed lotus or fly-whisk, he is ornamented in a similar fashion as the life-sized *dvārapāla*s (door guardians) carved on the facade of this cave. Both the attendant and the *dvārapāla*s wear a broad necklace encrusted with jewels, a belt worn around the rib-cage that has alternating circular and square gems, a pearl sash tied at the waist, a triple pleated *dhoṭī*, and multiple strands of pearls twisted together into a single band worn across the torso. Indeed, a direct visual connection is made between these figures through their shared ornamentation, stance, and proximity to one another, suggesting that the male figure at the *yakṣī*'s side may serve an apotropaic function as well as being an attendant.

The figure standing on the *yakṣī*'s proper left, however, is not a mirror-image of the other male as one would expect. The male to her left has a beard and moustache, long hair, and wears a long, plain *dhoṭī*. A flat band which may be a *yajñopavīta* (sacred thread) falls across his bare chest. He makes a gesture of homage to Kūṣmāṇḍinī with his proper right hand and holds a single *chattra* (parasol) over his head with his left. According to Tiwari (1989: 67), who is the only art historian to comment on this figure, the individual may represent "a bearded devotee (*sādhu*)." However, it is unclear whether Tiwari is referring to a generic religious holy man in the use of the term *sādhu*, or if he is suggesting that the figure is a Śvetāmbara monk, as monks in this sect are commonly referred to as *sādhu*s (as opposed to the Digambara nomenclature of *muni*s).

What is clear, however, is that this figure plays an integral part in the *yakṣī*'s presentation at Ellora as he is included in twelve other reliefs at the site.[19] His appearance is consistent in all of

[19] These are found in CK 3, J6, J10, J12, J13, J17, J19, J20, J23, J24, J25 and J26.

the sculptures: he has a beard and moustache, wears a long *dhoṭī* and *yajñopavīta*, and holds a *chattra*. In almost all of the images, he stands to the proper left of the *yakṣī* and holds up his proper right hand in homage. Of significance, nearly identical figures also appear in the Jain caves at Ankai-Tankai, located approximately fifty miles away. Created in the eleventh and twelfth centuries, these excavations are very closely modeled on Ellora. In the two caves that contain reliefs of this *yakṣī* at Ankai-Tankai, the bearded fellow stands to the proper left of the goddess. Although one of the images has been recently plastered and painted, the relevant attributes are still recognizable. In the other image, carved in Cave 3 at Ankai-Tankai, the bearded figure is depicted with long hair that is partially tied-up in an ascetic's knot. Apart from the sculptures at these two cave sites, there are *no other images* of this goddess-type that I am aware of that include this figure.

The limited representation of the bearded devotee within the corpus of Kūṣmāṇḍinī/Ambikā-type images across India immediately suggests that his inclusion is particular to both the rock-cut medium and to this specific geographical region. Furthermore, one of the twelve reliefs at Ellora stands out from the others and it may provide a clue to this figure's identity. This image is located on the rear wall of J26 (Figure 2). In this relief, the bearded figure next to the *yakṣī* holds the *chattra* in his proper right hand and holds his proper left hand in front of his chest. In the left hand, he holds a small round object between his thumb and index finger. Carved above his proper left shoulder is a bowl filled with similar round objects which may represent either sweetmeats, specifically *laḍḍū*s, or *piṇḍa*s, balls of rice and flour that are often used as offerings in the *śrāddha* ceremony.

While it could be argued that this bowl of offerings represents the food that Kūṣmāṇḍinī gave to the Jain monk to break his fast, it is highly unlikely that the figure represents the monk himself. Visual evidence at the site negates this identification as representations of Jain monks found throughout the caves depict them without facial hair and garments (Owen 2006). In addition, fragments of a thirteenth-century painting on the ceiling of J21 appear to depict the story of Kūṣmāṇḍinī and, in one particular panel, she is shown giving alms to a naked ascetic. The nudity of the monk indicates his Digambara affiliation as does the fact that he is accepting food in his cupped hands rather than an alms bowl which is prohibited for full-fledged Digambara *muni*s.

On the other hand, the bearded fellow could possibly represent a *bhaṭṭāraka*, a celibate but non-initiated religious figure that came to prominence during the medieval period, particularly in southern Digambara Jainism. According to Dundas (1992: 105-7), *bhaṭṭāraka*s in the medieval period were advanced laymen who served an important role between the monastic and lay communities. *Bhaṭṭāraka*s helped run the everyday affairs of the monastery where they permanently lived and supervised the vows undertaken by the lay community. They also conducted rituals and were considered to be representatives of the monastic community when dealing with non-Jain individuals. Of significance, *bhaṭṭāraka*s did not look like Digambara Jain monks since they could wear robes and they often traveled by some sort of conveyance such as a palanquin. Indeed, such a figure is painted on the bracket above the far right pillar on the veranda of J21. In this thirteenth-century painting, the *bhaṭṭāraka* is seated in a palanquin and a single *chattra* is held overhead. He is surrounded by a retinue of soldiers who carry large shields and spears. Although the figure in the palanquin appears to be nude, he does have long black hair. If the bearded devotee in Ellora's Kūṣmāṇḍinī reliefs is a *bhaṭṭāraka* then these sculptures represent the earliest art historical evidence of this institution which did not become firmly established in Digambara Jainism until the thirteenth through fifteenth centuries.[20]

A more plausible identification for this figure seems to be Kūṣmāṇḍinī/Ambikā's husband. Both Digambara and Śvetāmbara textual accounts refer to her brahmin husband and the food prepared for the *śrāddha* ceremony. However, in the Digambara accounts, specifically the *Puṇyāśravakathā*, the food is given a greater emphasis in the text as it is transformed from being polluted to being suitable for consumptive and ritual purposes. After the fire destroys the town, the brahmins come to Kūṣmāṇḍinī's house and request that her husband give them the ritual offerings which were "purified" and "blessed" by the touch of the Jain ascetic (who they figured must have been a god in disguise). Although the brahmins failed to see the true import of Kūṣmāṇḍinī's actions, they, along with the people of the town, were "universally gratified" as all had partaken in the divine food. The inclusion of the bowl of offerings in the sculpture of J26 may refer to this part of the story while simultaneously adding an additional element to the narrative: that of Kūṣmāṇḍinī's husband now making offerings to her.

In addition to the heightened role of food in the *Puṇyāśravakathā*, this text also diverges from Śvetāmbara accounts in that the husband actually communicates with his wife, asking her to forgive him.

[20] One could also possibly argue that the figure is a type of Śvetāmbara *tyāgī yati* known as a *śrīpūjya*. *Śripūjya*s are Śvetāmbara resident mendicants who have also taken lesser vows and who function in similar ways as the Digambara *bhaṭṭāraka*s. They also seem to have differed visually from initiated monks as some nineteenth-century representations depict them with long hair and moustaches. However, as *yati*s were not a dominant force in Śvetāmbara monasticism until the nineteenth century, this identification seems highly unlikely for Ellora's ninth and tenth century images. For a detailed examination of the distinctions between *yati*s and *sādhu*s in Śvetāmbara Mūrtipūjaka Jainism see Cort (1991: 651-671). For *yati*s depicted in two nineteenth-century paintings, see Pal (1994: cat. nos. 117 and 119B). These paintings are also briefly discussed in Cort (1996: 628-30).

When Kūṣmāṇḍinī becomes a *yakṣī*, she initially hides her divine form from her husband and children to avoid alarming them. At this point in the story, her husband approaches Kūṣmāṇḍinī and begs for her forgiveness. This differs from the narrative in the Śvetāmbara *Vividhatīrthakalpa* where the husband had this intent but never actually speaks to his wife. Instead, in this text, he jumps into a well and dies. Though these are only subtle differences, the Digambara text nonetheless highlights the husband's remorse. In fact, in the *Puṇyāśravakathā*, when the husband dies, he is reborn as a lion but does not immediately become Kūṣmāṇḍinī's *vāhana*. Before being accepted by Kūṣmāṇḍinī, he has to demonstrate his devotion to her in her new form by licking her feet. According to the text, only then did he become her *vāhana*. The images at Ellora seem to emphasize the husband's repentance and devotion to the goddess by including the figure of the brahmin making a gesture of homage to the *yakṣī*. He is shown in both human form and as the *vāhana*, suggesting the long duration of his veneration.

Another interesting presentation of the bearded devotee can also be mentioned at this point. The figure is found in the *yakṣī* relief carved on the north (right) end of the veranda leading into J25 (Figure 3). Unlike the image in J18 and J26, the *yakṣī* in J25 is elevated from the floor of the veranda by a rock-cut pedestal that measures approximately four and a half feet in height. The over-life-sized figure of the Jain goddess is deeply recessed within the niche. The niche itself is framed by pilasters that are crowned with decorative capitals. Carved on the left side of the relief, when facing the image, is the brahmin, identifiable through his long hair, bare chest, and plain *dhoṭī*. Although only roughly carved out, the staff of the *chattra* is visible in his proper right hand while the single parasol remains as an oblong shape over the back of his head. In addition to the *yajñopavīta*, he appears to wear the skin of an antelope over his proper right shoulder.[21] According to ancient *dharma* literature, both the animal skin and the *chattra* are common elements worn or utilized by a *snātaka*—one who has performed the required ritual lustrations upon finishing his time as a student and who will then enter into the life of a householder. For example, Baudhāyana (5.2-7) writes that a *snātaka*

> ... shall wear a lower and an upper garment; carry a bamboo staff and a pot filled with water; wear a double sacrificial cord, a turban, a skin as an upper garment, and shoes; carry an umbrella; maintain the sacred domestic fire; and offer the new-moon and full-moon sacrifices. On the days of the moon's change moreover, he should get the hair of his head, beard, and body shaved and his nails clipped. (Olivelle 2000)

[21] In a close examination of this sculpture, one can see the two forelegs and shape of the antelope's head.

Given the above description regarding the maintenance of the domestic fire, the term *snātaka* also appears to be applicable to an individual even after he is married. While this text is far earlier in date than Ellora's carvings, it can nonetheless assist us in identifying the *type* of figure that is represented.

Of great interest is the brahmin's position outside of the relief itself. He appears to be looking into the niche at the goddess and thus mirrors our own position in front of this sculpture. The body of the brahmin seems to lean against the left pilaster and he places his proper left hand under his chin. The object of his gaze and devotion is clearly the *yakṣī* herself as even her female *cāmara* attendants are relegated to the sidewalls of the niche. In contrast to the *yakṣī*'s immobile presentation, the lion twists its body towards the goddess and raises its paw. The interest in depicting the brahmin from the back as well as the complex spatial setting within the niche which includes foreground, middleground, and background elements is reminiscent of the mid-eighth-century panel of Ravana Shaking Mt. Kailāsa carved on the south-side of Ellora's Kailāsanātha temple. Indeed, other features of the J25 relief, such as the treatment of the throne, attest to its relatively early date among Ellora's Jain *yakṣīs*.

While the majority of *yakṣī* reliefs at Ellora include the bearded devotee and other attendant figures, the sculpture carved in J11 presents her as a solitary figure. In this image, carved on a tall pedestal to the right of the shrine door, the majestic and elegant features of the goddess are highlighted rather than her maternal qualities (Figure 4). Though the artist has included the child in this sculpture, he is barely visible behind her proper left knee. Instead, the viewer is drawn to the delicate rendering of the goddess's ornamentation, such as the small bells on her anklet and the folds of cloth that hang over her jeweled belt. The artist has taken great care to contrast the intricacies of her coiffure to the smooth surface of her halo. Surrounding the halo and serving in part as a throne motif are *makaras* (mythical aquatic creatures) and female *cāmaradharas*. Above these figures are divine couples making gestures of adoration while their bodies bend in similar ways as the *makara*'s tails. The energetic and almost frenzied panel above the throne crossbar visually (and literally) replaces the mango tree and its rich foliage which one would expect to find in such reliefs. Though the tree is absent, the *yakṣī* appears to be holding a mango, or some other fruit, in her left hand. Although this sculpture has sustained some damage, one can still acknowledge the artist's skill and attention to detail as seen in the embroidered design surrounding the button on the bolster, the curls of the lion's mane, as well as the graceful rendering of the *yakṣī*'s pointed foot. Indeed, the richness of her presentation and the visual emphasis on her ornamentation parallels later textual descriptions of this goddess and what she can offer the devoted worshipper. According to the legend of Ambikā in the *Vividhatīrthakalpa*:

> Adorned with every kind of ornament on every part of her body, sporting a crown, earrings, a pearl necklace, jewelled bracelets and anklets, she grants all the wishes of faithful Jains and prevents any harm from coming to Jain believers. She shows to those who are devoted to Jainism all kinds of spells and magic diagrams and displays before them many a wondrous power. Through her power, no evil spirit, ghost, goblin, or witch can work its magic on a devotee and the faithful grow rich, become kings, and have fine wives and sons. (Granoff 1993: 184)

Financial well-being and a general abundance in material goods may also be granted to the devotee who worships the pot-bellied *yakṣa* that is paired with the *yakṣī* at Ellora. There are seventeen images of this Jain *yakṣa* at the site and all of them depict him seated on an elephant *vāhana*. He wears a tall, conical crown that is heavily encrusted with jewels and pearls, a broad necklace, and circular earrings. In many of the sculptures, long curly hair falls across his back and shoulders. He wears armlets that are typically carved with a *kīrttimukha* (face of glory), alluding to his role as a deity who can dispel evil as well as grant boons.[22] Draped across his broad torso and corpulent belly is a long strand of twisted pearls. In many of the sculptures, this element falls across the elevated wrist of his proper right hand which holds a citron.[23] Clutched in his proper left hand is a mongoose-skin purse which hangs heavy by his side.

Forming a canopy over this *yakṣa* is a large banyan tree. Like the mango, the banyan is an important tree in India, for both practical and symbolic reasons. In addition to providing food, the banyan tree creates a great amount of shade as it is able to grow over large areas of land. The tree produces shoots from its branches which extend down to the ground and take root into the soil. These aerial roots form new "trunks" of the tree, and thus a single banyan can give the appearance of a small forest of trees. The unusual feature of this tree to multiply in great abundance—providing food, shelter, and shade for many people—reinforces the very same characteristics embodied by the *yakṣa* himself.

As in Ellora's *yakṣī* images, the male deity is often presented with attendant figures.[24] However, rather than simply holding fly-whisks, the *yakṣa*'s attendants often hold attributes that reinforce themes of well-being and protection. In the image in J18, for example, the

[22] According to the *Vividhatīrthakalpa*, the *yakṣa* Kapardin (who is quite similar in appearance to Ellora's Jain *yakṣa*) was known to "ward off all harm that might befall the faithful" (see Granoff 1993: 186). In Ponna's *Śāntināthapurāṇam*, Sarvāhṇa *yakṣa* with his elephant can "trample through all those who stand in the way of attaining the *siddhapada*," see Settar (1975: 37).

[23] The object, usually identified by scholars as a citron, might be a *seethaphal* (custard apple). These trees and their fruits are common within the Deccan plateau and can be found in abundance at Ellora today.

[24] Ten images of the Jain *yakṣa* include attendants. These are found in: J6, J10, J12, J13, J17, J18, J19, J20, J23, and J24. The reliefs in CK 3, J22, and J25 may have also included attendants but the sculptures are too damaged to be certain.

yakṣa is attended by two male figures (Figure 5). The attendant on the right, when viewing the relief, carries a mongoose-skin purse in his proper left hand. The size and shape of the purse matches the bag held by the main deity. Although the *yakṣa*'s purse hangs over his proper left knee and is partly obscured, the bag held by the attendant is carved some distance from the figure's body. In fact, the artist has partially isolated this element by carving the purse beyond the boundary of the sculpted niche. In this position, the mongoose-skin bag is completely visible and in fact is well-lit by light coming into the open veranda. On the left side of the relief, another male attendant leans on a large club. As in the male attendant in the accompanying *yakṣī* relief (Figure 1), this figure essentially replicates the large *dvārapālas* (door guardians) that are carved on the facade of this excavation. However, an attendant holding a club is found in at least seven other *yakṣa* images at the site.[25] Two of these images, found in J10 and J20, depict both attendants wielding this weapon. The inclusion of such attendant figures clearly suggests the *yakṣa*'s role as a protective deity within the caves.

While the club seems to be the most popular attribute held by the *yakṣa*'s attendants, the carving in J24 presents us with a different iconographical program. In this image, the male deity is flanked by four figures (Figure 6). Two females holding *cāmaras* stand slightly behind him, with the figure on the right side of the relief also making a gesture of homage. They are accompanied by two male figures who hold the same attributes as the *yakṣa*, namely a citron and a mongoose-skin purse. The repetition of these elements serves to emphasize the *yakṣa*'s role as a deity of abundance—in terms of both nourishment (i.e., productive harvests) and financial wealth. The number, gender, and position of the *yakṣa*'s attendants in the J24 relief mirrors those found in the accompanying *yakṣī* relief (Figure 7). In this sculpture, the *yakṣī* is also flanked by two female *cāmaradharas* and two male attendants. And, like the *yakṣa* relief, one of the females waves her hand at the goddess in adoration.

The presentation of these two deities *as a pair* is carried out even further in the way that the figures sit upon their *vāhanas* and in the shape and size of their respective trees. In both reliefs, the *vāhana*'s head is closest to the open veranda and the knee of the deity is bent and raised over it, allowing for a full view of the animal. The foliage of the trees is carved as compact clusters, thereby linking these two trees visually, though they clearly represent different species. Nestled amongst the branches of these trees are small animals, including chipmunks and birds. The presentation of these trees differs greatly from the elongate canopy of foliage that covers the heads of the deities in J18. Moreover, the J24 figures are seated

[25] These are: J6, J10, J12, J17, J19, J20, and J23.

beneath an undulating *toraṇa* (archway), an element that provides a rich and luxurious architectural setting for these deities.

Other aesthetic choices made by the artists to heighten the presentation of these figures as pairs can be seen in sculptures that are positioned outside the shrine door. The most elegant *yakṣa/yakṣī* pairing is found in the small excavation numbered J11. Like the sculpture of the *yakṣī* described earlier (Figure 4), the male deity is presented in all his finery (Figure 8). Every jewel in his conical crown is carved with great care as are his other accessories, including his armlets and necklaces. A thick strand of twisted pearls falls across his chest in an animated fashion and replicates the design of the necklace worn by his consort. In both cases, the length of the jewelry draws attention to the rounded forms of their bellies, physical reminders of the concepts of well-being and sustenance. Not only does their ornamentation and figural form coincide beautifully, but their overall presentation within the excavation further emphasizes their relationship as a pair. For example, both *vāhana*s are carved in profile and face the shrine door, prompting the devotee to enter. Rather than including the banyan and mango tree, which in essence distinguishes each figure, the artists have carved identical panels of *makara*s and *cāmaradhara*s above the throne crossbars. The seated positions of the deities also underscores their presentation as a compact unit as each figure bends the outside leg and points their foot towards the other.

The efforts put forth by the artists to compose complementary images of these deities can be seen in other caves across the site. Moreover, as a pair, these deities demarcate important liminal crossings within Ellora's cave-temples. They mark the transition into greater sanctified spaces—areas within the excavations that are in need of protection. Though rock-cut and literally part of the mountain, doors and/or other openings such as windows or verandas are generally considered to be the most vulnerable part of a sacred structure and thus in need of protection through the presence of deities and other apotropaic motifs. This is also the case for stairwells and transitional passages between halls, and, as we have seen, *yakṣī* and *yakṣa* images often occupy these spaces. Perhaps the most dramatic examples are the images in J18 (Figures 1 and 5) that become visible when the devotee reaches the top of the stairwell leading up to this excavation.

The inclusion of the *yakṣa/yakṣī* pair in the majority of Ellora's Jain caves, combined with their large size and prominent locations within the temple, clearly indicates the importance of these deities at the site. Although such a detailed examination of these figures is a good way to understand the nature of this pair, it is also fruitful to consider them within the fuller context of other Jain sites. For example, most active sites today have a local presiding deity, usually a goddess, who may be assisted by a male guardian figure (*kṣetrapāla*).

For example, Ambikā plays an integral role in worship activities at Śatruñjaya in Gujarat while the goddess Sacciyā presides over the Rajasthani temples at Osiāñ. Closer in time and proximity to Ellora's Jain caves are the monuments at Śravaṇa Beḷgoḷa in Karnataka that continue to serve as active spaces for lay and monastic devotional activities. Of importance, the presiding deity is Kūṣmāṇḍinī and in the many small temples built on the hillside of Candragiri, one finds eleventh and twelfth-century images of this goddess as well as that of a male *yakṣa*. Though Ellora's Jain caves have not been active for some time,[26] the *yakṣa/yakṣī* pair may have served as presiding deities in the past.

The importance of these deities in Ellora's Jain caves may also account for the increased interest in goddess imagery at the site during the late ninth and tenth centuries. At this time, independent images of the Jain goddess Cakreśvarī and Padmāvatī were added to pre-existing sculptural programs.[27] Of significance, a relief of an eight-armed Cakreśvarī was carved on the left wall of the sanctum inside the Choṭā Kailāsa. The inclusion of a Jain goddess alongside the main shrine Jina surely supports an increased role for these figures in devotional activities.

During the medieval period, goddesses were often associated with *vidyās*, magical spells or invocations that could be used to obtain material objects or to satisfy worldly concerns.[28] Worship to the goddess Padmāvatī, for example, was particularly advantageous as she could either grant material rewards or assist one in averting evil acts performed by *preta*s (hungry ghosts), *bhūta*s (generic ghosts), and *rākṣasa*s (demons).[29] When invoked in her six-armed form (wielding a noose, spear, sword, crescent, club and pestle) she would guarantee victory over one's enemies.[30] In the fourteenth century, worship to Ambikā/Kūṣmāṇḍinī resulted in similar benefits. In a number of medieval narratives, Jain goddesses come to the

[26] It should be noted, however, that a thirteenth-century image of Pārśvanātha continues to be worshipped at the site. This relief is enshrined within a modern temple that is located on the opposite side of the hill from Ellora's main complex of caves.

[27] Images of Cakreśvarī can be found in J20A, CK 1 and on the interior of the gateway leading into the Choṭā Kailāsa complex. An independent image of Padmāvatī is carved on the left side of the doorway leading into the transitional cell preceding J20A.

[28] According to Shah (1947a), by the late eighth and ninth centuries, sixteen goddesses (known as *vidyādevī*s or *mahāvidyās*) are enumerated in Digambara and Śvetāmbara textual sources.

[29] Shah (1987: 266-84) discusses a number of tenth through twelfth-century texts in his section on the goddess Padmāvatī. Epigraphs dating from the tenth through twelfth centuries in Karnataka also attest to Padmāvatī's popularity in worship, especially by members of ruling families. Padmāvatī was the tutelary deity of the Śāntaras, Raṭṭas and the Śilahāras in Karnataka. Twelfth-century inscriptions also associate the goddess with the founding of the Gaṅga dynasty. See Singh (1975: 54-5); Nandi (1973: 150-1); and Desai (1957: 72, n.2 and 171-2).

[30] The twelfth through thirteenth-century Digambara authors, Vasunandin, Āśādhāra, and Nemicandra refer to this form of the goddess, see Shah (1987: 275 and 277).

aid of kings and monks to grant various types of personal requests, whether it is the authority to rule, victory on the battlefield, or success in religious debate (Cort 1983: 248). Jain *yakṣa*s similarly intervene with their human devotees and are known in medieval texts to preside over single-word spells or *mantra*s (Shah 1947b: 850-51). Although the images at Ellora predate this textual material, it seems clear that these deities served to not only protect the sacred structure of the cave-temple, but extended this protection to their devotees.

In addition to their roles in devotional practices, Ellora's Jain *yakṣa*s and *yakṣī*s contribute to the overall celestial environment of the caves. By including these figures, the artists of Ellora's Jain monuments have transformed the main halls of the excavations into an assembly of deities who have gathered together to be in the presence of the Tīrthaṅkara. In essence, these Jain deities prepare the devotee to enter into the most sacred of spaces, the shrine chamber. Furthermore, with their rich ornamentation, purses of coins, offerings of fruit, and gestures of giving, these figures clearly express the glorious nature of Jain worship and its benefits.

Bibliography

Bhattacharya, B. (1924), *The Indian Buddhist Iconography* (London; Reprint Calcutta: Firma K.L. Mukhopadhyay, 1958).

Bhattacharya, B.C. (1939), *The Jaina Iconography* (Lahore; Reprint Delhi: Motilal Banarsidass, 1974).

Chatham, D. (1996), "Style and Composition in the Indra Sabhā and the Jagannātha Sabhā Caves at Ellorā," *Nirgrantha*, ed. M.A. Dhaky and J. Shah, vol. 2 (Ahmedabad: Sharadaben Chimanbhai Educational Research Centre), 73-86.

Cort, J. (1983), "Medieval Jaina Goddess Traditions," *Numen* XXXIV: 235-255.

_____. (1991), "The Śvetāmbar Mūrtipūjak Jain Mendicant," *Man*, n.s., 26.4: 651-671.

_____. (1996), "Art, Religion, and Material Culture: Some Reflections on Method," *Journal of the American Academy of Religion* LXIV.3: 613-632.

Desai, P.B. (1957), *Jainism in South India and Some Jaina Inscriptions* (Sholapur: Jaina Saṃskṛti Saṃrakṣaka Saṅgha).

Dhavalikar, M.K. (2003), *Ellora: Monumental Legacy* (Oxford: Oxford University Press).

Dundas, P. (1992), *The Jains* (London: Routledge).

Ghosh, A. (1974), *Jaina Art and Architecture*, 3 vols. (New Delhi: Bharatiya Jnanpith).

Granoff, P. (1993), "Of Mortals Become Gods: Two Stories from a Medieval Pilgrimage Text" in *The Clever Adulteress and Other Stories: A Treasury of Jain Literature,* ed. P. Granoff (Delhi: Motilal Banarsidass), 182-188.

Gupte, R.S. and B.D. Mahajan. (1962), *Ajanta, Ellora and Aurangabad Caves* (Bombay: B.D. Taraporevala Sons & Co.).

Jain, J. and E. Fischer (1978), *Jaina Iconography* (Leiden: Brill).

Leoshko, J. (1999), "Reviewing Early Jaina Art" in *Approaches to Jaina Studies: Philosophy, Logic, Rituals and Symbols,* ed. N.K. Wagle and O. Qvarnström (Toronto: University of Toronto Centre for South Asian Studies), 324-341.

Nandi, R.N. (1973), *Religious Institutions and Cults in the Deccan (c. AD 600-AD 1000)* (Delhi: Motilal Banarsidass).

Olivelle, P. (trans.) (2000), *Dharmasūtras: The Law Codes of Āpastambha, Gautama, Baudhāyana, and Vasiṣṭha* (Delhi: Motilal Banarsidass).

Owen, L. (2006), "Depicting a Jain Assembly: Representations of the *Samavasarana* at Ellora," *Jinamañjari* 34.2: 44-60.

Pal, P. (ed.) (1994), *The Peaceful Liberators: Jain Art from India* (Los Angeles: Los Angeles County Museum of Art).

Pereira, J. (1977), *Monolithic Jinas: The Iconography of the Jain Temples of Ellora* (Delhi: Motilal Banarsidass).

Ramachandran, T.N. (1934), "Tiruparuttikuṇṟam and Its Temples," *Bulletin of the Madras Government Museum* 1.3 (Madras: Government Press).

Rao, T.A. (1914), *Elements of Hindu Iconography* (Madras; Reprint New York: Paragon Book Reprint Corp., 1968).

Settar, S. (1971), "The Brahmadeva Pillars: An Inquiry into the Origin and Nature of the Brahmadeva Worship among Digambara Jains," *Artibus Asia* XXXIII: 17-38.

_____. (1975), "The Classical Kannaḍa Literature & The Digambara Jaina Iconography" in *Aspects of Jaina Art and Architecture,* ed. U.P. Shah and M.A. Dhaky (Ahmedabad: Gujarat State Committee for the Celebration of 2500th Anniversary of Bhagavān Mahāvīra Nirvāṇa), 25-48.

Shah, U.P. (1940), "Iconography of the Jain Goddess Ambikā," *Journal of the University of Bombay* 9.2: 147-69.

_____. (1947a), "Iconography of the Sixteen Jaina Mahāvidyās," *Journal of the Indian Society of Oriental Art* XV: 114-177.

_____. (1947b), "A Peep into the Early History of Tantra in Jain Literature" in *Bhārata Kaumudī* (Allahabad: The Indian Press), 839-854.

_____. (1955-56), "Bronze Hoard from Vasantagadh," *Lalit Kalā* 1.2: 55-65.

_____. (1959), *Akoṭa Bronzes* (Bombay: Dr. P.M. Joshi).

_____. (1961), "Introduction of Śāsanadevatās in Jaina Worship" in *Proceedings and Transactions of the All-India Oriental Conference*

20th Session, Bhubaneshwar, October 1959, ed. V. Raghavan (Poona: Bhadarkar Oriental Research Institute and All-India Oriental Conference, 1961), 141-152.
_____. (1972), "Yakṣiṇī of the Twenty-Fourth Jina Mahāvīra," *Journal of the Oriental Institute, Baroda* XXII.1-2: 70-78.
_____. (1987), *Jaina-Rūpa-Maṇḍana* (New Delhi: Abhinav Publications).
Singh, R.B.P. (1975), *Jainism in Early Medieval Karnataka (c. AD 500-1200)* (Delhi: Motilal Banarsidass).
Tiwari, M.N.P. (1983), *Elements of Jaina Iconography* (Varanasi: Indological Book House).
_____. (1989), *Ambikā in Jaina Art and Literature* (New Delhi: Bharatiya Jnanpith).

Figure 1. Jain *yakṣī*, Ellora J18
Photo by the author

Figure 2. Jain *yakṣī*, Ellora J26
Photo by the author

Figure 3. Jain *yakṣī*, Ellora J25
Photo by the author

Figure 4. Jain *yakṣī*, Ellora J11
Photo by the author

Figure 5. Jain *yakṣa*, Ellora J18
Photo by the author

Figure 6. Jain *yakṣa*, Ellora J24
Photo by the author

Figure 7. Jain *yakṣī*, Ellora J24
Photo by the author

Figure 8. Jain *yakṣa*, Ellora J11
Photo by the author

IV. (Re)considering Geographical and Conceptual Boundaries

Devin DeWeese

Spiritual Practice and Corporate Identity in Medieval Sufi Communities of Iran, Central Asia, and India: The Khalvatī/ʿIshqī/Shaṭṭārī Continuum

The problem of the corporate identities of medieval Sufi communities in the eastern Islamic world,[1] from the Mongol conquest through the Timurid era, is a central issue for understanding the emergence of important Sufi 'orders' that dominated Sufi thought and organization in subsequent times. As such, this problem is of significance for the history of Sufism in general, and for the social history of the Muslim world since the 15th century, but the problem has not received sufficient attention.

It has often been customary to assume that the labels we attach to particular Sufi lineages and 'orders,' such as Naqshbandī, Kubravī, Chishtī, Qādirī, and so forth, apply historically to discrete communities identifiable from the time of each 'order's' eponym. In the case of the Kubravī tradition, for instance, we often speak of the "Kubravīya" as having been in existence from the time of Najm al-Dīn Kubrā himself, in the early 13th century. We do this (1) even though we know that Najm al-Dīn did not set about to establish a 'path' or an 'order' named for himself; (2) even though we know that among the many figures

[1] As in the case of modern political boundaries, the contemporary academic borderlines of 'area studies' seldom correspond to traditional cultural patterns, and often obscure more than illuminate social and cultural links and continuities that prevailed in the past. Such is certainly the case with the regions classed today as 'Central Asia,' 'South Asia,' and the 'Middle East,' for which the lines drawn nowadays in governmental and academic circles conceal not only longstanding ties and commonalities among these regions, but entirely different ways of defining the 'regions' themselves. The present study is focused on one aspect of the shared religious history of the eastern Islamic world, involving Sufi communities that spanned Central Asia, eastern Iran, and India between the 14th and 16th centuries. It may serve, it is hoped, as a small token of gratitude and respect from a student who made his way from 'South Asian' to 'Central Asian' studies, to a teacher and scholar who, now more than 30 years ago, first taught me ways of reading and 'interrogating' texts, and ways of thinking about religious life, for which I remain in his debt.

identified as disciples or associates of Najm al-Dīn, there is a great diversity of activity and affiliation in their later lives, and only one or two can be reliably linked with a subsequent lineage that came to be characterized as "Kubravī;" and (3) even though we know that the very term "Kubravī" never appears in our sources until the 15th century (or the late 14th, at the earliest). Nevertheless, the habit of referring to anyone and anything even remotely connected with Najm al-Dīn as "Kubravī" remains deeply ingrained in scholarship on Sufism.

This habit of using such labels, however, is an obstacle to a better understanding of the historical development of Sufi communities within their societies precisely during the period in which the social role and impact of Sufi groups was dramatically expanding. I would argue that before we can grapple with the sorts of 'corporate' activity we associate with 'Sufi orders' within their social and historical context, we must grapple with the ways in which Sufi communities referred to themselves, and with the specific collective designations by which others referred to them. At issue, I would emphasize, is not simply the terminology we choose to refer to Sufi groups or traditions, and the problems posed by terms such as 'order' or '*ṭarīqa*' or 'brotherhood;' at issue, rather, are the specific labels applied by Sufi communities to themselves and to each other, the patterns discernible in the use of such labels, and what the labels were meant to indicate about the groups to which they were applied.

Do such labels apply to a particular sociological grouping? If so, what sort of continuity, or what venue of continuity, is implied by their use over several decades or centuries? Or, conversely, what kind of change is implied by a shift in the use of a given label over time? Do such labels instead apply to a ritual or disciplinary method, or to a complex of such methods, identified with a particular group, or stressed by that group as the core of its identity? If the terms are to be applied to disciplinary methods or other discrete elements of doctrine or practice, how and by what media are we to conceive of their transmission and continued identification by those terms (if not within a particular sociological vessel)? When and why do retrospectively-created communal labels (that is, labels applied collectively to all followers of an earlier master only several generations after that master's lifetime) come to be adopted by a particular community that claims a connection with that master's legacy (and do they then make sense only when viewed retrospectively)? How are we to understand shifts in the meaning of terms such as *silsila* (the "chain" of transmission that ideally connects a particular Sufi with the Prophet, in an unbroken lineage of masters and disciples), or *ṭarīqa* (which can refer to the mystical path in general, to specific paths defined initiatically or otherwise, or to communities)? In short, what exactly are we referring to when we label a person, a group, an initiatic chain, a book, a particular contemplative practice, or a social profile "Kubravī," or "Chishtī," or "Suhravardī," and so forth?

One answer is, of course, that we ought to be referring to different things at different times by the use of such labels, reflecting the ways in which the labels shift their meanings, their social referents, and their doctrinal and ritual referents as well. Too often, however, we use the labels without considering the shifting referents, and we go further and pretend that applying the label, or fitting a group or a practice within the classification scheme implied by the label, in itself serves somehow to explain and elucidate. Above all, we must be careful to note when particular labels are used in our sources, and when they are not. Even though our inclination to assign a particular label may rest on attested *silsila* ties, we must consider what it means to use a particular label if our 15th-century sources, for example, do not use it. If we extrapolate identifications and labels in this way, and in effect insert the labels into our sources, we risk inventing an organization, a corporate continuity, or even merely a continuity of practice and transmission that may never have existed.

It is true that sources from the late 14th and 15th centuries reveal a growing tendency to identify Sufi groups on the basis of a 'founding' figure who presumably defined a specific ritual or social profile that served to distinguish his followers from other Sufi communities. In Central Asia, we hear, for example, of the "'Abd al-Khāliqiyān," i.e., "the followers of 'Abd al-Khāliq [Ghijduvānī]," referring to the groups that are better-known under the designation "Khwājagān" (known as the precursors of the Naqshbandīs). We also hear of the "Zayn al-Dīnīyān," i.e., "the followers of Zayn al-Dīn," referring to those who attached themselves to Shaykh Zayn al-Dīn Khwāfī of Herat (d. 838/1435).[2] At the same time, we find a wide range of communal labels attached to Sufi groups organized hereditarily and named, in our sources, after a shaykh ("master") who was both a natural and a spiritual ancestor to the community.[3]

At the other extreme, however, we find frequent references, in the 14th and 15th centuries, to Sufis identified as belonging to the "Uvaysīya." The latter term looks like the name of other Sufi 'orders' emerging in this period. Its eponym, however, was not a local shaykh of the recent past, but a contemporary of the Prophet, who according to tradition adopted Islam without ever meeting Muḥammad in person. He thus became the prototype of Sufis who claimed to be following the mystical path without the benefit of guidance by a living master—a claim regarded in some circles, for obvious reasons, as giving free rein to innovation and deviation. The "Uvaysī" Sufis

[2] This label was no doubt the precursor of the label "Zaynī" used to refer to the order traced back to Khwāfī, which became prominent in the Ottoman world, but survived at least into the 16th century in Central Asia as well.

[3] These include groups labeled "Ismā'īl Atā'ī," "Badr Atā'ī," or "Sayyid Atā'ī," as well as others identified by a descriptive phrase rather than a simple label, e.g., "the descendants of Shaykh Aḥmad-i Jām."

are thus not an 'order,' and have no *silsila* in the normal sense of the term, as indicating a transmission from living master to disciple in an unbroken chain going back to the Prophet. Yet we know of Sufis who claimed to be Uvaysīs but nevertheless established the communal structures typical of other Sufi groups in this era (DeWeese 1993).

Still other groups in the same period claimed authority and legitimacy not on the basis of a direct spiritual encounter with a deceased shaykh (or prophet), but on the basis of a different sort of 'shortcut' back to the Prophet, through the notion of the *mu'ammarūn*, the "long-lived" saints. This notion was especially popular in the eastern Islamic world from the 13th to the 15th centuries. Perhaps the best known of the *mu'ammarūn* is the figure of Baba Ratan, an Indian saint of the 13th century whose great age allowed him to have met the Prophet in person and to transmit various spiritual (and more tangible) legacies from him. Here too we are far from the 'normative' type of Sufi community, but the names of some of these *mu'ammarūn* came to be attached to Sufi groups that otherwise looked very much like other Sufi communities of the time, marked by claims to legitimacy on the basis of natural heredity or of spiritual descent as framed in terms of a normative *silsila*.

Labels of these types were attached to a wide variety of communities and organizational principles, and reflect doctrinal and ritual transmission conceived in terms of a *silsila*, natural descent, or some other form of spiritual or quasi-hereditary relationship. Together with the predominance of later designations for 'orders' and *silsila*s that are clearly based on eponymous 'founders' of particular groups, they suggest the growing acceptance of the principle of identifying groups on a personal basis (since even the claimants to Uvaysī-style transmission or to receipt of a 'legacy' from a *mu'ammar* came to use a label linked to a holy person). Moreover, as noted, the tendency to define Sufi communities in terms of initiatic transmission from a prominent shaykh of the not-too distant past (e.g., Kubravī, Naqshbandī, Zaynī) came to be the dominant mode of communal labeling for such groups in later times. We also find, however, three interesting communal labels, prominent in 15th- and 16th-century sources from Central Asia, eastern Iran, and India, that appear to be based not on the name of a 'founding' saint, but on a style of mystical practice or experience. The three labels I have in mind—Khalvatī, 'Ishqī, and Shaṭṭārī—are of particular interest, moreover, because they appear to overlap in their social referents, in their experiential profile, and possibly in their communal origins.

The groups referred to by these three labels are more or less familiar in the settings in which they developed separately. Their earliest phases have not been seriously explored, however, and their overlap has not been noted. It is unfortunately impossible, in a brief article, to trace each of these groups' history in depth, or to fully explore the evidence and arguments in favor of their overlap or continuity. Instead, I will briefly lay out the basic profile of each group, and then focus on two issues relevant to the relationship between their corporate label and their social, doctrinal, and ritual profile: (1) the problem of the *silsila*s that were formulated for each group well after the earlier social continuum had been obscured, and (2) the meaning of the corporate labels applied to the groups, and the relationship between the labels and the distinctive ritual profiles of the various groups.

I. The Khalvatīya:

The best-known among these designations is that of the Khalvatīya, familiar as the name of a major Sufi order that developed primarily in the lands of the Ottoman empire from the 15th century down to the present. The history of the Khalvatīya, in Azerbaijan and Anatolia, as well as in Syria, Egypt, and the Balkans, has been studied extensively for the past half-century, by numerous scholars.[4] Most studies of the Ottoman Khalvatīya, however, have ignored the substantial evidence regarding the activity of other individuals, and Sufi communities, identified by the designation "Khalvatī," in various parts of Iran and Central Asia during the 14th and 15th centuries. In particular, sources from the 15th and 16th centuries preserve scattered but substantial information about Khalvatī shaykhs and communities active in Mawarannahr (Bukhārā), Khurāsān (including Herat and Quhistān, to the west of Herat), and Kirmān (in south-central Iran); the evidence from all these communities points consistently to Khwārazm as the place of origin of this eastern Khalvatī 'tradition.'

By far the most substantial and enduring 'eastern' Khalvatī community, to judge from our sources, was that of Herat. The Khalvatī presence there, both before and after that city's emergence as the Timurid capital, has not drawn much attention,[5] but is clear from two Persian works produced nearly 20 years apart—the *Nafaḥāt al-uns*, a famous hagiographical compendium compiled by the illustrious poet and Sufi, Nūr al-Dīn 'Abd al-Raḥman Jāmī, in the latter 1470s, and the *Maqṣad al-iqbāl* of Amīr Sayyid Aṣīl al-Dīn 'Abdullāh b. 'Abd al-Raḥmān al-Ḥusaynī al-Dashtakī, a guide to the saints' shrines of Herat completed in 864/1460. Jāmī mentions three generations

[4] The seminal studies of the Khalvatīya in the Ottoman environment include Kissling (1953 and 1956), and Martin (1972); see also the summary of De Jong (1978b). For more recent studies of the Ottoman Khalvatīya, see the thorough treatment of Öngören (2000: 27-116), and the recent studies of Curry (2005 and 2008). The important monograph of Clayer (1994) offers the best survey of the Khalvatīya in the Balkans. For later Khalvatī groups in Egypt, see Bannerth (1964-66); De Jong (1978a and 1987); and Chih (1998).

[5] The Khalvatī community of Herat was noted by Aubin (1967: 204, n. 3-6, and 216; Aubin's article deals with another Sufi community linked to the Khalvatī tradition, as discussed below). Based on Aubin's article, the Khalvatī community of Herat was mentioned briefly by Savory (1969: 196), and by O'Kane (1987: 91).

of Khalvatī shaykhs, in his entry on the latest of them, called Ẓahīr al-Dīn Khalvatī:[6]

> He combined the exoteric and esoteric sciences. Mawlānā Zayn al-Dīn Abū Bakr Tāybādī[7] used to say, "I know no one like Ẓahīr al-Dīn beneath the celestial vault." He was a disciple (*murīd*) of Shaykh Sayf al-Dīn Khalvatī, and was in his company and service for 15 years; Shaykh Sayf al-Dīn departed the world in the year 783/1381-82, and his grave is in the shrine of the Khalvatīs, at the head of the Gāzurgāh bridge. Shaykh Sayf al-Dīn was a disciple of Shaykh Muḥammad Khalvatī, of whom they say that whenever he would engage in the *dhikr* in Khwārazm, his voice would carry for four leagues.

Jāmī goes on to identify Muḥammad Khalvatī as a contemporary of another Khwārazmian saint from the first half of the 14th century, and includes two further anecdotes about Ẓahīr al-Dīn, one describing his recitation of the Qur'ān, the other affirming his ascetic prowess (once during a forty-day meditational retreat, he broke his fast only four times, taking boiled wheat broth once every ten days). Jāmī adds, finally,

> They say that whenever he went for *ziyārat* (pious visitation) to [the Khalvatī cemetery at] Gāzurgāh, he would go barefoot upon passing the Gāzurgāh bridge; for he said, "I would be ashamed before God's saints to tread upon them with my sandals." He departed the world in the year 800/1397-98, and his grave is in the shrine of the Khalvatīs, near the grave of his shaykh.

Jāmī's account thus confirms a short segment of a *silsila* and provides death-dates for two of the three shaykhs he mentions: Shaykh Muḥammad Khalvatī of Khwārazm > Sayf al-Dīn Khalvatī of Herat (d. 783/1381-82) > Ẓahīr al-Dīn Khalvatī of Herat (d. 800/1397-98).[8] The same segment, and nearly the same dates, are confirmed in the *Maqṣad al-iqbāl*. This work's entry on Sayf al-Dīn Khalvatī praises his austerities, his knowledge of the esoteric and exoteric sciences, and his miracles, but places his death in 785/1383-84 (agreeing with Jāmī, however, on his burial "at the shrine of the Khalvatīs near the Gāzurgāh bridge"). The account adds the details that he was born in Herat, grew up in Khwārazm, and settled in Herat, and confirms his status as a disciple of Shaykh Muḥammad Khalvatī, at whose hand he donned the *khirqa* (the Sufi 'cloak' typically indicating disciple-

[6] Jāmī, *Nafaḥāt*: 504.

[7] This figure, whom Jāmī describes as an Uvaysī (*Nafaḥāt*: 498-501), was a prominent shaykh of the time of Timur (he was famous for a story affirming that the shaykh's spiritual power made Timur tremble in his presence); he died in 791/1389.

[8] Ẓahīr al-Dīn Khalvatī is also mentioned briefly in a short treatise by the famous poet and Ṣafavid propagandist, Qāsim-i Anvār (d. 837/1433), who recalled a discussion with "Mawlānā Ẓahīr al-Dīn Khalvatī," in the year 779/1377-78, in a Sufi hostel (*khānqāh*) in Herat; see Qāsim-i Anvār, *Kulliyāt*: 402 (and on Qāsim-i Anvār, see Savory 1969).

ship and succession).[9] The account of Ẓahīr al-Dīn Khalvatī included in the *Maqṣad al-iqbāl*,[10] meanwhile, praises his skill in reciting the Qur'ān, cites the same comment about him by Zayn al-Dīn Tāybādī mentioned by Jāmī, and affirms his service, "for a long time," to Sayf al-Dīn Khalvatī. Like Jāmī's account, it mentions his death in 800/1397-98 and his burial at the shrine of the Khalvatīs, but says that his grave is near that of his father (there is no other evidence, however, that Ẓahīr al-Dīn was a son, as well as a disciple, of Sayf al-Dīn).

Other members of the Khalvatī community of Herat are known only from the *Maqṣad al-iqbāl*, through which we can trace altogether four generations of this Khalvatī lineage.[11] Perhaps of greater interest, however, are the references in this work to a district or neighborhood (*maḥalla*), a cemetery, and a *khānqāh*—the chief institutional center for most Sufi communities of this era—in Herat, each linked by name with the corporate presence of the Khalvatī shaykhs.[12] These references indicate a reasonably substantial institutional presence of the Khalvatīya in the major city of Timurid Khurāsān, and remind us of the tangible 'infrastructure' of Sufi organizations in this period. At the same time, it is likely that the later Khalvatī shaykhs—at least those active after the time of Ẓahīr al-Dīn Khalvatī—were part of the extensive Sufi networks characteristic of the cosmopolitan city of Herat. These networks, evident from Jāmī's *Nafaḥāt* and from other sources of this era, bound Sufi shaykhs and their followers together across the formal *silsila* lines that seem to have been just then taking shape, and involved distinctive patterns of association and training, without necessarily involving formal discipleship.[13]

[9] *Maqṣad al-iqbāl*: 46-47; the printed text here reads "Maḥmūd" instead of Muḥammad, but earlier in the work (43), "Shaykh Muḥammad Khalvatī Khwārazmī" is mentioned among the contemporaries of another shaykh of Herat who died in 738/1337-38 (other such contemporaries named here range from the famous 'Alā' al-Dawla Simnānī [d. 736/1336] to "Abū Bakr Tāybādī" [d. 791/1389]).

[10] *Maqṣad al-iqbāl*: 47.

[11] *Maqṣad al-iqbāl*: 72-73, 78, 83, 89. They include: another *murīd* of Sayf al-Dīn, namely Abū Sa'īd Khalvatī (d. 820/1418); 'Abdullāh Khalvatī (d. 833/1429-30), possibly a disciple of Sayf al-Dīn or of Ẓahīr al-Dīn, said to have dwelled in "the Sufi hostel of the Khalvatīs" (*khānqāh-i khalvatīyān*); Darvīsh 'Abdullāh (d. 838/1434-35), a disciple of Ẓahīr al-Dīn identified as the owner of a feed shop and as an inhabitant of "the district of the Khalvatīs" (*maḥalla-yi khalvatīyān*) in Herat; and a certain Sayyid Ghiyāth al-Dīn (d. 862/1457-58), whose master is not identified. All but the second are said to be buried in the "cemetery enclosure of the Khalvatīs" (*ḥaẓīra-yi khalvatīyān*).

[12] The shrine or cemetery is the aspect of the Khalvatī 'institutional' presence mentioned most often. Undoubtedly the references to the *mazār-i khalvatīyān* reflect the name by which the cemetery had become known by the second half of the 15th century, and should not be construed as confirming the existence of a Khalvatī community before the time of Sayf al-Dīn. The Khalvatī cemetery in Herat is noted by Allen (1981: 181, No. 588; cf. 150, No. 506), citing the *Maqṣad al-iqbāl*'s accounts.

[13] For example, just prior to the entry for Ẓahīr al-Dīn Khalvatī, Jāmī gives an account of Abū Yazīd Pūrānī (d. 862/1458), a prominent shaykh of Herat whom Jāmī knew personally; Jāmī notes his close connections with Sa'd al-Dīn Kāshgharī (d. 860/1456) of the early Naqshbandī community of Herat; with Zayn al-Dīn Khwāfī (d. 838/1435), a prominent shaykh of Herat and the 'founder'—and in this case not merely the eponym—of the

Many of the shaykhs of 15th-century Herat who are mentioned in Jāmī's *Nafaḥāt* are indeed portrayed as having associated with, and having been trained by, multiple masters, and although Jāmī is often more willing to assign these other shaykhs to particular *silsilas*, it is clear that neither their mode of practice, nor their circle of intimates, nor their 'communal' identification was yet firmly linked with a particular Sufi 'order' defined in terms of a shared *silsila*.

We do not know the fate of the Khalvatī circle of Herat; our sources lose sight of its members, or fail to trace any "Khalvatī" shaykhs after the middle of the 15th century. Moreover, while the Khalvatī shaykhs are prominent in the *Maqṣad al-iqbāl* and in Jāmī's *Nafaḥāt*, they are nowhere mentioned in the larger history of Herat produced a generation later by Mu'īn al-Dīn Muḥammad Zamchī Isfizārī, the *Rawżāt al-jannāt fī awṣāf madīnat Harāt* (finished in 899/1493-94). The Khalvatī community is also missing from the works of Khwāndamīr and from the *Majālis al-'ushshāq*, both reflecting the literary culture of Herat from the late 15th and early 16th centuries. Whether these works' silence on the Khalvatīya is to be attributed simply to the interests and tastes of the various authors, to the ascendancy, by the 1490s, of Naqshbandī circles hostile to the Khalvatī shaykhs, or to the actual disappearance (or relabeling) of the Khalvatī community by the time of the later works, is unclear.

The possibility of Naqshbandī hostility is suggested by one of our two brief references to a Khalvatī community of Bukhārā. The *Rashaḥāt-i 'ayn al-ḥayāt*, completed in 909/1503-04 by Fakhr al-Dīn 'Alī b. Ḥusayn al-Vā'iẓ al-Kāshifī al-Ṣafī as a biography of the eminent Naqshbandī shaykh Khwāja 'Ubaydullāh Aḥrār,[14] includes a story about that tradition's eponym, Bahā' al-Dīn Naqshband, that is not found in the earlier hagiographies devoted to him (*Rashaḥāt*: I, 98); the story prefaces the account of Bahā' al-Dīn's death (in 791/1389). One of his followers is said to have related that Bahā' al-Dīn had attended the funeral of Shaykh Nūr al-Dīn Khalvatī, who had died in Bukhārā. On that occasion the mourners wailed so loudly, and the women made such loud and disagreeable sounds, that others in attendance were disgusted and tried to quiet them. This, however, led only to more noise, as everyone was talking or wailing at the same time, prompting Bahā' al-Dīn to say, "When my time has reached its end, I will teach the dervishes how to die."

Contention over the degree of noisemaking that should be coun-

Zaynī order; with Bahā' al-Dīn 'Umar Jaghāragī (d. 857/1453), whose *silsila* was traced back to 'Alā' al-Dawla Simnānī; and with the devotee of the Ṣafavid house, Qāsim-i Anvār, mentioned above. At the same time, Jāmī affirms that Pūrānī frequented the company of Ẓahīr al-Dīn Khalvatī, and was "very devoted to his *ṭarīqa*, although he did not enter into the relationship of discipleship (*nisbat-i irādat*) with him;" and despite his many informal ties to the prominent shaykhs mentioned here, Pūrānī "had no *pīr* in the *ṭarīqat* in the external sense," and was, Jāmī concludes, an Uvaysī (Jāmī, *Nafaḥāt*: 502).

[14] On this figure, see now the introduction to Gross and Urunbaev (2002).

tenanced, and, more broadly, over the proper limits of passionate exuberance in expressions of religiosity, is of course a common issue in many religious communities, and controversy surrounding the propriety of wailing and loud mourning during funeral rites has long been an issue in the Muslim world. This particular story pits Bahā' al-Dīn, representing the 'reformist,' *sharī'a*-conscious, and 'sober' tradition of the Naqshbandīya, against the raucous profile of the followers of Nūr al-Dīn Khalvatī (as we will see, the Khalvatī shaykhs are consistently ascribed a penchant for noisemaking, above all in connection with their distinctive style of spiritual practice, based on the vocal *dhikr*). Yet the story also suggests a rivalry, to the point of outright hostility and contempt, between the followers of Bahā' al-Dīn and the Khalvatī community, if not in the actual lifetimes of Bahā' al-Dīn and Nūr al-Dīn, then at least by the time the *Rashaḥāt* was compiled. Such hostility is further suggested by an incidental reference, in a Central Asian source produced somewhat later in the 16th century, to a disciple of Nūr al-Dīn Khalvatī named Qādir Qulī Turkmān, who is criticized for constantly rejecting and slandering the *ṭarīqa-yi khwājagān* (Ḥāfiẓ Baṣīr, *Maẓhar*: 181b-182a).[15]

The Nūr al-Dīn Khalvatī who figures in this story is in fact mentioned in an earlier Bukharan source, known as the *Tārīkh-i Mullāzāda*, completed most likely in the 1440s. This work—a guide to saints' shrines, like the *Maqṣad al-iqbāl*—also mentions the grave of a certain Shaykh Sirāj al-Dīn Khalvatī (*Mullāzāda*: 39), who is not further identified or even linked with the other "Khalvatī" shaykh mentioned in it. Regarding Shaykh Nūr al-Dīn Khalvatī himself, however, the *Tārīkh-i Mullāzāda* adds the important detail that "he was among the successors (*khulafā*) of the lineage (*khānavāda*) of the great shaykh Najm al-Dīn Kubrā" (*Mullāzāda*: 74). With such phrasing, this account is historically plausible, but we find no other evidence regarding Nūr al-Dīn's place in a 'Kubravī' lineage.

What we do find, however, is evidence regarding a Shaykh Nūr al-Dīn Khalvatī who figures prominently in hagiographical lore about the city of Kirmān, in central Iran. A pattern of close ties between Sufi communities of Bukhārā and those of Kirmān (for example, involving descendants of Sayf al-Dīn Bākharzī, a prominent shaykh and jurist of Bukhārā best-known as a disciple of Najm al-Dīn Kubrā) suggests that the Nūr al-Dīn of Bukhārā and the Nūr al-Dīn of Kirmān were one and the same person. The material from Kirmān is significant for linking the Khalvatī profile with the performance of the vocal *dhikr*, and for identifying this Khalvatī shaykh as a Turk. It also points to the 1350s as the time of the Khalvatī shaykh's arrival in Kirmān, and

[15] The source in question is a work, written by Ḥāfiẓ Baṣīr of Khuzār, in Mawarannahr, based on the teachings of a female saint of his native town known simply as "Aghā-yi Buzurg" ("the great lady"), whose death may be placed in 929/1522-23. On this work, see my discussion in DeWeese (2008: 300-303).

affirms that this Shaykh Nūr al-Dīn had been trained in Khwārazm by Shaykh Muḥammad Khalvatī.

The earliest substantial account again comes from a shrine-guide, the work of Mihrābī Kirmānī, a seventh-generation descendant of Sayf al-Dīn Bākharzī. The work recounts Shaykh Nūr al-Dīn Aḥmad Khwārazmī's victory over a scholar who objected to the apparent blasphemy entailed by the shaykh's Turkic accent as he uttered the *dhikr*; the defeated scholar became Nūr al-Dīn's disciple (Kirmānī, *Tadhkirat al-awliyā*: 2-4).[16] The account also affirms that Nūr al-Dīn was a *murīd* of Shaykh Muḥammad Khalvatī and traveled the mystical path in his service in Khwārazm, thus clearly linking him with the Khwārazmian figure who was also the master of the first Khalvatī shaykh in Herat (Kirmānī, *Tadhkirat al-awliyā*: 16-17).[17]

The same Shaykh Nūr al-Dīn, assigned the *nisba*s "Khwārazmī" and "Khalvatī," also appears in the biographical materials focused on perhaps the most famous saint of Kirmān—Sayyid Ni'matullāh Valī (d. 834/1430-31)—published a half-century ago by the late Jean Aubin. A relatively early biography of Sayyid Ni'matullāh includes a single reference to "Shaykh Nūr al-Dīn al-Abdāl al-Khwārazmī al-Khalvatī," and hints at some rivalry between the two shaykhs by noting that a local *qāżī* of Kirmān who became a devotee of Sayyid Ni'matullāh had formerly been a companion of Nūr al-Dīn Khalvatī (Aubin, *Materiaux*: 91). A 17th-century source records a longer anecdote about the challenge posed to Nūr al-Dīn Khwārazmī by Sayyid Ni'matullāh, who had just arrived in Kirmān following his expulsion from Mawarannahr by Timur. According to this pro-Ni'matullāh account, Kirmān was part of the "domain" of Nūr al-Dīn Khwārazmī, but the latter, upon learning that Sayyid Ni'matullāh was soon to arrive, understood that he intended "to seize Kirmān from me," and realized that Ni'matullāh's "solar rank" rendered Nūr al-Dīn powerless to oppose the newcomer (Aubin, *Materiaux*: 177-178).[18]

In the case of Kirmān and Bukhārā, our sources show us clearly only a single Khalvatī shaykh (and the one in Kirmān may well be the same as the one in Bukhārā).[19] We may rightly infer the existence of a

[16] This work's account of Nūr al-Dīn Aḥmad Khwārazmī is noted in Aubin (1967: 207).

[17] Chronological indications in the account suggest that Nūr al-Dīn came to Kirmān roughly between 1353 and 1365.

[18] The account is preserved in the *Jāmi'-i mufīdī* of Muḥammad Mufīd Mustawfī Yazdī, completed in 1099/1679, which cites in turn a treatise by a certain Ṣun'ullāh Ni'matullāhī of Kirmān; see also Aubin's discussion of the work in his introduction (7-8).

[19] There is nothing explicit in these accounts to suggest that Nūr al-Dīn Khalvatī made his way to Bukhārā once he was displaced from Kirmān, but such a scenario is certainly plausible if we assume that one and the same figure is reflected in the accounts from Kirmān and Bukhārā. That same assumption is also of interest with regard to Nūr al-Dīn's connection with the 'lineage' of Najm al-Dīn Kubrā: the Kirmānī material links him with Muḥammad Khalvatī of Khwārazm, and another relatively early source (from the second half of the 15th century) identifies Muḥammad Khalvatī as a direct disciple of Najm al-Dīn Kubrā. While such a relationship is utterly anachronistic, two independent sources link-

circle of disciples in both localities, but we have no further information on the institutional foundations or corporate continuity of a "Khalvatī" presence in Kirmān or Bukhārā, as we have for Herat. Our last example of a Khalvatī shaykh, nevertheless, is again connected with a substantial 'infrastructure,' in the Khurāsānī region of Quhistān.

For the Khalvatī community of Quhistān we have a unique hagiographical source first explored over 40 years ago by Jean Aubin (Aubin 1967).[20] The source in question was written toward the end of the 15th century by a certain Qivām al-Dīn b. Muḥammad, and recounts the life and mystical career of Akhī Muḥammad-Shāh Shārakhtī. The work affirms that Akhī Muḥammad-Shāh was alive in 810/1408, and Aubin suggests that he must have died soon after that, around 1410. Aubin's description of the work allows us to place Akhī Muḥammad-Shāh in the Khalvatī lineage stemming from the same Shaykh Muḥammad Khalvatī of Khwārazm known from other sources. According to the text, Akhī Muḥammad-Shāh was for thirty years the *murīd* of "Sayyid Niẓām al-Dīn," who was in turn among the companions (*aṣḥāb*) of Shaykh Muḥammad Khalvatī; of the latter figure, this work reports the detail mentioned also in Jāmī's *Nafaḥāt*, namely that when he recited the *dhikr* in Khwārazm, his voice could be heard four leagues away (Aubin 1967: 204).[21] As Aubin noted, the "Sayyid" or "Shaykh" Niẓām al-Dīn mentioned as Akhī Muḥammad-Shāh's master is portrayed as dwelling in the vicinity of Jām. Given his dwelling-place and his link to Shaykh Muḥammad Khalvatī, he is undoubtedly to be identified with the "Shaykh Niẓām Khalvatī" whose death on 18 Rajab 775/3 January 1374 in 'Ishqābād-i Jām is reported in the *Mujmal-i Faṣīḥī* (Faṣīḥ, *Mujmal*: III, 106).[22]

The hagiography studied by Aubin does not apply the label "Khalvatī" to its subject, Akhī Muḥammad-Shāh, or even to his master, Niẓām al-Dīn; it nevertheless notes the move of one of Akhī Muḥammad-Shāh's sons to Herat and his burial in the "Khalvatī cemetery" there. This may suggest a broader network of loosely-linked 'Khalvatī' communities, as well as the emergence of a 'Khalvatī' communal consciousness shared by the Quhistānī group. At the same

ing members of the Khalvatī community, in some way, to a line of succession from Najm al-Dīn Kubrā should not be discounted; they may reflect traditions linking later 'Khalvatī' shaykhs with lineages traced to disciples of Najm al-Dīn.

[20] Aubin's study remains a model of the judicious use of hagiographical materials in conjunction with available historical, geographical, and documentary sources in pursuit of a detailed social history of a limited area and period. The manuscript he used is preserved in the library of Istanbul University (MS F 1163, ff. 38b-64a).

[21] Given Jāmī's cavalier treatment of his sources, it is not unlikely that the work described by Aubin was his source for this comment, though Jāmī does not mention Akhī Muḥammad-Shāh or any other figures known from the hagiography studied by Aubin.

[22] The text edition notes that the full *laqab* "Niẓām al-Dīn" appears in one manuscript; cf. the Russian translation of part of the work (Faṣīḥ, *Mudzhmal*: 97). The *Mujmal-i Faṣīḥī* is a chronologically-arranged collection of historical and biographical data from the eastern Islamic world, compiled in the mid-15th century.

time, the work makes it clear that Akhī Muḥammad-Shāh managed a *khānqāh* for his community, and suggests that controversy and quarrels developed over the corporate control of the Sufi community's institutional infrastructure. It recounts, first, Akhī Muḥammad-Shāh's conflicts with the descendants of the famous 12th-century Sufi Shaykh Aḥmad-i Jām (reflecting, again, the tension in the Timurid era between entrenched hereditary Sufi groups and 'upstart' *silsila*-based groups whose authority came not from heredity but from charismatic demonstrations). The work also mentions a certain Akhī 'Alī, identified as a Khalvatī shaykh, who came some twenty years after Akhī Muḥammad-Shāh's death and effectively seized control of the *khānqāh* he had begun building. And finally, it hints at conflict between two sons of Akhī Muḥammad-Shāh over succession to the community's leadership.

Space constraints preclude further examination of scattered evidence on other groups and individuals assigned the name "Khalvatī" during the 14th and 15th centuries, encountered well beyond the Central Asian homeland of the Khalvatī tradition (in Yazd, Tabrīz, and even Egypt). We must return, instead, to the additional early information we have on the figure of Shaykh Muḥammad Khalvatī of Khwārazm, to whom the hagiographical and biographical materials from Herat, Bukhārā, Kirmān, and Quhistān independently link the Khalvatī communities active in these regions. First, the *Mujmal-i Faṣīḥī* reports the death of "Shaykh Muḥammad Khalvatī" on 28 Jumādā I 751/3 August 1350, without indicating where or giving any further details (Faṣīḥ, *Mujmal*: III, 77; Faṣīḥ, *Mudzhmal*: 77). This date corresponds reasonably well with the dates given or implied for three figures identified as direct disciples of Shaykh Muḥammad Khalvatī: Shaykh Sayf al-Dīn Khalvatī of Herat (d. 1383), Shaykh Nūr al-Dīn Khalvatī of Kirmān and (probably) Bukhārā, who died prior to Bahā' al-Dīn Naqshband (d. 1389), and the Shaykh Niẓām al-Dīn (d. 1374) mentioned in connection with the Quhistānī community.

Second, the earliest known reference to Shaykh Muḥammad Khalvatī of Khwārazm is found in the *Khulāṣat al-manāqib*, a hagiography devoted to Sayyid 'Alī Hamadānī (d. 786/1385), compiled in 1387 by Hamadānī's disciple, Nūr al-Dīn Ja'far Badakhshī (Badakhshī, *Khulāṣat*: 257).[23] This work mentions Shaykh Muḥammad Khalvatī in a wholly negative light, as a hostile shaykh who sent *jinns* to torment Hamadānī's companion. The account does not specify where this encounter took place, but it is followed immediately by another story that may point toward Khwārazm; it recalls Hamadānī's anger when provoked by a similar display of supernatural torments, and the

[23] See also the older German paraphrase of the work, Teufel, *Lebensbeschreibung*: 118. The passage was noted in Aubin (1967: 204 and 216, citing Teufel), without details of the encounter. On the subject of this work, see DeWeese (1992).

shaykh blamed for inflicting them is explicitly linked, elsewhere in the same work, with Khwārazm (Badakhshī, *Khulāṣat*: 220-221).[24]

Third, our early sources offer virtually no information regarding the spiritual lineage of Shaykh Muḥammad Khalvatī himself. Several such sources allow us to trace two or three generations in a lineage stemming *from* Muḥammad Khalvatī, but pay practically no attention to the identity of his master, or to any *silsila* or group with which he was identified (except for sporadic intimations of links with the legacy of Najm al-Dīn Kubrā). As noted, this is not at all unusual for prominent Sufi figures of this era who were adopted as the 'founders' of particular communal traditions; it is quite common for lineages to be traced back only as far as a shaykh of the 13th or 14th century, whose own initiatic lineage does not become the subject of significant attention until it is addressed in sources produced in the late 15th or 16th century. What we find, instead of information on Muḥammad Khalvatī's spiritual lineage or training, is an interesting comment regarding his *natural* descent. Jāmī's *Nafaḥāt*, as noted, mentions Shaykh Muḥammad Khalvatī in its entry focused on the chief Khalvatī shaykh of Herat, Ẓahīr al-Dīn; but Jāmī also mentions him in his entry on a contemporary shaykh who performed numerous seclusionary retreats—using the term "*arba'īn*" here rather than "*khalvat*"—at the grave of the celebrated 12th-century Sufi, Shaykh Aḥmad-i Jām. This shaykh, whom Jāmī met as a boy, had affirmed that Aḥmad-i Jām "bestowed great favor upon all his descendants, to the point that even Khwāja Muḥammad Khalvatī, who was externally quite dissipated, enjoyed his considerable favor" (Jāmī, *Nafaḥāt*: 454-455).[25]

This intriguing comment not only reflects the general distaste for Muḥammad Khalvatī's spiritual style, as reflected also in a story from the *Rashaḥāt* reviewed below, but also would appear to indicate that Shaykh Muḥammad Khalvatī was a descendant of Aḥmad-i Jām, and may have owed his reputation to, and formed his spiritual legacy within, the world of hereditary Sufi charisma focused on Aḥmad-i Jām (which was a mainstay of the religious history of Khurāsān and Mawarannahr from the 12th to the 17th century, at least).[26] If so, this is particularly interesting in connection with Akhī Muḥammad-Shāh Shārakhtī's quarrels with descendants of Aḥmad-i Jām, noted in the hagiography described by Aubin, and suggests tensions, typical of the era, between claimants to a *silsila*-based transmission from Shaykh Muḥammad Khalvatī (i.e., Akhī Muḥammad-Shāh), and claimants to his legacy through natural descent.

[24] Cf. Teufel, *Lebensbeschreibung*: 106, 118.

[25] The passage was noted (based on an older publication of the *Nafaḥāt*) in Aubin (1967: 210, n. 2).

[26] On Aḥmad-i Jām, see Moayyad and Lewis (2004); a study of this figure's familial legacy is long overdue.

Our final story about Muḥammad Khalvatī is found in two of the biographies of Khwāja Aḥrār, the eminent Naqshbandī shaykh of Tashkent and Samarqand who died in 895/1490; one is known as the *Malfūẓāt* or *Masmū'āt* and was compiled by Khwāja Aḥrār's son-in-law Mīr 'Abd al-Avval Nīshāpūrī, and the other is the *Rashaḥāt*, cited earlier. The story they tell about Shaykh Muḥammad Khalvatī is essentially the same in both versions. It explains, in effect, how Muḥammad Khalvatī came to dwell in Khwārazm, and again evinces considerable hostility toward the tradition he represented (Nawshāhī, *Aḥvāl*: 278; *Rashaḥāt*: II, 371-372).[27]

The account involves a maternal ancestor of Khwāja Aḥrār known as Shaykh Khāvand-i Ṭahūr, a prominent saint of Tashkent whose shrine is still a popular pilgrimage site there. Shaykh Khāvand-i Ṭahūr was the grandfather of Khwāja Aḥrār's mother, and materials preserved in the Aḥrār biographies allow us to date his death to 755/1354 (corresponding well with the date we have for Muḥammad Khalvatī). According to the story, Shaykh Khāvand-i Ṭahūr once went to Turkistān to spend time with a certain Tonguz Shaykh, "who was among the eminent figures from the lineage (*khānadān*) of Atā Yasavī."[28] He was accompanied on the journey by one of his inferior pupils, Shaykh Muḥammad Khalvatī,[29] whom he clearly disdained and wished to be rid of. After the two visitors had spent several days with Tonguz Shaykh, the latter confided to Shaykh Khāvand-i Ṭahūr that Shaykh Muḥammad Khalvatī was not a worthy companion, and promised to bestow upon him a gift that would signal his base propensities. The gift was a tambourine, and as Shaykh Khāvand-i Ṭahūr parted company with Muḥammad Khalvatī, sending him off to Khwārazm, he declared to him, "The gift of [Tonguz] Shaykh is a sign that followers of defective mind will gather in your presence, just as children and slave-girls and madmen congregate at the sound of the tambourine." The *Rashaḥāt*'s version adds here that indeed, after this Shaykh Muḥammad "Khalvī" went to Khwārazm, "many of the ignorant and common people gathered around him and became his *murīds*."

The account is of interest for evoking the same penchant for noisemaking highlighted in the story about Nūr al-Dīn Khalvatī's funeral in Bukhārā, and, in a less derogatory way, in the comment about Muḥammad Khalvatī's voice being heard at a great distance. Beyond this detail, however, the account is clearly designed to portray Shaykh Muḥammad Khalvatī as little more than a charlatan

[27] The account edited by Nawshāhī is from the work of 'Abd al-Avval Nīshāpūrī.

[28] The phrasing may indicate either natural or spiritual descendants of the celebrated Khwāja Aḥmad Yasavī, eponym of the Yasavīya; *"tonguz"* is the Turkic term for "boar" or "pig," and his appellation suggests some ironic or provocative implications that are unfortunately obscured in the sources.

[29] Some manuscripts of both works give the form "Khalvī" for his *nisba*.

who attracted a following on the margins of society because of the clamor he made. This suggests hostility between the Naqshbandī and Khalvatī communities, projected back into the time of the figure who is consistently identified as the 'founder,' in effect, of the Khalvatī tradition based in Mawarannahr, Khurāsān, and Kirmān.

Before we leave the eastern Khalvatī shaykhs and groups, it should be noted that the best-known 'Khalvatī' community—the one that unfolded in the Ottoman domains, through several *silsila* lines based initially in Azerbaijan and eastern Anatolia—is the one that appears to be most tenuously linked with the 'Khalvatī' figure of Khwārazm; that figure, as we have seen, is consistently identified as the point of origin for the short *silsila*s that may be traced for the Khalvatī shaykhs of Herat, Kirmān, Bukhārā, and Quhistān, but his links, if any, with the 'western' Khalvatī lineage are much more obscure. In nearly every case, the branches of the Khalvatīya active in the Ottoman lands, from the Balkans to Egypt, trace their lineage back to a certain 'Umar Khalvatī, who is said to have died at the very end of the 14th century. This would make him chronologically suitable, if slightly late, to have been a disciple of our "Shaykh Muḥammad Khalvatī" of Khwārazm, and indeed some western Khalvatī sources identify 'Umar Khalvatī's master as "Muḥammad" and link him with Khwārazm. Other western Khalvatī sources, however, complicate the picture, assigning a different name and/or a different *nisba*[30] to the master of 'Umar Khalvatī, and virtually all western Khalvatī sources further link their tradition with Shaykh Ibrāhīm Zāhid Gīlānī (d. 700/1301),[31] despite the chronological stretch involved in inserting only one link between him and 'Umar Khalvatī (d. ca. 1397). To further complicate the issue, our earliest source to mention 'Umar Khalvatī—the *Ṣafvat al-ṣafā*, compiled in the mid-14th century (but edited in the 16th) as a hagiography devoted to Shaykh Ṣafī al-Dīn (d. 735/1334) of Ardabīl, the ancestor of the Ṣafavid dynasty—links him directly with Shaykh Ibrāhīm Zāhid; this work makes no mention of the enigmatic figure of "Muḥammad Khalvatī" who, though assigned different *nisba*s in

[30] It is worth noting that the various elements of medieval Muslim names add an element of uncertainty in identifying individuals: an individual might be known by just one of the elements (e.g., a given name [*ism*] such as Muḥammad, an honorific [*laqab*], e.g., of the form "Kamāl al-Dīn," an adjectival form indicating a place of origin [*nisba*], e.g., "Samarqandī," or one or more other sorts of honorifics and nicknames). The *nisba* itself, moreover, is particularly unstable, since more or less specific versions may be used for a given individual (i.e., a figure known as "Bukhārī" in general may be assigned a more specific *nisba*, such as "Rāmītanī," pertaining to another town or village of the Bukharan oasis), and since it may change as an individual moves from place to place (i.e., a figure was sometimes referred to by the *nisba* reflecting where he happened to come from most recently, not his place of origin).

[31] On this shaykh's life see Aubin (1991). Shaykh Ibrāhīm Zāhid's own *silsila* is typically traced back thus to the Suhravardī tradition: Ibrāhīm Zāhid Gīlānī < Jamāl al-Dīn Tabrīzī < Shihāb al-Dīn Maḥmūd Tabrīzī < Rukn al-Dīn Muḥammad Sajāsī < Quṭb al-Dīn Abharī < Abū'l-Najīb Suhravardī.

different sources, is typically placed in the Khalvatī *silsila* between these two shaykhs (Ibn Bazzāz: 215, 240-241).

We cannot fully explore here the various versions of the western Khalvatī *silsila*, for which our western Khalvatī sources are extremely vague, leaving the distinctly 'Khalvatī' phase of the lineage quite obscure. We may note, however, that the available sources leave little basis for (1) affirming direct links between the 'Ottoman' Khalvatīya and any of the Khalvatī groups explored above, or (2) affirming the historical plausibility of the Khalvatī *silsila*.

In the first regard, it is quite possible that the 'eastern' Khalvatī communities of Bukhārā, Kirmān, Quhistān, and Herat have nothing to do with the tradition that became known as the Khalvatīya in the west. In some cases a connection has been assumed, but most studies of the Ottoman Khalvatīya have ignored the eastern groups, even though the 'eastern' Khalvatīya is mentioned in sources well before the 'western' Khalvatīya is.[32] Our earliest source to give a full *silsila* for the western Khalvatī groups in fact insists that there was no connection between the Khalvatī shaykhs active in the Ottoman realm and the Khalvatī community of Herat. The source in question, Lāmi'ī Chelebī's Ottoman Turkish translation (and expansion) of Jāmī's *Nafaḥāt al-uns*, completed in 927/1521, adds the following note at the end of the biography of Ẓahīr al-Dīn Khalvatī of Herat:

> I have heard from some prominent figures who have been in Herat that the shaykhs of the Khalvatīya mentioned here are not the Khalvatīs who are famous in our own time in the country of Shīrvān and the land of Rūm. The exalted *silsila* of those mentioned here [from Herat] goes back to Shaykh Rukn al-Dīn 'Alā' al-Dawla al-Simnānī;[33] the *silsila* of those who are famous in our time goes back to the holy Ibrāhīm Zāhid Gīlānī (Lāmi'ī: 571-572).[34]

Lāmi'ī nevertheless traces the western Khalvatī lineage through a series of obscure figures, including one whose name is given so vaguely that he could indeed be identified with the Khwārazmian 'founder' of the eastern Khalvatī groups: Sayyid Yaḥyā Shīrvānī of Bākū (d. 868 or 869/1463-65, typically regarded as the true organizational founder of the Khalvatī groups in Azerbaijan and Anatolia) < Ṣadr al-Dīn Khiyāvī Shīrvānī < Ḥājjī 'Izz al-Dīn Khalvatī < Akhī M.r.m

[32] Previous scholarship has not addressed the question directly; students of the western Khalvatīs have rarely taken note of the eastern groups, while the (fewer) students of the eastern groups have either assumed their connection with the western groups (Savory 1969, O'Kane 1987), or noted the problem without exploring it further (Aubin 1967).

[33] Lāmi'ī's contention—or that of his unnamed informants—that the *silsila* of the Khalvatī shaykhs of Herat went back to 'Alā' al-Dawla Simnānī is of interest in view of the sporadic reports linking Muḥammad Khalvatī of Khwārazm (or Nūr al-Dīn Khalvatī of Bukhārā) to Najm al-Dīn Kubrā, who is a central figure in the *silsila* normally shown for Simnānī; however, there appears to be no other basis for linking the eastern Khalvatī groups with Simnānī.

[34] On Lāmi'ī's work, see Flemming (1994: 62-66).

Khalvatī < Pīr 'Umar Khalvatī < Akhī Muḥammad Khalvatī < Ibrāhīm Zāhid Gīlānī (Lāmi'ī: 572).[35] Moreover, Lāmi'ī goes on to cite a Naqshbandī source that in effect contradicts his earlier remark: it affirms that Sayf al-Dīn Khalvatī of Herat was in fact a disciple of the Pīr 'Umar Khalvatī who is typically identified as the origin of the western Khalvatīya. The comment runs counter to what is known from the *Nafaḥāt* and the *Maqṣad al-iqbāl*, but in any case clearly links the eastern and western Khalvatī lineages.[36]

Of equal significance for the general historicity of the western Khalvatī *silsila*, moreover, is the ascription of the western Khalvatī *silsila* to Shaykh Ibrāhīm Zāhid Gīlānī. Shaykh Ibrāhīm Zāhid is perhaps best known as the shaykh to whom the *silsila* of the Ṣafavid order and dynasty is traced. Since he is thus shared, as a spiritual ancestor, by the Khalvatīya and the Ṣafavīya, earlier students of the Khalvatīya such as Kissling and Martin referred to the two orders as "twin brothers" or as belonging to the same "blood group" (Martin 1972: 284; Kissling 1956: 245-246); they assumed, on the basis of Shaykh Ibrāhīm Zāhid's inclusion in the Khalvatī *silsila* beginning in the 16th century, that he must indeed have 'founded' the lineage in the 13th century—an obviously problematical assumption. Yet the same students of the western Khalvatīya did not hesitate to point out supposed manipulations of the Khalvatī *silsila*. Kissling and Martin, for instance, were willing to accept that five Shī'ite *imāms* who appear early in the Khalvatī *silsila*, in versions produced during the 16th century, might have been deleted in some later versions of that *silsila* in order to conceal the order's links with the Ṣafavīya, at a time when links with the Ṣafavid enemies of the Ottomans might have raised suspicions about Khalvatī shaykhs. I would argue, however, that a different scenario is equally plausible: Ibrāhīm Zāhid might have been grafted into the Khalvatī *silsila*, not to conceal ties with the Ṣafavīya, but to assert them for competitive purposes. That is, a Khalvatī link to Ibrāhīm Zāhid may have been stressed or invented, during the 15th century, precisely because the Khalvatīya faced competition from

[35] The *nisba* "Khalvatī" appears here with the names of the most obscure figures in the lineage, suggesting that it was attached to them by Lāmi'ī himself, rather than by the traditions he relied upon in compiling his accounts.

[36] The ambivalence evident in Lāmi'ī's account in fact recurs in many subsequent western Khalvatī accounts; many say nothing at all about the identity of the figures who appear in the *silsila* between Sayyid Yaḥyā Shīrvānī and Shaykh Ibrāhīm Zāhid Gīlānī, while others—beginning with an Ottoman hagiographical compendium completed in 1030/1621—flesh out the biographies and identities of those figures and link them directly with the Khalvatī shaykhs of Herat (but do so in a quite artificial way that belies any authentic transmission of reliable accounts). The 17th-century work in question has been published in a modern Turkish "simplified" rendering (*sâdeleştirme*): Hulvî, *Lemezât*: 319-385; the work clearly adopts Jāmī's account of the Khalvatī shaykhs of Herat, but transports them (and the entire "village of Harī" [i.e., Herat] itself, moved to Gīlān so as to accord with Shaykh Ibrāhīm Zāhid's native region) to the westerly environment in which the 'Ottoman' Khalvatīya emerged.

the Ṣafavīya in their common homeland and wished to portray itself, rather than the Ṣafavīya, as the legitimate lineage maintaining the authoritative legacy of the local saint Ibrāhīm Zāhid.

A *silsila* traced through Shaykh Ibrāhīm Zāhid Gīlānī may thus have served a primarily competitive purpose. To be sure, we cannot completely rule out the authenticity of his place in the Khalvatī lineage. After all, the sources are late; his putative 'successors' are thoroughly obscure; even the eastern Khalvatī groups trace their lineage back no further than Muḥammad Khalvatī; and it is quite possible that this Muḥammad Khalvatī spent time in Gīlān or Shīrvān or other parts of the Muslim world, his 'eastern' identification as a Khwārazmian notwithstanding. What must be acknowledged, however, is that the inclusion of Shaykh Ibrāhīm Zāhid Gīlānī in the western Khalvatī *silsila* can neither support nor refute a connection between the western and eastern communities and shaykhs that bore the Khalvatī label. It also cannot refute the likely connections between the eastern Khalvatī groups and the other communities to which we may now turn.

II. The 'Ishqīya:

The 'Ishqīya is mentioned in sources as a Sufi community of Central Asia (based near Samarqand) from the 15th century down to the 17th. As far as is known, the 'Ishqīya was active, under this appellation, only in Central Asia, and no doubt for this reason it has remained the least familiar of the three groups considered here. Nevertheless, in recent years a few scholars have begun to explore its history (Babadzhanov 1991 and 2001; Schwarz 2000: 97-101, 157);[37] the study of the 'Ishqīya is complicated by the fact that no 'internal' 'Ishqī sources have survived (if any were produced), and we are dependent upon brief accounts of 'Ishqī shaykhs preserved in sources whose sponsors were often quite hostile to them.

The 'Ishqī shaykhs of the 15th century are best known as rivals, even enemies, of the famous Naqshbandī shaykh Khwāja Aḥrār, whose biographers included several stories depicting them quite negatively. The biographies of Khwāja Aḥrār mention altogether four generations—with natural descent here coinciding with spiritual transmission—in the 'Ishqī lineage, but speak with finality of the death of the last of the four, and the destruction of the 'Ishqīya, as a result of the conflict with Khwāja Aḥrār.[38] A quite different picture of

[37] Babadzhanov (2001) and Schwarz (2000) survey the 'Ishqī lineage's history, based on Navā'ī and Nithārī (and on the epitaphs studied in Babadzhanov 1991); they both mention several of the figures discussed here, but they do not address the 'Ishqī-Shaṭṭārī connection.

[38] For anecdotes involving the 'Ishqī shaykhs beyond those cited below, see *Rashaḥāt*: II, 621 (recounting how Khwāja Aḥrār 'stole' a disciple who intended to attach himself to

the 'Ishqīya is found, however, in a slightly earlier source, the *Nasā'im al-maḥabba* of the famous Timurid official and patron, Mīr 'Alī-shīr Navā'ī; this work, a Chaghatay Turkic translation of Jāmī's *Nafaḥāt*, included additional biographies, written by Navā'ī himself, dealing with the "Turkic shaykhs," among whom the most prominent are shaykhs we may link with the Yasavī and 'Ishqī Sufi traditions (Navā'ī, *Nasā'im*: 387-388). Navā'ī's work covers six generations of 'Ishqī shaykhs. His accounts are quite brief, but are entirely respectful; it remains unclear why Navā'ī, with his Naqshbandī affiliation and his admiration for Khwāja Aḥrār, conveys none of the hostility toward the 'Ishqī shaykhs that is evident in the biographies of Khwāja Aḥrār.

Combining the evidence from Navā'ī's work with epigraphic data from the tombstones of several 'Ishqī shaykhs recorded by Bakhtiyar Babadzhanov (Babadzhanov 1991), we can trace the 'Ishqī lineage—again, combining both natural heredity and spiritual transmission—back from the latest 'Ishqī shaykh mentioned by Navā'ī: Shaykhzāda Abū'l-Ḥasan (d. 1488) < his father and master Ilyās Shaykh (d. 1472) < Muḥammad (d. 1451-52) < Khudāyqulī (d. 1419) < Abū'l-Ḥasan 'Ishqī < Bāyazīd 'Ishqī. Navā'ī's accounts of these shaykhs offer relatively few biographical details (and no dates), especially for the 'middle' of the lineage: Ilyās Shaykh is linked with Samarqand, and is said to have performed the *ḥajj* and to have been skilled in his knowledge of Arabic; of Muḥammad, Navā'ī recounts a story about how he silenced a learned man who harbored doubts about his legitimacy (a familiar theme in hagiographical anecdotes); and of Khudāyqulī, we are told only of his greatness and of his many miracles.[39]

Navā'ī offers slightly more information regarding the first and last figures from the lineage who are accorded individual biographical entries, both of whom are named Abū'l-Ḥasan. In the entry on the earlier Shaykh Abū'l-Ḥasan 'Ishqī, Navā'ī affirms that he was from Khwārazm, that he was trained by Shaykh Bāyazīd 'Ishqī, and that the latter's *silsila*—and hence, in principle, that of the 'Ishqīya as well—went back to "the *Sulṭān al-'ārifīn*, Bāyazīd Bisṭāmī." Of the later Abū'l-Ḥasan, called *shaykhzāda* in recognition of his status as the son, as well as successor, of Ilyās Shaykh, Navā'ī first notes his engagement in extreme austerities already in his youth, and then affirms that "after Ilyās Shaykh, all the people of this *silsila* confirmed their pact (*bay'at*) and renewed their discipleship (*irādat*) with him." Navā'ī next

Ilyās 'Ishqī), and II, 628-630 (revealing that Aḥrār's chief disciple, Mawlānā Muḥammad Qāżī, had previously been a disciple of Ilyās 'Ishqī before Aḥrār lured him away).

[39] Another biography of Khwāja Aḥrār, by his son-in-law Mīr 'Abd al-Avval Nīshāpūrī, includes an anecdote in which Niẓām al-Dīn Khāmūsh (one of Khwāja Aḥrār's masters in the Naqshbandī *silsila*) recalls seeing Shaykh Khudāyqulī 'Ishqī, whom he identifies as a Turk and blames for a problem in his concentration; see Nawshāhī, *Aḥvāl*: 193 (and see the editor's notes on the 'Ishqī shaykhs, 455-456).

mentions that this Abū'l-Ḥasan, while performing the *ḥajj*, stopped in Bisṭām and was given a Sufi cloak (*khirqa*) and cap (*tāj*, literally "crown") by descendants of the "*Sulṭān al-'ārifīn*"—implicitly evoking the mention of Bisṭāmī in the entry on the first Abū'l-Ḥasan. Finally, he notes that this 'Ishqī shaykh, returning from the *ḥajj*, passed through Herat, where Navā'ī's own friend and mentor, Jāmī, gave to Abū'l-Ḥasan one of his books, a prayer-rug, and a handkerchief.

It is unfortunate that Jāmī himself made no mention of this—or any—'Ishqī shaykh. Nevertheless, Navā'ī's accounts, despite their brevity, are valuable not only for establishing the sequence of shaykhs (he mentions a few other 'Ishqī shaykhs as well), but for the clues he offers regarding the 'origins' of the 'Ishqī tradition. The connection established between Abū'l-Ḥasan 'Ishqī—and, implicitly, Bāyazīd 'Ishqī as well—and Khwārazm is significant, but it is above all the 'symmetrical' references to Bisṭāmī, in the accounts of both Abū'l-Ḥasans from the 'Ishqī lineage, that are of special importance. Bāyazīd (or Abū Yazīd) Bisṭāmī (d. ca. 261/874-5) is a well-known figure in the early history of Sufism, famous for his ecstatic utterances that came dangerously close to blasphemy from an exoteric perspective.[40] He became emblematic of the 'intoxicated' Sufi, and the epithet *Sulṭān al-'ārifīn*—"King of the Gnostics"—became attached to his hagiographical image. He was thus a formidable figure to include in Sufi lineages; yet of greater significance, for present purposes, is the *way* in which Bāyazīd Bisṭāmī was typically incorporated into Sufi *silsila*s, and, by extension, what his appearance in the *silsila* given for a particular Sufi community may signal. In most *silsila*s in which Bisṭāmī appears as a link—including available versions of the 'Ishqī *silsila* and the much more commonly encountered *silsila* of the Naqshbandī Sufi order—he is shown as the 'master' of Shaykh Abū'l-Ḥasan Kharaqānī (d. 425/1033).[41] The obvious chronological gap between Bisṭāmī and Kharaqānī is in fact openly highlighted in many accounts of the Naqshbandī *silsila*, which affirm that Kharaqānī was born well after Bisṭāmī died, and that Kharaqānī was trained by the "spiritual being" (*rūḥānīya*) of Bisṭāmī.

The Bisṭāmī-Kharaqānī connection was therefore an example of the kind of relationship that came to be labeled "Uvaysī," in which one Sufi was initiated and trained not by a living shaykh, but by the spirit of a deceased shaykh or prophet. The mere appearance of this connection in a *silsila* immediately signals the 'ahistorical' character of the lineage, insofar as the tradition straightforwardly acknowledges, at least at this point, that there is no direct transmission from living master to living disciple. There is some justification for seeing the Bisṭāmī-Kharaqānī connection, as used in the

[40] On Bisṭāmī, see Ritter (1960); on the formation of his hagiographical image, see Mojaddedi (2003).

[41] On Kharaqānī, see de Bruijn (1978), Landolt (1983), and the introduction to Mīnuvī (1980).

Naqshbandī *silsila*, as also providing a model for a similar connection between a later pair of shaykhs, who also did not meet in person, namely Bahā' al-Dīn Naqshband, eponym of the Naqshbandīya, and 'Abd al-Khāliq Ghijduvānī, the 'founder' of the Sufi lineage known as the Khwājagān, whose legacy the Naqshbandīya claimed to continue. Bahā' al-Dīn is portrayed having a purely visionary, spiritual encounter with Ghijduvānī, their relationship thus paralleling the paradigmatic relationship between Bisṭāmī and Kharaqānī (DeWeese 2006).

In the case of the (relatively few) known examples of the 'Ishqī *silsila*, only one version (that of Ḥazīnī, reviewed below) explicitly identifies Abū'l-Ḥasan Kharaqānī as the "disciple" of—or even as the next link in the *silsila* after—Bāyazīd Bisṭāmī; other versions simply disregard the problem of linking Bisṭāmī with the 'Ishqī shaykhs of the 14th and 15th centuries. Given the paucity of sources on the 'Ishqīya, it is perhaps not surprising that we find no explicit discussion of the chronological gap signaled by Bisṭāmī's inclusion as the 'founder' of the 'Ishqī *silsila*. Nevertheless, Bisṭāmī's appearance in a *silsila* that is obviously anachronistic in effect preserves, in fossilized form, the disregard for *silsila*s that was quite common in the 15th century (as evidenced by the currency, in that time, of the Uvaysī notion as used to explain and legitimize essentially unaffiliated shaykhs).

It is possible, moreover, especially given the clear evidence of competition between 'Ishqī and Naqshbandī groups in the 15th century, that the 'Ishqī *silsila* (or at least that portion of it that stands in for the era prior to the 14th century) was itself constructed with conscious regard to the rivalry with the Naqshbandīya. Naqshbandī groups were likewise formulating their *silsila*, and were 'back-filling' the gaps evident in earlier recordings, during the 15th century, and they too accorded a significant role to Bāyazīd Bisṭāmī. Even if the Naqshbandī example was not the direct (competitive) inspiration for the inclusion of Bisṭāmī in the 'Ishqī *silsila*, the process of building the 'Ishqī *silsila* may well have followed a course similar to the parallel process within the Naqshbandīya. In the Naqshbandī case, accounts of a more recent example of spiritual, "Uvaysī"-style transmission, from Ghijduvānī to Bahā' al-Dīn Naqshband, may have been modeled on the Bisṭāmī-Kharaqānī paradigm, as both ahistorical links were incorporated into the *silsila*. In the case of the 'Ishqīya we find some hints that the figure of (the earlier) Abū'l-Ḥasan 'Ishqī was the focus of tales about ahistorical, purely spiritual transmission, echoing the ahistorical implications of Bisṭāmī's inclusion in the 'Ishqī *silsila*.[42]

We will explore, below, further considerations of the 'Ishqī *silsila*, but it is important to note here the already problematical character of Navā'ī's affirmation that the 'Ishqī lineage went back to Bisṭāmī.

[42] This is suggested by a story regarding Sayyid Aḥmad Bashīrī (see DeWeese 1993), claiming for him the status of rightful successor to Abū'l-Ḥasan 'Ishqī.

The point is not that Navā'ī himself invented such a claim (though he may have misconstrued or wrongly concretized it), but that, in highlighting their 'connection' to Bisṭāmī, the 'Ishqī shaykhs themselves may have intended something quite different from a 'typical' *silsila* transmission.

This caveat, in turn, is important to keep in mind in light of another early affirmation about the 'Ishqī lineage. It appears in the *Rashaḥāt*, which, as noted, includes several anecdotes involving shaykhs of the 'Ishqīya, and Khwāja Aḥrār's competitive zeal directed against them. For present purposes what is most important about these stories is the brief explanation, found at the beginning of two consecutive accounts of this sort in the *Rashaḥāt* (*Rashaḥāt*: II, 541-543), of exactly who the leader of the 'Ishqīya was. The passage deals with Ilyās 'Ishqī, and its account of his lineage accords well with the picture given by Navā'ī. It likewise accords well with the chronology outlined above, making the first Abū'l-Ḥasan 'Ishqī a contemporary of Bahā' al-Dīn Naqshband (d. 791/1389).

> Shaykhzāda Ilyās 'Ishqī was the shaykh and leader of a (Sufi) group at the beginning of his holiness [Khwāja Aḥrār's] appearance in Samarqand; he had a Sufi hostel (*langar*) in Kūh-i Nūr, in the environs of Samarqand, and he practiced the vocal *dhikr*. He was the grandson of Shaykh Khudāyqulī, and he in turn was the son of Shaykh Abū'l-Ḥasan 'Ishqī, who in the time of the holy Khwāja Bahā' al-Dīn (Naqshband) was the shaykh and circle-leader of the *silsila-yi Khalvīya*.[43]

The term used here to refer to the *silsila* represented by Abū'l-Ḥasan 'Ishqī, and, by extension, by Shaykhzāda Ilyās 'Ishqī—"Khalvīya"—reflects precisely the same 'abbreviated' form of the *nisba* "Khalvatī" used in the *Rashaḥāt* to refer to Shaykh Muḥammad Khalvatī (in the story, noted above, about his journey to Tonguz Shaykh with Shaykh Khāvand-i Ṭahūr). There can be no doubt that the *Rashaḥāt*'s author intended to identify Abū'l-Ḥasan 'Ishqī, and in effect the entire 'Ishqī lineage down to Ilyās Shaykh, as part of the Khalvatī *silsila* and, by extension, the Khalvatī community. He uses the same term to refer to the origins of the 'Ishqī community that he elsewhere applies to the Khwārazmian "founder" of the Khalvatī lineages of Central Asia and Iran.[44] This passage thus offers our most direct evidence on the continuity between the social referents of the Khalvatī and 'Ishqī communal labels. It seems likely, indeed, that the *Rashaḥāt*'s account of the buffoonish Shaykh Muḥammad Khalvatī,

[43] Other biographies of Khwāja Aḥrār portray the master of this Abū'l-Ḥasan (according to Navā'ī's account), Bāyazīd 'Ishqī, as a contemporary of Bahā' al-Dīn Naqshband, and of Timur; see Nawshāhī, *Aḥvāl*: 281 (from the work of Mīr 'Abd al-Avval Nīshāpūrī), 663-664 (from the work of Mawlānā Shaykh).

[44] Navā'ī's evidence on the Khwārazmian locus of the earliest 'Ishqī shaykhs offers yet another point of possible overlap between the communal referents of the two terms.

or "Khalvī," was designed to project the enmity between Khwāja Aḥrār and the 'Ishqī shaykh of his time into the past, to the break in relations between Khwāja Aḥrār's natural ancestor and the spiritual ancestor of the Khalvatī tradition.[45]

To be sure, the shared derogatory vehemence of the *Rashaḥāt*'s accounts of these 'Ishqī and Khalvatī figures cannot in itself establish the continuity of the 'Ishqī and Khalvatī traditions. We might insist, for instance, that the author of the *Rashaḥāt* was simply misinformed in his explicit affirmation that an "'Ishqī" shaykh belonged to the "Khalvatī" *silsila*. Alternatively, we might argue that he merely wished to link the 'Ishqī rivals of Khwāja Aḥrār with a Sufi community that already stood discredited in Naqshbandī lore (to judge from his inclusion of Bahā' al-Dīn Naqshband's disparaging comments following the funeral of Nūr al-Dīn Khalvatī, and the story of the charlatan Muḥammad "Khalvī"). However, the *Rashaḥāt*'s author was perhaps uniquely situated to understand the connections among Sufi communities, both in Khurāsān and Mawarannahr, that were becoming obscured by new communal labels (Hanaway 1995). He combined direct familiarity with Khwāja Aḥrār, with whom he spent time in Samarqand, with an intimate knowledge of Sufi society in Herat (which he knew much better than the authors of the other biographies of Khwāja Aḥrār), and for this reason his identification of the 'Ishqī forebear's 'Khalvatī' identity is particularly important. Indeed, it is quite doubtful that he would have used the term "Khalvatī" or "Khalvī" to explain the affiliation of an 'Ishqī shaykh of Mawarannahr without clear knowledge of the former term's meaning and ramifications in Herat.

As noted, the enmity between the 'Ishqī community near Samarqand and the Sufi circle led by Khwāja Aḥrār was so intense that the *Rashaḥāt* twice notes the destruction of the 'Ishqī community in the time of Shaykhzāda Ilyās. In one account, in which Khwāja Aḥrār is shown recalling how he had trampled other shaykhs underfoot like ants, Shaykhzāda Ilyās' *langar* is said to have been struck by a pestilence that left many of his children and relatives, and finally Ilyās himself, dead (*Rashaḥāt*: II, 541-543).[46] That the 'Ishqī community survived, however, is clear not only from the earlier work of Navā'ī, but from accounts in three 16th-century sources (and scattered evidence from still later times).

From the *Mudhakkir-i aḥbāb* of Ḥasan Nithārī, written in 974/1566 as a continuation of the 'bio-anthologies' of poets compiled at the end of the 15th century by Dawlatshāh Samarqandī and Navā'ī, we

[45] Yet another anecdote projects the rivalry into the time of Bahā' al-Dīn Naqshband, and is of further interest for implying that either Shaykh Abū'l-Ḥasan 'Ishqī or some of his followers had become established near Bukhārā at some point in the latter 14th century; see *Rashaḥāt*: I, 129.

[46] See the translation of the second of these stories, from a different source, in Gross (1992: 166-167).

learn of a son of the later 'Ishqī shaykh named Abū'l-Ḥasan: Nithārī gives a biographical entry on a certain "Ma'ṣūm Khwāja 'Ishqī" (Nithārī, *Mudhakkir*: 220-221), identified as a descendant (possibly a son) of Muḥammad Ṣādiq Shaykh b. Abū'l-Ḥasan Shaykh b. Ilyās Shaykh b. Shaykh Muḥammad Shaykh b. Khudāyqulī Shaykh 'Ishqī. Noting that he himself met Muḥammad Ṣādiq in Kesh (Shahrisabz), Nithārī affirms further that Muḥammad Ṣādiq belonged to the *ṭarīqat* of the "Sulṭān al-'ārifīn," clearly referring to Abū Yazīd Bisṭāmī, and declares that he held fast to the *sharī'a* and never permitted any innovation (*bid'at*) to his followers (as if there were some suspicions on this matter, with regard to him or the *ṭarīqat*).

The Muḥammad Ṣādiq mentioned by Nithārī was clearly the most important 'Ishqī shaykh of the first half of the 16th century; from epigraphic data it appears that he died in 952/1545 (Babadzhanov 1991: 94, 96). He is accorded an entry in a hagiographical compendium on shaykhs of Central Asia entitled *Adhkār al-azkiyā*, completed in 993/1585 (Sivinchī, *Adhkār*: 107b-110a),[47] and he figures prominently in the most valuable 16th-century source on the 'Ishqīya, the *Jāmi' al-murshidīn*, completed in 972/1564-65 by Ḥazīnī, a shaykh of the Yasavī order who had moved to Istanbul from his native region of Ḥiṣār (in present-day Tajikistan). Ḥazīnī's work provides descriptions, in Persian verse, of four Central Asian Sufi communities: the Yasavīya, Naqshbandīya, Kubravīya, and 'Ishqīya (Ḥazīnī, *Jāmi'*: 105b-107a). Ḥazīnī confirms the lineage known from other sources, and adds yet another generation, in the person of Muḥammad Ṣādiq's disciple, Bābā Shaykh. The account credits Muḥammad Ṣādiq with gaining devotees and "servants" among the rulers (*salāṭīn*) of Bukhārā, Samarqand, Ḥiṣār, Tashkent, and Balkh.

Ḥazīnī offers little evidence regarding the 'Ishqī-Khalvatī continuum as argued here,[48] but his account in the *Jāmi' al-murshidīn* is of particular importance for its presentation of the early segments of the 'Ishqī *silsila*: the account seems intent on affirming the purely spiritual connections of the early figures in the *silsila*. The account begins by affirming that the 'Ishqīya is part of the *ṭarīq-i bāyazīdī*, referring to it also as the *ṭarīq* of Ṭayfūr (another name of Bisṭāmī). The aim is clearly to present the 'Ishqī *silsila* as originating, in effect, with Bāyazīd Bisṭāmī, thus agreeing with Navā'ī's contention. Unlike

[47] He is called in this work "Muḥammad Ṣādiq Shaykh Langarī"); cf. Sivinchī, *Adhkār*: 239a, an entry devoted to a disciple of his, Mullā Khalīl Qarākūlī.

[48] In another of his works (the Ottoman Turkish *Javāhir al-abrār*), Ḥazīnī refers to a certain "Shaykh Maḥmūd al-Khalvatī," who eventually became a disciple of Yasavī shaykhs; he describes a vision evidently experienced by this Maḥmūd, and interpreted by him in terms of the transformative power of intense mystical ardor (*'ishq*) (see Ḥazīnī, *Javāhir*: 82-92). Elsewhere in the same work (93), Ḥazīnī refers to the same figure as "Shaykh Maḥmūd al-Khalvatī, later (*thumma*) al-Zāvrānī," and makes it clear that he dwelled near Samarqand; the *nisba* "Zāvrānī" is evidently based on a place-name rather than on a communal designation such as Khalvatī.

Navā'ī, however, Ḥazīnī then alludes to the figure of Abū'l-Ḥasan Kharaqānī, and expressly describes the relationship between Bisṭāmī and Kharaqānī in terms of the Uvaysī style of transmission. Lest it be suspected that only a general inspiration or specific doctrinal insights might have been passed on by the spirit of the deceased Bisṭāmī, Ḥazīnī affirms that Abū'l-Ḥasan Kharaqānī learned the "protocols of the Path" (*ādāb-i ṭarīqat*)—referring to the institutional precepts of the Sufi community—from the *rūḥānīyat* of Bisṭāmī.

It is at this point, however, that the thread seems to be lost, at least in any way that can be confirmed by other sources. After further discussion of Kharaqānī, Ḥazīnī refers next to "Bahā' al-Dīn of the Maghrib" (i.e., "of the West"),[49] who enjoyed the care and guidance of Kharaqānī; it was this Bahā' al-Dīn, he affirms further, who "established" the 'Ishqī order ("*ṭarīq-i 'ishqīyān ū kard bunyād*"). This "Bahā' al-Dīn of the Maghrib," in turn, is cast as the master of "Bū'l-Ḥasan-i 'Ishqīya" (i.e., Abū'l-Ḥasan), and herewith we find a clear discrepancy between Ḥazīnī's account and that of Navā'ī, who called the master of Abū'l-Ḥasan 'Ishqī simply "Bāyazīd 'Ishqī" of Khwārazm.[50] This leaves the full *silsila* presented for the 'Ishqīya by Ḥazīnī as follows: Bisṭāmī > Kharaqānī > "Bahā' al-Dīn from the Maghrib" > Abū'l-Ḥasan 'Ishqī > Khudāyqul [*sic*] > his son Muḥammad Shaykh > Ilyās 'Ishqī > his son Abū'l-Ḥasan > Muḥammad Ṣādiq > Bābā Shaykh. The net effect is to give essentially the same early 'lineage' as was given by Navā'ī, though differing with Navā'ī regarding the name of Abū'l-Ḥasan 'Ishqī's master. Yet Ḥazīnī's version is in one respect more troubling than Navā'ī's: where Navā'ī speaks only of Bāyazīd 'Ishqī as the master of Abū'l-Ḥasan 'Ishqī and then links both more vaguely with Bisṭāmī, Ḥazīnī posits a direct master-disciple connection between Kharaqānī (d. 1033) and "Bahā' al-Dīn from the Maghrib," and affirms a similarly direct connection between this Bahā' al-Dīn and Abū'l-Ḥasan 'Ishqī (whose death, to judge from the *Rashaḥāt*, must have come in the late 14th century, some 450 years after Kharaqānī). Ḥazīnī thus allows only one *silsila*-link to account for a span of 450 years; yet he makes no mention of the chronological problem, and posits no Uvaysī-style connection between Kharaqānī and Bahā' al-Dīn, or between Bahā' al-Dīn and Abū'l-Ḥasan 'Ishqī (and this after discussing at some length the purely spiritual relationship between the chronologically-challenged pair of Bisṭāmī and Kharaqānī!).[51]

[49] The term "*maghrib*" typically refers to North Africa, but may refer simply to the "west," with its specific referents unclear. It may be used here to refer to an otherwise unidentified figure known as Bahā' al-Dīn whose 'western' identity is understood in distinction to the more famous Bahā' al-Dīn of 'the East,' i.e., Bahā' al-Dīn Naqshband.

[50] As we will see, the *nisba* assigned to the master of Abū'l-Ḥasan 'Ishqī by Ḥazīnī is echoed in another source, produced a century earlier, and within the Shaṭṭārī community.

[51] The effect of Ḥazīnī's account is underscored, ironically, by a Bukharan hagiography from the late 17th century, the *Thamarāt al-mashā'ikh*, which includes interesting comments about the 'Ishqīya (noted below), but at one point gives a brief outline of the

In short, Ḥazīnī's account, like that of Navā'ī, affirms that the 'Ishqī *silsila* "goes back" to Bāyazīd Bisṭāmī; but both authors—and especially Ḥazīnī—leave little doubt that their affirmation about the 'Ishqī *silsila* means essentially nothing in terms of the historical continuity or succession in the 'Ishqī community. Regardless of the ways in which its *silsila* was devised or (re-)constructed—and the insertion of Bisṭāmī in it is not entirely without significance—the 'Ishqī community as such cannot be traced in any meaningful way before the lifetime of Abū'l-Ḥasan 'Ishqī, or at most that of his nebulous predecessor, be he "Bāyazīd 'Ishqī" or "Bahā' al-Dīn from the Maghrib" (or another variant found in Shaṭṭārī accounts). The earlier segments of the *silsila* devised for the 'Ishqīya are thus of no significance in arguing for or against some degree of communal overlap between the 'Ishqīya and the Khalvatīya. Such an overlap is 'allowed' by the fact that whatever community or tradition Abū'l-Ḥasan 'Ishqī (or his predecessor) may have belonged to, it was not yet termed "'Ishqī," did not yet have a defined *silsila*, and thus might well have been known by a different communal label. The most important evidence for that overlap is, however, the *Rashaḥāt*'s identification of Abū'l-Ḥasan 'Ishqī as the leader of the 'Khalvatī' community of his time (and with Abū'l-Ḥasan 'Ishqī identified as a contemporary of Bahā' al-Dīn Naqshband, we would be free to conjecture that he, or his predecessor—Bāyazīd 'Ishqī or Bahā' al-Dīn from the Maghrib—could have belonged to the first generation of Shaykh Muḥammad Khalvatī's spiritual descendants).

For additional clues regarding the nature of the 'Ishqī-Khalvatī overlap, we must turn, finally, to the third tradition noted above, one whose direct continuity with the 'Ishqīya is expressly stated in numerous sources.

III. The Shaṭṭārīya:

The Shaṭṭārīya is reasonably well-known as a Sufi order of India that emerged, out of Central Asian roots, in the latter 15th century. Its later history in India has drawn considerable attention, but its obscure early phase remains largely unstudied.[52] Unlike the eastern Khalvatī groups and the 'Ishqīya, however, its shaykhs produced a substantial

'Ishqī *silsila*. The account adds six more generations after Muḥammad Ṣādiq, down to the author's own time, but its earlier additions are of equal interest. The author—or his sources—has filled in the extensive chronological gaps in the lineage, adding 13 names between Bisṭāmī and "Abū Yazīd 'Ishqī" (the master of Abū'l-Ḥasan 'Ishqī, and equivalent to Navā'ī's "Bāyazīd 'Ishqī"). Most of the names are simply unidentifiable (and Kharaqānī is not among them), suggesting that their addition was indeed a response to the uncomfortably ahistorical character of the *silsila*—which clearly caused more discomfort in the 17th century than it did in the 15th (*Thamarāt*: 72a-73b).

[52] On the Shaṭṭārī tradition see the survey of Elias (1995); two recent studies focused on the 16th-century Shaṭṭārī shaykh Muḥammad Ghawth (Ernst 1999 and Kugle 2003); and the discussion, with a good bibliography covering earlier studies, in Behl and Weightman (2000: xix-xxv, liii-lv, 8-11, 247).

literary legacy, beginning in the 15th century, that is important for our understanding of the *silsila*s claimed for the Shaṭṭārīya, and of this term's meaning as a corporate label (we will return to these issues shortly). We cannot explore here the later development of the Shaṭṭārī tradition, but our earliest information on its emergence links it with both the 'Ishqī and eastern Khalvatī communities, and we must consider the evidence on the early Shaṭṭārī *silsila*.

Evidently the oldest extant version of the Shaṭṭārī *silsila* appears in the *Laṭā'if-i Ashrafī*, a voluminous compilation of Sufi lore inspired by the figure of Sayyid Ashraf Jahāngīr Sīmnānī (his death-date is uncertain, but most likely belongs in the late 1420s).[53] The *Laṭā'if-i Ashrafī*, apparently compiled in the mid-15th century, traces a Shaṭṭārī lineage down to Sayyid Ashraf Jahāngīr; the shaykh identified as Sayyid Ashraf's master in this lineage is also shown, in later sources, as the master of the figure usually regarded as the eponym, and the 'founder,' of the Shaṭṭārīya, namely Shāh 'Abdullāh Shaṭṭārī. The *silsila* given in the *Laṭā'if-i Ashrafī* is shown in the accompanying chart; it is clear that, with a few insertions and other minor differences, it corresponds reasonably well not only with other, later versions of the Shaṭṭārī *silsila*, but with the *silsila* we can reconstruct for the 'Ishqīya (*Laṭā'if*, lith.: I, 389; *Laṭā'if*, MS: 206a). What is perhaps most significant about this work's account, however, is its confirmation that the term *shaṭṭārī* was current as a communal label already before Shāh 'Abdullāh came to prominence. The label's early use is also suggested by the case of Ḥaydar Badakhshī, a Central Asian Sufi who became a disciple of Sayyid 'Abdullāh Barzishābādī (d. 872/1467-68), in a Kubravī lineage, and wrote the *Manqabat al-javāhir*, a hagiographical work focused on Sayyid 'Alī Hamadānī (d. 786/1385); Badakhshī affirms in this work that he had previously belonged to the Shaṭṭārī *ṭarīqa*, before joining the circle of Barzishābādī (DeWeese 1992: 127). In view of his Kubravī master's death-date, his Shaṭṭārī affiliation must have come relatively early in the career of Shāh 'Abdullāh Shaṭṭārī, if not before it altogether. The use of the label "Shaṭṭārī" prior to the career of the figure typically identified as the founder of the lineage should remind us that in this case, at least, the label "Shaṭṭārī" was attached retrospectively to the name of Shāh 'Abdullāh; it was not transferred from a figure bearing that name to the Sufi lineage, but vice-versa.

The next oldest extant sources to give versions of the Shaṭṭārī *silsila* are the writings of a 16th-century figure, Muḥammad Ghawth of Gwalior (d. 970/1563),[54] who traced his primary affiliation back through three intermediaries to Shāh 'Abdullāh Shaṭṭārī. The works

[53] On this figure, and the *Laṭā'if-i Ashrafī*, see Rizvi (1978: 266-270), Lawrence (1978: 53-55), and Ansari (1960).

[54] On this figure, in addition to the discussions in Ernst (1999) and Kugle (2003), see Muqtadir (1993); Nath (1978, erroneously attributing the *Gulzār-i abrār* to him); and Rizvi (1983: 12, 156-161).

of Muḥammad Ghawth are especially important for their information on doctrine, and especially on practice, and include little biographical information; they do, however, present versions of the *silsilas* through which Muḥammad Ghawth claimed initiations. In one of his works, known as the *Javāhir-i khamsa* (an important source on the spiritual practices of many Sufi groups), the portion of his *silsila* traced back from the 'eponym' of the Shaṭṭārīya (see the chart) differs in a few respects from that found in the *Laṭā'if-i ashrafī* (Muḥammad Ghawth, *Javāhir*: 102a). Though it is not entirely clear which work has preserved the lineage more faithfully (the earlier work seems to duplicate some names, while Muḥammad Ghawth clearly garbles others), there is no doubt that they reflect a common tradition. In another, later, work, known as the *Awrād-i Ghawthīya* (a collection of Sufi litanies to which several *silsilas* are added), Muḥammad Ghawth presented a more complex situation, claiming no fewer than 14 initiatic *silsilas*, including two going back through Chishtī masters, two through Suhravardī shaykhs, two through Firdawsī shaykhs, and assorted others (Muḥammad Ghawth, *Awrād*, lith.: 87-98; Muḥammad Ghawth, *Awrād*, MS: 134-150).[55] The first among them is that of the "Masters of the Shaṭṭārī affiliation of the 'Ishqī lineage," thus offering our first datable affirmation that the Shaṭṭārī and 'Ishqī *silsilas* are essentially the same. The lineage itself, like that given in the *Javāhir-i khamsa*, largely coincides with the 'Ishqī lineage (divergences from the 'Ishqī versions are relatively consistent among most versions of the Shaṭṭārī *silsila*).

More significantly, perhaps, the other, non-'Ishqī lineages recorded by Muḥammad Ghawth in the *Awrād* reveal an interesting pattern: most of them came to him already 'packaged' together for the three spiritual generations preceding him. Traced back from himself, that is, most of the *silsilas* he records pass through the same three figures, the earliest of whom was, in the Shaṭṭārī/'Ishqī lineage, a direct disciple of Shāh 'Abdullāh Shaṭṭārī. The latter is the fourth spiritual ancestor of Muḥammad Ghawth, but most of the other *silsilas* pass through a different figure in that fourth generation, while sharing the last three before Muḥammad Ghawth (in one other case, only one preceding generation is shared, and in yet another case, the last two generations coincide). Only three of the 14 lineages share the latest four generations, i.e., including 'Abdullāh Shaṭṭārī; in other words, the other lineages 'feed into' the line that reaches Muḥammad Ghawth at the point occupied by 'Abdullāh Shaṭṭārī. The first is the 'Ishqī lineage noted above; the second is, significantly, identified as a Khalvatī lineage; and the third reaches Shāh 'Abdullāh through "Sayyid 'Alī Muvaḥḥid." The latter two lineages clearly reflect accounts recorded in a 17th-century source reviewed below, and ascribed there to a work by Shāh 'Abdullāh Shaṭṭārī himself, as we will see.

[55] I am indebted to Scott Kugle for copies of both of these texts.

This work of Muḥammad Ghawth thus 'expands' the spiritual foundations of the Shaṭṭārī eponym, and shows an even broader range of spiritual influences and initiatic transmissions entering the 'Shaṭṭārīya' *after* the time of Shāh 'Abdullāh Shaṭṭārī. This pattern of multiple affiliations is in fact quite interesting with regard to subsequent trends in the history of Sufi communities, and is especially significant in terms of the broader issue of what the Shaṭṭārī label came to subsume as it developed in India. For present purposes, however, this pattern means that we may dispense with that later 'input' in exploring the earliest phase of Shaṭṭārī history.

For that earliest phase, finally, the most important source by far is an encyclopedic hagiography from the early 17th century, the *Gulzār-i abrār* of Muḥammad Ghawthī b. Ḥasan b. Mūsā Shaṭṭārī (a spiritual descendant of the 16th-century Muḥammad Ghawth). Dedicated to the Moghul emperor Jahāngīr, the *Gulzār-i abrār* was compiled between 998/1590 and 1022/1613, and preserves the earliest substantial material (such as it is) on the life of Shāh 'Abdullāh Shaṭṭārī. His entry, however, appears not in the section reserved for Shaṭṭārī shaykhs, but in the third section, on shaykhs of the 9th century A.H., between the biographies of the Naqshbandī shaykhs Sa'd al-Dīn Kāshgharī and Khwāja Aḥrār (*Gulzār*: 53a-54a).[56]

The account there in fact offers few biographical particulars about Shāh 'Abdullāh. It gives his natural lineage (he is said to have been a descendant, through only six generations, of Shihāb al-Dīn 'Umar Suhravardī [d. 632/1234]), but his birthplace is nowhere specified (his early life is usually assumed to have been passed in Mawarannahr or Khurāsān, in view of his *silsila*-links, discussed below). The *Gulzār-i abrār* mentions the shaykh's travels to Nīshāpūr, and in general in Khurāsān and 'Irāq, as well as a stay in Tabrīz, in Azerbaijan. It also recounts his sojourn in Bengal, and finally his establishment in Māndū in Mālwa, where he died in 890/1485 and was buried, to the south of the tombs of his royal patrons, the Khaljī *sulṭāns*.

More important, for our purposes, the *Gulzār-i abrār* gives two *silsilas* for Shāh 'Abdullāh, which link him with *both* the 'Ishqī and Khalvatī communities of Central Asia. In the case of the first *silsila*, this link is strengthened by the direct assertion of the equivalence of the designations "Shaṭṭārī" and "'Ishqī," and is further solidified by the remarkable coincidence of *silsila* segments. This first *silsila* (shown also in the chart) runs thus: Shāh 'Abdullāh < Shaykh Muḥammad 'Ārif < his father Shaykh Muḥammad 'Āshiq < his father Shaykh Khudāqulī Māwarā'n-nahrī < Shaykh Abū'l-Ḥasan 'Ishqī < Abū'l-Muẓaffar Turk-i Ṭūsī < Shaykh Abū Yazīd 'Ishqī 'Irāqī < Shaykh Muḥammad Maghribī < Abū Yazīd Bisṭāmī (*Gulzār*: 53a-b,

[56] See also Rizvi (1983: 151-154).

92a).[57] The account then adds that this *silsila* is known as the 'Ishqīya in "Īrān and Tūrān" (i.e., Iran and Central Asia), but as the Bisṭāmīya in Rūm (i.e., Anatolia); presumably it is understood that in India the name Shaṭṭārīya is the equivalent of both, and indeed elsewhere in the work, in the introduction to the fifth section (ostensibly devoted to the Shaṭṭārīya), Abū Yazīd Bisṭāmī is named as the "founder" (*sar-i daftar*) of this *khānavāda*, and the lineage is referred to simply as the *silsila-yi shaṭṭārīya-yi 'ishqīya* (*Gulzār*: 92a-b).

This account from the *Gulzār-i abrār* thus makes explicit what could be surmised from the earlier reports on the Shaṭṭārī *silsila*, namely that it was understood to be essentially the same as the 'Ishqī *silsila* known from Navā'ī's *Nasā'im al-maḥabba* and the other sources reviewed earlier (complete with the assertion, despite the 'abbreviated' lineage, of a connection with Bāyazīd Bisṭāmī). The direct assertion of the equivalence of the *silsila*s, combined with the striking coincidence of *silsila*s (which are obscure enough, and which show just enough divergences, to let us argue against the suspicion that Muḥammad Ghawthī borrowed directly from the earlier sources), leaves no room for doubt about a substantial overlap between the lineages, and the communities, indicated by the two labels.

We will return, shortly, to the issues raised by the various versions of the 'Ishqī and Shaṭṭārī *silsila*s. For now we may note that the *Gulzār-i abrār* is of further interest insofar as it refers to the development of the 'Ishqīya "in Arab and Persian 'Irāq and in Iran and Tūrān," and mentions "the master of this group, Muḥammad Ṣādiq Shaykh," who "unfurled the banner of religious direction and the standard of spiritual guidance" in Mawarannahr in the 930s A.H. (i.e., the latter 1520s and early 1530s). The work's mention of Muḥammad Ṣādiq 'Ishqī (d. 952/1545) suggests ongoing connections—and not merely a memory of common origins—between his 'Ishqī group and the Indian Shaṭṭārīya well after the time of Shāh 'Abdullāh Shaṭṭārī.

The second *silsila* given in the *Gulzār-i abrār* is even more interesting, inasmuch as it is cited from a work written by Shāh 'Abdullāh Shaṭṭārī himself. This is the *Laṭā'if-i ghaybīya*, cited twice in the *Gulzār-i abrār*, where it is noted that Shāh 'Abdullāh dedicated the work to Sulṭān Ghiyāth al-Dīn Khaljī, the ruler of Mālwa (r. 873/1469-906/1501).[58] It is thus one of our earliest accounts, and directly links the 'eponym' of the Shaṭṭārīya with the eastern Khalvatī communi-

[57] The principal difference between this version and the earlier recordings is the 'correction' of the *nisba* of the Abū'l-Ḥasan (i.e., from "Kharaqānī" to "'Ishqī").

[58] A single manuscript of a work entitled *Laṭīfa-yi ghaybīya* is mentioned in the 'union catalogue' of manuscripts in Pakistan, and is ascribed to an "'Abdullāh b. Ḥusām al-Dīn;" the genealogy given by the author matches the lineage, traced back to Shihāb al-Dīn 'Umar Suhravardī, that is given for Shāh 'Abdullāh Shaṭṭārī in available works. The manuscript, copied in the 19th century and preserved in Rawalpindi, has not been available to me; that it is probably a late copy of the work cited in the 17th-century *Gulzār-i abrār* is further suggested by the affirmation in the work's introduction, as cited in the catalogue,

ties reviewed above. According to the *Gulzār-i abrār*, Shāh 'Abdullāh wrote in the *Laṭā'if-i ghaybīya*, "I heard that Shaykh Muẓaffar Kattānī Khalvatī, who was in Nīshāpūr, led the Sufi to God in three days of seclusionary retreat (*ṣūfī-rā dar seh rūz-i khalvat be-khudā mīrasānad*), and without delay I hurried to him." After affirming that his progress was even faster than he had hoped, Shāh 'Abdullāh recorded this Shaykh Muẓaffar's *silsila*: his shaykh was Ibrāhīm 'Ishqābādī, who was a *murīd* of Sayyid Niẓām al-Dīn Ḥusayn, who was in turn a *murīd* of Shaykh Muḥammad Khalvatī, whose shaykh was Najm al-Dīn Kubrā.

This remarkable account not only hints at the signification of the label "Shaṭṭārī," but links that signification with a shaykh who was clearly associated with one of the eastern Khalvatī communities discussed above: Shaykh Muẓaffar himself was ascribed the *nisba* "Khalvatī," and his lineage was traced back to the same Khwārazmian figure, Shaykh Muḥammad Khalvatī, to whom nearly all our accounts of the Khalvatī groups in Bukhārā, Herat, Kirmān, and Quhistān looked as the namesake of the Khalvatī tradition. The account even echoes the link between Muḥammad Khalvatī of Khwārazm and Najm al-Dīn Kubrā, a link that was noted also, indirectly, in the *Tārīkh-i Mullāzāda*'s affirmation that Nūr al-Dīn Khalvatī of Bukhārā belonged to the "lineage" of Najm al-Dīn Kubrā; the claim of Muḥammad Khalvatī's direct discipleship under Najm al-Dīn is a gross anachronism, but may reflect an oversimplication of a tradition reflected more accurately, even if its details remain unrecoverable, in the 15th-century Bukharan source. In any case, the value of Shāh 'Abdullāh's testimony is heightened not only by his direct acquaintance (however brief) with Shaykh Muẓaffar in Nīshāpūr, but by the evidence that he himself spent time in Bukhārā: a slightly later source that likewise records this excerpt from the work of Shāh 'Abdullāh Shaṭṭārī includes this additional detail, affirming that Shāh 'Abdullāh was in Bukhārā when he learned of Shaykh Muẓaffar's reputation (*Jāmi' al-salāsil*: 57b-58a).[59]

Of even greater interest in terms of a direct link with a later figure in the 'Khalvatī' tradition, however, is this account's mention of Muḥammad Khalvatī's disciple, Sayyid Niẓām al-Dīn Ḥusayn. There can be little doubt that the figure intended here is the Niẓām al-Dīn Khalvatī, discussed above, whose death in 775/1374 is recorded in the *Mujmal-i Faṣīḥī*, and who was the shaykh of Aubin's Quhistānī saint, Akhī Muḥammad-Shāh Shārakhtī. There seems to be no other mention of Shaykh Ibrāhīm 'Ishqābādī, the link between this Niẓām al-Dīn and Shāh 'Abdullāh's Shaykh Muẓaffar, but his *nisba* clearly links him with the Khalvatī community of 'Ishqābād in Jām. It is possible that he should be identified with the "Khwāja 'Ishqābādī" mentioned

that it gives an account of the mystical path of the "*khānadān-i 'ishqīya*" (Munzavī 1984: 1840, Title No. 3379, MS No. 9913).

[59] The account here cites the "*Risāla-i ghaybīya*." The *Jāmi' al-salāsil*, a Kubravī hagiography from the mid-17th century, is discussed briefly in DeWeese (1992: 135).

in Aubin's text as a disciple of Niẓām al-Dīn and as somehow hostile to the familial succession among the descendants of Akhī Muḥammad-Shāh Shārakhtī. In any case, the association of these figures with the town of 'Ishqābād suggests a plausible trajectory whereby a local 'Khalvatī' community (or individual) might have become known also by the *nisba* "'Ishqī" (although we cannot link the historical 'Ishqī community of Mawarannahr with the region of Jām on the basis of available sources).

In this connection the authority and antiquity of the account preserved in the *Gulzār-i abrār* are worth stressing: the account is not only the shaykh's own direct testimony, but is earlier than the *Rashaḥāt*, and contemporary with the works of Jāmī and Navā'ī. Of our sources on the Khalvatī and 'Ishqī circles of Central Asia, indeed, only Aubin's hagiography and the scattered early references to Muḥammad Khalvatī of Khwārazm (and one mention of Niẓām al-Dīn Khalvatī) are earlier than the *Laṭā'if-i ghaybīya*. Given its antiquity, this work's presentation of the *silsila* of the Shaṭṭārī 'founder' bears authority at least equal to that of the overlapping Bisṭāmī/'Ishqī lineage reflected in the *Gulzār-i abrār*, and it is no doubt significant that the author of the *Gulzār-i abrār* did *not* cite Shāh 'Abdullāh's own words in affirming his 'Ishqī *silsila*.

It is remarkable, indeed, that the author of the *Gulzār-i abrār* offers not even the briefest of narrative accounts, whether his own or drawn from the work of Shāh 'Abdullāh, about Shāh 'Abdullāh's association with the shaykh through whom the work traces his 'chief' *silsila* (chief, that is, to judge from its repetition and emphasis, as the definitively Shaṭṭārī *silsila*, in later works). That is, he integrates his account of the Khalvatī *silsila* into the narrative of Shāh 'Abdullāh's life; he does the same with another affiliation he claims for the 'founder' of the Shaṭṭārīya, when, following the focus on the Khalvatī shaykh, Shāh 'Abdullāh is further cited recounting his travels to Khurāsān, 'Irāq, and Azerbaijan, and noting his association with Shāh 'Alī Muvaḥḥid, who, he says, was licensed by Shaykh Zayn al-Dīn Khwāfī in a lineage going back through four intermediaries to [Shihāb al-Dīn 'Umar] Suhravardī. Accounts of these two lineages are indeed included in Muḥammad Ghawth's *Awrād-i ghawthīya*, alongside the 'Ishqī lineage; but in the *Gulzār-i abrār*, the 'Ishqī lineage is simply presented as Shāh 'Abdullāh's *silsila*, and we are never told any details about his relationship with his 'Ishqī master, or about when, where, and why it came about (standard elements of hagiographical presentations). To judge from this handling of the respective lineages, we would be justified in arguing that it was Shāh 'Abdullāh's Khalvatī initiation and training that were crucial to his spiritual development. Why the 'Ishqī lineage was emphasized rather than the Khalvatī lineage may have had more to do with extraneous factors—e.g., with the malleability of the 'Ishqī *silsila* as received, with the absence of even conjectural information about the earlier links in the Khalvatī *silsila*, with the differential susceptibility of each to verification or refutation, or simply with the rhetorical or competitive ramifications, in specific contexts, of the 'Ishqī and Khalvatī labels—than with the actual significance of the initiatory links or training claimed for Shāh 'Abdullāh through the respective lines of transmission.

We may return, finally, to the Shaṭṭārī adaptation of the 'Ishqī *silsila*; the various versions are shown in the accompanying chart. Without exploring all the particular manipulations of the *silsila*s provided for the 'Ishqī and Shaṭṭārī Sufis, we may note a few patterns that stand out at once. One is the obvious similarity of the 'Ishqī and Shaṭṭārī *silsila*s in the 'later' phases, prior to the latter 15th century. In fact, with the exception of the "Shaykh Abū'l-Muẓaffar Turk-i Ṭūsī" intervening between Abū Yazīd and Abū'l-Ḥasan, the *silsila* given in the Shaṭṭārī sources is strikingly similar to the *silsila* of the 'Ishqīya as reflected in the *Rashaḥāt* and other sources. In that *silsila*, "Shaykh Bāyazīd 'Ishqī" is clearly the Abū Yazīd 'Ishqī 'Irāqī appearing in Shāh 'Abdullāh Shaṭṭārī's *silsila*; Abū'l-Ḥasan 'Ishqī, whom Navā'ī identifies as a Khwārazmian, appears with the same name in both *silsila*s; the "Khudāyqulī Shaykh" from the earlier sources is simply identified as "Māwarā'n-nahrī" in the *Gulzār-i abrār*; and the "Muḥammad 'Āshiq" of the later work may be either of two disciples of Khudāyqulī named in the earlier sources (that is, "Muḥammad Shaykh" or "Shaykh Muḥammad Ṣūfī," mentioned by Navā'ī), or yet another *murīd*. At that point the *silsila*s diverge, and both the sequence of the *silsila*s and the known chronologies agree in making Shāh 'Abdullāh Shaṭṭārī (d. 890/1495) a contemporary of Shaykhzāda Abū'l-Ḥasan, the son of Khwāja Aḥrār's rival Ilyās.

As for the earlier stages in the lineage, the Shaṭṭārī versions all share several other features. (1) They include just three links between Abū'l-Ḥasan 'Ishqī, who must belong to the 14th century, and the 9th-century Bāyazīd Bisṭāmī, whom they agree in identifying as the 'origin' of the Shaṭṭārī lineage, and offer no discussion of the enormous chronological gap entailed by their presentation. (2) In including Bisṭāmī, they omit the figure typically shown as his 'disciple' in other *silsila*s that include Bisṭāmī, namely Abū'l-Ḥasan Kharaqānī, an omission perhaps addressed in some versions by garbling the name of Abū'l-Ḥasan 'Ishqī, identifying him as Abū'l-Ḥasan Kharaqānī. (3) They insert, as Bisṭāmī's 'direct' disciple, a figure bearing the *nisba* "Maghribī" (echoing Ḥazīnī's portrayal of a man from the Maghrib as the disciple of Kharaqānī in the 'Ishqī *silsila*, 'adding' the name "Muḥammad" for him, but offering no hint of the *laqab* Bahā' al-Dīn attached to him by Ḥazīnī), but offer no basis for deciding whether this Maghribī should be placed, chronologically, closer to Bisṭāmī (in the 9th century!) or to the 'historical' 'Ishqī shaykhs of the latter 14th century.[60] (4) They assign to the disciple of this Maghribī a name clear-

[60] It is of course possible that the "Muḥammad Maghribī" of Shaṭṭārī formulations is an echo of the figure called "Muḥammad Khalvatī," and linked with Khwārazm, in

ly recognizable as a garbling of "Abū Yazīd 'Ishqī," recalling the name assigned by one of our earliest sources on the 'Ishqīya—Navā'ī—to the direct master of Abū'l-Ḥasan 'Ishqī. (5) They insert, between this echo of Bāyazīd 'Ishqī and Abū'l-Ḥasan 'Ishqī, a figure whose name, "Abū'l-Muẓaffar Turk-i Ṭūsī," is not found outside Shaṭṭārī versions of the *silsila*, but includes one element, "Muẓaffar," that recalls the name of the 'Khalvatī' shaykh sought out by Shāh 'Abdullāh Shaṭṭārī because of his reputation for rapid spiritual advancement (the latter Muẓaffar's association with Nīshāpūr is of further interest in view of the close proximity of Ṭūs and Nīshāpūr).[61]

The net effect of these considerations is to underscore the utterly ahistorical character of the earlier links in the 'Ishqī/Shaṭṭārī *silsila*, and to suggest considerable manipulation even of the more recent links. In both cases, the significance of the *silsila* as a marker of historical and communal continuity is undermined. Conversely, given the substantial evidence suggesting social and historical continuities among groups bearing the 'Ishqī, Shaṭṭārī, and Khalvatī labels, the *silsila* claimed by the later 'Ishqī and Shaṭṭārī communities should present no serious difficulty to suggesting the communal and historical continuity with the Khalvatīya (no more serious difficulty, that is, than posed by the later western Khalvatīya's reconstruction of its *silsila*).[62]

IV. Links, Lineages, and Labels:

The sources reviewed here suggest that despite the different labels and spheres of activity known for the groups indicated by these three separate names—Khalvatī, 'Ishqī, and Shaṭṭārī—there is considerable overlap in their earliest phases, and that the three communal labels reflect later regional (and perhaps schismatic)

accounts of the eastern Khalvatī groups (and of the "Akhī Muḥammad," sometimes linked with Shīrvān, in western Khalvatī sources); and we might thus suppose that this figure's inclusion in Shaṭṭārī formulations, between Bāyazīd Bisṭāmī and the lineage's *second* Bāyazīd (i.e., Bāyazīd 'Ishqī, whom some Shaṭṭārī sources link with 'Irāq while garbling his name, but whom Navā'ī insists was from Khwārazm), hints at a tradition that indeed linked Bāyazīd 'Ishqī with the Khwārazmian Muḥammad Khalvatī.

[61] "Abū'l-Muẓaffar the Turk of Ṭūs" is of course inserted in the *silsila* four or five generations prior to 'Abdullāh Shaṭṭārī; but the cavalier handling of figures such as Bisṭāmī, Kharaqānī, and the Maghribī shaykh suggests caution about rejecting the possible identity of "Abū'l-Muẓaffar the Turk of Ṭūs" with "Shaykh Muẓaffar Kattānī Khalvatī"—or at least the possible common inspiration of these two appellations by the same obscure historical figure.

[62] It is also significant, however, that within the fully developed Shaṭṭārī order, the manipulation of *silsilas* seems to have ceased relatively early, at least along the lines noted here. That is, as a historically reliable *silsila* grew in importance, some Sufi communities continued manipulating their lineage, inserting figures to close chronological gaps or explaining relationships in non-historical ways. The Shaṭṭārīya in India, by contrast, seems to have chosen to avoid the problems with its 'Ishqī lineage, and to have stressed other, less problematical *silsilas* through the claim of multiple initiations on the part of early Shaṭṭārī masters (this is suggested, in connection with regard to 'suspect' Shaṭṭārī practices rather than problematical *silsila* formulations, in Ernst (1999: 434).

developments of an original sociological and 'corporate' continuum. The only evidence *against* the common communal origins of the three groups labeled Khalvatī, 'Ishqī, and Shaṭṭārī—aside from the three separate labels—comes from the *silsila*s constructed for them. The eastern Khalvatī communities are ascribed a *silsila* going back to the Khwārazmian Muḥammad Khalvatī and from him directly or indirectly to Najm al-Dīn Kubrā. If the connection is understood to be direct, it is an obvious anachronism, but even if it is taken to be indirect, the claim finds no confirmation in the relatively substantial sources on the successors and legacy of Najm al-Dīn Kubrā. In any case, such a *silsila* seems clearly distinct from the *silsila* for the groups labeled 'Ishqī and Shaṭṭārī, which displays similar chronological gaps, but which assigns a central role to the figure of Bāyazīd Bisṭāmī. The latter figure's inclusion, however, may well signal a *silsila* contrived, in whole or part, on the basis of considerations quite apart from historical continuity and direct master-to-disciple transmission. In this regard, as noted, the *silsila* for the western Khalvatī groups of the Ottoman world may well have been similarly contrived, in this case devised in the context of competition with the Ṣafavīya, which was developing precisely in the area—Azerbaijan—in which the western Khalvatīya emerged.

I would argue, then, that precisely because these *silsila*s were in all likelihood formulated quite late, on the basis of sparse information, and for a purpose other than a historically accurate rendering of a series of master-disciple relationships, the apparent discrepancies in the earlier phases of the *silsila*s typically given for the three groups are of little significance in judging the likely communal overlap among them. The point is not, finally, that we can definitively parse the *silsila*s and recover their 'actual' links; the point is that the *silsila*s that were later cited as legitimizing features for a Sufi community were formerly not critical for that goal, and that existing versions of *silsila*s reflect constructions for different needs and with different assumptions of what a *silsila* represented. What is clear, in any case, is that however important it became for the groups explored here to formulate a respectable *silsila* for themselves by the 16th century, the *silsila* was not an important (much less exclusive) marker of communal identity in the early phases of those communities' development.

If the *silsila*s for these groups were not crucial to their legitimation in the 14th and 15th centuries, what *was* the basis of their claim to legitimacy and their appeal to would-be adepts? Important clues may lie precisely in the labels attached to them, and the style of practice or mystical experience they signified. Here too the evidence points toward understanding these groups as belonging, originally, to a single social continuum, however loosely it may have been bound together. In each case, the communal label would seem to have specific implications, or to be linked with a specific 'profile' of practice or experience. In the case of the Khalvatīya, the seemingly obvious implication of its appellation is the prominence of seclusionary retreats in its practice; the situation is not so simple, however.

To begin with, we find an interesting use of the collective term *khalvatīyān*, in a work produced during the lifetime of Shaykh Muḥammad Khalvatī of Khwārazm, to refer to a particular community that, while admired by no less a figure than the eminent Sufi shaykh 'Alā' al-Dawla Simnānī, remained outside the fold of Islam. In the *Chihil majlis* of Amīr Iqbāl Sīstānī, compiled as a collection of discourses by Simnānī, shortly after the latter's death in 736/1336, the term "*khalvatīyān*" is used, in words ascribed to Simnānī himself, to refer to a particular group of Buddhist monks, devoted to seclusion and the practice of austerities. One representative of this group, known as "Paranda Bakhshī" (i.e., the "flying monk"), was known to Simnānī personally at the court of his Mongol patron, the Ilkhanid ruler Arghun; the monk came to Simnānī's *khānqāh*, and Simnānī even sent one of his own disciples to this monk for help with a particular obstacle on his spiritual path (*Chihil majlis*: 70). The point here, of course, is not that Simnānī's use of this label makes Shaykh Muḥammad Khalvatī, or other contemporary Sufis accorded this label, crypto-Buddhists or 'borrowers' of Buddhist practices; the point is that Simnānī, in seeking Islamic terminology to label and identify the spiritual style of a specific Buddhist group with which he became familiar, used a collective term that highlighted a specific aspect of Sufi practice (an aspect employed, we may stress, as an almost routine component of spiritual training in the Sufi tradition inherited by Simnānī himself).

The use of the term "Khalvatī," moreover, and an emphasis upon the practice of *khalvat*, undoubtedly took on special significance in the competitive atmosphere prevailing among Sufi communities of Central Asia during the 14th century, when we find *khalvat* linked with a ritual and organizational complex involving the vocal *dhikr*, *samā'* (the use of music in ritual and devotional practice), and hereditary succession (DeWeese 1996a; 1996b; 1999). Herat, indeed, where we find the Khalvatī community active in the second half of the 14th century, is the setting for a story that frames this complex quite plainly, in the questions posed by Malik Ḥusayn, the Kart ruler of Herat, to Bahā' al-Dīn Naqshband (DeWeese 1996a: 197-198). Asked by the ruler whether his brand of Sufism employed vocal *dhikr*, *samā'*, *khalvat*, and hereditary transmission, Bahā' al-Dīn replied that it did not; he then went on to offer an explicit contrast to only one, as he explained the dictum *khalvat dar anjuman* ("seclusion within the crowd"), itself part of a rhetorical dialectic intended to undermine the stock assumptions of 'normative' Sufi practice, which became a famous element of the Naqshbandī meditative and social program.

Finally, and most tellingly, *khalvat* is not the element of Khalvatī practice that is noted most prominently in the sources; the element highlighted is, instead, the vocal *dhikr*, and a 'noisy' profile in general. One might even suggest that the vocal *dhikr* somehow does not fit with the solitary retreat and seclusion that is the hallmark of *khalvat* early on, though it is clear that by the 16th century at least, the notion of *khalvat* had been expanded to include the oxymoronic 'public *khalvats*' at which masses of participants would gather for performances of the vocal *dhikr*. Whether that was at work in the Khalvatī—or 'Ishqī—communities is not at all certain from the sources, however.

In the case of the 'Ishqīya, the label itself would seem to imply spiritual practice or experience distinguished in some way by mystical love or rapturous ecstasy. What the sources tell us, however, is that the 'Ishqī community, too, was known for the raucous performance of the vocal *dhikr*. Interpreting the meaning of the communal label is further complicated by the relatively limited range of its use, for the single community, based near Samarqand, that appears to have been marked by hereditary succession (paralleling the apparent 'localization' of the appellation "Khalvatī" in Herat). The laconic sources, moreover, suggest that that label might simply be derived from the individual appellation of the earliest 'historical' member of the lineage (though as we have seen, different sources identified different figures as the first to be called "'Ishqī"), and why he bore it remains unclear. The communal overlap we are suggesting here might offer some justification for conjecturing that this label reflects a 'founding' figure's association with the 'Khalvatī' community of 'Ishqābād, but in the end the evidence is simply not sufficient to establish this.

For the 'Ishqīya, however, we also have explicit statements characterizing the 'Ishqī path, not in 'internal' sources, but in accounts produced by shaykhs of other orders. Ḥazīnī's account of the 'Ishqīya (Ḥazīnī, *Jāmi'*: 105b-107a), from the 16th century, stresses the 'Ishqī emphasis upon the vocal *dhikr*, but also refers to the 'founder' of the 'Ishqī *silsila* as "the boldest of the bold" ("*zabardast-i zabardastān*"), and as exemplifying a tradition of "vigor and haste" (*karr-u-zūd*). It is perhaps the elements of boldness, intensity, and speed that are implied in a lost work, cited in the *Thamarāt al-mashā'ikh*, a Bukharan hagiography from the late 17th century, which offers brief encapsulations of the particular merits and character of five major *silsilas* (including the Khwājagān, the Yasavīya, the Kubravīya, and the "Khalvīya," the latter identified only as "followers" of the Kubravīya). The fourth *silsila* mentioned is the 'Ishqīya, and its characterization is quite startling (*Thamarāt*: 48b49a): the 'Ishqī *ṭarīqa*, the author affirms, is called "bloodthirsty," because of its "intensity" (*ṭarīqa-yi 'Ishqīya, ke khūn-khwār gufte-and binā bar shāqqa-i*).[63]

[63] The work cited here, by the author of the *Thamarāt*, is a *ḥāshīya*, or explanatory comment, found in a manuscript of an otherwise unknown work entitled *Riyāż al-'āshiqīn*. The comment is paralleled in Muḥammad Ghawth's *Awrād-i ghawthīya*, where he refers to "the genealogical tree of succession for the Shaṭṭārī masters of the lineage of the fire-eating 'Ishqīya" (*shajara-yi khilāfat-i pīrān-i mashrab-i shaṭṭār-i khānadān-i 'ishqīya-yi ātash-khwār* [Muḥammad Ghawth, *Awrād*, lith.: 87; Muḥammad Ghawth, *Awrād*, MS: 134]).

In the case of the Shaṭṭārīya, finally, we find both more interesting semantic developments and explicit statements on why the community bore that name, and on its implications for the group's mystical and experiential profile. To begin with, the term *shaṭṭār* (or more properly *shuṭṭār*, a plural of *shāṭir*) appears to have been used most widely to refer to highwaymen or vagabonds. This use is rooted etymologically in the connotations of the Arabic verb *shaṭara*, meaning to "cut off" or "separate" or "withdraw" (as well as to be clever or cunning), and by extension to move quickly and boldly. In the specific historical context of eastern Iran in the 14th century, however, there is reason to suppose that the term *shaṭṭārī* would have suggested, originally, a distinct social and even political profile, rooted in the use of *shaṭṭār* or *shuṭṭār* to refer to highwaymen. It was the traveler Ibn Baṭṭūṭa who linked the term *shuṭṭār* with the Sarbadārs of Khurāsān, the upstart, populist, religiously-tinged militant movement that carved out a short-lived state in Khurāsān as Mongol power disintegrated in Ilkhanid Iran during the 1330s and 1340s (Smith 1970). In specific terms, Ibn Baṭṭūṭa identified the term *shuṭṭār* as the equivalent, in 'Irāq, of the term used for the Sarbadārs in Khurāsān, and linked it more generally with other terms for groups, and their leaders, involved in popular resistance against the government (Ibn Baṭṭūṭa: 575). Given the century, at least, between our evidence for this social profile and the emergence of the Shaṭṭārī Sufi community, and given the lack of evidence for any distinct political profile on the part of the Shaṭṭārī Sufis (or the Khalvatīs or the 'Ishqīs) before the 16th century, it would most likely be a mistake to imagine that the name Shaṭṭārī indeed reflects a distinctly antinomian and rebellious social profile. Rather, it more likely reflects a rhetorical profile, and the self-consious adoption of a provocative term evoking the boldness and speed of a highwayman or rebel in the context of a different kind of path.

As to the adoption of the term in a mystical context, we know of a 14th-century Sufi of Iran, Rukn al-Dīn 'Abdullāh Shīrāzī (d. 769/1367), who is known to have traveled through the Golden Horde and Central Asia, and whose honorifics, inscribed on his tombstone, included the affirmation that he was "the abode (*maqām*) of the *shuṭṭār*" (Humā'ī 1980: 4).[64] Possibly earlier still is the comment on the "path (*ṭarīq*) of the *shuṭṭār*," identified as the path of "those who journey toward God and 'fly' to God" (*ṭarīq al-sā'irīn ilā'llāh wa'l-ṭā'irīn bi'llāh*); the comment is ascribed in Shaṭṭārī sources to Najm al-Dīn Kubrā (Muḥammad Ghawth, *Javāhir*: 101b). Both of these uses of the term suggest its application to a group of saints, if not yet to

[64] Prompted by this phrase on Shīrāzī's tombstone, Humā'ī includes a discussion of the term *shuṭṭār* (Humā'ī 1980: 19-29), with reference to Muḥammad Ghawth's *Javāhir-i khamsa*, among other sources, and with a brief discussion of the Shaṭṭārī *silsila*.

an actual social collectivity; the second, at least, suggests the term's association with speed.

We do have several explicit indications, however, from sources produced within the Shaṭṭārī community, regarding the meaning of the label applied to it, and the experiential profile of the 'Ishqī and Shaṭṭārī tradition. One is indirect, but appears in the account of the Shaṭṭārī 'founder's' own mystical training, as noted above: Shāh 'Abdullāh Shaṭṭārī was drawn to one of his masters, Shaykh Muẓaffar Kattānī Khalvatī of Nīshāpūr, by his reputation for leading the Sufi to God in just three days of *khalvat*. The emphasis upon speed is underscored elsewhere in Shaṭṭārī sources, but this brief passage is especially valuable for linking speed in mystical attainment with the environment evidently regarded as particularly conducive to such speed, namely *khalvat*.

As for other explicit explanations, the 16th-century Shaṭṭārī shaykh Muḥammad Ghawth himself writes, prior to citing the comment ascribed to Najm al-Dīn Kubrā, that whenever the Seeker wishes to pass beyond "pious deeds and good works and mysteries," he should "come to the watering-place (*mashrab*) of the *shuṭṭār*" (the term "*mashrab*," meaning literally a place where one drinks, is a common term for a school of thought or practice or, in Sufi contexts, an initiatic affiliation). Muḥammad Ghawth then affirms that the *mashrab-i shuṭṭār* is more exalted and of greater value than all other affiliations (Muḥammad Ghawth, *Javāhir*: 101b). The latter claim is not surprising, given Muḥammad Ghawth's own primary affiliation, but his first comment implies that the path of the *shuṭṭār* is reserved for an elite who seek to transcend both the ordinary obligations of Islam and the 'mysteries' of normative Sufism.

From somewhat later, we read in the *Gulzār-i abrār* that the *pīrs* of this *silsila* are called *Shaṭṭārī* because "their passage on the royal path of the *ṭarīqa* is faster and speedier than that of the shaykhs of other classes" (*sulūk-i shāh-rāh-i ṭarīqat az mashā'ikh-i dīgar khānavādahā tīz-tar va garm-raw-tar-and*) (*Gulzār*: 54a). The passage not only highlights the element of speed, linked to *khalvat*, that initially attracted Shāh 'Abdullāh Shaṭṭārī, but also recalls the emphasis upon "boldness" and upon "speed and vigor" in Ḥazīnī's account of the 'Ishqīya. Elsewhere the same work discusses the communal label at greater length, in the context of affirming the essential identity of what is called the *silsila-yi shaṭṭārīya-yi 'ishqīya*, and exploring the reasons for naming the lineage *shaṭṭārīya* (*Gulzār*: 92a-b). It affirms that the 'Ishqī "school," compared with others, belongs among the "forerunners" (*al-sābiqūn*)—spoken of in the Qur'ān (LVI.1011) as those who will be close to God—with respect to attaining the stages of *fanā* and *baqā*. It then cites, again, the *Laṭā'if-i ghaybīya* of Shāh 'Abdullāh in explaining the name Shaṭṭārī, which, it affirms, alludes to "speed" (*sur'at*) and to the group's "rapidity in passing through the stages of the mystical path" (*az rūy-i tīz-ravī-yi ū dar ṭayy-i manāzil-i ṭarīqat*).

Perhaps the most interesting passage, however, links the Shaṭṭārī path with a principle of spiritual transmission that looks very much like the Uvaysī style, though the term "Uvaysī" is not invoked here. Some of the eminent saints of this school, the account says, have affirmed that this group, "without the medium of service to and association with an earthly body," has "obtained training from the souls of the great saints who have unloaded the burden of form." The account thus links the Shaṭṭārī community directly with the principle, if not the name, of Uvaysī-style transmission, and in effect acknowledges the ahistorical character of the Shaṭṭārī and 'Ishqī lineage; here too, as noted earlier, the possible role of the Uvaysī paradigm in divisions among the Khalvatī and 'Ishqī groups suggests another point of contact among the three traditions.

The author adds, finally, the specific explanation that all the "*mashā'ikh-i shaṭṭār*" in India have received their share of this school through Shāh 'Abdullāh Shaṭṭārī, implicitly affirming that his appellation was now the proximate cause of the adoption of the communal label "Shaṭṭārī" by what is presented, still in the early 17th century, as an Indian 'branch' of the 'Ishqīya, but as one with a heavy input—precisely with regard to what was declared the distinguishing mark of the Shaṭṭārīya, namely an emphasis on speedy attainment—from a clearly Khalvatī lineage.

V. Conclusion:

The three labels we have considered appear, in the end, to reflect the application of different communal appellations to groups that shared common communal origins and a common approach to mystical practice and experience. The specific groups came to be distinguished in part on a regional basis, but also came to be differentiated in terms of their *silsila*s, as *silsila*s were retrospectively defined for each group on the basis of its later competitive needs. It seems likely, that is, that we have here examples of Sufi communities, linked more or less closely and defined on the basis of the distinguishing characteristics of the spiritual practice they enjoined and the mode of experience they promised, that came to differentiate themselves by communal labels, and were driven by the dominance of the *silsila* as a sine qua non of legitimation and authority to devise a respectable lineage. In doing so they worked on the basis of authentic, if sparse, information, on the basis of reasonable, if often misleading, conjecture and assumption regarding the identity of particular figures, and on the basis of the didactic or competitive needs they faced in their specific environments.

Both the manipulation of the *silsila*s, and the shifting application of the labels, reflect a period in which the legacy of an individual 'founder' and the importance of the *silsila* as a basis for organization and legitimation had not yet become firmly established. Both the Khalvatī and 'Ishqī labels, and the descriptions of the disciplinary profiles of the groups to which they were applied, stress above all an *intensity* of practice that was in turn linked to the *speed* of mystical attainment; the Shaṭṭārī label itself alludes to that speed, while explanations of the Shaṭṭārī path likewise explicitly link speed and experiential intensity. This in turn suggests, incidentally, a fundamental difference between these three groups, together, and a community such as the Naqshbandīya, which was emerging at nearly the same time and in the same area. The former were marked by intensity, and were above all *visible* (and audible) as arguably ostentatious manifestations of mystical experience. The Naqshbandīs, by contrast, claimed to so internalize the intensity of mystical experience as to be unremarkable in public view, and thus in effect were marked by an 'ostentatious' *concealment* of practice and experience (a spiritual and social profile that harks back, as has often been noted, to the Malāmatī tradition).

The various explanations of these communal labels, or of the mystical profile of the groups to which they refer, suggest that in addition to probably sharing a common origin in social and communal terms, the groups that appear in our sources under the designations "Khalvatī," "'Ishqī," and "Shaṭṭārī" shared also a distinctive way of asserting their legitimacy, or of 'advertising' their appeal: they claimed to deliver results, and to do so quickly. Such a claim resembles offers of speedy attainment or 'instant enlightenment' in other contexts, as well as specific assertions, in other Sufi sources from the 14th and 15th centuries, that mystical advancement could be had merely by attaching oneself to the community, or even to the lineage, of a particular shaykh (e.g., DeWeese 1992: 141, 145-146). And like those claims, the promise of speedy advancement on the Sufi path is implicitly (and sometimes explicitly) contrasted with the hard slog of service to, and slow, guided progress with an attentive master. The popularity of the Uvaysī notion in the same era no doubt reflects the same sort of appeal, i.e., the promise of a direct and instantaneous spiritual encounter that could obviate the need for 'serving' and associating with "an earthly body," as the Shaṭṭārī work explained it.

At the same time, the promise of quick attainment reflected, and perhaps also enhanced, an inattention to the sequence of masters and disciples engaged in the long preparation and training that constitutes, paradigmatically, the substance of the Sufi life. It is thus perhaps not surprising that communities originally intent upon highlighting the speed or efficiency of their method faced historiographical difficulties when they felt obliged to set forth the *silsila* that connected them with the Prophet. The results of these historiographical difficulties are evident from the various patterns in the manipulation of each group's *silsila*; their *silsila*s, after all, came to be attached to the particular communal labels that had earlier signified not a corporate body defined in terms of a *silsila*, but one defined in large measure by the assertion of a distinctively intense and efficacious mode of practice, experience, and attainment.

Shaṭṭārī *silsilas*:

Laṭā'if-i Ashrafī, 15th century	Muḥammad Ghawth, *Javāhir-i khamsa, Awrād-i Ghawthīya*, 16th century	*Gulzār-i abrār*, 17th century
Sayyid Ashraf Jahāngīr Simnānī	'Abdullāh al-Shaṭṭārī	'Abdullāh Shaṭṭārī
Shaykh Muḥammad 'Ārif	Muḥammad 'Ārif	Muḥammad 'Ārif
Shaykh Khudāqulī	Muḥammad 'Āshiq [b. Shaykh Khudāqulī]	Muḥammad 'Āshiq
Shaykh Muḥammad 'Āshiq		
Khudāqulī Māwarā'l-nahrī	Khudāqulī Māwarā'l-nahrī	Khudāyqulī Māwarā'l-nahrī
Abū'l-Ḥasan Kharaqānī ["'Ishqī" added in lith.]	Khwāja Abū'l-Ḥasan Kharaqānī	Abū'l-Ḥasan 'Ishqī
Abū'l-Muẓaffar [Mawlānā] Turk-i Ṭūsī	Abū'l-Muẓaffar Mawlānā Turk-i Ṭūsī	Abū'l-Muẓaffar Turk-i Ṭūsī
Khwāja A'rābī Mazīd 'Ishqī [a garbling of "Bāyazīd 'Ishqī"]	al-Khwāja al-A'rābī Mazīd 'Ishqī [Abū Yazīd 'Ishqī]	Abū Yazīd 'Ishqī 'Irāqī
Khwāja Muḥammad Maghribī	Khwāja Muḥammad Maghribī	Muḥammad Maghribī
Bāyazīd Bisṭāmī	Abū Yazīd Bisṭāmī	Abū Yazīd Bisṭāmī

Jāmi' al-salāsil, 17th century	*Simṭ al-majīd,* 17th century	('Ishqīya)
		Muḥammad Ṣādiq
		Abū'l-Ḥasan
Shāh Najm al-Dīn Shāh 'Abdullāh Shaṭṭārī	'Abdullāh Shaṭṭārī	Ilyās Shaykh
Muḥammad 'Ārif	Muḥammad 'Ārif	Muḥammad Shaykh
Muḥammad 'Āshiq	Muḥammad 'Āshiq	
Khudāyqulī Māwarā' l-nahrī	Khudāqulī Māwarā'l-nahrī	Khudāyqulī
Abū'l-Ḥasan 'Ishqī	Abū'l-Ḥasan Kharaqānī	Abū'l-Ḥasan 'Ishqī
Abū'l-Muẓaffar-i Turk	Abū'l-Muẓaffar Mawlā Turk-i Ṭūsī	
Abū Yazīd A'rābī Yazīd 'Ishqī	Shaykh al-A'rābī	Bāyazīd 'Ishqī / Bahā' al-Dīn Maghribī
Muḥammad Maghribī	Muḥammad al-Maghribī	
Bāyazīd [Bisṭāmī]	*rūḥānīya* of Abū Yazīd Bisṭāmī	Bāyazīd Bisṭāmī

'Ishqī *silsilas*:

Navā'ī: (1500)	*Ḥazīnī*: (1565)	*Nithārī*: (1566)	*Thamarāt al-mashā'ikh*: (1690)
		Ma'ṣūm Khwāja Ishqī	[5 more generations down to author's time]
	Bābā Shaykh		Ḥakīm Shaykh
	Muḥammad Ṣādiq	Muḥammad Ṣādiq Shaykh	Muḥammad Ṣādiq
	Abū'l-Ḥasan	Abū'l-Ḥasan Shaykh	Abū'l-Ḥasan
Ilyās Shaykh	Ilyās 'Ishqī	Ilyās Shaykh	Shaykh Ilyās
Muḥammad Shaykh	Muḥammad Shaykh	Shaykh Muḥammad Shaykh	Shaykh Muḥammad
Khudāyqulī	Khudāyqul	Khudāyqulī Shaykh 'Ishqī	Shaykh Khudāyqulī
Abū'l-Ḥasan 'Ishqī	[Abū'l-] Ḥasan ['Ishqī]		Abū'l-Ḥasan 'Ishqī
Bāyazīd 'Ishqī [Khwārazm]	"Bahā' al-Dīn from the Maghrib"		Abū Yazīd 'Ishqī
			Mukhtār al-Dīn 'Ishqī
			Qivām al-Dīn Khiyāvānī
			Jamāl al-Dīn-i aṣghar Bisṭāmī
			[5 links with *nisba* Bisṭāmī]
	Kharaqānī		'Abdullāh Dāstānī
			[4 unidentifiable links]
[Bāyazīd Bisṭāmī]	Bisṭāmī	Sulṭān al-'ārifīn	Bāyazīd Bisṭāmī

Bibliography

Primary Sources

Aubin, *Materiaux*: J. Aubin (ed.), *Materiaux pour la biographie de Shah Ni'matullah Wali Kermani* (Tehran: Institut Français d'Iranologie de Téhéran, 1956; repr. Paris: Librairie d'Amérique et d'Orient, 1982).

Badakhshī, *Khulāṣat*: Nūr al-Dīn Ja'far Badakhshī, *Khulāṣat al-manāqib (dar manāqib-i Mīr Sayyid 'Alī Hamadānī)*, ed. Sayyida Ashraf Ẓafar (Islamabad: Markaz-i Taḥqīqāt-i Fārsī-yi Īrān va Pākistān, 1374/1995).

Chihil majlis: Amīr Iqbāl-shāh b. Sābiq Sijistānī, *Chihil majlis, yā Risāla-yi iqbālīya*, ed. Najīb Māyil Haravī (Tehran: Intishārāt-i Adīb, 1366/1987).

Faṣīḥ, *Mujmal*: Faṣīḥ Khwāfī, *Mujmal-i Faṣīḥī*, ed. Maḥmūd Farrukh, 3 vols. (Mashhad, 1339-1341/1960-1962).

Faṣīḥ, *Mudzhmal*: *Mudzhmal-i Fasikhi (Fasikhov svod)*, tr. D. Iu. Iusupova (Tashkent: Fan, 1980).

Gulzār: Muḥammad Ghawthī b. Ḥasan b. Mūsā Shaṭṭārī, *Gulzār-i abrār*, MS Calcutta, Asiatic Society, D 262, described (with a full list of biographies) in W. Ivanow, *Concise Descriptive Catalogue of the Persian Manuscripts in the Collection of the Asiatic Society of Bengal* (Calcutta, 1924): 96-108, Cat. No. 259.

Ḥāfiẓ Baṣīr, *Maẓhar*: Ḥāfiẓ Baṣīr Khuzārī, *Maẓhar al-'ajā'ib*, MS Tashkent, Institute of Oriental Studies of the Academy of Sciences of Uzbekistan, Inventory No. 8716/I (ff. 3b-195b), described in *Sobranie vostochnykh rukopisei Akademii nauk Uzbekskoi SSR*, V, ed. A.A. Semenov (Tashkent, 1960): 406-407, Cat. No. 4137.

Ḥazīnī, *Jāmi'*: Ḥazīnī, *Jāmi' al-murshidīn*, MS Berlin, Staatsbibliothek Preussischer Kulturbesitz, No. orient. Oct. 2847, described in *Verzeichnis der orientalischen Handschriften in Deutschland*, Band XIV/1: *Persische Handschriften*, ed. Wilhelm Eilers, descr. Wilhelm Heinz (Wiesbaden: Franz Steiner Verlag, 1968): 274-275, Cat. No. 352.

Ḥazīnī, *Javāhir*: Hazini, *Cevâhiru'l-ebrâr min emvâc-ı bihâr (Yesevî Menâkıbnamesi)*, ed. Cihan Okuyucu (Kayseri: Erciyes Üniversitesi, 1995).

Hulvî, *Lemezât*: Mahmud Cemaleddin el-Hulvî, *Lemezât-i Hulviyye ez Lemezât-i Ulviyye (Yüce Velilerin Tatlı Halleri)*, ed. Mehmet Serhan Tayşi (Istanbul: Marmara Üniversitesi İlahiyat Fakültesi Vakfı Yayınları, 1993).

Ibn Baṭṭūṭa: Ibn Baṭṭūṭa, *The Travels of Ibn Baṭṭūṭa A.D. 1325-1354*, tr. H.A.R. Gibb, vol. III (London: The Hakluyt Society, 1971).

Ibn Bazzāz: Ibn Bazzāz Ardabīlī ["Tawakkulī"], *Ṣafvat al-ṣafā*, ed. Ghulām-riżā Ṭabāṭabā'ī-Majd (Tabriz, 1373/1994).

Jāmī, *Nafaḥāt*: Nūr al-Dīn 'Abd al-Raḥmān Jāmī, *Nafaḥāt al-uns*, ed.

Maḥmūd 'Ābidī (Tehran, 1370/1991).

Jāmi' al-salāsil: Majd al-Dīn 'Alī, *Jāmi' al-salāsil*, MS Aligarh, Mawlana Azad Library, Shāh Munīr 'Ālam Collection, Box 33 (F) (uncatalogued).

Kirmānī, *Tadhkirat al-awliyā*: Sa'īd Mihrābī Kirmānī, *Tadhkirat al-awliyā'-i Mihrābī Kirmānī, yā Mazārāt-i Kirmān*, ed. Sayyid Muḥammad Hāshimī Kirmānī and Ḥusayn Kūhī Kirmānī (Tehran, 1330/1952).

Lāmi'ī: Abdurrahman Câmî, *Nefehâtü'l-üns min hadarâti'l-kuds, Tercüme ve Şerh: Lâmi'î Çelebi* (Istanbul, 1289/1872-73; repr. Istanbul: Marifet Yayınları, 1980).

Laṭā'if, lith.: Niẓām al-Dīn Yamanī, *Laṭā'if-i Ashrafī*, lithograph (New Delhi, 1295/1878).

Laṭā'if, MS: Niẓām al-Dīn Yamanī, *Laṭā'if-i Ashrafī*, MS Hyderabad, Salar Jung, Tas. 145, described in *A Concise Descriptive Catalogue of the Persian Manuscripts in the Salar Jung Museum & Library*, ed. Ḥājī Muḥammad Ashraf, vol. 8 (Hyderabad: Salar Jung Museum & Library, 1983): 146, Cat. No. 3271.

Maqṣad al-iqbāl: Sayyid Aṣīl al-Dīn 'Abdullāh Vā'iẓ, *Maqṣad al-iqbāl*, ed. Māyil Haravī (Tehran: Intishārāt-i Bunyād-i Farhang-i Īrān, 1351/1972).

Muḥammad Ghawth, *Awrād*, lith.: Muḥammad Ghawth, *Awrād-i ghawthīya*, lithograph (Raichur, 1313/1895-96).

Muḥammad Ghawth, *Awrād*, MS: Muḥammad Ghawth, *Awrād-i ghawthīya*, MS Hyderabad, Oriental Manuscript Library and Research Institute, No. 487 Farsi Tasawwuf.

Muḥammad Ghawth, *Javāhir*: Muḥammad Ghawth, *Javāhir-i khamsa*, MS India Office, Ethé 3067, described in Hermann Ethé and Edward Edwards, eds., *Catalogue of the Persian Manuscripts in the Library of the India Office*, II (Oxford: Clarendon Press, 1937), col. 37.

Mullāzāda: "Mu'īn al-fuqarā," *Tarīkh-i Mullāzāda*, ed. Aḥmad Gulchīn-i Ma'ānī (Tehran: Kitābkhāna-yi Ibn Sīnā, 1339/1960).

Navā'ī, *Nasā'im*: Alî Şîr Nevâyî, *Nesâyimü'l-mahabbe min şemâyimi'l-fütüvve*, ed. Kemal Eraslan (Istanbul: İstanbul Üniversitesi Edebiyat Fakültesi, 1979).

Nawshāhī, *Aḥvāl*: 'Ārif Nawshāhī, ed., *Aḥvāl va sukhanān-i Khwāja 'Ubaydullāh Aḥrār* (Tehran: Markaz-i Nashr-i Dānishgāh-i Tihrān, 1380/2001).

Nithārī, *Mudhakkir*: Sayyid Ḥasan Khwāja Naqīb al-Ashrāf Bukhārī, "Nithārī," *Mudhakkir-i aḥbāb (Adab va farhang-i fārsī dar qarn-i dahum-i hijrī)*, ed. Najīb Māyil Haravī (Tehran: Nashr-i Markaz, 1377/1999).

Qāsim-i Anvār, *Kulliyāt*: *Kulliyāt-i Qāsim-i Anvār*, ed. Sa'īd Nafīsī (Tehran: Intishārāt-i Kitābkhāna-i Sanā'ī, 1337/1958).

Rashaḥāt: 'Alī b. Ḥusayn Ṣafī, *Rashaḥāt-i 'ayn al-ḥayāt*, ed. 'Alī Aṣghar Mu'īnīyān, 2 vols, (Tehran, 2536/1977).

Sivinchī, *Adhkār*: Mīr Sayyid Muḥammad, "Mīr Sivinchī," *Adhkār al-azkiyā*, MS Tashkent, Institute of Oriental Studies of the Academy of Sciences of Uzbekistan, Inventory No. 7582/III (ff. 84b-244b), described in *Sobranie vostochnykh rukopisei Akademii nauk Uzbekskoi SSR*, XI, ed. A. Urunbaev and R.P. Dzhalilova (Tashkent, 1987): 364-365, Cat. No. 7568.

Teufel, *Lebensbeschreibung*: J.K. Teufel, *Eine Lebensbeschreibung des Scheichs Alī-i Hamadānī (gestorben 1385): Die Xulāṣat ul-Manāqib des Maulānā Nūr ud-Dīn Ca'far-i Badaxšī* (Leiden: E.J. Brill, 1962).

Thamarāt: Sayyid Zinda-'Alī, *Thamarāt al-mashā'ikh*, MS Tashkent, Institute of Oriental Studies of the Academy of Sciences of Uzbekistan, Inventory No. 2619, described in *Sobranie vostochnykh rukopisei Akademii nauk Uzbekskoi SSR*, III, ed. A.A. Semenov (Tashkent, 1955): 353, Cat. No. 2669.

Secondary Sources

Allen, T. (1981), *A Catalogue of the Toponyms and Monuments of Timurid Herat*. Studies in Islamic Architecture, no. 1 (Cambridge, Massachusetts: Aga Khan Program for Islamic Architecture at Harvard University and the Massachusetts Institute of Technology).

Ansari, A.S. Bazmee (1960), "Ashraf Djahāngīr," *Encyclopaedia of Islam*, 2nd ed., I (Leiden: E.J. Brill): 702.

Aubin, J. (1967), "Un santon quhistani de l'époque timouride," *Revue des études islamiques* 35: 185-216.

_____. (1991), "Shaykh Ibrāhīm Zāhid Gīlānī (1218?-1301)," *Turcica*, 21-23 (= *Mélanges offerts à Irène Mélikoff par ses collègues, disciples et amis à l'occasion de son soixante-quatorzième anniversaire*), 39-53.

Babadzhanov, B. (1991), "Èpigraficheskie pamiatniki musul'manskikh mazarov kak istochnik po istorii sufizma (Na primere mazarov Astana-Ata i Katta Langar)" in M.M. Khairullaev (ed.), *Iz istorii sufizma: Istochniki i sotsial'naia praktika* (Tashkent: Fan), 89-98.

_____. (2001), "'Ishkiia," *Islam na territorii byvshei Rossiiskoi imperii: Èntsiklopedicheskii slovar'*, vyp. 3 (Moscow: Vostochnaia literatura), 46-47.

Bannerth, E. (1964-66), "La Khalwatiyya en Egypte," *Mélanges de l'Institut Dominicaine d'études orientales du Caire* 8: 1-74.

Behl, A., and Weightman, S. (trs.) (2000), Mīr Sayyid Manjhan Shaṭṭārī Rājgīrī, *Madhumālatī: An Indian Sufi Romance* (Oxford: Oxford University Press).

Chih, R. (1998), "Cheminements et situation actuelle d'un ordre mystique réformateur: la Khalwatiyya en Égypte (fin XVe siècle à nos jours)," *Studia Islamica* 88: 181-201.

Clayer, N. (1994), *Mystiques, état et société: Les Halvetis dans l'aire balkanique de la fin du XVe siècle à nos jours* (Leiden: Brill).

Curry, J.J. (2005), "Transforming Muslim Mystical Thought in the Ottoman Empire: The Case of the Şa'bâniyye Order in Kastamonu and Beyond," Ph.D. Dissertation, Ohio State University.

_____. (2008), "The Intersection of Past and Present in the Genesis of an Ottoman Sufi Order: The Life of Cemâl el-Halvetî (d. 900/1494 or 905/1499) and the Origins of the Halvetî *Tarîqa*," *Journal of Turkish Studies/Türklük Bilgisi Araştırmaları*, 32/1 (= *In Memoriam Şinasi Tekin III*): 121-141.

de Bruijn, J.T.P. (1978), "Khara ānī," *Encyclopaedia of Islam*, 2nd ed., IV (Leiden: E.J. Brill), 1057-1059.

De Jong, F. (1978a), *Ṭuruq and Ṭuruq-Linked Institutions in Nineteenth Century Egypt: A Historical Study in Organizational Dimensions of Islamic Mysticism* (Leiden: E.J. Brill).

_____. (1978b), "Khalwatiyya," *Encyclopaedia of Islam*, 2nd ed., IV (Leiden: E.J. Brill), 991-993.

_____. (1987), "Mustafa Kamal al-Din al-Bakri (1688-1749): Revival and Reform of the Khalwatiyya Tradition?" in N. Levtzion and J.O. Voll (eds.), *Eighteenth-Century Renewal and Reform in Islam* (Syracuse, New York: Syracuse University Press), 117-132.

DeWeese, D. (1992), "Sayyid 'Alī Hamadānī and Kubrawī Hagiographical Traditions" in L. Lewisohn (ed.), *The Legacy of Mediaeval Persian Sufism* (London: Khaniqahi Nimatullahi Publications/School of Oriental and African Studies), 121-158 (reprinted as *The Heritage of Sufism*, vol. II, *The Legacy of Medieval Persian Sufism (1150-1500)* [Oxford: Oneworld Publications, 1999]).

_____. (1993), "An 'Uvaysī' Sufi in Timurid Mawarannahr: Notes on Hagiography and the Taxonomy of Sanctity in the Religious History of Central Asia," *Papers on Inner Asia*, No. 22 (Bloomington: Indiana University, Research Institute for Inner Asian Studies).

_____. (1996a), "The *Mashā'ikh-i Turk* and the *Khojagān*: Rethinking the Links between the Yasavī and Naqshbandī Sufi Traditions," *Journal of Islamic Studies*, 7: 180-207.

_____. (1996b), "Yasavī Šay s in the Timurid Era: Notes on the Social and Political Role of Communal Sufi Affiliations in the 14th and 15th Centuries" in M. Bernardini (ed.), *La civiltà timuride come fenomeno internazionale* (= *Oriente Moderno*, N.S., 15 [76], No. 2), 173-188.

_____. (1999), "Khojagānī Origins and the Critique of Sufism: The Rhetoric of Communal Uniqueness in the *Manāqib* of Khoja 'Alī 'Azīzān Rāmītanī" in F. De Jong and B. Radtke (eds.), *Islamic Mysticism Contested: Thirteen Centuries of Controversies and Polemics* (Leiden: E.J. Brill), 492-519.

_____. (2006), "The Legitimation of Bahā' ad-Dīn Naqshband," *Asiatische Studien/Études asiatiques* 50/2: 261-305.

_____. (2008), "Orality and the Master-Disciple Relationship in Medieval Sufi Communities (Iran and Central Asia, 12th-15th centuries)" in M.F. Auzépy and G. Saint-Guillain (eds.), *Oralité et lien social au Moyen ge (Occident, Byzance, Islam): parole donnée, foi jurée, serment* (Paris: Collège de France - CNRS/Centre de Recherche d'Histoire et Civilisation de Byzance, Monographies 29), 293-307.

Elias, J.J. (1995), "Shaṭṭārīyah" in J.L. Esposito (ed.), *The Oxford Encyclopedia of the Modern Islamic World* (New York: Oxford University Press), 4: 50-52.

Ernst, C.W. (1999), "Persecution and Circumspection in Shaṭṭārī Sufism" in F. De Jong and B. Radtke (eds.), *Islamic Mysticism Contested: Thirteen Centuries of Controversies and Polemics* (Leiden: E.J. Brill), 416-435.

Flemming, B. (1994), "Glimpses of Turkish Saints: Another Look at Lami'i and Ottoman Biographers," *Journal of Turkish Studies*, 18 (= *Annemarie Schimmel Festschrift*), 59-73.

Gross, J. (1992), "Authority and Miraculous Behavior: Reflections on *Karāmāt* Stories of Khwāja 'Ubaydullāh Aḥrār" in L. Lewisohn (ed.), *The Legacy of Mediaeval Persian Sufism* (London: Khaniqahi Nimatullahi Publications/ School of Oriental and African Studies), 159-171 (reprinted as *The Heritage of Sufism*, vol. II, *The Legacy of Medieval Persian Sufism (1150-1500)* [Oxford: Oneworld Publications, 1999]).

Gross, J., and Urunbaev, A. (eds. and trs.) (2002), *The Letters of Khwāja 'Ubayd Allāh Aḥrār and his Associates* (Leiden: Brill).

Hanaway, W.L. (1995), "Ṣafī, Fakhr al-Dīn 'Alī b. Ḥusayn Vā'iẓ Kāshifī," *Encyclopaedia of Islam*, 2nd ed., VIII (Leiden: E.J. Brill), 800-801.

Humā'ī, J. (1359/1980), introduction to Rukn al-Dīn Mas'ūd b. 'Abdullāh Shīrāzī, *Nuṣūṣ al-khuṣūṣ fī tarjamat al-fuṣūṣ, sharḥ-i Fuṣūṣ al-ḥikam-i Muḥyī'l-Dīn Ibn 'Arabī*, ed. Rajab-'Alī Maẓlūmī (Tehran: McGill University/Tehran University, Insitute of Islamic Studies).

Kissling, H.J. (1953), "Aus der Geschichte des Chalvetijje-Ordens," *Zeitschrift der Deutschen Morgenländischen Gesellschaft* 103: 233-289.

_____. (1956), "Zur Geschichte des Derwischordens der Bajrâmijje," *Südostforschungen* 15: 237-268.

Kugle, S.A. (2003), "Heaven's Witness: The Uses and Abuses of Muḥammad Ghawth's Mystical Ascension," *Journal of Islamic Studies* 14: 136.

Landolt, H. (1983), "Abū'l-Ḥasan Ḵaraqānī," *Encyclopaedia Iranica*, I, fasc. 3: 305-306.

Lawrence, B.B. (1978), *Notes from a Distant Flute: The Extant Literature of pre-Mughal Indian Sufism* (Tehran: Imperial Iranian Academy of Philosophy).

Martin, B.G. (1972), "A Short History of the Khalwati Order of Dervishes" in N.R. Keddie (ed.), *Scholars, Saints, and Sufis: Muslim*

Religious Institutions since 1500 (Berkeley: University of California Press), 275-305.
Mīnuvī, M. (ed.) (1359/1980), *Aḥvāl va aqvāl-i Shaykh Abū'l-Ḥasan Kharaqānī* (2nd ed., Tehran: Kitābkhāna-i Ṭahūrī).
Moayyad, H., and Lewis, F. (trs.) (2004), *The Colossal Elephant and his Spiritual Feats: Shaykh Ahmad-e Jâm; The Life and Legend of a Popular Sufi Saint of 12th Century Iran* (Costa Mesa, California: Mazda Publishers).
Mojaddedi, J.A. (2003), "Getting Drunk with Abū Yazīd or Staying Sober with Junayd: The Creation of a Popular Typology of Sufism," *Bulletin of the School of Oriental and African Studies* 66: 1-13.
Munzavī, A. (ed.) (1363/1984), *Fihrist-i mushtarak-i nuskha-hā-yi khaṭṭī-yi fārsī-yi Pākistān*, vol. 3 (Islamabad: Markaz-i Taḥqīqāt-i Fārsī-yi Īrān va Pākistān).
Muqtadir, A. (1993), "Muḥammad Ghawth Gwāliyārī," *Encyclopaedia of Islam*, 2nd ed., VII (Leiden: E.J. Brill), 439-440.
Nath, R. (1978), "The Tomb of Shaikh Muḥammad Ghauth at Gwalior," *Studies in Islam* (New Delhi: Indian Institute of Islamic Studies), 15/1: 21-30.
O'Kane, B. (1987), *Timurid Architecture in Khurasan* (Costa Mesa, California: Mazdâ Publishers).
Öngören, R. (2000), *Osmanlılar'da Tasavvuf: Anadolu'da Sûfîler, Devlet ve Ulamâ (XVI. Yüzyıl)* (Istanbul: İz Yayıncılık).
Ritter, H. (1960), "Abū Yazīd . . . Bisṭāmī," *Encyclopaedia of Islam*, 2nd ed., I (Leiden: E.J. Brill), 162-163.
Rizvi, S.A.A. (1978), *A History of Sufism in India*, vol. 1 (Delhi: Munshiram Manoharlal).
_____. (1983), *A History of Sufism in India*, vol. 2 (Delhi: Munshiram Manoharlal).
Savory, R.M. (1969), "A 15th Century Ṣafavid Propagandist at Harāt" in Denis Sinor (ed.), *American Oriental Society, Middle West Branch, Semi-Centennial Volume* (Bloomington: Indiana University Press), 189-197.
Schwarz, F. (2000), *'Unser Weg schließt tausend Wege ein:' Derwische und Gesellschaft im islamischen Mittelasien im 16. Jahrhundert* (Berlin: Klaus Schwarz Verlag; Islamkundliche Untersuchungen, Band 226).
Smith, J.M. (1970), *The History of the Sarbadar Dynasty 1336-1381* (The Hague/Paris: Mouton).

Jason BeDuhn

Digesting the Sacrifices: Ritual Internalization in Jewish, Hindu, and Manichaean Traditions

In the words of Peter Brown, "the emergence of the holy man at the expense of the temple marks the end of the classical world" (Brown 1971a: 103).[1] That classical world extended further than we tend to think. One region of substantial cultural contact included all of the Semitic and Indo-European speaking peoples, who for millennia coexisted and influenced each other in every aspect of life. Certainly, other populations contributed to the mix in various locations within this continuum, but for the ritual development with which we are concerned here, these two major groups provide the essential context. Within this cultural environment, settled life and the rise of states had been closely associated with an organized priesthood and ritual sacrifice that made use of fire on an altar to transmit food offerings to the gods. The holiness of the priest was inextricably tied to his function in the sacrificial ritual. When such holy persons became the center of the ritual, rather than functionaries of it, something fundamental changed in the religious ideology of this world.

While the priest had always been supported by a portion of offerings made to the gods, this remanded or leftover portion was usually distinguished from that transmitted to the gods through the sacrificial ritual. In various places at different times we can observe an erosion of this distinction, by which the meal of the priests becomes conflated with the sacrifice itself, and the traditional place of the sacrificial fire is replaced by the digestive fire of the priest's body. A further transformation subsequently occurred in some settings when the internalized sacrifice of the priest came to be interpreted with varying degrees of metaphor as an entirely mental or "spiritual"

[1] On this fundamental shift, see further Brown (1971b), Smith (1978).

sacrifice no longer associated with food ritual per se. We thus can speak of three phenomenologically distinct modes of ritual: (1) in the first, the ritual is centered in the sacrificial altar and implements that transmit food to the gods, while the consumption of ritual leftovers by the priest amounts to a payment for ritual services and not part of the sacrifice itself; (2) in the second, the priest's body provides the means to deliver offerings to the sacred dimension for which they are intended, and so the meal is the sacrifice itself; (3) in the third, food is no more than alms to support the life of a holy person which is itself, metaphorically, a sacrifice of good thoughts, words, and deeds. Generally speaking, these three varieties of ritual arise sequentially in Semitic and Indo-European areas, and so give the appearance of logical development, even though at any one time they coexisted in various forms as ritual alternatives and rivals.

It is essential to maintain a clear distinction between the second and third forms identified above. There has been a great deal of discussion in modern religious studies of the holy person as competitor and displacer of the priest, and of the support of the holy person through alms as a rejection of and substitute for sacrificial ritual. Because sacrificial terminology and imagery were commonly transferred to the holy person, this development has been characterized as the "spiritualization" of sacrifice. Examples can be found in the Indian *śramaṇa* movement, as well as in the anti-sacrifice trend in the Hellenistic and Roman west. When examined alongside of classical sacrificial ritual, it is easy to see the "spiritualization" trend as a religious revolt, oppositional to traditional sacrifice. Yet there is a missing link between external rites of sacrifice and the supposedly anti-ritual support of the holy person to be found in the distinct set of ideas and practices associated with internalization of sacrifice in the feeding of the holy person. Distinguishing internalization from spiritualization depends upon identifying the boundary between what takes place metaphorically "within" a person in his or her thoughts, attitudes, intentions, etc., and what takes place literally within a person in the internal apparatus of his or her body—in either case, the boundary established by the culture concerned, not by our own constructs of human interiority.

Ritual internalization has been largely neglected in modern studies because it tends to be assimilated to "spiritualization" through a kind of metaphorical colonialism of one form by another. From the modern scientific viewpoint, while external rites are real and actually occur in space and time, internalized rites are imaginary and ultimately indistinguishable from the metaphoric transference of sacrificial language to the dedicated life of the holy person. If something is thought to go on "inside" a person, it is assumed that there is no practical distinction between an unseen physiological mechanism and an unseen psychological mechanism; and when people talk of one, they really mean the other. Such an interpretive attitude is completely antithetical to the principles of cultural research, because it projects the researcher's categories onto the people being studied, and in this way obscures the culture the researcher seeks to understand. The historical cultures we study know perfectly well what they are talking about within their own frames of reference. As we shall see, what they conceived as happening to the food once it had entered the body was no more or less imagined or metaphorical than what was assumed to happen to food in a sacrificial fire. It was really inserted into something the culture had designated a ritual apparatus, where it was transmuted by chemical processes just as real as those caused by fire. The ritual expert monitored the process of the sacrifice in both processes by observing relevant signs of its progress, by sight in the one case and by physical sensation in the other.

The concept of ritual internalization is based on an observed analogy between the cooking and consumption of food in a fire and the heating and digestion of food within the individual. In both cases, organic material is structurally and chemically transformed in a way that allows it to be transmitted as an essence or energy to its ultimate ritual destination. As the external ritual fire yields smoke that ascends into the air to sustain the gods, so the digestive fire of a holy person yields the physical energy that supports the sacred movements and actions that characterize the individual's holiness. To the degree that the holy person remains a priest, a mediator between the human and divine realms, and so not the ultimate destination of an offering, certain specific actions of the fed holy person are conceived of as transferring that energy on to the gods—e.g., prayers, hymns, prostrations, meditations, and so forth.

Manichaeism offers a clear example of a ritual system built around internalization of food ritual. The Manichaean Elect, wandering holy men and women supported by the alms of laypeople, were among the earliest manifestations of the trend to which Peter Brown alludes in its Persian and Roman setting. Of course, they were relative late-comers compared to the wandering ascetics of the Indian tradition; it has not been lost on modern researchers, just as it was not on the contemporaries of the Manichaeans, that there may be a substantial debt to India in the formation of the Manichaean tradition. Mani himself traveled to India early in his career, and established a permanent mission there. Primary Manichaean texts show knowledge of the Hindu, Buddhist, and Jain religions. The asceticism and mendicancy of the Elect closely resembled Hindu, Buddhist, and Jain models available through such contacts. It is easy to compare the surface appearance of the alms support of the Elect to that provided to Indian monks and *saṃnyāsins*, where we are dealing with a "spiritualization" of sacrifice with no more than metaphorical relation to ritual sacrifice. Yet the ritual and ideology associated with the Manichaean practices stand in the way of such a comparison, and point instead to the direct sacrificial connotations of the offerings and their handling. For this reason, the

Manichaean Elect cannot be looked upon merely as mendicants, but bear the marks of an uprooted priesthood with antecedents within their own more immediate environment of Near Eastern sacrificial systems. Judaism, for example, cannot be left out of account when considering the background of Manichaean internalization of sacrifice.

Jewish Internalization of Sacrifices

In the classical period of Jewish sacrifice, we find three distinct ways of handling the sacrificial offerings. First, "whole" or "burnt" offerings made to God in reparation for serious religious and social crimes were entirely burned on the fire altar, and the priests received no food portion from them. They did, however, get the skins of animal offerings of this type as payment for their services. Second, priests and offerers each received a portion (*terûmāh*) of voluntary offerings made on certain occasions not involving any offense. Third, a set of offerings known as *ḥaṭṭā't*, effecting purification or sanctification of individuals in a number of specific circumstances, were eaten entirely by the priests, while neither offerers nor person affected by the rite received a portion (Lev. 4:1 - 5:13, 6:17-23; Num. 15:22-29; Ezek. 45:19-23). "[S]ince the person offering the sacrifice admitted his guilt, he received no part of the victim, and everything reverted to the priests" (de Vaux 1997: 419). Likewise, even the priests were not allowed to partake when the sacrifice involved their own purification; in such a case the offering was disposed of without being eaten.

The *ḥaṭṭā't* offers the form of sacrifice most amenable to development into an internalized sacrifice in the meal of holy persons. The question is, did it already possess characteristics of internalized sacrifice in the classical period, when other forms of sacrifice coexisted with it? Why did the priests eat the *ḥaṭṭā't* rather than burn it on the altar? It has been suggested that since the *ḥaṭṭā't* was a "sin" offering, it would pollute the altar. The priests ate the sin-contaminated offering, and when they themselves were involved in the sin, the offering had to be disposed of in a remote, ritually segregated space to safely remove the sin from the community. Based on this manner of handling the offering, it would seem reasonable to accept the suggestion that the priests functioned as sin-eaters (Snaith 1967: 16-17, 57, 117).

There are problems with this conclusion, some more serious than others. The whole or burnt offering involves what are arguably even worse "sins," and yet they are entirely burned on the altar. Roland de Vaux contends that since the priests eat the *ḥaṭṭā't* meat as 'a most holy thing' (Lev. 6:22), the sacrifice cannot be loaded with the sin of the offerer (de Vaux 1997: 419). Yet the expression "most holy" (qōdeš qodāšîm) is used generally of any food consumed by the priests, and primarily serves to mark it as something prohibited to anyone else. Its holiness could involve the *tremendum* aspect of the holy, and such language would be perfectly appropriate for something so tainted with sin that it would not be safe for anyone other than the priests to eat it. This would seem to be the sense of the reference to priests bearing the burden of the community in the *ḥaṭṭā't* (Lev. 10:17). We need to be careful of our terminology here, for as recent study of the issue has demonstrated, the *ḥaṭṭā't* is not really a "sin" offering (Milgrom 1983: 67-69). Rather, the *ḥaṭṭā't* involves managing the boundary between ritual purity and impurity. It is performed in connection with the consecration of priests (Lev 8:2, 14-17), of Levites (Num 8), and of altars (Num 7), as well as for the periodic reconsecration of priests in the "eighth-day service" (Lev 9:2-3, 7-11, 15, 22). It is the appropriate rite for purification from childbirth (Lev 12:6-8), from skin disease (Lev 14:13, 19, 22, 31), from sexual discharge (Lev 15:15, 30), and from corpse-contamination (Num 6:11; 19).

Jacob Milgrom originally rejected the hypothesis that the priests were thought to eat the sin or contamination of the offerer in the *ḥaṭṭā't* rite. Following de Vaux, he argued that the priest, by definition, cannot come into contact with what is impure. The Yom Kippur goat for Azazel, for example, is driven out to an "inaccessible land" precisely so that no one can come upon it and eat it (Milgrom 1983: 70-1). He recognized the problems with the alternative of seeing the *ḥaṭṭā't* as a payment to the priests for carrying out a purification: the terminology of the priest's portion (*terûmāh*) is never used in connection with the *ḥaṭṭā't*. He also weighed the evidence that the meat of the offering continued to be seen as bearing impurity even after the ritual shedding and daubing of blood: those who carry the *ḥaṭṭā't* to the place of burning are contaminated by it (Lev. 16:27-28), just as are those who handle the Azazel goat (Lev. 16:26) whereas the removal of normal altar ashes does not induce impurity (Lev. 6:4). The priests must bathe after the burning of the *ḥaṭṭā't* (Lev. 16:23-24)—the only time this is prescribed for priests (Milgrom 1983: 73).[2] The *ḥaṭṭā't* offering is therefore in a condition of impurity (Milgrom 1983: 87). But Milgrom argued that only when the priests are caught up in the impurity is the offering carried out as an impure thing; when the priests eat the offering because they are not involved in the impurity, the offering has already been purified. The eating of the *ḥaṭṭā't* demonstrates that the offering is no longer tainted, that pardon has been achieved, and thus to refuse to eat it is to signal doubt about the pardon (Milgrom 1983: 74, citing Lev. 10:16-20). Milgrom considered these rules to be a priestly heightening of the more general concern about making expiation for killing any animal found in the Jewish tradition (Milgrom 1983: 96-103).

Yet Milgrom changed his mind in later publications. Noting that, unlike other priestly portions, the eating of the *ḥaṭṭā't* was manda-

[2] Milgrom points out that this is even more emphasized in the Qumran Temple Scroll, 26:10.

tory, he has conceded of the *ḥaṭṭā't* offerings that, "there is a strong possibility that they had to be eaten by the priests in order to complete the expiatory process ... it is precisely because the purification offering is associated with impurity that its ingestion by the priest becomes so crucial" (Milgrom 1991: 638). Rabbinic sources expressly state that in the *ḥaṭṭā't*, "the priests eat and [thereby] the offerers are expiated" (hakkōhănīm 'ōkĕlīm wĕhabbĕ 'ālīm mitkappĕrīm: *Sipra*, Shemini 2:4; *b. Pesah.* 59b; *b. Yoma* 68b; *b. Yebam.* 40a, 90a). Eating the sacrifice was integral to the rite, not a separate reward of the priest or a disposal of used offerings, as shown by the fact that eating the *ḥaṭṭā't* took priority over the eating of any other food that fell to the priest's portion, even that of offerings made before the *ḥaṭṭā't* if they had not yet been consumed by the time the *ḥaṭṭā't* was offered (Mishnah Zebahim 10.6). Milgrom abandons his earlier contention that the offering must be already pure for the priest to eat it, and now understands the eating of the *ḥaṭṭā't* as a kind of disposal of a "ritual detergent." The priests can dispose of the impurity passed to the offering from the lay community, but cannot do the same with impurity passed from themselves, because in the latter case they are in a state of impurity and need another means of disposal. "Thus the eaten *ḥaṭṭā't* no less than the burnt one has a purificatory purpose. They differ not in kind but in degree, the degree of impurity that they purge" (Milgrom 1991: 263). Even though Milgrom is inclined to regard these actions as purely symbolic, the clear parallelism between eating and burning as two alternate forms of completing the purifying sacrifice shows that the digestive system of the priest possessed a technical ritual function in the *ḥaṭṭā't*.

Modern researchers of ancient Jewish ritual are largely confined to extrapolating in this way from the bare facts of the ritual an underlying ritual theory that is not provided explicitly in the texts. The destruction of the Jerusalem temple in 70 CE, and the subsequent eclipse of the Jewish priesthood by lay Rabbis, has meant the loss of the sort of priestly exegesis of the inner workings of ritual that we have in abundance for India. The Rabbinic Mishnah, while closely interested in the ritual details of sacrifice, displays an utter "absence of explicit theorizing on questions of meaning" (Neusner 1979: 113). We must supplement the scant material in Rabbinic sources with non-Rabbinic Jewish commentators such as Philo, and careful use of related ritual traditions, such as those of Mesopotamia.

Philo of Alexandria, who wrote while the Jerusalem temple still operated, provides us with the closest thing to a Jewish ritual theory in the Hellenistic period. It might be cautioned that Philo's assimilation of Hellenistic philosophy renders his views unrepresentative of the traditional Jewish priesthood. Of course, the priests of the traditional civilizations around the eastern end of the Mediterranean were leading appropriators of Hellenistic culture, and in this respect Philo might be seen as entirely representative. At the same time, theories of internalized sacrifice were not one of the things Hellenism was contributing to their thought. Hellenistic influence can be seen in various ideas of "spiritualization" actively displacing sacrifice, at least among intellectuals; and Philo at times sounds this theme. But he maintains fidelity to the traditional ritual system, and passes on ideas about the internalization of sacrifice that cannot be attributed to his philosophical interests or sources.

Philo specifically characterizes the priest as a kind of sin-eater (*Spec. leg.* 1.190, 233). He says that the one who offers a sacrifice for his or her sin can have no part in it; it must be eaten by the priests or the servants of the priests (*Spec. leg.* 1.240). Eating the offering demonstrates, if it does not itself effect, a transmutation of sin into forgiveness. The fact that the ritually pure priests eat the sin-offering shows that it has been accepted; they could not safely eat it if they were not pure, nor could they eat it if the sin was not forgiven (*Spec. leg.* 1.242; eating the offering on the same day it is offered indicates the immediacy of forgiveness, *Spec. leg.* 1.243).[3] For these reasons, offerings made for the sins of priests cannot be eaten by anyone, but must be burned (although not on the altar, *Spec. leg.* 1.244). In fact, all offerings of the priests are so treated, and priests never receive a portion of their own offerings (*Spec. leg.* 1.256). Philo emphasizes the ability of the priest to act as a purifier in the ritual process, and describes the special character of priests that permits them to fulfill this important function. They are free from passions of the soul and from all vices (*Spec. leg.* 1.257ff.), endowed with a purified soul along with "the sacred chorus of the rest of the virtues" (*Spec. leg.* 1.269), and therefore are worthy to perform the rituals (*Spec. leg.* 1.270). The priests offer themselves as the "most excellent of all sacrifices" when they are imbued with "the most perfect completeness of virtue and excellence" and offer prayers and hymns (*Spec. leg.* 1.272).[4] These latter remarks show Philo well on the way to a "spiritualization" of sacrifice. Yet his earlier remarks on the conditions surrounding the priests' consumption of the *ḥaṭṭāʾt* (for that is the primary sacrifice under consideration in his exegesis) do not belong to such a "spiritualizing" interpretation, but show concern with ritual purity and the purifying function of the priests within a still fully functioning sacrificial system.

Internal processes peculiar to Judaism produced various sects that functioned independently of the Jerusalem temple. The late first century CE writer Josephus (*Wars* 2.8.119-161; cf. *Antiquities* 18.1.18-21) describes ritual meals of the Essene sect. Members of the sect were not permitted to eat food obtained outside of the group, but only pure Essene food they produced themselves (*Wars* 2.8.143);

[3] The prohibition of eating offerings while in a state of ritual impurity is found also in the Rabbinic tradition, *Tosefta Shebuoth* 1,8; *Sifra Hobah* 13,10.

[4] On sacrifices as external signs of an internal sacrifice of the soul, see *De migratione Abrahami* 89-93.

the same rule is attested in contemporaneous sectarian texts recovered from Qumran, and from Mani's description of the practices of the Elchasaite Jewish-Christian sect in which he grew up in the third century CE (*CMC* 79ff.). Members of the sect ate the food in formal, silent meals, while dressed in special garments and with blessings before and after. Philo provides a similar description of the meals of a religious association he calls the Therapeutae. They dressed in white garments, and sang hymns. Then younger members brought "the very holy food" (*De vita contemplativa* 81), of which Philo uses the same language applied to the sacrificial portions eaten by priests in the temple cult, and goes on to explicitly compare it to the shewbread of the temple. The meal was followed by a vigil with hymns and prayers. These communal rituals imitate priestly partaking of sacrifices, but without the temple and altar. They represent a detachment of the common practice of sanctified meals conducted in the temple precincts—found throughout the region in Hellenistic and Roman times—into independent ritual cells.

The texts discovered at Qumran derive from one or more such sectarian communities, and provide our only direct sources about their organization, operation, and ideology. They attest to the view that in such sectarian circumstances the community itself took the place of the temple as the locus of sacred ritual (1QS 5.5f., CD 4.18f., 1QpHab 9.4f., 11.12f.). Still unclear, however, is whether sacrifice per se was performed in these sectarian settings, or whether some sort of internalization or spiritualization of sacrificial practices occurred. The texts display a variety of views that reflect either ideological development over time within a single sect, or differences among multiple sects whose literary remains came to be gathered in the caves of Qumran during the upheavals of the Roman-Jewish war of 66-71 CE. Several texts look to the Jerusalem temple as the only proper place for sacrifice, and envision a future when the community will control and reform those rites, which were viewed as currently polluted and dysfunctional. In the interim, a kind of stop-gap ritual system operated in the sectarian community, with prayers and hymns in place of sacrifices (1QS 9:4-5, 26; 10:18, 22; CD 9.3-5). Elisabeth Schüssler Fiorenza maintains that the concept of spiritualization fails to capture what was going on here. She sees it as rather a "transference" of terminology and imagery from one practice to another within a still vital cultic system (Schüssler Fiorenza 1976). The sectarians at Qumran retained the distinction between priests and laypeople within a community that came together at its daily communal meals (1QS 6:4-5; 1QSa 2:17-18).

Jacob Neusner has demonstrated the common set of concerns with the consumption of meals in ritual purity shared by the Qumran community and the Pharisee movement. Both groups appropriated the rules of ritual purity encumbent on priests to their own sacred associations, and extended the conditions of the sacred priestly consumption of sacrificial portions to their own communal meals (Neusner 1975). Yet Neusner finds no evidence that either group endowed the meal with a sacrificial ideology (in this he agrees with van der Ploeg 1957). Rather, it was as if the sacrifice had been cut out of the ritual, leaving only the post-sacrificial eating of sacralized food in a state of ritual purity. While the intention "to recreate the conditions under which the priests ate the offerings in the Temple" is evident (Newton 1985: 34), there seems to have been no conflation of this ritual meal with the role of the external sacrifice, even when the latter was thought to be no longer functioning correctly in the Jerusalem temple. Because of the breakdown of purity in the temple from the point of view of the Qumran sectarians, the presence of God was transferred to their own community (see Newton 1985: 36-38); yet, for reasons left untold, this presence no longer needed to be sustained by sacrifice.

Looking further afield for hints of an ideology of internalized sacrifice behind ritual meals, we find them most closely associated with funerary ritual. This is an area of Jewish ritual that is poorly documented and little researched. E.S. Drower (1989: 38-41) found Mesopotamian Jews in the first half of the twentieth century observing ritual meals through which they believed human souls could be liberated from food by eating. Such a theory is tied up with ideas of transmigration of souls that have historically been widely embraced in popular Judaism. Within the same immediate Mesopotamian milieu, the Mandaeans practice the funerary ritual known as the *masiqta*, in which the ritual consumption of offerings is identified with specific effects on the condition of the soul in the afterlife. In this ritual system, it is specifically said that what the priests eat gets transferred to the soul of the dead in the afterlife (Buckley 1981: 147). The Mandeaeans have preserved a body of ritual commentaries that we are lacking for Judaism, and in this way may reveal some shared regional assumptions about the purposes connected to priests eating sacrifices rather than offering them in fire sacrifice.

Hindu internalization of sacrifices

The Indian ritual tradition experienced developments closely parallel to those within Judaism, even though Vedic ritual was not based in temples. Instead, the priests constructed temporary sacred spaces as ritual need arose. The priests received payment in food for their ritual expertise and labor, which belonged to the sacred obligations of the ritual system, while remaining clearly distinct from the offerings of the sacrifice per se. At some point, however, feeding the priests became imbued with the same sacrality and function as fire sacrifice. This development involved a concept of internalization of sacrifice which eventually paved the way for an abandonment of the fire ritual by wandering holy men, marking the same transition from classical to post-classical models of religious practice identified for the Mediterranean region by Peter Brown.

An elaborate theory of sacrifice surrounded Indian ritual and, unlike the case of Jewish ritual, has been preserved in an extensive exegetical literature. The oldest layer of ritual literature, the Vedic recitations, reflect a basic theory of sacrifice: feeding the gods, maintaining the world and its prosperity, and accumulating merit for the one who offers sacrifice. By the stage of development reflected in the *Brāhmaṇas*, a sophisticated system of ideas had formed that identified sacrificial ritual with the primordial sacrifices of the gods by which the universe came into existence; all things offered were considered a return of elements to their source, and so a reinforcement of cosmic order and prosperity (Heesterman 1987: 92). A great deal of thought was given to sacrifice as a channel of transmission of pure elements from this world to the heavenly one. The concept of sacrificial merit similarly became transformed into the idea that through sacrifice an individual supplies the makings of one's post-mortem body, into which one will be reborn in the afterlife (Bodewitz 1973: 304-305; Aguilar 1976: 44). "What he offers becomes his self in the hereafter; when he goes away from this world it calls after him, saying: come, here I am, your own self" (*ŚB* 11.2.2.5; cf. *MuU* 1.2.6). This self-constructing function came to be attached specifically to what was given to the priest as the *dakṣiṇā* (Heesterman 1959: 242-3, citing *ŚB* 4,3,4,5). Fasting, which always had a role in sacrifice as a condition of ritual preparedness, came to be seen as part of the sacrifice, and involved in the transmission of one's pure elements to the post-mortem embodiment to come (*ŚB* 11.1.8.4; *MS* 3.4.7:53.18; see Heesterman 1987). When the feeding of priests began to be considered not just a payment but an alternative form of sacrifice, this was anything but a "spiritualization" of sacrifice into mere acts of charity. The commentaries draw detailed analogies between the body of the priest and the design of the sacrificial altar, between the priest's digestive fires and the fire on the altar, and between the processes that go on inside the priest and the transformation and transmission of offerings in fire sacrifice.

The entire Indian ritual system was challenged by the rise of the *śramaṇa* movement, out of which emerged Jainism and Buddhism, whose origins cannot be explored here. The key element of this movement germane to our topic is its rejection of fire sacrifice. For those who became effectively independent religious communities, the turn against fire sacrifice entailed an abandonment of the Vedic religious tradition connected to it. Yet there was an "orthodox" side, if you will, to the movement that maintained its ties to the theological system of the Vedic tradition. While the conduct of holy persons in their way of life possessed fundamental similarities across the spectrum of the renouncer movement and universally involved abandonment of fire sacrifice, those who remained connected to the Vedic and Brahmanical tradition understood fire sacrifice to have been internalized and perfected within their own conduct and relations with laypeople.

> The non-ritual state of renunciation ... is often depicted as the ultimate perfection of the ritual. Within this context, the abandonment of rites and ritual accessories ... is regarded as a process of internalization. The abandoned fires, for example, are carried internally in the form of the breaths or the internal fire responsible for digestion. Whatever a renouncer eats, therefore, becomes a sacrifice offered in the internal fires... The renouncer's body thus becomes a sacred object; it is equal to the fire altar where the Vedic rites are performed. (Olivelle 1992: 68-69)

As in the Jewish case, we are dealing here with something distinct from what has been discussed as "spiritualization" of ritual. Ritual theory still governs the participants' understanding of what is taking place, rather than merely providing terms and images for metaphorical application to charitable support of holy persons. The holy person is not just an icon of the sacred, to be venerated and given symbolic offerings. The holy person's body is a ritual implement and not just an object of ritual devotion (*VDS* 30.2-3). The body must do work in the ritual since it takes the place of the ritual apparatus (*KS* 6.6; MS 1.8.7).

In making the switch from offering sacrifice in a fire to offering it as food for priests or other holy persons, the ritual participants carried forward the same intent of transmitting the essence of the sacrifice to the heavenly world, where it would serve the gods, the cosmos, and the offerer's own future happiness. The priest or holy person was conceived as connected to the gods, and to combine in himself both the divine recipients of sacrifice and the instrument of sacrifice itself (as *yajñapuruṣa*, sacrifice personified; see Bühnemann 1988: 197-199). This role was verbalized in spoken exchanges at the time of the ritual meal, with the offerer declaring recognition of the divine status of the priest, and the latter declaring blessings on the offerer. "An oblation deposited in a worthy brahmin will never miss its way to the deity" (*SG* 1, 2, 8; cf. *VDS* 30). The offering made through the mouth of a brahmin is superior to the *agnihotra* (*Manu* 7.84). Offerings given to an unworthy priest, on the other hand, bring dire consequences for the offerer, since they are misdirected from their intended heavenly goal (Heesterman 1959: 243). The worthiness of the offerer also gets sorted out in this ritual process.

> By means of various offerings and the *dakṣiṇās* which represent the parts of his body he disposes of his impure self ... Thus he is reborn pure, 'out of the sacrifice'... The function of the brahmin officiant is to take over the death impurity of the patron by eating from the offerings and by accepting the *dakṣiṇās*. By gifts and food evil and impurity are transferred and purity attained ... (Heesterman 1964: 3)

The Indian exegetes of internalized sacrifice applied to it ritual ideas originally dealing with alternative modes of sacrifice that could be used to perform the morning and evening *agnihotra* when one is traveling away from home or has become too debilitated to perform the actions of the external rites. This involved the absorption of the ritual fires into oneself (*Manu* 6.25,38; *BD* 2.18.8; on the earliest roots of this adaptation, see Olivelle 1992: 86-89). According to this theory, as a stop-gap the sacrifice can be considered to take place in the breathing of the priest, with the food consumed by the priest supplying the substitute offering that is transmuted in his digestive fire and transmitted through his exhalations rather than smoke. This is the *prāṇāgnihotra*, or offering in the breaths. It must be born in mind that when the *agnihotra* was adopted as well in non-priestly households, the same practice and theory applied. Because of this, the *prāṇāgnihotra* is not necessarily tied to religious virtuosi or especially holy persons, and becomes a kind of popularly embraced lay ritual (see Bodewitz 1973: 293-309; *BDS* 2.7.12). Nevertheless, it provided the basic metabolic theory operative when offerings were made to priests or renouncers.[5] In either case, as H.W. Bodewitz has argued, the *prāṇāgnihotra* is conceived as an actual ritual, necessarily involving an offering of food (Bodewitz 1973: 265), and should not be confused with various metaphorical reapplications of ritual language and imagery to a person's life or mental processes which also occurred in the Indian context (Bodewitz 1973: 318-321). The internalized sacrifice still served the function of feeding the deities to which the body of the holy person was ritually connected (Bodewitz 1973: 265-266), as well as continuing the ritual function of sorting out the pure from the impure elements of a person's embodied life ("The good which a man does during his life passes into his breaths, the wrong into his body," *JB* 1.15).

Changes in Indian ritual practice involved battles over the right to claim the traditional images, terms, and rights of ritual expertise.

> The question that occupies religious thought appears not to be: sacrifice or rejection of sacrifice, but rather what is the true sacrifice. Equally the question does not turn on brahmin superiority or its rejection, but on the point who is the true brahmin. On these points both orthodox and heterodox thinkers seem to agree to a great extent. (Heesterman 1964: 27)

[5] "The general idea of a sacrifice (to and) in the breaths as the substitute of the fires seems to have been transferred by the *Taittirīya*s to the *śrāddha* ritual, in which the invited brahmins act as substitutes for the fires." (Bodewitz 1973: 260). The offerer, addressing the offerings, says, "The earth is thy vessel, heaven is the lid. I offer thee in the mouth of brahman. I offer thee in the ex- and inhalation of learned brahmins."(BGS 2, 10, 36). Thus, "This sacrifice in the mouth of brahman seems to be regarded as a cosmic *prāṇāgnihotra* in which the five brahmins represent the five fires or *prāṇāḥ* of the eating brahman" (Bodewitz 1973: 261; see also 267, 320-1).

Buddhists and Jains sought to establish their mendicants as the true brahmins, encouraging the redirection of offerings from support of Vedic sacrifice to the support of their mendicant orders. But similar arguments appear within the Hindu tradition regarding the true brahmin and the original character of authentic sacrifice. The external *agnihotra*, it was asserted, was not practiced by the ancients, who offered instead internalized metabolic offerings where the purified element from food became an oblation in the breaths (*KU* 2.5).

Up to today, Hindu priests are considered able to consume the sins and impurities of offerers conveyed in their offerings (Hayley 1980: 114, 122-124, who explicitly compares Jewish temple priests eating the sin and guilt offerings). As we saw likely in the case of Judaism, funerary practices appear to conservatively preserve some of the basic ideas of internalized ritual in Hinduism. Feeding funeral priests feeds the dead, building and fortifying the latter's post-mortem body, while at the same time disposing of any sins that might negatively affect the deceased's state. Only the priests are pure enough to perform this ritual function with their digestion of food offerings (Parry 1985, esp. 617-618).

Manichaean internalization of sacrifice

Needless to say, Jewish and Hindu ritual systems operated with very little contact or influence between them, and their respective developments occurred independently of one another—at different times, under circumstances peculiar to themselves. We cannot say if some of their common characteristics reflect much broader cultural continuities or simply convergent parallel development. But a third religious community, arising historically later than Judaism and Hinduism and in contact with them both, observed what we have been observing about common points between them of practice and ideology. Mani and the early Manichaeans conducted their own kind of comparative religion project, and identified similarities in the practice and theory of ritual among all of the antecedent religions within the cultural area of West Asia. The Manichaeans interpreted these phenomenological similarities according to a theory of primordial religious revelation, and so saw them as remnants and echoes of a single ritual system, delivered by God to humanity through a string of ancient prophets (BeDuhn 2000b). Such points of contact between otherwise distantly related religions were taken to be the preserved elements of true religion corrupted by the accretions of time and malign intentions. By systematically sifting the world's religions for such common features, Mani believed he could discern the original common religion taught by all of God's prophets.

Mani had direct contact with both Hinduism and Judaism, broadly conceived, in his early days. Although Manichaeism dismisses Judaism as a false religion, Mani's own upbringing in a Jewish-Christian community, with clear connections to the sort of ritualism found among the Essenes and in the Qumran texts, shaped both his thinking and the form of his community in profound ways. Soon after leaving that community, he traveled to India, and the stamp of its religious culture on him is evident far beyond the subject of this study. Unlike Judaism, the "Brahmanic" religion is recognized in Manichaean texts as an authentic antecedent of Manichaeism; although, like all such antecedents, it is believed to have been corrupted (*TM 393*, in Henning 1944: 137-142).[6] In his experiences with both religions, Mani witnessed the centrality of ritual eating, and concluded that this was religious ritual *par excellence.* He found ready at hand theories of internalized sacrifice, by which holy persons were thought to transmit the sacred essence of the food they ate to the heavenly world. Other sacrificial techniques he encountered bore the hallmarks of evil, involving as they did the taking of life, the shedding of blood, or the pollution of pure elements such as fire.

Mani's religious innovation amounted, then, to a ritual reform. He declared the internalized sacrifice of the Manichaean ascetic Elect the only ritual technique actually capable of transmitting offerings to their heavenly destination (*Kephalaion* 87). Every other attempted means of making offerings to God delivered the sacred energies within the offering "to affliction and hardship and wickedness." A major part of Manichaean preaching involved dire warnings of the consequences of giving alms or offerings to religious figures incapable of doing the work of digesting the sacrifices. "False preachers who are errant and confused ... hold the name pious and take alms through deception and fraud. They themselves will go to hell and take the donor along with them" (*U 54*, Le Coq 1922, 29-30). Graphic torments in hell await "the one who takes as much *puṇya*-food as a grain of mustard and is not able to redeem it" (*M 6020*, Henning 1965). On the other hand, Manichaean food ritual worked because it was embodied in highly disciplined religious virtuosi who maintained a perpetual state of ritual purity and did not rely upon methods of sacrifice vulnerable to external pollution and which might actually inflict harm on the offerings. Mani was able to observe ritual behavior in all of the religions with which he came into contact that he could understand in terms of internalized sacrifice, and from those observations deduce a primordial universal ritual practice overlaid with various later corruptions. As in the traditional sanctity of the Jewish and Hindu priesthoods, only the Manichaean Elect were considered to maintain the degree of purity that allows them to serve as the ritual fulcrum in which both purification for sins and transmission of offerings to heaven is achieved.

Manichaeism shares with Hinduism the idea that sacrificial offerings form a kind of heavenly depository that support and sustain

[6] For a passage on the Brahmans from Mani's own *Living Gospel*, see Funk (2009: 120-122).

the offerer in the afterlife (*Kephalaion* 93 and 115; *Psalm-Book* 111). Manichaean texts from areas contiguous to India even adopt the term *puṇya* for the merit acquired by food offerings given to the ascetic elect (Parthian and Bactrian *pwn*). Offerings bring absolution for the offerer's sins (*Kephalaion* 115), and as in Hinduism can be made on behalf of the dead to assist their post-mortem condition. Manichaeism shares with both Hinduism and popular Judaism the notion of a transmigration of souls, agreeing with some Jewish traditions that souls are reborn into fruit and vegetables and can be liberated from them by ritualized eating (Augustine, *Contra Faustum* 5.10). As for the internalized processing of the eaten food, Manichaeism has a theory analogous to that associated with the Hindu *prāṇāgnihotra*: the food is refined in the digestive and metabolic processes, ultimately yielding "breath" (*pneuma*) which becomes the vehicle of its transmission to heaven (*Kephalaion* 114). As in Hindusim, this internalized sacrifice returns to the spiritual realm the divine elements that went into the creation of the cosmos, freeing them from mixture with impurity, and contributing to the eventual liberation of all living things to a divine condition.

Conclusions

The circumstance common to all the developments we have been examining is the emergence of non-sacrificial ritual practices within cultures where sacrifice provided the fundamental paradigms of religion itself. As Patrick Olivelle has discerned, in such circumstances the novel set of practices become invested with the ideology of sacrifice. The new ascetic virtuosi vie for the very same material support previously claimed by the traditional priests (Olivelle 1992: 36). Staking a rival claim involves both a critique and an affirmation of the sacrificial paradigm. On the one hand, reason must be given for innovation; on the other hand, the traditional paradigm must be claimed. In the Jewish and Hindu as well as Manichaean cases, sacrifice is challenged as defective, misunderstood, or misapplied. Non-sacrificial practices are at the same time promoted as the true realization of the intent of the gods. In the examples we have been studying, ritual terminology and imagery are resettled onto the ascetic's body, the sacrificial fires are deposited or discovered within the individual, and the ritual system becomes individualized, mobile, and internalized. What Olivelle says in regard to Hindu developments could serve equally well to characterize ideas that emerged among the Jews and Manichaeans:

> The internalized ritual is more permanent and more sublime. The renouncer's internal fires are permanently lit; he kindles them with every breath. His eating becomes a sacrificial offering. His body and bodily functions are transformed into a long sacrificial session. The renouncer's body thus becomes a sacred object; it is equal to the fire altar where the Vedic rites are performed. (Olivelle 1992: 68-69)

In such circumstances, then, we are dealing with what Durkheim called "a hypertrophy of the negative cult" (Durkheim 1965: 350), that is, an extension of the conditions of ritual preparedness to "a veritable way of life." Asceticism arises in all of these religious cultures from the intention to maintain a permanent condition of ritual purity. Ascetics are quite simply priests who take the entirety of time as the ritual period and the entirety of the world as the ritual space. This is particularly evident in those cases, such as the Hindu and Manichaean, in which the ascetics take up a wandering life in which their bodies constitute the portable ritual apparatus. The Jewish adaptation is of a different kind, wherein the sacrificial cult reserved for the temple is prohibited elsewhere, and must be replaced with a ritualized meal.

Because of the ideological continuity within each tradition, it is quite easy to be lured into thinking that first internalization and then spiritualization are somehow logical developments and outcomes of sacrificial thinking itself. Yet as Olivelle cautions, religious history is not driven merely by the inherent logic of religious ideas. All kinds of external factors and historical accidents contribute to the forces that push religious innovation. In the Indian case, as Olivelle has emphasized, the challenge of the anti-sacrificial *śramaṇa* movement stimulated the development of internalization ideas as a response that sought to retain the ideology of sacrifice, with all of its cosmological implications, while acceding in the displacement of fire sacrifice from its central place in ritual practice. In the Jewish setting, internalization received its prompt from a combination of the unique confinement of fire sacrifice to a single geographic location in combination with a desire to imbue rituals carried out elsewhere with some of the trappings and ideology of sacrifice, in some but not all cases involving a critique of the effectiveness of the temple fire sacrifice. Finally, in Manichaeism internalization was taken as a point of departure for the entire religious system, expressly in connection with a critique of fire sacrifice as an ineffective ritual technique. Yet as in the Jewish and Hindu cases, and unlike the more sweeping rejection of sacrifice in Buddhism and Jainism, Manichaeism retained the ideology of sacrifice as the fundamental framework of its food rituals.

It is possible to arrange a system of public support for religious virtuosi without any reference to sacrifice, as generally holds true in Buddhism or Jainism or, for that matter, in the support of Christian monastics. The need to specifically frame such a system within a sacrificial ideology arises only within cultures where sacrifice is the presumed underpinning of religious conduct.

> All Indian renouncers, both within and outside the Brāhmaṇical tradition, gave up ritual activities. They refused to use fire. It is only within the Brāhmaṇical tradition, however, that the renouncer's abandonment of fire and rites became the focal point for the theol-

ogy of renunciation. This theology considers the abandonment as the internalization and, therefore, the perfection of ritual life. (Olivelle 1992: 71)

In understanding such systems of renunciation, we must be careful to take seriously their investment of belief in a kind of technical apparatus within the body and connecting it with the larger cosmos. The reason why Hindu renunciation is not Buddhist is precisely because of this continued investment of belief in a sacrificial ideology and in the particular construction of the universe necessary to give purpose to that ideology. Participation in such sacrificially-framed systems of support for renunciates is motivated in part by belief in the existence of an apparatus that will actually process and transmit offerings to the spiritual dimension where they will produce specific results and benefits. Of course, there are other social and psychological motivations for participation, for example in heightened status and accentuated self-image. But to understand religions built around such support of holy people *as systems*, within which promoted actions and sanctioned rationales for those practices have an internal coherence and function of mutual reinforcement, we can afford neither to neglect the explicitly stated operative ideas in religious observance, nor to render them into mere metaphor by which religion itself becomes some sort of strange game of language no longer capable of explaining anyone's conduct.

Bibliography

Aguilar, H. (1976), *The Sacrifice in the Ṛg-Veda (Doctrinal Aspects)* (Delhi: Bharatiya Vidya Prakashan).

BeDuhn, J. (2000a), *The Manichaean Body: In Discipline and Ritual* (Baltimore: The Johns Hopkins University Press).

_____. (2000b), "Eucharist or Yasna? Antecedents of Manichaean Food Ritual" in *Studia Manichaica. IV Internationaler Kongreș zum Manichäismus, Berlin, 14.-18. Juli 1997*, ed. R.E. Emmerick, W. Sundermann, and P. Zieme (Berlin: Akademie Verlag), 14-36.

Bodewitz, H.W. (1973), *Jaiminīya Brāhmaṇa I, 1-65, Translation and Commentary, with a study of the Agnihotra and Prāṇāgnihotra* (Leiden: E.J. Brill).

Brown, P. (1971a), *The World of Late Antiquity* (London: Norton).

_____. (1971b), "The Rise of the Holy Man in Late Antiquity," *Journal of Roman Studies* 61: 80-101.

Buckley, J.J. (1981), "The Mandaean Tabahata Masiqta," *Numen* 28: 138-163.

Bühnemann, G. (1988), *Puja: A Study in Smarta Ritual* (Vienna: Institut für Indologie der Universität Wien).
Drower, E.S. (1989), "Evergreen Elijah: Ritual Scenes from Jewish Life in the Middle East" (J.J. Buckley, ed.), in J. Neusner and E. Frerichs, *Approaches to Ancient Judaism, Volume VI: Studies in the Ethnography and Literature of Judaism* (Atlanta: Scholars Press), 3-63.
Durkheim, E. (1965), *The Elementary forms of the Religious Life* (New York: Macmillan).
Funk, W.P. (2009), "Mani's Account of Other Religions according to the Coptic *Synaxeis* Codex" in *New Light on Manichaeism: Papers from the Sixth International Congress on Manichaeism,* ed. J. BeDuhn (Leiden: E.J. Brill), 115-127.
Gonda, J. (1980), *Vedic Ritual: The Non-Solemn Rites* (Leiden: E.J. Brill).
Hayley, A. (1980), "A Commensal Relation with God: The Nature of the Offerings in Assamese Vaishnavism" in *Sacrifice,* ed. M.F.C. Bourdillon and M. Fortes (London: Academic Press), 107-125.
Heesterman, J.C. (1959), "Reflections on the Significance of the *Dákṣiṇā*," *Indo-Iranian Journal* 3: 241-258.
_____. (1964), "Brahmin, Ritual and Renouncer," *Wiener Zeitschrift für die Kunde Süd- und Ostasiens* 8:1-31.
_____. (1987), "Self-Sacrifice in Vedic Ritual" in *Gilgul: Essays on Transformation, Revolution and Permanence in the History of Religions,* ed. S. Shaked, et al. (Leiden: E.J. Brill), 91-106.
Henning, W.B. (1944), "The Murder of the Magi," *Journal of the Royal Asiatic Society* 1944: 133-144.
_____. (1965), "A Grain of Mustard," *Annali dell'Istituto universitario orientale di Napoli. Sezione Linguistica* 6: 29-47.
Hermisson, H.J. (1965), *Sprache und Ritus im altisraelitischen Kult. Zur Spiritualisierung der Kultusbegriffe im Alten Testament* (Neukirchen: Neukirchener Verlag).
von Le Coq, A. (1922), "Türkische Manichaica aus Chotscho, III," *Abhandlungen der Preussischen Akademie der Wissenschaften* 1922, nr.2.
Milgrom, J. (1983), *Studies in Cultic Theology and Terminology* (Leiden: E.J. Brill).
_____. (1991), *Leviticus 1-16* (New York: Doubleday).
Neusner, J. (1975), "The Idea of Purity in the Jewish Literature of the Period of the Second Temple," *Acta Iranica* 5: 123-138.
_____. (1979), "Map without Territory: Mishnah's System of Sacrifice and Sanctuary," *History of Religions* 19: 103-127
Newton, M. (1985), *The Concept of Purity at Qumran and in the Letters of Paul* (Cambridge: Cambridge University Press).
Nikiprowetsky, V. (1967), "La spiritualization des sacrifices et le culte sacrificial au temple de Jérusalem chez Philon d'Alexandrie," *Semitica* 17:97-116.

Olivelle, P. (1992), *Saṃnyāsa Upaniṣads: Hindu Scriptures on Asceticism and Renunciation* (Oxford: Oxford University Press).
Parry, J. (1985), "Death and Digestion: The Symbolism of Food and Eating in North Indian Mortuary Rites," *Man: Journal of the Royal Anthropological Institute* 20: 612-630.
van den Ploeg, J. (1957), "The Meals of the Essenes," *Journal of Semitic Studies* 2: 163-175.
Schüssler Fiorenza, E. (1976), "Cultic Language in Qumran and in the NT," *Catholic Biblical Quarterly* 38: 159-177.
Smith, J.Z. (1978), *Map is Not Territory: Studies in the History of Religions* (Leiden: E.J. Brill).
Snaith, N.H. (1967), *Leviticus and Numbers* (London: Thomas Nelson).
de Vaux, R. (1997), *Ancient Israel: Its Life and Institutions* (Grand Rapids: Eerdmans).
Wenschkewitz, H. (1932), "Die Spiritualisierung der Kultusbegriffe Tempel, Preister und Opfer im Neuen Testament," *Angelos* 4: 70-230.

Manu Bhagavan

*The Hindutva Underground: Hindu Nationalism and the Indian National Congress in Late Colonial and Early Postcolonial India**

The destruction in 1992 of the Babri Masjid and the waves of violence that have followed it in India, coupled with the linked rise of the Bharatiya Janata Party (BJP) to political prominence, have led in recent years to a flourishing of studies on "Hindutva" or "Hindu nationalism." Yet for all these works, very few have examined the relationship between the Indian National Congress (INC) and the right-wing religious politics of the Hindu nationalist movement. What work has examined this nexus has largely focused on its two varying poles. The first has dealt with the link between nineteenth-century reform movements and the post-1920 emergence of militant Hindu religious organizations, most notably the Hindu Mahasabha and the Rashtriya Swayamsevak Sangh (RSS). Chetan Bhatt (2001), for instance, has carefully fleshed out the roles played by such mainstream nationalists and Congress stalwarts as Lala Lajpat Rai in developing the foundational ideological rationale bridging earlier ideas with the more rigidly communal ones that followed.

The second focus of scholarship has been on Congress activities of a more recent nature, post-Independence (primarily post-1980) when the party deployed "soft-Hindutva" for political gain. Generally, work in this group points to ways in which Congress-led governments succumbed to pressure from Hindu-right forces as

* This essay was originally published under the same title in *Economic & Political Weekly* (Sept. 13, 2008: 39-48). The content has remained the same, while the formatting has been modified and the bibliography updated. Research for this essay was made possible by a Fellowship from the American Council of Learned Societies and a PSC-CUNY Research Grant from the Research Foundation of the City University of New York. I would like to thank Judith Brown, V.N. Datta, Syed Akbar Hyder, Steven Lindquist, Gail Minault, Rupal Oza, Ambassador Philips Talbot, and Kamala Visweswaran for their assistance and advice. I am particularly grateful to the anonymous reviewers of EPW for their astute observations and cogent criticisms.

early as the fifties, eventually opening the door for some party members themselves to advocate and practice weaker, more "moderate" versions of Hindu nationalist policy.[1]

What is absent from both these approaches is a discussion of the Congress/Hindutva connection in the interim, mid-twentieth century (especially the forties), the high-water mark of Indian nationalism. This of course is not an accidental oversight. There is general consensus that this period, marked by the leadership of Mohandas K. Gandhi and Jawaharlal Nehru, was one in which the political spectrum was clearly delineated, the Congress on one side and religious nationalist parties on the other.

This paper seeks to counter this prevailing view by illustrating the way in which the Indian National Congress knowingly and intentionally sheltered and nourished Hindu nationalist ideologues, most notably Gujarat's K.M. Munshi, in the crucial moments before and after the midnight hour birthing the new nation-state. I hope to show that it was precisely because of this maneuver that Hindutva was salvaged from the abyss of political irrelevance and made part of the very fabric of postcolonial Indian political life.

I. Moplahs, the Mahasabha, and Munshi

The year 1919 marked a turning point in the development of Hindu nationalism in colonial India. While the Rowlatt Acts, the Montagu-Chelmsford reforms, and the Jallianwalla Bagh massacre all contributed to a perfect storm of Indian disaffection, Western machinations at the end of the first World War also contributed to a particular anger in the subcontinent. The victorious Allies moved to break up under a mandate system the old Ottoman Empire, which had sided with the Central Powers in the conflict. In India, many saw this as unwarranted Western imperial intervention, a threat to the Ottoman caliph, and an assault thereby on Islam as a whole. The brothers Muhammad and Shaukat Ali rallied in India and launched a campaign to "save the caliph" in India, the Khilafat movement. Gandhi supported this action and pitched it in the larger context of the other events as well, arguing that the time had come for a unified mass struggle against colonialism.

Gandhi's efforts coalesced into what became known as the Non-Cooperation movement, ranging in a series of activities that lasted until 1922. While Non-Cooperation as well as Khilafat eventually fizzled out, they also produced a long-term, unintended consequence.

Throughout the nineteenth and early twentieth centuries, the colonial state had radically transformed various land and labor

[1] Examples of such discussion may be found in Corbridge (1999) and Upadhyaya (1992).

relationships throughout the subcontinent. On the southwestern Malabar coast, such intervention had produced a highly oppressive landlord system, delineated along religious and caste lines. Upper-caste Hindus comprised the British-controlled property managers, while Muslim peasants, Moplahs, toiled under ever-harsher conditions. In 1921, tensions boiled over in a massive Moplah uprising. In the context of larger, subcontinental agitations, the Moplahs sought to establish their own "Khilafat king." The state responded with visceral force, and the entire rebellion resulted in bloody and brutal confrontations on both sides.

The Moplah challenge, like the larger Khilafat and Non-Cooperation movements, soon faded.[2] But it stuck in the craw of many right-leaning self-proclaimed defenders of Hinduism. For them, then as now, the events on the Malabar coast could and should be read only through a religious lens, as a manifestation of a Muslim "threat" that had to be militantly countered. Over the next several years, these "defenders of faith" organized and marshaled their forces, re-investing the dormant Hindu Mahasabha in 1922 as a first step. In 1923, Vinayak Damodar Savarkar published his seminal polemic, *Hindutva—or who is a Hindu?*, and a few years later (1925) Keshav Baliram Hedgewar established the RSS.

One of the central goals of this new brotherhood of saffron was to train Hindu men in various forms of physical fitness and martial arts, and so *akhadas*, or gymnasia, began to sprout all over the region for this purpose. Almost immediately upon its inception, the movement to create and run these *akhadas* was led in the Bombay Presidency in part by a fairly well-known if low-key political figure by the name of K.M. Munshi.

Kanaialal Maneklal Munshi was a Gujarati Brahmin who had trained under Aurobindo Ghose in Baroda College within the eponymous princely state. His politics leaned to the revolutionary right initially, but then moderated in the late teens. He came under the influence of Maharaja Sayaji Rao Gaekwad (of Baroda) and Mahatma Gandhi in the twenties and actively participated in their various campaigns. Munshi joined the Congress shortly after 1928, proclaimed himself a Gandhian, and participated in the famous Salt Satyagraha of 1930. Munshi was also a writer, prolific in Gujarati and English, and by the thirties he acquired a reputation as one of Gujarat's most famed litterateurs, aside from a more formal, and equally distinguished profession as a jurist. For many, this face is the only one by which Munshi is known.

Christophe Jaffrelot (1996), in one of the harsher indictments of Munshi to date, only considers him to be a "Hindu traditionalist"

[2] For more on the Moplah Rebellion, see Pannikar (1989); for more on Khilafat, see Minault (1982).

within the Congress Party. Jaffrelot distinguishes such figures from "Hindu nationalists," the former defined by what might be termed "Hindu chauvinism," but not outright subscription to Hindutva (Jaffrelot 1996: 84).

Jaffrelot argues that "[w]hile Hindu nationalism is built around opposition to the Other, whether Muslim or Christian, Hindu traditionalism is manifested simply by the promotion of culture, together with the interests of the community" (1996: 83-84). Thus, the question before us is whether Munshi's "promotion of culture," a task he saw as his primary mission, was built around an "opposition to the Other." Some initial answers may be found in a number of speeches and a variety of essays Munshi respectively delivered and wrote between 1938 and 1941 on the subject of "Akhand Hindustan (United Land of Hindus)."[3] In his essay "The Menace," Munshi argues that Hindus and Muslims had much in common, and that their overall good relations were spoiled only after British intervention. He also seems attentive to regional affinities, pointing out that the "Jat Hindu, the Jat Sikh, and the Jat Muslim in the Punjab were more allied to one another than the Jat Hindu of the Punjab and the Tamil Hindu of Madras" (Munshi 1942: 54). British rules overhauled this system however, and the result was the rise of the communal animosities that had come to dominate the landscape by the forties. On the face of it, Munshi's analysis is not that different from contemporary academic consensus on the matter.[4] But a strong undercurrent through the second half of the essay reveals virulent anti-Muslim sentiment. "Nationalism was thus to be destroyed; the Hindus were to be reduced to serfdom; and the Anglo-Muslim syndicate was to hold India in fee!" (Munshi 1942: 63). Munshi first blames the British for setting Muslims off against Hindus, but then claims that Muslims grew into a monster even their creator and master (the British) could not control. Munshi means this quite literally, since he explicitly states that "Britain, though it created this Frankenstein, is not equal to fighting it by itself" (Munshi 1942: 64). The "Muslim masses [had absorbed] as an anti-Hindu war-cry ..." (Munshi 1942: 64) the politics of disruption, a euphemism for the call for Pakistan, which was read merely as a vague obstructionism, an unfulfillable meta-demand deployed to force acquiescence on all other disputes. Munshi accepts and advocates an essentialized "Hindu versus Muslim" outlook, and argues that Muslims bore sole responsibility for any and all conflict. But these views are interlaced with more reasonable, and accurate, statements as the one illustrated

[3] Akhand Hindustan (AH) is often translated as "United India." But Hindu nationalists who used this term specifically conjoined land with religion, and also referred to the region as Bharat, a term meant to signify a pre-Muslim/pre-"foreign" "ancient past of (Hindu) purity." To better convey this meaning, I have chosen to translate "Akhand Hindustan" as "United Land of Hindus."

[4] Cf. Pandey (1992/1990) and Rai (2004).

earlier in the paragraph, creating the overarching impression of a careful and prudent thinker.

It is precisely Munshi's overall reputation as a reasonable and temperate intellectual that, I have argued elsewhere, gave him prominent status in what I have termed, building off the work of Chris Bayly, "the transgressive ecumene" (Bhagavan 2008). The transgressive ecumene constitutes a type of "physical and cultural debate" found in India in which "respectable men" who "could draw limits to the actions of government and also seek to impose their standards of belief and practice on the populace" used their status and their position to make a range of extremist, belligerent right positions acceptable to the mainstream.[5] That Munshi's overall ideology was, in fact, a dressed-up version of Hindutva is made clear in his correspondence in the forties. The General Secretary of the Bengal Hindu Students' Federation (the Students' Front of the Hindu Mahasabha) wrote: "I shall always try to keep you in touch with our activities. With regard to the aims and ideals of the Hindu Students Federation we had a long discussion with you and *your sympathy and encouragement has also strengthened our activities*... The aim of the Hindu Students' Federation is ... promotion of ... Hindu culture and Hindu nationalism.... A great danger threatens the Hindu nation at present and that is the menace of Pakistan. *You are doing an incalculable service to the country by rousing us to action in this time.*"[6] Another admirer wrote: "Hindus want leaders like yourself to protect their nation and culture. I want to draw your attention towards the organization 'Rashtriya Swayam Sevak Sangh'. I need not explain its ideology as you must be knowing about it as you once mentioned it in your lecture. Should I suggest you to join it ...?"[7] And Bhai Parmanand, a former President of the Hindu Mahasabha and the founder of its official propaganda tool, the *Hindu Outlook* newspaper, even noted in one column that Munshi had once been told that: "his ideas were just the same as that of the Mahasabha."[8]

Munshi, as mentioned above, was also a leader of the *akhadas* movement in the Bombay Presidency; while their initial purpose might perhaps have been difficult to discern, although I do not

[5] Bhagavan (2008) with quotations taken from Bayly (1996: 182, 204).

[6] Italics added. Letter from Amalendu Bagchi to K.M. Munshi, 6 September 1941, K.M. Munshi Papers, reel 34 (R-7987), file no. 59, pp. 71-74. Munshi's papers (MP) will hereafter be abbreviated as title, dd-mm-yy, MP, reel no., file. no.: pp.

[7] Letter from Raj Kishore Mediratta to Munshi (6-9-41, MP, 34 (R-7987), 58: 352). Munshi responded that he knew the leaders of the RSS well but that he could not join the RSS (Munshi to Mediratta, 13-9-41, MP, 34 (R-7987), 58: 351). I have argued elsewhere that his lack of membership in such organizations constituted an overall strategy to serve as a go-between between different camps. This was the means by which a certain type of pubic space, the "transgressive ecumene," was created that legitimized the discourse of the otherwise marginalized religious right. See Bhagavan (2008).

[8] Bhai Parmananda, "Mr. Munshi's Self-Defence," *Hindu Outlook* (16-9-41: 3). It is telling and significant that Munshi denied this and claimed greater affinity for the Congress than for any other organization.

believe this was so, by the early forties *akhadas* were unmistakably militant training camps associated with Hindu nationalism. The *akhadas* movement was so clearly affiliated with the Hindu nationalist cause that even Munshi's otherwise silver tongue could not persuasively defend the gymnasia as benign institutions.[9] This finally brought him to loggerheads in 1941 with the Congress High Command, most notably Gandhi, who was seemingly outraged by any Congress/Hindutva nexus. In the next section, we shall examine more closely this incident, significant because it led to Munshi's resignation from the Congress. If Munshi's one, unequivocal Hindu right activity brought him into conflict with Gandhi, and even ended in the former's departure from the INC, then how is it possible to argue that the Congress willfully retained Munshi (and figures like him) in their ranks at this time?

II. A Public Cleansing

Hindu nationalists' advocacy of violence for "self-defence" had become quite prevalent by the early forties. Gandhi took a public stand against such positions, and particularly any Congress support for them, in a letter to Bhogilal Lala, the Secretary of the Gujarat Provincial Congress Committee, published in *The Hindu* on the morning of 25 May 1941: "Those who favour violent resistance [against an opponent in defence of oneself or others] must get out of the Congress and shape their conduct just as they think fit and guide the others accordingly... [Also,] a Congressman may not directly or indirectly associate himself with gymnasia where training in violent resistance is given" (CWMG, vol. 80, 21-5-41: 267).

Munshi picked up on these comments and responded in a friendly letter to Gandhi on 26 May. He re-quoted the passages above, then in a moment of genuine self-reflection and anguish, stated;

> Since Pakistan has been in action at Dacca, Ahmedabad, Bombay and other places, it is clear that ... riots are going to be a normal feature of our life for some years. If ... the British machinery of maintaining

[9] Munshi's attempt to defend *akhadas* as neutral organizations of national self-defense will be discussed in the next section. In 1954, when his agenda was slightly different, Munshi used his position of authority as an eminent member of the Indian intelligentsia to glamorize *akhadas* and to streamline their position in Indian history: "The *akhadas* have a later origin. In about the thirteenth century, when religion and life were in danger from Islamic pressure, the Order set them up as its organized wings. They were mobile camps of ascetic warriors, not unlike the Knights Templar of medieval Europe.... Later, the *akhadas* played an important role in maintaining the spirit of the Era of Resistance. Brindavan was once saved from the iconoclastic fury of the Sultans of Delhi, by powerful hands of these *sadhus*. Being trained in arms, they also assisted Hindu kings in wars (Munshi, *Wolf Boy*, 25-7-54: 38)." Akhadas, in short, were long-standing tools meant to protect the Hindu population from the villainous Muslim Other (who were even, apparently, opposed to life itself!). This entire characterization fits in with the larger claims being made in this paper.

> order weakens, they will perhaps grow more frequent and intense if a division of India is sought to be enforced by internal or external agencies through organized violence ... Do you include 'akhadas' in the gymnasiums where training in violent resistance is given? I may inform you that for the last over fifteen years I have been associated with the 'akhada' movement in the presidency both directly and indirectly. I have still unofficial connection with several 'akhadas'. I deem them an essential machinery for training our race in the art of self-defence. During the last many years they have played a great part in giving us some self-confidence to resist *goondaism* ... I can, of course, keep quiet or can acquiesce in what you say or can, for fear of losing my Congress association and your confidence, both precious possessions in my life, voice your sentiments and go my way or do nothing. But something in me rebels against such a course. You have been the embodiment of truth... (Munshi to Gandhi, AH, 26-5-41: 262-263).

Munshi was here moved to confront Gandhi over *akhadas*, driven by the clear discrepancy between his political proclivities and his true affection for the Mahatma. Munshi saw Hindus blindly as one, homogenous "race," as doe-eyed innocents who had been victimized by *goondas*, gangsters and thugs out to steal and pillage. "Goondas" is used euphemistically but un-subtly to refer to Muslims, and to depict them as thieves and plunderers after India itself, to take pieces of it for Pakistan. For Munshi, *akhadas* were the only viable solution, merely self-defence institutes meant to protect a victimized populace. In a public statement issued shortly thereafter, Gandhi responded:

> Shri. K.M. Munshi came to me as soon as it was possible after his return to Bombay. In the course of discussion, I discovered that whilst he accepted in abstract the principle of Ahimsa [non-violence] with all its implications he felt the greatest difficulty in acting upon it, the more so as with his intimate knowledge of Bombay he was sure that he could not carry the Hindus with him, much less the Muslims and others ... I told him that there came a time in every Congressman's life when being a Congressman dragged him down. That was when there was conflict between thought and action; for the spring of non-violent action was non-violent thought. If the latter was absent, the former had subjectively little or no value. Therefore, it was good for him, the Congress and the country that he should resign and mould his action from moment to moment as he thought proper. And by this action, he would open the door for those Congressmen to resign whose practice could not accord with their thought. The Congress was conceived to be a non-violent and truthful organization in which there should be no place for those who could not honestly conform to these two conditions (Gandhi's statement, AH: 265-267).

Gandhi was primarily driven by his ethical concern for non-violence. But here this was wedded to a rejection of *akhadas*, the practical and material institutions that breached the moral code that should have governed them. Gandhi's gentle but firm suggestion that Munshi resign from the Congress was thus, on the face of it, a signal that Munshi had gone both ethically and practically astray.

Gandhi by the early forties, of course, was hardly the dominant voice in Congress politics that he once was. Nehru, writing in his prison diary at this time, noted that "It is very sad, this deterioration of a very great man. The greatness remains in many ways, but the sagacity and intuitive doing of the right thing are no longer in evidence."[10] To an extent, Gandhi himself recognized his increased marginalization, specifically naming Nehru as his successor in a speech on 15 January 1942 (Gopal 1976: 275).

Nevertheless, Gandhi remained a force to be reckoned with, for one thing because of the great esteem in which he was still held both by the High-Command and the general public. Nehru wrote the above comments under the duress of prison, and his other writing clearly conveys a continued affection and admiration for Gandhi.[11] Moreover, Gandhi re-entered the political scene with great flair in the late forties, in what is commonly regarded as his "finest hour," when he virtually single-handedly halted the communal bloodbath that had gripped India in the wake of Partition and Independence in 1947 (Hardiman 2003: 184-191).[12]

In such context, Gandhi's effort to nudge Munshi out of the Congress must be read carefully. Gandhi cannot be seen to simply represent the entire Congress, and the stand he takes here should not be seen to reflect on the organization as a whole. Nonetheless, it does appear quite straightforward that, upon learning of Munshi's role in the *akhadas* movement and his corresponding willingness to use force, Gandhi was unambiguous in disassociating the Congress from these right-wing positions, and both Munshi and the INC went along with his wishes. While this fact remains constant, the larger narrative clouds the picture considerably.

Gandhi, for one thing, was hardly consistent, changing his views and opinions on matters from time to time and instance to instance. In fact, in 1934 he famously proclaimed: "I have never made a fetish of consistency. I am a votary of truth and I must say what I feel and think at a given moment on the question, without regard to what I have said

[10] Nehru, *Prison Diaries* (in SWJH, 1943: 185-6). Nehru's is a telling statement, for it is around this same moment that Gandhi's alternative vision for a post-colonial India is sidelined, replaced by Nehru's own imagined preferences for India's future. See Chatterjee (1992: esp. 85-166) and Hardiman (2003: 66-85). Cf. Bhagavan (2008/2010).

[11] I am grateful to Judith Brown for bringing this point to my attention. Indeed, Nehru's writings make clear that he was particularly perturbed when he penned the earlier lines at a letter that Gandhi had reportedly written to the Viceroy regarding a 1942 All-India Congress Committee Resolution; Nehru regarded the letter as a daft political move. A few days later, Nehru learned that Gandhi's letter as not what he thought it to be, and his tone about the incident is noticeably different: "Some items in the papers, about the letter Bapu [Gandhi] is supposed to have written to Linlithgow [the Viceroy], pleased me. It was stated, apparently with some authority, that although he had written, there was no mention or question of withdrawing the August Resolution, or of fasting. He [Gandhi] is alleged to have written about the food situation." Nehru, *Prison Diaries* (in SWJH, 1943: 194).

[12] Cf., Pandey (2002).

before on it."[13] Thus his suggestion that Munshi depart the Congress in 1941 in itself does not necessarily imply that either Gandhi or the Congress, which still largely followed his instructions, reliably applied a constant policy in such cases.

Indeed, right-wing ideologues or their sympathizers were hardly the sole target of Gandhi's "polite purge" in this period. In the same spirit, if not the same breath, in which he castigated and cast out Munshi for his views, Gandhi also pressured M.N. Roy to depart. Roy, generally regarded as the founder of Communism in India, had been a prominent and vocal "leftist radical" within the Congress. While such targeting may seem, in fact, to prove that Gandhi was in fact consistent, and that fringe elements from either side of the ideological spectrum either towed the conventional line or were removed, the truth is that ideology was not the primary motivating factor in either the Roy or the Munshi cases.

What was troubling Gandhi more in this period was the emergence of the Second World War. The Congress had adopted an anti-war stance in its Haripura Resolution of 1938 arguing that the British were actually fighting to defend their imperialism, not the ideal of liberty. Additionally, Gandhi saw in Hitler not just the manifestation of violence, but the very embodiment of it: "[Hitlerism] means naked, ruthless force reduced to an exact science and worked with scientific precision. In its effect, it becomes almost irresistible."[14] Great Britain and the Allies, however, merely used and encapsulated violence in another form: "Supposing the Allies are victorious. The world will fare no better [than it would under Hitler]. They [the Allies] will be

[13] Gandhi, "Introduction to Varnavyavastha" (CWMG, vol. 65: 62).

[14] Gandhi, "How to Combat Hitlerism" (CWMG, vol. 78, 1940: 343). Of course, Gandhi had less than a month earlier, on 26-5-40, written to Lord Linlithgow, the British Viceroy to India, declaring: "I do not believe Herr Hitler to be as bad as he is portrayed. He might even have been a friendly power as he may still be" (Gandhi, "Letter to Lord Linlithgow," CWMG, vol. 78, 1940: 253). Many people have seen such statements as evidence of Gandhi's delusion, his gross misunderstanding of Hitler and Nazism, and an overall willful ignorance of *realpolitik*. See for example Dalton (1993: 135-138) and cf. Hardiman (2003: 60-61). I think these criticisms are hardly fair. For one thing, Gandhi was, if anything, a sly, pragmatic politician, very aware of when to compromise and when to hold out for something better. At the same time, marking in my opinion his greatness, he clearly believed in tactics and methods dismissed by others as "idealistic" or "unrealistic." As Ajay Skaria has brilliantly demonstrated, Gandhi's idea of satyagraha, often translated as "Truth Force," more correctly implied "the compulsion that, through the submission to the unilateral obligation to kinship, produced and sustained the neighbor-stranger" (Skaria in Bhagavan, ed., forthcoming). Gandhi felt *compelled* to reach out to *everyone*, placing no one, even Hitler, outside the bounds of (potential) kinship. Hitler confounded this desire more so than anyone else, certainly more than any Briton. This, I think, is the root cause of Gandhi's struggle in the early forties—his attempt to reconcile his belief in underlying kinship with his growing sense that Hitler represented his negative, his inverse, his mirror image in the true sense of that term. Moreover, as Hardiman rightfully points out, "civil resistance" was actually deployed with some success against the Nazis, indicating that Gandhi was not as far off the mark in advocating a non-violent solution to "Hitlerism" as some advocate. See Hardiman (2003: 61).

more polite but not less ruthless..."[15] To Gandhi, Hitler represented the ultimate challenge of his beliefs, the Moriarty to his Holmes. If Hitler was the incarnation of Absolute Violence, then for Gandhi the solution lay in Absolute Non-violence: "Hitlerism will never be defeated by counter-Hitlerism ... If my argument has gone home, is it not time for us to declare our changeless faith in non-violence...?"[16]

It is this conclusion that prompted Gandhi to take a hardline stance on membership in Congress, and to pen the very lines to Bhogilal Lala that in turn drove K.M. Munshi to admit the conflict within him to Gandhi. Roy in the meantime had taken a leading role in supporting the war, seeing it in a broader campaign against Fascism, and for this he was ostracized. For the pudding's proof, one need look no further than the fact that Gandhi even asked Sardar Vallabhbhai Patel, one of his closest lieutenants, to leave in a slightly different context on the same issue: "If the Congress adopts the policy of violence, I think you should resign."[17]

The cleansing of the early forties, in short, had little to do with ideological persuasion or general policy subscription. Instead, it had everything to do with individual faith in and commitment to Gandhi's supreme deity, non-violence.

III. Return of the Prodigal Son?

Gandhi, nevertheless, is not completely off the hook. Munshi notes in a commentary shortly after he left the Congress that "[s]everal Congressmen, while expressing the same views as I hold on the right of self-defence, have been making enquiries of me whether they should leave the Congress" (Munshi 1942: 270). But in his later recollections, speaking on the same subject, he states that

> Sardar Patel ... in a letter to Gandhiji, pointed out the danger of Congressmen leaving the Congress on this issue and organizing themselves as a separate party. Gandhiji got Mahadev Desai, his secretary, to issue an explanation to the effect that I had left the Congress because I had no faith in non-violence, but that those who had faith in non-violence, but only found it impossible to implement it, should remain in the Congress. Suddenly, those who had promised to come out with me, accepted this explanation and stayed with the Congress. That is how I began my lone campaign for Akhand Hindustan (Munshi 1967: 77).

The rather stunning conclusion we may draw from this admission is that Gandhi and Sardar Patel knowingly, actively, and successfully

[15] Gandhi, "Of What Avail is Non-Violence?" (CWMG, vol. 78, 1940: 180).

[16] Gandhi, "How to Combat Hitlerism" (CWMG, vol. 78, 1940: 344-45). I am grateful to my student, Alex Abell, for his astute observations on some of the material in this paragraph.

[17] Gandhi, "Letter to Vallabhbhai Patel" (CWMG, vol. 82, 14-4-42: 202).

maneuvered to keep within the Congress various individuals with political proclivities similar to Munshi, *including those who could not implement non-violence.* By Munshi's account, this was clearly a tactical decision, to maintain the hegemony of the Congress as an organization. For Gandhi, there remained the nuance of the utopic commitment to non-violence versus practical adoption of its practice, a distinction he apparently made between Munshi and those who were kept within the fold. Though this certainly seems more fig-leaf than a true, principled stand, Gandhi's position on non-violence is on the whole clear and consistent, and we should, I think, give him the benefit of the doubt in this instance.

Estranged from the Congress, Munshi became more active and open in his Hindu nationalist politics, becoming the leading voice of the Akhand Hindustan movement, and keeping the company of Hindutva stalwarts V.D. Savarkar, B.S. Moonje, and Shyama Prasad Mookerjee, among others. Despite this, Munshi remained in close contact with various Congress members, most notably Sardar Patel and Gandhi himself. And, remarkably, by 1946 all was forgiven.

On February 18, Gandhi asked Munshi in a private meeting to rejoin the Congress (Munshi 1967: 99). There can be no doubt that by this point Gandhi was fully aware both of Munshi's political views and of the company he kept. In a letter to Sardar Patel written shortly after his conversation with Gandhi, Munshi ensured that there could be no misunderstanding, that he was of the same mind as when he left: "I too have some idea of the difficulties Bapu and you would have to face in taking me back. Do I not know the trouble you had in getting the resolution for Akhand Hindustan accepted? Then, who can say how many would be hurt and how far that feeling would spread if a person like me is taken back?" (Munshi 1967: 100).[18] By 1946, the Akhand Hindustan movement was unquestionably equated with the Hindu nationalist cause, which in turn was unequivocally regarded as a violent movement bent on using all means necessary to achieve its goals.[19] How could Gandhi possibly welcome such a figure back into the Congress fold?

Returning to Gandhi's comments on his consistency: "It is for the reader to find out how far my present views coincide with those for-

[18] "Bapu," "Father," is a term of endearment used to refer to Gandhi. I could not uncover any Congress resolution on Akhand Hindustan pushed for by Gandhi and the Sardar. Munshi himself only makes reference to one Congress resolution passed in the early forties that complemented his position, one passed on 29 April 1942 by the All-India Congress Committee. Moved by Jagatnarain Lal and "not on the agenda," this decree "insisted on the unity of India (Munshi 1967: 80)," as a response to the infamous proposals made by C. Rajagopalachari through the Madras Legislature on 23 April 1942 supporting the idea of partition. Given that Gandhi and Patel had always maintained opposition to the idea of partition, though for very different reasons, I suppose that Lal's resolution is the one to which here Munshi is referring.

[19] In 1942, Gandhi had noted: "the Hindu Mahasabha is trying to rouse the Hindu mind for an armed conflict (Gandhi, "Interview to the Press," CWMG, vol. 82, 16-5-42: 288)."

merly expressed. Wherever he finds that whatever I have said or written before runs contrary to what I am writing now, he should without hesitation reject the former."[20] Though this perhaps suggests that we should conclude that Gandhi was acquiescent in Munshi's politics, Gandhi's reasons for welcoming Munshi back into the fold remain unclear. Gandhi as a general rule always reached out to those he saw as his opponents, making it a policy never to close off the kinship he felt towards all people.[21] His actions in the early forties were uncharacteristic, chosen in the context of the absolute dilemma, as he saw it, that Hitler imposed upon him. He remained conflicted over the war throughout the forties and likely leapt at the first opportunity once it was over to rescind any extreme measure he had earlier felt forced to take. In this sense, it is probably more accurate to say that Gandhi's decision to reinvest Munshi with Congress membership had little to do with Munshi himself.

We must note that Congress in the forties purged itself of communists and other leftists, while not enacting a similar eradication of its right-wing. Gandhi's invitation to Munshi thus remains peculiar, as it was not concomitant with any such re-inclusion of the left. We may discount this issue, however, I think for three reasons. First, Gandhi by and large was not personally involved with the leftist purge, as he was with Munshi, and thus could not retract anything in the formers' cases.[22] Secondly, Sardar Patel had by this point moved heavily to the right (Upadhyaya 1992: 826-27). Gandhi disagreed with his old friend, but still welcomed his counsel and his relationship. Patel and Munshi were very close friends, and so this may help explain one angle of Gandhi's action. Finally, Gandhi in this same moment reached out to his old respected opponent, Dr. B.R. Ambedkar and personally requested his participation in the Constituent Assembly.[23] Ambedkar's disaffection with mainstream nationalists largely stemmed from his confrontation with Gandhi,[24]

[20] Gandhi, "Introduction to Varnavyavasta" (CWMG, vol. 65: 62).

[21] Cf. n. 14.

[22] M.N. Roy becomes a sticking point however. I could find no indication that Gandhi ever reached out to him to re-invite his participation in the Congress.

[23] Author interview with Mohan Lal Gautam (2004).

[24] See Eleanor Zelliot (2001: 150-183). Ambedkar published in 1945 a volume entitled *What Congress and Gandhi have done to the Untouchables*, in which he asked and answered "What do the Untouchables say? Beware of Mr. Gandhi" (Ambedkar 1946: 250). Significantly for the argument of this paper, Ambedkar went on to say: "Congressmen never hesitate to impress upon the Untouchables that Mr. Gandhi is their saviour ... As an illustration of such propaganda, I refer to what one Rai Bahadur Mehrchand Khanna is reported to have said ... 'Your best friend is Mahatma Gandhi.... Dr. Ambedkar ... is just a creation of British imperialists...' If I refer to the statement of ... Khanna, it is not because he is worth taking notice of. For, there cannot be any one guilty of bigger blackguardism in Indian politics than this man. In the course of one year—not in very remote time *but in 1944*—he successfully played three different roles. He *started as Secretary of the Hindu Mahasabha*, turned agent of British Imperialism, went abroad to explain India's war effort to the British and American people *and is now agent of the Congress in N.W.F. Province*

so Gandhi's actions in this instance support the larger claim I am making that the Mahatma was interested in 1946 in salving wounds and returning to his favored, inclusive approach to politics (what Mouffe, 2000, has in another context called an "agonistic model" of politics).

Nevertheless, the elephant in the room remains the fact that the Congress thus reacquired and re-sheltered not just a vocal proponent of Hindu nationalism, but the very person who, as I illustrated earlier, used shifting rhetoric to legitimize the positions of the most belligerent and hostile of communitarians. The Congress as an institution endorsed such big-tent philosophy and therefore itself becomes implicated as the vehicle through which religious nationalists were able to break the barriers in which they were otherwise confined, entering in the process the corridors of power of the mainstream.[25]

IV. The Hindutva Underground

As alluded to earlier, Jaffrelot acknowledges the role of what he terms Hindu traditionalism in the Congress, but argues that this strategically allowed the Congress to cut off support to the Hindu nationalist organizations (Jaffrelot 1996: 98-108). In this sense, even if the High Command, including Gandhi and Nehru, were aware of Hindu nationalist ("traditionalist") infiltration of the Congress (this essay certainly indicates that Gandhi was aware), this should be read as a tactical maneuver meant to outwit and outlast their political opponents, to sap their strength and to disempower the Hindu right movement. Jaffrelot argues that the Congress was successful in this game, a point that is accurate, but that misses the short-term nature of these gains, since incorporating such elements into their command structure ultimately only weakened the edifice of the Congress' foundational and principled platform. Jaffrelot rightfully credits Jawaharlal Nehru with masterfully keeping both the nationalists and traditionalists (in Jaffrelot's distinction) at bay. I think, however, he overplays this, and is, as Nehru and Gandhi were themselves, unmindful of the tremendous influence wielded by the Hindu right from within *and through* the Congress. Three vignettes involving K.M. Munshi after his 1946 re-induction into the INC evince such influence.

The first, and most significant, operation in which Munshi participated was in the founding and initial leadership of the Bharatiya Vidya Bhavan, an academy launched in 1938 dedicated to the revitalization of "Indian culture." Munshi was the driving force behind the institution, and while the organization that emerged over the

[italics added]" (Ambedkar 1946: 250-251). Here, then, is another example of the cross-pollination between advocates of Hindutva and the Congress in the 1940's.

[25] I am grateful to K. Sivaramakrishnan and Biswamoy Pati for their thoughts on this conclusion.

years has taken on more diverse points of view, Munshi was quite clear from the outset what he wished the Bhavan to do and to stand for. At its 1938 inauguration, he proclaimed, "The Bhavan will be a new association which will organize active centres where ancient Aryan learning can be studied and where modern Indian culture will be provided with a historical background."[26] Munshi spent the next decades working to see his dream unfold in the incipient institution. That he saw himself as quite successful at this is seen in a solicitation letter written in 1951 by Lilavati Munshi, his wife and the Bhavan's Vice-President, and herself a dedicated advocate of the new institution: "Perhaps you have heard of the Bharatiya Vidya Bhavan... [I]t is today one of the foremost cultural institutions of the country. Its activities embrace all aspects of Indian culture..." (4-7-51, MP, 101 (R-8054), 295: 40).

The Bhavan's place as an eminent institution in India, with pronounced claims to represent and promulgate a latitudinarian Indian culture, then speak to the significance of its definition and deployment of that "culture." For instance, among the Bhavan's most important functions was the publication of books on "Indian history and culture," and imprinted in every one was an opening leaf explaining "What Bharatiya Vidya [Indian knowledge] Stands For." While most of the nine stated tenets have to do with the education of students and with methods of learning and teaching, one is particularly telling: "The ultimate aim of Bharatiya Shiksha [Indian teaching] is to teach the younger generation to appreciate and live up to the *permanent values* of Bharatiya Vidya which flowing from the supreme art of creative life-energy as represented by Shri Ramachandra, Shri Krishna, Vyasa, Buddha, and Mahavira have expressed themselves in modern times in the life of Shri Ramakrishna Paramahamsa, Swami Dayananda Saraswati, and Swami Vivekananda, Shri Aurobindo, and Mahatma Gandhi."[27] In short, the Bhavan, and *ipso facto* Munshi through his role as Founder and multi-decade *kulapati* (president) overseeing virtually every aspect of the Bhavan, large and small, took a rather narrow view of what "India" meant, indeed the self-same view as that espoused by the Hindutva movement. Only religious authorities "from the soil" were legitimate representatives of the "permanent values" of India; according to Hindutva, Buddha and Mahavira were part and parcel of the Hindu tradition, and were not "foreigners" to India. The complete absence of any purveyor of some of India's other historic traditions—Judaism, Zoroastrianism, Sufism, Islam, and Christianity—then held ideological resonance with the Hindu right.

In his most popular, and powerful, platform stemming from the Bhavan, Munshi wrote a series of widely-published "Kulapati's

[26] Munshi, quoted in Dave, et. al. (c. 1956, vol. 4: 124).

[27] Italics added, Munshi (*Swan Love*, 1958: opening leaf).

Letters," open-ended discourses that ranged from mundane daily occurrences to philosophical diatribes to memoir-moments recollecting events of significance in which Munshi participated. Here, Munshi made clear that the distinctly Hindu nature of the "permanent values" ascribed to Indian culture was part of his larger world-view.

> Nowhere have I found the genius of India reflected with greater beauty than in its literature and sculpture. *And nowhere has it been expressed with such unbroken continuity as in the latter* [italics added] ... Our outlook on life was based on an all-pervasive *Dharma* with four fundamental values or *Purusharthas*: *Dharma*, in the narrow sense of religious merit; *Artha* the attainment of desires; *Kama*, desire; *and* Moksha, the absolute integration of personality which released a man from the bondage of desires. Both the literary and plastic arts of India have, for their aim, the fulfilment [sic] of one or the other of the *Purusharthas*, which must be brought into a homogeneous pattern, with the integration of the human personality as its end ... Indian Art has to be viewed as associated with the spiritual needs of the hundreds of generations the [Hindu] temple was intended to serve. (Munshi, *Swan Love*, 15-1-56: 149-151).

The total conflation of India with Munshi's idea of Hinduism is hard to miss, as is the underlying sense that an Indian cultural purity rests on its Hindu-ness. Indeed the letters, written over the course of several years, 1952 to 1955, on the whole elide Hindu myth and history throughout, as in this account of Munshi's travels, where the real world became the site of one of the more fantastic episodes from the South Asian epic *Mahabharata*: "We reached Hanumanchatti where the pride of our sturdy hero Bhim in his superhuman strength was broken. It is an unforgettable episode. The giant of a man was suddenly not able to lift even the tail of an ancient monkey stretched across the path (Munshi, *City of Paradise*, 9 August 1953, p. 54)." Elsewhere, he spends a 1955 letter authoritatively discussing the *Mahabharata*'s historicity: "Suppose I were to tell you that I saw with my own eyes, the terracotta feeding bottle of Duryodhana; the painted grey pot which Draupadi served food; the little arrow with which Arjuna learnt marksmanship; the little stick with which Subhadra applied collyrium to her eyes, and the cutter with which Bhishma pared his ancient nails, you would laugh wouldn't you...? Well, you have lost the bet. I have seen these things or at any rate things that they would have so used. Now listen" (Munshi, *Wolf Boy*, 2-1-55: 138). While Munshi's somewhat playful blending of faith, fiction, and fact is not particularly unique to writers from his period, his influence through the Bhavan in shaping customs and community gave his musings an altogether different meaning.

> With the objects of the Bhavan before us, our College must develop an atmosphere in which a new tradition can be established. Our students should acquire faith in human dignity, in our cultural heritage, in the mission of our motherland and in God ... As regards the spirit, I would

> like more and more boys to take to the Gita examination. This year, we have decided to present a copy of the Bhavan's Book University edition of the *Mahabharata* to every student. You must not forget that the *Mahabharata* is the immortal book of life; there is nothing in life which it will not ennoble and strengthen (Munshi, *Janu's Death*, 2-6-52: 18).

In other words, the Hindu-izing of India's past, present, and future was very much the goal of the Bhavan, according to Munshi's vision and intent.[28]

This point is brought home in a few letters dedicated to Muslim aspects of India's past. Most of the space Munshi gives to discussing or mentioning the millennium of Islamic influence and encounters in the region is relegated to short, backhanded references to Muslims-as-foreign-invaders, as in this description of the "true Indian woman":

> A true Indian woman is an *Indian* first, ever old and ever new. In her old aspect, she stabilises society; in her newness, she shows the path to social strength ... she will just be *herself*: as much a daughter of Arundhati, Sita and Draupadi; as of Nayikadevi, who led an army which defeated Mu'z-ud-din Ghori; of Rudrammadevi, who fought the forces of Malik Kafur; of Lakshmibai, who defied the British, and of Mira of the loving heart and flaming idealism—good mothers, loyal wives, *and defenders of India's faith and freedom* (italics added to last phrase; Munshi, *City of Paradise*, 13-12-53: 123-124).

In one 1952 letter, Munshi seems to take a contrarian view, lauding the achievements of the Great Mughals (Akbar, Jehangir, and Shah Jahan): "Agra is one vast monument to the genius of Akbar ... Great as a warrior, ruler, organiser and statesman, he was also the fountain-head of a rich and fine culture ... It is equally a tribute to Jahangir that like his father, he too had inherited the Mongol indifference to sophisticated religions ... The most artistic monument in the Fort is Moti Masjid, built by Shahjahan. It is a marvelous structure ...." Yet Munshi's appreciation for these three figures stems from their Hindu-ness:

> To the left of the courtyard ... is the Golden House, where lived ... a Rajput princess ... mother of Salim [Jehangir]. Through her, a foreign Moghul became a son of the soil. On one of the panels in this Golden House ... [is] Shri Ramachandra ... with Hanuman in attendance; on another panel, there is what looks like the faded figure of Shri Krishna

[28] Munshi at various points displays a canny, and somewhat disarming, self-awareness of his problematic approach, while simultaneously strenuously rejecting all alternative approaches: "I know that what I am writing will not be accepted by the historians or the scientists or the politicians all of whom are busy about one thing, namely, trying to run the affairs of man without the aid of God. The materialistic interpretation of history, psycho-analysis, doubts and denials, have been woven into plausible theories which have rendered our existence purposeless (Munshi, *Wolf Boy*, 5-12-54: 125)."

> ... Then there is Jodhbai's palace ... In the centre of the courtyard is a Hindu temple where she worshipped. There is also a small stone tank where once grew the sacred Tulsi, which Shahjahan's mother worshipped at sunrise (Munshi, *Janu's Death*, 28-12-52: 135).

And while the great religious pluralism of Akbar, Jehangir, and Shah Jahan helped code them as Indian, they were the lone exception to the vastly applied rule, the inherent "foreign-ness" of all Muslims. Indeed, "Aurangzeb ... gleefully destroyed what Akbar arduously built (ibid.: 134)," so the syncretic Indian-ness of the Mughals ended there.

And this, in turn, has serious implications for Munshi's views of the contemporary state: "India's travails in history have not been accidental. They are the churnings from which her Mission has been born ... We want no foreign masters to teach us alien gospels. We want no novel ideologies from far-off lands. We would not barter India's soul for any illusory gospel, however alluring ... We must always remember that the Spirit for which India stands is there all the time (ibid.: 33-34)." Contemporary India, then, has no place for "foreign-ness," which Munshi again and again throughout the Kulapati Letters (and elsewhere) equates with Muslim-ness, and sometimes, though less so, with the British (and with Communism). Its mission, "spiritual leadership of the world," will only be secured by embracing its true spirit, its genius, mined only from its unpolluted heritage—its Hindu past. "Among the factors which contribute to create or strengthen the psychological bonds of nationhood," he himself noted, indirectly pointing out the importance of his own work, standing first were "the intellectuals, that is the class of men who think, speak and wrote, who teach, administer and govern, [and they] should develop the will to national unity" (Munshi, *Swan Love*, 17-7-55: 42). Munshi's writings on an "Indian culture" defined solely by a certain kind of Hinduism, then must be seen as a serious effort to bind religion and nation-state, the unequivocal goal of Hindutva as a whole.

Munshi's interest in the resuscitation of this pure Hindu past is what led him to take the leading role, with the blessings of his friend Sardar Patel, in the reconstruction of the Somnath Temple in Gujarat. Somnath was the famous temple that sat on the western shore and that had been raided and raised several times by Mahmud of Ghazni as he sought out riches to fund his campaigns to the west and north of his base in modern Afghanistan. As he embarked on his quest to rebuild the temple, Munshi requested the historical background of the temple from several scholars, virtually all of whom produced a narrative similar to this one:

> Few words invoke such poignant memories in the Hindu mind as Somnath... Indian history since the turn of the millennium itched [sic] its record in the stones of Somnath. It thus became a symbol. It thus became an outward image of a temple that each Hindu car-

> ries, privately, in his individual heart... The history of Somnath is the history of Hindu-Moslem relations since the turn of the millennium writ large. It represents the theory of thesis, antithesis and synthesis—creation, destruction, and rebuilding. The rebuilding of Somnath naturally coincides with the rebuilding of our nation (Shridarani, "Somnath: Emotion Enshrined," MP, 103 (R-No. 8056), 303: 318, 320).

Munshi himself was, in fact, considered quite an authority on Somnath. His most famed novel, *Jaya Somnatha*, published in Gujarati in 1937, dealt with the temple's destruction. Competing love interests between two Shaivite groups[29] leads a member of one to betray the temple and reveal a secret entrance to Mahmud's army, which had encamped nearby. Mahmud appears more interested in the surrounding fortress than in the temple itself, and is not depicted as virulently anti-Hindu. Of course, Mahmud specifically, and Muslims more generally, are still portrayed as outsiders and the engines of tragedy. But such portrayal is clearly controlled when contrasted with the more inflammatory rhetoric Munshi spread on Mahmud and on Somnath by the late forties and early fifties (Munshi 1937; Cf. Thapar 2004: 188-197).[30] For instance, after his successful effort to restore Somanth's temple by 1951, Munshi depicted a very different, if inadvertently equally fictional, history:

> The story of India's resistance to Mahmud's insatiable ambition is an epic of undying heroism... The story of internal feuds in India is a myth... Mahmud again [for a second time] invaded Jayapala's dominions, defeated him, and extracted tribute. Jayapala had the proud soul of a hero... Then the generous culture of Aryavarta impelled Anandapala ["heroic Jayapala's equally heroic son"] to send a foolish message to his ruthless foe [Mahmud] offering assistance... The tragedy of it was that Mahmud took the assistance ... and with his victorious army turned on the generous Shahi [Anandapala] in A.D. 1008. The conquest of India is the conquest of culture by those who lacked it... [After reaching Somnath], a terrible battle ensued... Mahmud captured the fort, entered the temple sanctified by centuries of devotion, broke the *Linga* to pieces, looted the temple and burnt it to the ground... A sacred city like that of Somnatha armoured principally by the devotion and reverence of the whole country, fell a prey to an army pledged to a fanatic destruction of alien shrines (Munshi 1976: 33-40).[31]

[29] Shaivities are worshippers of Shiva, for them the Lord of Existence. Other followers of Hindu traditions see Shiva as part of the Trinity: Brahma the Creator, Vishnu the Preserver, and Shiva the Destroyer. See Ramanujan (1973).

[30] Romila Thapar notes that "The depiction of Mahmud in this novel is not as negative as Munshi's later historical assessment of him, but that he was the anti-hero is evident. The segregation of Muslims was thought to be necessary to the purity of race and culture. Hence, the need to project a constant and visible distance between the Hindus and Muslims throughout history. It has been said that this novel brought together his [Munshi's] brahmanhood, family heritage, worship of Shiva, literary activity, and understanding of nationalism (Thapar 2004: 190-91)." I concur with this reading.

[31] A *linga* is a symbolic icon representing Shiva.

The caricatures made here, benevolent, generous Hindus categorically juxtaposed to devious, fanatic Muslims, are a considerable departure from Munshi's earlier stands. In an analysis published around the time of his correspondence with Gandhi, Munshi claimed to be more historical in nature and noted that

> Mahmud, no doubt, looted temples and broke idols when on his raiding incursion. But iconoclastic zeal was not his principal motive as suggested by Muslim chroniclers; it was conquest. First, he did annex the Punjab where he could do so; secondly, he was not a fanatic and not anti-Hindu... He allowed Hindus to observe their religious observances in Ghazni itself. Sewan Rai and Tilak were his trusted Hindu generals. Later annals written by enthusiasts to paint Mahmud 'the sword of Islam' evidently had to supply the motive of iconoclastic zeal to cover the basic fact that his raids, in spite of super-human efforts, did not result in conquests (Munshi, AH: 135).[32]

The point here is that Munshi's claims and depictions of Somnath's history at the time of its revival, going against Munshi's own analysis of the temple's past as well as against current academic thought on the subject (see Thapar 2004), required both a selective amnesia and a self-conscious act of historical reconstruction. But it was precisely his previous work, and his overall reputation as a Gandhian, as a member of the Congress, that lent his new view true weight and clout, a new view that strongly towed the Hindutva (and colonial; see Thapar 2004: 14) line of a South Asian past coded only by a never-ending Hindu-Muslim conflict.

Munshi's actions were to have long-standing consequences, for it was precisely the rebuilding of Somnath that the Sangh Parivar of the late twentieth century used to justify their campaign to build a Ram temple at the site of the Babri Masjid in Ayodhya. L.K. Advani, leader at the time of the BJP, "portrayed the 1950 rebuilding of Somnath as the first chapter in a journey to 'preserve the old symbols of unity, communal amity, and cultural oneness (Richard Davis in Ludden 1996: 43)." It would be anachronistic to claim that the future use of the Somnath event for communal purposes necessarily reverberates backwards through history to implicate the original rebuilding. Nonetheless, there is a clear continuity of logic that connects Munshi's activities with Somnath in the fifties and those of the Ram temple movement in the eighties and nineties,[33] supporting the overall argument of this paper that Munshi's writings and activities helped lay a solid foundation on which Hindutva could grow and prosper.

[32] This comment was made in a volume entitled *Akhand Hindustan* published in 1942, the year after Munshi left the Congress. But in the preface to the volume, Munshi claims that the book only contained reprints of essays published, or speeches made, between 1938 and 1942. His correspondence with Gandhi concerning Munshi's departure from the Congress comprises the appendix.

[33] Van Der Veer (1992) comes to a similar conclusion.

But while Munshi's actions with the Bhavan and with Somnath reflect his overall role as an intellectual somewhat removed from the hard-edged hand-to-hand combat of the political trenches, his role as the postcolonial Agent-General of Hyderabad from 5 January-21 September 1948 reveals someone who was also willing to be more directly involved in ground tactics advocated by the Hindu right. Here, Munshi played a central role in the "police action" in which the Government of India forcefully took over control of the Nizam's territory. As one newspaper columnist was reported to have said early in Munshi's tenure: "Munshi has been chosen to be the Trojan Horse in the siege of Hyderabad (Mukta 2002: 65)." Another despatch of a foreign correspondent noted: "If ever any blood is shed in Hyderabad, the first to be shed will be that of the bird-like Munshi (Munshi 1998: 239)." As always, Munshi justified his actions as a defense of "Hindus" from "Muslims," arguing that "It is a curious commentary on the foreign outlook of India that it was more interested in Nizam's bid for independence based on communal fascism than in the sufferings of the people of Hyderabad (Munshi 1998: 239)...." Not incidentally, the police action was widely considered essential to maintaining the unity of postcolonial India. While the take-over of Hyderabad is therefore complex, and certainly one of compelling interest for the Indian nation-state, even to so-called secular nationalists, we should not overlook the role of Hindu nationalists in this drama, nor of their long-standing desire to see this result, as I have illustrated elsewhere (see Bhagavan 2008 and also Kooiman 2002: 165-215). To wit, the local Hindu Sabha in Hyderabad passed the following resolution shortly after the government action: "The Hyderabad state Hindusabha on behalf of all the oppressed in the state send its hearty thanks to the Indian Government for its 'police action'... It pays special tributes to the State's Minister Hon'ble Sardar Patel and India's Agent General in Hyderabad Sjt. K.M. Munshiji who have acted wisely in coming to the rescue of the Hyderabadies before it was too late (V. Ramachandra Rao to Munshi, 4-10-48, MP, 47 (R-8000), 99: 70)." And illustrating that Munshi did indeed embrace the Hindu right in private, this representative of Hindutva went on to note:

> some members of the Mahasabha had come ... with a view to see you [Munshi] and convey in person our hearty thanks and appreciation for your services in Hyderabad. But unfortunately your D.C. objected to our seeing you even though we had come there after informing him a day before of our intention. I hope you [Munshi] will not forget the services rendered by the military personnel in the state forces ... *You had also promised to reward them and give them promotions if they worked to your expectations.* They have done their best and I need not say how valuable their information was to our armed forces (italics added; ibid.: 70-71).

The conspiratorial elements hinted at in this letter were not lost on everyone at that time. One foreign correspondent wrote:

"Munshi is the most hated Hindu in Hyderabad ... Almost alone, he is responsible for the spread of exaggerated reports of chaos in Hyderabad. The stories of attacks on Hindus, eagerly and naively reported by the Indian Press, nearly all came from the big house in Bolarum. There ten miles from Hyderabad city, Munshi used to curl up on a water-cooled verandah to gather the tittle-tattle from his own political agitators (Cheesewright, "He'll be Lucky to Get Out Alive...," *Daily Express*, 16-9-48, MP, 47 (R-8000), 98: 5)."[34] Munshi's role in Hyderabad in this context must be seen as part of Hindutva's historic effort to de-legitimize the Muslim Nizam and reclaim the state as their own.[35]

Munshi's activities in Hyderabad, along with the Bharatiya Vidya Bhavan and Somnath, then, represent a clear and purposeful form of Hindu nationalism. Munshi's long-running anti-Muslim bias is at the heart of all three cases, feeding off of and into this most fundamental of Hindu nationalist traits, and the defining characteristic by which Jaffrelot distinguishes such nationalists from "traditionalists." Munshi's efforts "to promote culture" as Kulapati of the Bhavan and through the rebuilding of Somnath clearly equated the modern Indian nation with resurgent, revivalist Hinduism and with a history in which "non-Hindus," a group defined apparently under the conditions laid forth by Veer Savarkar, were seen as the antagonists of the great motherland and "her people." His writing on various historical, political, and cultural subjects themselves represented a serious advancement of the Hindu nationalist agenda, as it gave the movement intellectual rationale and heft, and presented a serious challenge to countervailing "secular" philosophies and interpretations. In this, it was Munshi's position as a Congressman and a respected member of the overall intelligentsia that lent his positions all the more credibility and respect. But his role in Hyderabad reveals that he was also willing to leave the ivory tower when necessary.

[34] Cheesewright appears to be the journalist Munshi quotes in the line cited earlier in this paragraph, referring to "the bird-like Munshi." The exact line from Cheesewright's column reads: "In the blood that will flow in the State of Hyderabad, it will be a miracle if there are no drops from the veins of birdlike little K.M. Munshi, India's Agent-General" (MP, 47 (R-8000), 98: 5). Cheesewright also provides a specific instance of Munshi fabricating a report of a murder of four Hindus on a train, a report that was then made much of in "every Hindu paper." Cheesewright claims to have investigated the incident personally and found that, in fact, "no one had been murdered, or even seriously injured." There was some kind of assault, but that, Cheesewright claims, was "a reprisal for the murder of three Moslems on the same line the previous day" (ibid.).

[35] I deal with this point rather extensively in Bhagavan (2008). As a brief example, we might note that Nathuram Godse, in his courtroom statement, rather extensively airs his resentment of the Nizam's government, and expresses great satisfaction that the Indian Government had taken the state over. He also makes clear the key place of Hyderabad in the Hindutva imaginary, and ends with the words "Akhand Bharat Amar Rahe. Vande Mataram" ("Long Live Akhand Bharat [Akhand Hindustan/United India]. Glory to the Motherland"). See Godse (1977: esp. 112-113 and 117, but throughout as well).

Taking place after Gandhi's murder, all three examples in short indicate the way in which the Hindu right managed to operate and advance its positions, even in the most hostile of atmospheres. While the RSS was banned and the Mahasabha pilloried in this period, Munshi continued on with his work, a one-man insomniac sleeper cell using his inside position of privilege within the Congress to open successfully a back door through which the proselytizing of Hindu nationalism could proceed unobstructed. In blurring the boundaries between the Hindu right and secular left, Munshi brought the otherwise marginalized saffron movement back into the national dialogue. And by having the Congress endorse, if indirectly, such rightist positions, Munshi also created space in which the right could legitimately operate as an "ethical opposition" able eventually to voice the harsher aspects of their creed.

IV. Conclusions

Through K.M. Munshi, Hindu nationalism was reconfigured, made acceptable to mainstream nationalists in the Congress party. Munshi and other allies within the party utilized the power of this key organization to press forward an agenda in synch with the wishes of the religious right. And when overt Hindu nationalist bodies like the RSS and the Mahasabha were banned or marginalized following Gandhi's assassination, it was the Congress, then, that provided active ideologues safe harbor from the storm, a shelter in which they could regroup, re-plan, and eventually reemerge beginning in the 1960's as an accepted part of the political life of India.

Bibliography

Primary Sources

Ambedkar, B.R. (1946), *What Congress and Gandhi have done to the Untouchables*, 1st pub. 1945 (Bombay: Thacker & Co).

Dave, J.H., et. al. (eds.) (n.d., ca. 1956), *Munshi: His Art and Work, Volumes I-IV* (Shri Munshi Seventieth Birthday Citizens' Celebration Committee).

Gandhi, M. (1958-1984), *Collected Works* (Delhi: Government of India Publications), last accessed Dec. 14, 2005 online at http://www.gandhiserve.org.

Gautam, M.L. (2005), interview conducted by M. Bhagavan August 4.

Godse, G. (1977), *May it Please Your Honour: Statement by Nathuram Godse* (self-published: Pune).

Munshi, K.M. (1942), *Akhand Hindustan.* (Bombay: New Book Co.).
_____. (1955), *City of Paradise and Other Kulapati's Letters (Second Series)* (Bombay: Bharatiya Vidya Bhavan).
_____. (1967), *Indian Constitutional Documents, Volumes I and II* (Bombay: Bharatiya Vidya Bhavan).
_____. (1954), *Janu's Death and Other Kulapati's Letters (First Series)* (Bombay: Bharatiya Vidya Bhavan).
_____. (1976), *Jaya Somnath*, trans. H.M. Patel, first pub. 1937 (Bombay: Bharatiya Vidhya Bhavan).
_____. (1953), *Our Greatest Need and Other Addresses* (Bombay: Bharatiya Vidya Bhavan).
_____. (1961), *Replies to the Reader* (Bombay: Bharatiya Vidya Bhavan).
_____. (1976), *Somnatha: The Eternal Shrine*, first pub. 1951 (Bombay: Bharatiya Vidya Bhavan).
_____. (1956-1957), *Sparks from a Governor's Anvil, Volumes I and II* (Lucknow: Publications Bureau).
_____. (1958), *Swan Love and Other Kulapati's Letters (Fourth Series)* (Bombay: Bharatiya Vidya Bhavan).
_____. (1998), *The End of an Era (Hyderabad Memoirs)*, first pub 1957 (Mumbai: Bharatiya Vidya Bhavan).
_____. (1956), *The Wolf Boy and Other Kulapati's Letters (Third Series)* (Bombay: Bharatiya Vidya Bhavan).
_____. (unpublished), Private Papers of K.M. Munshi (New Delhi: Nehru Memorial Museum and Library).
Nehru, J. (1972-1982), *Selected Works of Jawaharlal Nehru*, ed. S. Gopal, volume thirteen (New Delhi: Orient Longman).

Secondary Sources

Bayly, C.A. (1996), *Empire and Information: Intelligence Gathering and Social Communication in India, 1780-1870* (Cambridge: Cambridge University Press).
Bhagavan, M. (ed.) (2008), "Princely States and the Hindu Imaginary: Exploring the Cartography of Hindu Nationalism in Colonial India," *The Journal of Asian Studies* 67.3: 881-915.
_____. (2010), "A New Hope: India, the United Nations and the Making of the Universal Declaration of Human Rights," *Modern South Asia* 44.2 (March): 311-347 (first pub. in *MAS* online, June 13, 2008).
_____. (forthcoming 2010), *Heterotopias: Nationalism and the Possibility of History in South Asia* (New York: Oxford University Press).
Bhat, C. (2001), *Hindu Nationalism: Origins, Ideologies and Modern Myths* (New York: Berg).
Bose, S. and A. Jalal. (2004), *Modern South Asia, Second Edition* (New York: Routledge).
Brown, J. (1991) *Gandhi*, first published 1989 (New Haven: Yale University Press).

_____. (2003), *Nehru* (New Haven: Yale University Press).
Chatterjee, P. (1994), *The Nation and its Fragments:Colonial and Postcolonial Histories* (Delhi: Oxford University Press).
_____. (2004), *Nationalist Thought and the Colonial World: A Derivative Discourse?* first pub. 1986 (Minneapolis: University of Minnesota Press).
Corbridge, S. (1999), "'The Militarization of all Hindudom'? The Bharatiya Janata Party, the Bomb, and the Political Spaces of Hindu Nationalism," *Economy and Society* 28.2: 222-255.
Dalmia, V. (1997), *The Nationalization of Hindu Traditions: Bharatendu Harischandra and Nineteenth-Century Banaras* (Delhi: Oxford University Press).
Dalton, D. (1993), *Mahatma Gandhi: Nonviolent Power in Action* (New York: Columbia University Press).
Gopal, S. (1976), *Jawaharlal Nehru: A Biography*, vol. 1, 1889-1947, (Cambridge: Harvard University Press).
Hardiman, D. (2003), *Gandhi in his Time and Ours: The Global Legacy of his Ideas* (New York: Columbia University Press).
Jaffrelot, C. (1996), *The Hindu Nationalist Movement in India*, first pub. 1993 (New York: Columbia University Press).
Kooiman, D. (2002), *Communalism and Indian Princely States* (Delhi: Manohar).
Ludden, D. (ed.) (1996), *Making India Hindu: Religion, Community, and the Politics of Democracy in India* (Delhi: Oxford University Press).
Mehra, P. (1985), *A Dictionary of Modern Indian History, 1707-1947* (Delhi: Oxford University Press).
Minault, G. (1982),*The Khilafat Movement* (New York: Columbia University Press).
Mouffe, C. (2000), *The Democratic Paradox* (New York: Verso).
Mukta, P. (2002), "On the Political Culture of Authoritarianism" in *Development and Deprivation in Gujarat (In Honor of Jan Breman)*, ed. Ghanshyam Shah et. al. (New Delhi: Sage Publications), 59-73.
Orsini, F. (2002), *The Hindi Public Sphere: 1920-1940: Language and Literature in the Age of Nationalism* (New York: Oxford University Press).
Pandey, G. (1992), *The Construction of Communalism in Colonial North India*, first published 1990 (Delhi: Oxford University Press).
_____. (2002), *Remembering Partition* (Cambridge: Cambridge University Press).
Pannikar, K.N. (1989), *Against Lord and State: Religion and Peasant Uprisings in Malabar, 1836-1921* (New Delhi: Oxford University Press).
Rai, M. (2004), *Hindu Rulers, Muslim Subjects* (Delhi: Permanent Black).
Sen, S.P. (ed.) (1974), *Dictionary of National Biography, Volume III (M-R)* (Calcutta: Institute of Historical Studies).
Thapar, R. (2004), *Somnatha: The Many Voices of a History* (New Delhi: Viking/Penguin).

Upadhyaya, P.C. (1992), "The Politics of Indian Secularism" in *Modern Asian Studies* 26(4): 815-853.
Van Der Veer, P. (1992), "Ayodhya and Somnath: Eternal Shrines, Contested Histories" in *Social Research* 59(1): 85-109.
Zelliot, E. (2001), *From Untouchable to Dalit*, 1st published 1992 (Delhi: Manohar).

Laura R. Brueck

Marking the Boundaries of a New Literary Identity: The Assertion of 'Dalit Consciousness' in Dalit Literary Criticism

> Through your literary creations cleanse the prescribed values of life and culture. Do not limit your objectives. Remove the darkness in villages by the light of your pen. Do not forget that in our country the world of the Dalits and the ignored classes is vast. Get to know intimately their pain and sorrow, and try through your literature to bring progress to their lives. True humanity resides there.
> Dr. B.R. Ambedkar[1]

Introduction

In just the last few years, scholarly attention to the subject of Dalit literature in India has increased almost as dramatically as the recent surge in the production of Dalit literature across India. The first significant example of Dalit writing in English translation appeared in Orient Longman's anthology of the literature of the Dalit Panthers, *Poisoned Bread* (Dangle 1992), and though for almost a decade afterwards there was no significant publication of Dalit literary texts outside of India, save for the lifelong work of scholars such as Eleanor Zelliot and Gail Omvedt, the dearth of Western access to Dalit texts and scholarly attention paid to them has recently turned around. English translations of Dalit literature now abound, thanks to a surge in interest by academic publishing houses in India and abroad as well as the rise of specialty publishing houses such as Navayana whose entire catalog focuses on matters of caste in literature and society.

[1] Ambedkar (1976) quoted in Limbale (2004: 50).

Scholarly focus on Dalit literature has emphasized the struggle of Dalit writers to "find their own voice" and to protest, through the medium of the written word, the marginal existence and code of silence that have been foisted upon them for centuries. In taking a closer look at the rhetorical strategies of Dalit literary critics, we understand the theoretical dexterity with which they not only articulate the right of Dalits to represent their own experience in a public medium, but also the ways in which they are establishing a system to exert control over their own representation in a literary mainstream. It is in Dalit literary critical texts that the boundaries of the growing genre of Dalit literature are being both constructed and carefully guarded and questions of identity and authenticity of experience and voice are being vigorously debated. I am particularly interested in the nature of what is at stake in these debates. The arguments in this paper concern issues facing Dalit literature as a whole, but are largely grounded in works of Dalit literary criticism in Hindi, reflecting the focus of my research. Such focus on Hindi Dalit literary criticism also proves helpful in understanding the ways in which regional Dalit literary traditions are determining and protecting their own socio-political identities not only as distinctly opposed to the standards of the 'mainstream' Indian literary sphere, but also as distinct from other regional language Dalit literary traditions across the country.

"Dalit literature" is a slippery term that is regularly applied to wildly diverse notions of what constitutes both "Dalit" and "literature". In their 1973 *Dalit Panther Manifesto,* the Dalit Panthers famously defined the meaning of Dalit broadly: "Who is a dalit? Members of scheduled castes and tribes, Neo-Buddhists, the working people, the landless and poor peasants, women and all those who are being exploited politically, economically, and in the name of religion" (in Murugkar 1991: 237). Hindi Dalit writer Kusum Meghval takes a less inclusive and more traditional stance in her book, *Dalit Society in Hindi Novels*: "The use of 'Dalit society' has been accepted for those traditionally thought of as Shudras in India. Dalit society consists of those castes who exist on a base level and who have been persecuted for centuries" (1989: 1). Similarly, the term "literature" has been applied variously to include Dalit renderings of traditional genres such as poetry, autobiography, short and long fiction, and drama, and is frequently extended as far as political tracts, histories of Ambedkar, and journalistic reporting of incidents of violence and discrimination against Dalits.[2] My own interpretation of "Dalit literature" elaborated throughout this work includes mostly texts of the more traditional genres—poetry, novels, short stories, and autobiography—created by their authors self-consciously as texts of Dalit literature. This Dalit

[2] For examples of Dalit pamphlet literature and a discussion of the multiple levels of Dalit literary discourse, see Narayan and Misra (2004).

literary sphere is attempting to make a significant intervention into what has traditionally been a literary culture reserved for the elite. As the following discussions will demonstrate, at the heart of this sphere is a commitment to changing the very nature of what is considered "literature" and who are considered "authors" in both Dalit and non-Dalit literary worlds. Many Dalit authors claim that they write only for a Dalit audience and that whatever impact their texts may have in a non-Dalit world is merely a secondary consideration. And yet the texts that I consider within the rubric of Dalit literature are not merely attempts to recover a Dalit voice, but rather to *incorporate* this Dalit voice into the Indian literary canon.

This essay will not suggest a definitive answer to the broad question, "What is Dalit literature?" To do so would be to fall into the same debates over identity and authenticity that continually inhibit more substantive discussions of content and form in Dalit literature. The term "authenticity" here refers to the question of who is *Dalit enough* to write "realistic" representations of Dalit experience, and debates over authenticity comprise the majority of public discussions over the nature of Dalit literature. The nature of these debates are political, rather than literary, and ultimately unresolvable for they come down to the ideological positioning of the critic, rather than an objective analysis of the literary expression of any particular text, or set of texts. For example, critic Digish Mehta describes Dalit literature as "writing contributed by members of the Dalit class, bearing witness in authentic terms to their experiences of deprivation" (1989: 83). Publisher and journalist S. Anand defines Dalit literature as "literature produced by Dalits in a conscious, defined, modern sense with an awareness of what it is to be Dalit" (2003: 1), while Marathi Dalit literary critic Sharankumar Limbale classifies Dalit literature as, "writing about Dalits by Dalit writers with a Dalit consciousness" (2004: 19). Such an emphasis on the "awareness of what it means to be Dalit" and the expression of Dalit experience in "authentic" terms suggests an essentialized prescription for a way of thinking and a way of writing that become crystallized in the concept of "Dalit consciousness" (*Dalit chetnā*).[3] Sharatchandra Muktibodh, in an essay entitled "What is Dalit Literature?" in the foundational anthology of Marathi Dalit Literature edited by Arjun Dangle, *Poisoned Bread*, also relies on the notion of texts produced by writers with a "Dalit consciousness" to serve as a definition for Dalit literature (1992: 267). It emerges immediately, then, that the question to ask is not, what is Dalit literature, but more aptly, what determines Dalit consciousness? How do you develop Dalit consciousness? Can non-Dalits have Dalit consciousness? Are there Dalits who do not? How does a Dalit writer express this consciousness in "authentic terms"?

[3] See Brueck (2006) for a discussion of *Dalit chetnā* in the context of the meetings and discussions of various Dalit literary organizations in Delhi.

The mission of this essay is less to provide answers to these questions than to establish the significance of asking them both in the form of criticism and creative text. With a brief discussion of the concept of Dalit consciousness in Dalit critical literature, I suggest the ways in which this theoretical concept functions as a central principle in the development of the Dalit literary genre. I suggest that the employment of Dalit consciousness in critical literature demands a strategic essentialization (following Spivak 1985) of the ideology of Dalit identity and strategies of representation. I also analyze the approach of Hindi Dalit literary critics to the construction of their own literary history, and consider both the role that Dalit consciousness plays in that project as well as the significance of constructing such a historical narrative in the context of both mainstream Indian literary history as well as in comparison with other regional Dalit literary and political histories.

"Dalit Consciousness" in Dalit Literary Criticism

In her important book, *Resistance Literature* (1987), Barbara Harlow codifies the shared aesthetic and ideological foundations of resistance literatures of liberation movements around the world through her readings of both poetic and narrative texts. Throughout, she emphasizes the political imperative as the driving force of resistance literature, and the characteristic that distinguishes it from other literatures. According to Harlow, "Resistance literature calls attention to itself, and to literature in general, as a political and politicized activity. The literature of resistance sees itself furthermore as immediately and directly involved in a struggle against ascendant or dominant forms of ideological and cultural production" (1987: 28). Dalit literature is the creative expression of a social liberation movement, a struggle not for independence from physical occupation but rather freedom from the tyranny of caste-based discrimination and exploitation. As I will demonstrate in the following discussion of Dalit literary criticism, Dalit writers regard themselves as inserting their previously silenced voices into the hegemonic canon of Indian literary history through the twin projects of creating a body of new literature along strict theoretical and aesthetic principles and turning their own critical gaze on canonical Indian literary texts.

I want to emphasize Harlow's categorization of resistance literature somewhat further, as her analytical framework proves helpful in creating a frame through which to read Dalit critical literature. Harlow conveys three fundamental concerns for resistance texts: "access to history for those who have been historically denied an active role in the arena of world politics; the problem of contested terrain, whether cultural, geographical, or political; and the social and political transformation from a geneology of filiation based on ties of kinship, ethnicity, race or religion to an affiliative secular order" (1987: 22). In the context of Dalits, their literature proposes to open for them access not only to history, but also to a world of self and community awareness and the means to construct a shared identity. First they must deconstruct the identity, amassed over centuries, of the powerless, the lowly, the untouchable, then replace it with a new kind of self-expression that will transform not only the way they see themselves, but also the way society sees them. The terrain they are contesting is that of representation, an area that is at once cultural, material, and political. It is to the emerging body of Dalit critical literature and its articulation of these struggles that I now turn.

The development of contemporary Dalit literature is commonly only traced as far back as the mid-1970s (and the formation of the activist-poet organization, the Dalit Panthers), and it has in these few short decades rapidly expanded from a largely poetic form into a broad catalog of short stories, novels, dramas, and autobiographies. It has only been within the last few years that a rich body of literary criticism has begun to accompany the literature itself in the pages of Dalit literary magazines and journals and in the introductions to anthologies of Dalit poetry and short stories. In most cases this critical writing is produced by writers who also write creative works of Dalit literature. In 2004, Canadian academic Alok Mukherjee translated Marathi Dalit writer Sharankumar Limbale's volume *Towards an Aesthetics of Dalit Literature: Histories, Controversies, and Considerations* (2004). Two book-length treatises on the history and aesthetics of Dalit literature in Hindi by two of the most prominent and prolific figures in Hindi Dalit literary circles include Omprakash Valmiki's *Dalit Sāhitya kā Saundāryshāstra* ("Aesthetics of Dalit Literature" 2001) and Mohandas Naimishray's *Hindī Dalit Sāhitya* ("Hindi Dalit Literature," forthcoming).

These critical studies attempt comprehensive evaluations of contemporary Dalit literature, both defending the social need for and value of Dalit literature as a transformative medium against nameless "upper caste" critics, while also creating a generic theoretical framework by which to define and manage the expanding boundaries of a growing literary genre. Like Harlow's principal assertion about resistance literature, these critical texts emphasize the singular political imperative behind Dalit literature. Valmiki asserts that Dalit literature is a "literature of action" committed to the struggle against the feudalistic mentality of society, emphasizing instead basic commitment to human values (2001: 15). Limbale goes so far as to suggest that the character of Dalit literature is univocal. He writes, "The experiences narrated in Dalit literature are very similar. Untouchables' experiences of untouchability are identical" (2004: 35). And while Harlow makes the point that resistance literature demands an "access to history" for its constituency, Valmiki stresses the value of recording contemporary Dalit experience in literature, experience that will ultimately become an alternative "Dalit history" for future generations. He bemoans the lack of contemporary Dalit awareness and understanding of their own history, blaming the complete monopolization of public narrative, both historical and literary, by the Brahminical castes,

> *Dalit racnākār kī apnī paristhitiyāṃ, anubhav-vaishiṣṭya bhale hī nijī hoṃ, phir bhī unkā sāmājik, aitihāsik arth hotā hai. Unko śabdbaddh karnā ānevālī pīḍhiyoṃ ke liye mahatvapūrṇ hotā hai. Hazāroṃ sāl se śoṣitoṃ, pīḍhitoṃ, dalitoṃ ke vicār, unkī bhāvnāeṃ apne mālikoṃ ke prati kyā thīṃ? … Yeh jāne kā koī rāstā hamāre pās nahīṃ hai … Sāhitya, jis par sāmantī aur brāhmaṇvādī soch kā prabhutva thā, voh hameṃ sirf unkī jo dhārṇāeṃ hamāre prati thīṃ.*
>
> No matter how particular a Dalit author's circumstances, or the features of his experience, they still have social and historical value. It is important to put them down in words for the sake of coming generations. What were the thoughts and feelings of those Dalits who were oppressed and exploited for thousands of years? … We don't have any way of recovering this information … Literature, which was ruled over by feudalism and brahmanism, offers us only those perspectives. (2001: 24)

In an effort to recover what Valmiki regards as a lost Dalit history, Mohandas Naimishray (forthcoming) has undertaken the project to construct an extended history of Hindi Dalit literature in an effort to reclaim those few voices of Dalit experience and perspective that have managed to make their way into more mainstream literary and cultural circulation. Beginning with north Indian bhakti poets like Ravidas and Kabir and continuing through the nationalist period with published poetry and pamphlet literature by authors such as Hira Dom and Swami Acchutanand, Naimishray constructs a loosely connected history of Dalit writers stretching back 500 years before the transformative politics of Ambedkar gave birth to modern anti-caste Dalit social and political ideology. The implications of constructing such a literary history will be considered more carefully in the second half of this essay.

The key concept around which Limbale, Valmiki, and Naimishray and indeed many other Dalit critics rally is the idea of Dalit consciousness. In the works of many Dalit critics, there is an emerging sense in their literary discourse of a singular "consciousness" that informs the production of Dalit literature and serves as a gauge for the authenticity of any given work. The function of the theoretical concept of Dalit consciousness is articulated in the expressive and interpretive practices of writing and reading. Dalit consciousness has emerged in recent years in a large body of Dalit literary criticism as a theoretical tool with which the architects of Dalit literary culture are able to set boundaries for the growing genre of Dalit literature as well as launch a distinctly Dalit critique of celebrated works of Hindi literature.

Dalit consciousness is a fundamental component of an emerging theory of Dalit aesthetics (*saundaryashāstra*). 20th century Dalit political leader and architect of the Indian constitution, Bimrao Ambedkar persists as the primary symbol and inspiration of struggle and freedom in Dalit political, social, and, as the epigraph at the beginning of this chapter suggests, literary imaginations. According to Valmiki, "Dalit consciousness obtains its primary energy from Dr. Ambedkar's life and vision. All Dalit writers are united with respect to this truth" (2001: 30). He lists several points of Dalit consciousness that reflect Ambedkarite ideology, including a rejection of the caste system and Hindu law and an embrace of rationalism and social equality. About literature specifically he lists, "disagreeing with the definition of 'great poetry' by Ramchandra Shukla" and "being against traditional aesthetics" (2001: 31).

Valmiki's points offer a hint of the deconstructive nature of Dalit consciousness as a tool for critical analysis. What is perhaps most interesting about such a formulation of Dalit consciousness is the suggestion of how the concept is being developed as a strategy for Dalit critical analysis, a kind of "test" by which Dalit critics can judge the "dalitness" of any work of literature, whether written by a Dalit or non-Dalit. Though I am not suggesting that the definition of Dalit consciousness is in any way fixed, or its tenets universally agreed upon, I do want to underscore that it is almost without exception regarded by Dalit writers as the ideal for all Dalit literature, and texts that purport to represent Dalit experience or identity are evaluated by how closely they adhere to this ideal. It is a concept that permeates readings of existing works of Dalit literature, and in such readings it is extremely important not just that a Dalit character is present, but rather how "authentic" the portrayal of the Dalit character, how "realistic" the narrative. It is a principle of Dalit consciousness that writings are made authentic only through the real-life experience of Dalit identity. For example, in an essay in his book chronicling the development of Dalit literary aesthetics, Valmiki emphasizes the importance of writing "the truth as one has experienced it, depicted just as it was seen and felt" for "pretension is impossible in a literal rendering" (2001: 50).

Hindi Dalit writers and readers do not only wield the concept of Dalit consciousness as an evaluative tool within their own literary circles, however, but increasingly are using Dalit consciousness as a critical lens to analyze "mainstream" works of literature that claim to represent them, works that have widely been heralded as progressive in Hindi literary circles.[4] It is about these works of literature that Dalit writers and critics are most interested in offering their own analysis, reconsidering their social and political stance in a position relative to Dalit consciousness. This kind of analysis is an effort to re-assert autonomy over their own representation, and simultaneously protect the boundaries of their own literary identity from disappearing,

[4] Iconic Hindi writer Munshi Premchand is one of the most frequent objects of analysis by Dalit critics, and frequently comes under severe criticism, though he is regularly celebrated in mainstream literary histories as an author who has displayed great empathy in his creation of Dalit characters. See Brueck (2006).

the emergent Dalit literary voice from being diffused and ultimately appropriated by agents of the dominant cultural sphere. The theoretical idea of Dalit consciousness thereby becomes an authoritative tool in the institutionalization of Dalit literature as its own textual genre, and the authority of Dalit literary critics to determine which authors and which texts may be included within the boundaries of the genre.

As rigid boundaries of this space are elaborated in the critical literature over what exactly having a Dalit consciousness entails, and a singular weight is given to Dalit consciousness as a determining factor not only of the critical success of a work of Dalit literature, but indeed of whether or not a work of literature can lay claim to the category of "Dalit" at all, arbiters of Dalit literature are constructing a critical framework based on the rhetorical practice of strategic essentialism. Dalit consciousness is the Dalit literary sphere's rendering of this practice for the political purpose of making an intervention into the mainstream literary-cultural sphere and claiming there a small space of their own in which they have the power to determine, by means of this essentialist concept, what authors and what texts may also share that space. The carefully guarded concept of Dalit consciousness and its essentialist application are powerful tools in the battle for self-representation and the authority of Dalits over their own literary and political voices.

Gayatri Spivak's (1985) concept of "strategic essentialism," articulated in her analysis of the Subaltern Studies collective's reconstruction of a subaltern consciousness from colonial historical records, allows us to understand the function of the calculated socio-political project behind the construction of authenticity and Dalit consciousness as critical categories in the Dalit literary sphere. An understanding of the power of strategic essentialism in the context of claiming space in the public sphere is essential for situating the socio-political project of Dalit literary criticism.

In her now-famous article, Spivak analyzes the self-stated goal of the academics in the Subaltern Studies collective to recover the "consciousness" of the colonial-era Indian subaltern subject through a "reading against the grain" of official and historical documents of the British empire in India.[5] According to Spivak, the subalternists are trying to uncover the (singular) "consciousness" of the (plural) subaltern, thereby looking for and ultimately establishing through their research a positivist subaltern consciousness. This kind of universal consciousness of the subaltern can be observed and tested but that is, in fact, insufficient to represent a complex and varied group of classes, castes, genders, languages, and locations. Yet she argues that the construction of this singular consciousness is a necessary fiction, since the true plurality of self-consciousnesses of diverse subalterns can never

[5] For elaborations on this project see Guha (1982) and Chatterjee (1989).

be reconstructed from their fragmentary appearances in records of insurgency in the documentation of the British Empire. Thus the overall project of the Subaltern Studies collective is a political one: to make serious interventions in the practices of history and historiography and to introduce the subaltern into the discourse of history, and the practice of essentializing identity is useful towards that end.

In a similar way, this is what Dalit writers, critics, and to a certain degree, academics of Dalit literature have been doing as well. There has been and continues to be so much focus on Dalit writers "finding their own voice" and *establishing* Dalit literature as a literary genre, as a vehicle of political and social change, and finally as an object of academic study that there has been a consistent practice of essentializing the textual practices of Dalit literature, from both within and without, in a conscious effort to establish a public voice and gain political ground. For example, in an interview with Arundhati Roy in which he challenges her authority to claim to authentically represent a Dalit character in her novel *The God of Small Things* (1998), S. Anand challenges, "I hope you agree that non-dalits cannot claim to produce 'dalit literature'. ... this is an issue of a long-suppressed community finding its own voice" (2003: 17). This challenge suggests how in the contemporary Dalit literary sphere such socially constructed categories as "Dalit" get transposed (strategically) onto actual identities. In safeguarding the category of "Dalit literature" only for authors born into one of the Dalit castes (and essentializing the nature of that experience), the inalienability that the caste system has imposed on social identities for centuries is re-appropriated as an exclusive and empowering category by Dalit writers. Spivak illustrates a similar empowerment of the category of class among subaltern societies,

> 'Class' is not, after all, an inalienable description of a human reality. Class-consciousness on the *descriptive* level is itself a strategic and artificial rallying awareness, which, on the *transformative* level, seeks to destroy the mechanics which come to construct the outlines of the very class of which a collective consciousness has been situationally developed. (1985: 342)

Spivak's analysis here of class not as an inalienable reality but as a descriptive and transformative category hearkens Harlow's earlier assertion of resistance literature's establishment of an affiliative identity for its constituents. Like the Marxist category of class, the category of "Dalit" too is a category created to unite a diffuse population of oppressed castes[6] under a single descriptor meant to denote both the system of oppression under which they struggle, as well as the insurgent spirit and self-awareness to overcome that oppression. Suggesting the transformative possibilities inherent in the term

[6] For a thorough description of the development of the term in Marathi and its various meanings depending on the political perspective of the speaker see Zelliot (1998: 268-269).

Mukherjee writes, "'Dalit' is a political identity, as opposed to a caste name. It expresses Dalits' knowledge of themselves as oppressed people and signifies their resolve to demand liberation through a revolutionary transformation of the system that oppresses them" (2003: xix). Rather than a moniker bestowed from above, such as the demeaning "untouchable," the administrative "scheduled caste," or Gandhi's condescending "harijan," Dalit is an expansive, positivist ideology of identity that was created within the community "from below" and subsequently has permeated the public sphere so as to become the unofficial, and politically correct, standard.

What I would like to suggest here is that there is an emerging sense in the discourse surrounding Dalit literature of a singular consciousness that informs the production of Dalit literature and serves as a measure for the authenticity of a given literary work. This singular consciousness is tied to an exclusive politics of identity that shuns those who may have been born into an untouchable caste, but who refuse the affiliative Dalit identity of the level of their own self-consciousness. Ranajit Guha explains that among subaltern societies any member of the community who does not choose to "continue in such subalterneity," or who does not embody a commitment to the collective subaltern in their own self-consciousness, is seen as an enemy to the collective. "The task of the 'consciousness' of class or collectivity within a social field of exploitation and domination is thus necessarily self-alienating" (in Spivak 1985: 342). So too in Dalit society, anyone who does not espouse the normative demands of exhibiting a carefully-defined Dalit consciousness is rigorously secluded from the public persona of the Dalit literary sphere. The bitterly ironic "Dalit Brahmin," for example, is a common epithet for Dalits who try to distance themselves from their caste identity, or who put more emphasis on personal material success than community improvement, perhaps inhabiting a middle class or elite class position. These Dalits are looked at with great derision by politically activist and community-oriented Dalits. Arjun Dangle, one of the founders of the Dalit Panthers, writes about some members of the Dalit community who reacted negatively to the emergence of Dalit literature,

> ... some educated people from amongst the Dalits too viewed Dalit literature very negatively. They wanted to forget their past, could not face the harsh social realities surrounding them and were filled with an inferiority complex. They took all the benefits of the concessions resulting from Dr. Ambedkar's movement, but the movement made no impact on them. They believed that with their individual prosperity society had also prospered.
>
> These 'Dalit Brahmins' felt (and feel even today) that Dalit literature was something dirty which had tarnished the image of their society. They wanted to speak, write, and live like Brahmins and missed no opportunity to ridicule Dalit literature. (1992: 249-250)

Dangle's description of the "Dalit Brahmin" who seeks to distance himself from the political progress and cultural expression of his caste community drips derision. Dangle's Dalit Brahmin is educated, yet beset by an inferiority complex. He is individually opportunistic, and unmoved by the communal spirit of freedom and struggle of the Dalit movement. Dangle continues, "When one examines the views of these 'Dalit Brahmins' who equate the depiction of the pitiable conditions of the Dalits with their derogation ... one gets an idea not only of their middle class attitude but also of their mental impotence" (1992: 250). This passage suggests how little room there is for criticism and debate over the nature of Dalit literature and narrative representation of Dalit life and experience in Dalit literary circles. Dissenters are viewed as enemies, as a threat to the collective consciousness, and are isolated with epithets like Dalit Brahmin. The strategic essentialism of defining a concept of "Dalit consciousness" is, we might consider, a conscious and calculated initiative to establish a public space for Dalit literature, and once established, may allow the boundaries of that space to be opened to embrace many more diverse understandings of the Dalit experience.

Writing the History of Hindi Dalit Literature

I turn now to the second strategic project of the dominant critical voices in the Dalit literary sphere, that of writing the history of Dalit literature. I will focus here specifically on Hindi Dalit literary histories and the significance for the Hindi Dalit literary community of constructing for Hindi a pride of place among other regional language Dalit literary traditions across India.

Hindi Dalit literature, in its contemporary avatar, is generally understood to have been established in the early 1980s with the early autobiographies, poetry, and short stories of eminent writers such as Omprakash Valmiki and Mohandas Naimishray.[7] Due to this late start, it is also supposed that Dalit literature in Hindi continues to lag behind the more "mature" Dalit literary traditions in Marathi and Tamil. This is in large part, critics say, due to the lack of an organized Dalit political movement in north India until the late twentieth century, and the absence of influential leaders such as Ambedkar in the West and Periyar in the South. While contemporary Hindi Dalit writers acknowledge enormous credit to Marathi Dalit literature in particular, and the influential centrality of Ambedkar, Phule, and the Dalit Panthers, they are increasingly engaging in projects of historical and critical reconstruction of a specifically Hindi literary lineage that reaches as far back as the fifteenth century. Foremost in this project is Mohandas Naimishray, and much of his forthcoming *Hindī Dalit*

[7] See Basu (2002).

Sāhitya is dedicated to the construction of a Hindi Dalit literary history, with separate chapters dedicated to Dalit literature before and after Independence.

Fifteenth-century *bhakti* poets Kabir and Ravidas represent the most important cache for distinguishing north Indian Dalit literary history from other regional languages.[8] Similar to the resurgence of Buddhism in India led by the post-Ambedkar neo-Buddhist movement, the contemporary Dalit reclamation of Ravidas, a member of the *Chamār* caste, has led to a renewed symbolic significance and physical presence in shrines and Dalit political centers across north India.[9] And Kabir was, according to Ambedkar, one of his primary influences in the ideology of social equality along with the Buddha and Phule.[10] The claim on these *bhakti* poets as part of a north Indian literary heritage, and the recognition of their influence on Ambedkar, is extremely significant for Hindi Dalit writers. Mohandas Naimishray, in his forthcoming *Hindī Dalit Sāhitya* (21), refers to an argument made by some Dalit writers that Hindi language society is actually "two steps ahead" of other states because it was in the north Indian linguistic sphere that these *bhakti* poets were produced. Recent writings by Dalit literary critics testify to the project of reclaiming the spirit of these *bhakti* poets as their own. Kanwal Bharti and Dharmavir, two prominent Dalit literary critics, have complained about the co-option of Kabir by the brahminical elite who have turned his legacy into one of "mysticism" (*rahasyavād*) rather than social equality.[11] According to author Namwar Singh, though Kabir may not have written anything like what we now consider Dalit literature, the heart of the Dalits yet resonates in his voice (2003: 24).

Many scholars also argue that the north Indian *bhakti* heritage may have actually fostered a particular ideological mindset among north Indian Dalits that is unique from that of other regions. Chroniclers of Dalit pamphlet literature Badri Narayan and A.R. Misra (2004) suggest that the *bhakti* poets are more than eminent literary forebears whose reclamation brings credibility to Hindi Dalit literature, but rather formed through their writings an ideological basis for the very development of the north Indian Dalit consciousness. While the Dalit literary lineage of western India is based on the development of the ideology of constitutionalism and other western notions of equality promoted by Ambedkar, Dalit society in the Hindi belt of Uttar Pradesh and Bihar "derived its ideological roots from

[8] Two special issues of the Hindi Dalit literary magazine, *Apekṣā*, are devoted to the two major *bhakti* poets held in especially high regard by contemporary Dalit writers: Kabir and Ravidas. See Tej Singh (January-March 2003 and April-June 2003). See also Dharmavir (1997).

[9] See Hawley (2005: 23).

[10] See Ambedkar's "Annihilation of Caste" (Rodrigues 2005). Also see Hawley (2005: 276) and Naimishray (forthcoming: 21).

[11] See Bharti (2003: 11-16) and Dharmavir (2003: 17-23).

other sources, especially from the literature of the bhakti movement, to create an alternative ontologic paradigm of liberation" (2004: 9). Tej Singh suggests in his introductory comments to a special issue of *Apekṣā* devoted to Ravidas that both Kabir and Ravidas are the two founding poets of a Dalit renaissance (*punarjāgaraṇ*) that is also inclusive of the contributions of icons such as Swami Achutanand, Phule, and Ambedkar (2003).

Swami Achutanand (b. 1879) is the most prominent pre-independence north Indian Dalit literary icon and critics and scholars of Hindi Dalit literature are actively engaged in establishing his historical centrality alongside the figures of Phule and Ambedkar who hail from Maharashtra. Achutanand, a name derived from the Hindi word for untouchable—*achhūt*—and assumed when the young Arya Samāji abandoned the organization in 1912, was a *chamār* from U.P. who became the leader of the north Indian Ādi-Hindu movement in the 1920s and 1930s (Jaffrelot 2003: 201-202). According to Jaffrelot, after denouncing the Arya Samāj for their Hindu protectionism and the Congress party for their nationalist resistance of British occupation and influence, Achutanand developed and propagated an *Ādi-Hindu* ideology (lit: original Hindu, suggesting the lower castes are descendents of inhabitants of the Indus valley who predate the Aryans) of common origins and a united political struggle of Dalits, Shudras, and tribals (*ādivāsis*; 2003: 203). He promoted his philosophy through the establishment of the Ādi-Hindu Society and important forays into print and publishing with the founding of the newspaper *Achhūt*, and later, *Ādi-Hindu* as well as the monthly journal *Usha*. According to Narayan and Misra, "Through these papers Achutanand not only conveyed the philosophy of liberation from social castigation, but also established the significance of the print media in Dalit mobilization and identity formation" (2004: 18). Naimishray also emphasizes the importance of Achutanand's use of the print medium, using poetry, songs, speeches, and journalism to promote the cause of Dalit self-respect and liberation, and creating a growing "consciousness of publishing" among Hindi-speaking Dalit communities (forthcoming: 47, 50).

The example of Achutanand illustrates that questions of influence are extremely significant in Hindi Dalit literary histories, especially because the Hindi Dalit public sphere continues to be considered behind in both politics and literature, particularly with respect to Dalit mobilization and literary representation in Maharashtra and Tamil Nadu. Many Dalit literary historians and critics therefore embed in their historical narratives alternative readings of literary influence, creating a position of primacy for north India. For example, Naimishray suggests in a lengthy discussion of Swami Achutanand that perhaps Ambedkar's momentous public performance of burning the *Manusmṛti* at the Mahad demonstration in 1927 was influenced by one of Achutanand's poems:

> *Swāmī-jī ne Manusmṛti kī kaḍī ālochanā san 1925 meṃ 'Manusmṛti se jalan' nāmak kavitā meṃ kī hai jabki Baba Saheb Ambedkar ne Manusmṛti 25 December, 1927 ko jalāī thī. Baba Saheb ne bhāyavād Swāmī jī se prabhāvit hokar hī Manusmṛti jalāī haiṃ. 'Manusmṛti se Jalan' kavitā meṃ vah kahate hai:*
>
> *Nivādin Manusmṛti hamko jalā rahī hai.*
> *Ūpar na uṭhne detī, nīche girā rahī hai.* (forthcoming: 58)
>
> Swami-ji made a strong criticism of the *Manusmṛti* in a poem entitled "Being burned by the *Manusmṛti*" in 1925, and Baba Saheb Ambedkar burned it on December 25, 1927.[12] Perhaps Ambedkar was influenced by Swami-ji when he burned the *Manusmṛti*. In "Being burned by the *Manusmṛti*" he says,
>
> The *Manusmṛti* burns us night and day
> It does not allow us to get up, it only throws us down.

Suggesting a theory of the influence of Achutanand's poetry over one of Ambedkar's most infamous public acts, however tenuous, is a powerful testament to the importance in contemporary Hindi literary history-writing of attempts to recover modern Dalit political and literary innovation in north India from the margins, or at least to acknowledge the role of local and regional historical and literary figures by whose works the unique Hindi Dalit consciousness was raised.[13] Naimishray asserts further such a re-examination of the significant role of Achutanand in early twentieth-century Dalit political and literary society might suggest that he may, through the efforts of recovery and re-writing, even be lifted to the same stature as Ambedkar, at least with respect to his influence in the Hindi belt.

> *Agar dalit itihās tathya sangat punarlekhan hotā to śāyad Swāmī Achūtānand kī bhūmikā uttar bhārat ke sandarbh meṃ Ambedkar se kam kar nahīṃ dekhī jā saktī. Dūsre aupniveśik kāl meṃ chhoṭe chhoṭe staroṃ par in sthānīya chetnā puṇjoṃ kī atyant mahatvapurṇ bhūmikā dalitoṃ ko lekhan kī shakti se yukt samudāy ke rūp meṃ rūpāntarit kar rahī hai.*
>
> If there were to be a fact-based rewriting of Dalit history, then maybe Swami Achutanand's role in the context of north India cannot be seen as less than Ambedkar. Also, the extremely important role of accumulated local consciousness on small stages in the colonial period transforms Dalits into a united community with the power of writing. (forthcoming: 52)

[12] According to Jaffrelot, this poem was not read publicly until 1927, the same year that Ambedkar burned the *Manusmṛti* at Mahad (Jaffrelot 2003: 203).

[13] In a similar vein, it has been suggested that Premchand may have been inspired to write his short story, "*Thākur kā Kuāṃ*" (The Thakur's Well) by the 1914 Bhojpuri poem "*Acchūt kī Śikāyat*" (An Untouchable's Complaint) by north Indian poet Hira Dom (Pandey 2003).

Tej Singh, in an essay discussing the important figures of the early Dalit literary sphere in north India, explains that Ambedkar and Achutanand had parallel missions in politics and literature, respectively.

> *Ek taraf Dr. Ambedkar ne rājnītik star par samāj-sudhār āndolanoṃ ko ek nishchit dishā meṃ āge baḍhāyā to dūsrī taraf Swāmī Achūtānand ne sāhitya ke star par samāj-sudhār āndolan ke mūl caritra ko udghāṭit karnā śuru kar diyā thā.*
>
> On one hand Ambedkar moved social reform movements forward in a certain direction on a political level, while on the other hand Swami Achutanand began to reveal the basic character of these social reform movements on the level of literature. (2004: 5-6)

Regardless of the obviously central influence of Achutanand in north India in broadly utilizing the world of print and publishing to spread his Ādi-Hindu philosophy through not only political speeches but also poetry and drama, he is rarely referred to as a "Dalit writer" (*Dalit lekhak*), though he was by birth from an untouchable caste and devoted his life's work to the social and political advancement of the lower castes. The reason he is heralded, but does not bear the title of "Dalit writer" in Hindi Dalit literary histories, is inherently tied to the question of Dalit consciousness as discussed earlier in this chapter. A contemporary understanding of Dalit consciousness is necessarily grounded in the Ambedkarite principles of political liberation, renunciation of Hindu identity, and the eradication of caste from Hindu society. While both the *bhakti* poet-saints and Achutanand were radical and revolutionary in their social protest and critique of the oppression of those at the bottom of the caste hierarchy, none of their work envisions a disintegration of caste altogether. Jaffrelot explains that Achutanand's critique of caste was "problematic" because he expressed himself in the same ideological manner as the bhakti poet-saints, searching for social equality within a religious framework rather than a secular one (2003: 203-204). Naimishray is somewhat more expansive in his characterization of Achutanand, asserting that he was the father of Dalit literature who provided courage, strength, and vigor to the early Dalit writers, fulfilling an unrivalled and important role in the early development of modern Dalit literature.

The question of naming also extends to another early twentieth century writer, Hira Dom, whose poem "*Achhūt kī Śikāyat*" (An Untouchable's Complaint) was published in Mahabir Prasad Dwivedi's legendary magazine *Saraswatī* in September, 1914. This poem is widely recognized and cited as the first work of Dalit literature in Hindi (Naimishray forthcoming; Navariya 2004; Narayan and Mishra 2004; Pandey 2003). Naimishray asserts that "scholars" (*adhyetā*) of colonial-era Dalit society have determined that this is the "first poem of Dalit consciousness" (forthcoming: 46). Narayan and Misra explain that this poem represented "the first description of alienation and subordination in written form of Dalit society, governed, as it was, by Brahminical society. It was an epoch-making event for it marked the first glimmerings of the arrival of the written medium for the propagation of the weals and woes of the Dalit community in a changed form" (2004: 16).

But there is some debate in Dalit literary circles about whether or not Hira Dom, like Achutanand, should actually be considered a "Dalit writer." Like Achutanand, Hira Dom's ancestral credentials are secure; he was born into an untouchable community among whose traditional occupations include working in cremation grounds. But Naimishray traces a debate in his book about the nature of the Dalit literary lineage centering on the common practice of referring to Hira Dom as the first Dalit poet. He cites a lengthy discussion by contemporary Dalit writer Kanwal Bharti who questions the 400-year gap in most Hindi Dalit literary histories who herald the bhakti poets for their spiritual and social revolution within the Hindu religious sphere, and Hira Dom, whose work, he argues, is in the same ideological vein (forthcoming: 45-47). In these pages Bharti asserts that the establishment of modern Dalit consciousness, and modern Dalit writers, comes only from the work of Ambedkar, and we should not confuse this post-Ambedkar, enlightened social and political consciousness with literature that belongs to the older tradition of *bhakti*. But as we have seen already, many contributors to the Hindi Dalit literary tradition would be loathe to give up the claim to Hindi literature of a modern Dalit consciousness dating back almost 100 years. Naimishray is conciliatory on this topic, while he refers to Hira Dom repeatedly as the "first poet with a Dalit consciousness," he also allows that the humanistic literature between the fifteenth and twentieth centuries that addresses issues of social justice and "the common man" (*ām ādmī*) is not generally considered Dalit literature in the modern sense. And yet he questions slightly the wisdom of this convention of naming within the Hindi Dalit literary sphere, and emphasizes that though modern Dalit consciousness cannot be said to have been present in literature before Ambedkar, the Bhojpuri/ Hindi literary tradition encompasses many writers who have worked tirelessly in the direction of this consciousness (forthcoming: 16).

The most significant Dalit writer and activist working in north India from the 1930s on who was directly influenced by Ambedkar and incorporated his developing ideology into his own work was Biharilal Harit. Born into a *Jātav* community near Delhi in Shahdara, Harit reportedly only attended a few years of schooling at a Baptist mission school, and honed his poetic writing skills through his exposure to the folk songs and poetry of the north Indian *Jātav* community (Naimishray forthcoming: 60). Active in Dalit literary and political movements from the early thirties until his death in 1999, and the author of 40 major works of poetry, some of which remain unpublished but have been uncovered by a few Delhi-based contemporary Dalit writers,[14] Harit adopted the title of "*Jankavi*" (people's poet) for his attention to the problems of the working class and laborers in his poetry, as well as his extensive use of the rural idiom and folk forms of song and verse, including *bhajan*,[15] *khayāl*,[16] *pad*,[17] *doha*,[18] and *caupaī*.[19] Naimishray lists Harit's poetry anthology, *Achhūtoṃ kā Paigambar* (Messenger of the Untouchables, 1946), as the first published collection of Dalit poems.

A special volume of *Apekṣā* (vol. 9, October-December 2004) is devoted to Harit's legacy. In his introductory essay to this volume, editor Singh, like Naimishray, traces the major milestones of the north Indian Dalit "renaissance" (*punarjāgraṇ*) since the *bhakti* period, and asserts that the decade of the 1930s was especially significant because this is when Harit established himself through his writings as a *jankavi*. According to Singh,

> *Jankavi voh hotā hai jo śoṣit-utpīḍit garīb jantā se juṛtā hai, uske dukhoṃ ko apnā dukh māntā hai, jantā kī bhāṣā meṃ jantā kī ākāṇkśāoṃ-icchāoṃ aur samvedanāoṃ ko abhivyakti detā hai aur lok-chandoṃ ko apnākar sahaj aur saral rūp meṃ apnī bāt kahetī hai.*
>
> He is a people's poet (*jankavi*) who is joined with the exploited and oppressed poor people, who believes their miseries to be his own, who expresses the ambitions, desires, and sympathies of the people in the language of the people, and who, adopting popular speech, speaks his own words in a simple and straightforward style (4).

Singh's definition of a *jankavi* is very similar to the earlier discussion of the various facets of modern Dalit consciousness, including authenticity of experience and struggle, and a rejection of elite literary language. Dalit literary critic Ish Ganganiya explains that Harit's work represents the crucial bridge between the lineage of bhakti-inspired poets and writers, and modern, Ambedkarite Dalit consciousness. He argues that Harit's attitude and style was that of the saint-poets of the bhakti tradition, but his contemporary social philosophy was based on the Ambedkarite model (Ganganiya 2004). This interpretation makes him a very important writer in

[14] *Dalit Lekhak Sangh* and Center for Alternative Dalit Media (CADAM) member and feminist Dalit writer Anita Bharti has spearheaded this effort to recover Harit's work and re-establish the significance of his legacy in contemporary Hindi Dalit literary histories. See Bharti (2004: 91-95).

[15] Devotional song.

[16] "A north Indian style of singing, or instrumental music, said to date from the fifteenth century, consisting of variations on a short phrase." (McGregor 1993: 515, n. 18).

[17] Devotional verse.

[18] "A rhyming couplet, in which each line consists of half-lines made up of feet of 6+4+3 and 6+4+1 syllables respectively." (McGregor 1993: 229, n. 16).

[19] "A quatrain, usually printed as two rhyming lines of verse, each containing 16 syllables." (McGregor 1993: 333, n. 19).

the Hindi Dalit literary canon not only for the fact that his writings represent many of the exigencies of a contemporary understanding of Dalit consciousness and authenticity, described above by Singh, but also because he is the necessary link that connects contemporary Dalit writing to a centuries-long north Indian Bhojpuri/Hindi literary tradition.

Conclusion

I want to reiterate the twinned endeavors of Hindi Dalit literary criticism: first, in conceptualizing and wielding the concept of Dalit consciousness as a kind of critical perspective and flexible literary category, some Hindi Dalit literary critics are both effectively re-imagining the category of Dalit literature and re-claiming authority over its boundaries; and second, constructing a sort of critical loom upon which to weave several strands from 500 years of north Indian literary history in a search for the origins of Dalit consciousness in pre-Ambedkarite literature, thereby producing the thick fabric of the "canon of Dalit consciousness." Such a fabric challenges the usual practice of Dalit historiography that routinely represent the twentieth-century north Indian Dalit sphere as lacking in import and influence. The construction of such a literary history is a reflection of the social forces behind the creation of a body of resistance texts as explained by Harlow: by establishing a centuries-long lineage of Dalit writers and tracing the development of a contemporary sense of Dalit consciousness, Dalit writers and critics are inserting themselves into a shared cultural history from which they have traditionally been excluded. Further, they are building what Harlow calls an "affiliative secular order," superimposing an intellectual history of social resistance over the more commonly assumed non-history of centuries of silent subservience based on the unquestioning assumption of a lowly caste identity from above.

The act of embodying an identity that is authentically and thus essentially "Dalit" is viewed as critical by the arbiters of the Dalit literary sphere in order to gain access to authoritative discourse of a hegemonic public sphere which regularly excludes Dalits from the processes of the exchange of ideas.[20] In the Hindi Dalit counterpublic Dalits make the privilege of authoritative discourse solely one which

[20] The continued refusal to allow Dalit voices to freely engage in the public mass communication despite their increasing economic and political power has been explicitly observed by many proponents of the Hindi Dalit counterpublic. As Dalit journalist Chandrabhan Prasad explains colorfully, "Ask a liberal newspaper editor to choose between allowing a Dalit writer to write on his opinion page or be shot dead and it is quite possible that for a fraction of a second, he might consider the latter option. A liberal captain of Indian industry, a post-modern Bollywood filmmaker and a subaltern academic don might just turn out to be like the editor in their own ways, with a few exceptions." ("A New Order for Today." *The Pioneer*. September 27, 2005).

belongs to Dalits themselves, fiercely protecting the very existence against dilution from non-Dalits, or Dalits who lack an authentic Dalit consciousness, as well as a subsequent weakening of its functions as a space of identity formation and agitation for the Dalit community. Dalit consciousness today is a thoroughly modern critical concept in the mode of deconstruction. It is an expression of denial, a theoretical tool that contributes to the destabilization of traditional notions of social hierarchy and cultural authenticity. Dalit consciousness is elemental in opposing the cultural inheritance of the upper castes, the notion that culture is a hereditary right for them, and one that is denied to Dalits. The concept of Dalit consciousness is deconstructive in its ability to clear the way for a new understanding of Dalit identity. To quote Valmiki again,

> *Dalit kī vyathā, dukh, pīḍā, shoṣaṇ kā vivaraṇ denā yā bakhān karnā hī dalit chetnā nahīṃ hai, yā dalit pīḍā kā bhāvuk aur aśru-vigalit varṇan, jo maulik chetnā se vihīn ho, chetnā kā sidhā sambandh dṛṣṭi se hotā hai jo dalitoṃ kī saṃskṛtik aitihāsik, sāmājik bhūmikā kī chavi ke tilasm ki toṛtī hai. Voh hai dalit chetnā. Dalit matlab mānavīya adhikāroṃ se vanchit, sāmājik taur par jise nakārā gayā ho. Uskī chetnā yānī dalit chetnā.*
>
> Dalit consciousness does not just make an account of or give a report on the anguish, misery, pain, and exploitation of Dalits, or draw a tear-streaked and sensitive portrait of Dalit agony; rather it is that which is absent from "original" consciousness, the simple and straightforward perspective that breaks the spell of the shadowy cultural, historical, and social roles for Dalits. That is Dalit consciousness. 'Dalit' means deprived of human rights, those who have been denied them on a social level. Their consciousness is Dalit consciousness. (2001: 29)

But as I suggested before, *this* notion of Dalit consciousness is essentialist in its very nature, positing a singular idea of how Dalits should think and write and cultivate political and personal awareness and struggle. It does not represent the alternative concerns of Dalit women, for example, who struggle within the confines of patriarchy as well as caste, nor does it represent the identity and consciousness of those materially advantaged Dalits who Dalit journalist Chandrabahn Prasad heralds as the "Dalit bourgeoisie." But the meaning of Dalit consciousness and the avenues of its theoretical application is the normative model, the one that is infiltrating the pages of Hindi literary magazines as well as the public meetings of Dalit writers in Delhi. If we are therefore to think of this essentialist representation as a strategic effort to create a unique and powerful presence of Dalit identities and voices in the fields of mainstream literary and socio-political discourse, then we must recognize the singular importance of the emergence of such a theoretical concept within the Hindi Dalit literary sphere.

Bibliography

Anand, S. (ed.) (2003), *Touchable Tales: Publishing and Reading Dalit Literature* (Chennai: Navayana).

Basu, T. (ed.) (2002), *Translating Caste: Stories, Essays, Criticism.* Vol. 2, Studies in Culture and Translation (New Delhi: Katha).

Bharti, A. (2004), "Bhimāyan: Ek Kāljayī Rachnā," *Apekṣā* 9 (Oct-Dec): 91-95.

Bharti, K. (2003), "Kṛpayā Kabīr ko Rahasyavād nā Banāye...," *Apekṣā*, 2 (Jan-March): 11-16.

Brueck, L. (2006), "Dalit Chetna in Dalit Literary Criticism," *Seminar* 558 (Feb.): 28-32.

Chatterjee, P. (2004), *The Politics of the Governed: Reflections on Popular Politics in Most of the World* (New York: Columbia University Press).

Dangle, A. (ed.) (1992), *Poisoned Bread: Translations from Modern Marathi Dalit Literature* (Hyderabad: Orient Longman).

Dharamvir (2003), "Kabir se Kati Bahas," *Apekṣā* 2 (Jan-March): 17-23.

Ganganiya, I.K. (2004), "Ambedkarvādī Rāh ke Musāfir - Jankavi Bihari Lal Harit," *Apekṣā* 9: 67-73.

Harlow, B. (1987), *Resistance Literature* (New York: Methuen).

Jaffrelot, C. (2003), *India's Silent Revolution: The Rise of the Lower Castes in North India* (New York: Columbia University Press).

Limbale, S. (2004), *Towards an Aesthetic of Dalit Literature: History, Controversies, and Considerations,* trans. A. Mukherjee, Modern Indian Writing in Translation Series (New Delhi: Orient Longman).

McGregor, R.S. (1993), Oxford Hindi-English Dictionary (New Delhi: Oxford University Press).

Meghwal, K. (1989), *Hindī Upanyāsoṃ Meṃ Dalit Varg* (Jaipur: Sanghi Prakāṣaṇ).

Mehta, D. (1989), "Differing Contexts: The Theme of Oppression in Indian Literatures," *New Comparison* 7: 79-87.

Muktibodh, S. (1992), "What Is Dalit Literature?" in *Poisoned Bread,* ed. A. Dangle (Bombay: Orient Longman), 267-70.

Naimishray, M. (Forthcoming), *Hindī Dalit Sāhitya.*

Narayan, B., and A.R. Misra (eds.) (2004), *Multiple Marginalities: An Anthology of Identified Dalit Writings* (Delhi: Manohar).

Rodrigues, V. (ed.) (2002), *The Essential Writings of B.R. Ambedkar* (New Delhi: Oxford University Press).

Singh, T. (2000), *Āj kā Dalit Sāhitya* (Delhi: Atish Prakāṣaṇ).

_____. (ed.) (2002), *Āj kā Samay: Samkālīn Dalit Kaviyoṃ kī Kavitāoṃ kā Saṇkalan* (Delhi: Sangīta Prakāṣaṇ).

_____. (2003), "Dalit Punarjagraṇ Aur Ravidās," *Apekṣā* 3: 2-8.

_____. (2004), "Jankavi Bihari Lal Harit," *Apekṣā* 9: 4-13.

_____. (2005), "Bīsvī Sadī kā Kathā-Nāyak Dalit 'Rangbhūmi' kā Sūrdās," *Apekṣā* 10 (Jan-March): 4-15.

Spivak, G.C. (1985), "Subaltern Studies: Deconstructing Historiography" in *Subaltern Studies IV*, ed. R. Guha (New Delhi: Oxford University Press), 330-63.

Valmiki, O. (2001), *Dalit Sāhitya Ka Saundaryashāstra* (Delhi: Rādhakrishna).

Zelliot, E. (1998), "The Roots of Dalit Consciousness," *Seminar* 471: 28-32.

KARLINE MCLAIN

*Young Śvetaketu in America: Learning to be Hindu in the Diaspora**

Scholars of religion have long focused their studies on sacred texts, and in this process have cast their inquiries backwards in time to seek out the oldest and, therefore, presumably the most authentic and authoritative texts. But, in so doing, they have often overlooked the contribution of later religious texts and narratives to the formation of religious beliefs and identities. This point has been astutely made by Patrick Olivelle in his article "Young Śvetaketu: A Literary Study of an Upaniṣadic Story":

> Scholars whose main goal is to uncover the most ancient versions of texts often tend to ignore later versions, even though it is these versions that provide insights into the religious, intellectual, and social history behind the texts. The story is told not just in the oldest but in the changes we can see from the older to the newer (Olivelle 1999: 47).

Śvetaketu is a character whose story is told in three different Upaniṣads: the Bṛhadāraṇyaka, the Chāndogya, and the Kauṣītaki. Whereas previous scholars were concerned with uncovering the oldest, most "authentic" account of the Śvetaketu story among the three versions, Olivelle's intervention was to demonstrate that each of these three Upaniṣadic narratives of Śvetaketu is authoritative, in that each version "has its own narrative logic from the viewpoint of the respective author, and the additions, subtractions, and modifications can be viewed as part of the narrative strategy of each author" (Olivelle 1999: 48).

* The title of this essay is inspired by Patrick Olivelle's article "Young Śvetaketu," and I thank Dr. Olivelle for working through the Upaniṣadic stories about Śvetaketu with me in great detail in our Sanskrit seminar in the fall of 1998. I also thank the comic book producers, especially Anant Pai and Dev Nadkarni, and the comic book consumers, who are cited anonymously here in order to protect their identities.

In this article, I will examine a much later version of the Śvetaketu story: the version told in the *Tales from the Upanishads* comic book (no. 392, 1987), which is part of the popular *Amar Chitra Katha* Indian comic book series. In extending this inquiry into the modern period, I intend to examine what changes have occurred in the transmission of this story over time and in the translation of this story into a new medium. Although comic books and other popular media have until recently been regarded with suspicion by many scholars of religion, I believe that by studying the narrative logic of this comic book from the point of view of its producers, and the reasons for its popularity among consumers, we can learn a lot about the meaning of the Śvetaketu story to modern-day Hindus, and, in particular, the modern practice of Hinduism in the American diaspora.

Śvetaketu in Amar Chitra Katha *Comics*

The *Amar Chitra Katha* comic book series is known and loved by millions of fans throughout India and the South Asian diaspora. It was founded as an English-language comic book series in 1967 by a pioneer named Anant Pai, who conceived of this series as a means of teaching Indian themes and values to middle-class Indian children enrolled in English-medium schools. These children, he feared, were learning Western mythology and history at the expense of their own. In 1978, the Union Minister of Education, Dr. Pratap Chandra Chunder, endorsed the use of this comic book series in the Indian school system, stating, "there are biographies of great men from different parts of the country; there are tales from Sanskrit; classics and folktales of various regions—all of which could help in promoting national integration" ("The Role of Chitra Katha in School Education" 1978: 2). Since this time, *Amar Chitra Katha* has dominated the flourishing Indian comic book market, selling over 440 titles and more than 86 million issues. In India, these comic books can be purchased at posh bookstores in urban cities, and at roadside stalls in smaller cities and villages. They have been endorsed by numerous politicians and educators, and are increasingly being used in English-medium schools. In North America, these comic books can be found in Indian grocery stores, restaurants, community centers, and Hindu temples; they are also regularly purchased online for direct international mail order by the parents and grandparents of Hindu children at www.amarchitrakatha.com and at the websites of other online retailers.

Amar Chitra Katha means "Immortal Picture Stories," and this comic book series has captured the attention of so many children, parents, and educators because these comics were the first to feature India's own immortal heroes—its mythological gods and historical leaders—as protagonists. The first comic books in the series were mythological in nature, recasting classical Sanskrit narratives of Hindu deities like Ram, Krishna, and Hanuman in the comic book format.

Over the years, the series has expanded to include issues on a variety of other subjects: celebrated Hindu kings such as Shivaji and Rana Pratap; medieval bhakti poets like Tulsidas; modern Hindu sages like Swami Vivekananda; animal fables from the *Pañcatantra*; and colonial-era nationalist heroes including Subhas Chandra Bose, Lokamanya Tilak, and Mahatma Gandhi. Although there are issues on Sikh gurus and Mughal emperors, the comic book series is predominantly Hindu.[1]

Within the *Amar Chitra Katha* corpus there are several issues that retell Upaniṣadic stories, including *Nachiketa and Other Stories* (no. 201, 1979) and *Tales from the Upanishads* (no. 392, 1987). Both of these comic books have been reprinted numerous times, and have been renumbered as part of the reprinting of "deluxe editions" (with fancier covers, better paper stock, and higher prices) of successful comics in this series that has been ongoing since 1994. When I interviewed Anant Pai, he stated that of these comics, *Tales from the Upanishads* has been the most successful, and he attributed its success in part to the use of the word "Upanishads" in the title:

> *Tales of the Upanishads* has done well because people want to learn about the Upanishads. These are the basis of Hinduism, they teach about the unity of atman and brahman—do you know "tat tvam asi?" "That art thou." Atman is the self, but it is really the same as brahman, the Godhead that is the root of everything. So, people see the title and they think, "I should read this and learn about the Upanishads"; or, "I should buy this for my child." That is why I make these comics, to educate (Pai, interviewed by the author in 2002).

Anant Pai felt that having the word "Upanishads" in the title of this comic book was so important in terms of customer appeal that when *Nachiketa and Other Stories* was reprinted in the deluxe edition format, he modified the title to *Nachiketa and Other Tales from the Upanishads* (no. 702). But in Anant Pai's opinion, the appeal of *Tales from the Upanishads* goes far beyond the title, as he revealed when I asked him who his intended audience was for this comic book—Hindus specifically, or Indians more generally:

> All Indians should be proud of the Upanishads, not just Hindus. Of course, they are sacred texts for Hindus, but anyone can learn from the Upanishads—not just in India, but anyone in the world can learn from Shvetaketu's example. Shvetaketu teaches children not to think that there is ever a time to stop learning, that you should be learning from your elders for your whole lifetime. This is a universal value (Pai, interviewed by the author in 2002).

[1] For an in-depth discussion of the *Amar Chitra Katha* comic book series, see McLain (2009b). On the production of the *Krishna* (no. 11) issue in the *Amar Chitra Katha* series in particular, see McLain (2005); on the issues about Mahatma Gandhi, see McLain (2007); on the *Tales of Durga* (no. 176) issue, see McLain (2008). For a discussion of *Amar Chitra Katha* as compared with another Indian comic book series, *Vivalok Comics*, see McLain (2009a).

For Anant Pai, the classical Sanskrit stories of Śvetaketu are clearly still worth telling, to both Hindus and non-Hindus. After examining the narrative strategy of the comic book version of this story, I will return to the subject of its meaning and value to Hindus today.

In the *Tales from the Upanishads* issue, "Shvetaketu" is the first story, followed by three others: "Raikva the Cartman," "When the Devas were Humbled," and "The Bold Beggar." The title of each story is marked with an asterisk, which explains at the bottom of the page which Upaniṣad each story is drawn from. The third story is drawn from the Kena Upaniṣad, and the rest are based on the Chāndogya Upaniṣad. When I interviewed the author of this script, Dev Nadkarni, nearly twenty years after it was originally written, he could still recall some of the sources he'd used in conducting the research for this issue, and primary among them was R.E. Hume's classic translation of the Upaniṣads, which was first published in 1921 and has been reprinted dozens of times:

> I referred to several texts, but the main source was *The Thirteen Principal Upanishads*. I think it was R.E. Hume who edited it. Incidentally, this was the book given me by a thoughtful colleague as a birthday gift just as I was beginning to write the script. I also recall having referred to Dr. S. Radhakrishnan's and R.D. Ranade's works—can't recall which ones though. Additionally, I had the important advantage of consulting my father, who has a Master's degree in Sanskrit literature and Indian philosophy (Nadkarni, interviewed by the author in 2006).

Mr. Nadkarni stated that in writing this script, he chose to focus primarily on the Chāndogya Upaniṣad because he was drawn to its narrative nature, and especially to the story of Śvetaketu:

> Chandogya happens to be one of the most important Upanishads and is also one that is replete with stories, unlike Isa and Kena. Its stories also seek to dwell on that connection between what Indian commentators like to describe as the "gross" and the "subtle" nature of things—what appears and does not, what is and is not, the fundamental singularity that we fail to see as a result of the interplay of our senses that attach us to all things worldly. Shvetaketu's dialogue with Uddalaka Aruni is one of the most beautiful conversations in all Upanishadic literature—the idea of how a mighty tree, "the gross," can spring out of nothingness, "the subtle," cannot be put across more simply (Nadkarni, interviewed by the author in 2006).

The "Shvetaketu" comic book story is based on the sixth chapter of the Chāndogya Upaniṣad, and this chapter does indeed contain conversations, metaphors, and—perhaps most importantly—characters that can be translated into a mixed (textual and visual) medium. In fact, the character Śvetaketu is one of the best-known characters from the Upaniṣads; according to Patrick Olivelle, young Śvetaketu is the "quintessential 'spoiled little brat' of ancient Indian literature" (Olivelle 1999: 69).

The first page of *Tales from the Upanishads* opens with the scene of an idyllic forest hermitage, where an elder sage—Uddālaka Āruṇi—is seated on the front porch studying scriptures, while a boy—the young Śvetaketu—chases a butterfly through the flowers. In the next panel, Uddālaka Āruṇi glances up at Śvetaketu, and decides that he is now old enough, at twelve years of age, to pursue the study of the sacred scriptures. Āruṇi calls Śvetaketu to him and tells him, "Dear child, every one in our family has without exception studied the scriptures and imbibed their meaning" (p. 1). He then sends young Śvetaketu away to study under another sage, with instructions to "Go forth son, and come back bright and resplendent, with the knowledge of the Brahman" (p. 2). The next several panels show us how Śvetaketu spent the next twelve years: reading scriptures, learning the sciences, and mastering the arts. In the large panel on the bottom of the second page, Śvetaketu is seated, with scriptures spread out on the floor in front of him. Here he is now clearly no longer a boy of twelve, but a young man of twenty-four, for he has an adult's stature and has grown a mustache. The narrative text at the top of this panel tells us that "At the end of twelve years, Shvetaketu had learnt all that there was to learn—at least, so he thought" (p. 2). This text forewarns us of Śvetaketu's arrogance, as does the thought balloon emanating from Śvetaketu, who is no longer reading the scripture in front of him, but is instead thinking to himself, "I have now mastered nearly everything that a man can study" (p. 2)!

After Śvetaketu returns to his father's hermitage, he falls at Āruṇi's feet and then proceeds to tell him how his studies went, stating that he has "mastered all the arts and sciences" and that he knows "everything that can be known" (p. 3). Upon hearing this, Āruṇi is alarmed at Śvetaketu's arrogance. The panel after Śvetaketu's outburst shows a close-up shot of a pensive Āruṇi, thinking to himself, "What pride! Such conceit is born only out of ignorance… This boy has not grasped the essence of the supreme knowledge—Brahman" (p. 3). Āruṇi, therefore, decides to give Śvetaketu a pop quiz about the nature of *ātman* and *brahman*, asking him if he possesses the knowledge by which "what is unknown becomes known; what is unseen becomes seen" (p. 3). In the next panel, Śvetaketu suddenly falls at his father's feet upon realizing that he cannot answer this question and therefore does not know everything. At the top of the fourth page, Śvetaketu begs Āruṇi to share this advanced knowledge with him.

Despite the spatial and textual limitations of the comic book medium, which usually mandate a substantial reduction or simplification of narrative storylines, these first three pages of the *Tales from the Upanishads* comic book are based fairly closely on the first verses of the sixth chapter of the Chāndogya Upaniṣad, as they are here translated by Patrick Olivelle (6.1.1-3):

> There was one Śvetaketu, the son of Āruṇi. One day his father told him: 'Śvetaketu, take up the celibate life of a student, for there is no one in

> our family, my son, who has not studied and is the kind of Brahmin who is so only because of birth.' So he went away to become a student at the age of 12 and, after learning all the Vedas, returned when he was 24, swell-headed, thinking himself to be learned, and arrogant. His father then said to him: 'Śvetaketu, here you are, my son, swell-headed, thinking yourself to be learned, and arrogant; so you must have surely asked about that rule of substitution by which one hears what has not been heard before, thinks of what has not been thought of before, and perceives what has not been perceived before?' (Olivelle 1996: 148).

In the comic book version, the core plot of this story is kept in tact, as are the emotions—Śvetaketu's arrogance, and his father's deep concern with that arrogance. Furthermore, in the Chāndogya Upaniṣad, after Āruṇi has asked his son about the "rule of substitution," Śvetaketu politely inquires (6.1.4): "How indeed does that rule of substitution work, sir?" (Olivelle 1996: 148). Śvetaketu's verbal politeness here in the original text is mirrored by his physical politeness in the comic book, where he falls at Āruṇi's feet to express his respect for his father and his sincere desire to learn from him. Patrick Olivelle has pointed out that this transformation of Śvetaketu's character in the sixth chapter of the Chāndogya Upaniṣad—from an arrogant know-it-all or "spoiled little brat" into a good student—is noteworthy, in that it is unique to the telling of Śvetaketu's story in this Upaniṣad. He argues that for the authors of the Chāndogya Upaniṣad (unlike the authors of the Bṛhadāraṇyaka and Kauṣītaki Upaniṣads), Uddālaka Āruṇi was both a good student and a great teacher, and thus was able to eventually teach even a difficult student like Śvetaketu: "Instead of acting like the spoiled brat of the earlier story, here Śvetaketu becomes a 'good student,' able to confess his ignorance and to learn from his teacher" (Olivelle 1999:67).

For the remainder of the "Shvetaketu" story in the comic book, Āruṇi illustrates the nature of *ātman* and *brahman* to Śvetaketu using an array of examples that are drawn from the Chāndogya Upaniṣad, and Śvetaketu proves to be an ideal student. First, as the two sit in their modest house, Āruṇi points out the clay pots and toys that are lined up against one wall. He explains to Śvetaketu that these pots and toys were created out of one essence, clay: "toys and vessels are merely different names given to it" (p. 4). Together, father and son then leave the hermitage and set out on a walk, where they pass by an artisan working at a potter's wheel. Āruṇi pauses in his tracks in the next panel in order to explain that as it is with clay, so also it is with gold and iron. Āruṇi then begins walking again, while he concludes, "Therefore, my child, you must get to know the essence of all things—the one thing that exists in everything in this universe" (p. 4).

This first example about the nature of ultimate reality in the *Tales from the Upanishads* comic book is derived from verses 6.1.4-6 of the Chāndogya Upaniṣad, wherein Āruṇi begins to instruct Śvetaketu after he has asked his father to explain the rule of substitution:

> 'It is like this, son. By means of just one lump of clay one would perceive everything made of clay—the transformation is a verbal handle, a name—while the reality is just this: "It's clay."
> 'It is like this, son. By means of just one copper trinket one would perceive everything made of copper—the transformation is a verbal handle, a name—while the reality is just this: "It's copper."
> 'It is like this, son. By means of just one nail-cutter one would perceive everything made of iron—the transformation is a verbal handle, a name—while the reality is just this: "It's iron."
> 'That, son, is how this rule of substitution works' (Olivelle 1996: 148).

In the comic book, the producers have worked to translate this conversation into a sequence of visual images. By inserting images of Āruṇi and Śvetaketu looking at clay toys in one panel, and an artisan hard at work creating pots out of clay in another panel, they have inserted visual activity into an otherwise static dialogue. But in doing so, the author and artist have worked together to preserve the core message that a potter can indeed create any number of things from a lump of clay—a large water pot, a small vessel, a clay toy—but ultimately, all of these things share a common nature.

After this first lesson, however, Śvetaketu states that he doesn't yet understand the nature of ultimate reality. So, as the "Shvetaketu" comic book story continues, Āruṇi and Śvetaketu proceed on their walk, and at the top of page five they arrive at a riverbank. Here, Āruṇi explains to his son that just as rivers eventually merge into the ocean and lose their individual identities, so too are we part of a larger truth. Then, walking further, Āruṇi and Śvetaketu happen upon a large tree, which is being struck by a man with a knife and a pail. Āruṇi takes advantage of this scene to explain that when one strikes a tree, it discharges a little sap, but continues to live and draw upon the earth for its nourishment. However, Āruṇi continues as they next walk by a dead tree, "when life forsakes one of its branches, it dries up" and "when the entire tree is forsaken by life, the whole tree dries up" (p. 6). In the next panel, a group in mourning is depicted walking down the road, carrying a corpse on a bier. Āruṇi continues the lesson: "Similarly, my son, when life forsakes the body, it dies. But life does not die… That which does not die is atman. You are that atman, which is all-pervasive" (p. 6).

On these two comic book pages, the lessons about the nature of ultimate reality are taken from passages 6.10 and 6.11 of the Chāndogya Upaniṣad. These are short and simple passages that translate well into such a visual medium. For instance, in verses 6.11.2-3, Āruṇi describes the nature of *ātman* using the example of the tree:

> 'When, however, life (*jīva*) leaves one of its branches, that branch withers away. When it leaves a second branch, that likewise withers away, and when it leaves a third branch, that also withers away. When it leaves the entire tree, the whole tree withers away.'
> 'In exactly the same way,' he continued, 'know that this, of course, dies

> when it is bereft of life (*jīva*); but life itself does not die.
> 'The finest essence here—that constitutes the self of this whole world; that is the truth; that is the self (*ātman*). And that's how you are, Śvetaketu' (Olivelle 1996: 153-4).

In this section of the comic book dealing with the tree and the corpse, the scriptwriter has cleverly divided up Āruṇi's lesson, placing a verse in each of seven panels, either as the spoken dialogue balloon in the panels depicting Āruṇi, or as the narrative text at the top of the panel when Āruṇi is not depicted. Thus, the lesson is brought to life visually. Multiple panels of stark tree branches cutting across dark skies—followed by the creative insertion of a panel featuring mourners walking along a barren road carrying a corpse on a bier—are poetic images that provoke an emotional response to the harsh reality of death on the part of the reader. And yet, the last panel on this sixth page is reassuring. Here we return to our protagonists, Āruṇi and Śvetaketu. While Śvetaketu watches the mourners walk into the distant horizon, Āruṇi comforts him—and the reader as well—with his lesson that *ātman* does not die, and that Śvetaketu—and presumably the reader too—is that *ātman.*[2] Comforted, but also curious, the reader will ideally continue on to the next lesson on the nature of reality along with Śvetaketu.

In the next panel, on the top of the seventh page, Śvetaketu asks his father to explain further why this *ātman* is all-pervasive, but can't be seen. At this point, Āruṇi looks around and points to a banyan tree that is nearby, asking his son to bring him one of its fruits. Śvetaketu does so, and then his father tells him to break it in half, and asks him what he sees. Śvetaketu holds the split fruit in his hand, and then peers into it in the next panel, telling his father that he sees many tiny seeds. Āruṇi next tells Śvetaketu to break a seed in half, and then tell him what he sees. Again, a close-up of Śvetaketu's hand is shown, this time with miniscule seeds in it: seeds that are so small that nothing can be seen in one that has been split in two. Śvetaketu reports this to his father. Āruṇi then asks his son, "If there is nothing in the seed, how can that nothing give rise to a mighty banyan tree?" (p. 8). He goes on to explain to Śvetaketu that it is this "something" that we cannot see that "is the essence of all things—the atman—that pervades the universe, you too are that, O Shvetaketu!" (p. 8).

Here the scriptwriter, Dev Nadkarni, has based this scene on the conversation that he found so beautiful in section 6.12 of the Chāndogya Upaniṣad, wherein Āruṇi teaches Śvetaketu about the mighty tree that springs out of nothingness:

[2] One significant philosophical difference emerges here in the translation of the Sanskrit phrase *tat tvam asi,* rendered by the comic book producers as "you too are that," which builds upon the most common translation of the phrase as "that art thou"; while Patrick Olivelle translates it as "and that's how you are." For a discussion of the significance of this phrase and its interpretations, see Brereton (1986).

> 'Bring a banyan fruit.'
> 'Here it is, sir.'
> 'Cut it up.'
> 'I've cut it up, sir.'
> 'What do you see there?'
> 'These quite tiny seeds, sir.'
> 'Now, take one of them and cut it up.'
> 'I've cut one up, sir.'
> 'What do you see there?'
> 'Nothing, sir.'
> Then he told him: 'This finest essence here, son, that you can't even see—look how on account of that finest essence this huge banyan tree stands here.
> 'Believe, my son: the finest essence here—that constitutes the self of this whole world; that is the truth; that is the self (*ātman*). And that's how you are, Śvetaketu' (Olivelle 1996: 154).

At this point in the comic book story, Śvetaketu and Āruṇi arrive back at their forest hermitage at the conclusion of their walk. But Śvetaketu still has a question for his father, one that requires one final metaphor. Śvetaketu asks his learned father about this essence that cannot be seen: "...if we cannot see the essence, how do we know that it exists?" (p. 8). In response, Āruṇi points to a lump of salt, and tells Śvetaketu to put it in a nearby pot of water, and then to look at it the next morning. After Śvetaketu wakes up the next day, he eagerly peers into the pot, but cannot see the salt. His father tells him to take a drink of water from the top, the middle, and the bottom of the pot. In three separate panels, Śvetaketu does so, reporting each time that the water is salty. Yet, he still cannot see the salt, for it has dissolved. On the top of the tenth page, Āruṇi finally explains the lesson, that *ātman* is like the salt that has dissolved in the pot of water: "... you cannot see the essence. But it is always present everywhere ... This omnipresent essence is atman, that pervades everything. You too are that, O Shvetaketu" (p. 10).

This final lesson involving the saltwater is derived from section 6.13 of the Chāndogya Upaniṣad. In this short section, Āruṇi does tell Śvetaketu to throw a chunk of salt in a pot of water, and then check on it the next morning, once it has dissolved: "'Now, take a sip from this corner,' said the father. 'How does it taste?'" (Olivelle 1996: 154). Śvetaketu takes a sip from the centre and from another corner, and after each sip reports that the water is salty. His father replies:

> "You, of course, did not see it [the salt] there, son; yet it was always right there. The finest essence here—that constitutes the self of this whole world; that is the truth; that is the self (*ātman*). And that's how you are, Śvetaketu" (Olivelle 1996: 155).

As in the previous lessons, the comic book scriptwriter and artist have brought this lesson about the nature of reality to life by transferring the text of the Chāndogya Upaniṣad into the dialogue balloons in the sequential panels, and by drawing out the imagery implicit in the text: the pot of water that sits on the front porch of the forest hermitage, and Śvetaketu's curious face as he peers into that pot of water again and again.

At the conclusion of the "Shvetaketu" comic book story, Śvetaketu once again falls at his father's feet, this time to express his gratitude for these lessons on the nature of *ātman* and *brahman*: "You have helped me gain the knowledge with which the unknown becomes known, the unseen becomes seen" (p. 10). In the Chāndogya Upaniṣad, at the conclusion of each lesson Śvetaketu politely asks his father, "Sir, teach me more"; and Āruṇi's response is, "Very well, son." After the final lesson, when Āruṇi again tells his son, "and that's how you are, Śvetaketu," the author concludes the chapter with this comment (6.16.3): "And he did, indeed, learn it from him" (Olivelle 1996: 156). The authors of the Chāndogya Upaniṣad don't mention that Śvetaketu fell at Āruṇi's feet in gratitude; however, the text does present Śvetaketu as a person who has clearly come to respect his father and his father's wisdom. In both the comic book and the sixth chapter of the Chāndogya Upaniṣad, Śvetaketu is transformed from an arrogant young man into a deferential adult, who is full of respect for his father's wisdom.

Thus, the comic book producers have been perhaps surprisingly faithful, given the spatial and textual limitations of this medium, to the Chāndogya Upaniṣad as they have recast the "Shvetaketu" story in the *Tales from the Upanishads* comic book. They have used the text of the Chāndogya Upaniṣad as the clear basis for the narrative text and dialogue balloons in the comic book panels, and as the inspiration behind such visual images as the forest hermitage, artisan, tree, and corpse. However, in creating the "Shvetaketu" comic book story, the scriptwriter and other producers selectively chose the passages from the sixth chapter of the Chāndogya Upaniṣad that they wanted to portray. As we have seen, sections 6.1 and 6.10 to 6.13 are the basis for the comic book narrative, while 6.2 to 6.9 and 6.14 to 6.16 are left out. What happens in these passages? Why did the scriptwriter decide not to include them? It is important to briefly examine the passages that have been excluded, in order to better understand the editorial decisions made in the making of the *Tales from the Upanishads* comic book.

In passages 6.2 to 6.4, Āruṇi delivers a cosmological discourse on the creation of the universe and the creatures within it. In these passages, Śvetaketu is a passive recipient of this wisdom; he does not appear even to ask for more instruction or clarification. In fact, it is not until the very end of 6.5, when Āruṇi has moved on to a discussion of the nature of food, that Śvetaketu speaks up once again, asking to be taught further. Hence, Āruṇi goes on to discuss food, its function in the human body, and the nature of hunger and thirst in 6.6 to 6.8. At the end of 6.8, Śvetaketu speaks up once more, again asking his father for further instruction. These passages present a lengthy monologue, one that cannot be easily converted to the comic book medium that relies upon dialogue as a narrative technique. Furthermore, in these complex passages there are few images for an artist to grasp hold of in order to translate the text into a series of visual panels. For instance, how would one illustrate verse 6.8.3, on the nature of hunger and thirst?

> Son, learn from me about hunger and thirst. When one says here: "The man is hungry", then the water drives away with what he has eaten. So, just as one calls someone a "cattle-driver", or a "horse-driver", or a "man-driver", similarly one calls water "hunger"—the "food-driver" (Olivelle 996: 152).

It is only with passage 6.9 that Āruṇi begins to use natural metaphors in order to teach Śvetaketu about the nature of the self and ultimate reality. In 6.9, Āruṇi begins with the example of bees preparing honey, explaining that although bees take nectar from many different trees, the honey that is produced is one undifferentiated existence. This then leads to 6.10, wherein Āruṇi discusses how different rivers merge into one ocean, thereby losing their individual identities. And like the honey or the ocean, we, too, are part of a larger truth. It is here—with tangible, natural metaphors like the rivers and the ocean, the dying tree, the banyan fruit seeds, and the saltwater experiment—that the comic book producers have found their inspiration for the "Shvetaketu" story.

Passages 6.14 to 6.16 in the Chāndogya Upaniṣad stray from this focus on the natural environment surrounding the forest hermitage. Instead, they shift to an urban scene, using a different human metaphor in each passage to further elaborate upon the nature of the self: a blind man from the land of Gandhāra, an ill man, and a handcuffed man who is perhaps a criminal. In excluding these passages, as well as passages 6.2 to 6.9, the "Shvetaketu" comic book story clearly does not tell the full story of Śvetaketu's lesson as it is found in the sixth chapter of the Chāndogya Upaniṣad. And in so excluding these passages, the comic book certainly cannot convey the extent of the philosophical discussion in this chapter of the Upaniṣad. However, if one of the fundamental messages of the Chāndogya Upaniṣad is the importance of vedic studentship (*brahmacarya*)—the importance of learning how to be a good student and how to recognize a good teacher—as Patrick Olivelle has argued (Olivelle 1999: 66), then the comic book creators have indeed retained this focus in their modern retelling of Śvetaketu's story.

Śvetaketu as a Modern Role Model

As we've seen, it was this very lesson about the importance of being a good student that made the Śvetaketu story so appealing to Anant Pai, the founding editor of the *Amar Chitra Katha* series, in the first place. Scriptwriter Dev Nadkarni, who first proposed this comic book title, also believed that young comic book readers could easily understand this lesson through Śvetaketu:

> When I first mooted the idea to the editorial team, it was viewed a bit skeptically because my senior colleagues—I was 23 then and that was my first job!—wondered how such abstruse philosophical concepts could be put across to children in the comic book format. But I was encouraged to try it out and wrote a couple of stories which appeared to read well. Actually, it was surprisingly straightforward because the original writers themselves had adopted the time-tested technique of wrapping philosophical concepts in the alluring format of the parable. It is amazing how much well-told stories can convey. Upanishadic characters like Nachiketa and Shvetaketu are both youngsters with a keen desire for the acquisition of knowledge—characters that are not difficult for young readers to identify with (Nadkarni, interviewed by the author in 2006).

Śvetaketu is held up as a role model for today's children by these comic book producers because he is able to shed his arrogance and realize that he has much to learn from his father, Āruṇi. Like "Shvetaketu," the following three stories in the *Tales from the Upanishads* issue—"Raikva the Cartman," "When the Devas were Humbled," and "The Bold Beggar"—also highlight this central theme of the Chāndogya Upaniṣad: the importance of being a good student.

In his discussion of the centrality of studentship to the Chāndogya Upaniṣad, Patrick Olivelle has pointed out that one of the central motifs particular to this Upaniṣad is the idea that "knowledge can come from unexpected and unlikely places":

> So, the great humanitarian Jānaśruti has to beg the comic character Raikva of uncertain ancestry to instruct him (*CU* 4.1-2); Jābāla is taught by bulls and birds (*CU* 4.4-9) and Upakosala by the sacred fires (*CU* 4.10-15); Baka is taught by a dog *CU* 1.12), and, of course, brahmins are taught by kings (*CU* 1.8-9; 5.11-24) (Olivelle 1999: 66-67).

This focus on knowledge being located in unexpected places is a theme that unites all four of the stories that the producers chose to feature in *Tales from the Upanishads*. The introduction to the comic book stresses this fact:

> The stories selected for this volume amply illustrate the fact that the sages in those bygone days were imbued with the spirit of scientific enquiry and there is also implicit acknowledgement of the fact that knowledge is not the monopoly of any select group. For example, in one of the stories, Raikva, a cart driver, is approached with humility by one of the great kings of his time, Janashruti, with the request to impart knowledge about Brahman (inside front cover).

Following "Shvetaketu," the second story in *Tales from the Upanishads* is "Raikva the Cartman," which is based on passages 4.1 to 4.2 of the Chāndogya Upaniṣad. In the comic book telling of this story, King Jānaśruti eventually finds his teacher in the commoner Raikva, who agrees to instruct the king in the nature of ultimate reality only after he learns humility and sheds his "royal ego" (p. 18). Whereas the first story, "Shvetaketu," taught respect for one's parents and elders more generally, this one teaches the reader to respect people no matter their class or occupation.

The third story, "When the Devas were Humbled," is based on chapters 3 and 4 of the Kena Upaniṣad. In this bold story, it is the gods themselves who must learn humility. After a victorious battle with the asuras, the gods are "intoxicated by their success" (p. 21) and believe their powers are invincible. It takes a complete stranger—who is the universal essence *brahman* in disguise—to teach them the limits of their powers and the nature of ultimate reality. Here, the reader learns that any stranger could possess great wisdom.

Finally, the fourth story in *Tales from the Upanishads* is "The Bold Beggar." Based on verses 4.3.5-8 in the Chāndogya Upaniṣad, this short story relates the tale of two wise old sages, Śaunaka Kāpeya and Abhiprātin Kākṣaseni, who are ultimately taught a lesson about the nature of ultimate reality by a young vedic student who appears on the doorstep of their forest hermitage begging for food. The comic book ends with these final words: "And the sages, who so far had only understood the literal meaning of the scriptures, realized then the spirit behind the words. Ashamed at their ignorance, they gladly shared their food with the young brahmana [brahmin student]" (p. 30).

Overall, these four stories teach the young comic book reader that like Śvetaketu, they too must overcome their arrogance and learn to be good students. And being a good student entails recognizing that wise teachers can be found in some unexpected places: they can be our parents, they can be working-class folks, they can be strangers, and they can be our juniors in society. Thus the moral of the *Tales from the Upanishads* comic book is that all of these people deserve our attention, for any one of them may be able to instruct us in the nature of ultimate reality. This theme is present in the *Nachiketa and Other Stories* comic book as well, where (in a story based on the first two chapters of the Kaṭha Upaniṣad) the young boy Naciketas finds a teacher in perhaps the most unexpected of persons: Yama, the God of Death.

But for scriptwriter Dev Nadkarni, the importance of retelling the Śvetaketu story in the comic book format is twofold: First, it teaches children who read this comic book the important moral lesson of good studentship. This is a lesson that he and founding editor Anant Pai both feel is universal—a child of any religion or cultural background can read this comic book and understand this lesson. Second, it teaches Hindu children, in particular, some of the basic philosophy of the sacred Upaniṣadic scriptures:

> The Upanishads, like the Vedas, are considered revered works by most Hindus. But few would be as familiar with them as they would be with

> epics like the Ramayana or the Mahabharata—or the Hindus' most holy book, the Bhagavad Gita. The Gita, in fact, incorporates many of the ideas discussed in the Upanishads and for many Hindus, this is perhaps their only exposure to Upanishadic and Vedantic thought (Nadkarni, interviewed by the author in 2006).

As Mr. Nadkarni points out, most Hindus today have not learned Sanskrit and have not studied Hindu sacred scriptures—indeed, it is a very small percentage of the Hindu population that undergoes vedic studentship, as Śvetaketu did. Nor do many Hindus read the Upaniṣads in English translation. Instead, the religious scriptures that the majority of Hindus are familiar with today are those stories that they learn through everyday encounters: epic stories about the Hindu gods from the Mahābhārata and the Rāmāyaṇa that are performed during important Hindu festivals, that are told to children as bedtime tales by their parents and grandparents, that are cast in the filmic medium or serialized in Indian TV shows, and that are recast in comic book format.

For Hindus living outside of India, where there is often not a temple and a priest just around the corner, it can be especially difficult to receive a religious education. In America, this is now beginning to change. Hindu temples have been constructed in dozens of cities during the past several decades, and these temples now act as sites for the celebration of major Hindu festivals, the regular worship of Hindu gods, and the religious education of Hindu children.[3] Furthermore, advances in satellite television and DVD technology have recently made available mythological films and television shows to Hindus throughout the diaspora. However, my own research with Hindus in the American diaspora has shown that for two generations now, the *Amar Chitra Katha* comic books have been a central component in their religious education. Long before they could be purchased over the Internet, and before there was a local Hindu temple, Indian community center, or grocer to stock them on their shelves, these comic books began to arrive in America: grandparents shipped them from India to their grandchildren; parents and children lugged them home in their suitcases after summer visits to India; and children passed each precious issue around to share them with their cousins and friends. For the past two generations, these comic books have played a key role in teaching Hindu children in America and elsewhere what it means to be a good child, and, more specifically, what it means to be a good Hindu (see McLain 2009b).

A mother of two Hindu children raised here in America expressed the importance of the *Amar Chitra Katha* comic books to me in these words:

[3] Two recent and excellent studies of Hindu temples in the American diaspora include Waghorne (2004) and Dempsey (2005).

> We as parents raised two children with stories from *Amar Chitra Katha* comics, and till this day we reminisce with them about moral stories to see how much impact these stories have had on their upbringing. These comic books when read to children will make them without drugs, hate, and juvenile crime. They make them proud of their Hindu culture. After our children left home, we have donated them to temples (interviewed by the author in 2001).

Again and again in the interviews that I conducted with Hindus in America, I was told of the moral value of these *Amar Chitra Katha* comic books. Here I cite another American Hindu, a young man in his twenties who grew up reading these comic books:

> I have been reading them since I was a toddler. My mom says I was gifted a few of the comics for my second birthday and I used to browse through them and pester my mom to tell the story. In a nutshell, I think these comics convey the morals and succinct values of Hinduism and the traditions and cultures of India. My appreciation of the rich and glorious history and tradition of India and Hinduism has been bolstered primarily by *Amar Chitra Katha* comics. I am sure many others of my generation feel the same (interviewed by the author in 2001).

Indeed, many Hindus of his generation do agree that the *Amar Chitra Katha* comic books have been one of the foremost sources in their religious and moral education. One nineteen-year-old explained to me, "We new generation of kids find [the] Indian past and thoughts outdated, but these comics beautifully depict our stories, giving us a lot of information!" (interviewed by the author in 2002). Another, a twenty-four-year old Indian-born Hindu man who now lives in Texas, stated: "I didn't really buy into worship like most devoted Hindus, though I didn't want to offend my parents trying to be different either. I'd strongly think my moral yardsticks would probably be attributed to comics like these instead of those visits to the temple or religious instruction" (interviewed by the author in 2002). For many of these teenage, twenty- and thirty-something Hindus living in America, the *Amar Chitra Katha* comic books are so important not just because they depict sacred events and figures, but because they are themselves sacred artifacts! On this point I cite one more comic book consumer, an Indian-born Hindu woman, in her early thirties, who now lives in Illinois:

> *Amar Chitra Katha* has been with me from when I was a little child. It continues to be my most favorite. Nothing matches up to it! *Amar Chitra Katha* makes an Indian proud of his or her heritage. First among the values taught, love and trust in God—how many stories of this in *Amar Chitra Katha*! Next, the stories of valor, sacrifice, courage, humility set an example for all people to follow. My eyes become moist thinking of the good that *Amar Chitra Katha* has done to India's children. *Amar Chitra Katha* is not just a book. It radiates a spiritual force (interviewed by the author in 2002).

For millions of Hindus in America, as in other diaspora communities and even in urban India, the *Amar Chitra Katha* comic books are an important means by which they have encountered the sacred in their everyday lives, and also learned more universal morals and values. If we as scholars were to simply dismiss these comic books because they are popular culture, because they are not the oldest, most "authentic" versions of sacred Hindu scriptures, then we will fail to understand how Hinduism is practiced today, and what these classical scriptures and stories mean to modern Hindus.

What, then, does the Śvetaketu story in the *Tales from the Upanishads* comic book issue mean to modern Hindus? In my interviews with American Hindus, several of them brought up the Śvetaketu story; each time, the moral of the story was either said to be respect for one's parents or elders, or being a good student, or some combination thereof. Here is one man's discussion of the moral value of the *Amar Chitra Katha* series in general, and the Śvetaketu story in particular:

> *Amar Chitra Katha* [*ACK*] was my first comic and whenever I get a chance I still read them. I am 32, still I enjoy the illustrations, the stories and the message which *ACK* gives in each story without loosing the essence. It is the only value-for-money comics which brings our glorious culture and tradition back to life for normal people. A picture is worth a thousand words, of course. *ACK* teaches the basic Hindu values of respecting the elders and humbleness, like the story of Shvetaketu; truthfulness, like the story of Harishchandra; and vegetarianism to an extent by making us love animals too, with the Panchatantra tales (interviewed by the author, 2002).

Here is another comic book consumer, a reader in his twenties who has lived in India, Australia, and now America, and who continues to collect these comic books and keep them with him whenever he moves:

> I have a huge collection of *Amar Chitra Katha* comics which has been growing and which I have been reading since I was 2 years old. They teach the values arising from the original Vedic culture ... *Amar Chitra Katha* is about bringing facts of Vedic history to the masses ... Like in *Tales from the Upanishads*. It teaches the Upanishads, and the moral values of Vedic Indians, that we too should respect today. Like Shvetaketu, who learns that he doesn't know everything, that he must learn from his father, and when he finally learns to respect his father then he learns what life is really all about (interviewed by the author, 2002).

Thus, for both the comic book readers, as for the comic book producers, the Śvetaketu story is still relevant today because the simple lesson of being a good student is just as important now as it was in classical India. And this lesson—which may have universal appeal—is perceived by many to be a distinctly Hindu value because it has been preserved in Hindu scriptures and passed on from one generation of Hindus to the next.

Conclusion: Śvetaketu in America

In recent years, several scholars have raised concerns about the potential of popular media to severely impact or even eliminate the tradition of narrative liberalism that undergirds Hinduism in particular and South Asian culture more generally. For instance, in addition to Vālmīki's Rāmāyaṇa, the Sanskrit epic story that scholars believe to be the earliest narrative of the Hindu god Ram, there are hundreds of other versions of this story in South Asia and beyond—from early Buddhist versions that redefine Ram as the Buddha himself in a previous life to anti-colonial Bengali versions that turn Ram into the villain and the antagonist Ravana into the hero; from women's oral songs about the hardships that Ram's wife Sita must endure to Hindu nationalist versions that transform the Hindu god-king Ram into a national hero; from epic scenes carved on classical temple walls and premodern Ram Lila plays to modern televised, filmed, and comic book renditions of the story.[4] However, when the televised "Ramayan" serial (directed by Ramanand Sagar, 1987) aired on India's state-run network, Doordarshan, Romila Thapar feared that the overwhelming popularity of this new rendition of the narrative could overshadow the pluralistic Rāmāyaṇa tradition. This was particularly troubling, she argued, because the state was presenting a version of the Rāmāyaṇa as part of India's "national culture" that really represented only "the middle class and other aspirants to the same status" (Thapar 1989: 74). Paula Richman and other scholars have argued that, on the contrary, they "take the popularity of the televised *Rāmāyaṇa* not as heralding the demise of other tellings but as affirming the creation of yet another rendition of the *Rāmāyaṇa*, the latest product of an ongoing process of telling and retelling the story of Rama" (Richman 1991: 5).

In a recent article about the Sri Venkateswara temple that was consecrated in 1976 in Penn Hills, Pennsylvania, Vasudha Narayanan raised this concern about the potential of popular media to eliminate the pluralism of Hindu narrative traditions within the specific context of the American diaspora. Narayanan lamented the fact that Hindus in America are receiving their education in Hinduism through such popular media as the *Amar Chitra Katha* comic book series and temple pamphlets:

> Thus we may have an entire generation of young Hindus growing up in this country, educated on the myths recounted by *Amar Chitra Katha*—where again, *one* story line is presented and ratified as "true" unlike the oral tradition which may present alternative versions of a story—and on symbolic meanings of temples, deities and rituals. The

[4] On the diversity of the Rāmāyaṇa tradition, see Richman (1991) and Richman (2001).

> effects of this controlled diet will have to be judged in future years (Narayanan 1992: 169).

Narayanan's primary concern is that the religious education of Hindus in America tends to ignore the pluralism of the Hindu tradition—especially its rich oral, textual, and visual narrative heritage—in favor of a simplified symbolic theology which reduces multiple versions of sacred stories to one dominant storyline that teaches a simple moral lesson about what it means to be Hindu.

Does the *Tales from the Upanishads* comic book by *Amar Chitra Katha* reduce the pluralism of the Upaniṣadic tradition into one storyline that presents a pithy lesson on Hinduism? The Upaniṣads are arguably some of the most important sacred texts of the Hindu tradition. Furthermore, they are also some of the most complex texts to interpret, as Patrick Olivelle has pointed out in the introduction to his English translation of them:

> These documents were composed over several centuries and in various regions, and it is futile to try to discover a single doctrine or philosophy in them. Different theologians, philosophers, and pious readers down the centuries both in India and abroad have discovered different 'truths' and 'philosophies' in them (Olivelle 1996: xxiv).

In this way, the Upaniṣads are an excellent example of the tradition of narrative liberalism within Hinduism. The story of young Śvetaketu, for instance, is told in the Bṛhadāraṇyaka, Chāndogya, and Kauṣītaki Upaniṣads. Olivelle has demonstrated that in each version, the authors have deliberately recast the story of Śvetaketu in accordance with their larger theological goals:

> [T]he author of *BU* [Bṛhadāraṇyaka Upaniṣad] intends to teach a theology of sexual intercourse as a fire sacrifice, while the author of *CU* [Chāndogya Upaniṣad] pursues a theology of the fire sacrifice offered to one's breath ... The intent of the author of the *KṣU* [Kauṣītaki Upaniṣad] is more difficult to determine; it appears that his purpose was somewhat narrow and limited to recasting the path after death ... into a narrative of an epic or puranic type describing a man's journey to the world of Brahman (Olivelle 1999: 48-49).

In addition, versions of the Śvetaketu story appear in several other classical sources: the Jaiminīya Brāhmaṇa (2.329), the Śāṅkhāyana Śrautasūtra (16.29.6-16.29.11), the Mahābhārata (3.132-3.134), and even a Buddhist Jātaka tale (Jātaka 377) where he goes by the name Setaketu and is humbled by an outcaste (Olivelle 1999: 67-68). Each of these versions of the Śvetaketu story is quite different from the next, depending on the authors' intentions. And yet, in each of these stories, the character Śvetaketu remains an arrogant youth who must learn how to be a good student. Olivelle concludes his article on young Śvetaketu with a brief discussion of the continuity of this theme in later versions of this story, including the version presented in the fourteenth century by Mādhava-Vidyāraṇya: "The image of Śvetaketu as an arrogant and irascible young man puffed up by a little learning has endured in the Sanskrit literary tradition" (Olivelle 1999: 69).

Thus, it would appear that throughout time, operating alongside a pluralism of narratives about Śvetaketu, there has also been a simple theme that has connected the many stories of this character: the theme of youthful arrogance being humbled. The theme of a young know-it-all being taught a lesson is an appealing one that has been applied to teach many different moral truths, from the need to respect your parents (if it is Āruṇi who teaches Śvetaketu that lesson), to the need to recognize that knowledge isn't the monopoly of the brahmin caste (if it is a kṣatriya king or an outcaste who teaches Śvetaketu that lesson). And it is this theme of youthful arrogance being humbled that the creators and the consumers of the *Tales from the Upanishads* comic book have found so appealing. For these Hindus, the "Shvetaketu" comic book story teaches universal values such as being a good student and respecting your elders, but wraps these universal values in a specifically Hindu story that is cast into the child-friendly comic book medium.

The *Tales from the Upanishads* comic book does, indeed, present only one storyline about Śvetaketu. As we have seen, the "Shvetaketu" story is based on the sixth chapter of the Chāndogya Upaniṣad—the chapter that is unique to this Upaniṣad, in which Śvetaketu begins to outgrow the infamous arrogance of his youth and transforms into a good student. As we have also seen, the limits of the comic book medium make it nearly impossible to do justice to a complex philosophical scripture. Thus, although we do learn from reading this comic book something about the nature of ultimate reality as taught in the Upaniṣads, and about the stories of characters like Śvetaketu and Raikva, we certainly don't learn anything about the larger theology of the fire sacrifice offered to one's breath that is the context for the Śvetaketu story in the Chāndogya Upaniṣad (see Olivelle 1999: 48). Furthermore, the lesson that, like Śvetaketu, the comic book reader too can transform into a good student and learn to respect his or her elders is a rather simple moral lesson. In this way, then, Narayanan's comment that the comics of the *Amar Chitra Katha* series reduce the pluralism of Hindu narratives into one storyline that teaches a simple moral lesson is certainly valid.

But does this necessarily mean that the religious education of Hindus in America, where these comic books are so central, is in danger? Does it mean that Hindus who grow up reading these comic books regard the "Shvetaketu" story as it is told in the *Tales from the Upanishads* issue as the authoritative Śvetaketu story—that is, does the comic book version become the dominant version? What about Paula Richman's argument, in reference to Sagar's televised "Ramayan," that televised epics and comic books and other popular products are just the latest version in the ongoing process of telling and retelling Hindu stories? I submit that we can't begin to have this much-needed conversation until we more fully investigate what the *Amar Chitra Katha* comic books and other popular versions of classical Indian narratives mean to Hindus in America and elsewhere around the globe.

My research has shown that for the past two generations of Hindus in America, these comic books are regarded as authoritative sources—they are sacred scriptures that "radiate a spiritual force," in the words of one comic book reader. For many of these Hindus living in the diaspora, these comic books have been so important, so authoritative, because they were a rare link to Hinduism and Indian culture more generally; the "Shvetaketu" story of the *Tales from the Upanishads* issue has simply become the dominant version for many Hindus in America because there was no other version of the story easily available. But as temples continue to be built throughout America, as further advances in technology are made, as more Hindus immigrate to the country, and as more colleges offer historical surveys of Hindu religious traditions, these comic books are increasingly becoming just one of many available sources from which Hindus in America can learn about the diversity of Hindu narrative traditions, and what it means to be Hindu. One American-born Hindu, now nineteen, explained to me how he learned the story—or stories—of Śvetaketu during our interview at the library of the Shiva-Vishnu temple in Livermore, California:

> I love *Amar Chitra Katha*! I read so many of them here [at the library of the Shiva-Vishnu temple in Livermore, California]. They tell stories about Hindu culture and they teach about good qualities that one should have. This is how I first learned about Shvetaketu. Then, in class a couple of years ago [as part of the temple's Youth and Education program], we learned about the Upanishads. We talked about how Shvetaketu is a good role model, because he learns how to listen and learn. And we also read some of the Upanishads, a little bit in Sanskrit in class on Sundays, and then more in English. So that way we read a couple of Upanishads that tell the story of Shvetaketu (interviewed by the author, 2005).

When I asked this young man if he knew what English version they read, he went to the bookshelf and returned with Patrick Olivelle's translation. The library of the Shiva-Vishnu temple boasts a nearly complete collection of the entire *Amar Chitra Katha* series, as well as many other academic and non-academic books about Hinduism, and there these comic books are regarded as an authoritative source on "Vedic literature, religion, and Indian history and culture"—but they are now one source among many.[5] As scholars of religion, we need to

[5] Interview with the librarian of the Shiva-Vishnu temple in 2005. Also see the Youth & Education page of the temple's website at www.livermoretemple.org for more information on the library and on religious education classes for children.

continue to study these modern tellings of classical Hindu stories—the stories found in comic books and films and temple pamphlets, as well as the impact of newly available English translations by respected scholars—in addition to casting our glances backwards in search of the earliest versions of these sacred stories, if we want to better understand Hinduism as a living religion.

Bibliography

Brereton, J. (1986), "'Tat Tvam Asi' in Context," *Zeitschrift der Deutschen Morgenländischen Gesellschaft* 136.1: 98-109.

Dempsey, C. (2005), *The Goddess Lives in Upstate New York: Breaking Convention and Making Home at a North American Hindu Temple* (New York: Oxford University Press).

McLain, K. (2005), "Lifting the Mountain: Debating the Place of Science and Faith in the Production of a *Krishna* Comic Book," *Journal of Vaishnava Studies* 13.2: 22-37.

_____. (2007), "Who Shot the Mahatma?: Representing Gandhian Politics in Indian Comic Books," *South Asia Research* 27.1: 57-77.

_____. (2008), "Holy Superheroine: A Comic Book Interpretation of the Hindu *Devi Mahatmya* Scripture," *Bulletin of the School for Oriental and African Studies* 71.2: 297-322.

_____. (2009a), "Gods, Kings, and Local Telugu Guys: Competing Visions of the Heroic in Indian Comic Books" in *Popular Culture in a Globalised India*, ed. K. Moti Gokulsing and W. Dissanayake (New York: Routledge), 157-173.

_____. (2009b), *India's Immortal Comic Books: Gods, Kings, and Other Heroes* (Bloomington: Indiana University Press).

Nachiketa and Other Stories, (1979), no. 201, Amar Chitra Katha (Bombay: India Book House Pvt. Ltd.).

Narayanan, V. (1992), "Creating the South Indian 'Hindu' Experience in the United States" in *A Sacred Thread: Modern Transmission of Hindu Traditions in India and Abroad*, ed. R.B. Williams (Chambersburg: Anima Publications), 147-176.

Olivelle, P. (tr.) (1996), *Upaniṣads* (Oxford and New York: Oxford University Press).

_____. (1999), "Young Śvetaketu: A Literary Study of an Upaniṣadic Story," *Journal of the American Oriental Society* 119.1: 46-70.

Richman, P. (ed.) (1991), *Many Rāmāyaṇas: The Diversity of a Narrative Tradition in South Asia* (Berkeley: University of California Press).

_____. (ed.) (2001.), *Questioning Rāmāyaṇas: A South Asian Tradition* (Berkeley: University of California Press).

Tales from the Upanishads (1987), no. 392, Amar Chitra Katha (Bombay: India Book House Pvt. Ltd.).

"The Role of Chitra Katha in School Education." (1978), (Bombay: India Book House Education Trust).
Thapar, R. (1989), "The *Ramayana* Syndrome," *Seminar* 353: 71-75.
Waghorne, J. (2004), *Diaspora of the Gods: Modern Hindu Temples in an Urban Middle-Class World* (New York: Oxford University Press).

List of Contributors

Jason BeDuhn
Professor, Department of Comparative Cultural Studies, Northern Arizona University, AZ

Manu Bhagavan
Associate Professor, Department of History, Hunter College and the Graduate Center, CUNY, NY

Brian Black
Senior Teaching Associate, Department of Religious Studies, Lancaster University, UK

Daniel Boucher
Associate Professor, Department of Asian Studies, Cornell University, NY

Laura R. Brueck
Assistant Professor, Department of Asian Languages and Civilizations, University of Colorado at Boulder, CO

Donald R. Davis, Jr.
Associate Professor, Department of Languages and Cultures of Asia, University of Wisconsin – Madison, WI

Devin DeWeese
Professor, Department of Central Eurasian Studies, Indiana University – Bloomington, IN

Oliver Freiberger
Associate Professor, Department of Asian Studies, The University of Texas at Austin, TX

Robert A. Goodding
Lecturer, Department of Religious Studies, University of Tennessee, TN

Steven E. Lindquist
Assistant Professor, Department of Religious Studies, Southern Methodist University, TX

Timothy Lubin
Professor, Department of Religion, Washington and Lee University, VA

Karline McLain
Assistant Professor, Religion Department, Bucknell University, PA

Lisa N. Owen
Assistant Professor, Department of Art Education and Art History, University of North Texas, TX

Federico Squarcini
Associate Professor of History of Religions, University of Florence, Italy.

Jarrod L. Whitaker
Assistant Professor, Department of Religion, Wake Forest University, NC

Robert A. Yelle
Assistant Professor, Department of History and the Honors Program, University of Memphis, TN

www.ingramcontent.com/pod-product-compliance
Lightning Source LLC
Chambersburg PA
CBHW021815300426
44114CB00009BA/191
* 9 7 8 1 7 8 3 0 8 0 6 7 0 *